Slavery and Human Progress

SLAVERY and HUMAN PROGRESS

David Brion Davis

OXFORD UNIVERSITY PRESS
New York Oxford

Oxford University Press
Oxford New York Toronto
Delhi Bombay Calcutta Madras Karachi
Petaling Jaya Singapore Hong Kong Tokyo
Nairobi Dar es Salaam Cape Town
Melbourne Auckland

and associated companies in
Beirut Berlin Ibadan Nicosia

Copyright © 1984 by David Brion Davis
First published in 1984 by Oxford University Press, Inc.,
200 Madison Avenue, New York, NY 10016
First issued as an Oxford University Press paperback, 1986

Oxford is the registered trademark of Oxford University Press.

All rights reserved. No part of this publication may be reproduced, stored in a retrieval system, or transmitted, in any form or by any means, electronic, mechanical, photocopying, recording, or otherwise, without the prior permission of Oxford University Press, Inc.

Library of Congress Cataloging in Publication Data

Davis, David Brion.
Slavery and human progress.

Includes index.
1. Slavery—History. 2. Progress. 3. Slavery—Emancipation—History. 4. Slavery and the church.
I. Title.
HT861.D38 1984 306′.362′09 83-25115
ISBN 0-19-503439-2
ISBN 0-19-503733-2 (pbk.)

Printing (last digit): 9 8 7 6 5 4 3 2 1
Printed in the United States of America

For

ADAM JEFFREY DAVIS

and

NOAH BENJAMIN DAVIS

ACKNOWLEDGMENTS

While working on this book during the past decade I have accumulated a great many personal and institutional debts that I can never adequately acknowledge. The research and writing were immeasurably aided by Yale University's policy of triennial leaves, by a National Endowment for the Humanities–Henry E. Huntington Library fellowship in 1976, and by the opportunity in 1980–81 to hold the French-American Foundation's Chair in American Civilization at the École des Hautes Études en Sciences Sociales in Paris. National Endowment for the Humanities research grants, awarded in 1980 and 1981 to support work on a companion project, "The Problem of Slavery in the Age of Emancipation, 1820–1890," made it possible to treat British West Indian emancipation and related subjects in much greater depth.

Any historian who ventures to trespass on the fields of so many distant specialists is bound to step on broken glass or even unexploded bombs scattered by controversies he only dimly understands. My ignorance, misconceptions, and foolhardiness are in no way the fault of the scholars who generously read portions of the manuscript, who saved me from many errors of fact and judgment, and who contributed to my continuing education. For a multitude of criticisms and suggestions I want to thank Ramsay MacMullen, Robert S. Lopez, Harry Miskimin, Gavin R. G. Hambly, Jonathan D. Sarna, Michael Meyer, Jacob R. Marcus, Sidney W. Mintz, Philip D. Curtin, C. Vann Woodward, David Eltis, Lewis C. Perry, and Fiona E. Spiers. I am especially grateful to Stanley L. Engerman, who read various versions of the entire manuscript. For countless historians of slavery and the slave trade Professor Engerman is an all-giving database who can be counted on to reply faster than a computer but in painstaking longhand.

Marcia Libes, Richard Leder, Mark Micale, and Jodi Saposnick helped me with various kinds of research and bibliographical assistance. Although Fiona E. Spiers and Christiane Dichamp did research for "The

Problem of Slavery in the Age of Emancipation," some of the materials they gathered proved to be invaluable for this preliminary book. I am grateful to the Curators of the Bodleian Library for allowing me to consult and photoduplicate the papers of Thomas Fowell Buxton, and to the Wesleyan Methodist Missionary Society for granting access to the Society's archives which are on loan to the School of Oriental and African Studies, London. Research for this book was made possible by the generous assistance of the following other libraries and institutions: the British Library; University College, London; Lambeth Palace Library; the British and Foreign Bible Society; Rhodes House, Oxford; the Institute of Commonwealth Studies; the Public Record Office, London; University of Durham, Department of Palaeography and Diplomatic; University of London Library, Manuscript Division; the Hull Museums; Buckinghamshire County Record Office, Aylesbury; the John Rylands Library, Manchester; Dr. Williams's Library, London; Friends House Library, London; Archives Nationales, Section Outre-Mer, Paris; Bibliothèque Nationale, Paris; Archives of Jamaica, Spanish Town; the Institute of Jamaica, Kingston; Perkins Library, Duke University; Henry E. Huntington Library, San Marino, California; Boston Public Library; New York Public Library; Yale University Libraries; Houghton Library, Harvard University; and Cornell University Library.

I was fortunate in being able to test some of the themes of this book in papers presented at a meeting of the Organization of American Historians, at Florida State University, the University of the West Indies, Rice University, the University of Cologne, the University of Paris, and other institutions. I am grateful for the criticisms I received on such occasions and profited especially from the interaction with other scholars at a conference on religion, antislavery, and reform held in the Rockefeller center at Bellagio, Italy, in July 1978. Preliminary papers, which contain some material revised in this book, have been published in *Anti-Slavery, Religion and Reform: Essays in Memory of Roger Anstey,* edited by Christine Bolt and Seymour Drescher (Dawson Publishing: Folkestone, England, 1980); *Bulletin of the Center for the Study of Southern Culture and Religion,* June 1979; *Rice University Studies,* 67 (Winter 1981); and *Oceans Apart? Comparing Germany and the United States,* edited by Erich Angermann and Marie-Luise Frings (Klett-Cotta: Stuttgart, 1981).

I want to thank Jonathan Mandelbaum and Mary Whitney not only for expert typing but for the kind of understanding care of the manuscript that one has no right to expect in this progressive age. In Paris, where I used up several American typewriters, the day was saved at critical moments by Susan and Rick Bradley and then by Jim Hedges, who generously volunteered their own machines for hazardous duty at the front. Meanwhile, my wife Toni kept me aware over the years that there is a world beyond slavery and that slavery is not the end of human life. I am grateful to Otto Sonntag for his expert copy editing and to Richard von Glahn for typing the index into a computer. Finally, I feel extraordinarily fortunate in belonging to the privileged group of historians who are lucky enough to have Sheldon Meyer as an editor. Without his continuing encouragement, I might well have abandoned what seemed at times a hopeless task. I can only hope that the book I have finally written justifies his almost extraterrestrial patience.

D.B.D.

Orange, Connecticut
May 1984

CONTENTS

Introduction xiii

PART ONE
HOW "PROGRESS" LED TO THE EUROPEANS' ENSLAVEMENT OF AFRICANS

1. A Black Slave Revolt in the Fertile Crescent 5
2. Problems of Definition and Comparison 8
3. Slavery and Imperial Expansion 23
4. The Expansion of Islam and the Symbolism of Race 32
5. From White to Black: European Expansion and the Changing Sources of Slaves 51
6. Jews and the Children of Strangers 82

PART TWO
REDEEMING CHRISTIANITY'S REPUTATION

1. Emancipation as Proof of Progress 107
2. Sacred Inspiration and Secular Power 116
3. New World Slavery as Christianity's "Fortunate Fall" 129
4. The Idea of Progress and the Limits of Moral Responsibility 154
5. British Emancipation: A Deceptive Model, Part One 168
6. British Emancipation: A Deceptive Model, Part Two 192

PART THREE
ABOLISHING SLAVERY AND CIVILIZING THE WORLD

1. The War Against Barbarism: Part One 231
2. The War Against Barbarism: Part Two 259
3. A Century of Progress 279

Epilogue 317
Notes 321
Index 365

INTRODUCTION

For many modern readers the juxtaposition of slavery and human progress may seem bizarre if not perverse. We have been told that belief in historical progress has long been extinct in the "West" and is a cynical joke in communist countries. But the concept still stirs positive emotions; it has hardly disappeared from political propaganda and commercial advertising intended for a global audience. "Slavery," on the other hand, still stands for what everyone abhors, or pretends to abhor, even if the term has been extended in discomforting and often illegitimate ways. If we doubt the genuine freedom of our so-called Free World, we are reassured by the knowledge that it is not, except perhaps in limited regions we would rather not think about, a Slave World. Almost three centuries ago John Locke began his famous *First Treatise of Government* by proclaiming that "Slavery is so vile and miserable an Estate of Man, and so directly opposite to the generous Temper and Courage of our Nation; that 'tis hardly to be conceived that an *Englishman,* much less a *Gentleman,* should plead for 't." When he wrote these lines Locke was not thinking of the slavery of blacks on American plantations, which unfortunately he was all too eager to plead for; but his choice of terms in a debate over English constitutional theory shows that "slavery" hardly had a progressive image.

Some readers may expect me to reformulate and defend one of the theories regarding slavery and *economic* progress that have gained currency since the time of Locke. On the most elementary level, such theories fall into two broad categories: the classic liberal and fundamentalist Marxian wisdom which holds that slavery, however understandable as a stage in human evolution, has always impeded technological innovation as well as social and economic growth; and the disconcerting view of various modern economists who suggest that slavery was compatible with nineteenth-century technology and high rates of growth, and was abolished when its contribution to Western capitalism was just beginning to matter. The former view conveys the comfortable assurance that slavery was doomed by impersonal laws of historical progress, and that economic development ensured, with or without violent revolution, social and moral betterment. The latter view, far from being an apology for human bondage, raises new questions about the motives for emancipation and the systems of labor that replaced plantation slavery.

When one surveys the literature interpreting modern slavery, these bipolar positions can be separated into four distinct arguments: (1) From the time of such eighteenth-century social theorists as John Millar, various writers including Auguste Comte, Karl Marx, Friedrich Engels, and a number of Christian abolitionists have perceived slavery as a necessary but primitive stage in the evolution of human institutions. Thus the enslavement of prisoners-of-war was a marked advance over killing them. By enforcing social discipline on otherwise ungovernable savages, bondage might also serve a progressive purpose at an early stage of civilization where a sparse population, together with a plenitude of land and food, prevented a "combination of labor." Despite important differences in emphasis, the writers who advanced such historicist arguments generally agreed that slave labor was inherently wasteful and inefficient and that well before the nineteenth century it had become a monstrous anachronism. In some respects this position resembled the argument of orthodox Biblicists who looked upon the slavery sanctioned by the Old Testament as part of a just and necessary "dispensation" preparing the way for universal freedom.

(2) A variant on this theme which deserves special attention is the argument of the late Eric Williams and numerous followers who maintain that the Europeans' enslavement of Africans was indispensable for conquering and settling the New World, and then for amassing the capital that financed the industrial revolution. According to this still popular thesis, white Americans and Europeans progressed only at the expense of black slaves whose labor built the foundations of modern capitalism. At a crucial turning point, however, slave labor became uneconomical and a drag on further capitalist development. At this point, which varied chronologically because of different stages of local and national evolution, capitalists decided that black slavery was "unprogressive" and determined to abolish the institution. For the Williams school the seeming "necessity" of black slavery for Western progress in no way implies moral justification. An analogy would rather be the discovery that the fortune of a highly respected family had originated in burglary, prostitution, and selling narcotics, and that the family, once established, had then led moral crusades against those very crimes.

(3) The third theory derives from the abolitionists and classical

economists who maintained that slave labor always retards long-term economic growth as well as social and moral progress. The underlying assumption was that oppressors cannot violate the immutable laws of nature without paying a heavy price. This view tended to dominate American historiography until very recent times. Drawing on such seemingly contradictory sources as Frederick Law Olmsted, who wrote vivid and hostile descriptions of the South in the 1850s, and Ulrich Bonnell Phillips, who in 1918 published what was long taken as the definitive (and apologetic) account of "American Negro Slavery," numerous historians and popularizers agreed that black slavery was a fatal impediment to incentive, innovation, and self-improvement. If it created fortunes for a few rich planters, it blighted the South as a region. When not temporarily sustained by the African slave trade and by expansion into fresh and fertile land, black slavery supposedly brought declining profits, soil exhaustion, and general economic and social stagnation. Advocates of this theory also held that the low quality of slave labor, coupled with the indolence of free whites who regarded most kinds of work as suitable only for blacks, had led to an impoverished, backward South that presented a shocking contrast, by the 1850s, to the bustling cities, factories, railways, and prosperous farms of the North. Historians who accepted these assumptions differed over the harshness of southern slavery and the possible debilitating effects of the blacks' racial characteristics, as distinct from the characterological damage inflicted by lifelong oppression. For the Phillips school, the heavy economic costs of slavery were partly offset by a paternalistic system of racial control that helped to "civilize" an inferior "stock" of immigrants from a savage continent.

(4) The final theory, advanced in its most extreme form by Robert William Fogel and Stanley L. Engerman's *Time on the Cross* (1974), is simply a reverse image of the fourth set of propositions defined above. In their assault upon even the covertly "racist" assumption that black slaves were inefficient workers and poor learners, Fogel and Engerman portray slavery as an unmistakably "progressive" institution, at least with respect to the benefits of economic growth. While acknowledging that slaves suffered cultural and psychological deprivations, they contend that the typical field hand received during his lifetime approximately 90 percent of the income he produced; that far from being "lazy, inept, and unproductive," he was "harder-working and more efficient than his white counterpart"; that southern slave agriculture was 35 percent more efficient than the northern system of family farming; that "far from stagnating, the economy of the antebellum South grew quite rapidly. Between 1840 and 1860, per capita income increased more rapidly in

the South than in the rest of the nation."[1] Although economists and historians have disputed most of the points Fogel and Engerman make, the scholarship of the last decade tends to support the view of slavery as a flexible and adaptable institution that was not incompatible with high rates of economic growth. As a result of the continuing controversy, scholars are now more reluctant to speak of a slave system becoming "moribund" or being doomed to "inevitable decline." Apart from economics, numerous recent studies have dramatized the capacity of the black family and of Afro-American culture in general to change, adapt, and develop under the most adverse conditions. Such works by no means imply that slavery itself was an instrument of progress; yet the recent tributes paid to the strength of black religion, folklore, art, and "nationalism" necessarily suggest that slavery did not bring universal retrogression and decline.

It is not my purpose to evaluate these conflicting theories or to argue that slavery has either furthered or retarded human progress. Quite frankly, I am not at all sure what "progress" really means. We shall have occasion throughout this book to consider changing conceptions of the term, ranging from the advance of a particular religious faith to the moral improvement of humankind. Historically, the concept of progress has been irresistibly associated with technological and economic growth, material improvements, and a rising standard of living. But I am far from confident that such quantitative progress is an adequate measure of qualitative progress, of the highest aspirations of the human soul. If the term once seemed as self-evident as the God it in some ways replaced, I am an agnostic on both counts.

On the other hand, I am well aware of the awesome power transmitted by the conviction that certain beliefs, customs, institutions, and even races stand in the way of "progress" and must be consigned to the rubbish heap of history. The theories described above illustrate some of the ideological uses of "progress," which have made slavery appear both as an intolerable obstacle to human betterment and as an institution that could conform to modern standards of efficiency, productivity, and material improvement. Few people today would deny that the eradication of the oceanic slave trade and the emancipation of millions of slaves were steps toward that which is better or more desirable for humanity as a whole. The very idea of progress owes much to ancient bondspeople who made manumission or escape the universal symbols for deliverance, redemption, resurrection, and divine mission. Yet one must not forget that enslavement has usually been seen by the enslavers as a form of human progress. When Prince Henry of Portugal reviewed in the 1440s the first shipments of slaves brought from the African coast, he "reflected with great pleasure upon the salvation of those souls that before were lost."[2] And as I shall try to suggest later on in this book, emancipators can be as coercive and oppressive, in subtle ways, as enslavers. It was not the enslavers who colonized and subjugated Africa, but the European liberators.

This is a study of the momentous shift from "progressive" enslavement to "progressive" emancipation. The first phrase refers to the fact that the early expansion of Islam, of Christianity, and of mercantilist Europe involved the enslavement of millions of pagans and infidels for their own supposed benefit as well as for the benefit of a "superior civilization." The spread of black slavery from the Mediterranean to the Atlantic islands and finally to the West Indies and Brazil was closely tied to the expansion of European trade, technology, and religion, and hence with Europe's gradual strategic gains over the rival Islamic world. Plantation slavery, far from being an aberration invented by lawless buccaneers and lazy New World adventurers, as nineteenth-century liberals often charged, was a creation of the most progressive peoples and forces in Europe—Italian merchants; Iberian explorers; Jewish inventors, traders, and cartographers; Dutch, German, and British investors and bankers. From the colonization of Madeira and other sugar-producing islands off the coast of West Africa to the westward extension of the "Cotton Kingdom," black slavery was an intrinsic part of "the rise of the West."

The second phrase refers to the new conception of "progress" that gained momentum in the late eighteenth century. The transformation was most dramatic in Britain, which during the eighteenth century led the world in transporting a record number of African slaves to the Americas and in developing from Maryland to Guiana the most populous and prosperous collection of slave colonies in modern history. In the nineteenth century, however, Britain led the world in attempting to suppress the African slave trade, in emancipating her own slaves, and in exerting diplomatic, economic, and even military pressure to secure universal emancipation. Since nineteenth-century Britain was also the unquestioned exemplar of commercial and industrial expansion and hence of modern progress, this shift in ideology and public policy in effect defined every slaveholding society as retrogressive. To complete the ironic cycle, after Cuba and Brazil had freed their slaves in the 1880s, the final targets of antislavery interventionism were within the Middle East and Africa, the regions from which Europeans had originally derived both sugar plantations and black slaves. The persistence of various forms of bondage supposedly proved that these societies were still living in a primitive age and required tutelage from the world's most progressive peoples. The British, having taken the lead in repentance and antislavery commitment, were by self-definition the people best equipped to assume such a task.

I do not mean to blur the crucial moral distinction between defending and abolishing slavery in the name of human progress. As I shall argue later on, the impetus behind British antislavery policies was mainly religious, though devout Victorians assumed that good economics was consistent with good religion. But if religious mission could originally justify the enslavement of millions of Africans for the good of their souls, it could later justify the subjection of "backward" peoples to colonial rule for the good of their civilization. As a premonition of the power of antislavery ideology, consider the meaning and global context of the following words. On December 6, 1846, Lord Palmerston, the British foreign secretary, was so outraged by reports of slave-trade atrocities in Zanzibar that he sent off this dispatch to Atkins Hamerton, the British consul:

> Captain Hamerton should take every opportunity of impressing upon these Arabs that the nations of Europe are destined to put an end to the African S.T. and that Great Britain is the main instrument in the Hands of Providence for the accomplishment of this purpose. That it is in vain for these Arabs to endeavour to resist the consummation of that which is written in the Book of Fate, and that they ought to bow to superior power, to leave off a pursuit which is doomed to annihilation, and a perseverance in which will only involve them in losses and other evils; and that they should hasten to betake themselves to the cultivation of their soil and to lawful and innocent commerce.[3]

Conditions in Zanzibar were clearly deplorable, since commercial "progress" had begun to encourage plantation slavery in East Africa as a means of producing cloves for overseas export. If Hamerton's efforts temporarily reduced the flow of slaves to the Persian Gulf and Oman, they probably increased the supply of slave labor in Zanzibar.[4] What needs to be emphasized, however, is that Palmerston's warning came only eight years after slavery had been truly abolished in the British West Indies, three years after ineffectual restrictions had been laid on slavery in British India. Yet by 1850 British cruisers had been authorized to seize suspicious ships within Brazilian territorial waters and even harbors. And the government of the United States, fearing that Britain's antislavery pretensions cloaked a plot to take over Cuba, Mexico, and California as a means of blocking the spread of republican institutions, had taken what some officials regarded as preemptive moves to seize California and northern Mexico, and to prepare the way for the annexation of Cuba.

As these examples suggest, the connections between slavery and "progress" are so fluid, ambiguous, and far-reaching that it would require a shelf of volumes by numerous scholars to do the subject justice. This is an exploratory study which pays a necessary price in selectivity for a broadly comparative overview that extends from antiquity to modern times. I have touched on the theme of progress in two previous books, *The Problem of Slavery in Western Culture* (1966) and *The Problem of Slavery in the Age of Revolution, 1770–1823* (1975). I shall view the subject in other contexts and from a somewhat different perspective in the concluding volume, *The Problem of Slavery in the Age of Emancipation, 1815–1890*. It was only after finishing the 1975 volume, however, that I saw the value of recomposing the entire history of Western slavery and emancipation around the theme of changing conceptions of progress. In Part One this has meant reviewing certain continuities between ancient and modern slavery as well as the transition in various regions from white to black manual labor. I covered some of this ground in *The Problem of Slavery in Western Culture*, but now have the opportunity to make important revisions in the light of recent scholarship. Parts Two and Three are mostly based on primary sources and constitute a pilot study for *The Problem of Slavery in the Age of Emancipation*. In this preliminary work I skip over certain central issues that I plan later to explore in some detail and also give more thorough analysis to subjects that should be peripheral to the more comprehensive though time-limited future work.

This is, in short, a transitional book that stands on its own and is not really part of a "series." It presumes little if any knowledge of the history of slavery on the reader's part, but is also addressed to the growing number of students of slavery and related institutions, some of whom will doubtless discover errors or misconceptions in their own fields of specialization. I should add that this is not a study in economic history, imperial history, black history, or even institutional change. I am less concerned with "underlying causes" than with the ways in which slavery and emancipation were perceived, understood, explained, symbolized, and related to larger frames of reference. But as I have already indicated, this purpose necessitates an interpretive account of the origins of New World slavery in order to provide us with our own frame of reference.

PART ONE

How "Progress" Led to the Europeans' Enslavement of Africans

". . . for all tame animals there is an advantage in being under human control, as this secures their survival. And as regards the relationship between male and female, the former is naturally superior, the latter inferior, the former rules and the latter is subject.

By analogy, the same must necessarily apply to mankind as a whole. Therefore all men who differ from one another by as much as the soul differs from the body or man from a wild beast (and that is the state of those who work by using their bodies, and for whom that is the best they can do)—these people are slaves by nature, and it is better for them to be subject to this kind of control, as it is better for the other creatures I have mentioned. For a man who is able to belong to another person is by nature a slave (for that is why he belongs to someone else). . . . Assistance regarding the necessities of life is provided by both groups, by slaves and by domestic animals. Nature must therefore have intended to make the bodies of free men and of slaves different also; slaves' bodies strong for the services they have to do, those of free men upright and not much use for that kind of work, but instead useful for community life. . . ."

Aristotle, *Politics*, 1.5.

"Owners often have to be reminded that this is actually a golden age for the family dog—far and away the best that he has ever known. And especially for the old dog. There was a time, more recently than you think, when by present standards all dogs were miserably treated. . . . Old dogs live well today. They are cherished and preserved and protected. They are comfortably housed and generously (too generously) fed. They are healthier and stronger and they live longer and more happily than they ever had in the past. Far from being outcasts, they have become the most privileged characters in every household."

George D. Whitney, D.V.M.,
The Health and Happiness of Your Old Dog.

1. A BLACK SLAVE REVOLT IN THE FERTILE CRESCENT

In the middle of the ninth century A.D., six hundred years before Portuguese voyages initiated an oceanic slave trade from West Africa to the Iberian Peninsula, eight hundred years before African slaves displaced white agricultural workers in Barbados and other British West Indian colonies, a full millennium before the issue of restricting or extending black slavery precipitated the American Civil War, many thousands of black slaves worked in regimented gangs on the tidal flats of southern Iraq.

Much of the Tigris-Euphrates delta, interlaced with ancient dikes and canals, had become abandoned marshland overgrown with tall reeds that sheltered wild game as well as various kinds of rebels and outlaws. As peasants had migrated to the thriving towns of the Abbasid Empire, rich farmland had been repeatedly flooded and encrusted with salt and other mineral sediment. Although the Abbasid Empire (750–1258) long preceded the "idea of progress" as understood by early modern philosophers and historians, Arab entrepreneurs knew that intensive labor could reclaim this wasteland, remove the mineral deposits, and prepare the subsoil for cultivation. What crops were to be cultivated is unclear, though rice, barley, millet, sorghum, onions, and melons were all grown in the region, and it is tempting to note that sugar, a luxury unknown to Europe before the Crusades of the eleventh and twelfth centuries, was already becoming an important export from Shushtar, in neighboring Khuzestan. In any event, in Basra, the region's commercial, financial, and agricultural center, wealthy proprietors had received extensive grants of tidal land on the condition that they would make it arable.[1]

This task of land reclamation, involving the extraction and removal of mountains of salty debris, required a kind of labor force that may have been unique in early Islamic history. But the sources for that history are fragmentary and often consist of later compilations of oral traditions attuned to genealogical and religious disputes, not to the economic institutions that arose in the wake of Islam's lightning strokes of Eurasian and African conquest. Our limited knowledge of slave labor in southern Iraq derives from the fortuitous event of a massive slave revolt that could not escape commentary. Most of the slaves were Zanj, or blacks of East African origin. While some of these Zanj and other black slaves had been transported across the Red Sea and by caravan across Arabia, it seems probable that for an indeterminate period slave ships had followed the northeast monsoons from the coast south of Somali to the Persian Gulf's inland port of Basra, from which Sindbad sailed on his legendary adventures in the Spice Islands and East Africa.[2]

Most of the Zanj were apparently owned by absentee proprietors in Basra, who delegated authority to drivers and overseers of various kinds. These "véritables 'capitalistes,' " as Alexandre Popovic terms them, were an anomaly in the Islamic world, which generally defined slavery as a domestic or military institution. But the evidence suggests that the Zanj suffered from labor conditions as oppressive as those in the West Indies some eight or nine centuries later. As early as the late seventh century, slave insurrections, apparently involving mainly blacks, were quickly and ruthlessly crushed. Then, in September 869, the Zanj rose in what was to become the greatest slave revolt from the Roman servile wars of the second and first centuries B.C. to the black revolution of the 1790s that destroyed France's most lucrative colony, Saint Domingue.

The Abbasid Empire, like revolutionary France, was preoccupied with internal fiscal and political conflicts that threatened both the authority and survival of the Baghdad caliphate. Such superficial parallels should not be pressed, and it would be highly misleading to liken Shiite or Kharijite rebels to eighteenth-century Jacobins. We have little verified knowledge concerning Ali b. Muhammad, who precipitated and led the Zanj revolt. A poet and teacher at the royal court in Samarra, he was versed in occult sciences and claimed for a time to be a direct descendant of Ali, Muhammad's son-in-law, and to have received supernatural revelations. At Bahrain, Basra, and Baghdad he recruited followers for abortive uprisings. There is no firm evidence that Ali b. Muhammad was a Shiite or Kharijite or that he adhered to any specific social or political vision. Having failed to mobilize Bedouins and other potential allies, he may have turned to the Zanj out of sheer opportunism. It is clear that he exploited the many grievances of the slaves, promising them worldly possessions and demanding the beheading of their masters for violating the Qur'an's injunctions against cruel treatment. It is also clear that the blacks produced their own military leaders who displayed tactical skill as well as remarkable perseverance. On the canals and reedy lakes, the rebels ambushed the imperial armies, sinking boatloads of troops and slaughtering or enslaving prisoners. The Zanj forces were augmented by Bedouins, local peasants, and black soldiers who deserted the Arab armies. After failing in an initial assault on Basra, the Zanj established what may have been the first "maroon" community in recorded history—that is, protected, self-sufficient communities of fugitive slaves.

For years the Zanj continued to repel government attacks, to raid the countryside, and to retire safely into their marshland stronghold. In the autumn of 871, after severing communication between Baghdad and the Persian Gulf, the rebels finally seized Basra, killing thousands of Arab men and enslaving the women and children. The government forces, like their later French counterparts in Saint Domingue, were decimated by tropical illness and distracted by war on another front. The Zanj advanced northward as the government pulled back troops for the defense of Baghdad. In 879, after ten years of bitter fighting, the thousands of former slaves appeared unconquerable.

As late as 882 the blacks successfully beat off attacks on their villages, using tactics similar to those of the later maroons of Surinam, Jamaica, and Palmares, in Brazil. But during a final siege of the Zanj capital, the Arabs lured many blacks away with promises of amnesty and reward and then used the turncoats to encourage more desertions. Engineers succeeded in clearing river channels for the imperial warships, and in bombarding the Zanj fortifications with Greek fire. After a fierce battle in 883, the Arabs finally crushed the main Zanj force, though isolated groups of rebels continued for a while to resist. In Baghdad, some three hundred miles from Basra, the authorities paraded Ali's head on the top of a pole.

It is clearly a mistake to interpret this dramatic rebellion as primarily a racial conflict or as part of a continuing revolutionary struggle of slaves against masters. As recent scholars have insisted, the Zanj revolt must be understood within an Islamic social and political context that has little relevance to later Western ideologies. Ali b. Muhammad sought neither to abolish slavery nor to establish an egalitarian state; the Zanj villages, sometimes seen as models of primitive communism, were geared to limited goals of plunder and survival. Nor can one interpret the development of slavery in southern Iraq as a precedent that contributed in any way to the plantation systems created by the later expansion of Europe. Indeed, there is evidence that the Zanj revolt discouraged further Arab experiments in amassing foreign slaves for large-scale projects of land reclamation and protoplantation agriculture. The Zanj who survived were apparently enlisted in Abbasid armies or dispersed as personal servants.

On the other hand, the magnitude and duration of this system of slavery present an "exception" significant enough to cast doubt on the conventional thesis that Islam irresistibly fostered a contempt for land and agriculture, an indifference to the economic functions of labor, and an insistence on "domestic" forms of servitude regulated by religious norms and traditions. Although black captives had appeared in Egyptian iconography in the third millennium B.C. and were portrayed with increasing frequency and realism from the fifteenth century B.C. through Hellenistic and Roman times, the Arabs and their Muslim allies were the first people to develop a specialized, long-distance slave trade from sub-Saharan Africa. They were also the first people to view blacks as suited by nature for the lowest and most degrading forms of bondage.[3] As we shall see, this point requires further refinement and qualification. For the moment it is sufficient to stress that even by the eighth and ninth centuries A.D., religious and commercial expansion could create a slave "colony" remarkably similar to those established in the New World. It is also noteworthy that this protoplantation system was destroyed when a radical religious vision, the nature of which is still obscure, became fused with the accumulated grievances of an uprooted and oppressed mass of slaves.

2. PROBLEMS OF DEFINITION AND COMPARISON

The more we learn about slavery, the more difficulty we have defining it. The difficulty is compounded by a waning faith in theories of history that view slave labor as a mode of production or an "industrial system" created by certain economic or political conditions and sentenced to extinction by the laws of human progress. The late nineteenth and early twentieth centuries generated a profusion of confident theories explaining the rise and fall of slavery in ancient and modern societies. Whether Marxist or positivist, specialized or broadly comparative, these bold studies took for granted the objectivity of slavery as a categorical and transcultural concept. If they differed on the causes and functions of bondage in the stages of human evolution, such scholars a Giovanni Abignente, J. K. Ingram, Ettore Ciccotti, C. J. M. Letourneau, and H. J. Nieboer never doubted that slavery was a discrete and fundamentally premodern institution.[4]

For reasons that deserve further study, scholarly interest in slavery and related forms of servitude languished from the First World War to the 1950s, a period that set new records for the mobilization, degradation, and extermination of millions of unfree workers. Pioneering studies, such as Eric Williams's *Capitalism and Slavery* (1944), Frank Tannenbaum's *Slave and Citizen* (1946), and Bernard J. Siegel's "Some Methodological Considerations for a Comparative Study of Slavery" (1945),[5] attracted widespread attention only by the 1960s, when an upsurge of interest in American Negro slavery set off a chain reaction that led to explosive debates over the meaning of slavery in antiquity, precolonial Africa, Asia, the Islamic world, and even Nazi Germany. It should be stressed that much of the basic research for this great slavery boom was done before 1960 and was unrelated to the American civil rights movement. This is not the place to analyze the rich and often combustible interaction of various forms of Marxist, Althusserian, structuralist, and cliometric theory that have contributed to the continuing controversies. The issue of slavery remains a testing ground for social theory and hence for the presumed "progress" of social science. Yet our striking gains in empirical knowledge have not been matched by a widely accepted paradigm or theoretical model. The problem posed by Claude Meillassoux in 1975, after he summarized the extraordinary diversity of African slavery, is still unresolved:

> In the present state of research, there is really no general theory that allows us to identify slavery or the objective conditions for its likely emergence. Recognition of the phenomenon is still empirical or implicitly comparative. Empirical recognition is based on pinpointing one or more terms applied to servile states (but such terms are not always exclusively applied to slaves); on the condition of legal subordination to the absolute authority of a master (but a condition shared with other persons not classed as slaves); on a legal and economic condition that allows masters to sell such people and/or claim their total produce (but a condition that is also shared with the masters' dependent kin, with people

pledged for debts, etc.). No formal criterion has been brought to light that allows us to make a categorical distinction between slaves and all the comparable social components.[6]

While Meillassoux by no means agrees with the extreme nominalists who question the usefulness of "slavery" as a transcultural or universal term, his point deserves elaboration in order to emphasize the danger of imposing an abstract concept on incomparable institutions and of then tracing the supposed history of the reified term. The word for slaves has been applied to captives held for ceremonial sacrifice; to household servants who were part of a *familia* and under the domination of a *paterfamilias;* to the concubines and eunuchs of a harem; to children held as pawns for their parents' debts; to female children sold as brides; and, by analogy, to subject or conquered populations; to the industrial proletariat; to the victims of racial or political tyranny; and to men or women supposedly dominated by drugs, alcohol, sexual passion, mental disease, or sin. In some societies, slaves have enjoyed a higher status than the lowest castes of free workers. They have been given honored posts in royal courts, armies, and government bureaucracies. They have been allowed to enter the arts and professions, to marry free spouses, to become members of their owners' families, and to travel or conduct business with minimal interference. The rulers of some Muslim societies were customarily recruited from the male children of female slaves. And, of course, there are many examples of monetary payment being given for the total economic, sexual, or social dominion of nominally free persons, especially women. Thousands of nominally free workers have been transported across the seas to labor in mines or on plantations; they have been subjected to systematic debasement, dishonor, racial discrimination, and corporal punishment; they have been stripped of the most elemental civil rights; contract and convict laborers, predominately male, have often been denied the opportunity for parenthood and family life; their children, though technically freeborn, have sometimes had no chance of escaping their parents' status.

These difficulties do not preclude a theoretical model that succeeds in distinguishing superficial variables from the essential elements of slavery and even in accounting for different forms of servitude in different historical situations. The most ambitious and promising attempt to meet these goals is Orlando Patterson's recent book, *Slavery and Social Death.* This is the first systematic analysis in over eighty years of slavery as a global institution that was "firmly established in all the great early centers of human civilization and, far from declining, actually increased in significance with the growth of all the epochs and cultures that modern Western peoples consider watersheds in their historical development." Patterson offers a preliminary definition of slavery, on the level of personal relations, as "the permanent, violent domination of natally alienated and generally dishonored persons." These abstract and somewhat enigmatic phrases, which notably omit any reference to property, services, or labor, take on rich layers of meaning as Patterson examines sixty-six slaveholding societies selected from George P. Murdock's *Ethnographic Atlas*, as well as an additional list of forty-odd "large-scale slave systems" (the precise number depends on how one classifies a "system"). For Patterson slavery is preeminently a relationship of power and dominion originating in and sustained by violence. It is a state of "social death" substituting for a commuted physical death from war, capital punishment, starvation, or exposure. One aspect of such social death is natal alienation from ancestors, relatives, and descendants—in short, from membership in a recognized lineage, community, and culture. A second aspect, which Patterson brilliantly illuminates, is symbolic and ritualistic dishonor. In many societies masters acquired slaves for the sole purpose of enhancing their own honor and prestige, a goal that required obsequious behavior and self-contempt from even the most privileged and nonproductive dependents. Patterson emphasizes that these "constituent elements" of slavery were never static and can be understood only with reference to specific socioeconomic contexts and the institutional processes of recruitment, enslavement, incorporation, and manumission. It is too early to say how Patterson's schematic and dialectical analysis will fare when scrutinized by specialists in ancient, medieval, Asian, African, and precolonial American history. Fortunately, the present study makes no claims as social science and has no need of a single, comprehensive definition in order to point to changing connections between slavery and progress, as those terms have been understood at different historical periods.[7]

At the outset, however, it is important to call attention to several common fallacies that often distort comparative discussions of human bondage. The first misconception is to assume that the institutions of numerous societies can be amalgamated into "ancient slavery," "Muslim slavery," "Latin American slavery," or "North American slavery," without reference to time, place, and changing socioeconomic conditions. Even within a relatively circumscribed region, such as the British Caribbean in the eighteenth century, differences in climate, topography, soil, demographic structure, and stages of economic development contributed to significant variations in the institution of black slavery.[8] As Orlando Patterson and other recent scholars have demonstrated, slavery was never a static or uniform system; it was not the automatic result of a few simple conditions, such as political consolidation or the scarcity of free labor in relation to "free land"; and it cannot be understood apart from a matrix of variables including kinship and economic structures, social stratification, cultural values, and ethnic, religious, or racial ideologies.

A second fallacy is to assume that the slave's juridical status defined his actual condition. For many years this bias distorted generalized comparisons between North American and Latin American slavery. But given our present and increasing knowledge of North American slavery—and we have richer and more diverse evidence about slavery in the United States than about slavery, serfdom, or even working-class culture in any previous or contemporary society—it is clear that laws and judicial decisions can be highly misleading. As one might expect, laws intended to protect slaves from assault, cruelty, and injustice were seldom enforced. But it is noteworthy that nineteenth-century southern courts not only upheld the conviction of whites for killing or abusing slaves but also vindicated the right of slaves, in extreme circumstances, to self-defense. As Eugene D. Genovese has perceptively concluded:

> The slave codes of the southern United States came from the slaveholders themselves and represented their collective estimate of right and wrong and of the limits that should hedge in their own individual power. Their positive value lay not in the probability of scrupulous enforcement but in the standards of decency they laid down in a world inhabited, like most worlds, by men who strove to be considered decent. These standards could be violated with impunity and often were, but their educational and moral effect remained to offer the slaves the little protection they had.[9]

No less striking is the fact that, contrary to law, a few privileged American slaves were allowed to own guns and hunt game; to acquire literacy; to assume trusted positions of management, occasionally even over hired white laborers; to purchase their own freedom; and most important, since this practice was far more widespread, to establish a meaningful, if vulnerable, control over their familial, religious, and cultural lives. Recent scholarship, mostly attributing such gains to the indomitable strength of the Afro-American heritage, has produced brilliant studies of the slave family, the slave community, and slave folklore and culture—all of which should have been obliterated, according to earlier theories of American slavery as a "total institution."[10]

A third and related danger is to exaggerate the moral distinction between the supposedly benign paternalism of traditional household slavery and the supposedly absolute exploitation of plantation slaves producing staples for a capitalist world market. Admittedly, these two forms of bondage served different purposes in societies that must conceptually be kept distinct. But as we shall see, apologists for modern plantation slavery repeatedly invoked the model and precedent of domestic servitude sanctioned by the Old Testament. It is a grave mistake, as Eugene Genovese has shown, to interpret planter paternalism either as mere rationalization or as incompatible with cruelty and oppression. "Wherever paternalism exists," he points out, "it undermines solidarity among the oppressed by linking them as individuals to their oppressors." There is no reason to assume that premodern forms of bondage were more benign or free from every species of violence and exploitation. "There is no known slaveholding society," Orlando Patterson writes, "where the whip was not considered an indispensable instrument." Even the slaves who rose to the rank of Ottoman grand viziers were subject, as Daniel Pipes points out, "to the merest whim of their masters," the sultans, who "could reduce the grand vizier to a kitchen aide or have him executed; yet, at the same time, the grand vizier directed the government of a world power."[11]

Finally, it was not uncommon for diverse forms of slavery to coexist within a single premodern society. As Suzanne Miers and Igor Kopytoff note with respect to precolonial Africa:

> There is nothing to prevent the use of some "slaves" as chattels on agricultural estates or in a workshop even while others are simultaneously closely integrated into kin groups and still others serve as aristocratic warriors or bureaucrats. Industrial "slavery" need not, after all, preclude familial "slavery"; increased complexity merely creates more specialized types of servitude.[12]

But such complexity and specialization appear at the very beginning of recorded history—that is, in Mesopotamia in the third and second millennia B.C., where slaves served as concubines, court eunuchs, domestic servants, artisans, construction workers, miners, and agricultural laborers. The truly striking fact, given historical changes in polity, religion, technology, modes of production, family and kinship structures, and the very meaning of "property," is the antiquity and almost universal acceptance of the *concept* of the slave as a human being who is legally owned, used, sold, or otherwise disposed of as if he or she were a domestic animal. This parallel persisted in the similarity of naming, branding, and even pricing slaves according to their equivalent in cows, horses, camels, pigs, and chickens.[13] Yet the same premodern societies considered the slave sufficiently responsible to be punished for escape or other crimes and to be rewarded by positions of trust and prestige, manumission, or eventual assimilation to his owner's family and society.

From the Ur-Nammu tablet, one of the oldest surviving records of human law, to the Hammurabi Code and fragments of early Egyptian judicial decisions, it is clear that the most "advanced" societies in the eyes of the later Western world shared a generalized concept of slavery that Greek philosophers and Roman jurists later systematized and refined. Retrospective analysis can demonstrate that slavery had very different meanings in ancient Mesopotamia, fourth-century Greece, and the Roman Empire. In most premodern societies, for example, the ownership of any property was bound up with customary claims and powers over people; Roman private law was distinctive in conceiving property as a relationship between owners and things and in recognizing an absolute and exclusive ownership of things, including slaves. Despite such differences in sociolegal contexts, it seems likely that the authors of the Hammurabi Code would have assented to the definitions of slavery propounded by Aristotle and by the Roman *Lex Aelia Sentia*—even though they might have been mystified by Aristotle's doctrine that certain people "are slaves by nature, and it is both to their advantage, and just, for them to be slaves"; and by the dictum of Gaius, the Roman jurist, that "all human beings are either free men or slaves."[14] Many historical tragedies stemmed from the illusion that everyone understood what slavery meant, that it was part of what the Romans termed *ius gentium,* or the law of nations. The illusion was fostered by the seeming universality of the concept and by the fact that most slaves were originally procured by war or interstate trade. Yet the sellers of slaves, whether in Asia, Europe, or Africa, could seldom begin to imagine the future status of their captives in a wholly foreign society.

In a sense, slaves were the world's first "modern" people. The archetypical slave was a foreigner, an outsider torn from her or his protective family matrix by capture, treacherous sale, greed, debt, the threat of famine, or punishment for crime. The vulnerability of young women is suggested by the fact that in the earliest protoliterate tablets, the sign for "slave girl" appeared before the word for "slave," which in ancient Sumerian meant "male (or female) of a foreign country." Although such acquired outsiders were assimilated in varying degrees to the culture and even kinship structures of the possessive society, there is a profound meaning to James Vaughan's description of bondage as the "institutionalization of marginality." This concept applies to slaves of internal origin who had fallen into a state of "social death" as a result of poverty or crime. It can also be applied to a spectrum extending from the "closed" societies of Asia, which barred the descendants of slaves from membership in lineage systems based on the control of valuable land, to the "open" societies of Africa, which sought slaves as a means of augmenting social and political power. According to Miers and Kopytoff, the central problem of slavery, at least in African societies, was the " 'rehumanization' of the nonperson in a new social setting." Yet, even in the most "absorptive societies," this process took several generations and always fell short of complete integration. Judging by the case studies assembled by Miers and Kopytoff, even the most assimilated descendants of slaves never acquired the status of authentic kinsmen. In times of crisis or famine, they were the first to be sold.[15]

Hence the "modernity" of the slave lay in his continuing marginality and vulnerability, in his incomplete and ambiguous bonding to a social group. As a replaceable and interchangeable outsider faced with the unpredictable need of adjusting to wholly alien cultures, he was the prototype for the migratory labor and confused identity that have accompanied every phase of human progress. Moreover, as Orlando Patterson points out:

> . . . the liminality of the slave is not just a powerful agent of authority for the master, but an important route to the usefulness of the slave for both his master and the community at large. The essence of caste relations and notions of ritual pollution is that they demarcate impassable boundaries. The essence of slavery is that the slave, in his social death, lives on the margin between community and chaos, life and death, the sacred and the secular. Already dead, he lives outside the mana of the gods and can cross the boundaries with social and supernatural impunity.

On a somewhat different level, Patterson adds, the pressing needs of the Roman bureaucracy for specialization, efficiency, and assignment by merit could best be met by "natally alienated persons who could most readily be employed in this way: ever ready to move physically, and occupationally, not only upward but laterally, downward, and out; ever ready to retrain for entirely new positions and to accept, without complaint, whatever was offered in remuneration."[16]

Today, however, we automatically contrast slavery with free wage labor or with various modern ideals of individual autonomy. Through most of history such antonyms would have appeared absurd or contradictory. In earliest Saxon law, for example, the "autonomous" stranger who had no family or clan to protect him was automatically regarded as a slave. Similarly, in most of Africa, according to Miers and Kopytoff, "the antithesis of 'slavery' is not 'freedom' qua autonomy but rather 'belonging.' Significantly, the Giriama of the Kenya coast, when asked to name the opposite of *mtumwa* ('slave'), invariably replied 'Mgiriama,' meaning simply a Giriama."[17] In premodern societies the salient characteristic of slavery was its antithetical relation to the normal network of kinship ties of dependency, protection, obligation, and privilege, ties that easily served as a model for nonkinship forms of patronage, clientage, and voluntary servitude.

Of course, the slave also "belonged" to a master or household, but in a fortuitous and artificial way. In practice, the claims to a slave's services and even to his person might differ little from those purchased by a bride-price or bridewealth and exercised over wives and children. But the acquisition of a slave short-circuited the kinship systems that defined and prohibited incestuous relationships while assuring the continuing identity and perpetuation of family lines. In theory, the slave stood alone in being alienated from his natal lineage, including ties with ancestors, living kin, and descendants. His identity did not grow from family tradition or organic cultural roots; it depended on the hazards of fate and on an "artificial" loyalty to authorities who were not his kin. This point helps to explain why Roman law could apply the same juridical term to captives who labored in Spanish silver mines and to privileged urban craftsmen and merchants whose *peculia* allowed them to engage in business on their own. It also helps to illuminate an ancient religious metaphor. To become a "slave" to Yahweh or Christ was not simply to imitate the humility and subservience of a bondsman. It was also to acknowledge the transference of primal loyalties and obligations to a new and awesome power, in the hope of gaining a new and transcendent freedom.

From a psychoanalytic view, all notions of authority and dependence originate in the family. Not only do parents or parental figures provide the prototypes for all relationships involving love and power but the child achieves liberation from "enslavement" to the pleasure principle by internalizing, through psychological ties with its parents, the norms of a given society. According to Freud, this socialization is bought at a heavy cost and might be described as an enslavement of instinctual needs to the reality principle. We need not take the theory literally or debate the universality of the oedipal phenomenon in its more restricted and culture-bound sense. The relevant point is that the family, whether nuclear or extended, is the prime agent of socialization and the source for later concepts of authority, subordination, security, rebellion, and identity.

This general orientation helps one understand the paradox of the slave who is given an important role within a family's domestic economy but who stands outside the delicate dynamics of kinship psychology. Deracinated from his own kinship group, the slave discovers that his own fate depends on adventitious circumstance. No brethren can protect him from arbitrary oppression or avenge his murder or sexual violation. Hence the biblical horror over a sibling rivalry that exceeded normal bounds and, stopping short of fratricide, led Judah to propose selling Joseph to Ishmaelite slave dealers. But as the story of Joseph also shows, in a lesson that would influence Islamic thought and culture, fortune could smile on even a slave, especially one who had contracted an earlier bond with the Lord.

In Egypt, Joseph was regarded as an alien and outsider, as the accusation of Potiphar's wife makes clear (she seems to have held the common assumption that a household slave was fair game for sexual exploitation, whereas Joseph seems to have regarded the overture as in some sense incestuous, or oedipal). Yet Joseph, like many later Mamluks and other Muslim slaves, became a trusted counselor, administrator, and wielder of power, all of which depended on his "freedom" from kinship ties and obligations. His eventual confrontation with his brothers and reunion with his family simply underscore the centrality of deracination. Whether the slave was degraded to the status of chattel property or elevated to that of governor of Egypt, he could be thought of as the extension of his owner's will. Such a relationship, unmediated by family restrictions or by the normal stages of generational succession, gave masters the illusion of omnipotence, of escaping the bonds of kin. It was not accidental that the concept of slavery was extended to concubines, who complemented the legal allotment of wives, or to eunuchs, whose seed could not pollute the lines of legitimate kinship descent.

If the master-slave relationship can often be described as "paternalistic," as Genovese and numerous other scholars maintain, such paternalism should not be confused with the ambivalent bond between father and child. For at least in the abstract model of "perfect slavery," the slave stands apart from the oedipal system, a fact that gave him special value in certain patriarchal and dynastic societies. By definition, he could not progress through the stages of dependency and self-assertion that would prepare him to replace his masters. His status as a fictive minor was perpetual unless suddenly ended by physical rebellion or by the transfiguring act of manumission. And as Orlando Patterson has brilliantly shown, manumission as the negation of an already negated social life could be conceived only as a sacrificial gift requiring continuing gratitude and obligations to the master and his successors. Hence "freedman status was not an end to the process of marginalization but merely the end of the beginning—the end of one phase, slavery, which itself had several stages."[18]

Nevertheless, in most societies slavery has been a domestic or household institution, an association that has not been wholly lost even in the exceptional instances where bondsmen have been regimented in labor-intensive industries. The ideal of *domesticating* captives, as we have already suggested, has always been a source of ambiguity and tension. On the one hand, there has been an almost universal pressure to assimilate bondage to a familial model of loyalty, protection, obligation, gratitude, and reciprocal duties and rewards. Over thousands of years masters have justified their dominion as natural and paternal, as if derived from biological or kinship ties. Given such an acknowledgment of their common humanity, slaves could not altogether resist the psychological processes of identification and introjection even though barred from the claims of family membership enjoyed by adopted and legitimate kin. In point of fact, the children or grandchildren of slaves were sometimes absorbed within the master's kin group even while being stigmatized as the descendants of slaves. When a master acknowledged paternity of a slave woman's children, Muslim law accorded the children freedom and full rights of inheritance. On the other hand, as the biblical example of Hagar and Ishmael suggests, such attempted assimilation could also evoke bitter conflicts over questions of legitimacy and succession. Legitimate wives and children have seldom welcomed the granting of kinlike privileges to favored slaves. And the slave who became a recognized part of the family tree ceased to be a slave.

Opposed to this assimilationist trend was the fact that the slave's chief value lay precisely in his detachment from familial structures and relationships, in his alienability and almost infinite vulnerability to the will of others. The presence of a slave, as a symbol of extreme and unmitigated dependency, could objectify the deepest human fears of loss of being, of belonging *to* instead of *in*, of becoming a nonperson, a thing. Hence the nominally free dependent could rejoice in the knowledge that he or she was at least not a slave—or be so reassured by those exercising power. The legal or formal contrast could thus mask areas of overlap between slavery and other forms of subordination and coerced labor, such as that of wives, children, clients, and serfs.

But this need for social differentiation, for a symbol of debasement that would give a shred of prestige to less total forms of subordination, was also qualified by a widespread linguistic impulse toward comparison and homogenization. From antiquity to modern times the concept of slavery has been encrusted with complex metaphorical, allegorical, and anagogical meanings. The terms for bondage and emancipation have been extended to other external conditions, as in Seneca's "A great fortune is a great slavery" or in Rousseau's "Man is born free, and everywhere he is in chains." They have also referred to an internal enslavement to sin, ignorance, passion, the will, or the unconscious id. When Jesus spoke to the Pharisees, who claimed exemption as Abraham's children from any form of slavery, he merged internal or moral freedom with the notion of legitimate succession: 'Verily, verily, I say unto you, Every one that committeth sin is the bondservant of sin. And the bondservant abideth not in the house for ever: the son abideth for ever" (John 8:31–35).

As a metaphor, slavery has been applied to the disabilities of the individual, of a collective group, and of mankind in general. Saint Paul could even speak of all creation's being delivered from slavish corruption into the liberty of the children of God. For our purposes, the most momentous tropes pertained to the history of human redemption. Early Christians, for instance, interpreted the stories of Israel's deliverance from bondage in Egypt and of Abraham's slave-born and freeborn sons as "prefigurations" of Christ's salvation of man. In more recent times Marx and Engels could proclaim with confidence that "the proletarians have nothing to lose but their chains."

Although metaphorical extensions can sometimes be dismissed as hyperbole or rhetorical artifice, it would be a mistake to think that Philo of Alexandria, for example, was merely employing figurative language when he insisted that a great king might be a slave, and a man in chains a freeman. Similarly, there was more at work than mere verbal play when Moses used the same word to refer to the Jews' slavery in Egypt and to their later bondage to Yahweh, or when Jesus announced that "he that was called in the Lord being a bondservant, is the Lord's freeman: likewise he that was called being free, is Christ's bondservant."[19]

From at least as early as the time of the Stoics, people have distinguished the literal and specific application of terms like "slavery" from the supposedly deeper meanings the terms contained. Without venturing into historical theories of language, one can affirm that virtually every vision of individual salvation or collective utopia has been defined as a release or emancipation from a genuine but final slavery. Perfect liberty, to be sure, even when conceived as security, power, or belonging, has been no more attainable than perfect and total submission. The point is that the objective example of slaves has provided a referent for symbolizing any form of constraint, dishonor, exploitation, or even socialization of mankind's pleasure-seeking instincts. If some men have seen slavery in other men's liberty, it is because the perfect antithesis of slavery can be found only in a freedom from all sense of alienation coupled with a fulfillment of all human wishes.

There is thus a wider psychological and cultural significance to the confusions surrounding the definition of "actual slavery." Metaphorical usage tells us nothing about the sociological character of particular forms of servitude. But sociological analysis and typology tell us nothing about the meanings people have attached to various kinds of dependency, constraint, and exploitation. The symbolic associations derived from slavery as an archetypal concept, a concept rooted in the notion of a human captive half domesticated to an alien household, became deeply embedded in religious and secular literature. They survived in societies such as those in western Europe where slavery itself had disappeared. Modern concepts of political, religious, civil, economic, and even psychological liberty were originally defined in reference to some form of slavery. For the institution of bondage suggested not only deracination, submission, and alienation but also "the state of War continued," in John Locke's phrase, between two antagonists with irreconcilable interests. As warfare sublimated, slavery could stand for an elemental struggle between exploiters and exploited; or for a necessary stage, as Hegel would have it, in man's individual and collective journey toward a free and autonomous consciousness; or as a model for converting people into commodities and objectifying all human relationships.

Although no antislavery protests appeared in the ancient or medieval worlds, the institution of slavery has always been a source of conceptual contradiction as well as of complex social tension. On one level, as Hegel masterfully demonstrated, the contradiction arose from the impossibility of transforming a conscious being into a totally dependent and nonessential consciousness—one whose essence is to be the mere instrument and confirmation of an owner's will. The moral problems generated by this impasse were imaginatively explored by Stoic, Jewish, and Christian thinkers, and received formal recognition in the Justinian Code. Thenceforth, Western jurisprudence acknowledged that slavery was the single instance of a practice justified by the law of nations that was also contrary to the law of nature. On a second level, as Orlando Patterson has recently argued, slavery epitomized the most extreme form of human parasitism, which necessitated deception, camouflage, and self-deception on both sides. (Patterson tends, unfortunately, to confine his discussion of self-deception to the ideology of the master class, apparently in reaction to controversial but plausible theories that many bondsmen, like many other exploited peoples, including soldiers and sailors, internalize the degraded image defined by their commanders.) Patterson goes on to make the crucial point that in most slaveholding societies "manumission became an intrinsic part of the process of slavery" as masters found it in their best interests "to exploit their slaves' yearning for freedom as a preferred form of incentive," and then to rely on cheap and easily obtainable replacements. He rightly emphasizes that the frequency of manumission usually "reinforced the master-slave relationship" and that "the volume of manumissions partly determined the number of persons to be enslaved." Yet he eloquently concludes that "the first [people in the world] to think of themselves as free in the only meaningful sense of the term, were freedmen. And without slavery there would have been no freedmen."[20]

But slavery was never simply a one-to-one relationship between conqueror and captive, as Hobbes, Locke, Hegel and other philosophers sometimes implied. While often dispersed through towns, fields, royal courts, and free households, slaves constituted a collective body or "class," even though excluded from the class or caste structures of a given society. Tensions also arose, therefore, from the ambiguous relationship between slaves and what normally was a much larger nonslaveholding population. This was especially true when military or commercial expansion brought an influx of foreign captives who displaced nominally free servants and workers while augmenting the wealth, power, and symbolic prestige of the rich. As William McKee Evans points out, such conditions frequently gave rise to a "solidarity myth" designed to affirm "the oneness of those who owned slaves and those who did not" and to assure "those whose importance had been reduced, whose labor had been cheapened, that they shared with the slaveholder a fundamental superiority."[21]

Such solidarity myths sometimes appealed to a common ethnicity or nationality, as in ancient Greece and the early Roman Republic, or to a common religious mission, as in Jewish Palestine in the period of the Second Temple. But as later Christians and Muslims would discover, religious distinctions were both impermanent and subject to conflicting pressures. During the Maccabaean wars, for example, the Jewish Tannaim, or interpreters of traditional oral law and jurisprudence (halakah), realized that the sudden increase in gentile or "Canaanite" slaves threatened the ritual purity of Jewish households. R. Eliazar affirmed the general rule "that possession of uncircumcised slaves makes it impossible for their master to participate in the paschal meal." Various halakic rulings insisted that as soon as a master acquired gentile slaves, he was obliged to circumcise the males and baptize the females. For Jews such ritual purification was a form of "progress" that transformed an unclean "Canaanite" into a "brother in the Commandments," a servant who could prepare meals, sacrifice the paschal lamb, or even vow property to the Temple. As. E. E. Urbach concludes, "slavery became an influence contributing towards proselytism, and there were many who were accepted into the Jewish faith *via* this route." Assimilation was qualified, however, by a solidarity myth based on the biblical curse of Canaan, a subject we shall discuss more fully later on. Although the emancipated slave could marry a freeborn Jewish woman and held the same legal and religious status as a proselyte, he could not escape the social stigma of his origins. As R. Eleazar b. Simeon explained:

> It would be but natural for the manumitted slave to take precedence over the proselyte, inasmuch as the slave has grown up in an atmosphere spiritualised by Jewish considerations . . . and the proselyte has not; but the ruling is because the slave had, as such, fallen within the category of the cursed (cf. *Gen.* ix 25), whereas the proselyte had never been included therein.[22]

The critical question was not whether religious conversion resulted in the slave's immediate emancipation, an expectation explicitly denied by Jews, Christians, and Muslims alike, but whether it represented the first step toward progressive and ultimately complete assimilation. As we shall see, all three faiths idealized the paternalistic household as a self-contained environment conducive to such rebirth and acculturation. But since slaves were acquired from or lost to the outside world of war and trade, the domestic sanctuary was inevitably affected by the changing fortunes of the slaveholding group. Palestinian Jews, for example, became far more fearful of manumitting or trying to assimilate foreign bondsmen after the Romans had destroyed the Second Temple, had enslaved tens of thousands of Jews, and had prohibited the circumcision of slaves. The danger of slave proselytes' appealing to Roman authorities or converting to Christianity intensified the need for in-group solidarity.[23] For people of rival faiths the household ideal was also compromised by the dramatic vicissitudes of Mediterranean war and commerce. Neither laws nor religious scruples could prevent Jews, Christians, and Muslims from selling captives and even coreligionists in the most lucrative foreign markets. Finally, the ideal of conversion and assimilation was further strained wherever slaves replaced the more traditonal forms of conscripted labor in such enterprises as mining, public works, and large-scale commercial agriculture.

3. SLAVERY AND IMPERIAL EXPANSION

From the time of Aristotle, numerous commentators felt the need to justify slavery not simply as a punishment prescribed for certain peoples but as a positive benefit for masters and slaves alike. This need was never felt so acutely as in the nineteenth-century American South, which confronted the libertarian heritage of the Enlightenment as well as the related and newer doctrine that bondage universally impeded the moral and material progress that was the birthright of the human race.

Although Southerners staked much of their case on the alleged inferiority of Africans—as Aristotle had done with respect to non-Greek "barbarians" of any kind—they felt that it was insufficient to argue that Negroes either were inherently incapable of freedom or would require many generations of servitude as training for the responsibilities of civilized life. In an age attuned to classical models and precedents, educated Southerners found their own way of life mirrored by passages from Aristotle, Plutarch, Polybius, Livy, Tacitus, Cato, and Pliny. They therefore invoked the examples of ancient Greece and Rome to show that slavery could provide the necessary foundation or "mudsill" for the highest achievements of freedom and civilization. Roman slaveholders, George Frederick Holmes pointed out, "conquered the world, legislated for all succeeding ages, and laid the broad foundations of modern civilization and modern institutions." As Holmes implied, ancient precedents could point the way toward even more glorious triumphs of the human will and spirit. In the words of William Henry Holcombe, "African slavery is no retrograde movement . . . but an integral link in the grand progressive evolution of human society as an indissoluble whole." Looking ahead, in 1860, to an age of empire building that would far surpass that of Rome, Holcombe hailed slavery as

> the means whereby the white man is to subdue the tropics all around the globe to order and beauty, and to the wants and interests of an ever-expanding civilization. . . . From this time forth, the subjugation of tropical nature to man; the elevation and christianization of the dark races, the feeding and clothing of the world, the diminution of toil and the amelioration of all the asperities of life, the industrial prosperity and the peace of nations, and the further glorious evolutions of Art, Science, Literature and Religion, will depend upon the amicable adjustment, the co-ordination, the indissoluble compact between these two social sys-

tems, now apparently rearing their hostile fronts in the northern and southern sections of this country.[24]

As it turned out, whites found other means of subduing and exploiting the tropics while formally condemning slavery as a "retrograde movement." Antislavery dogma consequently tended to obscure earlier historical connections between slavery and symbols of progress. Assuming that cultural achievement could never depend on moral evil, most historians and classicists tended to ignore ancient slavery or to regard it as a deplorable defect unrelated to the glories of Greece and Rome. In Part 2 I shall have more to say about this persistent impulse to relegate ancient slavery to a purely moral sphere.[25] At this point I should stress that it is not my purpose to suggest that slavery has been an unsuspected key to human progress, or even to analyze the actual effects of slavery on economic growth or on the development of science and technology.[26] It is sufficient to call attention, in a brief overview, to the ways imperial expansion encouraged mass enslavement as a means of consolidating the power and promoting the interests of civilizations that not only regarded themselves as the carriers of light and truth but that also made unquestionable contributions to modern conceptions of progress.

Before comparing three examples of such expansion, we must ask a preliminary question: Did the ancients themselves perceive any connection between slavery and human progress? According to the traditional view, expounded by Walter Bagehot and John B. Bury, this is an anachronistic question since the ancients had no "idea of progress" in the modern sense. More recently, however, Ludwig Edelstein and Robert Nisbet have challenged this belief. Marshaling innumerable quotations, ranging from Xenophanes to Seneca, they and other scholars have contended that the Greco-Roman world produced visions of intellectual and social improvement that anticipated the most optimistic assessments of Condorcet. Yet, as Eric R. Dodds reminds us, the same classical authorities recognized "the permanence of the irrational and unteachable elements in human nature" and often expressed their belief in the myth of eternal recurrence or their nostalgia for a mythical golden age. According to Dodds, it was only in fifth-century Greece that the idea of progress was "widely accepted by the educated public at large"—a period, we might note, in which a recent and dramatic increase in the number of foreign slaves had evoked or reinforced a general contempt for manual labor. And though the philosophers most attuned to science would continue to celebrate "the concept of *technē*—that is to say, the systematic application of intelligence to any field of human activity," most of the "optimists" cited by Edelstein and Nisbet also feared that technological advance would feed new desires, encourage moral decay, and lead to a day of catastrophe: "Cities that an age has built," wrote Seneca, "an hour obliterates."[27]

Ancient views of slavery and progress must be interpreted within this mixed context of pride in human achievement, respect for the vicissitudes of fate, and yearning for rustic or pastoral simplicity. For example, slave revolts and servile wars were sometimes seen as providential punishment for collective pride and greed, a threat unknown to the supposedly virtuous inhabitants of a lost golden age. On the other hand, Athenaeus quoted from Pherecrates' play *The Savages* a presumably commonplace observation: "For in those days there was no Manes and no Sekis to be anyone's slave, but women had to do all the hard work around the house themselves. And in addition they had to grind corn early in the morning so that the village would echo to the noise of the mills."[28]

It is often forgotten that Aristotle's famous defense of slavery is embedded within his discussion of human "progress" from the patriarchal village, where "the ox is the poor man's slave," to the fully developed polis, where advances in the arts, sciences, and law support that perfect exercise of virtue which is the goal of the city-state. Barbarians, according to Aristotle, make no distinction between slaves and women, for they are, in effect, a "community of slaves" who lack a natural leader. But while nature has obligingly designed barbarians to be slaves, such natural, animate "tools" are also indispensable for the well-being of the household and the polis. Aristotle admitted that "if every tool were able to perform its particular function when it was given the order or realised that something had to be done (as in the story of Daedalus' statues or Hephaestus' tripods which Homer describes as 'entering the assembly of the gods of their own accord'), so that shuttles would weave cloth or harps play music automatically, then master craftsmen wouldn't need assistants, nor masters slaves." For some modern readers this passage has seemed to anticipate automation, or at least the displacement of slaves by technology, and thus undercuts the need for believing in "natural slaves." But since Aristotle envisioned slaves as an elemental and permanent constituent of the household—in contrast, for example, to the changeable constitutions of civil government—he no doubt intended the image of automata to suggest no more than the *instrumental* character of the ideal slave. In the household this meant knowing how to carry out every command in order to provide slaveholders with the leisure necessary for politics, philosophy, or simply the good life of happiness and virtue. Under ideal circumstances, Aristotle also affirmed, the land should be cultivated *only* by slaves, preferably by men who were not from the same tribe or nation and who were not "too courageous."[29]

Ancient concepts of progress focused on the cumulative advance of knowledge, including the applied arts and sciences. Since most writers took slavery for granted, they seldom made explicit connections between what Marxists would later term the "base" and "superstructure" of their societies. Insofar as Athenians dated their progress toward political freedom from Solon's reforms of the early sixth century, there was an implicit connection between the exemption of citizens from enslavement for debt and an increasing reliance on the labor of foreign captives. From the perspective of the late fifth or early fourth century, it was clear that the freedom and prosperity of Athenians had advanced as foreign bondsmen had increasingly replaced Greeks in the most arduous and degrading occupations. Thus Xenophon, after noting the immense private fortunes made from the labor of slaves in silver mines, offered a proposal that would bring more equal benefits to the entire free community: "just as private individuals who buy slaves are provided with a continuous income, so the community too should acquire public slaves, until there would be three for each Athenian citizen."[30]

Livy and other Latin historians could also look back to a turning point, in the fourth century B.C., when the abolition of debt bondage had brought "a new birth of freedom" to the Roman people. While debtors were sometimes still imprisoned or even sold on the other side of the Tiber, the need for conscripturing soldiers from the population of peasant farmers contributed to a solidarity myth that differentiated Roman citizens from the various groups of foreigners who could be enslaved with impunity. It is true that Posidonius and other Stoic philosophers expressed concern over the lethal conditions in Spanish silver mines, where slaves were forced to labor night and day in underground excavations in order to produce "unbelievably large revenues for their masters." Some of the philosophers who exulted over the promise of science and technology were also alarmed by the Romans' ostentatious display of slaves and wealth. The heroes of the early republic, it was said, had been content to travel with a few personal servants. Yet such attacks on extravagance seldom questioned the desirability of profits from improvements in productivity. The "ancient consensus," according to Thomas Wiedemann, "was that, as long as the farm manager was competent, slaves would produce greater surpluses everywhere except on marginal land, and on land so far away that the owner could not supervise it regularly." From Plato onward, even the visions of a utopian society toward which humans might evolve assumed the continuing existence of slaves. There is no indication that the Cynic, Stoic, and Epicurean critics of a corrupt or "sick" society ever contemplated the abolition of slavery. Progress, however conceived in the ancient world, was fully compatible with human bondage.[31]

Moving on from such questions of moral and symbolic meaning, we should note that the history of slavery in the Western world was profoundly affected by three explosive surges of imperial expansion. In the two and one-half centuries following the First Punic War, of the mid-third century B.C., the Romans won mastery of an empire that extended from Syria to England and from the Black Sea to Morocco. In approximately one hundred years, beginning with the Arab conquests of Iraq, Syria, and Egypt in the 630s and 640s A.D., the Arabs and their Muslim converts conquered an area that reached from the Pyrenees to the Indus and that included Spain, southwestern France, North Africa, Armenia, Caucasia, Iran, and much of modern Pakistan. Again, in approximately one hundred years, beginning with the explorations of the West African coast in the mid-fifteenth century, Portugal established a seaborne empire comprising forts and trading posts in Japan, Malaysia, India, and along both eastern and western African coasts, and sugar colonies in Madeira, São Tomé, and Brazil. Meanwhile, in less than half a century, Spain conquered a New World empire extending from Santo Domingo to Santiago and Buenos Aires.

Neither the Romans nor the Arabs nor the Iberians established empires for the purpose of acquiring slaves. None of the invading powers enslaved, en masse, the nations they conquered. But while statistics can be little more than guesses, especially for the chaotic and sparsely documented period of early Islamic expansion, there can be little doubt that the three epic periods resulted in the enslavement of captives on a scale unmatched in previous human history.[32] To be sure, one can point to equally ruthless slaughter and enslavement in various continents; from antiquity to the great Mongol invasions of the thirteenth century, the steppes of central Asia were especially vulnerable to raiders who captured and displaced populations over vast geographic areas. What really distinguished the Romans, Arabs, and Iberians was their long-term success in administering and integrating their empires, and in transforming the institutions and cultures of many of the regions they conquered. The Roman Empire, which survived as a single political unit for at least six hundred years, bequeathed to Christian Europe the juridical and philosophical foundations for modern slavery. The Islamic empires, though soon divided by schism and civil war, diffused normative rules and expectations regarding slavery that persisted to the mid-twentieth century. The Iberians, who drew on both Roman and Islamic models, not only established the institutions of black slavery and plantation agriculture in the New World but also sustained them for nearly four hundred years. Whatever the relation between slavery and material progress, these examples unmistakably linked the institution with the spectacular accumulation of private wealth and power.

Before proceeding further, we must note certain fundamental differences. Although slaves were ubiquitous in the Islamic world, the Arab conquests did not lead to genuine slave societies except perhaps in a few regions that specialized in mining or intensive agriculture. In distinguishing a "genuine slave society," I follow the criteria of M. I. Finley, who argues that it is not so much the number or even the proportion of slaves that counts but rather their role in basic production and their central place in a given social structure. Hence the universal presence of slaves in Muslim harems, households, and armies cannot be equated with the slave labor force on which the ancient Italian and early modern Brazilian economies depended.[33]

The Iberian governments tried to be more discriminating than the earlier Romans and Arabs in protecting various ethnic groups from enslavement. Beginning in the early sixteenth century, for example, Spanish authorities devised elaborate and only partially successful rules to prevent the wholesale enslavement of Amerindians. Somewhat later the Portuguese crown tried to prohibit its subjects from capturing or buying Japanese and Chinese slaves. Although Portuguese adventurers began capturing their own black or Moorish slaves in Mauretania as early as the 1440s, and Iberians forcibly enslaved tens of thousands of Amerindians in the first half of the sixteenth century, both Portuguese and Spaniards increasingly relied on captives purchased from people who were not their subjects. It is true that the Romans, after the conquests of the middle and late republic, also bought slaves from specialized merchants, from pirates, and even from their barbarian enemies, although a much more important source seems to have been foundlings from the provinces. Muslims, too, after the era of intercontinental conquest, purchased slaves from Christian and Jewish traders; in the sixteenth and seventeenth centuries, such middlemen bought from the Crimean Tatars hundreds of thousands of Polish and Russian captives who were dispersed throughout the Ottoman Empire.[34] But the Iberians were the first whites to gain direct access by sea to the populations of sub-Saharan West Africa. They and their successors from northwestern Europe never confronted the problem of a dwindling supply of slaves (as the Ottomans did after the Russian conquest of the Crimea). A further point of contrast is that the Iberians transported African slaves across the Atlantic to depopulated and uncultivated regions, whereas Romans and Muslims normally imported slaves into regions that had long been settled.

A slave society emerged at the very center of the Roman Empire, that is, in central and southern Italy and Sicily. In this region the influx of perhaps two million foreign captives provided the fuel for an agrarian revolution that freed landlords from a competitive labor market. The importation of slaves enabled landowners to consolidate large estates and to evict the small farmers who supplied the manpower for military conquest but who also vastly increased the population of plebeian Rome. According to Keith Hopkins, the elite recognized the hazards of reducing citizens to a state of quasi-bondage; but "slavery allowed the rich to enjoy the fruits of conquest by exploiting outsiders instead of insiders, without provoking a sharp break in the political culture."[35] In contrast, a vast ocean separated modern European states from most of the social consequences of their colonial labor systems. Though for a time Portugal and Spain imported considerable numbers of African slaves, during the sixteenth and seventeenth centuries the gap continued to widen between the labor systems and social institutions of the metropolitan and colonial societies. The expansion of Islam produced a third and wholly distinct variant as prisoners of war, representing every social rank and a diversity of ethnic and religious groups, were enslaved and melded within new Islamic polities. Jihads, or holy wars against the infidels, helped to maintain slavery as an accepted part of Muslim societies. But as symbols of prestige, patriarchal power, and sexual affluence, Muslim slaves became integrated for the most part into the economy of households and into the military and administrative structures of various dynasties.[36]

During one period Roman imperial slaves performed administrative functions rather similar to those of the trusted slaves of later Muslim caliphs and sultans. But whereas Muslim slaves augmented the military power and thus the independence of rival dynasties from Spain to Bengal, the Roman government kept a close check on the independence of wealthy, slaveholding magnates and relied on a military force constituted in part of citizen peasants, many of whom had been displaced on the land by slaves. Only the Muslims chose on a regular basis to recruit large numbers of professional soldiers through enslavement. Slave soldiers sometimes proved indispensable for the defense of Iberian and other Christian colonies, but they were always used with reluctance and fear, as a last resort. And while slaves increased the power and local autonomy of Iberian planters, they played no appreciable role in the imperial bureaucracy, which was centrally administered by the metropolitan governments.[37]

Our knowledge of the barbarities of West Indian and North American slavery depends largely on evidence supplied by foreign travelers, by abolitionists, and by slaves or ex-slaves themselves. Such sources are rare or nonexistent for periods before the eighteenth century. Nevertheless, there can be no doubt that slaves were often treated with inhuman cruelty by Romans, Muslims, and Iberians alike. The Romans institutionalized the torture of slaves as a normal part of judicial interrogation and even as a spectator sport (it should also be noted, however, that various African, Amerindian, and Asian societies gloried in the ritual torture and killing of slaves). Yet the Iberians never looked upon certain classes of slaves as carriers of culture and refinement, as the Romans looked upon the more educated captive Greeks. And though Muslim masters often manumitted large numbers of slaves as a demonstration of religious peity, they do not seem to have rivaled the Romans in massive emancipations or in according full citizenship to many former slaves. Finally, the Iberians deserve the dubious credit for gradually *restricting* bondage, for the first time in history, to peoples of African descent, and thereby broadening the category of "nonenslavable peoples."

Apart from these and other critical differences, the three periods of imperial expansion exhibit certain striking parallels. Within a relatively brief period, a militant, expansive power enslaved tens or even hundreds of thousands of foreigners of diverse geographic origins. The scale alone, coupled with centralized slave markets and a continuing demand for slave labor, distinguishes the Roman, Arab, and Iberian examples from earlier or contemporary societies, with the possible exception of Athens during the classical period. Exception might also be made for the various Mongol and Turkish conquests in the east and for the expansion of Mali and other African states in the western Sudan. In both cases, however, the growth of a slave trade became closely linked with the geographic extension and power of Islam.

The point to be emphasized about the Roman, Arab, and Iberian conquests is that the expansion of slavery, even when taken for granted, was part of what later writers perceived as a miraculously rapid expansion of civilization and light. As we have seen, nineteenth-century Southerners made much of the argument that a not-so-peculiar institution had underpinned the glories of Greece and Rome. A modern scholar agrees at least that "democracy in Athens and plebeian privileges in Rome were made possible by the combination of imperial conquest and slavery."[38] With certain qualifications the point can be extended to later historical links between slavery and the growth of long-distance commerce, of urban crafts and industries, and of large-scale agricultural production. Though far less numerous than in ancient Athens and Rome, slaves were ubiquitous in the Byzantine Empire; in the great Muslim seats of learning, science, and art; in Spain during the brilliant Umayyad dynasty of Cordoba; and in Renaissance Spain and Portugal. The importation of tens of thousands of slaves into Venice and Tuscany, in the late fourteenth and fifteenth centuries, was partly a response to devastating epidemics that led to labor shortages and economic contraction; yet the presence of such "domestic enemies," as Petrarch termed them, hardly stymied cultural and intellectual achievement in Renaissance Italy. Although slave labor seldom increased the output of Islamic economies—and Egypt's continuing importation of Mamluks probably contributed to a balance-of-payments crisis in Egypt's foreign trade, aggravating the general economic depression of the fifteenth century—the various periods of Islamic resurgence depended on imperial conquests by new converts, such as the Almoravids, Seljuk Turks, and Songhay, all of whom revivified human bondage.[39]

One should add, as a qualification, that since slaves were commonly traded along with gold, ivory, spices, salt, wine, and other luxury goods, it was only natural for them to appear in the major international markets, in the more thriving towns and cities, or wherever long-distance commerce flourished. If the astonishing medieval demand for pepper and salt reflected a lack of refrigeration and an impoverished cuisine, the demand for slaves reflected a world in which there were few purchasable commodities that signified private wealth, leisure, and power. In the Mediterranean basin, whether under Christian or Muslim rule, the continuing transfer of slaves was more often the result than the cause of commercial growth.

On the other hand, one cannot lightly dismiss the remarkable coincidence of slavery with commercial expansion, particularly in view of the nineteenth-century ideology that pictured all bondage as inherently subversive to human progress. There is no clear evidence that slavery prevented technological innovation in Roman mining and agriculture, as antislavery dogma later maintained, or that it contributed to the decline and fall of the empire. The institution did not stifle science, learning, or urbanization among the Arabs; nor did it disappear from the more prosperous and "culturally advanced" portions of medieval Europe. Indeed, slavery was closely associated with the commercial transactions between Muslim and Christian states, with the rise of Venetian and Genoese trading ventures and Mediterranean colonization, and with the voyages and settlements that prepared the way for Columbus and Vasco da Gama. And by the beginning of the sixteenth century, a momentous change had already occurred. Instead of being symbols of luxury, slaves were producing articles of luxury for a new consumer class. Paramount among such luxuries was an exotic commodity—sugar. By the time of Columbus's fateful voyages to America, much of Europe's sugar came from Portuguese plantations on which the majority of workers were black.[40]

4. THE EXPANSION OF ISLAM AND THE SYMBOLISM OF RACE

In some ancient languages the word for "slave" simply connoted labor or service. In other languages, however, the word referred at first to the foreign origin of captives, even if it later extended, as in the Third Dynasty of Ur (2345–2308 B.C.), to in-group debt slaves and children who had been sold by their parents. In ancient India the word *dasa* originally referred to the dark-skinned Dravidian people conquered by Aryan invaders. It later came to mean "slave," even though fewer Dravidians seem to have ended up in slavery than in the lowest rungs of the caste system or, worst of all, in the ritually unclean category of untouchables. By the Buddhist period slavery had lost its ethnic connotations and a *dasa* could well be light-skinned.[41]

The origin of the European variants of "slave" presents a somewhat different transition from ethnic reference to a generalized category of "enslavable barbarian." During the late Middle Ages, the Latin *servus* and other ethnically neutral terms gradually gave way to *sclavus,* the root of *schiavo, esclavo, esclave, sclau, Sklave,* and "slave," all meaning a person of "Slavic" origin. According to Charles Verlinden, *sclavus* had as early as the tenth century become legally synonymous with "slave" in the parts of Germany through which pagan Slavic captives were transported to Muslim Spain. But this usage virtually disappeared with the decline of the Umayyad dynasty and the eclipse of the overland trade in slaves to the west. Italian merchants continued to buy large numbers of genuinely Slavic prisoners along the Dalmatian coast, but only in the thirteenth century did they begin to tap one of the most continuously productive sources of slaves in human history—the peoples from Caucasia to the eastern Balkans who were repeatedly subjugated by invaders from Central Asia. Representing a multitude of languages and cultures, these captive Armenians, Circassians, Georgians, Abkhazians, Mingrelians, Russians, Tatars, Albanians, and Bulgarians were no more a distinct people than were the "Negroes" who later ended up as American slaves. By the early thirteenth century, however, these "Slavs," who were highly prized in Egypt, Syria, Cyprus, Sicily, Catalonia, and other Mediterranean markets, had begun to transform the European words for chattel slaves, as distinct from native serfs. Italian notaries applied the label *sclavus* not only to non-Slavic peoples from the Black Sea but also to Muslim captives from such reconquered regions as Majorca and Spain. In 1239 a Corsican notary used *sclava* in recording what Verlinden interprets as the sale of "une négresse captive." The rapid extension of *sclavus* to people of non-Slavic origin suggests a growing assumption that true slavery was appropriate only for pagans and infidels who shared the supposed characteristics of "Slavs," which were almost identical with the later "sambo" stereotype of North American blacks. Since Portugal remained on the periphery of the Slavic slave trade but became increasingly involved in religious warfare with Muslim North Africa, the word *escravo* had to compete with such terms as *mouro, guineu,* and *negro.* Later on, the French *noir* and English "black" became virtual synonyms for "slave." Much earlier, the Arabic word for slave, *'abd,* had come to mean only a black slave and, in some regions, to refer to any black whether slave or free.[42]

In antiquity, however, bondage had nothing to do with physiognomy or skin color. It is true that various Greek writers insisted that slavery should be reserved for "barbarians," but they considered Ethiopians no more barbarous than the fair Scythians of the north. Skin color and other somatic traits they attributed to the effects of climate and environment. Although it would appear that the ancients put no premium on racial purity and were unconcerned with degrees of racial mixture, we still have much to learn about the changing origins and status of black slaves. The first difficulty arises from the vagueness of such ancient designations as "Ethiopian" and "Kushite" as well as the more modern label "Negro." As a result of nineteenth-century racist theories, scholars have long contrasted the supposedly superior craniology of "Nilotic types" with the prognathism and facial angle of "pure Negroes." Such a "mismeasure of man," to use Stephen Jay Gould's phrase, is not only arbitrary but generally assumes that cultural differences are determined or can be explained by physical traits.[43] Of all the myths surrounding slavery and human progress, none has been more insidious and enduring than the image of sub-Saharan Africans as a single, benighted race condemned to a perpetual coma of savagery except when infused, on the northern fringes of the Dark Continent, with the blood or inspiring example of Eurasian peoples.

We now know that the peoples of prehistoric Africa, like those of other continents, migrated over immense geographic regions, created rich and highly diverse cultures, and developed trading networks that spanned much of the continent. The desiccation of the vast Sahara region had, by the third millennium B.C., increasingly isolated the central and western Sudan from the early civilizations of the Mideast. But African farmers south of the Sahara were the first to domesticate the sorghums and millets that later became valued crops in the Mideast. The southward diffusion of agriculture and cattle husbandry, to say nothing of the rapid spread of metallurgy, especially ironworking, throughout West Africa, provide ample evidence of adaptive and intercommunicating cultures. For the Egyptians, Phoenicians, Greeks, and Romans, however, sub-Saharan Africa remained a land of legend and fantasy, sharply differentiated from the familiar North African states and colonies from the Nile to the Maghrib.[44]

It is of considerable importance that the Nile offered the only corridor between the Mediterranean and the African tropics, providing continuous contact with blacks who had long interacted with the urban civilizations of Egypt and the Mideast. Judging by the surviving iconography, blacks exhibiting a diversity of physical traits were numerous in Egypt after the fifteenth century B.C. Many of these blacks were portrayed as enemy warriors or captive slaves. But dark-skinned Nubians ruled Egypt during the Twenty-fifth, or "Ethiopian," Dynasty and later built temples and pyramids at their capital city, Meroë, above the fifth cataract of the Nile. As the crossroads of African, Asian, and Mediterranean cultures, the Nile valley clearly hastened ethnic and genetic intermixture; but only in racially conscious modern times would it seem important to insist that Nubians, Kushites, or even Ethiopians were not "true Negroes." If some classical writers looked upon blacks as primitive people who lived in a torrid land inhabited by crocodiles, giraffes, and leopards, they saw nothing incongruous about armies of disciplined black warriors or such black pharaohs as Taharqa, whose features later generations would identify as unmistakably "Negroid." The crucial point, which was transmitted to medieval Europe, was the association of blacks with ancient Egypt.[45]

In Egyptian and especially Hellenistic sculptures, murals, mosaics, plaquettes, masks, phials, vases, and jewelry, one encounters a complete spectrum of "Negro" types. They include musicians, dancers, acrobats, boxers, jugglers, grooms, gladiators, charioteers, household servants, and soldiers. Insofar as these images depicted actual models and were not mere variants on artistic conventions, most of the models may well have been slaves. If so, the dignity and expressive individuality with which they were usually portrayed stand in marked contrast to the racist stereotypes of later slave societies. Such iconographic evidence does not prove that the ancient world was free from racial prejudice. It does suggest, however, that there was no conventional equation between blackness, slavery, and limited human capability. Throughout antiquity, of course, black slaves were an exotic rarity amid massive populations of Asian and European captives.[46]

The eventual diaspora of African slaves depended on innovations in transport, such as the Arab dhows and Iberian caravels and three-masted carracks that opened the East and West African coasts to long-distance seaborne trade. Although the evidence is fragmentary, the initial innovation may well have been the westward spread of the camel and North Arabian saddle. Camels had been domesticated in southern Arabia and Somalia as early as the third millennium B.C., but, according to Richard W. Bulliet, it was sometime between 500 and 100 B.C. that the invention of the North Arabian saddle provided riders with a secure mount above the camel's hump, bracing them for combat with swords or spears. Though horses were superior for warfare, camels could traverse deserts where horses might perish; for carrying heavy loads camels also proved to be cheaper and more efficient than horse-drawn carts. Throughout the Mideast camels gradually replaced wheeled vehicles as the ordinary means of transport, and camel-breeding nomads gained control of commercial networks that stimulated the growth of such caravan cities as Mecca. During the first centuries of the Christian era, this camel-breeding nomadism appears to have spread westward from the Upper Nile along the southern tier of the Sahara to Darfur, Borku, Tibesti, and on to Mauretania. In Roman North Africa camels were sometimes used for plowing or for hauling carts, but the trans-Saharan caravan trade was developed by Bedouins, Berbers, and other camel-riding nomads who transported gold, ivory, and exotic African commodities from the Sudan to Egypt, from the Fezzan to Tripoli, and from the upper Niger to Morocco, to name only three of the shifting commercial routes. Despite the paucity of direct evidence, it is probable that well before Islam these desert caravans included black slaves who traveled mainly on foot but who were dependent on food and water carried by camel-riding merchants. The camel (often combined with horse cavalry) gave nomads a military advantage over the sedentary peoples of the Sahel and the upper savanna, and also provided the means for long-distance travel across deserts that had blocked the various Mediterranean invaders of North Africa.[47]

Religions of Mideastern origin tended to spread along the southern and western routes of trade. For example, merchants in search of aromatic gums carried Judaism and Christianity into Ethiopia; much later, Islam advanced southward in Africa mainly as a traders' religion. Although all three faiths helped to justify the enslavement of nonbelievers, as distinct from foreigners, neither the Talmud and rabbinic Mishnah, nor the Christian patristic literature, nor the Qur'an and Muslim holy law suggested that blacks were inferior beings suited by nature for bondage. Indeed, rabbinic sources distinguished the cursed descendants of Canaan from the black descendants of his brother Cush, who had supposedly established prosperous kingdoms south of Egypt. Ephraim Isaac notes that "in some Jewish sources both the children of Shem (including the Israelites) and the children of Ham [the father of Cush, Mizraim, Put, and Canaan] were described as black; the first as 'black and beautiful', the latter as 'black like the raven.' " Rabbis spoke of the beauty of Moses' Kushite (or Ethiopian) wife, of the black Queen of Sheba, and of Solomon's Kushite scribes. The famous passage in the Song of Songs "I am black but beautiful, O ye daughters of Jerusalem," appears to have read, in the Hebrew and earliest Greek versions, "I am black *and* beautiful." According to Jean Marie Courtès, Origen established the framework for later Christian exegesis when he interpreted this black "bride" as the Church of the Gentiles, prefigured by Moses' marriage to an Ethiopian wife, a symbolic "union of the spiritual Law with the Gentile nations, which in turn foreshadowed the universal Church." The rabbis were no less inclined to associate the conversion of Ethiopia with the glorious Day of Judgment. Commenting on the passage in Psalms "Gifts shall come out of Egypt; and Ethiopia shall soon stretch out her hands ['or offerings'] unto God," they imagined Ethiopians asking, in Ephraim Isaac's translation, "If the Messiah received gifts from the Egyptians who enslaved [the Israelites] how much more will he not receive from us who have never subjected them to slavery? In reaction to this, other nations will follow the Ethiopians in bringing our gifts and paying homage to the Messiah."[48]

For early Christians, Ethiopia represented the most remote and dramatically "other" nation of the known world. In the New Testament the first baptism of a non-Jew occurs when Philip the deacon, traveling south through the Gaza desert, encounters an Ethiopian eunuch riding in a chariot. The eunuch, who held "great authority" under Ethiopia's

Queen Candace and was in charge of her treasure, had been to Jerusalem to worship at the Temple. Philip's conversion and baptism of the Ethiopian became an enduring symbol for Christianizing the world. The theme appeared in Christian iconography from the third century on and was especially popular in northwestern Europe in the sixteenth and seventeenth centuries. The mixture of races in early Christian Egypt probably reinforced the appeal of universal evangelism. For example, Saint Menas, the patron saint of Alexandria, was sometimes depicted with "Negroid" features on the ampullae sold to pilgrims; in the Nubian states, which became Christianized during the seventh and eighth centuries, Menas appeared for a time as a black warrior-protector, similar to Saint George.[49] By the end of the fourth century, Ethiopian Christians were making pilgrimages to the Holy Land. Ethiopian Christians also captured infidel white slaves in the Arabian Peninsula and supplied black slaves to the labor markets of the Lower Nile. By the seventh century, when Islam began expanding beyond Arabia, the presence of numerous black slaves in Egypt and the Mideast by no means suggested that bondage was becoming a racial institution. And for Muhammad and his early Arab followers, some of whom referred to themselves as "black," all human beings were potential converts and brethren; skin color could not signify either a sinful or a pious soul.[50]

It is probable that color symbolism derived in part from astrology, alchemy, Gnosticism, or various forms of Manichaeism influenced Christian and Muslim attitudes toward black people. Until far more research has been done on this subject, one must be extremely cautious in relating black demonology to any changes in the actual enslavement or treatment of Africans. It is clear that patristic writers equated "Ethiopians" with the cosmic forces of sin and darkness and hence with the human struggle for redemption and salvation. Origen, the head of the catechetical school in Alexandria in the early third century, introduced into patristic literature the allegorical themes of Egyptian blackness and spiritual light. Didymus the Blind, who in the fourth century held the same position in Alexandria that Origen had previously occupied, asserted that "those who fall beneath the stroke of God's sword are the Ethiopians, because they all share in the malice and sin of the Devil, from whose blackness they take their name." He also spoke of the necessity of "wounding" the Ethiopians for their own good and pictured their loss of "sonship with the Devil" as a cleansing and washing that would make them "whiter than snow." Jean Marie Courtès and Jean Devisse have documented the prevalence in early Christian symbolism of Ethiopian demons and tempters, often described as ugly and evil smelling, who represented the spirit of vanity, idolatry, or fornication.

The fact that Nubian and Ethiopian Christians adhered to the Monophysite doctrine that Christ has a single nature strengthened the image of heresy in Byzantine and Roman eyes, an image later confirmed by Africa's association with Islam. As Devisse puts it: "The linking together of the four ideas—black, other, sinner, dangerous—runs throughout all the manifestations of medieval Western Christian thought. The Saracen, the 'enemy' in the epic poems, and the bird that distracts the saint at prayer are black." Gernot Rotter has also shown that Arab writers, sometimes drawing on astrological theories, depicted terrifying demons with "Negroid" traits and described gigantic Africans "as black as Satan."[51]

But the association of blackness with death, danger, evil, and grief has been common to many cultures, and it is simplistic to assume that such symbolism accounts for the growing Muslim and Christian conviction that black Africans were in some way "made" to be slaves. The first objection, as we have already seen, is that "Slavs" and other light-skinned peoples were said to have all the slavish characteristics later attributed to black Africans. The second objection is that color symbolism is usually abstract, ambiguous, and reversible. The black devils and demons of early Christian iconography were usually pure fantasies, as devoid of ethnic traits as the medieval Black Madonnas; yet in medieval Europe, which Islam had largely sealed off from Africa, specifically "Negroid" blacks were depicted among the resurrected saints on the Day of Judgment and as camel drivers or attendants in scenes of the Adoration. By the early fifteenth century one of the Magi or Kings had become an ethnically recognizable "Negro," a transformation extended in the thirteenth century to Saint Maurice, protector of the Holy Roman Empire. As Ladislas Bugner has shrewdly observed:

> Only the Devil is totally black. The whole dialectic of the black-white symbolism was developed out of an unrealism based upon the sense of salvation which allowed the possibility of passing from black to white as well as that of falling back from white to black. The black Ethiopian illustrated the state of sin insofar as the literary metaphor supported the image of an Ethiopian turned white by the grace of repentance and baptism. Could art follow the concept? . . . Was not the only way to render the image of the black Ethiopian, the figure of sin, to deny him any sort of human face in order to recognize in him the horned, fantastic creature of the Devil?
>
> On the other hand an Ethiopian purified by conversion and relieved of his blackness would no longer be distinguished from a white man. The sarcophagi of the early Christian centuries show us the Ethiopian Eunuch converted by Philip without any distinctive ethnic feature, whereas, in a parallel way, the images of demons eliminate all precise reference to a particular human type. In this case we would have the invisible "Ne-

gro" at the center of the debate, but passed over and denied from either side by the white man, in function of his idealized image on the one hand and his phantasmal image on the other.[52]

With such cautionary points in mind, it still seems likely that the derogatory meanings of blackness were intensified by religious cosmologies that envisioned spiritual progress as the triumph of the children of light over the pagan or infidel children of darkness. Color symbolism, like the garbled interpretations of the biblical curse of Canaan, provided additional justification for new patterns of enslavement shaped by the Islamization of the trans-Saharan caravan trade. For devout Muslims the crucial and troublesome question was who could legally be enslaved. Apart from Christian enemies who might be ransomed by their brethren, the answer increasingly focused on pagan Africans or on blacks of presumably pagan origin. Ironically, by enslaving or converting so many blacks and by imposing a barrier to Europe's direct knowledge of sub-Saharan Africa, Muslims contributed to Christian ignorance, mythology, and the tendency to identify blacks with Christianity's mortal and "infidel" enemy.

Islam, like Judaism and Christianity, acknowledged that bondage was an exceptional condition, a deviation from the norm of freedom that required juridical sanction and regulation. Indeed, Islam went further than Christianity, specifically forbidding its adherents to enslave fellow Muslims by force and providing detailed laws governing the relations between slaves and free persons. Like Jews and Christians, whose practices they often assimilated, Muslims regarded manumission as a pious and meritorious act. And though the Qur'an defined the slave as the absolute property of his owner, the *Shari'a,* or religious law, also emphasized the slave's human capabilities. Islamic norms accorded the domestic slave an undeniably human status in his master's household. With his master's permission, a male slave could legally marry another slave or even a free person, including his master's daughter. And while even Muslim ascetics and reformers never questioned the right of masters to copulate with as many slave concubines as they could afford to maintain, the acknowledged children of such unions were generally deemed to be free. As in ancient Athens and Rome, slaves were often entrusted with business and administrative responsibilities. Ideally, the male household slave occupied a position analogous to that of an adopted son and retained a clientlike bond with his patron even after manumission. Yet there was often a sharp discrepancy between the ideals expounded by Muslim clerics and the actual treatment of slaves, which varied according to social and economic circumstance. The ideology of religious conversion and eventual acculturation often helped to mask the realities of social and economic exploitation.[53]

Before elaborating on this point with respect to the enslavement of pagan and even Muslim blacks, we must emphasize the crucial role Islam played in opening up a vast world unknown to antiquity. Though later Christian empire builders seldom acknowledged it, Muslims initiated the expansionism and claims to universalism that later Christians associated with historical progress. As Peter Brown reminds us, "At the time when Columbus sailed to the New World, Islam was the largest world religion, and the only world religion that showed itself capable of expanding rapidly in areas as far apart and as different from each other as Senegal, Bosnia, Java, and the Philippines." Even more impressive than such intercontinental expansion was the continuing ability of Islamic culture to hold together the decentralized fragments of former empires in "a vast Islamic galaxy, pulsating with energy at innumerable points." The unifying forces that transcended continuing schisms, warfare, and dynasties included the sacred Arabic language of the Qur'an, the Hajj, or pilgrimage to Mecca, and a dedication to scholarship and cumulative knowledge that would fill all gaps in the classical Great Chain of Being. As Brown points out, "A scholar might publish in Samarkand the definitive work on arithmetic used in the religious schools of Cairo. Or, in a dialogue with colleagues in Baghdad and Hamadan, he could claim to have recovered the unalloyed teachings of Aristotle in the libraries of Fez and Cordoba."[54] Obviously, medieval Muslims never imagined that they would eventually receive grudging credit for preserving classical science and philosophy for a later and more "progressive" Christian Europe; nor did they view their impact on black Africa as a preparatory stage for the slave societies of the New World.

The triumphant Arabs of the Middle Ages, like the triumphant Europeans of the nineteenth century, never questioned their own ethnic superiority or their historic mission to carry religious truth and scientific learning to the farthest corners of an indivisible world. Having won hegemony over a major part of the former Hellenistic and Roman empires, they saw themselves as the legitimate heirs of classical civilization. The "civilized world" extended, as it had in antiquity, from the Iberian Peninsula eastward across the Mediterranean and North Africa to Egypt, Syria, and Iran. By the mid-eleventh century the only non-Muslim lands that had any claim to civilization, in Arab eyes, were those in the rival Byzantine Empire and in the distant Orient. To the north of this latitudinal belt of art, learning, and refinement lived various tribes of white barbarians—the Franks, Germans, Slavs, and Turks. To the south lived peoples no less wild and uncivilized, peoples distinguished by their black skin.[55]

Muslim concepts of race and progress were actually part of a complex and systematic "human geography," recently reconstructed by André Miquel, which related the fascinating diversity of human customs and cultures to the climatic zones and celestial spheres of a perfectly ordered cosmos. While drawing on the knowledge and conceptual categories of such late classical authorities as Ptolemy, the Alexandrian astronomer, geographer, and mathematician, Muslim geographers benefited from the detailed ethnographic reports of Muslim merchants and travelers whose inexhaustible curiosity about *Dar al-Harb,* the lands of infidelity, arose from the certitude of men who have found the ultimate religious truth. As Miquel has shown, this encyclopedic vision of human geography ranged from the mathematics of creation to the sciences of the heavens and earth; from cartography and the classification of exotic plants and animals to the history of Rome; from descriptions of the customs and government of the British Isles and infidel Spain to those of India, China, and Indonesia. To understand the standards by which Africa would be measured, one should note the Muslims' immense respect for the civilizations of India and especially of China, which stood in striking contrast to the "savagery" of the islands to the south. The Indians and Chinese, supposedly the descendants of Noah's son Japheth, had succeeded in combining science and the refinements of luxury with extensive social order and a responsible public life. For Muslim merchants, who profited from the protection of powerful states, the Asian monarchies were self-evidently just and legitimate; Muslim visitors considered any enemy of the Chinese emperor a public enemy.[56]

Although Muslim geographers corrected and amplified much of the knowledge accumulated by Ptolemy, Miquel concludes, as late as the tenth and eleventh centuries black Africa remained largely a continent of legend and mystery. Paulo Fernando de Moraes Farias goes further, showing how Arabs used empirical evidence to construct formal categorical models, such as *Zanj, Barbara,* and *Habasha,* that conformed to stereotypes of the "enslavable barbarian." Arab maps pictured the "land of the Zanj" extending eastward below the Indian Ocean but also westward along the branch of the Nile that supposedly ran from Kanem toward Ghana and the Atlantic (actually, the Upper Niger). This mixture of specific geographic and ethnic references with "free-floating" classificatory labels contributed to the ideological justifications for enslaving sub-Saharan peoples.[57]

Arab writers, especially the physicians who wrote manuals on the slave trade, elaborated on the ten traits of African blacks that had originally been specified by Galen, the most celebrated medical authority of antiquity, who in the second century A.D. had resided for a while in Alexandria. This catalog of ethnic stereotypes included blackness of skin and kinky hair; thin or sparse eyebrows; wide nostrils; thick lips; sharp, white teeth; "chapped" hands and feet; an offensive odor; eyes with large, black pupils; inferior intelligence; and an oversized penis. Black females, at least from Nubia and Ethiopia, were sometimes described as models of feminine sexuality: "a beautiful face, clear complexion, supple body, upright breasts, a slim wasit, broad shoulders, ample buttocks, and a vagina as tight and pleasurable as that of a virgin."[58] Yet the positive image of black women was limited almost exclusively to Arabic poetry in which the poet typically justified his ardor for a black concubine—much as Bryan Edwards, the eighteenth-century Jamaican historian, interrupted his defense of black slavery to sing of a "sable queen of love" whose "skin excell'd the raven plume,/ Her breath the frangrant orange bloom/ Her eye the tropick beam."[59]

By the eighth and ninth centuries, Arabic literature was already merging blackness of skin with a variety of derogatory physical and characterological traits. A presumption of color prejudice is revealed in the defensive formulas of several black poets who came to be known as "the crows of the Arabs": "Though I am a slave my soul is nobly free/ Though I am black of color my character is white"; "even though I am totally black, musk is black too, and there is no cure for my color"; "blackness doesn't hurt me as long as I possess this tongue and firm heart."[60] Rotter's pioneering work, supplemented by the research of Bernard Lewis and André Miquel, shows that for medieval Arabs, as for later Europeans, the blackness of Africans suggested sin, damnation, and the devil. Although Arab and Iranian writers usually followed classical authorities in attributing the blacks' physical traits to climatic and other environmental forces, including the astrological effects of the planet Saturn, they increasingly invoked the biblical curse of Canaan to explain why the "sons of Ham" had been blackened and degraded to the status of natural slaves as punishment for their ancestor's sin. The precise origins of this argument, which was later taken up by European Christians and expounded as unshakable dogma in the nineteenth-century American South, are still obscure. We have already noted that early rabbinic teachings distinguished the innocent black descendants of Cush from the accursed descendants of his brother Canaan; later on we shall have more to say about the significance of Jewish and Christian definitions of "Canaanites." Since all three religions accepted the genealogy presented in Genesis, in which all nations evolved from the progeny of Noah's three sons, they faced similar difficulties in interpreting the extraordinary anomaly in Genesis 9:22–27: Noah's curse fell not against his offending son Ham but against one of Ham's four sons, Canaan. When Muslim writers extended the malediction to the "sons of Ham," they devised various strategies to exempt such peoples as the Egyptians and Berbers, who had traditionally been classified as the descendants of Mizraim, a son of Ham. By the tenth century some Muslim writers reduced such complexities to the simple assertions that "Ham begot all blacks and people with crinkly hair" and that "Noah put a curse on Ham, according to which the hair of his descendants would not extend over their ears and they would be enslaved wherever they were encountered."[61]

This religious mythology, so contrary to the universal promise conveyed by the Qur'an and the *Shari'a,* was part of a wider ideological trend to identify all blacks with the most inferior and contemptible of peoples, the Zanj. One aspect of such racist stereotyping concerned physical and mental deficiencies. According to an Arabic account of the early tenth century, for example, the infants of the Zanj, Ethiopians, and other blacks were burnt by the heat while still in the womb and came out "something between black and murky, malodorous, stinking, woolly-haired, with uneven limbs, deficient minds and depraved passions." Arabic literature repeatedly emphasized the blacks' physical repulsiveness and mental inferiority, themes that merged with the geographers' descriptions of the "primitivism" of sub-Saharan peoples. In contrast to the civilized nations from the Mediterranean to China, the blacks in the tropical zone had supposedly produced no sciences or stable polities; instead, they went naked, practiced cannibalism, and lived more like animals than like human beings. Rotter shows that Arab writers frequently associated blacks with the apes, and Lewis quotes a thirteenth-century Iranian who concluded that the Zanj differed from animals only because "their two hands are lifted above the ground," and that "many have observed that the ape is more teachable and more intelligent than the Zanjī."[62]

From these premises it followed that the enslavement of blacks was as natural as the domestication of beasts of burden. According to Ibn Khaldun, the great fourteenth-century Arab historian who was born in Tunis and lived in Egypt, "the only people who accept slavery are the Negroes *[Sūdān],* owing to their low degree of humanity and their proximity to the animal stage. Other persons who accept the status of slave do so as a means of attaining high rank, or power, or wealth, as is the case with the Mameluke *[mamlūk]* Turks in the East and with those

Franks and Galicians who enter the service of the state [in Spain]." Black kings, it was alleged, sold their subjects without even pretext of crime or war. But the victims were incapable of resentment since they gave no thought to the future and had "by nature few cares and worries; dancing and rhythm are for them inborn."[63]

From the accursed "sons of Ham" to the image of carefree blacks dancing an Arabic equivalent of "the long-tailed blue," one encounters in the Middle Ages the same stereotypes used to justify North American slavery to an age increasingly attuned to spurious connections between race and human progress. Or almost the same, since nineteenth-century Americans, unlike medieval Muslims, tried to deny recognition of the blacks' military and sexual capabilities. Muslim writers often praised black slaves for their patience, piety, loyalty, benevolence, courage, and subservience, but they also amplified the other side of the stereotype: blacks were stupid, vicious, dishonest, dirty, and dominated by uncontrollable sexuality. The frequent castration of black males for Muslim masters has been described as "a complete and barbarous amputation, 'level with the abdomen.'" On whites the operation was performed with more generosity.[64] Bernard Lewis argues convincingly that the only unqualified and full-scale defense of black Africans, an essay by Jahiz of Basra, "must be understood as a parody of Shu'ūbiyya tracts [written by Persians and other non-Arabs who resented Arab privileges], intended to throw ridicule on Persian pretensions by advancing similar arguments on behalf of the lowly and despised Zanj." In other writings Jahiz stated categorically that "we know that the Zanj are the least intelligent and the least discerning of mankind, and the least capable of understanding the consequences of actions. . . ."[65]

Since most white Muslims knew blacks mainly as slaves who performed the most menial and degrading services, one must attach special significance to the diary of Ibn Battuta, who in 1352 visited the Islamic kingdom of Mali, having previously traveled from his native Morocco to India, China, Sumatra, and East Africa. Ibn Battuta was a remarkably candid and tolerant observer who had recorded his impressions of Christian and pagan states as well as cultural diversities throughout the entire Islamic world. But upon arriving at Walata, after a two months' caravan journey from Sijilmasa, south of the Atlas Mountains, he "repented" having come into the land of the blacks "because of their lack of manners and their contempt for whites." After first refusing to enter the house and accept the hospitality of a Malinke official, he concluded after the meal that there was "no good to be hoped for from these people" and decided to return at once to Morocco. He then changed his mind and even began to exclaim over the "surpassing beauty" of the Malinke women, though as a pious Muslim he was shocked by their sexual freedom and by the fact that they "go about in front of everyone naked, without a stitch of clothing on them." As Battuta saw more of the empire of Mali, he applauded the black Muslims for their punctilious observance of prayer, their insistence on wearing clean garments on Fridays, their study of the law and memorization of the Qur'an. No other people, he decided, so greatly abhorred injustice; in Mali neither travelers nor inhabitants had anything to fear from robbers or men of violence. But these virtues Battuta found difficult to reconcile with such heathen practices as matrilineal descent, the eating of carrion, and sexual permissiveness. Moreover, the pagans who lived in the gold-mining country south of Mali, Battuta pointed out, were genuine cannibals. A delegation who returned to thank the sultan for the gift of a slave girl had appreciatively smeared their faces and hands with her blood.[66]

While Ibn Battuta's moral sensibilities confirmed some of the negative stereotypes of black Africa, he expressed no revulsion at the sight of both male and female slaves working in a copper mine near Takedda or at traveling northward in a caravan that included six hundred black female slaves (earlier he had purchased a young female himself). The similarity between Muslim and later Christian racial imagery tells us less about black Africans than about the common pressures felt by a "white" ruling race intent on celebrating its own progressive civilization while keeping slaves or an underclass of freedmen in a state of permanent subordination. Racial stereotypes, in both instances, were clearly nourished by a long-term flow of slave labor from sub-Saharan Africa.

Given the scarcity and unreliability of quantitative evidence, the magnitude of the Islamic slave trade cannot be measured with any precision. We know that after the Islamic conquests of Egypt and Tripoli, the Nilotic and central Sudanese states regularly delivered slaves to the north as part of a commercial pact or as a form of tribute. Muslim domination of the long Red Sea coast ensured a continuous shipment of black slaves to Yemen, Arabia, Iraq, Iran, and eventually Muslim India, a trade that was greatly supplemented by the establishment of Qanbalu and other commercial centers south of the Horn of Africa on the Swahili coast. Meanwhile, as Berber tribes gradually converted to the new faith, the trans-Saharan caravan trade became Islamized. Ralph A. Austen, who has made the most sophisticated attempts to assess the sources of supply, the demand for black military and domestic slaves, and the fragmentary demographic evidence, estimates that in the period 900–1100 the number of black slaves exported by the trans-Saharan trade rose from a previous annual average of approximately 3,000 to 8,700, or to a total 1,740,000 persons for the two centuries. Austen also concludes that from 850 to 1000 the number of blacks exported across the Red Sea or Indian Ocean to Islamic Asia rose from an earlier yearly average of 2,400 to 9,257. For the period 1000–1200 his estimate drops to an average of 7,200 per year, which still means a total of 1,440,000 slaves for two centuries. As Austen makes clear, these are no more than informed and systematic guesses. The key point is that the importation of black slaves into Islamic lands from Spain to India constituted a continuous, large-scale migration that in total numbers may well have surpassed, over a period of twelve centuries, the African diaspora to the New World.[67]

But one can easily be misled by the fact that medieval Muslims and later Christians both looked upon blacks as primitive and inferior people especially suited for enslavement. Even apart from crucial distinctions between the economic and social needs of slave-importing regions, the relations with sub-Saharan Africa were very different. The spectacular military triumphs of the early Muslims tend to obscure the limitations of Islamic expansion. It took nine centuries and the final stimulus of a modern, European-dominated world market before the Arabs ventured out from such protected trading posts as Zanzibar, Kilwa, and Sofala into the heartland of East Africa. Supreme at times as soldiers and merchants, the Omani Arabs were anything but aggressive entrepreneurs. In East Africa they genially intermixed with native populations, contributing to a syncretized Swahili culture. To their Somali and Swahili converts they left the task of spreading Islam along with inland trade. The gold, ivory, and slaves were brought to the Arabs on the coast. Similarly, while occasional Arab travelers visited the kingdoms of the Upper Niger, the spread of Islam in the west depended on black or dark-skinned converts whose military and commercial power seemingly proved the superiority of the Arabs' deity. As Nehemia Levtzion has shown, Islam advanced in West Africa by a system of generally peaceful relays, passing from the Berbers to the Soninke and then to Malinke-speaking traders who spread the faith southward across the Sahel, or pastoral "shore" of the desert, to the fringes of the forest. The complex symbiosis between Islam and traditional native religions meant that "the Islamization of Africa became more successful because of the Africanization of Islam."[68]

This persistent mixing of races and cultures helped prevent the emergence of rigid color barriers. Mansa Musa, the fabulously wealthy black king of Mali, won fame throughout the Islamic world and even in Christian Europe for his lavish pilgrimage to Mecca in 1324, which cost a fortune in gold and slaves (in Egypt, where he was drained nearly to bankruptcy, Mansa Musa purchased Turkish slaves for his court in

Mali). Although only a small number of blacks could afford the cost of such a long pilgrimage to Mecca, many thousands benefited from the religious encouragement of manumission as an act that would be rewarded in heaven. Black slaves sometimes achieved extraordinary military and political power—as in fifteenth-century Bengal, where on occasion they controlled the throne, and in early-eighteenth-century Morocco, where they became kingmakers. The Maliki school of Muslim law, dominant in West Africa, upper Egypt, and other regions, accorded slaves unusual rights, privileges, and protections. Above all, neither the values nor the social structure of most Islamic societies encouraged capitalist enterprise—though, as we shall see, this did not preclude an indirect absorption in intercontinental commercial markets.[69] It would be a mistake, therefore, to conclude that the racist views we have found in Arabic literature were ever systematized in discriminatory laws and institutions.

On the other hand, after all such allowances are made, we are still left with some inescapable facts. The Arabs and their light-skinned converts from Morocco to Iran were the first modern people to create a continuing demand for large numbers of foreign slaves, a demand that persisted from the seventh century well into the twentieth. Muslims sought to prohibit the enslavement of conquered free Muslims and of resident Jews and Christians under the protection of Muslim states. In contrast to the practice of later Christians, such distinctions never implied that *whites* should be exempt from bondage. On the contrary, Muslims in Egypt and especially in the Maghrib (extending from Morocco along the Barbary Coast to Tunis or even Tripoli) rejoiced for many centuries in their strategic access to Christian captives, who were often seized by corsairs and sometimes sold by rival Christian merchants. Depending on the times, markets, and circumstances, Circassians, Turks, Greeks, Italians, and Spaniards were prized as concubines, servants, soldiers, and galley oarsmen. In the thirteenth century the tables were somewhat turned by Mongol invasions of the Islamic empires east of Egypt and by the Christian reconquest of Sicily, Sardinia, the Balearics, and most of Spain. A growing respect for the white barbarians of Europe is evidenced by the safe conducts that Muslim states granted to various Christian religious orders in search of slaves to be redeemed. Both in Christian Spain and in the Maghrib, the ransoming of captives became a major business as well as a source of revenue for sultans and kings. No less revealing is the fact that caliphs and sultans allowed Christian chaplains to minister to Christian mercenaries and presumably slaves, who were valued precisely because they were free from the conflicting religious loyalties that divided Islam.[70] From the first crusades to the gradual Christian repossession of the Mediterranean, European and North African states fought and traded as roughly equal powers. This circumstance helped raise both the price and the status of white slaves.

Although Christian slaves sometimes received cruel and brutal treatment (as did Muslim slaves in Europe), they were often regarded as hostages held for ransom or prisoner exchange. Unlike blacks, they were not customarily transported by caravans across hundreds of miles of desert or by lethal shiploads to the Persian Gulf and to markets as far away as Canton. Muslim travelers took it for granted that the slaves laboring in Saharan salt and copper mines and on oasis plantations would be black. In towns and households it was also assumed that the most degrading labor would be reserved for blacks. In discussing this tendency to identify the lowliest forms of bondage with blacks, Bernard Lewis notes the "complaints by black Muslim rulers about 'holy wars' launched against them to take captives, and by jurists—usually black jurists—at the enslavement of free black Muslims contrary to law."[71] Such racist tendencies might well have been reversed if the sub-Saharan peoples had been in a position to send out missionaries to ransom captives, or armies to threaten the Muslim states.

This is not to say that black Africans were the passive victims of Arab and Berber exploitation. As early as 720 the Nubians repelled an attempted Muslim invasion, agreeing to an armistice that provided for the annual delivery of several hundred slaves in exchange for wheat and other commodities.[72] In the western Sudan a tradition of strong kingdoms long preceded the arrival of Islam. Ancient Ghana, which succeeded the still earlier Soninke kingdom of Wagadu, became known to the Arabs of the late eighth century as "the land of gold." As Kharijites, Ibadites, and other religious dissidents sought refuge in the west, the Sudan also became, in Nehemia Levtzion's words, "something like the 'New World' to which people travelled to become rich." Sudanese rulers welcomed peaceful Muslim traders but were alert to ideological threats to the existing structures of authority. They were also sensitive to the usefulness of Muslim amulets, prayers, and jihads against traditional foes. In Ghana, as in other African states, blacks made selective use of Islamic beliefs and practices. Devout Muslims, who were mostly merchants and clerics, lived in segregated quarters; the rulers, as Ibn Battuta discovered in the later and more Islamized kingdom of Mali, adhered to traditional customs and symbols of power. South and southeast of Mali, it took centuries for Islam to make significant advances into the well-developed commercial towns of Hausaland and among the peoples of the Akan forest. Farther east, the "stateless" peoples south of the kingdom of Kanem continued to resist Islamic penetration, which took the form of undisguised slaving raids for the Zawila-to-Tripoli caravan trade. From one perspective, therefore, the preeminent fact appears to be the resilience of black cultures, which assimilated and Africanized Islam only along the edges of the Sahara and the Sahel, within the powerful states west of Lake Chad, and near the trading posts along the Swahili coast. Benin and the Yoruba states are prime examples of technologically advanced cultures that remained untouched. But it is also true that medieval Muslim traders had encircled the head of black Africa, from modern Tanzania to northern Nigeria, drawing slaves from distant interior regions and preparing the way for things to come.[73]

The main incentive to "progress" was gold, not slaves. In the mid-eleventh century, Almoravid expansion greatly increased the flow of gold from the western Sudan to the Maghrib and Muslim Spain. A militant and reformist Berber dynasty, the Almoravids conquered Morocco and much of Spain, destroyed the capital of Ghana, pushed the sedentary Sudanese populations southward, and enslaved large numbers of blacks in the Upper Niger region. By extending commercial and cultural networks from Spain to the Sudanese savanna, the Almoravids and their Almohad successors encouraged both the development of new goldfields and the consolidation of Mali, which controlled access to the southern sources of gold and slaves as well as the importation of horses, salt, metals, and other commodities desired by the pagans to the south. The Muslim rulers of the Sahel recognized that the supply of gold would be jeopardized by any attempts to conquer or dominate the non-Muslim blacks who actually mined (or whose slaves mined) the gold. In contrast to the central Sudan, Mali and other western states sought to protect peaceful trade as a cornucopia of revenue and local power. Still, the purchase and export of "Lamlam," as Arabs called the vulnerable stateless blacks of the south, was second in importance to gold. And such trade was especially insidious because it appeared to be reciprocal, built upon indigenous systems of labor recruitment and servitude, and because it formed a small but growing part of an invigorating intercourse with the wider world.[74]

It was more than coincidence that the northward flow of West African gold expanded when Europe's extraordinary economic growth of the eleventh and twelfth centuries led to significant exports of grain, hardware, and especially textiles. Before this era of technological and economic progress, Europe had little to offer Islamic societies besides wood, hides, and slaves. But the "rise of the West," it is now abundantly clear, was nourished by continuous interchange with the East, including distant parts of Asia, for which Muslim traders served as middlemen. Despite almost constant warfare between Christians and Muslims, North African states customarily granted Italian merchants free access to their ports. By 1253 the pursuit of gold had led Genoese merchants as far as Safi, a terminus of the caravan trade well south of Casablanca on the Moroccan Atlantic coast. In 1252 Genoa and Florence began reintroducing gold coinage to western Europe, providing a stable medium of international exchange after an extended period of economic expansion, monetary confusion, and scarcity or debasement of the standard silver coinage. Montpellier, which was part of the seafaring kingdom of Aragon, specialized in minting Arab pieces of gold for use in foreign exchange. Europe's gravitation toward the gold standard greatly increased the value of a rare metal traditionally coveted by kings, bishops, nobles, and the richer merchants. The prosperity of Mansa Musa's Mali empire owed much to the growth of an insatiable European market for gold.[75]

This point illuminates the significance of the famed Catalan Atlas, or "map of the world," which the infante Juan of Aragon presented in 1381 as a gift to the newly crowned Charles VI of France. The map had been made in Majorca, then part of Aragon, by the great Jewish cartographer Abraham Cresques. In West Africa the map portrayed Mansa Musa as a crowned and stately king holding and contemplating an enormous gold nugget. The inscription described him as "lord of the Negroes of Guinea. . . . The richest, the most noble lord in all this region on account of the abundance of gold that is gathered in his land."[76] If the trans-Saharan trade was still a mystery to most Christians, the Catalan Atlas served notice to Europe of Aragonese knowledge and power.

From Roman and Visigothic times, Spain had maintained close ties with the Maghrib. It was only after 1212, however, following the decisive Muslim defeat at the battle of Las Navas de Tolosa, that the united realms of Aragon and Catalonia began to challenge Genoa, Pisa, Venice, and other Italian cities for control of the western Mediterranean. From the thriving Catalan port of Barcelona, expeditions conquered Majorca, Sicily, and Sardinia; Catalan commercial companies, which included nobles and bourgeois, Christians, Jews, and Muslims, established trading centers in the Maghrib and as far east as Greece. In one recorded period of fifty-three days, in 1284, thirty-one ships sailed from Majorca to the Maghrib. The Italians and eventually the Portuguese were no less enterprising in establishing trading posts that sometimes extended into the desert. Such competition increased the complexity of intercontinental trade. Along with gold, slaves, dates, sugar, and caraway seeds, the towns of the Maghrib distributed produce from Egypt and Syria; Majorca reexported similar goods to the Iberian coast and Italy. In the mid-fifteenth century the Venetian explorer Ca da Mosto reported that Arabs divided slave caravans at Wadan so that "one part was taken to Barca and then to Sicily, one part to Tunisia, another to the coasts of Barbary, and a fourth to the Portuguese in Arguin."[77]

The importation of black slaves into Europe at that time is less significant than the impact of European "progress" on the structure of sub-Saharan societies. The demand for gold evoked a reciprocal African demand for horses, fine textiles, and weapons—including, eventually, firearms. The states that profited most from intercontinental trade were the best equipped and most highly motivated to gather large numbers of slaves. When Diogo Gomes reached the mouth of the Gambia River, in the mid-fifteenth century, he found that the Islamized Malinke rulers had already established a long-distance trade with Timbuktu, shipping salt up river in exchange for gold and slaves.[78] If the Portuguese "discovery" of West Africa inaugurated a new era in the history of human bondage, it also extended patterns that long antedated the revolutionary expansion of Europe.

5. FROM WHITE TO BLACK: EUROPEAN EXPANSION AND THE CHANGING SOURCES OF SLAVES

If one takes the New World as a whole, one finds that the importation of African slaves far surpassed the flow of European immigrants during the first three and one-third centuries of settlement. From Brazil and the Caribbean to Chesapeake Bay, the richest and most coveted colonies—in terms of large-scale capital investment, output, and value of exports and imports—ultimately became dependent on black slave labor. Yet the enslavement of whites persisted and at times even flourished on both Christian and Muslim shores of the Mediterranean and the Black seas, in eastern Europe and Russia, and even in western Europe, where lifelong sentences to the galleys became an acceptable and utilitarian substitute for capital punishment. And as David W. Galenson reminds us, "the use of bound white laborers preceded the use of black slaves in every British American colony, and it was only after an initial reliance on indentured servants for the bulk of their labor needs that the planters of the West Indies and the southern mainland colonies turned to slaves."[79] Despite the gains of recent scholarship, a full explanation of the transition from white and Amerindian servitude to Afro-American slavery must await more detailed studies of every colony, of transatlantic transport, and of the changing labor markets in the Americas, Europe, and especially Africa. For the Africanization of large parts of the New World was the result not of concerted planning, racial destiny, or immanent historical design but of innumerable local and pragmatic choices made in four continents. The following discussion can do no more than trace some important continuities between such choices and point to the often bitterly ironic connections between the extension of black slavery and white concepts of progress.

The story begins, as I have already suggested, with the revival of the ancient Mediterranean slave trade that accompanied the early expansion of western Europe. Abolitionist historians and later believers in synchronized moral and material progress have tended to ignore this subject while making much of the indisputable decline in the number of slaves from the late Roman Empire to the tenth century. Although the causes of this earlier transformation are still a matter of controversy, the period was marked by a general decline in total population, commodity production, trade, physical security, and the status of formerly free peasants. Beginning in the tenth century, however, a population boom helped to stimulate an increase in productivity, the creation of an economic surplus, the rise of merchant and craft guilds, and the transformation of local markets and places of refuge into self-governing towns. Internal changes within the feudal hinterland, including innovations in agriculture and technology, enabled western Europe to take advantage of the commercial leadership of the Italian city-republics. Specifically, when the Pisans, Venetians, and Genoese gained control of much of the eastern trade that had earlier been monopolized by Greeks, Arabs, Syrians, and Jews, they could count on funds for investment as well as extensive internal markets for spices, silk, indigo, sugar, and slaves.[80]

The trade in foreign slaves was simply one manifestation of Italian cosmopolitanism and business enterprise. In the case of Genoa, as Robert S. Lopez observes, "it was the merciless Arab raids of the early tenth century that forced the fishermen and agriculturists to fight back, capture booty, and learn the advantages of robbing, buying, and selling commodities of foreign countries. Unlike many other fighters of the Christian frontier, who just became Crusaders or Junkers, the Genoese were quick learners."[81] As they scrambled to catch up with their Venetian rivals, the Genoese learned how to profit from the Castilian and Portuguese reconquests of southern Iberia, how to establish direct maritime trade with London and Bruges, and how to exploit commercial bases or colonies in the eastern Mediterranean. Genoese merchants bought and transported anything for which they could find new markets—grain, cheese, salt, fish, wine, sugar, alum; Senegalese gold; fine cloth and linen from northern Europe; silk, spices, and other luxury goods from the Orient; Moorish slaves from Spain and pagan or Christian slaves from the Balkans, Greece, and the Black Sea. Papal edicts were powerless in curbing an entrepreneurial spirit that led Genoese financiers to lend millions of ducats to the Spanish crown, and Genoese traders to sell thousands of Christian slaves to the Muslims of Syria and Egypt. What needs to be stressed is that such unscrupulous slave trading was part of a general defiance of traditional restraints and limits that made Genoa a crucible of economic and maritime innovation. According to Lopez, by the thirteenth and fourteenth centuries Genoa had also become a relatively open and egalitarian society that excluded noblemen from public offices and provided "plentiful opportunities for the humblest sailor and huckster to raise his income."[82]

The connections between slavery and commercial progress are most dramatically revealed in the rapid expansion and ultimate contraction of Mediterranean sources of foreign labor. From Palestine, where the rival Italian cities established their first colonial outposts, the crusading soldiers and entrepreneurs of western Europe encroached upon the domains of an enfeebled Byzantine Empire. In 1204 the capture and sacking of Constantinople, during the Fourth Crusade, opened the Aegean and Black seas to Italian merchant colonizers. The Venetians had long marketed slaves acquired along the Dalmatian coast, and now led the way in building colonial trading posts along the shores of the Black Sea. Tana, their main slave-buying entrepôt, stood at the mouth of the Don, on the Sea of Azov, a gateway to Central Asia. By promoting trade with the Tatars, who were eager to sell slaves and other commodities, Venetians established direct links with the Far East, thereby overleaping the barrier of Muslim middlemen. For the first time European Christians, the most famous being the Venetian Polo family, began traveling overland from the Black Sea to the Chinese court of the Great Khan. At approximately the same time, during the late thirteenth century, the Genoese were regularly sending ships westward into the Atlantic. As the allies of a revived Byzantine Empire, the Genoese also established their own colonial outposts in the Crimea and along the Black Sea coast. As Charles Verlinden has amply demonstrated, this combination of discovery, colonization, and commercial-military expansion provided the experience and models for Europe's later momentous ventures into the New World.[83]

The Italian colonies in the Levant and Black Sea were virtual laboratories, in Verlinden's apt phrase, for testing and developing the techniques of commercial companies, colonial administration and finance, long-distance trade, and plantation agriculture. To skip ahead of our account, it was not fortuitous that Genoese and other Italians should help colonize the Canary Islands in the mid-fourteenth century (we have already noted that by 1353 Genoese merchants had established contact with the caravan trade on the Moroccan Atlantic coast); that the Genoese, after being defeated by the Venetians in 1381 and suffering a succession of reverses in the Levant, should turn westward and ally themselves with Iberian imperial expansion; or that Genoese and other Italian sea captains, sailors, merchants, scientists, technicians, and bankers should play a central role in the exploration of West Africa, in voyages to America and the Far East, in establishing sugar plantations in the newly discovered islands of the Atlantic, and in helping to promote the New World colonies of Spain, Portugal, Holland, France, and England. It was a group of Genoese entrepreneurs, associated with merchants of Antwerp, who provided the capital that transformed Brazil into a sugar colony. Individual Genoese made a no less significant contribution in financing and developing the African slave trade that supplied labor to sixteenth-century Spanish America.[84]

To understand the significance of changing sources of labor, we must return briefly to the expansion of slavery in the Mediterranean. Beginning in 1347 the Black Death and subsequent famines and epidemics devastated Europe. In parts of northern Europe, where the plague suddenly reduced the population by at least one-third, the labor shortage hastened the erosion of various forms of servile dependency and encouraged attempts to regulate wages and compel the unemployed to work. But in Italy, where seaborne trade had long brought an influx of mostly female slaves from the Dalmatian coast and reconquered Spain, the population decline created a new and continuing demand for foreign slaves. The shortage of household servants and agricultural workers induced even northern Italians to tolerate the risks of buying Circassians, Georgians, Armenians, Turks, Bulgarians, Tatars, and a few Africans. In 1364 the priors of Florence permitted the unlimited importation of slaves as long as they were not Roman Catholics (they could thus be Eastern Orthodox Christians). Between 1414 and 1423 no fewer than ten thousand bondsmen (mostly bondswomen) were sold in Venice alone. This continuing demand for servile labor coincided with a mounting supply of captives offered to various buyers from the Ottoman conquests in central Anatolia, Thrace, and the Balkans and from the celebrated transcontinental invasions of Timur (Tamerlane).[85]

Slavery had always been pervasive and deeply entrenched in southern Italy, Sicily, Crete, Cyprus, Majorca, and Mediterranean Spain. These regions had all been subject to Muslim conquest and Christian reconquest; they remained frontier outposts, vulnerable to raids but also the closest beneficiaries of centuries of Christian-Muslim terrorism and trade. Sicily and the other Mediterranean islands were coveted prizes in the chesslike contests involving Normans, Germans, Aragonese, the Italian city-states, Byzantines, and the papacy. With respect to the history of "progress," these slaveholding and extraordinarily cosmopolitan societies were at the forefront of Western commercial, agricultural, and technological innovation, despite the ravages of war and political instability. Under the Norman kings of the twelfth century, Sicily may well have been the most prosperous and most efficiently governed realm in Europe; the thirteenth-century slaveholding and sugar-producing regime of Frederick II is renowned for its encouragement of science and learning, its struggles against special privilege, and its constructive constitutionalism based on Roman and Arabic precedents. In the thirteenth century, one must add, Sicilian proprietors could benefit from a relatively dense supply of nominally free labor; the slave population was largely Muslim and female—though recent comparative studies show that female slaves have seldom been exempt from the most grueling field labor. It is significant that Sicilian officials qualified the general designation for "Moor" or "Saracen" with the Latin terms for "white," "sallow," and "black." In thirteenth-century Aragonese Sicily, as in Venetian Crete, the small scattering of Moorish blacks were probably acculturated natives of Egypt, the Barbary Coast, and Spain.[86]

But in the fourteenth century, as the number of Moorish captives declined as a result of successful Christian reconquests and agreements between Muslim and Christian princes to reduce piracy and encourage mutually beneficial commerce, the Black Sea trade profoundly transformed the ethnic composition of slave populations from Cyprus to Catalonia. It is astonishing to discover that in the early fourteenth century most of the slaves in Crete, which in commercial agriculture was the most important of the Italian colonies in the Levant, were Greek. The native Greeks of Crete, Cyprus, Chios, and other islands (to say nothing of Italian proprietors) seem to have had no scruples about buying Christian brethren of the Orthodox faith. By the 1380s, however, Greek slaves were greatly outnumbered by Tatars, Bulgarians, Russians, Circassians, and Alans. Slaves of Black Sea and Balkan origin also took the place of Moorish captives in Sicily, Majorca, and Catalonia-Aragon. Charles Verlinden maintains that these regions had become genuine slave societies well before the population loss following the Black Death. By 1328, for example, slaves appear to have constituted 36 percent of the Majorcan population, about the same proportion as that of the combined southern United States in the decades preceding the Civil War. In Majorca, as in Sicily, coastal Catalonia, and even Genoa, masters included artisans and small shopkeepers as well as the proprietors of estates. Bondsmen worked at a variety of commercial, industrial, and agricultural occupations.[87]

The turning point came with the Ottoman capture of Constantinople in 1453. While the Venetians struggled for some decades to preserve their commercial access to the Black Sea, the Turks soon diverted the flow of Black Sea and Balkan captives to Islamic markets. Mediterranean Europe was thus cut off from its major source of slaves, and for most potential buyers the price of slaves became prohibitive. The only alternative to the Crimea and the steppes of western Asia was sub-Saharan Africa. As early as 1430, Sicilian notaries began distinguishing black slaves *(sclavi nigri)* as a category separate from "black Saracens." The constriction of the Black Sea trade gave temporary stimulus to the Arab caravan trade, which had already begun transporting sub-Saharan blacks to the shores of Libya. In Sicily, Naples, Majorca, southern France, and Mediterranean Spain, officials noted that such blacks came from the mountains of Barca, in Cyrenaica. The picture is complicated, in the second half of the fifteenth century, by the gradual diversion of the caravan trade to Arguin Island and other Portuguese posts on the African Atlantic coast and by the subsequent dispersion of black slaves from Portugal to Mediterranean Europe. Notarial deeds in the second half of the fifteenth century indicate that blacks accounted for 83 percent of the servile labor force in the Aragonese realm of Naples. Verlinden concludes that, "as in Naples, slavery in Sicily at the end of the fifteenth century was preeminently black slavery." The size of Sicilian slaveholdings was relatively small—the baron de Cadera, for example, owned only twenty bondsmen, eighteen of whom were black. The significant points pertain to sex ratio and employment. The new population of black slaves was predominately male. Unlike the black household servants and page boys in the courts and cities of Europe, the blacks in Sicily, Majorca, and other plantation areas worked mainly in the fields and vineyards and on sugar plantations. As Verlinden has concluded, the Mediterranean had developed an "American" form of slavery several decades before America was discovered.[88]

The critical factor appears to have been the supply of labor available from regions that were ravaged by warfare or that lacked the political power and stability to protect their subjects. The plantation-oriented economies of the Mediterranean eagerly absorbed Moorish, Greek, and Caucasian slaves as long as they could be obtained at a tolerable price, though the price multiplied many times as a result of the demographic crisis and escalating labor costs of the fourteenth century. When Ottoman conquests later closed off the traditional sources of foreign labor, the Christian slaveholding regions turned to blacks from sub-Saharan Africa until that flow of labor was increasingly diverted to more profitable markets to the west.

For various reasons, the trends that had been dimly visible in the Mediterranean became fully manifest in Portugal. The Christian reconquest of Portugal, completed by the mid-thirteenth century—a century and a half before the Muslims were finally driven from Spain—brought an end to a direct supply of slaves from warfare. Unlike Catalonia and other lands facing the Mediterranean, Portugal could not easily import slaves from the Levant and the Black Sea. Yet Portugal's harbors were ideally situated for the small ships of Italian merchants carrying commodities from the Mideast to England and western Europe.[89] As early as 1317 Dom Diniz (king of Portugal, 1279–1325) promised a Genoese merchant one-fifth the value of all slaves brought back from the Moroccan coast. This venture was premature and unsuccessful; and it must be stressed that catching slaves amounted to little more than an incidental reward for the later Portuguese who dreamed of humbling Islam, of spreading the true faith, of finding the rich sources of gold south of Mali, of forging an alliance with Prester John's legendary Christian kingdom somewhere south of Islamic Africa, and of breaking the Arabs' monopoly of the spice trade. Nevertheless, realizing these objectives would put the Portuguese in direct contact with black Africa at a time when the Muslims had not only organized a thriving slave trade across the Sahara but also begun transporting blacks by ship along the west Moroccan coast.[90]

By the turn of the fifteenth century, the Portuguese house of Avis, strongly supported by mercantile interests, had achieved political stability; national independence had been secured by a decisive victory over Castile; a commercial and dynastic alliance had been cemented with England. Genoese capital and technology had also helped to strengthen Portuguese sea power. In 1415 Dom João I (king of Portugal, 1385–

1433) took the offensive against Islam. The king's son Henrique (later known as Henry the Navigator) took part in the capture of Ceuta, in northern Morocco, where he acquired the informed determination to send out fleets that could bypass the caravan trade and find the direct sources of African gold. Five years later, after Prince Henry's voyagers had discovered or rediscovered the uninhabited Madeira Islands, Portugal founded a small Madeiran settlement. By the 1450s various expeditions, aided by Italian seamen, had raided the Canary Islands and the Mauretanian coast, rounded the dreaded reefs at Cape Bojador, discovered the Cape Verde Islands, and explored the outlets of the Senegal and Gambia rivers. After a lull occasioned by political conflicts over commercial and military priorities, Portuguese explorations advanced at breathtaking speed: by 1475, across the equator; 1483, the mouth of the Zaire; 1487, around the Cape of Good Hope; 1497–98, Vasco da Gama's voyage around the Cape to Moçambique, Mombasa, Malindi, and India. Leading a partially overland expedition from Egypt to India, Pedro de Covilhã returned in 1487 by way of East Africa, exploring the coast as far south as the Zambezi. In 1501 Pedro Cabral arrived in Lisbon laden with spices from the East, having officially taken possession of Brazil on his way to India. During the next twenty years the Portuguese secured Goa, on the Malabar Coast of India; gained temporary control of the Persian Gulf and Red Sea; conquered Malacca, guarding the entrance to the South China Sea; and finally won dominance in the Moluccas, the main source of Arab wealth in spices. One can still see magnificent Japanese screen paintings depicting the arrival in the 1540s of gigantic, long-nosed Portuguese merchants, who are shaded from the sun by parasols held by barefooted African slaves. Within a century after the first Portuguese caravels had rounded Cape Verde, this diminutive nation containing little more than one million people had established a seaborne empire extending from Brazil to the East Indies; apart from materialistic concerns, the achievement enabled Portuguese priests to convert tens of thousands of heathen, including the Kongolese king Nzinga Nvemba (who became Dom Alfonso I) and the lords of Bungo and other Japanese states.[91]

In this first stage of European imperialism, the history of slavery became inextricably tied to the history of sugar. Sugar cane had spread in ancient times from Southeast Asia to India, where its cultivation was commonplace by the fourth century B.C., at the time of Alexander's invasion. From India, however, the Puri or Creole cane moved very slowly to the west until the Arabs seized control of Iran. The Arabs developed sugar industries in Egypt and Syria, and extended cane cultivation to Cyprus, Crete, Malta, Sicily, the Barbary Coast, and southern Spain. Little is known, unfortunately, about the type of labor employed on the early Arab estates. The primitive technology available for milling and boiling imposed severe limits on productivity. Yet the cutting and processing of cane must be done without delay and thus requires a fairly concentrated labor force. It is clear that Muslim as well as later Christian proprietors often relied on free or corvée labor. But Noel Deerr, though not always consistent in his judgments, concludes that "the intimate connection between sugar and slavery must be looked on as having its roots in the wave of Arab expansion which spread over North Africa from the seventh century onwards, and which also extended into Southern Europe."[92]

It would have been better for the Christians' morals if they had remained content with honey, which was the only sweetener they had known except for a few obscure references to sugar in classical literature. But when the crusaders founded their feudal kingdom in Palestine, they discovered the joy of sugar and other unknown condiments. One chronicler described Arab sugar as "this unsuspected and inestimable present from Heaven." The cultivation of sugar by the chivalric Hospitalers and Knights of the Teutonic Order symbolizes a paradoxical alliance that would long characterize European expansion and "progress"—the merger of feudal forms and ideals with business enterprise. Italian bankers and merchants provided long-term credit, shipping, and profitable markets for the sugar grown on crusader-owned estates near Tyre, Acre, Sidon, and Tiberias.[93]

As Sidney M. Greenfield points out, "of all the exotic items to which Europeans were exposed in the Holy Land, and for which a demand developed on this continent [Europe], the only one whose production they came to master was sugar cane." Consequently, even when the Mongol conquests of the thirteenth century shut off the westward flow of sugar from Iran and other eastern centers, and when the Franks finally withdrew from Palestine in 1291, Europeans could cultivate their own sugar in Cyprus, Crete, and Sicily. In Cyprus, the Venetian entrepreneurs managed their sugar plantations by "capitalist" methods, importing expensive copper boilers from Italy, using hydraulic mills to press the cane, and employing a mixed labor force of local serfs and Muslim slaves. It must be emphasized that the use of sugar was still often medicinal; that until the nineteenth century the condiment remained an expensive luxury, at least on the Continent; and that large-scale demand depended on the appearance of many relatively affluent consumers eager to sweeten their drinks. On the other hand, the drastic shrinkage of European populations in the second half of the fourteenth century brought a no less drastic decline in the price of wheat and other foodstuffs. Survivors of the plague, especially in urban centers, could thus afford new luxuries. In Sicily and southern Italy landed proprietors turned increasingly to sugar and sweet wines as substitutes for low-priced grains. Cane sugar, either pure or as an ingredient of *siropate, paste,* and other sweetened foods, gradually acquired a new importance in the international network of trade and finance. Genoese merchants, for example, began transporting bulk shipments of sugar to markets as distant as England. During the century or so following the Black Death, there was a significant if temporary increase in the daily calories that Europeans consumed. The demand for sugar continued to rise with the monetary expansion and population recovery of the second half of the fifteenth century, largely because Ottoman conquests constricted sources of supply from the East. There was thus sufficient incentive for Italians to introduce an improved Sicilian sugar press to Spain, to promote sugar cultivation in southern Portugal, and to provide the capital, cane, and technology for plantations in Madeira and the Canary Islands.[94]

It seems likely that even if there had been little European demand for sugar, Portugal would have imported large numbers of African slaves. As we have seen, Portugal had been largely cut off from Moorish and Mediterranean sources of cheap labor. There was papal sanction for destroying Islamic power and establishing Christian hegemony over the pagan peoples theoretically subject to Islamic rule. Papal briefs of the 1450s authorized the Portuguese king or Order of Christ to conquer and reduce to perpetual slavery the infidels, pagans, unbelievers, and enemies of Christ from the Maghrib to the Indies. In the interest of subjecting this non-Christian world to militant Christian rule, it was a short step from attacking Mulsims in Morocco to seizing black captives on the Mauretanian coast. In 1441 one of Prince Henry's household knights led two landing parties in nighttime assaults on coastal villages and then paraded his black captives before his appreciative patron, who as the grand master of the Order of Christ then or on a similar occasion "reflected with great pleasure upon the salvation of those souls that before were lost."[95]

More then a century earlier, Castilians and Normans had begun raiding and plundering the Canary Islands, enslaving the pagan Guanches, who were not black, on the ground that any resistance to the true faith was in effect a war against all Christendom. During the early fifteenth century the Portuguese launched their own attacks against the stubborn Canary Islanders, who were sold in Madeira and the slave markets of the Mediterranean before becoming the victims of literal genocide. Initially, the Portuguese also likened the seizure of black captives to the chivalric exploits of the Iberian reconquest, shouting, "Portugal!" or "Saint George!" as they shot crossbows at terrified villagers. They then discovered that successful trade depended on acquiring the trust and meeting the terms of the powerful and well-organized states of West Africa. In Senegambia this meant fitting into a commercial role already defined by Muslim traders and their hosts. Indeed, the Portuguese and their various European agents became increasingly enmeshed with Muslim culture from Morocco to the Moluccas. South of Morocco, as they began tapping the sources of the caravan trade in gold, ivory, and slaves, the Portuguese gradually adopted Muslim patterns of barter and religious conversion in lieu of knightly ideals of heroic conquest.[96]

Although Portuguese rulers were primarily interested in precious metals that could help pay for expensive imports from Asia, the evidence indicates that in the period 1441–70 up to one thousand black slaves may have arrived in Portugal every year; in the period 1490–1530 between three hundred and two thousand slaves were annually imported into Lisbon. From Lisbon, which would soon become Europe's main, if temporary, port of entry for the spices and treasures of the East, tens of thousands of black slaves were dispersed through southern Portugal, Spain, and the western Mediterranean. Agrarian interests in Portugal feared that such slave exports would raise the cost of labor, but the crown received considerable revenue from the profitable sale of blacks abroad. By the early sixteenth century black slaves performed much of the manual labor in Lisbon itself and constituted roughly 10 percent of the city's population. Castilian ships also engaged in a direct trade with West Africa until the Treaty of Alcáçovas (1479) validated Spanish claims to the Canaries in exchange for recognition of Portuguese rights to the Madeiras, Azores, and Cape Verdes, and to a nominal monopoly of the trade with West Africa.[97]

But apart from the temporary Iberian and Mediterranean demand for black slave labor, it was clearly sugar and the small Atlantic islands that gave a distinctive shape to New World slavery. Today it is difficult to appreciate the importance of the rugged, volcanic Atlantic islands as crucibles of New World institutions. The pattern of trade winds and ocean currents made all the islands crossroads of navigation, landmarks and stopovers for the ships of every maritime nation engaged legally or illegally in trade with West Africa, Asia, the West Indies, and Brazil. The Portuguese government understood the strategic value of permanent settlements along the vital sea lanes from the Azores to São Tomé, in the Gulf of Guinea close to the equator. The Cape Verdes and São Tomé were also ideal bases for trading ventures along the disease-ridden African coast. But in fifteenth-century Portugal, in contrast to England of the late sixteenth and early seventeenth centuries, there was no "excess" population of unemployed and dangerous laborers. Sidney M. Greenfield persuasively suggests that the only migrants who could be induced to settle Madeira were a few artisans and other workers who aspired to escape manual labor and achieve landholding and "noble" status. The colonists probably relied on captives from the Canary Islands to construct a system of irrigation canals from teacherous mountain ravines to the fertile but arid lands below. By the 1440s black slaves had begun to supplement or replace the Guanches. For some decades the colonists cultivated mainly cereals, but by the mid-fifteenth century there was sufficient sugar production to warrant the use of a hydraulic mill, or *engenho,* in place of hand presses. Twenty years later, when European markets were feeling the full impact of Ottoman conquests in the eastern Mediterranean, Madeiran sugar was being shipped directly to Antwerp, which soon would become the major entrepôt not only for sugar but for Portuguese spices and other luxury imports from Asia. Antwerp, it should be noted, also exported much of the copper that was exchanged for slaves on the West African coast. The technological revolution in the mining industries of Hungary and central Europe greatly increased the production of copper (and silver) and thus became closely linked to West Africa and the Atlantic islands via Portugal. By the 1490s Madeira had become a wealthy sugar colony wholly dependent on the labor of African slaves. As the first true colony committed to sugar monoculture and black slave labor, it was the transitional prototype for later mercantilist ideals of empire. Madeiran sugar, outstripping the production of the entire Mediterranean, was being shipped or reexported by the late 1490s to England, France, Italy, and even the eastern Mediterranean. Columbus, who lived for over a decade in Madeira, had the foresight to take sugar plants from the Canary Islands on his voyages to the "Indies."[98]

Despite encouragement from the Portuguese crown, Italian entrepreneurs failed to convert the uninhabited Cape Verde Islands into another Madeira. But the islands' arid climate and the difficulty of attracting European settlers contributed to a path of development that was no less useful. The Treaty of Tordesillas (1494) gave Portugal a supposedly permanent monopoly over the supply of labor and other commodities from West Africa. By the time Spanish colonization had created a new demand for labor in the Caribbean, the Cape Verdes had become a staging center for the seasoning and reexport of African slaves, enabling purchasers to escape some of the hazards of sickness and prolonged negotiation on the Guinea coast. Accordingly, African workers in the Cape Verdes produced rum and fine textiles with which the Portuguese or their mulatto offspring bought more slaves.[99]

Because the Atlantic islands were convenient stopovers on the easiest routes to or from Spanish America, they soon acquired a racially mixed and cosmopolitan population. Funchal, in Madeira, was a center of acculturation where sailors and slave traders of various complexions mingled with a merchant community that eventually included a high proportion of Englishmen, Scots, and Flemings. By the 1480s Bristol fishermen were selling the Madeirans fish that may well have been caught off the Newfoundland banks. Even before English privateers saw Spanish sugar plantations in the Caribbean or began capturing cargoes of Brazilian sugar in the sea warfare of the late sixteenth century, northern Europeans had been directly involved in the Madeiran sugar boom. São Tomé occupied an equally strategic site, roughly one hundred miles west of Cape Gabon at the junction of wind systems that powered both northbound and southbound Atlantic traffic. After a long period of experiment and disappointment, Madeiran planters aided by the ubiquitous Genoese finally took advantage of São Tomé's fertile and well-watered soil. As early as 1495 Antwerp had begun receiving sugar from São Tomé, which during the first half of the sixteenth century imported more African slaves than Europe, the Americas, or the other Atlantic islands. The spectacular success of São Tomé and neighboring Príncipe made it clear that sugar and slaves could become the keys to imperial wealth and power.[100]

To be sure, sixteenth-century Europe was more dazzled by the gold, silver, and pearls that cascaded into Spain, to say nothing of the pepper, cloves, nutmeg, cinnamon, rubies, sapphires, emeralds, coral, damasks, and silks that continued to flow into Lisbon and Antwerp. England and France, scorning the papal division of the world between Spain and Portugal, sought to rob the Spanish galleons of their treasure and to carry on lucrative, if illicit, trade with the Spanish Empire. When the Dutch embarked on imperial adventures, they attacked São Tomé, Príncipe, and Brazil and then headed for Portuguese Asia. In 1580, the year before the United Provinces proclaimed their independence from Spain, Portugal fell under the Spanish throne. The Dutch therefore had the excuse of subverting their Spanish enemies when they began in the seventeenth century to crush Portuguese power in the Far East and to establish an eastern empire extending from the Spice Islands to the Cape of Good Hope.

In the meantime, however, sugar had become for Portugal an even more valuable import than spices. The sale of African slave labor to Spanish America had also become a means of earning the silver needed to pay for Asian luxuries, since the value of Western commodities sent to the East never approximated the value of Eastern imports. Moreover, the *asientos,* or licenses for delivering shipments of slaves, provided a cloak for smuggling European manufactures that could be exchanged for silver, hides, sugar, and other commodities in Spanish American markets. While the Dutch later gave priority to the East Indies, they also seized the rich sugar-producing regions in northeastern Brazil, most of the Portuguese forts and slave-trading settlements in Africa, and Caribbean bases from Surinam to Aruba. The Hollanders' eagerness to retain control of the Atlantic slave trade, even after they had been expelled from Brazil in the mid-seventeenth century, underscored the preeminence of sugar and slaves in the struggles for mercantilist power. Black slavery took root in the Americas in a slow, spasmodic, and seemingly haphazard way, but even the last three-quarters of the sixteenth century gave ample and cumulative evidence that the fortunes of the New World depended on Africa.[101]

To account for this fact historians have given increasing attention to disease environments and "virgin soil epidemics." In the fourteenth century, as we have seen, plagues of Asian origin created a widespread labor shortage that stimulated a demand for slaves throughout the Mediterranean. A century later, when the Portuguese began exploring tropical Africa, they suffered mortality rates as high as 50 percent within a few months. Lacking immunity to falciparum malaria, yellow fever, and other diseases endemic to tropical Africa, European traders, sailors, soldiers, and missionaries died in appalling numbers until quinine and other prophylactics began to reduce mortality in the mid-nineteenth century. This persistent reality not only deterred effective European settlement but also raised the average mortality of slave-ship crews, while on the African coast and at sea, above that of slaves on the Middle Passage (though a fairer comparison would include the ghastly death rates of 20 percent or more suffered by slaves while being marched to the coast and held in barracoons). Accordingly, Europeans spent as little time as possible on the West African coast and welcomed a commerce that would move available labor to more salubrious regions.[102]

Pre-Columbian America had been isolated from the microbial infections that had swept through Asia, Europe, and much of Africa; Amerindians had also been spared from most of the diseases common to pastoral societies and transmitted by livestock. The New World environment was thus "virgin soil" for pandemics of smallpox, influenza, measles, and other infections that were especially lethal to infants and to adults in their most productive years. According to the now classic estimates of Sherburne F. Cook and Woodrow Borah, the population of central

Mexico fell from a precontact level of over 25.0 million to 1.9 million in 1585 and slightly over 1.0 million in 1605. Much earlier the Arawak on Hispaniola, the first Spanish New World colony, had been virtually exterminated by disease, mass murder, and oppressive labor. A pre-Columbian population that Cook and Borah estimate at between 7 and 8 million plunged to approximately 10,000 by 1520 and to fewer than 500 survivors by the 1540s. Cook and Borah stress that this dramatic decline "conformed to a general pattern for the tropical Caribbean islands and coasts of America." The less extreme decimation of Andean Amerindians has long been known; it now appears that population losses in North America may also have been catastrophic, thereby giving the first European settlers the impression of a relatively "empty" continent even before they began to exterminate hostile villages in the Indian wars of the seventeenth century.[103]

There can be no doubt that both the Spanish and Portuguese turned to African labor as a more reliable and durable substitute for captive aborigines, who seemed in the sixteenth century to be on the path to extinction. Philip D. Curtin notes that in the tropical lowlands such African diseases as malaria and yellow fever not only increased the mortality of Amerindians but also long prevented the formation of a self-sustaining population of European immigrants. "Slavery," he adds, "became the dominant form of labor organization wherever the impact of disease was most critical. . . . Non-European immigrants from Africa [became] epidemiologically preferable to Europeans." Peter H. Wood has also suggested that the English settlers in South Carolina found Africans particularly desirable for rice cultivation because of their relative immunity to malaria and yellow fever as well as their native experience in cultivating rice.[104]

Without disputing the importance of epidemiology, one must be wary of a "medical" explanation of the New World's transition to black slavery. During the first centuries of colonization whites, blacks, and Amerindians all suffered extraordinary mortality rates, but certain peoples were always considered more expendable than others; much ultimately depended on the supply and cost of alternative forms of labor. For example, young British indentured workers flocked to Barbados during the colony's initial tobacco era of the late 1620s and 1630s. In 1640, just before Barbadian landowners began switching from tobacco to sugar, the island contained fewer than one thousand blacks and approximately nine thousand whites, mostly bound laborers; even this recently reduced estimate slightly exceeded the contemporary white population of Virginia, which had been settled twenty years earlier than Barbados and was populated mainly by the same kind of aspiring young indentured servants. Although mortality was generally much higher in the West Indies than on the North American mainland, Barbados was fairly salubrious by seventeenth-century standards. Early colonists were relatively isolated from bubonic plague, smallpox, influenza, and other European killers; malaria did not appear in the seventeenth century, and yellow fever, possibly introduced by slave ships, did not strike until 1647. There was also an abundance of food. Even in the sugar-boom decade of 1650–60, the net white migration to Barbados rose to 16,970, only 553 below the combined net white migration to Virginia and Maryland in the same decade. But in Barbados white workers were increasingly displaced by black slaves. White workers began to avoid the West Indies, and freed servants began an exodus to the North American mainland, only after the islands were becoming wholly transformed by sugar and black slaves.[105]

The historical epidemiologists also tend to overlook the fact that long before Virginia became committed to black slavery, the colony had been a "death trap," as Edmund S. Morgan puts it, for Englishmen foolhardy enough to settle there. From 1625 to 1640 it probably took fifteen thousand English immigrants to add fewer than seven thousand to the cumulative white population. Yet a plantation economy developed and flourished with white indentured labor; planters continued to favor importing white servants when an alternative supply of black slaves was available and after white mortality had been significantly reduced. By the time Virginia turned decisively to African labor, in the 1680s, the colony had already overcome most of the "seasoning" hazards for blacks as well as for whites.[106]

The most telling point, however, is the mortality of African slaves themselves in every colony south of the Chesapeake. While Africans were not as vulnerable as Amerindians to Old World diseases, the Amerindians were not subjected to thousands of miles of land and sea travel under the most oppressive conditions. The assumption that Africans were somehow "hardier" necessarily omits the unrecorded death tolls from place of capture or initial sale even to the African coast. Planters could disregard such losses unless the cumulative costs inflated the price of slaves to a prohibitive level. But from about 1680 to 1780, despite a fourfold rise in real prices offered for slaves on the African coast, the tropical colonies affirmed that it was cheaper to import a productive slave from Africa than to raise a child to working age. Philip Curtin suggests that since African captors and middlemen could sell trade slaves for much less than the cost of reproduction, the appropriate economic "model" is burglary, and highly sophisticated burglary at that. Moreover, in the period 1640–1700 British planters in Barbados, Jamaica, and the Leeward Islands apparently accepted a loss of 164,000 slaves in order to increase their holdings by a bare 100,000. According to Richard S. Dunn, who works from Curtin's estimates, "between 1708 and 1735 the Barbadians imported 85,000 new slaves in order to lift the black population on this island from 42,000 to 46,000." While various factors accounted for the failure of slave populations to reproduce themselves, similar conditions prevailed throughout the Caribbean and Brazil. One can hardly conclude, therefore, that colonists chose African labor in order to minimize the loss of life.[107]

In parts of the Old World, as we have seen, black slavery was an established institution by the beginning of the sixteenth century. There was nothing inevitable, however, about the transfer of the same institution to the various colonies of the New World. In view of the Iberians' extraordinary and unprecedented attempts to halt the enslavement of Amerindians, it was not inconceivable that African captives would eventually be accorded a protected status above chattel slavery. No one could have predicted that black chattel slavery would flourish in Mexico and Peru until the mid-seventeenth century and then gradually give way to other and more subtle forms of coerced labor; or that the institution would languish in Cuba until the sugar boom of the early nineteenth century. Here we can do no more than outline some of the developments that tended to associate the expansion of New World slavery not only with mercantile and imperial "progress" but also with warped, one-sided societies that seemed to be doomed to moral and social decay.

Black slaves and sugar plants were introduced into the New World within the decade after Columbus's first voyage; the early development of plantation slavery was clearly encouraged by immigrant planters and traders from the Canary Islands, Portugal, and Portuguese possessions, knowledgeable people who sought to make quick fortunes in Hispaniola, Cuba, and other Spanish settlements. This direct transfer of institutions was retarded and modified, however, by the Spanish crown's insistence on quarantining the Amerindians from any religious faith other than orthodox Catholicism; by early alarms over the propensity of blacks to escape; by the temporary availability of Amerindian labor; and by the fact that seizing or mining gold and silver had far more appeal than agriculture. When in the 1520s substantial numbers of black slaves did begin replacing Amerindians, they were often put to work mining gold and silver. But whether engaged in mining, agriculture, or stock-raising, the Iberians took it for granted that whites would be exempt from physical labor. As William L. Sherman puts it:

> Europeans who shipped to the New World during the sixteenth century sought opportunity, but not at the end of a hoe. Cortés spoke for them all when he stated that he had not left Spain to plow the land. Spanish artisans of course came to ply their trades, merchants negotiated, law-

> yers, physicians, and other professionals established practices, and a burgeoning bureaucracy spread to all corners. Indeed, Spaniards representing practically every type in Spain migrated to perform all kinds of work—except common labor.[108]

Accordingly, beginning with Hispaniola in the 1510s, Spanish colonists kept clamoring for more African slaves to fill the void created by Amerindian mortality. In 1518 the crown responded by allowing the direct importation of *bozales,* or Africans who had not been spiritually and culturally purified by residence in Spain, and by granting a succession of slave-trading contracts, which were then sold or resold to European merchants. Given the paucity of early records and the high incidence of smuggling after the mid-sixteenth century, it is impossible to determine the actual volume of the African slave trade to Spanish America. For the period 1521–94, Colin A. Palmer cautiously estimates a total importation of 73,000 black slaves, half of whom went to Mexico; for the period 1595–1639 his estimate for the Spanish colonies rises to 151,205, again with approximately half the slaves ending up in Mexico. Although in the sixteenth century Spanish America probably imported fewer black slaves than the small island of São Tomé, these estimates overturn the still common impression that black labor was relatively insignificant in the first century of Hispanic-American colonization. In 1560, black slaves greatly outnumbered whites in Hispaniola and Cuba; a decade later they at least equaled the number of whites in Mexico City and Vera Cruz. From 1593 to 1640, blacks constituted one-half the population of Lima. What deserves special notice is the concentration of black slaves in sugar-producing regions, in food production generally, in coastal pearl fisheries, in mining areas where Amerindians were in short supply, and in such commercial centers as Havana, Cartagena, Panama, and Lima. According to Kenneth R. Andrews, wherever in the Caribbean the Spaniards achieved "a certain precarious prosperity it was usually created by the African slaves, while the continuance of existing enterprise and development of new alike depended heavily upon imports of Negroes. . . ."[109]

This point was well understood by Portuguese smugglers and by the French corsairs, mostly Huguenots, who from the 1520s onward captured, killed, and sold black slaves while raiding Spanish commerce and besieging Hispanic-American settlements. It was also understood by Sir John Hawkins and the eminent adventurers, including Queen Elizabeth, who backed his famous slave-trading expeditions from the Canary Islands and West Africa to the Spanish Caribbean. By the 1620s the connections between slaves, plunder, and wealth were even better understood by the Dutch West India Company, which won naval hegemony throughout the Caribbean. From the outset, Spanish colonists had not received the number of slaves they wanted. Though dependent on Portugal for African labor, Spain was obsessed with maintaining a monopoly over commerce with the New World, excluding the Brazilian coast east of the treaty line. Continuing friction between Spanish and Portuguese commercial interests made it impossible for the depopulated Caribbean to receive an adequate supply of labor. It is true that Portugal's merger with Spain from 1580 to 1640 eliminated certain administrative problems. But for a variety of other reasons—including the costs of defense, Brazilian competition, and a shortage of capital and credit—the boom that accompanied the initial decades of colonization gave way to economic decline. By the early seventeenth century the Spanish Caribbean had fallen into poverty and decay. After the 1620s even Mexico began importing far fewer African slaves as the Amerindian population started to recover and as Brazil and then the northern European colonies absorbed most of the supply. Without sufficient replenishment from Africa, the black populations in most of Hispanic America tended to die off or gradually merge as a result of increasingly frequent manumission into a mestizo underclass of marginal and dependent labor.[110]

The "failure" of black slavery to become part of a sustained, secure, and prosperous plantation system has often distracted attention from the crucial role Africans played in the conquest and settlement of Hispanic America. In retrospect it often appeared that Spanish slavery was simply part of the "Black Legend" that made the Caribbean, in Orlando Patterson's phrase, the "theater of European imperial horrors." On the one hand, as J. H. Elliott observes, "the almost miraculous sequence of events which led to the discovery, conquest and conversion of the New World did much to reinforce the linear and progressive, as against the cyclical, interpretation of the historical process in sixteenth-century thought." On the other hand, these very events evoked a profound ambivalence from the writers of the late eighteenth century who were most attuned to historical progress. Referring specifically to the philosophes' preoccupation with slavery, Elliott notes that their hesitancy on the meaning of America's discovery "sprang precisely from the dilemma involved in attempting to reconcile the record of economic and technical progress since the end of the fifteenth century with the record of the sufferings endured by the defeated societies."[111]

The discrepancy, however, was not so much between Old World and New as between the standards and expectations of two eras. The Mediterranean, to quote Patterson again, was also from the viewpoint of human oppression "a vortex of horror for all mankind." In the age of

Philip II, according to Fernand Braudel, "privateering, like America, was the land of opportunity and the wind of prosperity was unpredictable."[112] It is easy to miss the simple fact that Europeans behaved in the Caribbean much as they had behaved in the Mediterranean and the Canary Islands. To the Caribbean and South America they simply transferred customary patterns of piracy, banditry, plunder, cruelty, and ruthless reprisals, along with slavery. It is true that Amerindians were generally more vulnerable than Saracens and were slaughtered and enslaved with incredible ferocity, from sixteenth-century Hispaniola and Brazil to seventeenth-century Virginia and New England. Europeans of all nations continually expressed horror at the Amerindians' sadism, sodomy, idolatry, and cannibalism, but they hardly needed tutoring, as the later cantos of Dante's *Inferno* vividly show, in any conceivable sin. What was so terrifying about sixteenth-century America was the escape from any sense of spatial or even temporal limits—from the structured universe that Dante took for granted. Even in medieval Europe, after the long era of Viking raids, it would be difficult to find examples that match the Spaniards' uninhibited ravage of the Greater Antilles or the prolonged devastation wrought by the Paulistas' slave-raiding expeditions in the backcountry of Brazil. In Central America, where the conquistadores were disappointed by the cheapness of tribute, they found some compensation in branding Amerindian slaves on the face and shipping perhaps sixty-seven thousand to Panama, Peru, and the Caribbean.[113] Feudal traditions and royal edicts meant little in an environment in which tens of millions of people had recently perished and in which every European hoped to strike it rich. Spanish sovereigns were troubled by the lack of restraints on the self-made caudillo obsessed with looting and raping (and above all with cheating the crown of revenue). But for many decades neither the crown nor the church had the effective power to stabilize these distant and isolated societies, where robbery and slaughter had become the way of life.

The links between New World slavery and Spanish depredations fit the needs of later Protestant and abolitionist authorities on moral and economic retrogression. Because the slave trade had originally been promoted by conquistadores and Caribbean pirates, it seemed only fitting in 1820 for the United States to declare the trade piracy and for Britain to demand, without success, that the Catholic maritime nations do the same. From the sixteenth to the nineteenth century, however, the African slave trade was sanctioned by international law as well as by the highest clerical and temporal authorities in Catholic and Protestant states alike. As Holland, France, Britain, Sweden, Denmark, and the North American colonies acquired increasing wealth and maritime power, they all became involved in what Philip D. Curtin terms the "South Atlantic system." The most revealing connection between slavery and national progress is the eagerness of the most "progressive" peoples to join the system. To refrain from acquiring slave colonies or from engaging in the triangular trade was almost as unthinkable as spurning nuclear technology is in the world of today.

It was Brazil rather than Hispanic America that provided the model. Of the nearly ten million Africans who survived the voyage to the New World, well over one-third landed in Brazil and between 60 and 70 percent ended up in the sugar colonies.[114] As early as the 1520s sugar cane was being cultivated in the Pernambuco region of Brazil, but despite the aid of experienced planters from Madeira and São Tomé, the industry developed very slowly. It took time for the Portuguese to clear the coast of French Huguenot settlers, to subdue hostile Amerindians, and to experiment with Amerindian slaves sold by the Paulista *bandeirantes* until an adequate supply of Africans became available. Sugar production, as we have noted, required a concentrated force of productive and dependable workers who had little opportunity to flee and join fellow tribesmen in the interior, as Amerindians were often able to do. It was only in the 1570s, after the growth of Portuguese influence in the Kongo Kingdom and the founding of Portuguese Luanda in Angola, that northeastern Brazil began to receive massive numbers of African slaves (some of whom managed to escape to *mocambos,* or organized settlements of fugitives). In 1570 Brazil was still producing less sugar than Madeira; thirty years later production had increased almost sevenfold, and Brazil had become one of the wealthiest colonies in human history.[115]

This spectacular sugar boom attracted swarms of white colonists who aspired to become rich *senhores de engenho* and to outdo even the planters of Madeira and São Tomé in living lives of sybaritic luxury. By the 1590s the boom was also attracting English privateers, who captured enough Brazilian sugar, then destined for enemy Spanish domains, to make the price reportedly lower in London than in Lisbon. As the Dutch won independence from Spain and dominance in the Baltic, the refining and marketing centers for European sugar shifted to Amsterdam, London, Hamburg, and Rouen. In the 1630s the Dutch conquest of northeastern Brazil temporarily damaged the sugar industry but also resulted in improved technology and methods of production, which were extended to the Dutch colonies on the Essequibo and Berbice rivers, in Guiana.[116]

Meanwhile, during the relatively peaceful interlude of the early seventeenth century, Europe had acquired an insatiable taste for tobacco, as the Virginians were quick to learn. Until the Thirty Years' War aligned Spain against France, Holland, and most of Protestant Europe, traders had to rely on smuggling tobacco from the Spanish colonies or on precarious French and Anglo-Dutch ventures near the Amazon. The resumption of open warfare in the early 1620s allowed the French, Dutch, and English—who were all temporarily allied, despite England's isolation from the struggles on the Continent—to move beyond buccaneer bases and to found permanent settlements along the entire eastern perimeter of the Spanish Empire, in the Lesser Antilles.

Protected by Dutch naval power, the British and French fought off the native Caribs and by 1635 had taken possession of the chain of islands from Saint Kitts to Martinique as well as outlying Barbados. While the initial objectives were largely military and strategic, mercantilists were beginning to see the connections between privateering, settled colonies, and imperial power. In the Lesser Antilles the English, French, and Dutch also smuggled slaves to the Spanish Main. As early as 1619 it was a Dutch ship that unloaded the first blacks known to have arrived in Virginia. From their later-acquired possessions in Brazil, the Dutch also supplied slaves and sugar technology to the British settlers in Barbados and other islands. The Barbadian "sugar revolution" was already well advanced in 1654 when a largely black and mulatto army finally expelled the Dutch from Brazil, resulting in an exodus to the Caribbean of émigrés experienced in buying and managing slaves and in maximizing the output of sugar. Two years later a British expedition implemented part of Cromwell's "Western Design" by capturing Jamaica, which in the next century would become Britain's most valued colony.[117]

There is no need here to summarize the stages of growth that transformed the Lesser Antilles and then Jamaica and Saint Domingue into the main sugar-producing regions of the world. One point that is often overlooked, however, was the fortuitous character of West Indian development. In the 1630s an English Puritan settlement on Providence Island (Santa Catalina), off the coast of Nicaragua, was rapidly becoming a prosperous tobacco and cotton colony based on black slave labor; in 1641 the Spaniards wiped it out. Before conquering Jamaica, the expedition dispatched by Cromwell had failed to take over Hispaniola, although French buccaneers from Tortuga gradually gained control of the western part of the island, called Saint Domingue, which in 1697 was ceded to France as a minor part of the Treaty of Ryswick. Until the end of the Napoleonic era, West Indian acquisitions would depend not only on the fortunes of risky military ventures but also on the outcome of European battles and diplomacy. Various obstacles, ranging from maroon resistance to shortages of capital, labor, and effective administrators, also delayed the development of Jamaica and Saint Domingue, the two centerpieces of the eighteenth-century British and French slave empires. Yet, from the late seventeenth century onward, no one could doubt the striking correlation between the soaring importation of African slaves and the unprecedented wealth of the sugar colonies.[118]

Forty years ago, in his brilliant, provocative, and enormously influential *Capitalism and Slavery,* Eric Williams maintained that the wealth produced by the slave trade and by black slave labor in the colonies provided the capital that financed the British industrial revolution. Historians and economists have discredited this thesis by showing that even on the basis of the most generous calculations, the combined profits from the slave trade and West Indian plantations could not have come to 5 percent of the British national income at a time when planters were prospering and the industrial revolution was getting under way. There is still considerable controversy, however, over the contribution of the slave colonies to the economic growth of eighteenth-century Britain, France, and mainland North America. The debate, often highly technical and involving conflicting models of economic development, would concern us here only if we were trying to assign quantitative weight to the role of black slavery in the economic "progress" of the Western world. The more elemental point, which is easily obscured by abstract cost-benefit analysis, is that the vast majority of eighteenth-century policymakers and commentators equated slaves with wealth and national greatness. Their perception is confirmed by the value of slave-colony exports, by the per capita wealth of the slave colonies themselves, and by the simple fact that there was a demand for black slaves in every colony from Canada to Chile. Until the 1820s the transatlantic flow of African slaves was at least four times greater than the total flow of white immigrants to the New World.[119]

Turning first to trade, we find that by 1725–34, when slaves already constituted 90 percent of Jamaica's population, the official value of British West Indian exports to England was worth approximately fourteen times the value of exports from the colonies north of the Chesapeake. Although the northern colonies' exports to Great Britain increased dramatically after midcentury, in the period 1765–74 they still amounted to less than one-tenth the value of British West Indian exports. Given the disparity in population sizes, in 1765–74 the per capita value of West Indian exports was more than thirty-one times that of the largely nonslaveholding North. In the same pre-Revolutionary decade, the southern mainland colonies' exports to Britain were worth five times more than those from the North. Of course, the mainland colonies developed their own internal markets, and their total imports from Britain surpassed those of the West Indies (though not when measured per capita); yet the northern colonies also became increasingly dependent on legal and contraband trade with the British and foreign sugar islands.[120]

No less striking are Seymour Drescher's figures on the British West Indian share of the total British trade. From 1713 to 1822 the British West Indies continued to lead Asia, Africa, Latin America, and North America in the value of commodities sent to Britain; they also led Africa, Latin America, and even Asia (except for a few years in the mid-eighteenth century) as a market for British exports. Far from declining, the British West Indian share of non-European British imports rose from 24.0 percent in 1763–67 to 30.3 percent in 1808–12, dropping only to 25.8 percent in 1818–22. Even when we take British overseas trade as a whole, combining the value of imports and exports, the British West Indies accounted for 15.3 percent in 1763–67; 20.8 percent in 1803–07; 16.1 percent in 1818–22 (to the United Kingdom); and still 12.3 percent in 1818–32 (to the United Kingdom).[121]

The Brazilian and Caribbean example was not disdained in the far north. Only a few years after the English settlement at Massachusetts Bay and expansion into Connecticut and Rhode Island, the resulting "Pequot War" led not only to the extermination of Pequot villages but also, in 1638, to William Pierce's voyage to the Puritan colony at Providence Island, where Pequot captives were exchanged for black slaves. Seven years later, when the Barbadians were just beginning to purchase large shipments of Africans, John Winthrop, the founding father and aging but restored governor of Massachusetts, received the urgent proposal from his brother-in-law that a "just war" against the Narragansetts would afford a providential opportunity to exchange Amerindian men, women, and children for West Indian "Moores": "for I doe not see how wee can thrive untill wee gett into a stock of slaves sufficient to doe all our business, for our children's children will hardly see this great Continent filled with people, soe that our servants will still desire freedome to plant for them-selves, and not stay but for verie great wages. . . . I suppose you know verie well how wee shall mainteyne 20 Moores cheaper than one Englishe servant."[122]

This apprehension, later muted or forgotten by the champions of free labor, was echoed everywhere in the New World. As late as the 1830s and 1840s, it permeated Edward Gibbon Wakefield's influential theories of empire; it waned only when starvation and the disruptions of a global market economy created a mobile force of "voluntary" labor from Ireland, Germany, Italy, eastern Europe, India, China, and Southeast Asia. But in 1688 even the governor of French Canada begged

Louis XIV to end the manpower shortage of New France by authorizing direct shipments of black slaves. The promoters of Canadian slavery received official approval to import blacks, and continued into the eighteenth century to project visions of a slave-plantation society in the Saint Lawrence valley producing wheat and other commodities for West Indian markets. In 1716 the intendant of New France even attributed the progress of New York and New England to black labor! This assumption was not quite so farfetched as it may seem, since by 1690 approximately one out of every nine Bostonian families owned at least one black slave. It is true that New England, except for a prosperous stock-farming region in southern Rhode Island, never became dependent on black slave labor. Even the zones of commercial agriculture supplied foodstuffs mainly to local markets, and there were few labor needs that could not be met by the high rate of natural population growth. Even so, from 1710 to 1742 the number of black slaves in Boston increased fourfold while the white population only doubled. Gary B. Nash estimates that "by the second quarter of the eighteenth century about one-fifth of all Boston families owned slaves."[123]

In New York City, which had been 20 percent black when surrendered by the Dutch in 1664, some 42 percent of the heads of households owned slaves in 1703. Four years earlier the provincial governor had reported to the Lords of Trade that users of labor "have no other servants in this country but Negroes." From 1700 to 1774 New York imported at least 6,800 black slaves, and until the 1740s the colony's slave population grew at a more rapid rate than the white population; the increase in blacks was especially pronounced in New York City, parts of Long Island, and in the wealthy farming districts east of the Hudson. For comparative purposes it is enlightening to note that in North Carolina slaves constituted only 6 percent of the population in 1710 and 14 percent in 1720. Even in Virginia and Maryland the proportion of slaves rose from a mere 7 percent in 1680 to 15 percent in 1690 and 22 percent in 1700. Yet in New York and New Jersey black slaves made up 12 percent of the population from 1720 to 1740; in New York City the proportion rose to more than 21 percent in the late 1740s, and in Kings County to over 34 percent. As Gary Nash points out with respect to New York City, "If we exclude from the 'laboring class' the 30 percent of white males who functioned as government officials, lawyers, doctors, teachers, clergymen, shopkeepers, merchants, and others who did not work with their hands, it appears that of every one hundred persons in the laboring ranks, fifteen were slaves in 1703 and about thirty in 1746."[124]

It is somewhat startling to discover that even Pennsylvania and Delaware, which ordinarily could rely on a sizable flow of white immigrants, led Maryland and Virginia until 1670 and North Carolina until 1690 in the proportion of slaves in their provincial populations. In 1690 the proportion of slaves in the northern port towns still approximated that in tobacco-growing Virginia and Maryland, and greatly exceeded that in North Carolina. By the 1760s three out of every four of Philadelphia's servants, free and slave, were black. The proportion of slaves in New York City in the mid-eighteenth century was higher than the comparable figure for Jamaica and Antigua in 1660, for South Carolina in 1680, for North Carolina in 1730, and for Georgia in 1750. These comparisons simply underscore the willingness of every colony to turn to black slaves, despite universal fears of insurrection, complaints from white artisans and servants, and desires for racial and ethnic homogeneity, when the demand for cheap labor could not be met otherwise. Throughout the British New World colonies, the regions that drew the greatest total immigration relative to their existing populations also imported the greatest proportion of black slaves.[125]

Whatever view one takes of the "progress" of the New World, it is clear that black slavery was indispensable not only for regions capable of producing agricultural staples but also for the port cities and neighboring commercial farms and livestock-raising centers from Newport to Buenos Aires. The long-term costs for blacks, whites, and society in general should obscure neither the initial preference for white indentured servants in all the staple-producing societies nor the relative eagerness of northern urbanites to accept African slaves—as late as 1763 New York City absorbed two large shiploads from Africa, more slave imports than the colony had received in any year since 1731. What finally differentiated the borderland Chesapeake colonies, despite a continuing but reduced influx of white indentured servants, was the fact that African slaves were cheaper and more plentiful than white servants and that tobacco exports expanded from approximately thirty million pounds in the early 1720s to one hundred million pounds by the 1770s. Available statistics tend to confirm Allan Kulikoff's conclusion that "if the Chesapeake planters had not cultivated a marketable staple its [the colonies'] population would have been as racially homogeneous as New England's."[126]

In marked contrast to the Caribbean, Brazil, and even South Carolina, the Chesapeake's slave population began to grow naturally by the 1720s, despite the sexual imbalance associated with continuing importations from Africa. Climate, the plentitude of land and provisions, and the relative ease of tobacco cultivation made the Chesapeake more salubrious than the rice and sugar colonies. Although recent studies question the effect on slave demography of planter intentions, it appears that Chesapeake planters showed increasing interest in establishing self-sufficient plantations, in becoming less dependent on the African slave trade, and in encouraging stable family life among their bondsmen. While Virginia's white population rose from 61,198 in 1720 to 259,411 in 1770, the black population shot up from 26,559 to 187,605, a more than sevenfold increase. By the latter year, nearly one-half of all white Chesapeake families owned one or more slaves. Edmund S. Morgan has persuasively argued that the movement of black slaves into positions formerly occupied by an underclass of unruly and despised white servants converted Virginia into a remarkably "free" and affluent society of whites, led by an enlightened planter oligarchy, who not only dominated every phase of the War of Independence and national confederation but also articulated ideals of liberty and inalienable rights that would continue to inspire revolutionary sentiments in the hearts of whites and blacks alike.[127]

Alice Hanson Jones has recently shown that the pre-Revolutionary South was far wealthier than New England or the middle colonies, whether private physical wealth is measured in the aggregate "or is averaged per free capita . . . , per free wealthholder . . . , or by the conceptually more dubious per capita measure [including slaves as sharers in the use of wealth as well as human capital]." The South also "led all regions on the basis of estimated net worth, when financial assets and liabilities are taken into account." Stanley L. Engerman concludes that in about 1770 the per capita wealth of Jamaica was above that of the mainland colonies even when one excludes the value of slaves but includes slaves in the total population. By the same criteria, which exclude one-third of the South's total physical assets, the southern colonies equalled New England but fell somewhat below the middle colonies in private wealth per capita. As Engerman adds, "if we measured the value of wealth per free person the differences would appear more dramatic in favor of the South"—again, even excluding the value of slaves.[128] Although these estimates must be treated with some caution, they point to an unmistakable conclusion: by the eve of the Revolution, the most productive and wealthiest regions of British America (and of French, Portuguese, Dutch, Danish, and probably Spanish America) were the staple-producing economies dependent on slave labor. And one may add that the urban, mercantile centers and suppliers of West Indian provisions were hardly less dependent, directly or indirectly, on the labor of black slaves.

In some ways the slave systems of the New World suffered irreparable damage from the traumas of the American Revolution, the disruption or loss of protected markets, the wars of the French Revolution, and the resulting instability and breakup of the Spanish Empire. After winning independence from Britain, the South suffered a sharp, if somewhat temporary, decline in its proportional shares of national wealth and exports.[129] Moreover, during the Age of Revolution hundreds of thousands of black slaves won freedom through revolt, military service, or escape. Revolutionary ideology, reinforced by fear and gratitude for loyal service, encouraged widespread manumission in Virginia, the Caribbean, and Spanish America. The rise of industrialism, accompanied by new religious and humanitarian values that we shall consider later on, undermined traditional sanctions for human bondage. Yet none of these forces met the New World's chronic need for more and cheaper labor. The cataclysms of the Age of Revolution simply opened new opportunities for Brazil, Cuba, Louisiana, and the Caribbean territories conquered by Britain.

What transformed the entire balance of power was the almost total destruction of Saint Domingue, a colony only slightly larger than New Jersey, even counting mountains and rain forests inhabited by fugitive maroons, but one that by 1790 contained up to two-thirds the number of slaves in the entire American South and that produced more than 30 percent of the sugar imported by the North Atlantic economies as well as increasing supplies of cotton, coffee, and other tropical staples. The Haitian revolution of the 1790s terrified American and European whites and was disastrous for the North American merchants who had supplied provisions for the French West Indian expansion of the 1780s. But the eclipse of Saint Domingue was a godsend for British, Brazilian, Cuban, and North American planters. After a series of post-Revolutionary economic setbacks, the southern United States soon recovered. Historians have customarily attributed this recovery to the providential (or satanic) invention of the cotton gin and to the no less providential removal of French power from New Orleans and the Gulf of Mexico. More credit needs to be given to the enterprise and adaptability of planters who were capable of taking almost immediate advantage of these opportunities. As southern whites and blacks began cultivating the fertile territories southwest of the Appalachians, they at least matched the productivity and growth in per capita income of the rest of the nation. By about 1840 the South was growing 60 percent of the world's cotton and providing some 70 percent of the cotton consumed by the British textile industry. Accounting for well over half the value of all United States exports, slave-grown cotton paid for a substantial share of the imported capital, iron, railroad rails, and manufactured goods that contributed to the nation's economic growth. Southern cotton was equally vital for the northern textile industry and for the growth of New York City, in particular, as a distributing and exporting center that drew income from commissions, freight charges, interest, insurances, and other services connected with marketing America's most valuable commodity.[130]

Economic historians will probably never agree on the precise contribution of black slavery to the economic growth of the Western world. There has been a recent tendency to downgrade the importance of long-distance trade as a factor in national income before the nineteenth century. Slave-grown produce made only a marginal contribution to the national income of Britain and other Western states until the rise of the cotton-textile industry. But from an elevated overview, one is struck by the role of innovative "carriers" who helped to transfer plantation slavery from one frontier zone to another: the Genoese and other Italians who converted the Atlantic islands into plantation colonies; the planters and slaves from Madeira, the Canaries, and São Tomé who promoted sugar production in Hispanic America and then ignited the first great sugar boom in Brazil; the Dutch and Jewish émigrés who brought selected slaves, cane, and expertise to the Caribbean colonies acquired by Britain, France, and Holland; the Barbadians and their slaves who initiated the settlement of South Carolina (and it is now clear that slaves themselves were often indispensable carriers of technical and even managerial skills); the planters from the Leeward Islands and Barbados who later opened up new frontiers in the Windward Islands, Trinidad, and Guiana; and most numerous of all, the white and black migrants from the Atlantic seaboard who extended the Cotton Kingdom across Georgia, Alabama, Mississippi, Louisiana, and southern Arkansas to northeastern Texas. Such a roll call of entrepreneurs, which could be greatly amplified, suggests a kind of progression in the history of slavery toward always more promising frontiers. These frontiers differed, however, from the idealized North American frontier celebrated by Frederick Jackson Turner. No regenerating benefits flowed backward from the Black Belt to the stagnating Chesapeake, to Barbados and the Leeward Islands, to northeastern Brazil, or to Madeira and Sicily.

It is true that the older, displaced regions often profited by selling slaves to areas of expansion. H. A. Gemery and J. S. Hogendorn have also presented an interesting theory concerning a "backward linkage" from non-innovative sugar plantations to the highly inventive and adaptive techniques for gathering slaves in Africa. They argue, essentially, that while the planters' single-minded reliance on increasing supplies of labor diverted attention from possible technological improvements to step up productivity, this limited vision shifted the burden of innovation to black and white entrepreneurs who could profit by creating an elastic supply of labor from Africa. But whatever the innovations in slave gathering and transport, it would be perverse to conclude that such processes contributed to the "progress" of Africa, however defined.[131]

There is still much debate over how much slavery itself was responsible for a pattern of boom-and-decline that was by no means confined to slaveholding economies. In the West Indies, as in the American South, the major declines in output and wealth came *after* emancipation, not before. Regional depressions can often be attributed to self-defeating mercantilist restrictions on trade, the effects of war, hurricanes, rising production costs, temporarily glutted markets, a shortage of currency or credit, foreign competition, and numerous other exogenous factors. As early as the mid-eighteenth century, however, slave societies were acquiring the image of social and cultural wastelands blighted by an obsessive pursuit of private profit. The negative image was popularized by Anglo-American magazines, newspapers, poetry, plays, and treatises on political economy. The stereotype became part of the accepted public geography in taverns and coffeehouses in London and Philadelphia, among the radical artisans and cognoscenti of Birmingham and Manchester, the Calvinist clergy of New England, the farmers and merchants of Vermont, and Quakers everywhere. According to the rapidly emerging view, the slave colonies were lands of tyranny and decay where private extravagance extinguished public virtue; where reckless improvidence led to mountainous debts, impoverished soil, bad roads, ramshackle buildings, spavined and degenerate livestock, and unpainted fences; where one could travel for a day without seeing a school, a church, a public square, or an institution for civic improvement; where the indolence of whites stifled ambition while black slavery degraded the worth of labor; and where self-indulgence, coupled with brutal and arrogant exploitation, drained the very springs of human progress.[132]

Such stereotypes usually have at least some grounding in reality, but the slave colonies had certainly not become *more* violent, wasted, and depraved than in earlier times. What had changed were the values, sensibilities, and ideological needs of certain sectors of Anglo-American society. In previous works I have tried to map out the complex emergence of antislavery sentiment; there is no need to retrace that ground except where it bears on certain themes in Part 2. The point to be stressed here is the gradual divergence from attitudes and social patterns that had once been almost universally accepted. As we have seen, black slaves (and slave codes) had been as ubiquitous in northern coastal towns as in the comparable cities of eighteenth-century Hispanic America. It was estimated by the 1760s that, because of the continual travel between colonies and metropolitan centers, there were at least twenty thousand blacks in Britain; many were held as slaves, but an increasing number lived in the most destitute slums of London, Liverpool, and other port cities. Through much of Christendom, as in the Islamic world, black slaves were by no means confined to plantation societies. But during the last third of the eighteenth century, free-labor societies became increasingly alarmed over intrusions from the slaveholding colonial world. Much of this animus arose from the kind of racism that would long be directed against foreign immigrants who threatened to reduce wages and disrupt the behavorial norms of ethnically cohesive communities. The antiblack prejudice that erupted in London and Philadelphia was in many ways similar to the hostility toward Irish immigrants and, in the case of Philadelphia, earlier German "redemptioners." There was something new, however, about the public sympathy for Granville Sharp's successful efforts in 1771–72 to free a slave who had been brought to London from Virginia, who had tried to escape, and who had then been locked in chains aboard a ship bound for Jamaica. There was also no precedent for the movements in England and Rhode Island to deport free blacks to a "free" colony in West Africa. In 1777 a French royal decree went so far as to prohibit the further entry of blacks, in order to promote public security and prevent miscegenation.[133]

Until the 1760s, roughly speaking, black slavery was generally assumed to be a necessary and "progressive" institution, accepted or tolerated in cities like Boston, New York, and London, which were far removed from the booming peripheral zones of plantation agriculture. But during the next thirty years there occurred a profound change in the basic paradigm of social geography—a conceptual differentiation between what can only be termed a "slave world" aberration and the "free world" norm. I am not referring to anything as specific as the first abolitionist literature or the first signs of sectional discord in the new United States. I have in mind a much vaguer and more general consensus that black slavery was a historical anomaly that could survive for a time only in the plantation societies where it had become the dominant mode of production. This invidious demarcation seemed so compellingly self-evident by the late eighteenth century, despite the persistence of black bondage in the American North and even parts of Europe, that it sapped the morale of the more cosmopolitan southern leaders and of West Indian proprietors who could afford to live in England. According to modern statistical analysis, New World slavery had never been more successful; the great years of North American, Cuban, and Brazilian expansion still lay ahead. During the next eighty or more years, the burgeoning consumer societies of the Western world would rely on slave labor for cotton textiles, sugar, coffee, cocoa, rice, hemp, leather, and a variety of foodstuffs, metals, and even manufactured goods. Yet, within this consumer world, few people doubted that free labor was the irresistible wave of the future. The political leaders who continued to warn against precipitous social change still looked upon slave labor as the uneconomical vestige of a barbarous age. Its perpetuation imperiled, as an anonymous American writer put it in 1797, not only civilized man's "improvement of three thousand years" but also the emergence of "the present heathen world . . . from their native darkness, to the knowledge of arts and sciences—of christianity, and of future glory."[134]

6. JEWS AND THE CHILDREN OF STRANGERS

By the mid-nineteenth century, disputes over the sinfulness or the biblical sanction of New World slavery had divided the Protestant world, exacerbating older theological conflicts over scriptural interpretation. This issue could not be ignored by young Jewish intellectuals, trained in German universities, who confronted the challenges of assimilating philology and humanism and of relating their religious heritage to the modern world. In 1859, for example, Moses Mielziner, a future acting president of Hebrew Union College in Cincinnati, submitted to the University of Giessen a learned doctoral dissertation entitled "Slavery amongst the Ancient Hebrews." Mielziner, the son of a rabbi, was a talmudic scholar, trained in philology at the University of Berlin; in 1859 he was a teacher and ordained rabbi in Denmark. His dissertation begins with a ringing and unequivocal affirmation:

> Among the religions and legislations of antiquity none could exhibit a spirit so decidedly averse to slavery as the religion and legislation of Moses;

> nor could any ancient nation find, in the circumstances of its own origin, such powerful motives to abolish that institution as the people of Israel. A religion which insists so emphatically upon the exalted dignity of man as a being created in the image of God, a legislation which bases its laws upon that dignity of man, and which enjoins, in all its enactments, not only the highest justice, but also the most tender kindness and the most considerate forbearance, especially toward the needy and the unfortunate; a people, lastly, which had itself pined under the yoke of bondage, and had become a nation only through its deliverance from servitude; all these must have made it their object to abrogate, if possible, the unnatural state of slavery, so degrading to the human being.[135]

On 4 January 1861, a national fast day proclaimed by the outgoing President James Buchanan as the United States had begun to fall apart, a prominent New York rabbi delivered a very different kind of sermon. Morris J. Raphall, who also held a doctoral degree and had been educated in Denmark and Germany, excoriated "the Biblical critics called Rationalists" who twisted Scripture to fit modern fashion; invoking Noah's curse and "prophecy," Raphall upheld the conservative Christian view that the African race, as "Ham's descendants," had been condemned to bondage "upwards of 4,000 years ago," and proclaimed that abolitionist preachers were guilty not only of inciting civil war but "of something very little short of blasphemy." Raphall's sermon provoked a stinging rebuttal from Dr. David Einhorn, a Baltimore rabbi who had known Mielziner in Germany; it also led Francis Lieber and other New York liberals to circulate a translation of Mielziner's dissertation, which abolitionists greeted with enthusiasm. As Einhorn made clear, the issue involved not only fidelity to Jewish tradition but also the fate of American Jews:

> We are vividly reminded of Jewish clowns who delighted wedding guests with all sorts of leaps in the domain of the Draschah [homily]. . . . The spotless morality of the Mosaic principles is our pride and our fame, and our weapon since thousands of years. This weapon we cannot forfeit without pressing a mighty sword into the hands of our foes. . . . Would it not then be justly said, as in fact it has already been done . . . *Such* are the Jews! Where *they* are oppressed, they boast of the humanity of their religion; but when they are free, their Rabbis declare slavery to have been sanctioned by God, even mentioning the holy act of the Revelation on Sinai in defense of it.[136]

This bitter controversy serves as a reminder that there was no official "Jewish position" on slavery or on any other social issue. In the early nineteenth century Moses Judah, a Jewish merchant, served on the standing committee of the New York Manumission Society, the second antislavery organization in human history. Yet, even in the northern colonies and states, many Jews had emigrated from South Carolina and the Caribbean. Mordecai M. Noah, for example, had spent much of his youth in Charleston before becoming a Tammany Hall Democratic party leader, newspaper editor, United States consul to Tunis, surveyor of New York Port, and self-appointed spokesman for the American Jewish community. Noah was also one of the North's most vocal defenders of black slavery. The first American Jew to rise to national political eminence was Judah P. Benjamin, the brilliant attorney general, secretary of war, and then secretary of state of the Confederate States of America. Born in the British West Indies, Benjamin had moved as a child to Charleston and later to New Orleans, where he became a wealthy sugar planter, railroad promoter, and advocate of southern secession.[137]

But like earlier Christian and later Muslim liberals, Mielziner and Einhorn were clearly wrong in detecting a basic antipathy toward slavery and even an incipient trend toward abolitionism in the premodern history of their faith. After carefully surveying sources of the period of the Second Temple, the Mishnah, and the Talmud, E. E. Urbach concludes that there is not "the slightest suggestion of any notions of the abolition of slavery. On the contrary, the fundamental distinction between bond and free is present throughout. . . . A humane concern for the lot of the slave was occasionally aroused, but only after the economic situation had brought about a continual deterioration in his legal and social status." On the other hand, Mielziner's point about the dignity of life receives support in one crucial respect: "The Rabbis . . . equated the law regarding bodily injury to the Canaanite or gentile slave of another person with the law regarding bodily injury to a free man. . . . This absolute equality of slave and free man in all matters regarding the judicial safeguarding of their lives has no parallel in either Greek or Roman Law."[138]

As a result of their own bondage in Egypt and their sense of historical mission, the ancient Hebrews also sought to limit and mitigate the servitude of their own people. Moses called on every Jew to remember "that thou wast a bondman in the land of Egypt, and the Lord thy God redeemed thee." Therefore, "if thy brother, a Hebrew man, or a Hebrew woman, be sold unto thee, he shall serve thee six years; and in the seventh year thou shalt let him go free from thee. And when thou lettest him go free from thee, thou shalt not let him go empty." The Torah provides specific rules for the redemption of indigent Hebrews who sold themselves to strangers living under Jewish jurisdiction: "And if he be not redeemed by any of these means, then he shall go out in the year of the jubilee [every fiftieth year], he, and his children with him. For unto Me the children of Israel are servants; they are My servants whom I brought forth out of the land of Egypt: I am the Lord your God."[139] The ritual observance of Passover has reminded Jews in all times that bondage is an affliction from which people long to be redeemed.

But to assume that the religious ideals of Judaism reflected social reality, especially when such ideals have been refracted through a modern antislavery lens, is equivalent to taking Jefferson's Declaration of Independence as a description of the Virginian and American social order at the time of the Revolution. In both cases, to be sure, the ideals took on new meaning as they outlived the conditions of their birth. Yet in both cases there is now abundant evidence that later "progressive" scholars have softened the truth about their fathers. Frank Moore Cross's recent translation of Samaritan papyri indicates that the Jewish lords of Samaria made no distinction between slaves bearing Hebrew and non-Hebrew names and held both categories of servants in perpetuity.[140] This discovery confirms the argument of Urbach and other scholars that foreign slaves were scarce and expensive in the pre-Maccabean period, that the majority of Hebrews in Judea and Galilee were smallholders, tenants, or landless laborers whose debts could easily lead to enslavement, and that the six-year limit was either not enforced or never applied to the majority of Hebrew slaves who were forced to sell themselves or their children into perpetual bondage. Urbach shows that the enslavement of Jews by fellow Jews was not only common during the period of the Second Temple but also persisted in Babylonia, in the fourth century A.D., "in the *entourage* of wealthy rabbinic circles." It is also clear that, despite continuing prohibitions against selling fellow Jews to foreigners, merchants during the fourth to the first century B.C., could not resist the high prices offered for slaves in Egypt and in the "Canaanite" slave-trading centers of Tyre and Sidon.[141]

Urbach contends that the motive for redeeming such Jewish slaves was not the tie of kinship, "but the clear presentiment that the sale of a Jew to a Gentile as a slave meant, in the end, his assimilation; the whole Jewish community thus became subject to the injunction *'suffer him not to assimilate.'* " Since the acquisition of Jewish slaves could be an incentive for paying ransom, the Halakah permitted the retention as bondsmen of "redeemed" Jewish slaves. Urbach surmises that the majority of such ransomed Jews remained in a state of servitude, augmenting the principal labor force of the landholding class until the time of the Maccabees. But after this important point is granted, the fact remains that Jews took in-group obligations more seriously than did later Christians and Muslims. During the late Roman Republic, by which time tens of thousands of Jews had been shipped to Rome as captives and many had then won their freedom, they pooled their efforts to buy and free their fellow Jews. Similarly, in the later Byzantine Empire Jewish merchants utilized their commercial contacts with the Muslim world to ransom Jews enslaved by Arab corsairs. In Fatimid Egypt, when Jews were able to systematize the flow of charitable contributions from Spain and other distant communities to their seats of learning in Jerusalem and Baghdad, there were even fewer barriers to the redemption of enslaved coreligionists. No organizational effort was too great or costly to rescue Jews from another Egyptian or Babylonian captivity.[142]

But what of the "Canaanites," a term that was extended generally to non-Hebrew bondsmen? Since many of the Hebrew Scriptures came to be regarded by Christians and Muslims as the word of God, two texts in particular exerted a profound, though highly confused, influence on the history of human bondage. We have already referred to the mysterious passage of Genesis 9:24–25, in which Noah awakened from his drunkenness "and knew what his youngest son had done unto him. And he said: 'Cursed be Canaan; a servant of servants [the meanest servant] shall he be unto his brethren.' " In the second text, Leviticus 25:44–46, it is God Himself who tells Moses that since the Hebrews should not sell their own brethren or rule over them "with rigor," they should buy their slaves "of the nations that are round about you":

> Moreover of the children of the strangers that do sojourn among you, of them may ye buy, and of their families that are with you, which they have begotten in your land; and they may be your possession. And ye may make them an inheritance for your children after you, to hold for a possession: of them may ye take your bondmen for ever.

As numerous scholars have shown, many societies have thought of slavery as a degrading and contemptible condition suitable only for aliens and enemies who were ethnically distinct. The ancient Hebrews simply validated this widespread tendency by creating extremely potent myths concerning their original Canaanite enemies. Ephraim Isaac suggests that after the Hebrews had conquered parts of Canaan, and the Canaanites (or Phoenicians) had come to dominate Mediterranean trade:

> . . . the Canaanites were said to be cursed because their father Canaan violated the divine ordinance of land distribution and usurped the dwelling and inheritance of the Israelites. . . . Moreover, the fact that in later times the Canaanites, a formerly agricultural people, were traders, sailors, and businessmen of the world of Israelite peasantry, may have caused them to be stereotyped as exploitative, commanded by their forefather to be "robbers, adulterers and lazy". . . .[143]

What is so perplexing about the story of Noah's curse is that Canaan himself appeared to be innocent. It was his father, Ham, who aroused Noah's rage. Gerhard Von Rad surmises that the original Yahwistic narrative made no mention of Ham and was meant to reflect the horror of the newly arrived Israelites over the sexual depravity of the Canaanites. Von Rad thinks that a later redactor inserted the name of Ham as the father of Canaan in order to harmonize the story with the later "table of nations." However this may be, the early rabbis never doubted that it was Canaan who bore the curse, even if they differed in their speculations about God's purposes and and the possibility that Canaan himself had been guilty of castrating or sexually abusing his grandfather. We have already discussed Ephraim Isaac's arguments against the theory that early rabbinic sources extended the curse of Canaan to the descendants of Cush, the blacks of Africa. It is true that scattered midrashic and talmudic sources say that Ham had castrated his father, Noah; that because Ham had had sexual intercourse on the ark, in violation of a divine command, he had been punished, "in that his descendants, the Ethiopians, are black"; and that Noah had proclaimed that "since you have disabled me from doing something [cohabitation] in the dark, Canaan's children shall be born ugly and black!" But these conflicting legends concerning blackness of skin never implied that the black descendants of Cush were singled out, like the Canaanites, for perpetual bondage. Augustine and other patristic authors invoked Noah's curse to justify slavery in general and referred to Ham as the "wicked son" who could be compared to Cain. It was not until the Middle Ages, however, that Jewish, Muslim, and Christian writers began to identify the Noachian curse specifically with the black "children of Ham."[144]

Meanwhile, the Maccabean wars and conquests of the Jewish Hasmonaean kings greatly increased the supply and economic importance of "Canaanite" slaves, a label that by then included all gentile bondsmen. Since foreign captives were plentiful in Judea and since various legal protections diminished the value of Hebrew slaves, the bondage of Jews virtually disappeared. Pressures of religious and ethnic solidarity therefore magnified the inherent gap between free people and slaves. Yet, as we have already seen, there were countervailing pressures to circumcise, baptize, and assimilate gentile servants in order to avoid household contamination. One finds a similar tension in many premodern societies, but the records show that Jews agonized over every conceivable question and possibility regarding semi-emancipation, degrees of ritual purity, liability, and the property rights and precise religious status of slaves and freedmen. One sample Baraita, of rabbinic teaching "external" to the Mishnah, will suffice:

> It can happen that a man can sell his own father in order to enable his mother to have her marriage settlement paid over to her. How? A Jew buys a male and female slave on the market, the two of them [already]

> having a son (*who is not also bought*—Rashi's gloss). He manumits the female slave, marries her himself, and then takes the step of making over all his property to her son. (*He dies, and his widow claims her marriage settlement out of the estate*—Rashi). The result is that the son sells his father, the slave, in order to find fluid capital for his mother to collect her marriage settlement.[145]

Like other slaves in the ancient Mideast, the slaves of Jews were both the beneficiaries and the victims of an elaborate body of law that required written documents for every sale, manumission, or other transaction. Rabbis, like later Muslim and Christian clerics, admonished masters to treat their slaves with humanity and respect, but there is no reason to assume that such strictures were any more effective among Jews than among other peoples. Manumission and assimilation were common as long as Judaism remained a strong and proselytizing religion. But Jews faced a wholly new universe after the destruction of the Second Temple in 70 A.D., the disastrous rebellions against Rome, and the resulting mass enslavement and impoverishment of their own people. After Roman legislation prohibited the circumcision of slaves, masters increasingly pressured rabbis to permit pagan slaves to dwell in Jewish households. Urbach finds some indication that the rabbis who disallowed the retention of uncircumcised slaves also tightened the rules against manumission. What linked the two issues was the growing isolation and vulnerability of Jewish communities. The "conservative" teachers feared that the internal presence of pagans would undermine religious purity and solidarity and that frequent manumissions would disperse those slaves who had accepted the covenant or relax the standards governing authentic assimilation.[146]

That these concerns persisted to the twelfth century and beyond is shown by the rules spelled out in Maimonides' *Code*. Drawing a sharp distinction between Hebrew and gentile slaves, Maimonides ruled that heathen slaves could be worked with "rigor" (though they should be treated with mercy and never abused or disgraced); that masters were forbidden to teach slaves the Scriptures and that such illegal teaching could never be grounds for freedom; that a child born of a heathen female slave and sired by her Israelite master "has the status of a heathen in every respect and can be bought and sold and employed forever as other slaves are." Maimonides also held that "if the slave stipulates at the outset that he will not be circumcised the master may retain him as long as he wishes, even as a heathen, and then he may sell him to a heathen or to a foreign land"; but that a slave purchased without such specifications should be given a year to consider conversion and, if still refusing to be circumcised and to accept the religious duties of a Jew, should be sold to a heathen or foreign land.[147]

Medieval Christians greatly exaggerated the supposed Jewish control over trade and finance and also became obsessed with alleged Jewish plots to enslave, convert, or sell non-Jews. To keep the question in perspective, one must recall that in the thirteenth century the church officially held that the Jews themselves had been condemned to perpetual slavery as punishment for their crucifixion of Christ. This doctrine sometimes sanctioned the confiscation of Jewish property and even the sale of Jews as chattel slaves. Though various popes sought occasionally to protect Jews from murder and violence, they also insisted that Christ's supposed slayers, like Cain, had been condemned to be fugitives and wanderers. Most European Jews lived in poor communities on the margins of Christian society; they continued to suffer most of the legal disabilities associated with slavery. Even after conversion to Christianity, an act legally analogous to the emancipation of a slave, they were subject to scrutiny and interrogation when suspected of secret Judaizing practices. As late as 1739, Portuguese authorities incinerated twelve men and women who were accused of practicing Jewish rites after their supposed conversion to Christianity.[148]

It is true that from the ninth to the twelfth century Jews played a central role in the expansion of Mediterranean commerce and in pioneering long-distance trade. According to Robert S. Lopez, the Jews for a time provided the sole link between Catholic Europe and the more advanced civilizations of China, India, and the Byzantine and Islamic empires.[149] Before the Italian commercial expansion of the twelfth century and the Italian invasion of the Black Sea after 1204, Jewish merchants occupied strategic centers of strength in the Byzantine Empire, Muslim Spain, and Fatimid Egypt. Thanks to their interlocking communities and far-reaching networks of communication, they could supply the interior of Europe with precious luxuries from the East as well as with salt, wine, and textiles. As intermediaries between Christian and Muslim worlds, Jews seemed to be in a position to develop and dominate the Mediterranean slave trade. Yet they did not.

There were two major restraints. First, most Jews lived in disciplined communities in which surveillance and group solidarity subjected every aspect of life to talmudic law and to the specific *responsa* of judicial authorities. It was normal for Jews in Spain or France to refer controversial questions to the Jewish seats of learning in Baghdad, Jerusalem, or Cairo. Deeds for the sale or manumission of a slave had to conform to the strict standards of Jewish law, which in Egypt was recognized by Muslim courts. Indeed, in an era when the concept of territorial law had not yet developed, Jewish and Muslim courts cooperated to a remarkable degree, mutually enforcing the principle that each person should be subject to the norms of his own religious community.

A Jewish slaveholder might thus be required to show why a servant had not been baptized and brought into the covenant of Israel; or been sold to a non-Jew; or been forced to work on the Sabbath; or been sexually exploited, Jewish law differing sharply from that of Islam on the sinfulness of a master's sexual relations with his slaves. The slave of a Jewish master could seek emancipation on any number of legal grounds. If he did not wish to win de facto liberty by becoming assimilated into a Jewish community, he could profess allegiance to Islam or Christianity, and then appeal to outside authorities for liberation.[150]

The second restraint on Jewish slave dealing lay in the determination of Muslims and Christians to keep their own peoples from becoming Judaized through the agency of slavery. Muslims had always been insistent on this point. And whereas Jews had to rely on ransoming their own captive brethren, the Muslims had the power within *Dar al-Islam* to free any professing Muslim held by an infidel. Christians, who had originally been forced to accept and tolerate the enslavement of fellow Christians in the Roman world, were for a time more equivocal in forbidding the bondage to Jewish masters of their coreligionists or potential converts.[151]

The restraints on Jewish slave dealing were most effective in the well-ordered communities of the eastern Mediterranean. The rulers of the early Byzantine Empire prohibited Jews from engaging in the slave trade, which continued to flourish as a result of wars with Persians, Bulgars, Magyars, Arabs, and Seljuks. In the eighth century, however, Byzantine Jews were forcibly, though temporarily, required to profess Christianity. As "New Christians," occupying a position similar to that of the later Marranos of Spain and Portugal, they appear to have taken a minor part in the slave traffic. During later centuries of relative religious toleration, the authorities sometimes failed to enforce stringent laws forbidding Jews from owning or circumcising non-Jewish slaves. A ninth-century account refers to Jews' purchasing slaves in Bulgaria and selling them in Venice to an envoy of Basil I, the Byzantine emperor. By the eleventh century the Jews in Cherson, in the Crimea, seem to have bought Christian slaves with impunity. For the most part, however, the Byzantine rulers were successful in reserving to their Christian subjects the lucrative slave trade of the eastern Mediterranean.[152]

In his masterly study of Jewish commercial communities in the Arab world, S. D. Goitein has confirmed David Ayalon's view that Jews played no appreciable role in the Egyptian slave trade. It is possible that the documents from the Cairo Genizah, which present such a rich and detailed picture of economic life from the mid-tenth to the mid-thirteenth century, may be unrepresentative of the merchant community at large.

The business records that have survived were left by Jews whose religious scruples forbade the destruction of Hebrew written characters. But if slave dealing was limited to the nonreligious, it must have been considered a marginal and less than reputable undertaking. The significant point is that while the Genizah records contain numerous references to the sale, purchase, manumission, and marriage of individual slaves, there is no evidence of slave trading as a specialized or organized activity. Yet Egypt stood at the center of what Goitein portrays as a booming "free-trade community" in which Muslims, Jews, and Christians traveled on the same ships and did business with one another. The Jewish merchants, whose integration into Egyptian society extended to business partnerships with Muslims, were predominant in the silk industry and in the production and sale of sugar. But the only slaves appearing in the Genizah records are domestic servants and various kinds of stewards and business agents who were accorded extraordinary privileges and responsibilities.[153]

Jewish merchants became more directly involved with slave trading in central Europe and the western Mediterranean. The Jewish population was smaller in the west than in the east, and religious discipline appears to have been less strict. In Spain, for example, Jewish moralists repeatedly denounced concubinage with slave girls, a practice sanctioned by Muslims but apparently rare among Jews in Egypt. As intimated by Maimonides, western rabbis in effect legitimized slave trading by excluding uncircumcised slaves from the talmudic ban on selling servants to Gentiles. They provided a further loophole by affirming that Jews had no duty to persuade slaves to be circumcised if noncircumcision had supposedly been a condition of purchase. Since Christian authorities everywhere outlawed the circumcision of slaves of non-Jewish origin, a Jewish merchant could at least feel free to buy slaves for the purpose of eventual resale. Indeed, even Saint Thomas Aquinas recognized the need for compromises that would encourage Jewish merchants to allow the Christianization of their slaves. For a time the church permitted Jews to purchase Christian slaves for purposes of trade, so long as the slaves were sold to Christian owners within three months—a requirement, as Aquinas observed, that was not enforced.[154]

Christian princes had a more forceful interest in protecting property rights and ensuring adequate supplies of labor and revenue. As early as the ninth century, Louis the Pious specifically allowed Jews to import and sell slaves within the Holy Roman Empire. But such policies frequently clashed with the evangelizing aims of the church. In the ninth century, Archbishop Agobard created a furor in Lyons when a prominent Jewish merchant took legal action to reclaim a slave woman whom

Agobard himself had baptized. The church sought to enforce a fixed price as compensation to infidels and Jews whose slaves had been converted to Christianity, and repeatedly complained that secular authorities upheld a much higher market price. In the late fourteenth century the king of Aragon defended the right of Jews in Sicily to hold Muslim slaves, a practice that brought mounting fire from the clergy. It was only in the latter half of the fifteenth century, however, that the secular authorities in Sicily finally gave way to the crusading zeal of the church, acquiescing in the forcible baptism of slave children and ultimately in the confiscation of all slaves owned by Jews. The issue contributed to waves of anti-Semitism that culminated, as in Spain, in the expulsion of Jews in 1492.[155]

The actual extent of Jewish slave dealing is still highly debatable. In the tenth and eleventh centuries, Jewish slave dealers were prominent in Prague, which had become a major transit point for the shipment of Slavic captives to Germany, France, and Spain. Hebrew literary sources refer to the pagan Slavonic countries as "Canaan," citing the fact that the people sold their own kinsmen as slaves. Along with Christian and Muslim merchants, Jews transported captives from the eastern German frontiers to western Europe and increasingly to Spain. In Spain itself Jews were frequently in a position to sell Muslim slaves to Christians, and Christian slaves to Muslims. Although castration was cause for immediate emancipation according to talmudic law (and was similarly prohibited by Islamic law), both Jews and Muslims found others to perform the distasteful operation. Eunuch "manufacturers" included Christian merchants who gave relics to their local church. Salo W. Baron, who contends that Verlinden exaggerates the extent of Jewish slave dealing in Spain, admits that despite all religious and legal barriers, Jews played an active role in supplying eunuchs and other slaves to *Dar al-Islam.*[156]

The Christianization of Slavonic Europe and the Christian reconquest of Spain ultimately reduced the supply of infidel slaves and thus limited the opportunities for slave merchants of whatever faith. In Muslim and particularly in Christian countries the vast majority of Jews had no contact with slavery in any form. Even the Jewish slaveholders, who were far more numerous than slave traders, appeared mainly in Mediterranean lands from Egypt to Spain where economic development and an intermingling of cultures had produced a state of relative religious tolerance. In Majorca, for example, Jewish planters owned large estates equipped with gangs of Muslim slaves. In Sicily, where Jewish and Muslim scholars contributed to the high civilization of the court of Frederick II, slaveholding was a facet of culture and opportunity. For as late as the second half of the fifteenth century, Sicilian records show an increasing number of Jews buying and selling unbaptized slaves. Yet for most European Jews the late Middle Ages were a time not of widening opportunity but of violent persecution and massacre, of new discriminatory laws, of being forced to wear a visible badge of infamy—originally introduced by the Muslims—and finally, in late thirteenth-century, England, in late fourteenth-century France, and in late fifteenth-century Spain, of facing mass expulsion or extermination.

The decline of Jewish involvement with the slave trade coincided with the Crusades and with Italian commercial expansion in the eastern Mediterranean and Black Sea. It may have been more than coincidental that Christian governments became obsessed with the specter of Jewish slaveholders at precisely the time when Italian merchants were displacing Jews from the more honorable branches of eastern trade and were also developing the highly commercialized Black Sea slave trade. No simple hypothesis can account for the explosive eruption of anti-Semitism in thirteenth-century Europe or for its later consequences in the western Mediterranean. The alarm over religious heresy, exemplified by the Albigensian Crusade, clearly played a part. But it is worth noting that as Christians took over various economic activities that had long been proscribed and delegated to Jews, the activities could partly be legitimized by proscribing everything Jewish. In other words, a crusade to purge Europe of a supposedly polluting and diseased element could serve to disguise Christian borrowings from a real or stereotyped Jewish tradition. There can be no doubt that the massive enslavement of diverse peoples from the Black Sea, who were a new counterpart to the biblical "children of strangers," was accompanied by an increasing sensitivity to the rights of Christians. According to the emerging consensus, free Christians could not legally be enslaved except as punishment—on Mediterranean galleys, for example—for a specific crime. Although baptism never entailed automatic emancipation, except for the slaves of infidels, it was agreed that only Christians could righteously enslave others, for the purpose of saving their souls. These propositions, confirmed by numerous edicts of the fourteenth and fifteenth centuries, were a transmogrification of Jewish doctrine from the time of the Diaspora. It is thus conceivable that the new Christian slave trade gave added force to the ancient fantasy that Jews plotted to kidnap or otherwise enslave the children of strangers in order to circumcise them or drink their blood. While such matters are never subject to historical proof, the evidence suggests psychological links between the emergence of a new slave trade in fifteenth-century Spain and Portugal and the culminating expulsion of the Jews.

The supreme irony, with a view to the history of human "progress," is that this closing ring of persecution opened the way for the Jewish contribution to the Atlantic slave system. To be sure, this contribution was relatively minor and depended on such dramatic adaptations as conversion to Christianity and emigration to the New World. It also drew on centuries of cultural development that had little to do with persecution. The great Portuguese discoveries of the fifteenth century owed much to Jewish science, technology, capital, and geographic knowledge. Even during the Roman Empire, Jewish communities had become widely dispersed through North Africa and the Maghrib. Later invading Muslims treated Jewish merchants with contempt but accorded them privileges denied to any Christian. Though massacred in Tuat and Tlemcen, Jewish goldsmiths and traders won official positions in Morocco and built commercial networks that extended eventually to Timbuktu. Arabs respected the Jews' geographic knowledge of the Sahara; Jews acquired an important role in the Catalan maritime trade with the Maghrib, and Spanish kings chose multilingual Jews as their envoys to Muslim lands. Like the Muslim Kharijite rebels and refugees, the Jews found the Maghrib and western Mediterranean a frontier of opportunity. By the fourteenth century, Christian Majorca was prospering as a result of an African trade initiated between resident Jews and their brethren in Morocco. The Majorcan Jews, expert in the manufacture of clocks, quadrants, and other nautical instruments, began producing accurate maps based on information supplied by their African coreligionists. These fourteenth-century cartographers divulged caravan routes that Muslims had long regarded as closely kept secrets. At a time when Europe hungered for the gold needed to pay for expensive imports from the East, the Majorcan and Catalan maps focused attention on Africa. I have already mentioned the famous Catalan Atlas of the world made by Abraham Cresques, whose apprentice son, Jafuda, became a "New Christian" after the anti-Semitic riots of 1391. Ronald Sanders presents the intriguing hypothesis that Jafuda (who became Jaime Ribes or "Master Jacome") helped to chart the Portuguese explorations of the early fifteenth century and that he and other Jews or Marranos were inspired by the hope of discovering the "lost tribes of Israel," an event that would end religious discord and inaugurate the messianic age.[157]

Sugar was another factor that contributed indirectly to Jewish involvement in the Atlantic slave system. The Genizah documents show that producing or selling sugar was one of the common occupations of Egyptian Jews from the eleventh to the fourteenth century. Other records indicate that Jews were prominent as sugar exporters from Crete and as owners of Mediterranean sugar refineries. Fernand Braudel points out the parallels between the Jews' "network of intelligence and collaboration" and that of French Protestants after the revocation of the Edict of Nantes. From Turkey to Naples and Portugal, Jews responded to discriminatory barriers by discovering or creating new commercial opportunities, which included the international trade in sugar. Marranos or "New Christians" were leaders in establishing sugar plantations in Madeira, the Azores, and São Tomé, and in, as Braudel puts it, preparing the way for the Dutch and "marking the beginning of Amsterdam in world history." Brutal coercion played a part in this transformation. In 1493, when Portugal was flooded with Jewish refugees from Spain, the children of Jews who refused to convert were forcibly baptized and shipped off to São Tomé. It was assumed, as a later chronicler put it, that "being separated, they would reasonably be better Christians; and it was a result of this that the island came to be more densely populated, and on account of this it began to thrive exceedingly." There is evidence, however, that as the children matured and became planters, many "reverted" to Judaism. The early Brazilian sugar industry owed much to Marrano initiative and for a time remained dependent on the technical skills of Marrano foremen and artisans. According to Arnold Wiznitzer, "New Christians played a leading part in organizing the export of sugar from Brazil through their family and business connections with the Marranos in Portugal and the former Portuguese Marranos who had escaped to Amsterdam and lived there as open professing Jews." By the seventeenth century, Jews had come to own many of the sugar refineries in both Antwerp and Amsterdam.[158]

But to what extent can the Marranos be considered Jews? This controversial question leads back to the theme of persecution and to the bitter ironies of Jewish involvement with black slavery. Tens of thousands of Spanish Jews professed Christianity in the face of mounting persecution, particularly after the epidemic of anti-Semitic massacres in 1391. Although the church ostensibly offered conversion and assimilation as a final solution to the Jewish problem, the Marranos came under increasing suspicion of duplicity. Beginning in 1480, the Inquisition finally unleashed a reign of terror designed to purge the Marranos of the last secret taints of Judaism. The confessions extracted by torture and threat of death simply reinforced Christian fantasies and led to the decision of 1492 to expel all nonconverted Jews, who were regarded as the source of continuing contamination. Jacob R. Marcus concludes that many of the Marranos, even those who confessed to secret Judaizing practices, had lost all knowledge of their religious heritage. Yet even assimilation and intermarriage could not protect persons of Jewish descent from suspicions of heresy. It was said by an inquisitor that Marrano homes could immediately be distinguished from a hilltop on any chilly Saturday—no smoke rose from their chimneys! A trace of Jewish blood, according to the Spanish doctrine of *limpieza,* was sufficient to alert the Inquisition to evidences of impurity. In short, the Marranos were Jewish to the extent that they were never free from persecution as crypto-Jews. And when given the opportunity, especially in seventeenth-century Holland and Dutch Brazil, some Marranos sought to recover and reaffirm the identity that the Inquisition had sought to detect.[159]

Professing Jews could play no part in the early history of the Americas, since they were outlawed from all Spanish and Portuguese domains. In 1497, after considering the economic disaster that would result from expelling the large Jewish population, the Portuguese crown ordered their forcible conversion to Catholicism. Many of the Portuguese Marranos, who may have constituted as much as 20 percent of the country's population, sought to emigrate to safer sanctuaries, especially after 1547, when the pope sanctioned the Portuguese Inquisition. The crown tried periodically to stop emigration but also recognized the need for skilled artisans, technicians, and merchants in the expanding empire. Accordingly, Marranos flocked to Madeira and São Tomé; in the Kongo Kingdom and Angola some became prominent as contractors for slave cargoes destined for Spanish America; in Brazil they took a lead in the early hardwood industry and then prospered as merchants, surgeons, bankers, and sugar planters. Agents of the Inquisition followed the Marranos to the colonies, spying out secret rites and sending offenders to Europe for trial. But despite this harassment Marranos found freedom and opportunities in the Portuguese colonies that were unobtainable in the metropolis. And during the seventeenth century such freedom and opportunities became increasingly tied to the slave system and to the related international struggles for power.[160]

As the Dutch won independence from Spain and then took the offensive against the exposed colonies of their united Spanish and Portuguese enemies, they welcomed Marrano refugees, who often possessed intimate knowledge of the Luso-Hispanic empires. Granted relative religious freedom, a thriving Jewish community emerged in seventeenth-century Amsterdam. The Jews' knowledge of different languages and of the intricacies of international finance, and their business contacts in Brazil, Africa, and the Islamic world, aroused the interest of Dutch and eventually of English imperialists. No doubt the Inquisition exaggerated the conspiratorial role of Jews and Marranos in preparing the way for Dutch imperial triumphs. Yet there was no reason that Brazilian Marranos should not have corresponded with their freer brethren in Flanders and Holland. It was only natural that Marranos and Jews should accompany the Dutch expedition that captured Recife and that some Marranos, living under a Dutch edict of toleration, should strive to recover their religious heritage.

Dutch authorities did much to encourage Jewish emigration to Brazil. Jews constituted a substantial proportion of the white civilian population of Recife and Dutch Brazil. In 1639, however, professing Jews owned only about 6 percent of the sugar mills in Dutch Brazil. According to Arnold Wiznitzer, they were far less notable as planters than "as financiers of the sugar industry, as brokers and exporters of sugar, as suppliers of Negro slaves on credit, accepting payment of capital and interest in sugar." Jewish merchants could not become directly involved in the African slave trade, which was monopolized by the Dutch West India Company. Yet the company, Wiznitzer adds, "sold slaves at public auctions against cash payment. It happened that cash was mostly in the hands of Jews. The buyers who appeared at the auctions were almost always Jews."[161]

Warfare and rebellion gradually disrupted the Dutch sugar industry in Brazil, leaving it virtually in ruins by 1654, at the time of the Dutch exodus. Up to this point, three observations deserve emphasis with respect to Jewish involvement with the Atlantic slave system. First, the initial participants were all nominal Christians, many of whom had lost any sense of Jewish identity except for the peril of being persecuted as the descendants of Jews. Second, the Portuguese colonies were frontier areas that offered Marranos temporary security as well as economic opportunity. Though Dutch Brazil was by no means free of anti-Semitism, it was one of the few spots in the world where some Marranos could recover their Judaism and where Jews could freely practice their religion while engaging in a wide range of vocations. Unparalleled freedom and opportunity thus coincided with a social world dependent on the African slave trade. Finally, Jews apparently had no difficulty in adapting talmudic precepts and values to the institution of black slavery. There is no evidence of an incipient antislavery tendency in Jewish thought. Indeed, the Diaspora of New World Jewry from Brazil to the Caribbean and from the Caribbean to North America was intimately tied to the expansion of the slave system.

Again, religious persecution gave the impetus to migration and to a deepening commitment to black slavery. Brazilian Jews looked with terror upon the return of the Portuguese, who promised death to Marranos who had reverted to Judaism or had collaborated with Dutch heretics. In the early 1650s Marrano and Jewish refugees fled from Brazil to the Caribbean and as far north as New Amsterdam; a larger number returned temporarily to Holland but then gravitated to the West Indies. "Wherever they went," writes Jacob R. Marcus, "these Dutch Jews brought with them skills as businessmen and their experience as sugar planters, refiners, and brokers. It was out of this Diaspora that would emerge the new Jewish communities of Surinam, the Caribbean islands, and North America."[162]

The Dutch Jews did not initiate the sugar boom in the West Indies. Except in Surinam, they never constituted a planter class. But despite their small numbers and initial lack of wealth and power, they played a vital role in helping to transform the Caribbean from a Spanish lake into Europe's great cockpit of imperial aspiration. When the Dutch dispatched an expedition to capture the strategic island of Curaçao, they recruited a Sephardic Jew as an interpreter. Knowledge of Spanish enabled the Sephardim to develop networks of illicit trade, breaking through Spain's mercantilist barriers and making Curaçao the great entrepôt of the Caribbean. To one Dutch Jew, Philippe Henriquez, the Board of Admiralty even granted the concession to ship blacks directly from Africa to Curaçao. The other Jews in Curaçao were obliged to buy slaves from the Dutch West India Company. They frequently sold slaves, together with manufactured goods from Holland, along the Spanish Main or to purchasers from the various Caribbean islands. During the eighteenth century Jews accounted for approximately one-half of the white population of Curaçao. Founded by Marranos in 1651, Curaçao acquired a synagogue eight years later and has had the longest continuous history of any Jewish settlement in the New World. Until 1825 it was also the largest Jewish community in the Americas. Although virtually all the Curaçao Jews owned black slaves, their holdings were proportionately smaller than those of the Protestants, who owned the larger plantations. Nevertheless, most of the Jews' commercial wealth derived from the reexport of slaves, from the sale of slave-grown produce, or from credit mechanisms that lubricated the gears of the plantation system. And thanks to their affluence and close ties with North America, the Curaçao Jews were able to send generous contributions to the first eighteenth-century synagogues in New York and Newport.[163]

Curiously, the one region where Jews pioneered as sugar planters was along the Guianese coast of South America, a region that never fulfilled its extraordinary promise. There are various explanations for the belated development of the Guianas. The rich alluvial soils of the coastland lay beneath the sea at high tide, guarded by mangrove swamps and finally accessible only thorough the technical feats and capital outlays of Dutch engineers. There were no natural fortresses, as at Cartagena, for defense against inevitable assaults from the sea. Accordingly, in the early and mid-seventeenth century, British and Dutch settlers moved far up the yawning mouths of the Guianese rivers. Geographic isolation, a shortage of slave labor, raids by hostile Amerindians and fugitive blacks, and frequent capture by warring European nations—all retarded expansion of a plantation economy. It was only in the eighteenth century that British and especially Dutch colonists began moving downriver to build the dikes essential for coastal plantation agriculture. In the meantime, however, the remote upriver settlements provided Jews with a rare opportunity for plantation ownership.[164]

In seventeenth-century Surinam, Dutch Jews built their own self-governed town, Joden Savanne, in the interior jungle. Joden Savanne was the center of a Jewish planter class that depended on sugar and slaves. During the late seventeenth and early eighteenth centuries, Jews apparently owned a large share of the slaves and plantations in Surinam; they seem also to have taken a lead in developing the sugar industry along the Essequibo and other rivers to the west. Even in the late eighteenth century, by which time the Surinamese Jews had turned to the timber trade and were less involved with sugar plantations, they represented one-third of the colony's white population. At that time more Jews lived in Paramaribo, the capital of Surinam, than in all of North America. And the Guianese synagogues invested their surplus funds in black slaves. One might hastily explain the Jews' acculturation to Caribbean ways as the result of lawless frontier conditions. The Sephardim, to say nothing of the Marranos, had presumably strayed far from Jewish tradition. Even in the mid-seventeenth century, however, the Sephardic Jews of Surinam had established their own synagogue, school, and cemetery, and continued to maintain close ties with the mother synagogue in Amsterdam. Moreover, by the 1690s 13 percent of the Surinamese Jews were Ashkenazim—a proportion that rose to 50 percent by 1750. If the Ashkenazim tended to stick to the urban trades, leaving the sugar and vanilla plantations to the Sephardim, it would appear that neither religious tradition nor communal solidarity had any effect on the unquestioning acceptance of a slave economy.[165]

Since the Guianas failed to develop as a major sugar-producing region until the nineteenth century, they serve mainly as a limiting case proving that, in the absence of discriminatory conditions, Jewish communities could become totally enmeshed in the plantation system. The Caribbean islands offered fewer opportunities to own choice land. Unlike the embattled Hollanders, the French and English had never welcomed the Jews as allies and had less need of recruiting foreign white colonists. Nevertheless, even the Catholic French winked at laws that would have excluded Jewish refugees from settling in Martinique, Guadeloupe, and Saint Domingue. With an eye to Dutch achievements, Jean Baptiste Colbert, Louis XIV's minister of finance, even legalized the presence of individual Jewish merchants in the French Antilles and congratulated Jews for their agricultural innovations. Religious prejudice prevented Jews from acquiring more than a marginal place in the French West Indies. But despite various edicts of expulsion, a handful of Jews prospered as planters in the French islands. The Gradis family of Bordeaux gained considerable wealth and power in eighteenth-century Saint Domingue. And the ties between French Caribbean Jews and their brethren in British North America contributed to the illicit trade that brought the French plantation system to its ultimate grandeur and doom.[166]

The importance of Jews in the British slave colonies is still open to dispute. Authorities in Cromwellian England were alert to Dutch precedents and to the value of Marranos in providing intelligence on the Hispanic Empire. Despite continuing legal discriminations, England by the eighteenth century was probably the freest European country that a Jew could find. The British West Indies, removed from the strictest Anglican or Puritan constraints, presented an even more promising haven. The Jewish and Marrano refugees from Dutch Brazil aided British colonial expansion in a number of ways. Raphael de Mercado, a Brazilian physician, invented an improved sugar mill that he brought as an emigrant to Barbados and that helped to make him a wealthy planter. More important than technology was the Jewish experience with international trade and the devices that allowed the purchase of slaves and other commodities on credit. Yet Jews did not emerge in the British West Indies as prominent slave traders. They lived for the most part in town ghettos, subject to discriminatory taxes but close to the synagogue, school, and friends that sustained cultural identity. They managed retail shops and engaged in moneylending, but were hardly on a level of affluence with the great planters. The Barbados census of 1680 lists 54 Jewish households out of a total of 405 in Bridgetown; the Jews collectively owned 163 slaves (an average of 3 per household); the non-Jews, 1,276 (an average of 3.6 per household). Like other townsfolk, most Jews in the British Caribbean owned a few personal slaves and often hired out skilled workers and artisans, or looked for minor profits from individual sales. Although some historians have contended that Jews treated their slaves more humanely than did non-Jews, Jacob R. Marcus concludes that Jews had no higher or lower scruples than their gentile counterparts. Yet their slaves enjoyed Saturdays free from work, in addition to Sunday market days, which no Jewish merchant could afford to miss.[167]

Whatever the Jewish refugees from Brazil may have contributed to the northwestward expansion of sugar and slaves, it is clear that Jews had no major or continuing impact on the history of New World slavery. In Newport, Rhode Island, Aaron Lopez and Jacob Rivera engaged in the African slave trade as late as the 1770s, and a few Jewish merchants in New York, Philadelphia, and Charleston imported slaves along with other commodities. But this is to say no more than that Jewish merchants were in tune with their time.[168] The significant point is not that a few Jewish slave dealers changed the course of history but that Jews found the threshold of liberation in a region dependent on black slavery. It has been said that the more enlightened rulers of Europe were much swayed by the early achievements of enfranchised Jews in Dutch Brazil, the Caribbean, and North America. It has less often been noted that those achievements were intertwined with the enslavement of another people who, like the Jews, would long be feared as a contaminating disease, regarded as candidates for conversion, considered a threat to civilization, loathed as a peril to sexual and racial purity, and seized as objects for either expulsion or extermination.

PART TWO

Redeeming Christianity's Reputation

"For when I have heard much talk of the world's growing worse, I have known that this was indulged in by persons who had thought that it could grow better."

Kenneth Burke,
Towards a Better Life: Being a Series of Epistles, or Declarations

"I can hardly help wishing that the war might go on and on till it brought us suffering and sorrow enough to quicken our consciences and cleanse our hearts."

Charles Eliot Norton
to George William Curtis
11 May 1862

1. EMANCIPATION AS PROOF OF PROGRESS

The Society of Friends, having enjoyed decades of increasing prosperity, influence, and colonial expansion, experienced a deep trauma during the Seven Years' War (1756–63). From colonial war zones to the British metropolis, Quakers interpreted their suffering and persecution as a divine chastisement calling for collective efforts at self-purification. In 1758 Philadelphia Yearly Meeting cautiously resolved to exclude from business meetings any members who subsequently bought or sold black slaves; the meeting also authorized a committee to visit Quaker slaveholders, beginning a quiet, charitable, and ultimately effective campaign to persuade all Friends to manumit their slaves. In 1761 London Yearly Meeting ruled that henceforth Quaker slave dealers should be disowned.

In the 1760s, as for many decades to come, black slavery was sanctioned by Catholic, Anglican, Lutheran, Presbyterian, and Reformed churchmen and theologians. No modern church or sect had sought to discourage its members from owning or even trafficking in black slaves. From Canada (under both French and British rule) to the southern limits of Spanish America, colonial governments took the legality of black slavery for granted. The governments of Britain, France, Spain, Portugal, Holland, and Denmark all openly supported the African slave trade.

By the 1750s, to be sure, the classical justifications for slavery, already discredited by Montesquieu and Hutcheson, were being demolished by the arguments of Rousseau, Diderot, and other philosophes, to say nothing of the calculations of Hume and Franklin regarding the effects of slavery on population growth and the productivity of labor. On the level of abstract political philosophy, John Locke, a shareholder in the Royal African Company, was the last major thinker to seek justifications for enslaving foreign captives. And Locke's strained arguments were more than counterbalanced by his more famous and influential celebration of human liberty. Yet the Enlightenment's indictments of slavery were scattered and desultory. Often they left loopholes for a defense of colonial slavery on grounds of expediency and public interest. As late as the 1770s, when the Quaker initiative finally led to a rash of militant antislavery publications on both sides of the Atlantic, no realistic leader could seriously contemplate the abolition of New World slavery—except, on the analogy with European slavery and serfdom, over a span of centuries.[1]

Yet in 1807, only thirty-four years after a delegation of British Quakers had failed to persuade the Lord of Trade to allow Virginia to levy a prohibitive tax on further slave imports, Britain outlawed the African slave trade. Twenty-six years later, Britain emancipated some 780,000 colonial slaves, paying £20 million compensation to their supposed owners. Only ninety years separated the first, cautious moves of the Philadelphia Quakers from the emancipation edicts of France and Denmark (1848), which left Brazil, Cuba, Surinam, and the southern United States as the only important slaveholding societies in the New World. It was barely a century after the founding of the London Society for Effecting the Abolition of the Slave Trade (1787) , sixty-one years after the final abolition of slavery in New York State (1827), that Brazil freed the last black slaves in the New World. By then antislavery had even found a champion in the great African missionary Cardinal Lavigerie and had won public endorsement from Pope Leo XIII.

From any historical perspective, this was a stupendous transformation. To be sure, for the black slaves themselves, of whom there was an increasing number through the early nineteenth century, sixty or ninety years seemed interminable. The gradual extension of "free soil" did nothing to lighten the burdens of slaves in the more dynamic plantation societies, and it can even be argued that in many regions "emancipation" was little more than a cosmetic change in legal status that failed to improve the blacks' basic conditions and quality of life. The chronology of reform also had a different meaning for abolitionists, who experienced a succession of delays, defeats, excuses, and compromises and who, lacking the benefit of hindsight, could never be certain of the future. From the distance of the late twentieth century, however, the progress of emancipation from the 1780s to the 1880s is one of the most extraordinary events in history. One can easily think of more rapid transformations in the realms of science, technology, and economic structure—and, of course, some historians have insisted that the abolition of slavery can be explained only as a by-product of technological and economic change. One can debate the question of underlying causes, but no one can deny the striking and probably unprecedented shift in public attitudes toward an established institution. In our own time the only comparable, and still incomplete, transformation pertains to racial and sexual discrimination, both of which the more radical abolitionists of the nineteenth century attacked as forms or offshoots of slavery.

By the 1830s, following Britain's emancipation act and roughly midway between the first organized antislavery agitation of the 1780s and the abolitionists' final triumphs in Cuba and Brazil, the Western world was beginning to view slave labor as an intolerable obstacle to human progress—as an economic anachronism as well as an offense against Christian morality and human rights. This consensus, however qualified by an insistence on gradual and orderly change, was clearly part of a much broader transformation in manners and moral sensibility. An adequate analysis of this transformation would have to move beyond such labels as humanitarianism, evangelicalism, romanticism, egalitarianism, and utilitarianism. It would need to clarify the later reformers' ambivalent response to the American and French revolutions, to the period when hundreds of thousands of black slaves won or were granted their freedom in the United States, the Caribbean, and Latin America while millions of others were becoming locked within plantation economies. A causal explanation would also have to relate the antislavery sensibility to the triumphant hegemony of a capitalist worldview and particularly to capitalist views of labor, while avoiding any temptation to reduce the rise of abolitionism to the interests of an entrepreneurial class—a class that for the most part detested abolitionists. But here we are less concerned with underlying causes than with the linkage between antislavery and conceptions of human progress, a linkage that became a powerful ideological force in its own right.

For nineteenth-century liberals it was precisely the altruistic and disinterested character of the antislavery crusade, pitted against the selfish interests of both slaveholders and capitalist "lords of the loom," that seemed to prove that public virtue and enlightenment could keep pace with material advance. John Stuart Mill, for example, invoked the example of British emancipation to show that "one person with a belief is a social power equal to ninety-nine who have only interests." Arguing against the "naturalistic theory of politics," which pictured all historical change as the inevitable outgrowth of social and economic circumstance, Mill contended:

> It was not by any change in the distribution of material interests, but by the spread of moral convictions, that negro slavery has been put an end to in the British Empire and elsewhere. . . . *It is what men think that determines how they act;* and although the persuasions and convictions of av-

erage men are in a much greater degree determined by their personal position than by reason, no little power is exercised over them by the persuasions and convictions of those whose personal position is different, and by the united authority of the instructed.[2]

If altruism and benevolence were in the long run conducive to material advance, as Emerson and other liberal idealists happily conceded, this in no way diminished the sublime achievement. The British knew, Emerson pointed out:

> Slavery is no scholar, no improver; it does not love the whistle of the railroad; it does not love the newspaper, the mail-bag, a college, a book or a preacher who has the absurd whim of saying what he thinks; it does not increase the white population; it does not improve the soil; everything goes to decay. For these reasons the islands proved bad customers to England.

Such material considerations simply demonstrated that the laws of progress rewarded virtue and that slavery was in every way detrimental to both virtue and progress. After making a few gibes about "shop-keeping civility," Emerson graciously concluded that self-interested motives had not carried "excessive or unreasonable weight" in Britain's decision to free her slaves, a decision vindicating the cause of human rights and reflecting "infinite honor on the people and parliament of England."[3]

Addressing a somewhat skeptical French public, Alexis de Tocqueville was no less impressed by the "hazardous and singular task" that the British had just completed:

> We have seen something absolutely without precedent in history—servitude abolished, not by the desperate effort of the slave, but by the enlightened will of the master; not gradually, slowly, through successive transformations which by means of serfdom led insensibly towards liberty; not by successive changes of mores modified by beliefs, but completely and instantly, more than a million men simultaneously passed from the extremity of servitude to complete independence, or better said, from death to life. What Christianity itself did only over a number of centuries has been accomplished in a few years. If you pore over the histories of all peoples, I doubt that you will find anything more extraordinary or more beautiful.[4]

Tocqueville contemptuously dismissed the popular French theory that Britain's only aim in abolishing West Indian slavery was to "crush others' colonies, and thereby to gain a monopoly of sugar production for its own establishments in India." Pointing out that India produced only one-fifteenth as much sugar as the Dutch "free-labor" colony of Java and one-fifty-fifth as much as the British slave colonies at the time of emancipation, Tocqueville scoffed at the absurd claim that "England, in order to strike at other nations' sugar colonies, has started out by ruining its own, several of which were in a state of extraordinary prosperity. That would be the most insane Machiavellianism imaginable." The truth was, Tocqueville insisted, "that the emancipation of the slaves was a parliamentary reform, the act of the nation and not of its rulers." The government, by which Tocqueville meant the successive English ministeries, had resisted emancipation until "the popular torrent prevailed and swept it along." Even the "violence, deceit, hypocrisy, and duplicity" that the British had characteristically displayed in trying to suppress the slave trade of other nations could not detract from "the philanthropic and especially Christian conscience *[sentiment]*" that had produced the great event of British emancipation.[5]

By the mid-nineteenth century, liberals throughout the world cited the progressive abolition of slavery as proof of a transcendent purpose in history, a purpose gradually revealed and made manifest through human enlightenment. Interpreting contemporary emancipations as the culmination of centuries of struggle against barbarism, prejudice, and oppression, they tended, like Tocqueville, to divide the progress of liberty into two dispensations that resembled but were not to be confused with the conventional Hebrew and Christian dispensations. The first epoch included ancient slavery and medieval serfdom, subjects on which there was little systematic knowledge. The second epoch centered on the history of colonial slavery, making little allowance for the actual persistence of serfdom in eastern Europe and even in parts of western Europe.

Ancient slavery had long posed a problem for humanists and orthodox Biblicists. Because nineteenth-century Southerners made specious appeals to classical and biblical precedents, we have tended to minimize the force of such precedents for writers who had no material or social interest in defending slavery. For example, from the fifteenth century onward humanists of the stature of Pontano, Grotius, Herder, and Wilhelm von Humboldt continued to find justifications for an institution accepted by Aristotle and Seneca and inseparably associated with the glories of Greece and Rome. In the words of Arnold Heeren, the early-nineteenth-century Göttingen philosopher and historian:

> But one should not try to deny the truth that, without the instrument of slavery, the culture of the ruling class in Greece could in no way have become what it did. If the fruits which the latter bore have a value for the whole of civilized mankind, then it may at least be allowed to express doubt whether it was bought at too high a price in the introduction of slavery.[6]

Similarly, while antislavery churchmen ridiculed biblical justifications for modern black slavery, most of them conceded that the twenty-fifth chapter of Leviticus, authorizing Jews to buy and keep "the children of strangers" as "your bondmen for ever," at least meant, in the hedged words of a Scottish abolitionist, "that slavery is not of *such a nature, as to preclude the possibility of the Divine Being himself, in any circumstances whatever, tolerating its existence*."[7] Historians have not generally appreciated the importance of the tedious and repetitious debates over "the Bible and slavery," debates that set the stage for the better-known controversies over Darwinian evolution and the so-called Higher Criticism. Even after the American Civil War some orthodox Jews as well as Christian biblical scholars continued to insist on the abstract lawfulness of human bondage as an ordinance of God.

In general, however, nineteenth-century writers neutralized the force of precedent either by denying the significance of ancient slavery or by relegating the subject to a purely moral sphere. Both strategies served to isolate modern slavery as a monstrous aberration, unrelated to the central trends of history or the larger patterns of economic and political life. For the classical philologists who dominated the academic study of antiquity, modes of production had no relevance to the timeless achievements of the human spirit; slave labor was simply an unfortunate, if peripheral, aspect of ancient society, a subject best left to the antiquarians.[8] The moralists, for their part, tended to stress the incomparability of modern plantation slavery to the benign, domestic servitude of biblical and even Hellenic societies. If the "Oriental despotism" of Rome had produced a more malignant and truly comparable form of bondage, this was a moral corruption that had helped bring on the decline and fall of the empire. According to William Blair, in a history of Roman slavery published in the year of British emancipation: "The influence of Slavery upon the Romans themselves, may be seen in the character and manners, of both the high and the low ranks of freemen. Licentiousness in the former; idleness in the latter; and cruelty in both. . . ." Henri Wallon, who in 1847 published the first comprehensive and authoritative history of slavery in antiquity, had no doubt that in ancient times "slavery decimated nations rather than saved them, corrupted morals rather than refined them, ruined rather than benefited the family and the state. . . . The bad points were the direct results of slavery, the good ones of freedom."[9]

It is true that from the late eighteenth century onward, a few historians and social theorists diverged from the prevailing moralistic dualism. William Mitford's multivolume *History of Greece* attributed the evils of Athenian slavery to excessive democracy. Johann Friedrich Reitemeier interpreted Greek slavery as a stage in the evolution of various forms of dominance and submission, an evolution governed by the landowners' demand for luxuries, urban investments, and cheap urban labor. Reitemeier was indebted to John Millar, the great Scottish social theorist who in 1771 identified changing property relations as the key to the progressive stages of human development. For Millar, a student and later a colleague of Adam Smith's, economic activity, the authority of fathers, the position of women, social rank, laws, customs, and the uses of leisure were all functional expressions of an interrelated social system. In ancient societies slavery had become a necessary means of social discipline and capital accumulation, enabling primitive men to progress from the poverty and insecurity of earlier hunting and pastoral stages. Millar believed that no revolution in history had advanced human happiness as much as the abolition of slavery in Europe. He insisted, however, that this momentous transformation had nothing to do with religious or moral opinion. European slavery had been destroyed by impersonal social and economic forces, which had then been ratified by liberal laws and customs. It followed that the revival of chattel slavery in the American colonies was an irrational regression, a violation of the laws of political economy induced by the lust for power and that "blind prepossession which is commonly acquired in favor of ancient usages."[10]

At the risk of oversimplification, one may think of a "scientific" tradition concerning slavery that extends from the writings of Benjamin Franklin, David Hume, Adam Smith, and John Millar to such later figures as Auguste Comte, Karl Marx, and Friedrich Engels. Despite their profound differences in other respects, these writers viewed slavery as an institution that could be understood only in terms of its social and economic utility and its relation to the laws of historical progress. Beginning with Franklin and Hume, such theorists took it for granted that slave labor was less efficient and normally more expensive than free labor and that slave societies inhibited the growth of population and thus of industry and national wealth. Accordingly, slave societies could arise only under special circumstances—in a primitive stage of social organization and property accumulation; where the supply of free labor was inadequate to exploit the resources of extensive new land, as in the American tropics; or where artificial protections and monopolies allowed the lust for power to supersede economic self-interest. Modern slavery, from this viewpoint, was less a moral evil than a senseless anachronism, an affront to social science. On the one hand, it seemed certain that such a "disgraceful anomaly," as Comte termed it, would yield to the same impersonal forces that had brought liberty to Europeans. On the other hand, since all history was in a sense self-justifying, modern slavery might persist as long as special circumstances required it.[11]

The dominant Christian view was no less ambiguous on the lessons to be learned from antiquity. Christians had traditionally argued, with respect to Old Testament ordinances, that God had allowed the Jews certain extraordinary and temporary privileges, such as slavery and divorce, which had then been abrogated by Christianity. Most abolitionists, supported by such historians as Henri Wallon, Edouard Biot, Augustin Cochin, and Paul Allard, presupposed an irreconcilable conflict between slavery and the Christian message that all men were equal before God. According to the prevailing nineteenth-century dogma, it was Christianity that had first softened the harsh laws and manners of the Roman world and that had then improved the condition of slaves until, gently and almost imperceptibly, they had been elevated to a state of freedom. This was the grand theme of Wallon and Biot, who both won prizes in a competition sponsored by the Académie des Sciences Morales et Politiques for the best explanation of the abolition of ancient slavery. What such Christian apologists shared with Comte and Marx—who represented opposing ideological positions—was the belief that the abolition of ancient slavery had depended on the unfolding of an immanent historical design. From both perspectives masters and slaves were only the agents of social or moral forces they could not comprehend. In the words of Augustin Cochin, who popularized the Christian historiography: "All of this work of transformation is due much less to the external changes of governments, institutions, and laws than to an internal change in souls. Sentiments of equality are born, and this suffices, before the laws sanction progress, before words express it." Edouard Biot articulated precisely the ideology that dominated antislavery thought until it was finally repudiated by radical abolitionists. Explaining why Christianity had accepted ancient slavery as a "given condition," directing its efforts less to remedial legislation than to "the morality of men," Biot concluded:

> It is evident that laws too favorable to the slaves would have strongly tended to upset the whole social edifice, already crumbling under the repeated blows of foreign invasions. It was preferable, in order to maintain public tranquility, that improvement in the lot of the slave be brought about progressively through improvements of the master.[12]

This faith in the indirect benefits of Christianization—like the faith in the indirect benefits of political and economic freedom—gave way only slowly and incompletely to the belief in a new or second dispensation, distinguished by conscious decision, collective effort, and mobilization of public opinion. As described in 1823 by the new Liverpool Society for the Abolition of Slavery, the great discovery that made "the present age . . . remarkable beyond any that has preceded it, for the rapid and surprising improvement which has taken place in the moral character and disposition of mankind," was "the practice of combining society itself in intellectual masses, for the purpose of obtaining some certain, defined, and acknowledged good, which is generally allowed to be essential to the well-being of the whole."[13] This discovery owed much to the eighteenth-century voluntary associations for civic improvement, and even more to the liberating precedents of the American and French revolutions. The description of the Liverpool abolitionists could be applied not only to most of the radical and revolutionary causes of the nineteenth century but also to the Bible and tract societies and to the organizations for the promotion of temperance, Sunday schools, and foreign missions. Whatever the goal, the "intellectual masses" were emboldened by the promise of rational planning, coordinated effort, and division of labor, to say nothing of the availability of cheaper and more efficient methods of printing and distributing propaganda to an increasingly literate public.

But if the methods of achieving progress had changed, there was still confusion and controversy over the actual dynamics of social transformation. For most Anglo-American abolitionists, the new dispensation had not abrograted the more reassuring features of the earlier Christian dispensation that had peacefully transformed European slaves into serfs, and serfs into free peasants. Emancipation still pertained primarily to "moral character and disposition"; it implied no basic change in land ownership, economic decision making, or the dependency of agricultural labor; it precluded and would indeed prevent, according to abolitionist doctrine, the kind of revolutionary struggle and racial warfare that had ravaged Haiti.

When even the most radical British abolitionists sought to refute the popular mythology regarding the Haitian revolution, a mythology that long infected and debilitated antislavery thought, they elaborated a countermythology stressing the social order and labor discipline that had followed emancipation. For example, in 1833 the journal of the Agency Anti-Slavery Society attributed Haiti's years of bloodshed and destruction to the French Revolution and especially to Napoleon's efforts to exterminate the blacks. The blacks themselves, according to the British abolitionists, had remained peaceful and industrious after the French Convention had granted them immediate emancipation. Despite long and costly resistance to French tryanny, the Haitian people had by the

1820s shown striking moral improvement; their population had more than doubled (in contrast to the slave population in the British islands); the rights of property in Haiti were inviolable; free peasants worked cheerfully on the large estates of paternalistic proprietors.[14]

Yet British and American abolitionists created a collage in which they repeatedly juxtaposed such images of peaceful and orderly evolution with apocalyptic rhetoric demanding the death of a satanic institution. Although their conception of progress included elements of continuity, it was more centrally attuned to a moment of collective rebirth and transfiguration. As in ancient times, slave emancipation would ultimately depend on divine Providence as manifested in the Christian spirit. But now the efficacy of Christianity could be proved, in the face of competing worldly pressures, only by a dramatic worldly act. Providence could reveal itself only through a new human ability—the ability of an enlightened and righteous public to control the course of events.

2. SACRED INSPIRATION AND SECULAR POWER

Before we turn to some of the specific historical connections between abolitionism and ideas of progress, it will be useful to gather clues by examining the extraordinary response to Britain's abolition of the slave trade in 1807 and to its slave emancipation in 1833. The former, according to the bishop of London, would soon bring "a total change in the condition of one quarter of the habitable globe," exterminating a greater quantity of evil and producing a greater quantity of good than any act since the beginning of the world. The duke of Norfolk agreed that in the history of the world no human legislature, at least, had passed such a "humane and merciful Act," and observed that it could not be coincidental that the 1807 triumph had occurred in Passion Week, when the Son of God displayed "that stupendous instance of Mercy towards

Mankind, the redemption of the world by his Death upon the Cross."[15]

For British, American, and some later Continental and Latin American reformers, it was Thomas Clarkson's canonical *History of the Rise, Progress and Accomplishment of the Abolition of the African Slave-Trade by the British Parliament,* published in 1808 in two volumes, that spelled out the redemptive message of this "Magna Charta for Africa." While Clarkson rejoiced at the removal of "one of the greatest sources of suffering to the human race," he considered this a minor benefit compared with Britain's liberation from a contagion that had poisoned "the moral springs of the mind" and jeopardized Christian salvation. Because the twenty-year crusade for abolition had coincided with the French Revolution and the Napoleonic wars, Clarkson thought that by arousing and sustaining "generous sympathies" and a "spirit of benevolence," it had probably saved Britain from barbarism. Threatened by the Napoleonic Antichrist and by "barbarous opinions" that substituted the law of force for moral accountability, Englishmen could at least take comfort "that, at this awful crisis, when the constitutions of kingdoms are on the point of dissolution, the stain of the blood of Africa is no longer upon us . . . that we have been freed (alas, if it be not too late!) from a load of guilt, which has hung like mill-stone about our necks, ready to sink us to perdition."[16]

For Clarkson the glorious contest had stripped away the deceptive conventions of secular society: "It has unmasked the vicious in spite of his pretension to virtue. . . . It has separated the moral statesman from the wicked politician. It has shown us who, in the legislative and executive offices of our country are fit to save, and who to destroy, a nation." In 1792, when public enthusiasm for abolition had reached a high pitch, "the good were as distinguishable from the bad, according to their disposition to this great cause, as if the divine Being had marked them; or . . . as we may suppose the sheep to be from the goats on the day of judgment." Opponents of abolition, "through vicious custom and the impulse of avarice, had trampled under-foot the sacred rights of their nature, and had even attempted to efface all title to the divine image from their minds." In contrast, Clarkson imagined that even Charles James Fox, considered hopelessly ungodly by the evangelicals, had died in 1806 while contemplating the imminence of abolition and experiencing a "joy ineffable, from a conviction of having prepared the way for rescuing millions of human beings from misery." Whatever his previous sins, Fox's final efforts as prime minister had raised his spirit to the "fittest state" as it went "gliding from its earthly cavern, to commix with the endless ocean of benevolence and love."[17]

Speaking to the future, Clarkson prophesied that "emancipation, like a beautiful plant, may, in its due season, rise out of the ashes of the abolition of the Slave-trade." Like many Americans, he was struck by "the wonderful concurrence of events as previously necessary for this purpose, namely, that two nations, England and America, the mother and true child, should, in the same month of the same year, have abolished this impious traffic; nations which at this moment have more than a million subjects [slaves] to partake of the blessing. . . ."[18] In future decades, the prophecy and religious message would inspire countless young reformers in both countries.

In 1833, when Clarkson was seventy-three, half blind, and suffering from a painful accident, he expressed astonishment to his aged co-worker William Smith that both had "lived to see those two great days for our country, and for Humanity, the abolition of the Slave-Trade and of W. Indian or rather Colonial Slavery. Having seen this we may depart in peace, for we may leave the world with an assurance that slavery has now received what will be its Death Blow in every part of the world."[19] Though many abolitionists had bitterly opposed monetary compensation to planters as well as the coercive system of black "apprenticeship," their doubts soon evaporated in a chorus of self-congratulatory rhetoric that exceeded, if anything, the extravagance of eighteen-seven.

As in 1807–08, wider concerns contributed to the outpouring of relief and thanksgiving over national regeneration. If there was no sense of having averted the retributive disaster of a French invasion, the French revolution of 1830 had ignited a fuse leading to a powder house of domestic discontents. On one rampart, the Church of England faced an increasingly militant and powerful alliance of Dissenters who threatened to join forces with Catholics, Utilitarians, and anticlerical radicals in demanding the abolition of tithes, church rates, ecclesiastical abuses, and remaining religious disabilities. When it appeared that the Anglican bishops could be blamed for defeating the parliamentary reform bill of 1831, the burning of the bishop's palace in Bristol seemed to be a portent of the violence to come. On another rampart, the government faced a succession of working-class riots, trades-union manifestos, rural insurrections, and demands for universal suffrage, to say nothing of near anarchy in Ireland. The passage of the Reform Bills of 1832, followed by the harsh Irish coercion act of the following year, left many observers with the impression that England and especially Ireland had narrowly escaped revolution.

It would be absurd to claim that Parliament emancipated West Indian slaves in order to divert attention from domestic oppression. The most obvious objection is that slave emancipation was not politically feasible until the domestic crisis had been largely resolved. Moreover, the political impulse for emancipation came from the large urban centers, the regions of mobilized religious dissent, and the newly enfranchised boroughs—not from the bastions of traditional privilege.[20] On the other hand, Parliament succeeded in appeasing this antislavery public while rejecting its demand for immediate and uncompensated emancipation, much as the English Reform Bills of 1832 had appeased the prosperous middle class while reinforcing the political power of the landed aristocracy. Later on we shall give closer attention to the details of West Indian emancipation. For the moment it is sufficient to emphasize the symbolic importance of an act that simultaneously demonstrated Parliament's independence, both from the crown and from popular agitation; its sensitivity to human rights and to "respectable" public opinion; its devotion to liberty and commitment to the rights of property. Above all, the slave emancipation act was designed to restore public confidence in the disinterested virtue and justice of the newly reformed Parliament. In this respect it is worth noting that Edward Stanley, a valued member of Lord Grey's Whig administration, became a political liability as the secretary for Ireland and as the author of the unpopular Irish coercion act. After threatening to resign in response to the liberals' attacks, Stanley succeeded in transferring himself to the Colonial Office, where he quickly redeemed his reputation by sponsoring and championing the slave emancipation bill. By the spring of 1833 any public association with this cause was an enviable political asset.[21] The final, ecstatic response to slave emancipation drew resonance from deeper yearnings for national unity, for benevolent leadership, and for reassurance that Britain had weathered the worst of a dangerous storm.

In one of the most significant sermons delivered on emancipation day, 1 August 1834, Ralph Wardlaw showed how a seemingly political and secular act helped to fulfill the eschatological promise of Christianity, prefiguring an era of universal freedom and harmony. A well-known minister and reformer in Glasgow, Wardlaw was a leader of the Congregationalists or Voluntaries, who tended to dominate Scottish abolitionism. Like many Scottish reformers, he was a devout evangelical but had also been nourished on the doctrines of Francis Hutcheson, Adam Smith, Thomas Reid, and other luminaries of the Scottish Enlightenment. Since 1832 he had worked openly for the disestablishment of the Church of Scotland, claiming that any state religion inevitably led to corruption, rationalism, hypocrisy, and secularization.[22] In other words, it was in the interest of Protestant orthodoxy and religious purification that Wardlaw supported the principle of voluntarism. The success of religious voluntarism, as the American example had shown, depended on vigorous enterprise. Among British Dissenters, in particular, abolitionism had proved to be an extremely effective instrument for exciting and mobilizing popular enthusiasm, though at the cost, as Wardlaw admitted, of considerable contention and a "war of controversy." Fortunately, an act of wholesale emancipation marked a specific day of "Jubilee," when preachers like Wardlaw could appeal for a closing of ranks:

> Let the heat of anger, and the coldness of estrangement, and the distrustful surmises of reciprocal jealousy, be on either side frankly and for ever dismissed. Let the Negroes become the object of a common interest and a common effort for their well-being. . . . Let the day, which imparts liberty abroad, be the restorer of amity at home![23]

In hailing emancipation as a literal Jubilee, Wardlaw took his text from the verses of Leviticus describing the day of emancipation and atonement in the seventh month following seven sabbatical years. This allowed him to expand on the political aspects of Jewish law, which had set divine limits to human ownership of land and persons; he could then move on to the "typical" or eschatological aspects that prefigured Christian redemption. For example, the ancient Hebrew Jubilee prefigured Christ's mission "to proclaim liberty to the captives, and the opening of the prison to them that are bound." This passage from Isaiah, which Jesus "stood up to read," according to Saint Luke, in the synagogue at Nazareth, was for Wardlaw and many other abolitionists the essence of the Gospel message. Few of them realized that it also had a special and somewhat different meaning for thousands of black slaves.

As might be expected of a devout evangelical, Wardlaw interpreted the Gospel's "proclamation of freedom" to be primarily a "freedom from Sin, from Satan, from Death, from Hell." But by 1833 these terms had become so intertwined with West Indian slavery that dissenting ministers, in particular, saw nothing profane in assimilating the British emancipation act to the traditional framework of Old Testament types and New Testament antitypes. Indeed, for Wardlaw the Jubilee occasioned by Parliament's political decision was nothing less than the harbinger of Christ's final salvation of the world:

> The trumpet has sounded through all the colonial dependencies of our country, which proclaims "liberty to the captives."—O! what heart is there so cold, so seared, so dead, as to feel no thrill of exulting emotion at the thought, that on the morning of this day, eight hundred thousand fellow-men and fellow-subjects, who, during the past night, slept bondmen, awoke freemen![24]

Not only had Britain averted "a gathering storm of divine retribution" for a national sin; by accepting the national sacrifice of £20 million as the price of freedom, the British people had also exerted on the world a mighty "*moral power*": "the influence of high-minded example,—the influence ever imparted by the manifestation of disinterested self-denying principle." Wardlaw was confident that British emancipation would be "but the first day of a Jubilee year,—of a period of successive triumphs . . . of continuous and rapidly progressive prosperity, to the cause of freedom." For the most "grievous reproach to Christianity," in the eyes of the vast pagan world, had at last been rolled away.

Wardlaw claimed that the colonial freedmen, many of whom had already been converted in spite of the impediments of slavery, would soon make "admirable missionaries" to their former brethren in Africa. To the remaining freedmen, who still suffered from spiritual bondage, Britain owed the greatest possible reparation for wrongs for which "we have all, as members of the community, been indirectly chargeable": "While, as Britons, we gave our millions to compensate the master; as Christians, we will send to the slave the 'unsearchable riches of Christ.' " Above all, Wardlaw rejoiced at the thought that "Britain's trans-Atlantic daughter" had already caught the spirit of British philanthropy; and that once America joined Britain in setting "the united example of the entire, peaceful, and final extinction of slavery,—the world will be shamed into imitation:—and in no long period, there will not be found on earth a remnant of it, to attest its existence, and indicate its nature, to posterity." This triumph, in Wardlaw's millennial vision, would prepare the way for the final Jubilee of universal love and mercy.[25]

The themes that Wardlaw elaborated appeared in countless other commentaries on the meaning of West Indian emancipation. What are we to make of this rhetorical response? The liberation of innocent captives, as a metaphor for social progress, hardly suggests social legislation prescribing the rights and duties of an underclass. One thinks rather of an army of liberation, the storming of the Bastille, the dramatic restoration of a preexisting freedom and social identity. Yet this was a liberation without liberators, without visible agents or institutions of any kind, even though it had been decreed initially by the British Parliament. Wardlaw spoke as if a divine breath had passed over the West Indies immediately after midnight on 1 August 1834, infusing freedom into the breasts of 800,000 slaves and releasing the British people from an accumulated burden of guilt. The imagery suggests a spiritualizing of the heroic ideals of the Age of Revolution, when liberty and equality were to be won on the barricades or on the field of battle. Wardlaw and his audience could simply take it for granted that the West Indian blacks would continue to perform the same kinds of labor for the same masters.

But though Wardlaw described emancipation as an essentially spiritual and moral process, it was by no means synonymous with the traditional Christian concept of an inward freedom that transcends one's external worldly condition. Slave emancipation unleashes the forces for universal progress. It removes impediments, opening the minds and souls of the freedmen to the full benefits of Christian civilization. At the same time it purifies and strengthens Christian civilization, endowing Britons and eventually Americans with the mission to liberate and save the world. One should note that emancipation also destroys any conception of the black West Indians as a corporate group, entitled by race or a common ill fortune to their own way of life. The worthiest freedmen will become Christian missionaries. Others will prove their merit, individually, by their willing industry, obedience, and Christian piety. If some freedmen retreat to the bush and revert to barbarism, the problem can be blamed, as with English pauperism, on defective character. For it was the very essence of emancipation, as Wardlaw and other reformers conceived it, to remove the arbitrary constraints that stifled responsibility and concealed individual worth.

Historians have sometimes been puzzled by the apparent anomaly of a British Parliament granting "liberty to the captives" in 1834 and in the same year enacting the New Poor Law, designed to incarcerate British paupers in workhouses where husbands would be separated from wives and where both sexes would be subjected to slavelike labor, regimentation, surveillance, and discipline. But one must avoid the mistake of projecting modern conceptions of autonomy into the minds of the early emancipationists. Ralph Wardlaw, for example, was an ardent champion of penitentiaries and asylums, and devoted one of his pamphlets to the uplifting cause of imprisoning all British prostitutes for the purpose of reformation.[26] From his sermon on liberating the captives, one would never suspect that Parliament had allowed West Indian courts and legislatures to spell out the regulations governing labor, vagrancy, and standards of maintenance—and hence the practical meaning of emancipation—or that special magistrates, analogous to the "guardians" appointed under the New Poor Law, had been empowered to inflict corporal punishment at their own discretion.

Again, we must avoid the retrospective indignation that can only serve to congratulate the present world while obscuring our understanding of the past. The important point is that celebrations of British emancipation affirmed a new congruence between the conditions of West Indian life and the values of the Protestant ethic. As slaves the West Indian blacks had been beyond the reach of such supposedly universal values; when they rose in insurrection, for example, British society increasingly blamed their masters. But the chorus of praise lavished on the behavior of the newly freed apprentices—testifying to their "worthiness" for freedom—meant that they could now be judged by the standards of the mother country and that they were individually responsible for their own fate.

Although abolitionists eventually concluded that apprenticeship was as oppressive as slavery, they were at first dazzled by the radiant reports from West Indian missionaries and government officials. Despite their confident public predictions, Thomas Fowell Buxton and other abolitionist leaders had privately feared that widespread disorder followed by the blacks' refusal to work might partly confirm the warnings of their opponents. Buxton, who for a decade had led the parliamentary campaign, anxiously prayed on emancipation day for "My 700,000 Clients."[27] By 29 August he could inform the Cromer Missionary Society that emancipation "has succeeded to the utmost & beyond the utmost of our expectations—I have various sources of intelligence—I have been favoured with the information Govt. Missy Soc's & private correspondence & one and all write in declaring that it has been crowned with complete and glorious success. . . . I speak on the authority of letters from the Planters themselves that never was there a period in which so much work was done, in which the Laws were so well obeyed in which so much security & such enterprise prevailed." On 28 December, Buxton was still expressing his private thanksgiving that the government could report no act of violence on the part of the blacks. By the following March he was ebullient. Lord Aberdeen had assured him "that every thing was going on marvellously well in the West Indies. The Negroes quiet dutiful diligent. 'It is quite amazing.' ' 'Tis contrary to reason' 'It cannot be accounted for'—but so it is." Edward Stanley had volunteered the further happy news that even in Jamaica "the Negroes had all returned to their work in good humour" after the Christmas holiday, and that they "appear the most orderly & the most industrious of menkind."[28]

Buxton and other evangelicals were particularly moved by the accounts that "the Jubilee Day," as one missionary put it, "and the Sunday following, were festivals in Religion, rather than in common rejoicing." Emancipation day "past off very quietly," wrote Mrs. Dawes from Antigua. "It was observed as a day of solemn thanksgiving in consequence of the Governor's proclamation to that effect; business was suspended, and all the churches and chapels in the island open for Public Worship." In another letter that Buxton also drew on for public speeches, Charles Thwaites told how the slaves had filled the local chapel, which was hung with palm and coconut branches, "to usher in the important day. . . . The feelings of the people were of a sanctified nature, and the meeting had a high moral tendency. I cannot describe my feeling at the close of the meeting at 12 o'clock at seeing the numerous company before me, who had entered the Place as Slaves but were now free. To God be all the glory." Nothing excited the missionaries as much as the "glorious Resolution" of the British and Foreign Bible Society to give a copy of the New Testament and Book of Psalms to every freedman who could learn to read by Christmas: "to behold Ethiopia stretching out her hands on that day, to receive the Book of God—the charter of their eternal freedom! This will be 'Magna Charta' indeed! the Magna Charta of eternal freedom, furnished by the British and Foreign Bible Society!"[29]

In America Ralph Waldo Emerson, though a rebel in theology, made use of such missionary reports in his influential speech commemorating the tenth anniversary of the Jubilee, "an event singular in the history of civilization; a day of reason; of the clear light; of that which makes us better than a flock of birds and beasts: a day, which gave the immense fortification of a fact,—of gross history,—to ethical abstractions." It especially impressed Emerson that "the negro population was equal in nobleness to the deed." Meeting in churches and chapels on the night of 31 July, they had welcomed their emancipating moment with prayers and tears of joy, "but there was no riot, no feasting" and, according to one report, " 'not a single dance . . . nor so much as a fiddle played.' " The next morning, Emerson assured his listeners, "with very few exceptions, every negro on every plantation was in the field at work." That the ensuing decade had witnessed a public crusade to abolish apprenticeship in no way diminished Emerson's reverence for the initial emancipation. Since apprenticeship was also abolished on 1 August, in 1838, the second emancipation was easily subsumed in the first. Like Ralph Wardlaw, Emerson stressed that "other revolutions have been the insurrection of the oppressed; this was the repentance of the tyrant," the harbinger of a new era, when "the masses" would awaken and apply an absolute moral standard to every public question.[30]

One might well ask how the masses can awaken when tyrants repent, and in America some black abolitionists like J. McCune Smith and Robert Hamilton would have preferred honoring "some day in which some enslaved black man in our own land swelled beyond the measure of his chains and won liberty or death." But for most free blacks the First of August became a far more significant holiday than the Fourth of July. It was a day of promise when both black and white abolitionists could deliver orations, odes, and sermons that not only condemned the evils of slavery and racial discrimination but also reminded the world that Britain, the tyrant symbolically overthrown every Fourth of July, must still teach white Americans the meaning of freedom.[31]

It should now be clear that the responses to the British abolitionists' triumphs of 1807 and especially of 1833 were genuine rituals designed to revitalize Christianity and atone for national guilt. For various liberal and evangelical segments of Anglo-American society, West Indian emancipation was a rite of passage that evoked fantasies of death and rebirth, enabling it to function, to borrow Anthony F. C. Wallace's terms, "almost as a funeral ritual; the 'dead' way of life is recognized as dead; interest shifts to a god, the community, and a new way."[32] One aspect of this regenerative renewal was its emphasis on the "death struggles" of West Indian slavery or, as Buxton put it, "the death of the old parent Dragon," which would make it easier to slay the "posthumous brood."[33] Less obvious was the way in which Buxton's culture, by annihilating its supposed "antithesis," acquired the attributes of omnipotence and universality.

The implications of this point become apparent in a remarkable anthology published in 1834, containing "prose and verse, illustrative of the evils of slavery, and commemorative of its abolition in the British colonies." Its title, *The Bow in the Cloud,* refers to the rainbow now spanning the seas from Africa to the West Indies, after the passing of a Noachian storm. Many of the selections had been written during the abolitionist struggle and were included to remind readers of the evils still flourishing in "that land of *boasted* freedom," the United States. In the verse, nationalism mixes with sentimentality: according to Lord Morpeth, the heirs of Runnymede, Trafalgar, and Waterloo have now proved that being mighty to rule means being mightiest to relieve and save.[34]

The funereal theme emerges in the Reverend Richard W. Hamilton's "Description of Jamaica, in Its *Most* Modern Statistics," supposedly dated 2 May 1934. The twentieth-century author, who as a child had heard from his abolitionist grandfather terrifying accounts of West Indian cruelty and torture, travels to Jamaica to see the remnants of history's most barbarous institution. Wardlaw, we may recall, looked forward to the day when "there will not be found on earth a remnant of it, to attest its existence, and indicate its nature, to posterity." Of course, such literal annihilation would raise problems by effacing all remembrance of Christianity's redeeming struggle. Buried within a Kingston museum, our author finds the relics he seeks. The model of a slave ship and the instruments of torture curdle his blood, overwhelm him with guilt, and validate his grandfather's tears. The Jamaican blacks, however, have long since forgiven and forgotten, though they have not forgotten their benefactors. On the bay where the author lands, they have erected a magnificent statue of Wilberforce, who even in marble exudes a "holy, kindly air." In this thoroughly Christianized elysium, the blacks seem to spend most of their time singing hymns, praising everything English, and expressing their eternal gratitude to Wilberforce, Brougham, Clarkson, and the county of Yorkshire. They are especially keen on sending missionaries to Borneo.[35]

By burying slavery, the British also eliminated all crime and violence. In Jamaica there are no troops or prisons, nor is there any "frivolity." The people are meek, pious, cheerful, and courteous—in short, "civilized"—the "husbandman" (there is no mention of industry) happily earns his bread by the sweat of his brow. Not only has racial prejudice disappeared, but amalgamation is a publicly accepted ideal. Consequently, the Jamaican physiognomy has changed and *now* exhibits the image of man's Creator: "The brow which receded now rises into a mass of power and sublimity; the chin which, in consequence of this deformity, once protruded, now fixes the right angle of the facial line; the lips have lost their sensual thickness, the nostrils their brutal dilation. . . ." Here is "progress" indeed! The burial of slavery has also buried the Negro. Even so, the white governor who addresses a mostly dark-skinned senate and assembly is an English peer.

Parts of this fantasy may have seemed ridiculous even to abolitionists, but the central hopes and contradictions pervaded their responses to British emancipation. Two points deserve special emphasis: there is a transfiguring event that overcomes and buries the Antichrist, leading to a millennium of peace, harmony, and unity in Christ Jesus; there is also a continuing dependence on the part of the freedmen, who are as cheerful, dutiful, and deferential as the planters had claimed slaves to be. Indeed, portions of the above "Description of Jamaica" read almost like a caricature of the proslavery idylls published some years earlier by West Indian apologists. The image has simply been refracted through an abolitionist lens; the removal of all emblems of coercion is sufficient evidence of the blacks' consent and of the absence of social conflict. On the level of political action, as we shall see, the British abolitionists were capable of realistic assessments of social change. But such assessments were framed by a larger worldview in which their black "clients" became the symbolic projections of fears and hopes, deeply embedded in Western culture, concerning sin, liberation, and redemption.

It should be expected that an event like West Indian emancipation would evoke a displacement of wishes and fears from an internal to an external position, from an inner to an outer world, or "from centre to periphery."[36] Dependency can make a colonial frontier as valuable for psychological as for political and economic exploitation. At the outset, however, it was the cultural *independence* of the slave colonies that enabled British reformers to define a new collective mission and identity. In this connection it is useful to recall Hegel's use of lordship and bondage as metaphors of mind containing, in M. H. Abrams's phrase, "a sustained inner as well as outer reference."[37] For our purposes there is no need to summarize Hegel's extremely complex argument, which deals with the impact of dependence and independence on the evolution of self-consciousness. As in Hegel's primal scene, Britain "discovered" in the slave colonies a wholly independent culture, analogous to an independent consciousness. The very existence of such a culture challenged the presumed universality of Britain's emerging religious and economic values. For example, the obviously unfair and arbitrary qualities of West Indian slavery challenged the assumption that wealth, power, and rank were distributed in accordance with natural justice. The existence of such an antithetical model was especially aggravating when English laborers claimed to be even more oppressed than West Indian slaves. In Hegel's paradigm the threatening "Other" must either be killed or enslaved. In point of fact, West Indian whites warned repeatedly of the dangers of being "enslaved" by Parliament, echoing the rhetoric used half a century earlier by their North American brethren. But despite their blustering threats, the West Indian whites recognized that resistance could easily lead to racial warfare and to their own extermination. They therefore submitted, by their own definition, to a form of political and cultural bondage.

Although it may seem bizarre to speak of slave emancipation's "enslaving" the British West Indies, there is something to be learned from the planters' perception. Like Hegel's bondsman, they preferred Britain's version of "the truth," of the nature of moral being, to their own annihilation. Henceforth they would have no protection against policies that would shatter their economy and eventually deprive them of their traditional institutions of self-government. Meanwhile, the "killing" of slavery helped to validate Britain's own self-image, confirming her mission to lead the world, including her errant "trans-Atlantic daughter," toward a new era of justice and Christian brotherhood. In 1839 British abolitionists could remind a sympathetic foreign secretary of the "noble attitude which Great Britain has taken before the world on the great subject of slavery," and insist on the government's "plain and imperative obligation" to use "its mighty moral influence, for diffusing through other countries the same freedom which at so much cost has been happily . . . established in the dependencies of our own."[38] By the 1840s abolitionists and government officials alike were avowing such objectives as "a general emancipation of the Negro race" and "the abolition of slavery throughout the world." It is significant that Buxton, at the time of his maximum influence on government, spoke metaphorically of Britain's tightening two "chains" for the "deliverance of Africa": "a chain of vessels on the coast to capture Slavers, a chain of native Powers in Africa acting in concert with us, abandoning the trade themselves, and prohibiting slaves from being passed through their dominions."[39] The more that Britain achieved such new emancipations and the more that her white and dark-skinned missionaries triumphed over the last vestiges of barbarism, the more certain it seemed that the British version of civilization was universally valid and rooted in what Wardlaw termed "disinterested self-denying principle." Such self-perceptions ultimately depended, as the *Bow in the Cloud* fantasy suggests, on the humble gratitude of increasing numbers of "clients." But such undying gratitude is seldom evoked by even the most generous social legislation. It is the gratitude of the captive who has been liberated from tyranny, of the redeemed sinner who has been delivered from hell.

The writings we have discussed contain an implicit tension between two attitudes toward human history and destiny. The first is a basically secular belief in the possibility of continuous, gradual improvement in accordance with the natural laws of cause and effect—the underlying assumption being that morality, justice, and happiness are capable of the same cumulative advances as science and technology. The second attitude is oriented to what Paul Tillich has called *kairos,* "a decisive moment" of qualitative change that must be distinguished from *chronos,* that is, chronological or "watch time." The new things or fulfillments that happen in the *kairoi,* the great moments of history, are "not in a progressivistic line with the other new things before and after [them]." For Tillich the *kairoi* are never inevitable or predictable, nor are they total fulfillments; they represent a "victory over a particular power of destruction, a victory over a demonic power which was creative and now has become destructive."[40]

The British antislavery triumphs were perceived in precisely this way, but they were also assimilated to a faith in continuous and universal progress, a progress conforming to social and economic laws. The issue, it must be stressed, was how to comprehend the liberation of oppressed peoples, how to project the concepts of an inherited Christian culture into a heathen world of darkness. In our preceding examples, the *kairos* appears as an eschatological leap that overcomes a "demonic power" and then transcends the limits of previous political, racial, and economic history. Emancipation, according to the vision in *The Bow in the Cloud,* eliminates all political, racial, and economic conflicts of interest. Because the once exotic sugar islands were so remote and so marginal to British life, they served as an ideal experimental theater for imagining the consequences of liminality, the essence of which is a "release from normal constraints." Slave emancipation inevitably led to such a liminal, threshold state, whose very indeterminacy aroused anxiety as well as creative hope.[41] Utopian dreams often half conceal a latent nightmare. It is clear that many reformers feared that the revitalizing *kairos,* once unleashed, would bring on the very disaster predicted by the slaveholders: that after being liberated, the blacks would reject Christianity and "civilization," turn against their benefactors, and become lazy, violent, barbarous, and ungovernable. On an important psychological level, this negative image is the true subject of *The Bow in the Cloud.* The antidote, designed to stabilize change and keep the image positive, is a dose of *chronos*—an insistence on continuity, dependence, and progress without disorder. This mixture reveals the central strategy and mission of nineteenth-century evangelical reform: the attempt to fuse these two conceptions of change, channeling sacred inspiration into the controllable world of secular power.

3. NEW WORLD SLAVERY AS CHRISTIANITY'S "FORTUNATE FALL"

New World slavery provided Protestant Christianity with an epic stage for vindicating itself as the most liberal and progressive force in human history. Of course, not all Protestants aspired to be liberal and progressive; the very aspiration was in large part a response to the Enlightenment's sweeping attacks on institutional religion and the Christian view of history. One of the philosophes' most damning charges had been that Christians, with the exception of a few Quakers, continued to defend colonial slavery. And what could be more vulnerable to a philosophe's ironic wit than the *Code noir*'s solemn requirement that all French slaves be instructed in the Catholic faith, or Christianity's role in justifying the enslavement of Africans for the good of their souls?

Looking back from 1843, Alexis de Tocqueville credited eighteenth-century France with having "spread those ideas of freedom and equality which shatter and destroy servitude throughout the entire world" and with having "propagated, led, and illuminated that unselfish but passionate love of humanity which suddenly made Europe alive to the cries of slaves." Courting the national pride of a French audience, Tocqueville claimed that the British were simply applying French principles and "behaving in accord with what we still have the right to call *French* sentiment. Are they to be more French than us?" If this argument was somewhat disingenuous, it included an important insight into the Enlightenment's effects on Christianity—or to be more precise, on Anglo-American Protestantism:

> After having long struggled against the egoistic passions that caused slavery to be re-established in the sixteenth century, Christianity tired and became resigned. Our philanthropy took up the work of Christianity, revived it, and brought it back into the fray as its auxiliary. It is we who have given precise and practical meaning to the Christian idea that all men are born equal and we, too, who have applied it to the realities of this world. Finally, it is we who developed new obligations for government, and have made its most important responsibility that of coming to the aid of all the unfortunate, of protecting all the oppressed, of supporting all the weak, and of guaranteeing every man an equal right to freedom.[42]

Although there is much to be said for this theory, Tocqueville glossed over the actual process by which the Enlightenment revived Christianity and brought it "back into the fray"—not as an auxiliary but as a deadly rival. From the 1770s, when Granville Sharp and Benajmin Rush linked antislavery to a defense of religious orthodoxy, most Anglo-American abolitionists recoiled from the kind of secular "philanthropy" that had led Voltaire to proclaim that "every sensible man, every honorable man, must hold the Christian sect in horror." Christian reformers were especially sensitive to the French Enlightenment's exposure of the so-called treason of the clerks, the liberal Christians' concessions, in Peter Gay's words, "to modernity, to criticism, science, and philosophy, and to good tone."[43] In Britain and America, to be sure, it was much easier to make such concessions while claiming to preserve one's orthodoxy. The important point, however, is that Anglo-American reformers succeeded in appropriating many of the principles and arguments of "the modern paganism" while insisting that a secular philanthropy was necessarily spurious and self-defeating.

As Tocqueville well knew, the Enlightenment's actual verdict on colonial slavery was anything but clear-cut.[44] For Anglo-American abolitionists, Napoleon finally revealed the true tendencies of French rationalism when he reinstituted the slave trade as well as colonial slavery. What else could one expect from a secular culture that worshiped power and utility; that denied universal moral truth, divine judgment, and heavenly reward; and that tended, after dismissing the biblical account of creation, to treat racial differences as a subject for zoology? On the last point it was not a Frenchman but David Hume, Britain's truest philosophe, who cemented a connection between racism and religious infidelity. Hume made himself an ideal target by advancing the suspicion that blacks were "naturally inferior to whites" and by sneering that a supposedly learned Negro in Jamaica was probably "admired for very slender accomplishments, like a parrot, who speaks a few words plainly."[45]

Hume's words enabled orthodox Christians to make a defense of the Africans a defense of religion itself. John Wesley, for example, called Hume "the most insolent despiser of truth and virtue that ever appeared in the world." Though Wesley in general thought of primitive people as bestial idolators, his *Thoughts upon Slavery,* published in 1774, quotes descriptions of Africa suggesting an "image of pure nature," "the idea of our first parents . . . the world in its primitive state." He warned that by seizing these unoffending Africans and enslaving them to labor in the New World, Britons were stained with such blood and guilt that nothing but repentance and emancipation could prevent divine retribution. Similarly, early antislavery writers like James Ramsay and Granville Sharp repeatedly identified the theory of racial inferiority with Hume, Voltaire, and materialistic philosophy in general; they explicitly presented their attacks on slavery as a vindication of Christianity, moral accountability, and the unity of mankind. James Beattie, the Scottish philosopher who won enduring acclaim for defending the immutability of truth and moral sentiment against the "sophistry and skepticism" of Hume and Voltaire, warned that the inferiority of Negroes had become a favorite topic for writers whose real target was the authority of Scripture. This claim was questionable, but it provided Beattie with the chance to demolish Hume's specious reasoning on racial inferiority. Beattie's *Elements of Moral Science,* long a popular text in America as well as Britain, made it clear that the question of Negro slavery posed a decisive test for religion and moral philosophy:

> It is impossible for the considerate and unprejudiced mind to think of slavery without horror. . . . If this be equitable, or excusable, or pardonable, it is vain to talk any longer of the eternal distinctions of right and wrong, truth and falsehood, good and evil.[46]

Beattie's attack on Hume was part of a wider debate on the Negro's capacity for progress. Since the debate involved the anthropology and physiology of racial differences and elicited arguments from such diverse figures as Buffon, Kames, Hume, Jefferson, Rush, Kant, Blumenbach, Herder, Samuel Stanhope Smith, Charles White, and the abbé Grégoire, even a brief summary would distract us from the theme of Christianity and moral progress. The complexities of racial theory should not obscure the continuing ideological importance of the biblical account of a single human race descended from common parents. Even when qualified by racist stereotypes or by strained interpretations of the curse of Canaan, the belief in a common origin implied that all peoples share a common nature and destiny. For example, the article "Negro" in the 1797 edition of the *Encyclopaedia Britannica* drew on the latest "scientific" authorities and repeated the most derogatory stereotypes:

> Vices the most notorious seem to be the portion of this unhappy race: idleness, treachery, revenge, cruelty, impudence, stealing, lying, profanity, debauchery, nastiness, and intemperance, are said to have extinguished the principles of natural law, and to have silenced the reproofs of conscience. They are strangers to every sentiment of compassion, and are an awful example of the corruption of man when left to himself.

But as the last sentence intimates, such an extreme moral and physical "degeneration" from a common, presumably white ancestral type implied the capacity for a no less spectacular "improvement." For the Christian environmentalist author, probably Colin MacFarquhar, the very vices of the blacks, whether exhibited in savage Africa or under the despotic rule of New World slavery, were sufficient to explain their own perpetuation. To refute the theory of natural inferiority, the author pointed to the French Revolution as proof of the corrupting effects of tyranny and superstition even in a supposedly civilized nation. Why should anyone be surprised that

> the negroes of Africa, unacquainted with moral principles, blinded by the cruellest and most absurd superstitions, and whose customs tend to eradicate from the mind all natural affection, should sometimes display to their lordly masters of European extraction the same spirit that has been so generally displayed by the lower orders of Frenchmen to their ecclesiastics, their nobles, and the family of their murdered sovereign![47]

By turning the environmentalism of the Enlightenment against the speculations of Hume and Jefferson, such writers could attribute every instance of Negro depravity either to "the influence of climate and the modes of savage life" or to the degrading effects of slavery. Moreover, the *Britannica* author characteristically undercut his initial racist remarks by arguing that "the ill qualities of the negroes have been greatly exaggerated" and that "there is good reason to believe that their intellectual endowments are equal to those of the whites who have been found in the same circumstances." Evidence of "native ingenuity" could be seen in the fabrics and dyes of West African textiles. The final proof of a capacity for progress lay in the achievements of West Indian carpenters, watchmakers, physicians, and even poets who made it impossible to doubt "that 'God, who made the world, hath made of one blood all nations of men,' and animated them with minds equally rational."[48]

For Britons, at least, the long struggle with "infidel France" reinforced the conviction that Christianity, if unadulterated and wedded to free institutions, would inevitably promote the moral and material progress of every human race. By 1805 the doctrine of inherent black inferiority had become so disreputable that a young abolitionist like Henry Brougham could gleefully review and publicize a recent French book that argued that Negroes were a separate, inferior species, fit only for a state of slavery. Writing anonymously in the *Edinburgh Review,* Brougham expressed delight that the French author had at least openly and consistently set forth the doctrines upon which a defense of slavery had to rest but which few British apologists "can be brought to acknowledge." Such an explicit reformulation of Aristotle's theory that some men are born to be slaves gave Brougham the chance to associate the theory with French despotism. For example, after quoting a long description of the tyranny, butchery, terror, and violent discontinuities of African life, Brougham drew the predictable comparison with "the happy and enlightened empire of France."[49]

Brougham's main concern, however, was not the Napoleonic aberration but rather the great nineteenth-century theme of race and progress. Like the *Britannica* essayist, he attributed examples of the blacks' "apparent inferiority" either to the European slave trade or to the African soil and climate, which encouraged indolence: "How can a people, placed in such circumstances, advance in civilization, or even in habits of industry, unless they are stimulated by new desires, and excited to the attainment of difficult objects?" Considering the similar barbarism and immorality displayed by the Russians only a century ago, Brougham thought it remarkable that Negroes had progressed as much as they had in the face of far worse disadvantages: "insulated by the deserts of Africa from all communication with other nations, or surrounded by the slave factories of the Europeans, or groaning under the cruelties of the West India system." Brougham did not really differ with the defenders of that system in his assessments of the Negro's present character and need for disciplinary controls. The difference turned on inherent racial capability. Brougham noted that in the interior of Africa, where the slave trade inflicted less harm, travelers had found that Negroes were generally "mild, gentle, and amiable in an extraordinary degree," and had made impressive progress not only in "the more refined arts" but also in creating "political societies of great extent and complicated structure, notwithstanding the grievous obstacles which are thrown in the way of their civilization. . . ." The benefits of European influence, Brougham thought, had largely been nullified by the slave trade, which had unfortunately taught blacks "the tyrant's vices"; yet he boldly acknowledged that the history of Haiti presented irrefutable evidence of "negroes organizing immense armies; laying plans of campaigns and sieges, which, if not scientific, have at least been to a certain degree successful against the finest European troops; arranging forms of government . . . entering into commercial relations with foreigners, and conceiving the idea of contracting alliances. . . ." The telling proof, in short, of the "presumptuous arrogance, which would confine to one race, the characteristic privilege of the species," could be found "in our losses." The real question, which metaphysical theories of inferiority could only obscure, was "how long they will suffer us to exist in the New World."[50]

The specter of black revolution reinforced Brougham's conclusion that "there is nothing in the physical or moral constitution of the Negro, which renders him an exception to the general character of the species, and prevents him from improving in all the estimable qualities of our nature, when placed in circumstances tolerably favourable to his advancement." This unshakable belief in a universal capacity for progress, opposed only by those who "deny the authority of the Bible, and laugh at the precepts of all religions, when they interfere with the interest of the planters," underpinned Brougham's vision of gradual emancipation—a controlled removal of the "impediments" that prevent "the general improvement of the slaves in their habits of voluntary exertion," leading at first to their status as "serf tenants, paying a proportion of their crops to the lord of the land," and finally to full freedom. Brougham also envisioned a subsidence of racial prejudice, similar to that "which has made the European baron cease to look down upon his serf as an inferior animal," and perhaps a gradual mixture of races.[51]

These two essays express the views of race and progress that governed British discussions of slavery in the era of slave-trade abolition and emancipation. Even West Indian apologists seldom maintained that blacks were inherently inferior and incapable of intellectual and moral progress. In this respect it is worth noting that from the time of Paracelsus and Giordano Bruno to that of the *Journal des savants* and Voltaire, it was the heterodox or the champions of anticlerical science who dismissed biblical authority and who suggested that Negroes, having a separate origin, were a species separate from man. During the Victorian period British racist theory was evidently nourished by the declining faith in revealed religion and the growth of secular social science, as well as by disillusion over the consequences of various slave emancipations. By 1884, to cite only one example, the *Encyclopaedia Britannica* was propagating the most flagrant variety of "scientific" racism: when the Negro child reaches puberty, explained Prof. A. H. Keane of University College, a "premature closing of the cranial sutures" stops further growth of the brain, and "all further progress seems to be arrested." In the classic, eleventh edition, of 1911, Thomas A. Joyce, a noted ethnographer and anthropologist, affirmed that "mentally the negro is inferior to the white" and stands "on a lower evolutionary plane"; though black children sometimes show a capacity for intellectual progress, the subsequent "arrest or even deterioration in mental development is no doubt very largely due to the fact that after puberty sexual matters take the first place in the negro's life and thoughts."[52]

The point of this digression is to stress that the abolitionist view of progress depended on a Christian and an essentially prescientific, pre-Darwinian anthropology. To avoid misconceptions, we should remember that antiblack stereotypes long predated modern science and that racial ideology reflected the needs and historical experience of concrete social groups. Many white Americans had little difficulty in reconciling an abstract belief in the unity of mankind with a more visceral conviction that blacks were inherently unfit for freedom. It is also true that even the most devout abolitionists were indebted to the Enlightenment for their assumption that environment is preeminent in shaping human character. Although Brougham was a serious Christian, his views on Negro capability were similar to those of Diderot and Condorcet, and probably owed as much to Montesquieu as to Christianity. On the other hand, it is clear that a different intellectual tradition extends from Hume, Voltaire, and Jefferson to the scientific racism of the mid-nineteenth century and that the impeachment of revealed religion opened the way not only for social science in general but also for a science of human capability based on measurable physical traits. The samples we have just quoted from the *Encyclopaedia Britannica* were part of a much wider movement to classify, objectify, and differentiate human "types"—with the avowed objective of making a science of human progress. Abolitionists were fortunate in not having to confront this new ethnography and physical anthropology until most black slaves had been emancipated, at least in the New World. They were also fortunate, during the first decades of the nineteenth century, in being able to identify theories of natural inferiority with Napoleonic France, which happened to be a seedbed for the later physiological social science. In other words, even though abolitionism was part of a broad movement for Christian revitalization, it never acquired the fundamentalist traits of a movement pitted against science and enlightenment as such. For several decades, at least, most Anglo-American reformers never doubted that true science and enlightenment were at one with the Word of God or that the diffusion of pure religion would guarantee the universal progress of mankind.

To understand the eventual outcome of such beliefs, it is necessary to look more closely at the evangelical background of the early antislavery movement. Genuine abolitionism, as distinct from isolated protests against human bondage, originated in the great Quaker revival that moved from an ideal of quietistic spirituality and self-annihilation in the mid-eighteenth century toward a later reaffirmation of both the sinfulness of natural man and the mercies of Christ the Redeemer. From the work of early American Quaker missionaries like John Churchman and John Woolman to the transatlantic efforts of Anthony Benezet, the Dillwyns, Pembertons, and Gurneys, testimony against slavery became a crucial symbol of "serious religion" and self-renunciation in a continuing war against worldliness, infidelity, and religious declension. If the Society of Friends' benevolence impressed Voltaire, the Encyclopedists, and the later founders of the French "Friends of the Blacks," it was their demonstrative piety that impressed John Wesley and various groups of evangelicals in the southern United States, some of whom formed associations named "Friends of Humanity." In Maryland, Virginia, and North Carolina the Quaker example influenced Baptists, Presbyterians, and Methodists who were striving to recover the antiworldly zeal of the Great Awakening of the 1740s.

The precise extent of Quaker influence is difficult to measure and is of less importance than the widespread appearance, by the 1780s, of common views of sin and religious duty. None of the leaders of the Great Awakening had denounced slaveholding as a sin or even as an evil, although revivalists had often urged that black slaves be Christianized and treated in accordance with New Testament ideals. In contrast, for both Quakers and southern evangelicals like Freeborn Garrettson, David Rice, Carter Tarrant, and James Meacham, slaveholding could no more be sanctified than the vices of gambling, drinking, horse racing, and Sabbath breaking that infected the planter class. Religious rebirth required, along with other renunciations, the voluntary manumission of slaves—a purification ritual analogous to baptism, circumcision, or dietary prohibitions that at once severed true believers from a former life of corruption and marked them off from unregenerate Gentiles. Like the Quakers, the southern Baptists and Methodists of the 1770s and 1780s were victims of religious ridicule and persecution. Of generally humble background, they were far less restrained than the Quakers in denouncing the luxury, high living, and religious indifference of the southern elite. By no means all evangelicals demanded slave emancipation as a sign of individual and national repentance in the midst of Revolutionary crisis. But for men like Garrettson, who actually owned black slaves, the decision to sacrifice immoral wealth was a double emancipation, signifying new identities for both master and slave. The decision culminated Garrettson's conversion experience in 1775, finally freeing him from Satan's temptations: "all my dejection and that melancholy gloom, which preyed on me, vanished in a moment: a divine sweetness ran through my whole frame. . . ."[53]

Benjamin Rush, the first non-Quaker to make an important contribution to antislavery in the middle colonies, illustrates some of the complex connections between abolitionism, the Enlightenment, and the desire to vindicate revealed religion. Though of Pennsylvania Quaker heritage, Rush found his religious identity in the teachings of "New Light" Presbyterians of the Great Awakening. His lifelong hostility to deism was not lessened by his medical study in Edinburgh or by his youthful acquaintanceship with Franklin, Hume, Diderot, Mirabeau, and a host of philosophes. Indeed, later in life Rush fretted over Franklin's susceptibility to deism and denounced Thomas Paine's *Age of Reason* as one of the most dangerous books ever written. In 1776, however, it was the unpopular cause of antislavery that first drew Rush and Paine together in a temporary alliance (Rush then encouraged Paine to write the revolutionary pamphlet *Common Sense* and helped to get it published). Rush had earlier attacked black slavery, at the prompting of Anthony Benezet, as a means of vindicating divine Scripture and proving that natural justice and revealed religion always speak the same truths. In particular, he had challenged John Millar, the Scottish moral philosopher, who held that the Bible nowhere condemned slaveholding and that free labor was the natural outgrowth of economic progress. Rush acknowledged that his antislavery writings of 1773 had brought ridicule from the faculty of the College of Philadelphia, a "set of freethinking gentlemen." His concerns were similar to those of his English correspondent Granville Sharp, who in 1776 combined denunciations of American slavery with alarm over the increase of religious infidelity and the "open declarations of Deists, Arians, Socinians, and others, who deny the Divinity of Christ, and the Holy Ghost."[54]

In New England there was little Quaker influence outside Rhode Island; and the Baptists and later the Methodists, who were viewed as religious subversives, were conspicuously silent regarding black slavery. Instead, for a brief period beginning in the 1770s, it was the established Congregationalist clergy who took the lead in proscribing slaveholding as a heinous crime and the "capital sin of these States." These "New Divinity" ministers, all heirs of the Great Awakening and disciples of Jonathan Edwards, were fervent believers in the sinfulness of natural man; in the dependence of redemption on a new birth or saving experience; and in God's retributive judgment of sinning nations. Desperately fearing such divine judgment during the crisis of war and early nationhood, they cooperated with less godly reformers in various antislavery activities. By the 1790s, however, the earliest and most radical opponents of black slavery were at the forefront of New England's crusade against deists, illuminati, and other religious infidels.[55]

In Britain the relation between antislavery and the evangelical reaction to the Enlightenment was complicated by the polarization between established church and religious Nonconformists. The Dissenters, ranging from pious Quakers and Baptists to freethinking rationalists, were united at least by their common disabilities and by their opposition to the Test and Corporation acts, which barred them from public office, the universities, and most professions. By the late eighteenth century some Nonconformists had combined evangelical religion with republican ideology, a mixture that appeared far more radical in Britain than in America. Conservatives became alarmed when even Methodists spoke of slavery's violating the natural and unalienable rights of man. A few sectarians, mostly of the artisan class, adopted the heresies that disturbed Granville Sharp and that made them a receptive audience for Paine's *Age of Reason*. But to illustrate the political and religious conservatism of the English establishment, it is worth noting that by the mid-1790s even Sharp, Clarkson, and Wilberforce—all devout Anglicans—were accused of being in league with Paine and the French Jacobins.

One of the reasons the anti-slave-trade campaign elicited massive public support in the early 1790s was that its petitions provided an opportunity for mobilizing the opinion not only of towns and various corporations but also of dissenting groups that ordinarily had no means of exerting influence. Hence the cause enlisted a considerable amount of diffuse anti-establishment feeling from people who were primarily dedicated to religious liberty and parliamentary reform. The Manchester Abolition Committee, which initiated the anti-slave-trade petitioning in 1787, was led by political radicals who had closer ties with Paine and the Enlightenment than with evangelical religion. Because antislavery became an important political issue in Britain in the 1790s—half a century earlier than in the United States—even such conservative reformers as Wilberforce welcomed the parliamentary support of closet Unitarians like William Smith and liberal Whigs like Charles James Fox, Samuel Whitbread, and Sir Samuel Romilly. But this political dimension should not obscure the crucial points: from the 1770s onward, devout Quakers were always the backbone of active antislavery organization and communication; from Sharp and Wilberforce to Buxton and Joseph Sturge, religion was the central concern of all the British abolitionist leaders; the grass-roots support, especially after 1823, came overwhelmingly from Baptist, Methodist, and Presbyterian Dissenters.[56]

Thomas Clarkson, the first reformer to make abolitionism a professional career, showed unusual tolerance for rationalism and religious diversity. But Clarkson was also the son of an Anglican curate who as a young man had died from a fever contracted while visiting the sick. Headed originally for the ministry, Thomas Clarkson found a more challenging, dangerous, and "useful" mission on the Liverpool docks, where he interrogated seamen and tracked down witnesses who would testify to the evils of the Atlantic slave trade. Like his Quaker and evangelical co-workers, Clarkson insisted that "to Christianity alone are we indebted for the new and sublime spectacle of seeing men going beyond the bounds of individual usefulness to each other—of seeing them carry their charity, as a united Brotherhood, into distant lands."[57]

When Clarkson searched as a historian for the original "streams" of benevolent influence that had finally converged in the abolition movement, he found the headwaters represented not by secular men but rather, "where it was most desirable, namely . . . the teachers of Christianity in those times." Providence had evidenced an ecumenical spirit by selecting such representative agents as Morgan Godwyn, an Anglican; Richard Baxter, a Nonconformist; and George Fox, a Quaker. Clarkson even suspected that denominational rivalry had helped to advance the humanitarian cause: the pioneering Quakers had not only shown that abolitionism was not "dangerous" but had also set an example that made other Christians seem "less worthy." The Quaker ethic of self-denial and nonviolence had helped to expose the temporizing tendency of the established churches. On the other hand, the simultaneous development of antislavery in Britain and America had proved that Christianity was "capable of producing the same good fruit in all lands."[58]

For both British and American evangelicals, it was William Wilberforce who came to symbolize the noblest spirit of Christian abolitionism and who spelled out the larger significance of making such "practical benevolence" the vehicle for religious revitalization. Looking at the actual practice of "professed Christians in the higher and middle classes" in late-eighteenth-century Britain, Wilberforce discovered an all-absorbing preoccupation with worldly and commercial interests coupled with a perfunctory acceptance of the mere forms of Christianity. Given the growth of skepticism and the decline of true faith, Wilberforce concluded, "the time is fast approaching when Christianity will be almost as openly disavowed in the language, as in fact it is already supposed to have disappeared from the conduct of men; when infidelity will be held to be the necessary appendage of a man of fashion, and to believe will be deemed the indication of a feeble mind." The final consequence of such degeneration was readily apparent in France: "manners corrupted, morals depraved, dissipation predominant, above all, religion discredited. . . ." The only remedy lay in reviving and promoting what Clarkson termed the heart of Christianity, "practical benevolence"—but remembering, as Wilberforce cautioned, that benevolence, unless originating in Christian humility, "dispenses but from a scanty and precarious fund; and therefore if it be liberal in the case of some objects, it is generally found to be contracted toward others. . . ."[59]

Crusades for religious revitalization are often less concerned with the devil than with fellow priests who have made peace with the devil. For Quakers and early Methodists, for example, public testimony against slavery helped to expose the self-serving expediency of the established churches. Under the banner of "practical benevolence," the evangelical party led by Wilberforce and the Clapham Sect challenged the complacency and worldly system of patronage within their own Church of England. By the 1820s abolitionism was serving similar purposes for evangelicals like Thomas Chalmers and Andrew Thomson within the Church of Scotland. In the northern United States the disciples of Charles Grandison Finney concluded that silence or undue "prudence" regarding slavery epitomized the "Satanic doctrine of expediency" that had morally enervated the Presbyterian and Congregationalist churches. The reformers' sense of a common, international cause strengthened their self-confidence in the face of mounting counterattacks. On the first anniversary of British emancipation, George Thompson reminded the Massachusetts Anti-Slavery Society that Clarkson and Wilberforce had also once been branded as fanatics: "All the filthy channels of the dictionary were turned upon a Wilberforce, and they fell like water upon the back of a swan, leaving its purity and loveliness unspotted and unruffled." Vilified to the day of his death, Wilberforce had then been honored by the tributes of royalty, nobility, bishops, and the entire British nation: "Who does not now wish to struggle for the mantle of Wilberforce?"[60]

Until 1833, at least, many British conservatives had feared that slave emancipation would encourage assaults upon their own privileged interests. In the spring of 1833 the abolitionist *Christian Advocate* ridiculed such efforts to link the colonial question with "every tenure of real estate" and with the churchman's "divine right to tithe," a self-defeating strategy that could appeal only to old-school tories who had insulated themselves from the generous feelings of an entire nation.[61] In America, however, it was the abolitionists who remained insulated from both public opinion and the centers of power. Unlike their British brethren, they were challenging a vital national interest; there were no political or legal agencies, short of revolution, that could fulfill their objectives; and in "this heaven-favored, but mob-cursed land," as George Thompson described it, public opinion had by the mid-1830s become a *"demon of oppression."* Thompson, who had canvassed Britain as a professional lecturer for the Agency Anti-Slavery Society and who had then been hounded in America by anti-abolition mobs, assured an Edinburgh audience that the struggle in Britain had never been "so sublime . . . our sacrifices were never so great; our temptations to swerve were never so strong. . . . It was never necessary that we should suffer in our reputation; that we should lose our friends . . . or that we should be deprived of the substance and amount of our profitable trade."[62] Such persecution encouraged the tendency of many abolitionists to move from an initial concern with the reformation of morals to outright attacks on hierarchy, inequality, intolerance, and any restriction on freedom of discussion. William Lloyd Garrison, for example, who in the 1820s had echoed all of Wilberforce's censorious protests against atheism, deism, profanity, Sabbath breaking, lewdness, and intemperance, was by the 1840s sounding like a philosophe committed to the uncompromising goal of discovering the truth:

> I know of no safer, higher, or better way, than to leave the human mind perfectly untrammelled to contend for unlimited investigation, to vindicate the supremacy of reason, to plead for unfettered speech, to argue from analogy, to decide upon evidence, to be governed by facts, to disclaim infallibility, to believe in eternal growth and progress, to repudiate all arbitrary authority, to make no body of men oracular, to learn from the teachings of history, to see with our own eyes and hear with our own ears. . . .[63]

Understandably, religious conservatives interpreted such language as proof that abolitionism inevitably gravitated toward the most dangerous doctrines of the "infidel Enlightenment." This view seemed to be dramatically confirmed by the career of reformers like Henry Clarke Wright. Until his mid-thirties, Wright appeared destined to remain within the Calvinist ranks of New England's clerical elite, continuing his earlier warfare against Unitarianism, gambling halls, grog shops, secular public schools, and other evidences of moral disintegration. At Andover seminary, where Edwardsian theology had been fortified by heavy doses of hermeneutics and biblical scholarship in original Greek and Hebrew texts, Wright had been expertly trained for his later responsibilities as a minister and traveling agent for the American Sunday School Union. But in 1835 Wright became a Garrisonian abolitionist. Outraged by the establishment's complicity in persecuting Garrison and Thompson and in stifling free discussion, he struck back with what his recent biographer calls a "venomous anticlericism." The leading champion of radical nonresistance, Wright also affirmed that "Christ is the Prince of moral reformers—the great Captain of agitators in aggressive warfare, as well as the Prince of Peace." Denouncing the Sabbath and professional clergy as frauds perpetrated by self-serving priesthoods, he wrote a tract entitled "The Bible, If Opposed to Self-Evident Truth, Is Self-Evident Falsehood." When Wright reexamined the archfiends of his theological education, he discovered that Thomas Paine had actually sought to vindicate God from the barbarous vestiges of a primitive religion. "In *spirit* and in *practice*," Wright concluded, "Voltaire was nearer the kingdom of heaven than the slaveholding clergy of America."[64]

But as Lewis Perry has brilliantly shown, Wright's odyssey was anything but a direct voyage toward secular reason. His superficial reversal of old orthodoxies did not imply a tolerance of dissent or an acceptance of a pluralistic world. To the end of his life he "searched enthusiastically . . . for new religious authorities."[65] For a time, indeed, Wright insisted on his own unswerving orthodoxy as he continued to battle not only Unitarians and other theological liberals but also apostate puritans who had forgotten the absolute claims of divine sovereignty and who had been corrupted by "subserviency to the will of man." Wright's conversion to radical abolitionism did not mark a revolutionary break with his earlier religious concerns. Throughout his adult life he continued to abhor disorder, violence, and immorality and to demand the restoration of "the Order of God's creation" in which all human presumptions of dominion would give way to a common submission to the divine will. In Wright's eyes, Negro slavery was simply the most flagrant example of man's usurpation of divine authority. When respected leaders of church and state excused such a national sin by pointing to the similar subordination of wives and children and to the coercive foundations of all government, Wright and other nonresistants concluded that something was drastically wrong with the prevailing forms of marriage and civil society.[66]

Many historians, forgetting the roots of modern radicalism in the Protestant Reformation and the English civil wars, have tended to picture abolitionism as part of a broad and irresistible process of "secularization," as a bridge between purely spiritual reform and later secular struggles for social justice. But this model of unilinear progression obscures the complex and dialectical relation between Christianity and the Enlightenment, a relation suggested by the very title of Henry Wright's curious pamphlet *The Merits of Christ and the Merits of Tom Paine.* Even when abolitionists excommunicated their fellow churchmen and renounced all sacraments, arguing that no human ordinances can aid the individual in his quest for salvation, they perceived their movement as a purification and *extension* of Christian principles. What struck their opponents as a secularization of religion was for them a sacralization of social progress—the only point of agreement being that the boundary between sacred and profane had been redefined or, as the abolitionists would have it, restored. British and American abolitionists were both keenly aware that religious reformers had always been branded as heretics. In 1824 James Stephen compared the persecution of British abolitionists to the martyrdom of Hugh Latimer and Nicholas Ridley, who had refused to be intimidated by charges of instigating violence. Henry Wright wrote in the *Liberator* as "Wickliffe." In 1860 Garrison emphasized that abolitionists had been harassed with the same charges of treason, infidelity, blasphemy, and subversion that had been hurled at Jesus, Wyckliffe, Luther, Calvin, and Fox.[67]

But Garrison also insisted that the abolitionists had never contemplated the slightest conflict with church and pulpit. They had begun as solid church members, "tenacious of their theological views, full of veneration for the organized church and ministry," confident that both would render "efficient aid to their cause." They had never dreamed that consistent testimony against America's "distinctive, all-conquering sin" would ultimately require them to sacrifice "their church relations, their political connections, their social ties, their worldly interests and reputation." With grief and dismay they had then discovered

> that the religious forces on which they had relied were all arrayed on the side of the oppressor; that the North was as hostile to emancipation as the South; that the spirit of slavery was omnipresent, invading every sanctuary, infecting every pulpit, controlling every press, corrupting every

household, and blinding every vision; that no other alternative was presented to them, except to wage war with "principalities, and powers, and spiritual wickedness in high places. . . ."

In their struggle to unmask evil and restore clear vision to the people, the abolitionists had certainly not been "infidel" to the cause of the slave, to the cause of Jesus, or to what Garrison considered the cause of the true church:

> If, therefore, it be an infidel Society, it is so only in the same sense in which Jesus was a blasphemer, and the Apostles were "pestilent and seditious fellows, seeking to turn the world upside down." It is infidel to Satan, the enslaver; it is loyal to Christ, the redeemer. . . . It is infidel to all blood-stained compromises, sinful concessions, unholy compromises, respecting the system of slavery. . . . At the jubilee, its vindication shall be triumphant and universal. . . . Genuine Abolitionism is not a hobby, got up for personal or associated aggrandizement; it is not a political ruse; it is not a spasm of sympathy, which lasts but for a moment. . . . It is an essential part of Christianity, and aside from it there can be no humanity. Its scope is not confined to the slave population of the United States, but embraces mankind. . . . It is the spirit of Jesus, who was sent "to bind up the brokenhearted, to proclaim liberty to the captives, and the opening of the prison to them that are bound; to proclaim the acceptable year of the Lord and the day of vengeance of our God."[68]

Here there is no trace of the philosophe or of "secularization," as that term is generally understood. If Garrison was atypical of abolitionists in some respects, he eloquently typifies the general inclination to fuse slave emancipation with the Christian vision of resurrection and redemption. From the material goal the vision acquired concrete immediacy, but the vision's power still depended on faith in its sacred origins.

The fusion of emancipation and redemption was secular only in the sense that Christianized science and the "Baconian method"—as celebrated by Scottish moralists and American Presbyterians—promised to bring millennial dreams within the "practical" realm of historical possibility. Thus, according to the American Theodore Weld, any theological student "who would preach in the nineteenth century, must *know* the nineteenth century," which for Weld meant "gathering facts, and analyzing principles, and tracing the practical relations of the prominent sins and evils and all-whelming sorrows of his own age." But this was simply to say that Christianity could not keep pace with the world's expanding capacities for evil unless it employed the new intellectual and organizational powers of the age. The providential significance of a subject like slavery, in Weld's eyes, was that it could not "be investigated and discussed intelligently and thoroughly, without amplifying and expanding the intellect and increasing the power of its action upon all subjects." As soon as American seminaries and other institutions freely discussed and addressed themselves to subjects like slavery, they would "introduce a new era in mind—the era of *disposable* power and practical accomplishment." Neither Weld nor his co-workers doubted for a moment that in struggling for this new era in mind, "theirs is the cause of God, and that God is with them."[69]

The conviction that abolitionism was, in the words of the militant British Quaker Elizabeth Heyrick, a "*holy* war,—an attack upon the strong holds, the deep intrenchments *[sic]* of the very powers of darkness"—depended on a belief in the infinitude of slavery's evil. Only such a belief could justify the assurance of the British Anti-Slavery Society that it was the "providence of Almighty God, who has, from the beginning to the end, been the true DOER of the glorious work; originating it in the hearts of its advocates,—lifting it over the all but insurmountable obstacles of its early days . . . providing means, providing instruments, unexpected, diverse, conflicting, yet under the skillful guidance of the DIVINE HAND, all urging forward to the same conclusion. . . ." Only an infernal evil sprung from a "bottomless perdition," in Milton's memorable words,

> Where peace
> And rest can never dwell, hope never comes
> That comes to all,

could warrant Garrison's description of George Thompson's American mission as being "physically and spiritually, intellectually and morally, the identical mission of the Son of God—to bind up the broken-hearted, to preach deliverance to the captive. . . ." Long before Thomas Fowell Buxton became an abolitionist, he instinctively quoted Milton after describing in a speech the horrors of the Middle Passage: "Then think of his [the Negro's] arrival at the scene of his captivity. The chief of our Poets has described the Den to which the Rebellious Angels were driven, but had he known the Slave Trade, he might have spared his fancy in the description of fact." It required more than a finite, temporal evil to lead Wilberforce, upon his retirement in 1821, to anoint Buxton as parliamentary leader of "this Holy Enterprise . . . this *blessed service,*" trusting that after God's purposes had been fulfilled, the two men would at last meet in heaven "and spend an Eternity of Holiness and Happiness complete and unassailable."[70] The sublimity of such rewards was directly proportional to the iniquity of slavery and to the heroic struggle required to overthrow it.

This point brings us to the heart of the controversy between abolitionists and their Protestant opponents who had long acknowledged that slaveholding might be conducive to sin and contrary to the public interest but who resisted the idea that any institution sanctioned in the Bible could be intrinsically sinful. As Henry Clarke Wright noted in his journal, the New England clergy also feared that if reformers concentrated their attacks on a specific embodiment of sin, then "that sin will assume such an importance that every body will think nothing is necessary to make them christians but abstinence from that particular sin." Calvinists, in particular, were suspicious of attempts to impute unconditional evil to abstract "essences" or categories, such as slaveholding and corporal punishment, considered apart from the mixed good and evil of all human relationships.[71] Convinced that sin pervades every human enterprise, Calvinists had traditionally mistrusted people who looked for salvation in various holy causes or who sanctimoniously shunned the painful callings and responsibilities of life. It was a papist delusion to think that salvation could be won by celibacy, monasticism, or meritorious works, and radical sectarians were equally deceived in thinking that evil could be incarnated in institutions that, however imperfect, were intended by God to be improved and rendered useful by pious human authority.

It is nevertheless true that a remarkable number of abolitionists, in both Britain and America, came from Calvinist backgrounds and continued to profess at least a modified Calvinist faith. But whatever they retained of their theological heritage, such reformers contemptuously rejected the myth that had always rationalized black slavery—the myth that such servitude could be ennobled by Christian love and reciprocal obligation. What remained, in abolitionist eyes, was the unlimited dominion of one human being over another—a sacrilegious assumption, in Theodore Weld's influential definition, of "the prerogative of God," "an invasion of the whole man—on his powers, rights, enjoyments, and hopes, [which] annihilates his being as a MAN, to make room for the being of a THING."[72] For Weld, as for most abolitionists, it was still the slave's immortal soul that made him a "God-like being" protected by God's prerogatives. But the soul was now inseparable from human "powers, rights, enjoyments, and hopes," so that external dominion over the *body* was synonymous with spiritual annihilation. To combat such an evil was clearly virtue, whatever the insidious disguises of sin. The existence of such an evil enabled even Calvinists to discover an element of goodness in the human heart—in the disposition to "practical benevolence."

Ironically, though, it was the belief in the infinite depravity of the human heart—a belief shared by most evangelicals—that underlay the abolitionist argument that unlimited power opens the way to every forbidden desire and imaginable transgression. In 1762 John Woolman, the pioneer Quaker reformer, had expressed doubts whether any man could be saintly enough to exercise such power with Christian charity; yet Woolman had refrained from judging slaveholders as a group. Most Quaker and Anglican abolitionists moved slowly and cautiously toward the position that having the power to do evil necessarily meant doing evil. By 1830, however, British and American abolitionists were coming to view black slavery as a Dantean inferno, a microcosm of the sinful human condition. Enticed by every temptation, deprived of the redeeming discipline of labor and self-improvement, the planters—whether in the West Indies or the American South—were exhibited as living representations of every human vice. The moral ambiguities of orthodox Protestantism were thus dichotomized into "all good" and "all bad" objectifications. This is not to suggest that abolitionists were "borderline personalities" engaged in a pathological process of "splitting."[73] When flagrant injustice has long been concealed and protected by all the psychological mechanisms of a cultural system, some kind of splitting may be essential for ethical integrity. There are times when it is pathological to dwell on the good associated with all evil or on the sin associated with all virtue.

For our purposes it is more important to reemphasize that the splitting of traditional Protestant concepts also involved the naturalization of the ultimate moral dichotomy: heaven and hell. Here, beginning with the antislavery poems of Cowper and Blake, abolitionist literature surely contributed to some of the central preoccupations of nineteenth-century Western culture. It can be no accident that during the period from the French and Haitian revolutions to the emancipation of Russian serfs and North American slaves, the themes of captivity and bondage permeated the writings of Schiller, Fichte, Kleist, Blake, Shelley, Wordsworth, Coleridge, Scott, Dickens, Hegel, Marx, and Turgenev, to name only some representative examples. Slavery, even when portrayed more figuratively and ambiguously than in *Uncle Tom's Cabin*—which was probably the most sensational literary success of the nineteenth century—presented the perfect symbol for all modern defiances of natural and supernatural limits. If the bondsman could symbolize the parameters of alienation and dehumanization, the master could stand for all satanic transgressions against society's attempts to circumscribe and control the aggrandizements of the individual ego.

One can even argue that the abolitionists, in their own cultural and religious sphere, were engaged in an enterprise parallel to that of the romantic poets and philosophers: the transposing into "nonpolitical areas," as M. H. Abrams has described it, of key concepts of the Enlightenment and ideals of the American and French revolutions. But where the poets and philosophers focused on "metaphors of mind," following biblical and classical precedents "to import from the social into the moral order of experience the contraries of freedom and submission, mastery and servitude, in reference to the act of the human will in choosing between the good and the bad," the abolitionists moved outward in search of social correlatives that would validate their inner moral experience.[74] Buxton, it should be recalled, said that knowledge of the slave trade would have allowed Milton to spare "his fancy in the description of fact" (but he then proceeded to quote Milton's "fancy"). Henry Wright, who filled his private journals with romantic posturings inspired by Goethe, Byron, and Scott and who portrayed his abolitionist travels as a Childe Harold's pilgrimage, retained a puritan mistrust for fiction:

> Novel reading his produced in me a kind of sickly, morbid sensibility, that unfits me to feel a deep interest in human suffering. . . . It cannot be right for any one to expend the energies of his feelings and sympathies on fictitious joys and sufferings, when there are so many living men, women and children who might be blessed if the same were given to them. This passion for novels I'll set myself resolutely to subject to righteousness.[75]

Faced with the same revolutionary events that stirred the romantic poets and philosophers—the Enlightenment's challenge to the traditional Christian view of history and human nature, and the continuing disintegration of the preindustrial social order—the abolitionists recovered moral certainty by confronting the objective existence of human slavery. For Clarkson the history of the British abolition of the slave trade, both as an event that happened and as a nonfictional subject for contemplation, aroused sensations of horror, indignation, and pleasure that corresponded with the magnitude of the evil overcome. Such moral exercises proved that good and evil were not illusions and that the Creator had endowed human nature with the capacity for historical redemption.

But this activist virtue, like the evil it was designed to vanquish, also involved transgression. It was all very well to talk of obedience to conscience or to the "higher law" of nature, which, according to Blackstone and an ancient tradition of jurisprudence, took precedence over all human laws. But jurists and theologians had always warned that this fortified gate was the very one that Satan was most likely to breach. Especially in America, as we have already suggested, abolitionists discovered that their holy struggle required the repudiation not simply of a tyrannical monstrosity but of a whole system of rules, laws, and proprieties interwoven with the political and social order—a system based on the traditional assumption that slavery was part of the finite, imperfect world of human institutions. Except for a few radicals like Henry Clarke Wright, abolitionists were able to prevent their commitment to liberty from expanding into a perfectionist or anarchistic assault upon all authority. Their seemingly limited demand was that worldly power could not be allowed to curb the free will necessary for a servant's self-improvement and moral accountability. Yet, in so far as Negro slavery incarnated infinite sin, it could be countered only by an institutionalized protest that incarnated infinite virtue. If the root of slavery lay in a disposition to transgress divine limits on human power and self-indulgence—as Wright, Clarkson, Buxton, and virtually all Anglo-American abolitionists agreed—the sin necessarily called forth a contrary disposition of sympathy and benevolence transcending all personal and worldly interests.

The abolitionist movement, however constrained and differentiated by local circumstances, could not avoid this transgression or "natural supernaturalism," to use Abrams's phrase, an overleaping of boundaries between the sacred and profane. Wright simply illustrates, in a strikingly clear and magnified way, how abolitionism could lead from Calvinist revivalism to the view, as summarized by Lewis Perry, that "each human being was its own system of law . . . men and women were their own saviors and gods."[76] Wright's search for worldly embodiments of the diabolical and divine attracted many readers and disciples both in Britain and in America. The search led to the sacralization of sexual love and motherhood; to lectures on "the Abolition of Death" and the advocacy of "anti-Death societies"; and to a preoccupation with health and a "science of body" that merged spiritualism with water cures, promising to expel morbid secretions from the body's system much as abolitionism hoped to ensure social health and progress by purging the "morbid matter" of slavery. The wider faddishness of spiritualism and water cures should not obscure important links with the abolitionists' concern for the sacredness of the human body, the physical embodiments of sin, and the material signs or tests of progress. What needs to be emphasized is not the covert materialism and secularization but the fact that this merger of sacred and profane opened the way for an extravagant idealization of the self. Wright, who was considered an expert on children and child rearing, loved to play educational games that would instill lessons of nonresistance, common brotherhood, and common paternity. In doing so, as Perry points out, Wright slipped easily into the role of God (or slaveholder, one might add), exhibiting the very traits of manipulation, aggression, and vengeance that he had repudiated in the traditional image of his Creator. Few Christians could go as far as Wright in acknowledging the "errors" and "imperfections" of Jesus (mainly celibacy). But when Wright celebrated the powers of conscience and human improvement, he spoke for his own and future generations. For Wright there could be no self-aggrandizement in freeing slaves or in teaching children to turn the other cheek. Similarly, there could be no sensuality in endorsing the holiness of matrimonial love. The motto of Wright's model husband and wife sums up the reformers' "transgression": "Progress, not pleasure, is our aim."[77]

Given this broader eschatological context—that of reconstituting Christian culture in the wake of the French Revolution and in the face of the rising tide of industrial capitalism—one sees that New World slavery bore an ironic analogy to Adam's "fortunate fall," or *felix culpa,* which according to traditional doctrine had set the necessary stage for human redemption through the death and resurrection of Christ. Abolitionist historians made it unmistakably clear that black slavery represented a historical decline from a previous state of relative purity, not simply the perpetuation of an evil from earlier, barbarous times. Clarkson, for example, insisted that the popes and princes of Europe would never have approved a practice so contrary to natural truth and morality as the African slave trade. After exonerating Emperor Charles V, Pope Leo X, Queen Elizabeth, and Louis XIII, he argued that Cardinal Ximenes and even Bartolomé de Las Casas had done their best to prevent the Edenic New World from becoming corrupted by black slavery. It was only because the Christian rulers of Europe had been deceived and kept in ignorance that fraud and avarice had finally triumphed.[78]

In America the problem of the fortunate fall was complicated by the Founding Fathers and the War of Independence. Even the most radical abolitionists could not free themselves from the reverential awe with which their generation looked back upon the demigods of 1776. For all American reformers the Declaration of Independence was a symbolic bench mark dividing the ages of monarchic despotism from a new era of political liberty and self-determination. David Walker, the free black abolitionist and the author of the flaming *Appeal to the Colored Citizens of the World,* might attack Jefferson and the racism of American institutions in general, but he concluded his manifesto by quoting the Declaration of Independence and exclaiming, "See your Declaration, Americans! ! ! Do you understand your own language?" John Humphrey Noyes, the millenarian founder of the Oneida Community, might renounce all allegiance to the government of the United States, "a bloated, swaggering libertine . . . with one hand whipping a negro tied to a liberty-pole, and with another dashing an emaciated Indian to the ground," but he did so by signing his name to what he called "an instrument similar to the Declaration of '76."[79] Feminists, pacifists, temperance reformers, and abolitionists all drafted public pronouncements modeled on Jefferson's declaration. They pictured their own moral revolutions as the fulfillment of the political and military struggles of an earlier dispensation, much as the New Testament was said to have fulfilled and superseded the Old Testament. The reformers' testaments implied at least a moral superiority over forebears who had resorted to carnal weapons and who had resisted such comparatively minor oppressions as a tax on tea. Yet the reformers' language betrayed a psychological dependence on the fathers of a nation "conceived in liberty" and officially dedicated to an ideal of human equality. Especially when they traveled abroad, American reformers tended to reaffirm their faith that the United States, for all its sins and shortcomings, had at least escaped from the glacial tyrannies and injustices of the Old World.

Among American abolitionists William Goodell came closest to approximating Clarkson's role as the movement's historian. A political activist who had earlier traveled as a seaman to Europe and Asia, Goodell combined religious orthodoxy with a radical critique of racial prejudice and the "aristocracy of wealth." His interpretation of America's declension and revolutionary promise, published in 1852, illuminates the theme of a "fortunate fall." Like many abolitionists, including Henry Wright, Goodell drew on the old Federalist and Congregationalist imagery depicting a "general decline of pure religion and sound morality" that had followed the Revolution and that had contributed to a growing disregard for liberty and human rights, exemplified by such "flagrant iniquities" as the slave trade and slavery. Yet Goodell found flaws in both the Federalist and Democratic-Republican traditions: "Had the 'Federalists' been more democratic in their theory of civil government—had the 'Democrats' . . . reduced their own theory to practice, the system of American slavery would have been abolished at an early period of our history." He correctly noted that with respect to Negro slavery, the writings of Calvinist clergyman like Samuel Hopkins and Jonathan Edwards the younger had been "among the most radically democratic of their times." Although Thomas Paine had also advocated the abolition of slavery, his "infidel principles and lax morals" had aroused prejudices against his admirable democratic principles. Indeed, for Goodell nothing had furthered the decline of republican morality more than the excesses of the French Revolution, particularly "the open repudiation of Christianity and the Bible, and . . . the idea of the overthrow of all churches." In the resulting conservative reaction, "the doctrines of immediate and unconditional emancipation, as taught by Edwards, were systematically confronted with the 'Jacobinism of the first French Revolution'—a misrepresentation less excusable now, than during the dimness and confusion near the close of the last century."[80]

This commitment to democracy separated Goodell from earlier conservatives and contemporary southern evangelicals who also associated moral decline with increasing prosperity, with political demagoguery, and with what James Henley Thornwell termed a "loosening of the ties of moral restraint."[81] For Goodell it was nevertheless clear that the decline of early antislavery commitment could be chiefly attributed to the Americans' quest for wealth:

> The pursuit of wealth had begotten the inordinate love of it. . . . Inequality of possession, continually increasing and in striking contrast to earlier times, had undermined the spirit of equality, and introduced aristocratic tastes. Humanity and human rights were less valued than wealth. The concentration of capital created a new element of political power. . . . The possession of wealth, or of talents prostituted to the support of its claims . . . supplied passports to seats in the State and National Councils, to places of authority and power.[82]

Goodell proceeded to document the effects of such materialism on the American Protestant churches as they moved from frank opposition to slavery during the Revolutionary period through stages of embarrassment, apathy, and apology. He concluded that even religious revivals had "done little towards restoring the ancient standard of morals." Far from preserving an independent standard of moral judgment, the American church had become the most influential agent of declension—eagerly adjusting itself to "the unexpected profitableness of slave labor in the production of cotton"; to "the profitableness of the cotton manufacturer at the North"; and, above all, to the "mean," "infidel," "blasphemous," "murderous" prejudice that "virtually predicates humanity upon the hue of the skin, that disbelieves that 'God had made of one blood all nations of men,' that arrogates to less than one-sixth part of the human race the exclusive monopoly of our common humanity. . . ." By the logic of the American jeremiad, the very totality of this fall from grace presented an unprecedented opportunity for total rebirth—a promise of emancipation for

> the ground tier of humanity, hid under the rubbish of centuries of degradation—classes who have scarcely been thought of, as human, and to whom no Magna Charta . . . no Declaration of Independence, have brought even a tithe or a foretaste of their promised blessings. The houseless, the landless, the homeless—the operatives of Manchester and

> Birmingham, the tenantry of Ireland, the Russian serfs—above all, *the North American Slaves*—what have Christian civilization and democratic liberty and equality in reserve for these?[83]

In 1807 Thomas Clarkson had been writing the history of what he and other abolitionists considered an already triumphant cause (Goodell took pains to document the later disillusion of Clarkson and other British reformers who had overemphasized the importance of the slave trade). Clarkson could therefore look back upon a kind of cumulative and irresistible progress, punctuated by temporary setbacks, following Europe's initial fall from grace. But for Goodell, viewing the bleak American prospects following the Compromise of 1850, it appeared that only some decisive change, or *kairos,* could prevent republican government from deteriorating into "a ruthless despotism," or the church and ministry from becoming "handmaids of oppression," throwing themselves "as blocks under the chariot wheels of the Messiah."[84]

The two historians agreed, however, that the slave system was the essence of iniquity, the only satanic obstacle to the fulfillment of human dreams. Its existence was therefore "fortunate" at least in a providential sense. The paradise to be regained by its abolition would be a "far happier place," to borrow the phrase Milton's archangel used to reassure Adam, than any previous Eden. Christianity had been leached of its vitality by the Enlightenment and the treason of clerks; shocked into a reactionary hysteria by the French Revolution; contaminated by prosperity and worldly compromise—but it could still be redeemed and resurrected by its victory over black slavery. Cleansed and confident, Christianity as "practical benevolence" could then meet the demands of a new industrial age.

4. THE IDEA OF PROGRESS AND THE LIMITS OF MORAL RESPONSIBILITY

I

The idea of progress implies that a particular course of change leads toward that which is beneficial or desirable for humanity as a whole. Already in the 1760s colonial slavery seemed incompatible with this standard in the eyes of the progressive-minded cognoscenti of Paris, Edinburgh, Glasgow, Birmingham, Philadelphia, Boston, London, and even parts of Virginia. Some ninety years later the battle-scarred William Goodell could still speak hopefully of the "indefinite amount of latent, half-developed, incipient abolitionism" in the United States, and of a public mind that questioned neither "whether slavery *ought* to be abolished, nor *when* it should be—but, by what methods and motives should the people be brought up to the work."[85]

But, of course, methods and motives were at the very heart of the controversy, profoundly affecting the meaning of "when" and "ought," and of abolition itself. No doubt the abolitionist movement depended on the prior diffusion of the idea of progress and on the implicit assumption that bondage, in all its literal and metaphorical manifestations, was precisely what the progress of humanity must overcome. Yet, as both white and black abolitionists discovered, emancipation could be even more effectively blocked by men who believed in progress than by those who fatalistically resigned themselves to the sins of this world.

To speak of the idea of progress as an *obstacle* to emancipation may be troubling for people who would like to translate all historical problems into binary choices: for example, did the idea of progress (or the Enlightenment) make a positive contribution to the antislavery movement or did it not? Unfortunately, the questions we are exploring are much too complicated for yes-or-no answers. This is not to say that muddy thinking can be justified by references to life's confusions. For those of us who still think of history as a kind of moral philosophy teaching by examples, it is precisely the multiple character of truth—the varied angles of vision that are also the subject of imaginative literature—that one must seek to capture. If such inquiry has any "therapeutic" value, it arises from the discovery that the most comforting and reassuring facets of meaning, include those that conform to iconoclastic or ideological desires, are not the only dimensions of historical experience.

Discussions of the idea of progress commonly slip into the idealist fallacy of picturing ideas as autonomous forces that shape human history—or, equally misleading, as ahistorical cognitions that can be understood without reference to social and historical context.[86] At the outset we should remind ourselves that belief in progress is sometimes infused with messianic fervor and sometimes held with the cool detachment of a mathematical theorem. Since human moods and outlooks are seldom consistent, a faith in progress has often alternated with despair over impending decline or catastrophe. Appeals to progress have helped to inspire revolution as well as to reconcile people to prolonged suffering and injustice. It is also naïve to assume—as intellectuals and ideologues are inclined to do—that the actual behavior of a people will be determined by a "climate of opinion" that celebrates progress and singles out a particular practice, such as slaveholding, as a vestige of barbarism.

The so-called Scottish Enlightenment furnishes a sobering example of this point. The French philosophes and American Quakers were both indebted to the pioneering Scottish moral philosophers for theories that specifically linked the abolition of slavery to the political, moral, and economic progress of human society. C. Duncan Rice has recently shown why slavery acquired such symbolic importance for eighteenth-century Scottish moralists who were preoccupied with theories of social cohesion and who "filled a peculiar social position as a professional elite closely allied to the bar and the landed governing class." Belief in the immorality and inexpediency of slavery, expounded in sermons, lectures, treatises, and debating-club discussions, became the keystone of a larger ideological edifice. Rice concludes that "well before the American Revolution, there must have been few Scots educated above the level of basic literacy who were not familiar with the enlightened indictment of slavery." Yet he also convincingly shows that this indoctrination had no apparent effect on the hordes of young Scots who became slave traders or emigrant overseers in the slave colonies, men whose "high literacy and disciplined system of patronage gave them a disproportinate share of the posts as clerks, factors, bookkeepers, and managers on which the slave system depended." Scotland ultimately became warmly responsive to abolitionism, but only after a prolonged exposure to religious revivalism.[87]

The fact that ideas of progress can easily be compartmentalized does not mean that they should be dismissed as mere epiphenomena. People's conceptions of the past and future do matter. Ideas of progress have given direction and significance to concrete interests, conflicts, and life-and-death struggles. While engaged dialectically with historical experience, conceptions of progress appeal at least implicitly to a scale of values supposedly outside history—to transcendent standards by which all historical change must be judged. In this sense the belief in historical progress is an explanatory system, analogous to and often overlapping a system of theology, organizing and modifying arbitrary interests in accordance with certain coherent rules.[88]

No doubt there were economic and political forces that made both antislavery and the idea of progress increasingly congenial to the early modern age. But the close relationship and the parallel development of the two sets of thought also suggest internal connections rooted in the history of Western social and political philosophy—or, more precisely, in the ancient tendency to define the *individual's* progress toward authentic liberty and virtue as the antithesis of remaining a slavish soul, a soul obedient only to sin or to an owner's will.

From the time of Jean Bodin, in the late sixteenth century, to that of Turgot and Condorcet, in the middle and late eighteenth century, the writers who gradually formulated an antislavery philosophy were also major contributors to the theory that knowledge and even material welfare and social justice advanced in progressive stages governed by the laws of nature and human nature. Condorcet's ecstatic vision of irreversible secular progress—penned just before his death during the Reign of Terror—is often taken as the symbolic legacy of the last philosophe to the utopian socialists and reformers of the nineteenth century. Credited with sketching the first fully developed theory of the unlimited progress of all humanity toward peace, equality, and happiness, Condorcet also wrote one of the Enlightenment's most sweeping indictments of colonial slavery.[89] But except for the belief that slavery retarded human progress, there was little that united political absolutists like Bodin with egalitarians like Condorcet. It is therefore important to note what most advocates of antislavery and progress held in common: the belief in a "higher law" of nature that should govern human institutions but that had long been obscured by false systems of philosophy and theology; the conviction that these natural principles, like the laws of science, could be discovered by the right process of reason and by a study of universal history; and, most important, a willingness to apply the standards of expediency and "common sense" to the entire tradition of classical and scholastic thought, including the justifications for slavery passed down by Aristotle, Augustine, the Justinian Code, and canon law. Once the traditional worldview had been dismantled, liberals could rejoice that there was no divine or cosmic design opposing what Adam Smith described as the universal and uniform drive of "every man to better his condition."

An internal connection between antislavery and the idea of progress is also suggested by the hazier religious tradition that extended from Hellenistic Judaism and Joachim of Fiore through the various millennial sects of the late Middle Ages and the English civil wars. The point to be made here is simply that religious visions of a historical emancipation from sin—of the Third Age or imminent Kingdom of God—were characteristically described as a collective redemption from an epoch of slavelike submission, injustice, and inequality. Whether conceived as a final stage of history or as a cataclysmic break with the past, such collective redemption implied a repudiation of *chronos*—of faith in the continung amelioration or improvement of existing institutions. Though perfectionists and millenarians were concerned with their own freedom from sin and not with the freedom of slaves, their acts of symbolic purification tended to challenge every principle of servitude. It was not accidental that the Quakers, the only radical sectarians who managed to survive the English civil wars and Restoration, to combine piety with growing prosperity, and to become involved with colonial slavery, were the first Christians who renounced slave trading and slaveholding as a test of faith. Nor was it accidental that the Quakers were originally prodded to move toward this action by visionary "deviants" whose radical eschatology resembled that of the Anabaptists, Diggers, and Fifth Monarchy Men.[90]

Perfectionism and millennialism should not be confused with the secular idea of progress, despite the frequent indebtedness of secular theorists to earlier religious prophets. Yet the three elements were synthesized by eighteenth-century Anglican theologians intent on answering the deist challenge to Christianity. In response to the deists' arguments that Christianity was "as old as creation" and that nature is always governed by the same uniform laws, these apologists held that throughout history mankind had shown continuous progress toward enlightenment and moral perfection, achieving at successive stages an improved capacity to understand and fulfill God's revealed law. To prove that Christianity had enabled humanity to surpass the moral capability of the ancients, such writers commonly cited the abolition of slavery and serfdom in western Europe. Such a blend of progressive and millennial thought was of supreme importance to early Anglican abolitionists like Granville Sharp and the Reverend James Ramsay. Ramsay, who made much of serfdom's gradual disappearance, predicted that when the blacks in the colonies were finally emancipated, the way would be open to "the fabulous golden age, when mutual wants and mutual good, will & shall bind all mankind in one common-interest."[91]

But whether invoked by Christians or by philosophes, the model of Europe's emancipation of white slaves and serfs carried profoundly conservative implications. The process had taken many centuries. And as we have already suggested, it represented the supposedly irresistible fulfillment of a causal sequence that went even farther back in time. In other words, the crucial turning point or *kairos* lay in the distant past—for many Christians, in the initial reception of Christianity. The theory of incremental social progress also excluded any sharp break between past and future, between the Old World and the New, or between the experience of whites and of blacks. The goal of liberation might be furthered by enlightened legislation, but ultimately it depended on a process of progressive amelioration carried out by the slaveholders themselves.

These assumptions long dominated the thought of British, American, and French abolitionists who otherwise represented a wide spectrum of political and religious views. For example, James Ramsay, who was considered an abolitionist because of his insistence on immediate remedial legislation, looked forward to the gradual Christianization and amelioration of West Indian slavery—to replacing "artificial" and arbitrary power with a more effective, orderly, and lawful authority, based on nature and revelation and aimed at maintaining production while elevating the moral conduct of the black population. Condorcet, who rejected Ramsay's belief in permanent human (not racial) inequalities, outlined a program of social engineering that would gradually prepare blacks for freedom and emancipate them in carefully planned stages. Though Condorcet considered slavery a crime and liberty the restoration of a natural right, "not a gift or an act of charity," as a practical minded philosophe he also agreed with his fellow leaders of the *Amis des noirs* that a sudden restoration would be equivalent "to abandoning and refusing aid to infants in their cradles or to helpless cripples."[92]

David Rice, the fiery Presbyterian preacher from Virginia who fought to prevent Kentucky from becoming a slave state, held that bondsmen were in no way obligated to serve their masters, and he even applauded the blacks of Saint Domingue who were "bravely sacrificing their lives on the altar of liberty." Rice warned the Kentucky constitutional convention of 1792 that "as a separate state, we are just now come to the birth; and it depends upon our free choice whether we shall be born in this sin, or innocent of it." Nevertheless, when Rice contemplated the obstacles to a general emancipation in the southern states, he turned to the precedent of Christianity's abolishing slavery in Europe, "not by producing laws for its abolition, but its effects on the hearts of christians[,] disposing them to justice and mercy."[93] In 1791 Noah Webster appealed to the same historical example. Considering the "privileges" already won by American slaves, Webster said, "it is no ill-founded prediction, that slavery in this country will be utterly extirpated in the course of two centuries, perhaps in a much shorter period, without any extraordinary efforts to abolish it." As an ardent nationalist who celebrated the glorious achievements and promise of American life, Webster felt that such progress would be too slow for "the friends of humanity," for "the spirit of our governments," and for "our public prosperity." Hence it was "highly necessary that public measures and private societies should lend their aid to accelerate the progress of freedom, and with all convenient speed, banish the galling chains of bondage from the shores of our Republic." Yet Webster cautioned that humanitarians should always remember that "however unjustifiable the policy by which slavery has been introduced and encouraged, the evil has taken such deep root . . . that an attempt to eradicate it at a single blow would expose the whole political body to dissolution."[94]

As we shall see, it was precisely this line of argument that British abolitionists had repudiated by 1830, partly because it had been skillfully appropriated by their opponents. The attention devoted after 1830 to the distinction between "gradualism" and "immediatism" has tended to obscure the earlier and more fundamental distinction between a faith in progress that would only soothe the individual conscience, neutralize effective action, and thus protect the slave system; and a faith in progress that would provide assurance that individual action could be effective, in gear with the underlying thrust of history, and hence ethically mandatory. From the very outset, abolitionists discovered that their most dangerous opponents were not forthright defenders of black slavery but rather the "progressives" who were confident that Christianity and economic growth would inevitably "improve" the institution until it ceased to exist. Because abolitionists themselves shared much of this faith, they went through a long and painful search for tests of morally responsible action—tests that would distinguish authentic antislavery testimony from hypocrisy and self-deception.

Before we examine such changing tests or symbolic issues, it is important to know more about the intellectual obstacles the abolitionists faced. In the late 1780s, as soon as British reformers demanded legislation outlawing the African slave trade, their assumptions were challenged by champions of progress who also professed an abhorrence for any kind of human bondage. According to a scholarly treatise by G. J. Thorkelin, a professor at the University of Copenhagen and a member of the Royal Danish Academy of Science, the history of Europe from antiquity to the late Middle Ages showed that slavery was always the result of economic scarcity, "a necessary evil attending upon nations in a state of uncivilization and barbarism; and that very great efforts, for a continued length of time, are required to extirpate it." Instead of retarding progress by destroying a valuable branch of trade, the reformers should therefore work for ameliorative legislation ensuring the blacks humane treatment and eventual freedom. To abolish the slave trade without any such preparation would undercut the very economic and moral forces on which the progress of Africa and the colonies depended.[95]

Such reasoning carried weight even with a man like Henry Thornton, the wealthy London banker and Anglican evangelical who was an intimate friend of Wilberforce's and the virtual founder of the Clapham Sect. As chairman of the directors of the Sierra Leone Company, Thornton confided to John Clarkson late in 1791 that while many of their colleagues favored immediate abolition of the slave trade, "I am rather inclined myself to aim at the introduction of general light and knowledge than the removal of this particular evil." He also advised Clarkson, who was about to command the company's fleet transporting North American free blacks to Sierra Leone, that he should insist on strict sexual morality but should not let his antislavery zeal offend neighboring African leaders and traders, on whom the success of the colony would depend.[96] As an MP, Thornton supported Wilberforce's abolition bills, but his preference for the more traditional and indirect means of spreading Christian light and knowledge long remained the dominant faith among Anglican evangelicals. Down to the American Civil War, it constituted the bedrock faith of the northern Protestant churches.

In 1788 one of Adam Smith's disciples pointed to a different kind of indirect means and articulated a theory of progress that would continue to undercut every specific plan that British and American abolitionists proposed. The anonymous author had no doubt that the entire slave system was cruel and oppressive or that it stifled economic growth and drained the nation of wealth. But as long as the colonists' demand for slaves remained at the present high level, he argued, laws prohibiting the trade would prove to be as ineffective as the earlier Spanish and Portuguese threats of capital punishment for anyone exporting gold and silver to the rest of Europe. Even if Britain succeeded in blockading the African coast, penalties could not be imposed on the French, Dutch, and other nationals who would quickly take up the British share of the market. As for the British colonies themselves, substantive remedial legislation would also be unenforceable. The author was clearly thinking of the recent American Revolution, but he accurately anticipated the problems faced by the special magistrates sent out to supervise the West Indian apprenticeship system in the 1830s. To enforce ameliorative legislation, he pointed out, tribunals would have to depend on British judges living in an alien setting far from home. Should it not be expected that such judges would

> be partial towards men with whom they will be in daily habits of social intercourse; with whom they will be forming the strictest connections of friendship and alliance; and whose influence, should they presume to do their duty with rigour, may be sufficient to remove them from their posts; than towards those whom, perhaps, they already consider as beings of an inferior species, and from whom they have, at least, nothing either to fear or to hope?[97]

On the one hand, the implementation of reform would probably be left to magistrates who identified their own interests with those of the planters; on the other hand, if the magistrates were men of "extraordinary integrity," they would arouse such violent resistance that the resulting uproar both at home and abroad would lead to a reactionary repudiation of reform. It was axiomatic, the author concluded, that legislation could never succeed in regulating the relations between two bodies of men "when the party in whose favour it was thought necessary to interfere, did not derive from other sources such a degree of weight and importance, as even to enable it to claim the protection of the very law that was made in its behalf."[98] This statement is especially striking because it touches the heart of the problem of various post-emancipation "reconstructions" and because it raises questions that were almost never discussed by abolitionists. But any implication that freedmen should be given enough economic power to enable them to claim the protection of law would have been anathema to the author, who proceeds to quote extensively from *The Wealth of Nations* on the futility of any state intervention in market activities. According to this doctrine of progress, if the West Indies were deprived of monopolistic privileges and subjected to the forces of free competition, the artificial demand for slaves would cease and the islands would soon be inhabited and cultivated by "a much more useful body of men."

There were obvious discrepancies between the evangelical reliance on Christian benevolence and the economists' reliance on free-market forces. The two schools of thought offered opposing explanations, for example, for the disappearance of slavery and serfdom from western Europe. Yet the two conceptions of progress also had much in common. Both viewed slavery as an anachronism that was certain to be destroyed by peaceful and indirect means unless well-meaning zealots, devoid of either Christian charity or economic wisdom, ignited flames imperiling the entire social order. In some respects Adam Smith's economic man was simply a secular version of the twice-born Christian, his self-interest being converted by an "invisible hand" into a force for the public good. The parallel becomes almost explicit in Smith's explanation of the essentially noneconomic (and therefore sinful) origins of slavery: "The pride of man makes him love to domineer, and nothing mortifies him so much as to be obliged to condescend to persuade his inferiors. Wherever the law allows it, and the nature of the work can afford it, therefore, he will generally prefer the services of slaves to that of freemen." In short, the same sin of pride that blinded slaveholders to Christian charity also blinded them to the principle of self-interest as revealed by the new science of economics. Unfortunately, according to Smith, the high profitability of cultivating sugar and even tobacco for an artificially protected market obscured the intolerable cost and low productivity of slave labor—because "a person who can acquire no property, can have no other interest but to eat as much, and to labor as little as possible."[99] In the long run, however, consumers would refuse to subsidize a system that rewarded waste, inefficiency, the careless management of labor, and a willingness to indulge in present gratifications at the expense of future progress.

When focused on slavery, this general faith was wholly compatible with the evangelical goal of amelioration through the spread of Christian light and knowledge. Economic sins gave scientific confirmation to Christian values; the common cause proved that self-interest, though always suspect in orthodox Protestant eyes, could promote Christian virtue. It is no exaggeration to say that this kind of synthesis, derived mainly from the Scottish moralists, became the dominant creed in antebellum America. Though challenged by southern defenders of slavery as a "positive good" and by abolitionists who demanded "immediate emancipation," a faith in the mellowing effects of religious and economic progress remained strong in the South as well as among northern churchmen, reformers, and community leaders.

But to be convincing, the belief in indirect means required periodic evidence that the slave system, in Abraham Lincoln's later words, had been put "in the course of ultimate extinction." On this point, given the contrary experience from the 1820s onward, it is easy to forget that the American prospects seemed for a time more favorable than the British. In Britain the original agitation against the slave trade exposed the planters' bitter hostility to any Christianizing of slaves or curtailment of colonial economic privileges. The abolitionists' defeats in the 1790s suggested that Britain's established order would protect the planters' interests even in the face of massive public demands for reform. In the contemporary United States, however, except for a few Georgians and South Carolinians, every national leader publicly condemned the slave trade; most of them also deplored the evils of black slavery. In 1787 Congress barred involuntary servitude from the vast territories north of the Ohio River, and by 1804 the nine states north of Delaware had either emancipated or provided for the future emancipation of all blacks. The African slave trade, earlier outlawed by every state except South Carolina, which had itself shut off slave imports before 1803, was prohibited in 1807 by congressional action. From the South, but not from the West Indies, came increasing reports that planters were encouraging the Christianization of their slaves. Suffering from the prolonged effects of depressed tobacco prices, Virginians in particular showed an interest in agricultural diversification. If market forces and evangelical Christianity worked inevitably for the amelioration and gradual eradication of chattel slavery, Americans had reason to be confident. They could draw added assurance from the supposedly liberating and enlightening influence of republican institutions and from the increasingly popular theory that slave labor was a temporary expedient occasioned by a low ratio of population to arable land—a ratio that was bound to change with the continuing growth of population and settlement of the trans-appalachian West.

James Wilson, one of the framers of the Constitution, was by no means alone in interpreting the Constitution's slave-trade clause, which allowed congressional prohibition after a period of twenty years, "as laying the foundation for banishing slavery out of this country; and though the period is more distant than I could wish, yet it will produce the same kind of gradual change which was pursued in Pennsylvania." Although the early abolition societies expressed alarm over various setbacks, their outlook was on the whole optimistic. Jonathan Edwards the younger probably expressed a widespread conviction in 1791 when he predicted that, at the present rate of progress, it would within fifty years "be as shameful for a man to hold a Negro slave, as to be guilty of common robbery or theft." Whether they spoke of fifty or one hundred years, early abolitionists were content to work for a goal beyond their own lifetimes—as long as they remained certain that no good effort was ever lost and that progress was irreversible. Even as late as 1829, when Garrison was denouncing southern intransigence and demanding emancipation in the District of Columbia, he cautioned:

> The emancipation of all the slaves of this generation is most assuredly out of the question. The fabric, which now towers above the Alps, must be taken away brick by brick, and foot by foot, till it is reduced so low

> that it may be overturned without burying the nation in its ruins. Years may elapse before the completion of the achievement; generations of blacks may go down to the grave, manacled and lacerated, without a hope for their children; the philanthropists who are now pleading in behalf of the oppressed, may not live to witness the dawn which will precede the glorious day of universal emancipation; but the work will go on.[100]

With the benefit of hindsight, we know that the premises of gradualism were often built on illusions (although a quarter of a century after *Brown* v. *Board of Education of Topeka,* we can hardly afford to be condescending toward early reformers who had no precedents or central administrative institutions). From the outset, southern planters were determined to prevent either Christianization or the abolition of the slave trade from undermining their system of labor. Between 1795 and 1810 the price of slaves continued to rise, reflecting the conviction that slavery was anything but a dying institution. British reformers, assuming that chattel slavery could not survive in the New World without the continuing importation of Africans, interpreted a self-reproducing black population as a significant step toward gradual emancipation—as evidence both of continuing amelioration and of an eventual land-labor ratio that would reduce wages below the cost of maintaining slaves. But the unprecedented natural increase in America's slave population was in fact a sign of the institution's vitality. It was the fertility of American slaves that ensured a continuing supply of labor for the westward expansion of cotton.

As we have seen, later abolitionists like William Goodell looked back upon the post-Revolutionary decades as a time of disastrous moral declension. After the mid-1790s, religious and political leaders were clearly less inclined to denounce the irremediable evils of slaveholding or to demand measures intended to destroy the system. But this growing caution, equivocation, and silence is easier to document than to explain. As in England, to be sure, reaction to the French Revolution deflated enthusiasm for reform. Politicians and journalists blamed antislavery agitation for igniting the black revolution in Saint Domingue (1791); for encouraging the Gabriel and Denmark Vesey conspiracies in Virginia (1800) and South Carolina (1822); and for directly promoting insurrections in Barbados (1816) and Demerara (1823). In the United States the extension of political equality to white males was accompanied by a sharp upsurge of Negrophobia and by what George M. Fredrickson has called "an ideological marriage between egalitarian democracy and biological racism." Until the mid-nineteenth century, at least, British abolitionists could safely decry biological racism as irreligious and beneath contempt. But since free blacks represented less than 2 percent of the North's population in 1820, their deteriorating condition and increasing persecution raised ominous questions regarding the fate of the mass of blacks in the South. Finally, the federal system of government discouraged reformers from looking beyond such local concerns as state emancipation acts and measures to prevent the kidnapping and out-of-state sale of free blacks. Beginning with a crucial compromise in 1790, such compelling special interests as the federal assumption of state debts led to bargains in which economic and political stability took priority over the implied powers of Congress to investigate and regulate various segments of the slave system. As a result of the "federal consensus" established in 1790, even the widespread protest against admitting Missouri as a slave state was easily stigmatized and dismissed as a sectional and politically motivated maneuver.[101]

One can also argue that the nature of evangelical abolitionism in the Revolutionary period virtually guaranteed a subsequent "declension." During the crisis of war and uncertain independence, many evangelicals insisted that renouncing slaveholding was a sign not only of individual purity but also of the collective repentance necessary to avert divine retribution. By absorbing the sin of slaveholding into the rhetoric of the jeremiad, these evangelicals equated manumission with a renunciation of impiety, intemperance, gambling, lewdness, and religious indifference. They also staked the urgency of reform on credible signs of impending catastrophe. When the United States, despite its notorious "inconsistency," survived and prospered during a period when the nations of Europe were engulfed in cataclysmic war; when the Second Great Awakening spread religious conversion like a contagion from frontier Kentucky to Georgia and Connecticut—it appeared that God had not forsaken His experimental Republic. Why should Northerners, who tend to express a smug pride in their own purification from slavery, take a less charitable view of the South's burden, or doubt that the blessings of Providence would ultimately provide the means for that burden's removal? Meanwhile, the southern Baptist, Methodist, and Presbyterian clergy, only a few of whom had ever denounced slaveholding as a sin, recognized that the triumph of God's Kingdom in America would depend on an unambiguous distinction between the things of Christ and those of Caesar. To bar slaveholders from communion or to follow the Quaker example of gradual internal purification would defeat the great purpose of the revivals—the diffusion of vital Christianity through all ranks of society. Isolated pockets of sanctity could do nothing to ameliorate the condition of slaves. Hence, instead of withdrawing into enclaves of impotent purity, even the more zealous antislavery advocates like the Methodist bishop Francis Asbury retreated to the ideal of Christian paternalism that had long been maintained by sectarians like the Moravians as well as by orthodox Catholics and Protestants: "What is the personal liberty of the African, which he may abuse," Asbury asked, "to the salvation of his soul, how may it be compared?" The goal of Christianity was to make slaveholders more godly.[102]

Ironically, British abolitionism was spared such declension precisely because it began with no revolutionary expectations. The British abolitionist leaders of the late 1780s and 1790s were attempting, in some respects, to catch up with the United States by freeing West Indian planters from their dependence on the African slave trade. Clarkson, Wilberforce, and the British Quakers assumed that by cutting off the "artificial" supply of labor, they could set in motion a chain of forces, sustained by economic self-interest, that would force planters to improve the treatment of existing slaves, leading slowly but irresistibly toward the creation of a free "peasantry." The crucial reforms would be carried out by the planters themselves.

But this limited and seemingly conservative approach also enabled the British abolitionists to focus national attention on a significant *political* goal: an act of Parliament outlawing a previously favored branch of trade. The rhetoric demanding this "immediate abolition" was radical, uncompromising, and charged with warnings of divine retribution. The test of true antislavery commitment, like a test of true sanctification, lay in a scornful repudiation of all counterfeit professions—such as proposals for "improving" the slave trade by strict regulation or for colonial legislation ameliorating the condition of slaves in order to increase the domestic labor supply before ending importations from Africa. Until Parliament outlawed the trade, abolitionists insisted, no reliance could be placed on either the planters' benevolence or their self-interest. As we have seen, the abolitionists' sudden triumph in 1807 was widely interpreted as a vindication of Christianity and a deliverance from national guilt.

One can easily be deceived by the similarities between British and American rhetoric, especially the evangelical obsession with national redemption. The West Indian colonies were dependent politically and militarily on a powerful metropolis and were marginal to English consciousness. Abolitionists never assumed that national redemption would begin with the voluntary change of heart of individual planters. Even government leaders, though responsive to pleas from the larger proprietors, tended to perceive West Indians as a special class who represented the narrowest "pecuniary interests," as the colonial secretary put it in 1833, and who were therefore subject to the most utilitarian manipulation. Such utilitarianism was more congenial to British than to American political institutions. And in Britain, abolitionists could take for granted the authority of Parliament to examine witnesses, weigh empirical evidence, and adopt whatever measures were deemed necessary for promoting the national interest. Even during the first "gradualist" period, from 1787 to 1807, the reformers contended that planters could never be expected to perceive or pursue their own best interests until Parliament had deprived them of an artificial and morally corrupting supply of slave labor. As the West Indian planters rightly feared, this view of progress and moral responsibility opened the way for unprecedented intervention if the abolitionists proved to be wrong in their expectations.[103]

As it turned out, the abolitionists had overestimated the impact of the 1807 law both on the international slave trade and on the treatment of West Indian slaves. By 1814 suppressing the former had become a point of national honor in Britain's diplomatic maneuvers to shape the post-Napoleonic world. Even British planters now hailed a policy of humanitarianism, enforced by British warships, that promised to deprive their Spanish, French, and Portuguese competitors of a cheap and plentiful supply of labor. But this new consensus on the slave trade concealed the abolitionists' radical reassessment of planter self-interest and of the need for further governmental intervention.

In 1804 the young Henry Brougham had summed up the then prevailing abolitionist dogma that once the slave trade has been outlawed

> there needs no further interference with the structure of Colonial Society, or the concerns of West Indian proprietors. Every man may now be left to pursue his own interest in his own way. Few will continue so insane as to maltreat and work out their stock, when they can no longer fill up the blanks occasioned by their cruelty, or their inhuman and shortsighted policy. . . . In a very few years all the Negroes in the West Indies will be Creoles, and all the masters will treat them with kind indulgence, for their own sakes.[104]

Eleven years later, Thomas Clarkson spelled out the new premises and conclusions. Since the colonists had stubbornly refused to enact ameliorative legislation, "it must be obvious that there *may,* and more probably that *there will,* be an alarming *Decrease* in the *Negro population.*" Here Clarkson openly faced a possibility that abolitionists had long been reluctant to discuss—that slavery might be eradicated by the slaves' inability to reproduce. While the planters would blame such an outcome on the abolitionists, Clarkson angrily accused the West Indian legislatures of subverting the principles of humanity and justice embodied in the abolition law of 1807, and of thereby subverting the British constitution. The colonists had *"forfeited their Charter over & over again,* and the Mother-Country has on this Ground, if on no other, a direct Right to interfere, and to substitute better Laws, and the British People have a Right to call upon their government so to do." From the beginning, Clarkson had struggled to overcome false conceptions of self-interest—in 1788, for example, he had tried to convince William Pitt that the supposed self-interest of traders gave no automatic protection to African slaves. By 1815 he was able to agree with James Stephen and other abolitionist leaders that the exercise of arbitrary power had insulated the planters' minds from the enlightening effects of the abolition law and hence from their own true interests as defined by the abolitionists: and "if the owners of Slaves, and the Colonial Legislatures are deaf to Reason, they must be *compelled to obey it.* They must be *over awed by the public Voice."*[105]

5. BRITISH EMANCIPATION: A DECEPTIVE MODEL, PART ONE

As we saw in the preceding discussion, by the early nineteenth century there was widespread agreement that Negro slavery was an unprogressive institution. Despite much evidence of the profitability of slave labor, at least in the short run, despite biblical defenses of paternalistic servitude, and despite various justifications for subjugating uncivilized or supposedly inferior peoples, the leading statesmen and legislators of the Western world professed to believe that chattel slavery, long an unacceptable status for whites, must inevitably give way to Christian freedom. This is a fact of considerable importance even though few statesmen or legislators were prepared to endorse measures that might conceivably threaten private property, economic productivity, or social order.

But if historical progress seemed to ensure the eventual emancipation of all slaves, there was sharp disagreement over the instrumentalities of progress, especially the political means required for morally responsible action. For a time the liberals who acclaimed the United States as history's revelation of the future could interpret the growth of black population and the spread of free soil in the North and Northwest as signs of progressive amelioration. But as the Cotton Kingdom emerged in the South and Southwest and as free blacks were subjected to harsher persecutions in the North, new doubts arose. American theories of moral declension suggested that religious revivals, political liberty, and economic self-interest were by themselves insufficient. By the early 1830s a sense of crisis had gripped a new generation of reformers who searched for an alternative to indirect amelioration. The British emancipation act of 1833 provided them with what appeared to be a model of decisive action—an "act of the nation and not of its rulers," as Tocqueville later put it. Because such interpretations exerted a profound influence on all future struggles against Negro slavery, it is important to examine with greater care the steps that led to the second mass emancipation of colonial slaves—always remembering that in the first emancipation, that of Saint Domingue, the French Convention essentially ratified the freedom that slaves had already won.

Despite their antiplanter rhetoric, most British abolitionists continued until 1830 to think of emancipation as the fruition of continuous improvement—of a process that would gradually prepare blacks for freedom, alleviate their suffering, and ween their masters from dependence on tyrannical authority. Although the reformers were quick to attribute slave insurrections to planter brutality, the specter of Haiti haunted their minds and strengthened their determination to repudiate any measures that might undermine law and authority or endanger the long-term productivity of colonial labor.

Late in 1823 Zachary Macaulay bitterly noted that George Canning's private secretary had publicly accused "Wilberforce, Buxton & Company" of instigating the recent slave insurrection in Demerara, when in fact it had been Canning and other cabinet ministers who had disregarded the abolitionists' detailed plans for "silent and progressive improvement . . . preparing the slaves, gradually and in no long time, for the grand change of substituting a moral impulse to labour, for that of the whip." The government itself had recklessly ordered the governors of Demerara and other crown colonies to begin "amelioration" by outlawing the whip as a symbol of authority in the fields. The whip, Macaulay reminded Thomas Fowell Buxton,

> is the grand badge of slavery in the West Indies. Its use is identified with the servile state. It is the symbol of it. And if, in Baptism, even our Bish-

> ops can mistake the symbol for the thing it represents, can we wonder that the poor slaves should confound this prominent and ever present symbol of slavery with slavery itself . . . [?] Govt however *begins* with saying "you must lay aside the whip." The slaves might naturally enough say "Lay aside the whip? Why this is giving our freedom. If the whip is abolished we are no longer slaves." And then what substitute has Govt provided?[106]

Apart from such caution—and it should be noted that in 1823 Macaulay had no fear of even an "instant emancipation, if the due and obvious precautions were taken"—the British abolitionists had long agreed that effective progress depended on some kind of direct governmental intervention.

It was James Stephen, the chief architect of the 1807 slave-trade abolition act, who first alerted his co-workers to the inadequacy of their original expectations. "The legal mastermind of the campaign for abolition and suppression," in Ann M. Burton's apt phrase, Stephen was both a devout member of the evangelical Clapham Sect and an expert on maritime law who could draw on years of legal experience in the British West Indies.[107] As he rose to the positions of master in Chancery, member of Parliament, and intimate adviser to two prime ministers, Stephen probably acquired more direct governmental influence than any other abolitionist ever achieved. Since this influence depended in large measure on Stephen's extraordinary ability to link abolitionism with British interests in the global war with Napoleonic Europe, his power waned with the onset of peace. But since Stephen also formulated and revised the basic strategy for governmental intervention and since his sons James and George later tried to emulate him, it is worth examining the personal background that led to such an important family commitment.

Deeply repentant over his youthful irreligion and sins of the flesh, the elder James Stephen was almost obsessed with the snares of self-deception and with the "special Providences" that had narrowly saved him from becoming a West Indian planter. The first providential intervention occurred in 1781, when Stephen was twenty-three, poor, and sexually entangled with three women, one of whom was about to give birth to his illegitimate child (much later, after a first wife had died, he married Wilberforce's sister). At the moment of bleakest guilt and poverty, news arrived that his elder brother, William, who was in Saint Kitts, had inherited the fortune of their uncle—a Scots planter who had started out as a slave-ship surgeon and had then made a modest fortune by buying "refuse negroes" at "Guinea yard sales," giving them medical treatment, and then reselling them at a large profit. The financial assistance Stephen now received from his brother allowed him to save his baby's life, resolve his sexual conflicts, and resume his legal training. For the rest of his long life, he remained keenly aware that tainted money had enabled him to escape disaster and enter a respected and lucrative profession (as a child, he and his mother had spent several months in a squalid prison, nursing his father who had been confined there for debt).

But despite this "temporal deliverance," Stephen still faced almost certain spiritual corruption when he sailed off in 1783 to join his brother, by then a planter in Saint Kitts. Like many other young Scots, Stephen believed in the abstract injustice of slavery, and at Aberdeen had been impressed by the antislavery lectures of James Beattie; but he soon discovered that even the most enlightened West Indians had become "indurated by the system they administered." What spared Stephen was a second providential intervention. During an unscheduled stopover at Barbados, before he had become "indurated," he witnessed the horrifying judicial procedures that led to the conviction for murder and burning alive of two probably innocent slaves. From that moment, Stephen resolved never to own a slave himself, a decision that protected him from the morally anesthetizing environment during his years of legal practice in Saint Kitts. Responding later to the charge that his abolitionism was the product of religious zeal, Stephen maintained that it would be much nearer the truth to say that it was his enmity toward slavery, acquired from his experience in the West Indies, that finally made him a Christian.[108]

During his decade in the Caribbean, Stephen had become an expert on colonial slave law and on the intricacies of smuggling and international trade that sustained the plantation system. He was also the first abolitionist to move beyond images of individual dominion and to think of slavery as a truly social system based on economic oppression—on a "merciless excess of forced labor exacted by means as merciless." For Stephen, the more publicized moral and spiritual evils of black slavery were all derivative; the central and invariable reality was that slaves were worn down, malnourished, overworked, and continually punished for not producing enough. No moral "amelioration" could be effective as long as such economic oppression continued. Nor could reformers expect moral exhortation to change the hearts of slaveholders:

> . . . it is natural for Planters to feel their own personal credit for humanity virtually arraigned, when that system is represented as cruel and inhuman, not in its occasional only, or incidental, but, as I maintain, in its ordinary and even its necessary effects.

Stephen insisted that his quarrel was not with "those who *conduct* the system" but with the system itself. Since the system necessitated oppression for the personal benefit of competitive proprietors, no individual planter could institute effective reforms without suffering ruinous losses. Only radical intervention from the outside—analogous, one may suggest, to the "special Providences" that had saved Stephen himself—could break through the nexus of evil and give planters the freedom of will to pursue their own best interests.[109]

Stephen's first opportunities to influence colonial policy arose early in the Napoleonic wars when he was practicing law in the Prize Appeals Court of the Privy Council. He shrewdly concluded that the epic struggle with France, the outcome of which depended increasingly on control of the high seas, could be used as an instrument for suppressing the entire Atlantic slave trade, an objective equivalent to severing the aorta of New World slavery. Stephen's conviction that the war had been "concerted in the cabinet of heaven to bring forth its long oppressed, degraded children with a mighty hand and with an outstretched arm" may strike the modern ear as almost medieval.[110] His strategy, however, was based on a wholly modern conception of economic warfare and naval power. He knew that previous attempts to outlaw the British slave trade had been subverted by the reasonable argument that foreign competitors would simply appropriate the British share of the trade. Although the war had enabled Britain to sweep most enemy ships from the Atlantic, Stephen also knew that the neutral American flag had given protection to a flourishing trade of slaves and provisions to enemy colonies, to say nothing of the far more vital shipment of colonial produce to Napoleonic Europe. The obvious answer to this *War in Disguise: or The Frauds of the Neutral Flags,* Stephen's immensely influential polemic of 1805, was to widen the definition of contraband trade and of belligerent maritime rights. It has often been said that Stephen helped to precipitate the American War of 1812, and there can be little doubt that he initiated the policies embodied in the famous orders in council of 1807, which blockaded enemy ports and allowed the British navy to seize neutral ships trading with the French, Spanish, Dutch, or Portuguese colonies. For our purposes, however, the important point is Stephen's plan to exploit the self-interest of warfare—both the national interest of Britain and the personal interest of British captains and crews who would be eligible for prize money—as a means of eradicating the Atlantic slave trade.[111]

It is true that Stephen barely mentioned the slave-trade issue in *War in Disguise,* but Roger Anstey and Ann M. Burton have convincingly argued that this was a tactical maneuver. From 1798 to 1815 Stephen worked tirelessly as the abolitionists' professional watchdog, cautioning them to mute humanitarian arguments and to focus on questions of national security. He seized every opportunity to prevent British ships and capital from supplying the enemy with slave labor, either directly or by reexport from British colonies; to block or postpone orders in council authorizing a trade in slaves to such conquered territories as Trinidad, Demerara, Berbice, Essequibo, and Surinam, which might revert to the enemy; and to extend economic warfare to the neutral American flag, which allowed ships of various nations to supply the enemy with slaves. This is not to say that a rather obscure adviser, even when well informed and skillful at exploiting political divisions, determined British maritime policy during the critical Napoleonic years. Yet Stephen's intimacy with Wilberforce, Grenville, and especially Spencer Perceval enabled him to achieve some momentous victories: in 1805, an order in council barring the importation of African slaves into the conquered territories; in 1806, supposedly "supplementary" acts of Parliament that strictly limited the transport of slaves from the older colonies to the rich and undeveloped lands of Trinidad, Saint Vincent, and Guiana and that also prohibited British subjects from selling slaves to foreign territories, a measure that annihilated perhaps two-thirds of the British African slave trade. Stephen helped to shape the famed abolition law of 1807, which was frankly advanced as a humanitarian measure, as part of a larger strategic vision in which God's decrees would be enforced by British power.[112]

Stephen revealed his underlying assumptions about Providence and British power when he privately exhorted Perceval to use the 1807 orders in council for "the total liberation of Africa from the slave trade." It was not by accident, he assured Perceval, that Napoleon had provided Britain with such an unexpected opportunity:

> Wise righteous & wonderful Providence . . . to make this great foe of the African race [Bonaparte] the instrument of their own compleat deliverance and that in conjunction with the very event he most abhors, the triumph of British commerce and British power over confederated Europe. Who durst have hoped that when we abolished the Slave Trade last spring we should be so soon in a situation to compel all other Powers to renounce it too? & that merely by the use of a maritime system, which our own interest & self-preservation prescribe to us, which every party in the country is prepared to acquiesce in, if not loudly applaud, & which even the British West Indies will be the first to rejoice in & commend. . . .
>
> Think what ought to be done in relation to the Portuguese slave trade & settlements on the coast—Advert to the unmeasurable importance now of the system we adopt towards America in respect of the colonial trade. The whole supply of Portuguese & Spanish America is undoubtedly your own if you choose—& by shutting out the supply of . . . *Slaves to Brazil Cuba etc.* you will keep in check the sugar planters of those Colonies, the

> only true means of finally saving our own. If you allow a single flag called neutral now to carry slaves from Africa, these benefits will be lost. . . .
>
> You must plant in England one foot of this bridge over which you may compel all the commerce of the earth to pass & pay toll, but then you must look well to the foundation. Would that you were dictator, and I your sole advisor. I would then if necessary cry in your ear incessantly—you have the happiest & most glorious game to play that ever presented itself to the ruler of a great nation. You may set your foot on the neck of France, great & proud as she is. You may lay the whole world under contribution for the support of your war against her, & that without violating one of those sacred principles which ought to govern the conduct of nations.[113]

As it turned out, these hopes were largely defeated by the exigencies of Britain's new alliance with Portugal and Spain, by the repeal of the orders in council, and by the necessity of relying on treaties for the suppression of the foreign slave trade. Stephen's central contribution was to focus attention, with a view to national security, on the conquered and eventually ceded colonies, especially Trinidad and Guiana (Demerara, Berbice, and Essequibo). Already in the late 1790s, when the price of sugar was soaring, there was enormous pressure from speculators to sell the fertile crown lands of Trinidad—and according to some contemporary estimates, the clearing and cultivation of Trinidad might have required as many as one million new slaves from Africa. During the same Napoleonic period the speculative development of new frontiers in the American South and of a new plantation system in Cuba prepared the way for a massive influx of slave labor—either from the older American states or, in Cuba's case, from Africa. By delaying the sale of crown lands and by helping to curtail the flow of slave labor from the older colonies to the new British frontiers, Stephen and his allies prevented an incalculable strengthening of the British slave system. Moreover, Stephen was instrumental in preventing the ceded colonies of Trinidad, Saint Lucia, and Guiana from acquiring British constitutions and representative assemblies.[114] The creation of this crown colony system was a long and complex process, but it is illuminating to imagine the rough analogy of Alabama, Mississippi, Louisiana, and Arkansas being denied representative government, being subjected to free-labor experiments on federal land, and being ruled by a succession of secretaries of state who relied on the expertise of a permanent abolitionist bureaucrat—for it was Stephen's son James who in 1813 became legal counsel to the Colonial Office and whose influence over the details of administration increased until, as assistant undersecretary and as permanent undersecretary in the 1830s, he helped to rationalize and reorganize the entire colonial system. While in 1833 George Stephen, another son and eminent lawyer, orchestrated the public agitation of the radical antislavery Agency Committee, his brother James drafted the government's emancipation bill.[115]

This division of labor dramatizes the remarkable contrast with the situation in the United States, where a Stephen family (and one can think of likely counterparts) could never have found the institutional tools, even during Reconstruction, to exert such influence over the regulation of labor, race relations, credit, land tenure, and other crucial "colonial questions." Unfortunately, the contrast also tends to reinforce traditional stereotypes that distort our understanding of British and American perceptions of progress and moral responsibility. Historians have often been misled by the British abolitionists' own illusion of continuity—of an unbroken and persevering "movement" that arose, providentially, in the 1780s; gathered cumulative sanction from prestigious converts, from "the public voice," and from the government's commitments; and steadfastly overcame a succession of obstacles, ruses, and halfway measures culminating in the abolition of the West Indian apprenticeship system in 1838. This legend of coherence drew support from the abolitionists' reflections on their own private lives—on the often trivial and fortuitous circumstances that had led them to a holy cause and that unmistakably revealed a providential plan. The endurance and longevity of such figures as Sharp, Wilberforce, Clarkson, Stephen, Macaulay, Stephen Lushington, and Buxton made it all the easier to think of abolitionism as a single and consistent crusade, which adopted new tactics only in response to the endless and diabolical evasions of their opponents. In 1833 Edward Stanley, the new colonial secretary, exploited this mythology in behalf of the Whig government's emancipation plan, cleverly quoting Fox and especially Burke as a way of emphasizing the Whiggish pedigree of antislavery thought. Yet, in actuality, British abolitionism was always torn by disputes over tactics and strategy. Burdened by despair, defections, and distractions, the "movement" virtually disappeared in the late 1790s, the late 1810s, and the late 1820s. In response to changing circumstances and to their own miscalculations, especially regarding planter self-interest, the abolitionists radically redefined their fundamental premises and objectives.

We can briefly illustrate these points by returning to the career of the Stephen family. Even before 1812 the elder James Stephen promoted the idea of using the ceded colonies as governmental "yardsticks"—to borrow the term Americans applied to the TVA in the 1930s—which would provide examples to the older chartered colonies of model slave codes and closely supervised experiments with free labor. The goal, which won at least temporary support from such political leaders as George Canning and Spencer Perceval, was to demonstrate that humanitarianism was compatible with material progress and that the British colonies did not need a continuing supply of African labor in order to keep pace with their foreign rivals. In practice, however, such social engineering collided with West Indian traditions of self-government and soon became ensnarled in disputes between contending governors, commissioners, courts of policy, and British political factions.[116]

Stephen increasingly invested his hopes in a single panacea—a centralized registry, administered by the British government, which would furnish precise statistics on all slave births, deaths, and sales: any unregistered black would be presumed to be free. Backed by the prestigious members of the African Institution, an organization formed to further the purpose of the 1807 abolition act and to encourage the Christianization and civilization of the "Dark Continent," Stephen advertised registration as the only effective means to prevent British colonists from illicitly importing African slaves. This concern was not unreasonable, especially after Britain restored neighboring colonies to France without requiring an immediate end to the African slave trade. But the argument was also shrewdly designed to bypass the predictable furor over any "unconstitutional" intervention in the colonists' internal affairs. A centrally administered registry of slaves could be justified as nothing more than a supplementary enforcement of a parliamentary act regulating imperial trade. Stephen was confident, however, that his plan would lead to the reasonably rapid and painless emancipation of all British slaves. An accurate registration system would present the public with irrefutable evidence of the low fertility and ghastly mortality necessitated by the existing slave system. The revelation of such facts would finally awaken planters to their own true interests and induce them to enact the ameliorative legislation that should have resulted immediately from the abolition act of 1807. If the colonists remained recalcitrant, the plan would provide the administrative mechanism for direct governmental intervention.[117]

In 1812 the abolitionists agreed to postpone a parliamentary bill for registration; in exchange, the Perceval administration allowed Stephen to draft an order in council instituting registration in Trinidad. In the same year, however, the assassination of Perceval deprived Stephen of further direct influence. Lord Liverpool's long administration (1812–27) tried to avoid any infringements on the internal affairs of the chartered colonies—although all ministers continued to defend the theoretical supremacy of Parliament that had been affirmed before the American Revolution. In 1815 Wilberforce, spurred on by his brother-in-law

Stephen, finally introduced a registration bill in Parliament, thus igniting a furious battle with West Indian interest groups, who now consolidated their power and devised more subtle strategies for exerting political influence. Alarmed by news of a slave insurrection in Barbados, the Liverpool administration persuaded Wilberforce to withdraw his motion and to settle for the government's compromise, which simply encouraged the colonial legislatures to establish their own systems of slave registration.

Totally disillusioned by this impending defeat, Stephen resigned his seat in the House of Commons. His son James continued to work as permanent counsel for the Colonial Office, reviewing colonial slave legislation and devising ingenious schemes to link slave registration with colonial debts and mortgages, which were increasing at a rapid rate. But James Stephen the elder regarded the colonially administered registries as worse than useless and as proof that the West Indians had scored a decisive victory. The son, working within the government, tended to mute his antislavery principles, to avoid contact with antislavery organizations, and to wait patiently for opportunities when he could persuade his superiors to veto colonial laws and press for tangible reforms. During the 1820s and early 1830s, his father and eventually his younger brother George viewed West Indian slavery from a radically different perspective. In 1830 the elder Stephen admonished his fellow abolitionists to accept no compromise and to propose no measure short of "a general, entire, immediate restitution of the freedom wrongfully withheld." Although the elder Stephen denied any change in the abolitionists' objectives and outlook, he and other leaders now contended that piecemeal reforms could only delude the British public and strengthen the slave system. Nothing could be expected from the white colonists until Parliament had imposed its will by a direct act of emancipation.[118]

There is no need here to review the full history of British emancipation, except as it furnishes a case study of rapidly evolving and sometimes contradictory ideas of progress. The question to be kept in mind is how changing political circumstances, combined with changing abolitionist demands and expectations, led to a kind of compartmentalization or double vision. We already touched on this phenomenon in our discussion of *kairos* and *chronos*. The elder James Stephen exemplified one aspect of such double vision when he called on the British public to chant in unison a demand as "simple" as that of Jehovah's messenger to Pharoah, "LET THE PEOPLE GO," and then leave the practical means to Parliament.[119] As we shall see, government leaders as well as abolitionists accepted this conceptual demarcation between the formal act or command of emancipation, with all its religious overtones, and the "practical" regulations to give the command effect. There was a parallel dichotomy between the "voice" of the British public, interpreted as a pure and spontaneous expression of Christian morality, and the political arts of compromise that were needed to balance contending interests and to advance the common good. Even within the Stephen family the younger James sought to ensure the ordered progression of *chronos,* whereas his father and especially his brother George invoked the imagery of holy warriors annihilating a demonic power.

In trying to mediate between these two realms, the abolitionists were sometimes skillful bargainers who knew that rhetoric denouncing "wretched temporising expedients" and "miserable compromises between God and mammon"—phrases used by the elder Stephen—could prepare the way for concessions. Yet the duality was something more than a pragmatic choice of rhetoric to fit different audiences and situations. It was a means of viewing social engineering in Christian millennial terms, of linking redemptive theology with social science. As the most "modern" and yet traditional of Western nations, Britain could represent radical social change as the restoration or preservation of social order. The formula helped to incorporate into British culture a shared sense of public responsibility and righteousness that could not easily be exported to other societies, such as the United States, where a chasm separated immediatist rhetoric from the realities of power. Since everyone involved saw the crisis of 1833 as a test case not only for Britain but for the rest of the world—as a great experiment in *legislated* progress affecting labor productivity, incentives to work, and the religious and moral uplift of a supposedly backward people—it is important to examine the nature and origins of abolitionist illusions.

The first point to bear in mind is that British abolitionists had no realistic chance of obtaining even effective ameliorative measures from the conservative ministries that preceded the enactment of parliamentary reform. Sensitive still to the mistakes that had led to the American Revolution and to simultaneous upheavals at home, government leaders were determined to avoid any disruption in the existing system of imperial rule. They took for granted that any reforms affecting the internal affairs of the colonies depended on the voluntary cooperation of colonial legislatures and absentee proprietors. In both houses of Parliament the West Indian faction was stronger in the 1820s than it had been in 1806 and 1807, when it had been defeated on the issue of the slave trade. Even in the Commons, the colonists' friends decisively outnumbered abolitionists; and as late as 1833, West Indians could count on overwhelming opposition in the House of Lords to any measure unacceptable to the absentee-planter interest.[120] The very fact that the colonies were suffering from acute economic distress, that slave prices were falling, that the white population was declining at an alarming rate, and that resistance was becoming more overt among all classes of nonwhites aroused sympathetic fears in a tense and almost equally embattled English aristocracy. Despite the West Indians' pessimism and cries of doom, from 1815 to 1832 the British abolitionists were repeatedly defeated or outmaneuvered. During most of this period the British government was no more successful in negotiating effective international agreements to suppress the African slave trade. As the elder Stephen warned, the failure of reform on both fronts could only accelerate the economic decline of the British West Indies and divert the flow of British investment to the more profitable slave systems of France, Cuba, Brazil, and the United States.

As we have seen, the abolitionists rejected the belief that Christianization could by itself lead to gradual moral improvement and desirable social change within a slave society. They also rejected the alternative of revolution, except as a prophecy of the colonists' certain fate, as Stephen put it, "if our peaceful endeavours fail."[121] Aside from administrative pressure from the Colonial Office, this left the two alternatives of direct parliamentary intervention and of fiscal policies that, by undercutting the profitability of slavery, would encourage the substitution of free labor. From the 1820s onward, British abolitionists vacillated between these two distinct and at times incompatible views of governmental responsibility.

On the one hand, the new Society for the Mitigation and Gradual Abolition of Slavery throughout the British Dominions was a product of the disillusioning experience with registration. The society's leaders, who constituted the London Anti-Slavery Committee, agreed that only authoritative intervention by Parliament could prepare the way for slave emancipation and hence for the presumed benefits of a free-labor economy. Although abolitionists like Stephen and Macaulay would have been content initially with various "ameliorative" laws, they recognized that direct legislation governing the conditions of labor, punishment, and social welfare would evoke resistance and thus require a willingness to coerce the colonists and subject them to increasingly stringent controls. Stephen was confident, however, that there was no risk of a white rebellion that might necessitate military force. In 1825 he gently rebuffed his co-worker James Cropper for seeking to propagate their enemies' myth of "a dangerous resistance." Even in Jamaica, Stephen pointed out, the whites "are so utterly impotent that the smallest British garrison ever maintained there would suffice to deter them from so insane a project; or the feeblest squadron on that station would starve them into submission by shutting their Ports without shedding a drop of blood." Indeed, the government could call the colonists' bluff simply by threatening to take away British troops, instead of sending more, since then, "to use their own favourite figure, they would feel the knife at their throats if bereft of the protection of that Power which they preposterously affect to menace." In short, the planters were so fearful of their own slaves that they would have no choice but to submit to the will of Britain, unless well-meaning abolitionists like Cropper undermined that will by taking the planters seriously.[122]

On the other hand, the new movement for West Indian emancipation owed much of its impetus to James Cropper, a devout Quaker, a wealthy Liverpool merchant and importer of East Indian sugar, and a fervent disciple of Adam Smith's. The differences between Stephen and Cropper went beyond the issue of governmental intervention and planter resistance. As a Dissenter and a prototype of the self-made entrepreneurs who were transforming the British economy, Cropper had agonized over the moral implications of his own success, especially during the Napoleonic wars, when few commercial transactions could meet Quaker tests of "innocent" trade. But Cropper's doubts over the incompatibility of Christianity and profit were largely resolved by his discovery of *The Wealth of Nations.* The book became for him a second bible, whose laws were to be no more questioned than the Ten Commandments. Though still acutely aware of the corrupting power of wealth, Cropper now saw the hand of God in the flow of goods toward their natural markets, in the unfettered interplay of capital, labor, and resources, and in the contribution of individual self-interest to the irresistible march of human progress. Instead of retiring to a country refuge for a life of quietistic devotion, as he had often dreamed of doing, Cropper began attacking commercial restrictions with the zeal of a missionary. He worked vigorously, for example, in the campaign to repeal the 1807 orders in council, which James Stephen had done so much to promote. This circumstance should not obscure the fact that Stephen and Cropper shared a commitment to civilize and Christianize Africa and to atone for the sins of the African slave trade and colonial slavery; they also shared a providential view of history in which seemingly fortuitous and secular forces were intended by the Creator to be exploited for the purpose of human redemption. But whereas Stephen looked to laws, regulations, magistrates, evidence, and enforcement, Cropper initially hoped that no laws would be necessary to force the West Indians to see their own true interests. As he wrote Macaulay in 1822, "Our cause is great, we only seek to second or to remove impediments out of the way of the free operation of the Laws which the Creator has fixed in the nature of things. . . ."[123]

Although historians have often treated Cropper as a marginal figure, he was instrumental in shifting national attention from the African slave trade to West Indian slavery; in organizing the first British societies specifically dedicated to slave emancipation; in raising funds, mostly from Quaker sources, to finance the activities and publications of the Liverpool and London societies; and in establishing communication with various American antislavery groups. Cropper launched his personal antislavery crusade in 1821, in response to a West Indian move to increase duties on East Indian sugar and open British Caribbean markets to North American commerce. As a leading member of the Liverpool East India Association, he was aware that self-interest made his own motives highly suspect. He was prepared, however, to endure the martyrdom of suspected hypocrisy; in his own heart, he knew that he had "neither wish nor intention ever to add one more shilling" to his property and that personal motives could have no bearing on his facts and arguments, which stood "on the same firm ground as the multiplication table or any other mathematical truth." Cropper's axioms, though supported by a maze of statistics on costs, prices, bounties, drawbacks, and the volume of trade, were simple: free labor and free trade in "legitimate" commodities were the divinely appointed engines of moral progress; the British slave system had always depended on the protection of discriminatory duties on sugar imports and bounties on sugar exports, which constituted an annual subsidy of some £1.2 million paid by British consumers; slave labor was thus a moral and economic anachronism that could be abolished most effectively by free-market forces—specifically, by the competition with free labor that would result from equalizing duties on East and West Indian sugar.[124]

In order to propagate this redeeming message, Cropper at first prodded and then joined forces with the London abolitionists who looked less to the laws of the market than to ameliorative laws prescribed by a paternalistic government. The precise nature of this alliance is difficult to assess. Although Cropper's first objectives were economic, he clearly abhorred slavery and sincerely believed that free trade would lower the price of sugar, increase the world's demand, and force suppliers, in the interest of efficiency and productivity, to turn to the incentives of free labor. On a tactical level, Cropper had discovered that the purely commercial arguments of the East Indian merchants had little chance of persuading Parliament to equalize sugar duties—in 1822 he had headed an East Indian deputation that had futilely presented their case before a parliamentary commission. Yet few of Cropper's East Indian associates wished to involve themselves in the potentially hazardous and radical cause of antislavery. There was thus a tactical aspect to Cropper's appeal for moral support from such well-known philanthropists as William Allen, Wilberforce, Macaulay, and Clarkson. Cropper's larger strategic planning focused on two objectives: to promote a popular movement for West Indian emancipation by gathering and disseminating evidence on the intolerable cruelities of slavery; then to persuade this growing antislavery public that no measures for mitigating the evils of slavery could be effective as long as slaveholders continued to benefit from bounties and preferential duties. Although the London abolitionists resisted the second proposition, and some of them feared that Cropper's commercial self-interest would taint a humanitarian cause, they welcomed his initiative and cooperation in the first objective. They especially welcomed his aid in putting at their disposal a special fund originally raised by the Society of Friends to combat the slave trade, and his offer to advance £500 out of personal funds to finance Clarkson's 6,000-mile tours of 1823–24, which produced hundreds of petitions to Parliament and led to the organization or coordination of hundreds of provincial antislavery societies. Cropper had not only proposed such a tour to Clarkson and to the London Anti-Slavery Committee but had also planned the itinerary and supplied an extensive list of names obtained from correspondence with the Bible Society, the Church Missionary Society, and the Wesleyan Methodists. In accordance with his larger strategic plan, he counted on Clarkson to arouse antislavery sentiment from the nation's wellsprings of moral and religious indignation. Meanwhile, he secured the approval of the London Anti-Slavery Committee to make a follow-up tour, at his own expense, in order to provide the newly formed provincial societies with detailed and practical information. The London abolitionists surely knew that Cropper had obtained, by brilliant maneuvering, a national forum for publicizing his views on free trade and East Indian sugar.[125]

It is important to note, in view of the abolitionist schisms and fragmentation of the 1830s and 1840s, that this period witnessed no overt division over economic or political ideology. We may also note, without pretending to explore the question further, that Cropper was flexible enough to support his colleagues' moves for legislative amelioration and gradual emancipation as concomitants to more-fundamental economic reforms and that his colleagues, faced with insurmountable obstacles and burdened by traditional habits of political deference, were in no position to reject such aid. But while Cropper influenced abolitionist thought regarding the mechanisms of emancipation, he failed, at least in the short run, to make emancipation dependent on an elimination of West Indian commercial privileges. He also failed to convert most of his Liverpool and Lancashire associates, including East India importers, wheat merchants, and rising industrialists, to his antislavery doctrines. By the mid-1840s, however, Cropper's free-trade and antislavery ideology had become an almost official British creed. His connections with the British and American antislavery movements are thus complex enough to warrant more extended examination, even if this necessitates later backtracking to take up other themes.

In 1824, when the London abolitionists became disheartened by the results of their initial parliamentary campaign for slave amelioration, Cropper's ideas won growing endorsement from the Anti-Slavery Committee, which conducted the day-to-day business of the Anti-Slavery Society. Cropper had predicted and hoped for such an outcome. During the next seven or eight years, it became increasingly apparent that only meager results could be expected from parliamentary speeches or negotiations with cabinet ministers. Almost by default, Cropper became the unofficial philosopher and strategist of the antislavery movement. The committee's publications emphasized the economic evils of slavery, the hidden costs paid by British consumers, and the need for mobilizing consumer power in favor of free-labor sugar. Meanwhile, Cropper focused his own efforts and financial resources on mobilizing public opinion.[126]

In a decade of reactionary politics, conservative abolitionists were no doubt alarmed when their opponents charged that Cropper was adopting the methods of the rabble-rousing Major Cartwright and that his pamphlets were being circulated among slaves in the West Indies and the southern United States. Cropper, who still hoped at most for the adoption of a plan that would extinguish West Indian slavery within thirty years, was troubled himself when Elizabeth Coltman Heyrick, a fellow Quaker, published an inflammatory pamphlet that denounced the principle of gradualism, attacked the government for conspiring with slaveholders, and called for a massive consumers' boycott of slave-grown produce in order to achieve immediate, unconditional emancipation.[127] But despite the embarrassment of such unwanted allies, the Anti-Slavery Committee supported an experiment to market East Indian sugar and urged its friends to avoid slave-grown sugar, regardless of origin. Cropper expressed admiration for the moral scruples that led some people, mainly Quakers, to abstain from any produce of the slave system, although he knew as a realistic merchant and investor that he himself was deeply dependent on such produce and that a general boycott would paralyze British commerce and industry and lead to bankruptcies, unemployment, and the starvation of both British workers and black slaves. It is possible that Cropper and other abolitionist leaders recognized that radicals like Heyrick had helped them appear more moderate. By the 1830s, at any rate, the hazards of being tarred with the brush of radicalism were more than outweighed by the advantage of telling the government, in effect, that if the official abolitionist proposals were rejected as being too revolutionary, there were women as well as men who were eager to address the slaves on their right to immediate emancipation. The crucial point, which held profound significance for future conceptions of emancipation and human progress, was that Cropper's innovative measures for appealing to the people—the strategy of commissioning well-informed agents to mobilize public opinion, of converting petition gathering to a science, of pledging political candidates to slave emancipation, and of planning a nationwide campaign to exert "pressure from without"—was attuned to an essentially antigovernment ideology of laissez-faire.[128]

Meanwhile, in 1824, Cropper's antislavery travels led him to the most impoverished districts of Ireland, where he came to the startling recognition that in regard to food, clothing, and housing these "civil, kind-hearted, and generous-minded poor people . . . must be infinitely worse off than many of the slaves." This discovery confirmed his conviction that Irish poverty and West Indian slavery, the two dark shadows that thwarted Britain's progress, were intimately related. Both evils were the result of monopoly and special privilege, which stunted initiative, encouraged single-crop agriculture, and depleted human and natural resources. If Irish leaders could only be made to see this connection, Cropper thought, they could be enlisted in an invincible crusade for economic liberalism that would elevate Irish peasants and West Indian blacks to a life of genuine freedom and well-being. In Cropper's mind, as we have seen, the science of political economy was primarily a search for the ingenious means that God had designed for the advancement of the human race. Ireland's rushing streams, for instance, were clearly meant to be harnessed to textile mills that would provide employment, at the lowest cost, for the crowds of idle, starving men. But where would this second Lancashire find an infinitely expansive market for cheap cotton fabrics? Obviously in India, where free trade would encourage millions of peasants to cultivate unlimited supplies of sugar and eventually of cotton. The desire to purchase Irish textiles would provide East Indians with the competitive incentive that would ultimately destroy West Indian slavery. Cropper was admittedly ill at ease regarding the source of cotton that would put this beneficient chain of events in motion. He had been one of the first British importers of American slave-grown cotton, a point repeatedly exploited by John Gladstone and other West

Indian adversaries. Though clearly troubled by the westward expansion of American slavery, Cropper drew comfort from the thought that no artificial subsidies protected the institution from the competition of free labor. He agreed with the somewhat later verdict of Edward Gibbon Wakefield that the profitability of American slavery was the temporary result of a "superabundance of land in proportion to people," that the system was both more efficient and more humane than West Indian slavery, and that it would disappear as soon as population increased on the American frontier and prices and wages fell accordingly. America's gravitation to such a "normal" condition of land scarcity and low wages—or of what Wakefield called a "combination of power"—would presumably be accelerated by eventual competition with East Indian cotton.[129]

Intoxicated by this vision of providential design and global progress, Cropper promoted Irish antislavery committees, invested in a textile mill in Limerick, and made overtures to Daniel O'Connell, the popular champion of Irish rights. Although O'Connell had various motives for giving public support to the London Anti-Slavery Society, English abolitionists were well aware that his "conversion" seemed to have been triggered by Cropper's Irish tour. Indeed, by the spring of 1825, members of the London committee were publicly eulogizing Cropper, and the committee's official *Report* simply restated his argument that West Indian slavery could not be abolished by parliamentary resolutions or royal orders in council as long as the system continued to benefit from a protected British market. Nevertheless, the committee's conservative members increasingly opposed Cropper's proposals for public meetings and for employing itinerant agents to arouse public feeling—this was a time when the issues of Catholic emancipation, parliamentary reform, and labor unrest divided and frightened British reformers. The Anti-Slavery Committee finally refused to give its sanction to Cropper's extensive tours through the English Midlands, the North Country, and the West. Although Cropper himself had doubts about the wisdom of presenting technical economic arguments to large audiences, he addressed Dissenter congregations of a thousand or more (two thousand, reportedly, in Birmingham). He also spoke to scores of smaller groups of "influential citizens" in such towns as York, Hull, Manchester, Sheffield, Leeds, Bath, Exeter, and Plymouth, encouraging the formation of women's antislavery societies and enlisting the active support of such future abolitionist heroes as Joseph Sturge—like Cropper, a Quaker of rural origin, and a young entrepreneur who had already become a major wheat merchant in Birmingham. Unfortunately, we know far too little about the activities of such daughter-confidantes as Eliza Cropper and Priscilla Buxton, who played a central role in antislavery history. Suffice it to say that Eliza Cropper, who accompanied her father on many of his otherwise lonely tours, married Joseph Sturge, who was soon to become one of England's leading capitalists and a founder of the Agency Anti-Slavery Committee, the Central Negro Emancipation Committee, the British and Foreign Anti-Slavery Society, and the Anti-Corn Law League.[130]

In the late 1820s Cropper had become deeply discouraged by the apparent hopelessness of the emancipation cause, but by 1831 he was joined by a host of young allies, new converts who were apparently unaware of his much earlier proposals to arouse the general public, to exact pledges from parliamentary candidates, and to coordinate efforts with American abolitionists. The rekindling of antislavery zeal, especially among Dissenters in the provinces, evoked increasing criticism of the cautious and deferential tactics of the London abolitionists. Such places as Manchester, Birmingham, and Dublin took the lead in public agitation and political commitment. Although the London committee had earlier accepted the principle of employing itinerant agents, it was not until the spring of 1831, after he had recovered from a long illness, that Cropper enlisted the aid of George Stephen in organizing the special Agency Committee, which at first had the status of a subcommittee of the Anti-Slavery Society. Cropper promised the new group an initial £500, to which Sturge added £250 and Cropper's two sons £100 apiece. After the Agency Committee demanded its independence from the London committee's supervision and control, Cropper served as an effective mediator between the two groups, a role made easier by his own financial power and by his influence in disbursing official Quaker funds. He played a leading part during the last, critical months of the struggle for emancipation, chairing meetings, summoning deputies to London from the provincial societies, writing pamphlets that fused the new doctrine of "immediatism" with his former economic theories, and helping Charles Stuart expose the malicious character of the American Colonization Society.[131]

As early as 1823 Cropper had publicly opposed the idea of sending America's free blacks to Africa. Having close commercial and religious ties with American Quakers, he was well-informed about the issues of race and slavery in the 1820s—he was an agent for Benjamin Lundy's *Genius of Universal Emancipation,* and the London abolitionists acknowledged that correspondence with the United States, as well as with Cheshire, Lancashire, Yorkshire, and Ireland, fell within the jurisdiction of Cropper's Liverpool Anti-Slavery Society. From his American informants Cropper had learned that the Colonization Society, while attracting support from numerous well-meaning foes of slavery, exploited the racial prejudice that was coming to dominate American thought. As he studied the question further, he recognized that it was precisely such prejudice that had prevented the growing population of free blacks from competing with slaves, especially in the West, and thus from proving the economic superiority of free labor. Nothing could strengthen American slavery more effectively than the "diabolical scheme" of the Colonization Society, which proposed to remove the very population that could lower labor costs, bring down the price of cotton, and force slaveholders to confront the wholesome realities of a free market.

This question acquired a sudden urgency in 1831 when the Colonization Society commissioned a Quaker agent, Elliott Cresson, to raise £100,000 from the apparently inexhaustible sources of British philanthropy. Although Cresson won a sympathetic hearing from influential Quakers and from Wilberforce, Buxton, and especially Clarkson, he soon encountered his nemesis in Charles Stuart, one of the founders and original full-time lecturers of the Agency Committee. A former army officer in India, Stuart had been converted to evangelical religion in New York State and had then become an abolitionist lecturer in Ireland, where he had applied the revivalistic techniques of Charles G. Finney to the cause of immediate emancipation. From 1831 to 1833 he conducted a crusade throughout England to discredit Elliott Cresson and demolish the reputation of the American Colonization Society. Stuart was soon aided by Nathaniel Paul, a black Baptist minister and abolitionist from Albany, New York. Cropper helped to ensure the success of this crusade by warning the London committee not to be deceived by Cresson's pretensions and by writing a public letter rebuking Thomas Clarkson for having endorsed a society founded on racial prejudice and dedicated to the perpetuation of slavery. In 1833 Cropper presided over public meetings at which William Lloyd Garrison excoriated the American colonizationists, and in the following year he contributed to a fund that would enable Stuart to return to America as an antislavery agent.[132]

Since communications between Anglo-American abolitionists owed so much to Cropper's various initiatives, his somewhat idiosyncratic aims and assumptions help to illuminate misperceptions on both sides. It was natural that Cropper, the only British abolitionist leader attuned to American events, should have congratulated the obscure group of Garrisonians for organizing in 1831 the New England Anti-Slavery Society, and that two years later Garrison should proceed to "Dingle Bank," Cropper's "delightful retreat," immediately after landing in Liverpool. There, conversing with Cropper's friends and family and reading newspaper accounts of the crucial parliamentary events that had drawn Cropper to London, Garrison was elated to learn that "slavery has received its death-blow," that the day of Jubilee was at hand. To his *Liberator* readers he exclaimed over the incredible news of an emancipation petition "signed by EIGHT HUNDRED THOUSAND ladies!!!" Garrison was outraged, however, to discover that some abolitionists were prepared to accept the "heresy" of monetary compensation to planters—"an unconditional surrender of the whole ground of controversy," an "obliquity of moral vision, or something worse"—when "the slaves only, are entitled to remuneration," and when the planters deserve only "punishment proportionate to their crimes." A month later, after Cropper had introduced him to the abolitionist leaders gathered in London, Garrison assured his New England colleagues that the payment of compensation "excites universal reprobation among the people, and is justly viewed not only as money bestowed where no loss can be proved, but as an abandonment of the high ground of justice." As we shall see, however, knowledgeable abolitionists had realized all along that emancipation without some form of compensation was politically inconceivable. Cropper himself had proposed that since England had "nursed the West Indians into these difficulties and must help them get out of it," immediate emancipation should be linked with an equalization of sugar duties and with a £15 million public loan at an interest rate low enough to enable planters to pay off their oppressive mortgages. As a tactical measure, Cropper and other leaders insisted on postponing any compensation until the planters could prove genuine financial loss or until the abolitionists' demands had been met. For a time, opposition to the unexpectedly large grant of £20 million seemed to be the only promising weapon for pressuring the government to reduce or eliminate the term of apprenticeship. But attacks on the principle of compensation were largely confined to Charles Stuart and other Agency Committee radicals who had little understanding of the patient and skillful bargaining required for any significant social legislation.[133]

As the first intermediary between British and American abolitionists, Cropper helped to focus the Americans' attention on the extraparliamentary activism that he had long encouraged. He thus contributed to the common American illusion that no government could resist the united voice of a righteous and indignant Christian public. Of course, this was what the American reformers wanted to believe, wholly apart from Cropper, and it was to be expected that, after 1833, leaders of the Agency Committee and the more militant provincial societies should turn their eyes to America and to the goal of "universal emancipation"; that American abolitionists should look to such successful itinerants as Charles

Stuart and George Thompson for guidance on how to follow Britain's "noble example"; and that Buxton and Lord Suffield, both veteran leaders of parliamentary abolitionism, should warn that such interference in American affairs was likely to excite resentment and retard progress.[134] The less obvious point is that by 1831 Cropper, George Stephen, and other strategists of popular agitation could demand "immediate emancipation" with the assurance that members of Lord Grey's cabinet were committed at least to gradual emancipation and that James Stephen the younger, together with Henry Taylor, the head of Colonial Office's West India division, would be instrumental in shaping and implementing any legislation.

For Cropper, to be sure, it was essential that any paternalistic regulations be regarded as a temporary expedient to cushion the possibly turbulent transition to a free-market economy. It is crucial to understand that Cropper's seeming radicalism—his opposition to ameliorative laws, apprenticeship, and African colonization; his reliance on public agitation, pledging candidates, and petitioning—rested on his unswerving assumption that the laws of economics would soon replace laws requiring physical coercion and that the West Indies would soon enjoy normative conditions in which the fear of starvation and then the desire for superfluities would induce freedmen to increase their output of agricultural staples. Although most of the anti-institutional radicals were evangelicals who simply denounced the sinfulness of halfway measures, giving little thought to the practical conditions of postemancipation life, this very absence of theory made them congenial agents for philosophies of progress akin to Cropper's. Garrison, for example, was clearly influenced by Lord Howick's "sensible speech" attacking the underlying principles of Stanley's original emancipation plan. What especially struck Garrison was Howick's account of his conversion from gradualism to the view "that there were only two possible courses to be adopted—*we must recognise perfect slavery or perfect freedom.*" But Howick's speech was actually a brilliant presentation of laissez-faire and free-labor ideology, heavily indebted to Edward Gibbon Wakefield and committed to the thesis that Parliament had no right to intervene in the relations between colonial proprietors and employees. Once Parliament had taken the momentous step of abolishing "the right of the planters to the gratuitous services of the labouring population," Howick said, recognizing "that competition was the essence of free labour; that there is no intermediate state between slavery and freedom," Britain could safely entrust regulatory legislation to the planters' own self-interest: "while the great principle of allowing the value of labour to be determined by competition is adhered to, there can be no objection to any laws which they may pass, however severe may be the restrictions they impose." The "competition" Howick had in mind required laws against vagrancy and especially measures to prevent freedmen from lapsing into subsistence agriculture on land of their own.[135]

Initially, at least, neither Parliament nor the British antislavery movement followed this ideological route. Cropper, unlike Buxton and the parliamentary abolitionists, therefore increasingly interpreted antislavery history as a series of disastrous blunders, beginning with misguided efforts to suppress the slave trade and to impose various meliorative laws that culminated with the monstrous system of apprenticeship—blunders that economic knowledge could easily have prevented.[136] Although it can be maintained that Cropper introduced a needed economic and "practical" dimension to the abolitionist argument, he exposed the movement to internal contradictions while failing to recruit allies from his own entrepreneurial class. For all his faith in redeeming the world by commercial and industrial expansion, Cropper equated slave emancipation with a lowering of labor costs and consumer prices, which meant surrendering the fate of West Indian blacks to the "invisible hand" of a world market in which they would supposedly compete successfully with foreign slaves.

Without exaggerating Cropper's later influence, we can say that he defined the issues that would preoccupy and divide British abolitionists in the 1840s; he also represented a mode of antipaternalist thought that would be developed and extended by his son-in-law Joseph Sturge, by Joseph Pease, and by some of the provincial antislavery societies most closely associated with American abolitionism. Here it is sufficient to note that by 1840 Garrison, Wendell Phillips, Henry Stanton, and other Americans had enthusiastically embraced the cause of the British India Society and the conviction, as stated by George Thompson, that "the battle-ground of freedom for the World is on the plains of Hindostan." Pease, the leading spirit of the India Society, quoted Cropper extensively to support his contention that fifty years of antislavery history simply proved that slaveholders were impervious to rational argument and appeals to justice. Had they been forced to compete with East Indian sugar and cotton, he claimed, slavery and the slave trade would have disappeared from the world long ago. These new free-produce champions had to deal with the troubling discovery that British India still contained possibly millions of slaves, and both the India Society and the British and Foreign Anti-Slavery Society launched a vast and partially successful campaign to remove all legal sanction for the diverse forms of Indian servitude. More revealing, however, was Pease's argument that the annual cost of maintaining slaves in Cuba and Brazil was five and one-half times the annual income of free laborers in Bengal. Indeed, he referred approvingly to a friend in Madras who paid only two shillings a day to have his fields cultivated by eight men, sixteen oxen, and eight ploughs. How could any Cuban or Brazilian slaveholder match that? he asked.[137]

The visions of economic progress associated with free labor and free trade confused and divided an antislavery movement primarily dedicated to religious revitalization. At the World Anti-Slavery Convention, held in London in 1840, the delegates endorsed resolutions proclaiming that free labor was cheaper than slave labor and therefore more profitable to employers. They also agreed that the most costly, most wasteful, and least productive form of slave labor was a system dependent on importing bondsmen from abroad. This traditional abolitionist dogma necessitated the somewhat awkward acknowledgment that slavery in the southern United States was a lesser of two evils, a fact supposedly confirmed by the lower market price of American as opposed to Brazilian cotton. But when the committee on free labor proposed expanding sugar production in Demerara in order to undercut the slave systems of Cuba and Brazil, knowledgeable voices warned that these systems, despite their dependence on the illegal slave trade from Africa, were "notoriously profitable speculations" that could market sugar for less than half the price, duty free, of British sugar produced by free labor. In 1841 the London abolitionist leaders would in fact join Tory protectionists in defeating the free-traders' drive to open British markets to the cheaper but "blood-stained" sugar from foreign slave societies. Until 1846, when the Whigs and free-traders finally triumphed, the issue divided and seriously weakened an antislavery movement committed in principle to the ideology Cropper had championed. Thus, while the 1840 World Anti-Slavery Convention was willing to stake the case for emancipation on the anticipated cheapness of free labor in the British West Indies, the delegates revealed significant uncertainties when they deleted clauses proposed by the committee on free labor referring to the rise in the salable value of estates and to the "rapid accumulation of wealth in the instance of individual proprietors."[138]

6. BRITISH EMANCIPATION: A DECEPTIVE MODEL, PART TWO

Before examining some other ambiguities of West Indian emancipation, especially as a model for the rest of the world, we must return to the 1820s and explain why the abolitionists' ideal of amelioration was so suddenly discredited and transformed. In the 1820s the owners of most West Indian estates lived in Britain and included some of the richest and most influential members of the landed and mercantile ruling class. Led by the Society of West India Planters and Merchants, these proprietors and investors could dissociate themselves from local Caribbean politics and prejudices and adjust their tactics to the British political scene. They understood the inflammatory power of British evangelical opinion and were genuinely fearful that a public debate over the abuses of colonial slavery would spark insurrections that could turn Jamaica into another Haiti. Some of the absentee "West Indians" were reformers at heart, eager to soften the brutalities of slavery if this could be done without endangering public order or a reasonable return on their investment. Accordingly, the standing committee of the Society of West India Planters and Merchants resolved early in 1823 to head off antislavery agitation by drafting their own detailed program for slave amelioration. The committee's proposals were hardly distinguishable from those of the abolitionists: concrete provisions for the religious instruction of slaves (if effectively implemented, this reform would strike at the heart of the abolitionists' appeal); prohibition of labor and communal markets on the Sabbath (a measure of extraordinary concern to British evangelicals but an unenforceable infringement on one of the few accepted liberties of black Creole culture); the legal regulation of all corporal punishment, including the protection of slave women from flogging; and legal procedures, modeled on Spanish precedents, allowing slaves a hearing for serious grievances and for claiming the right to manumission.[139]

When Thomas Fowell Buxton proposed resolutions in 1823 intended to free all slave children born after a fixed date and to prepare and qualify all other blacks for freedom, "by slow degrees, and in a course of years," "with as much expedition as may be found consistent with a due regard to the well-being of the parties concerned," George Canning quickly seized the initiative by proposing the government's own resolutions, which the House of Commons adopted without opposition. The elder James Stephen later suggested that the West Indians had virtually dictated Canning's resolutions, and it is clear that Lord Bathurst, the colonial secretary, worked closely with the West Indians and essentially incorporated their ameliorative program in the circular letters sent out to the colonies. While the Canning resolutions vaguely committed the government to emancipation "at the earliest period that shall be compatible with the well-being of the slaves themselves, with the safety of the colonies, and with a fair and equitable consideration of the interests of private property," Canning also insisted that the planters themselves were "the instruments through whom, and by whom, you must act upon the slave population." The government's strategy had two prongs: to appease the abolitionists with administrative measures just strong enough to sustain their hopes, and to give colonial agents the impression that such measures were a political expedient needed to keep the humanitarians at bay.[140] Nevertheless, government officials expected colonial legislatures to enact the reforms recommended by Bathurst and embodied in an 1824 order in council for Trinidad. They were troubled when the lieutenant governor of Jamaica, in an address to the Jamaican Council, was content to rely on planter paternalism—on the assurance that "the spontaneous kindness and humane disposition of their owners . . . a mild and discreet exercise of authority on one part[,] of a cheerful and willing obedience on the other[,] a reciprocity of good feeling will be established almost superseding the necessity of Legislative Control."[141] For the next eight or nine years, the contest between the Colonial Office and slave colonies essentially involved competing versions of paternalism—the "spontaneous" paternalism of planters as opposed to the paternalistic regulations of the "official mind."

The image of planter paternalism received immense support from the British West Indian interest, which financed a propaganda campaign to convince the public that most masters were now humane Christians who loved and understood their "servants"; that remarkable progress had already been made in improving the material and spiritual condition of the blacks, who should be the envy of the English and especially Irish working classes; and that anyone who continued to rail against "inhuman oppressors" and "cruel and unfeeling masters," invoking obsolete laws and shopworn legends of atrocity from the seventeenth and eighteenth centuries, was either a religious fanatic or a neo-Jacobin hoping to ignite an English revolution by lighting a West Indian fuse. This voluminous literature anticipated many of the themes of the somewhat later "proslavery argument" in the American South, and it is clear that South Carolinians, in particular, were attuned to the West Indian crisis and to the need for mounting a preemptive offensive against a possible coalition of Anglo-American abolitionists.[142] One should add that by the 1820s the southern states were already well ahead of the British colonies in adopting legal and procedural protections for slaves, however unenforceable in practice, and in developing a paternalistic ethos that drew strength from the fact that leading planters exercised personal authority over their own plantations and carried decisive weight in local courts and legislative bodies. Moreover, southern apologists knew that they could address a national audience increasingly convinced that blacks were inherently inferior to whites. With few exceptions, their British counterparts translated this belief, which was widespread in the West Indies, into the argument that Africans were a primitive people not yet prepared for freedom, that servitude had always been part of God's plan for ordered progress, the "stepping ladder" by which various races had advanced from barbarism to civilization.

For a time, the Society of West India Planters and Merchants succeeded in preempting the abolitionists' program for progressive amelioration. If the wealthiest West Indian proprietors had exercised a control over local courts and legislatures equivalent to that of resident planters in the southern United States, while also retaining their influential place in British public life, they might have continued to meet the prevailing tests of gradual progress. But the absentee owners were not only separated by vast geographic distance from their agents, employees, and the less successful planters; the two groups were also divided by class, culture, and political circumstance. Although the Society of West India Planters and Merchants purported to speak for "the West Indian interest," it had little power over the turbulent colonial assemblies that increasingly invoked American Revolutionary precedents in defying parliamentary interference. This recalcitrance and siege mentality clearly embarrassed the absentee lobbyists, although as late as 1833 the standing committee could warn discreetly of "those calamities which must result from a dissolution of the ties which connect the colonies with the British Empire." By then, however, "the West Indian interest" was so divided that some proprietors had privately proposed plans for slave emancipation and had exhorted cabinet ministers on the need for asserting parliamentary supremacy. Even the standing committee revealed its true colors when it claimed that the colonists "do not propose to vindicate the system of slavery"—a statement that must have astounded the colonial assemblies—and then proceeded to rely on Lord

Stowell's proposition that "if it be a sin, it is a sin in which the Country has had its full share of guilt, and ought to bear its proportion of the redemption." In other words, the absentee proprietors were prepared to settle for cash and let the colonists deal with the consequences.[143]

The issue that undercut the West Indians' propaganda, discredited the very concept of amelioration, and evoked a massive and irrepressible outcry in Britain was not slavery per se but religious persecution. Christianization, of both masters and slaves, had always been considered the key to amelioration of any kind. And the West Indian colonies had always been notorious for their godlessness—it was not until 1824 that Anglican bishoprics were established even for Jamaica and Barbados, although by that time Moravian, Methodist, and Baptist missionaries had converted thousands of colonial slaves and free blacks. The Moravians generally enjoyed the trust and cooperation of influential planters, and in Antigua, in particular, Methodist missionaries had benefited from planter patronage from the time of the eighteenth-century visits of John Wesley and Thomas Coke. But unlike the American South, which by the 1820s was already becoming a bastion of evangelical Protestantism, the British colonies resisted the idea that either Christianization or amelioration could strengthen and help perpetuate a slave system.[144]

There were a number of reasons for this crucial difference. In the Caribbean the religious reformers were not fellow colonists representing a white majority deferential to planter authority. They were outsiders, the agents of Nonconformist sects that Anglicans had long associated with fanaticism and sedition. To be sure, it was characteristic for the London Missionary Society to instruct the Reverend John Smith that "not a word must escape you in public or private which might render the slaves displeased with their masters or dissatisfied with their station. You are not sent to relieve them from their servile condition, but to afford them the consolations of religion."[145] But the founders of the LMS had included abolitionists eager to Christianize the new colony of Sierra Leone, and there had always been a significant overlap between the supporters of the various missionary and antislavery societies. More fundamental, from the viewpoint of white colonists, was the fact that Methodist and Baptist missionaries worked almost exclusively with slaves and free blacks. The whites, in so far as they professed any faith, were overwhelmingly Anglican. By the time of emancipation, estimates of slave membership in the sectarian churches ranged as high as 47,000, with many more "hearers or inquirers."[146] Although Christianity appealed especially to Creole slaves of relatively elite status, it is clear that the missionaries understood only dimly the process of religious syncretization by which black preachers blended Baptist hymns, vodun, crosses, Shango, and prophetic visions based on the books of Daniel and Revelation. "Baptist missionaries," as Michael Craton points out, "were among the last to recognise the truly revolutionary implications of the faith they taught. Their planter enemies understood it better, instinctively. . . ." For the planters the revolutionary implications became manifest in the Demerara insurrection of 1823, which began near the site of the Reverend John Smith's chapel and was led by Quamina, Smith's chief deacon. So many Baptist converts and deacons were involved in the great Jamaican insurrection of 1831 that it became popularly known as the "Baptist War." But the "revolutionary implications" that Craton has in mind pertain less to the slaves' desperate resort to violence than to their aspirations and new sense of identity and self-respect. As a result of their creolization and Christianization, slave leaders of the 1820s and early 1830s were attuned to the debates in England on their future status and were acutely aware of the planters' sense of crisis.[147] The Jamaican rebels were determined "to seize the initiative and switch from bondage to . . . the status of quasi-peasants—working their own land [that is, provision grounds held by customary right] much of the year, and for the estates for wages when they wished." To the extent that the revolts prepared the way for an eventual abandonment of plantation labor and the creation of "free villages" based on the slaves' "proto-peasant" system of internal markets, they were a success. The sectarian missions exerted a profound influence on this long-term erosion of plantation discipline, a fact that helps to explain the phenomenal appeal of Christianity, both as a source of respectability and as a source of prophetic justice, to West Indian blacks of the postemancipation era.[148]

Until the eve of emancipation, however, the missionaries insisted that their evangelizing efforts could teach slaves only to become more humble and obedient. In 1824 some Wesleyan missionaries in Jamaica drew up and publicized resolutions that sounded precisely like the concessions their American brethren were then making to proslavery ideology. But the Jamaican missionaries were replying to specific accusations that planters made in response to Methodist speeches and publications in England: that they believed slavery to be incompatible with Christianity; that their doctrines were calculated to produce insubordination among the slaves; that they were secretly attempting "to put in operation means to effect the emancipation of the Slaves"; that they were connected and were in correspondence with British abolitionists (still identified as members of the African Institution); that they were secret enemies of the West Indian colonies; and that they were enriching themselves by extorting money from the slaves. Unlike American

Methodists, the Jamaican missionaries depended on local magistrates for licenses to preach. They could look back on years of arrests, harassment, and jailings and feared that unless they conciliated planters, their chapel would be forcibly closed. With the exception of some Kingston merchants, mainly Catholics and Jews, they had few white allies. Some of their fellow missionaries who were more in touch with British Methodist opinion disavowed the proplanter resolutions. In England, Richard Watson and other leaders of the Wesleyan Missionary Society were infuriated by the unauthorized declaration that Methodism could be reconciled with "interminable" bondage. For Watson, an active abolitionist convinced that slavery could not long survive in the British Empire, the crucial question was whether the institution would be terminated by the operation of "principles destructive of order, and loyalty, and civil duty" or by the peaceful and benevolent principles of Christianity. Unlike toil and poverty, slavery in Watson's view was not one of the "*necessary* evils" imposed by the discipline of heaven on sinful men. The need to censure the Jamaican missionaries' concessions led to an official vindication of abolitionism and to the affirmation "that the degradation of men merely on account of their colour, and the holding of human beings in interminable bondage, are wholly inconsistent with Christianity." Southern evangelists were spared from such discipline and from having to reconcile such metropolitan edicts with the concessions to local prejudice needed to protect them from savage persecution.[149]

But British Nonconformists, still militant and embittered by their own struggles for religious freedom, thirsted for the blood of white martyrs. In Demerara, where about two hundred and fifty slaves were killed or executed under martial law following the 1823 insurrection (which had resulted in the deaths of only three whites), "missionary Smith" was court-martialed and sentenced to death for complicity in the revolt. On 9 February 1824 Buxton jubilantly wrote that the abolitionists had "a capital case as to the Demerara insurrection," since Smith was innocent, would refuse to give in, and would not be harmed.[150] But three days earlier Smith had died in a squalid Georgetown jail. As the "Demerara Martyr," he evoked hundreds of petitions to Parliament and provided Brougham with the occasion for sensational speeches attacking the colonial system and inflaming the religious public. Meanwhile, in Barbados mobs attacked a Methodist congregation, sacked a church, and threatened the life of a prominent missionary, whose replacement had to travel under a military escort. The reports of persecution and atrocity reached a climax with the bloodbath that followed the Jamaican insurrection of 1831. Hundreds of black Christians were tortured, flogged, and executed. The colonists jailed, tarred and feathered, and physically threatened English missionaries, whose stories were soon as well known in England as Foxe's *Book of Martyrs.* British Methodists could vividly remember their own militant campaigns against attempts to prohibit field preaching; Dissenters from the nonprivileged classes were familiar with employers' complaints that religious meetings distracted workers from their duties; they knew of Anglican squires who harassed or expelled Nonconformist tenants. It was this experience with a religious establishment that provided a bridge of empathy with the idealized West Indian slave—a "man and a brother" like Henry Williams, who was nearly flogged to death in a Jamaica workhouse for the crime of attending a Methodist chapel.[151] Incensed by such incidents, missionaries began to send their home societies evidence of slaveholder brutality and of complicity on the part of colonial officials. In England, Methodist and Baptist leaders, some of whom were already active in antislavery societies, transmitted this evidence to the Colonial Office as well as to their congregations. From the provinces, from Scotland and Wales, from the dissenting chapels and ladies' antislavery societies, from Methodist electors who demanded pledges from parliamentary candidates, a rising chorus condemned West Indian slavery as an unreformable sin, as "Treason against the whole human Race," as an unholy war against Christianity itself.[152]

This outburst of public protest, which included demands that Parliament be "compelled" to annihilate slavery immediately, astonished the leaders of the London Anti-Slavery Committee, who in 1830 were still considering plans for the emancipation of newborn children. Buxton emphatically denied that either he or the committee knew the authors of newspaper advertisements calling for petitions for immediate emancipation, but he blamed this "great revolution" in the public mind on the "savage defiance" of the West Indians, who had made a mockery of progressive amelioration. Recalling that he and Henry Brougham had attended a crowded public meeting at which they had received "a lesson & a lecture on the tameness & moderation" of their principles, he concluded that "the nation has run before the Anti S. & have come to the settled, & for ought I know the true conclusion that you can only mitigate S[lavery] by striking at Slavery itself. The petitions which crowd your table, are the spontaneous sentiments of the people of Eng & if they go, as you think, too far—thank the col. assemblies—those who will flog females indecently. . . ."[153]

According to the official interpretation affirmed by later parliamentary speeches, state papers, and countless histories, the newly reformed House of Commons soon responded to such "spontaneous sentiments" with a humanitarian act necessarily tempered by political realism. As we have seen, liberals like Tocqueville and Mill hailed this unprecedented example of disinterested public opinion's determining a momentous issue of state. And it is indisputable that by 1832 the strength of British antislavery sentiment dismayed and deeply concerned the members of Lord Grey's Whig cabinet, the West Indians, and even King William IV. It is also clear that neither the hundreds of thousands of abolitionist petitioners nor the MPs who favored emancipation can easily be categorized; certainly they represented no hidden or shadow "interest," such as East Indian sugar or free trade (James Cropper, as we have seen, was singularly unsuccessful in mobilizing such groups even in 1833, when government policies were fluid and when abolitionism opened the way for tactical gains). On the other hand, it is naïve to think that even the reformed Commons was a representative assembly bound in some way to enact whatever the people willed. To understand the ambiguities of the abolitionists' seeming triumph, it will be helpful to consider in some detail three distinct levels of thought and action that gave specific meaning to conceptions of progress and that prepared the way for the final emancipation act.

The first level, which is complicated by day-to-day details that we can only touch on here, concerns the rapid shifts in tactics, strategy, and expectations arising from (1) the efforts of Buxton, Lord Suffield, Brougham, and other parliamentary abolitionists to orchestrate public pressure with the changing keys struck within the Commons and the cabinet; (2) the counterefforts made by West Indian lobbyists and members of government; and (3) the attempts of the Whig cabinet leaders to delay a decision and then to find a compromise more or less acceptable to all parties. From the spring of 1830 to the summer of 1832, when the overriding issue of parliamentary reform was finally resolved, Buxton and Suffield (who led the abolition cause in the House of Lords) could only hope that the bare possibility of an embarrassing independent vote for emancipation in the Commons would induce the government to take more vigorous and effectual steps to fulfill its "pledge" of 1823. Early in 1830 Sir George Murray, the Tory's colonial secretary, had announced that the 1823 resolutions should be taken "as rather an opinion than a pledge," that the government had no intention of interfering with slavery in the chartered colonies, and that West Indians had assured him that public interest in the subject was subsiding. After talking with Murray, the abolitionist leaders had concluded that "if left to the government and the colonial legislatures, West Indian slavery may exist with very little mitigation for ages yet to come." Although the Whigs came to power toward the end of 1830, they were absorbed with other questions and initially content with cautious experiments intended to link slave amelioration with fiscal rewards. For well over a year, Buxton struggled with an impossible task: to exert tactful pressure on the Whig ministers; to mobilize public opinion at opportune moments; and to hold back militant agitation when it might do harm, admonishing antislavery leaders to take his advice "a little upon trust." Yet, early in 1832, after Britain had heard the grisly details of Jamaica's suppression of the slave insurrection, Lord Grey's administration authorized parliamentary committees to conduct formal investigations of West Indian slavery—an idea proposed by the West Indians, at least for the House of Lords, as a tactic for indefinite delay.[154]

The passage of parliamentary reform, whatever its limitations in remedying the inequities and corruptions of the traditional political system, revolutionized the prospects for slave emancipation. It is true that the Jamaican insurrection, the preliminary evidence given to the parliamentary committees, and the colonists' defiance of new orders in council had already convinced several Whig leaders that some kind of decisive action was urgently needed. Then the Reform Bills and the subsequent December election deprived the West Indians of many seats, reducing their representatives to some thirty-five MPs in the Commons as opposed to well over one hundred members pledged to support immediate emancipation. Even in November the government anticipated the danger of an independent abolitionist initiative and privately invited Buxton to put his cards on the table in the form of a specific plan. Buxton eagerly complied and was so flattered by Sir James Graham's deference to abolitionist power and to the "present state of feeling in this country" that he and Macaulay joyfully concluded that "things are ripe for obtaining nearly the full extent of our wishes. . . ."[155]

This confidence that the Whig administration would introduce a bill more or less conforming to abolitionist expectations explains Buxton's continuing admonitions that abolitionists should postpone public meetings and avoid militant agitation that might alarm conservatives, especially in the House of Lords. Of course, the caution and deference of the parliamentary abolitionists aggravated the divisions between the Agency Committee radicals and the dominant faction within the original Anti-Slavery Committee that ran the Anti-Slavery Society. As months went by, especially after the king omitted any reference to slavery in his speech opening the 1833 session of Parliament, Buxton maintained his rather tenuous leadership only by formally announcing his intent to introduce independent resolutions and, somewhat later, by agreeing to postpone such action only if the government publicly fixed a date for submitting its own plan to Parliament. But Lord Althorp and other government leaders knew they could put off the abolitionists, at least for a time, with private assurances of a "safe and satisfactory" measure. The cabinet's critical problem was to find a formula that could win maximal concessions from the West Indians, who had the active sympathy of the king as well as of powerful Whigs and Tories and without whose cooperation Lord Grey, the prime minister, was unwilling to act. In December 1832 the cabinet considered several specific plans, and in January a special cabinet committee recommended that the colonists be given a maximum of seven years in which to enact and prepare for the total abolition of slavery. But the pro-abolitionist ministers were apparently unprepared for the furious protests of the West Indians, who accused the government of betraying solemn commitments, such as Lord Goderich's earlier assurance that no measures would be proposed until the parliamentary committees had examined sufficient evidence to complete their assigned tasks. Although the cabinet's backtracking in February and March can partly be attributed to the accumulating objections to the leading emancipation plan—that of Viscount Howick, Lord Grey's son and the parliamentary undersecretary—at the crucial meetings no votes were taken, dissidents like Goderich did not feel free to express their individual views, and everyone but Howick apparently acceded to the necessity of an intermediate state of apprenticeship and to Lord Grey's view that no measure for slave emancipation could be proposed without first obtaining the West Indians' consent.[156] In short, on March 19, when Buxton finally succeeded in committing the government to a fixed date for unveiling an emancipation plan, the government had no plan. Yet the abolitionists, having been singularly unimaginative in drafting their own plans (in contrast, for example, to Henry Taylor and Lord Howick), relied in effect on the elder James Stephen's strategy of eliciting proposals from the government, which could then be remedied by unrelenting moral pressure.

But no one could foresee the events beginning in late March that shaped the foundations of the final emancipation act. Buxton and other parliamentary abolitionists were unaware of the substance of cabinet proceedings but were alarmed by rumors of Howick's impending resignation and of Goderich's replacement as colonial secretary by Stanley, a move that would necessitate further delay. In response, Buxton encouraged and gave his blessings to the militant public crusade for immediate emancipation, disregarding the duke of Wellington's threat that the House of Lords could defeat any precipitous move for the expropriation of private property. Meanwhile, Stanley had boldly confronted and overcome the first formidable obstacle—the West Indians' refusal to discuss formally any plan explicitly designed to abolish slavery in substance as well as name. While this breakthrough of 8 April required the pretense of a nonbinding, purely confidential discussion, and listening for three hours to the West Indians' demands for full monetary compensation, Stanley reported to Lord Grey at the end of a long day that he had easily persuaded Buxton, who had arrived minutes after the West Indians had left, to postpone any parliamentary initiative until 14 May. This background helps to explain Buxton's crushing despair on 7 May, when he returned home from a private interview with Stanley. Until then, his daughter Priscilla reported, "we had gone on hoping every thing from the Govt. plan. . . . I think I shall never forget his countenance on his return! We were at the moment in a great press—& Gentlemen here waiting to see him . . . & I only at home. However I did the best I could for him & very soon we left them all & went out on horseback. He soon told me all, 'As bad' he said 'as bad as can be' & indeed it appeared, its injustice only equalled by its folly. . . . He was strictly bound to secresy [*sic*] & told no one but me. . . . Mamma I think said 'Well others have had great disappointments &c.' He said 'I don't think anybody ever had such a one as I have.' " Buxton did not know that Stanley's plan had reduced Jamaica's agents to an even profounder state of despair. They were no less surprised by what they interpreted as a gross breach of faith and a "monstrous" subversion of constitutional rights.[157]

The double vision we have already discussed was never more apparent than in the events of 14 May, when Stanley fulfilled his promise to present the outlines of the government's revised plan to a House of Commons that had become something of a warehouse for hundreds of abolitionist petitions, including a monstrous roll that had been sewn and pasted together by a team including Buxton's daughter. Although Priscilla Buxton encouraged her father's threats to "declare war" and take a seat in opposition to the government, he was besieged by conflicting abolitionist pressure and advice—Macaulay approving the government's basic approach and urging Buxton to support it, George Stephen and the radicals suggesting that O'Connell should take the helm as the abolitionists' leader.

In his opening speech Stanley confirmed his reputation as a brilliant orator, paying tribute to Wilberforce and to the "sincere religious feelings" of the antislavery public, documenting the failure of the colonists to adopt ameliorative measures that could prepare the way for "the ultimate extermination of the system," and justifying Parliament's constitutional right, under such circumstances, to intervene. Priscilla Buxton, who attended the session, described Stanley's speech as "wonderfully good": "For the first two hours as excellent Antislavery doctrines as one would wish to hear. He spoke beautifully, his ease[,] clearness, & perfect self possession were astonishing as well as his acquaintance with the subject." She even enjoyed the colonial secretary's "clever attack upon my father," when Stanley affirmed that he could not be content with Buxton's earlier view that it would be sufficient to free all children born after a future date. After Lord Howick had delivered a devastating attack on the substance of Stanley's proposals, Buxton mildly objected to any provision that would require apprentices to subsidize a monetary loan to the planters. But to his more skeptical daughter he privately exclaimed, "Emancipation is effected, the thing is done." Despite his earlier despair over the details of Stanley's plan, Buxton revealed his double vision even before departing for the Commons debate on 14 May, when he delivered a private prayer thanking the Lord for His mercies, "that thou hast turned the hearts of those who have influence & power, & make them to be labourers in the cause of the oppressed. . . ." In other words, the government's remarkable willingness to endorse the *principles* of emancipation and moral progress took precedence over administrative details that could be adjusted during the parliamentary stages necessary for any legislation. Priscilla Buxton reported that after the speeches of 14 May, Stanley told Buxton, " 'Now don't go & lay the steam on again' 'Just a little' my father replied 'I must'. . . ."[158]

While Viscount Howick was a relative youth, not yet thirty-one, he had won distinction as a champion of Catholic emancipation, parliamentary reform, and utilitarian plans for colonial settlement and expansion. Having previously shown his lack of deference for "those who have influence and power" (as the third Earl Grey, he would later serve six stormy years as colonial secretary), he had finally resigned from his father's administration over the issue of slave emancipation, to which he had devoted some two years of intense study. In 1833 no abolitionist came close to rivaling Howick's grasp of the basic flaws of his party's program. Buxton and the more seasoned leaders of the Anti-Slavery Committee continued to assume that once the major objective of 14 May had been achieved—once the government had repudiated the hope of amelioration and had committed itself to an act of emancipation—there would be ample opportunity at later committee stages to strike out objectionable provisions and to eliminate or at least reduce the period of apprenticeship. But as Howick insisted in his prescient speech of 14 May, "no minor alterations" could possibly remedy a design that would inevitably lead to "the most fatal results."

Howick asked his audience to imagine the effect on the mind of the slave "when he is told that he is free, but finds that, for so long a period, his freedom is to make no difference whatever in his condition—that he is to go on labouring as before, without receiving any remuneration for his toil, beyond his accustomed and scanty supply of necessaries?" "Sir, twelve years is a long time in the life of any man. . . ." Under Stanley's plan, Howick pointed out, the so-called apprentices would still be subject to the "driving system" and would probably receive more lashes, even if perfunctorily authorized by magistrates, than under the existing system of slavery. Howick based this generally accurate prediction on the example of Demerara, where the crown's paternalistic regulations had in effect justified wholesale floggings as the only incentive for field labor. For twelve years, Howick argued, apprentices would have no other motive for the seven and one-half hours of daily labor supposedly owed to their former owners—labor worth fifteen times the value of the meager supplies provided by their masters (Howick rightly emphasized that most West Indian blacks were expected to produce their own food, in their "free time," and that the elderly, the infirm, and the small children were mostly dependent on the charity of the slave community). Moreover, unless the abolition act abrogated every constitutional right and privilege of colonial society, it would mostly be administered by judges and other officials recruited from the planter class and appointed by colonial assemblies. For a period of twelve years, Howick observed, the planters' main objective would be to extract the maximum amount of labor from apprentices without regard for capital losses occasioned by mortality. Howick focused his most withering sarcasm on Stanley's suggestion that "the negro will be encouraged to continue his industry and exertions, if out of his wages for the fourth of his labour [two and one-half hours in a ten-hour day], some deduction should be made . . ." for repaying the proposed £15 million loan to planters. Since the entire measure was based "upon an admission that slavery, (that is, the forced labour of one man for the benefit of another), involves a violation of justice and of natural equity," nothing could be more absurd and dangerous than to demand that apprentices should commit a portion of the small time at their own disposal to pay "a debt which they will feel they do not justly owe."[159]

Despite the struggles and revisions of the next three months, George Stephen was essentially right when he told Daniel O'Connell that if Stanley succeeded in committing the Commons to his broad resolutions, "no dextrity in committee will mend his odious scheme."[160] The West Indians actually won most of the major concessions and revisions: the conversion of the £15 million loan into a direct grant of £20 million compensation, an act of generosity to be contrasted with the parsimonious allowance of £300 per person a year for an absurdly small corps of 130 special magistrates, a salary so low as to attract mainly military officers already on half-pay and to ensure their dependence on planter hospitality; the provision that colonial legislatures would define the specific duties of the special magistrates as well as the details regarding the apprentices' labor, discipline, maintenance, and contractual obligations (James Stephen drafted the emancipation bill in such haste that he failed to specify minimal standards for the provisions and supplies owed to apprentices); finally, the House of Lords' specific empowerment of colonial authorities to compensate for "willful absence" by requiring additional work from delinquent apprentices for a period as long as seven years after the termination of apprenticeship. The abolitionists won two significant victories: the reduction of the term of apprenticeship to seven years for agricultural workers and five years for nonagricultural workers (to gain this concession from the West Indians, Stanley had to threaten to resign from office and thus jeopardize the agreement on compensation) and the abandonment by Stanley of the idea of requiring apprentices to make a direct monetary contribution to the fund for compensation. But since this proposal was what Buxton and others interpreted as making the Negro "pay for his own emancipation," its rejection obscured the fact that the apprentices' uncompensated labor was also a form of compensation and that apprentices were therefore required to subsidize a large share of the cost of their own emancipation.[161]

With this overview in mind, we can move on to a second level of analysis, which involves the extraordinary discrepancy between radical rhetoric, often based on realistic assessments of what was happening, and the abolitionists' ultimate conclusion that the emancipation act signaled a new Jubilee, an era when the "moral power" of disinterested public opinion would regenerate secular politics. The passage of parliamentary reform encouraged the latter vision, which the Agency Anti-Slavery Society exuberantly propagated during the last months of 1832. Yet in January 1833 George Stephen confided to the evangelical Lord Suffield that most of their colleagues were "chicken hearted politicians" who blindly and naïvely trusted the Whig ministry: "I would not undertake with such allies to release a slave within a century." Stephen's private thoughts are worth quoting at some length, since they poignantly summarize the view that the events of 1833 amounted to a disastrous failure, a view shared at least by Cropper and Sturge.

The great danger, Stephen warned Suffield, was that abolitionists would allow the government to take the initiative and then gratefully accept a plan requiring the slaves to subsidize their own emancipation as apprentices during a period when their masters would have no interest other than extracting the maximum amount of labor:

> I do not believe that the Whigs will grant to us immediate Emancipation, but I do believe that they will give Emancipation to a distant day perhaps five or seven years hence and thus quiet the country: the practical

effect of this will be to work the slaves to death before abolition occurs—& this, in spite of all measures however strong auxiliary to their protection.

In January, Stephen inferred that the ministry was still undecided "or decided against us" (this was when the cabinet was still considering Howick's plan for "immediate" emancipation at a fixed date) and that there was thus an urgent need to attack any apprenticeship scheme *"in anticipation"*:

> Moderation in this case becomes a crime. It will be too late to try out when the intentions of Government are declared. Then it will become a mere party-bone of contention. Resistance then will no longer be the resistance *of the country* but merely *of the opposition.*

Stephen was no more sanguine about the effects of Buxton's planned public meetings, which would be content with eloquence and self-congratulation:

> The whole [antislavery] world should have concentrated itself in a focus—and all the rank and talent and political influence that our party can boast should have been brought together to aid in placing slavery on its funereal pile . . . they should have imitated the Duke at Waterloo when he collected all his allies—all his veterans—all his power . . . formed them into line and shouted the grand victorious "Charge" which crowned his brows with eternal triumph and secured to Europe the peace she still enjoys! Such would have been our final struggle. The noble opportunity is lost. . . .[162]

The fascinating thing about this martial imagery, the post-Napoleonic obsession with finding a "moral equivalent to war"—to borrow the immortal phrase invented by William James a generation after America's own haunting trauma—is that it precisely anticipated the rhetoric applied to the actual event of West Indian emancipation, except, of course, for the point about the loss of a noble opportunity.

The developments of the spring and summer of 1833 only deepened George Stephen's gloom. Long angered by the caution and deference of Macaulay and Buxton, he expressed his disgust in late June to the enfeebled Wilberforce, whom he privately served as an attorney: "We might have gained all, & we have been 'let down' into being little better than nothing." To Joseph Sturge he confessed, "I am sick at heart with all the political apostasy which I see. What have *Anti-Slavery* men to do with politics? . . . but it is vain to look back & as to looking forward, all is dark & vexatious." Here we have the "anti-institutional" rhetoric that historians have identified with American abolitionists. Yet in July, even after Stanley informed George Stephen and a large delegation of abolitionist MPs that he could not "abate an hour of apprenticeship," even O'Connell and other immediatists refrained from the risk of defeating the bill and unseating the Whigs, whom Stephen termed a group of "rogues." Emancipation, however imperfect, was preferable to the indefinite continuation of slavery, especially after Buxton, Howick, and other parliamentarians had forced Stanley to reduce the term of apprenticeship.

In his later *Anti-Slavery Recollections,* published in the form of letters to Harriet Beecher Stowe, Stephen celebrated the revolutionary initiative of the "young England Abolitionists" who had organized the Agency Committee and broken free from the aristocratic prejudices of the entrenched old guard. Yet the message Stephen conveyed in 1854 was that the strategy of Buxton and Lushington had been "quite right" and that the cause had been blessed in having both ardent "young blood," capable of mobilizing a highly disciplined public voice, and "older heads to conduct the Parliamentary part of the conflict from which the youngsters were excluded." In retrospect, the events of 1833 seemed to have led to a heroic triumph: "though there was still work to be done in abolishing the apprenticeship . . . the great colonial controversy was now at an end, and our country had at length washed out the foulest blot that ever stained her escutcheon." Ironically, the substance of Stephen's recollections resembled Stanley's own professions that the time had come when an enlightened government could not disregard the people's "solemn conviction that things wrong in principle cannot be good in practice."[163]

In other words, the government essentially disarmed its opponents by endorsing and absorbing two ideologies—the abolitionist ideology, which called for a wholly new dispensation attuned to moral principles revealed by the collective voice of the Christian public, and the proprietor ideology, which insisted on gradual change, minimal interference with local self-government, and compensation for pecuniary losses. This unstable mixture inevitably led to continuing controversy, notably the abolitionists' final major crusade, in the mid-1830s, against the barbarities of apprenticeship. But as we saw in our earlier discussion of West Indian emancipation and conceptions of moral progress, the need for this renewed agitation in no way diminished the heroic image of 1833, any more than the latter achievement had reduced the stature of Wilberforce and the other victors of 1807. Publicly, at least, there was a broad consensus that the abolitionists' triumphs were all the moral equivalents of Waterloo as well as demonstrations of the irrepressible will of the British people. The persistence of the slave trade or of West Indian atrocities simply proved one of the abolitionists' central contentions: that men "indurated by the system," as the elder James Stephen put it, would find cunning ways to evade the law.

It certainly cannot be said that British abolitionists were content with the mere external forms of emancipation. The younger James Stephen quickly saw that Jamaica's laws intended to implement the emancipation act were actually designed to convert apprenticeship into a kind of slavery, and he futilely implored Stanley to veto the legislation. By 1835 Buxton had compiled a volume of evidence comprising a "Black Case" against apprenticeship, documenting instances of murder, torture, overwork, and the infliction of more corporal punishment than in the days of slavery. Having received private assurances that the government hoped the anti-apprenticeship campaign would succeed, Buxton nevertheless cautioned the radicals who by 1837 had rallied around Joseph Sturge that a crusade against the abstract *principle* of apprenticeship would divert attention from the far more crucial question regarding "the ultimate condition of the negro population after its expiration."[164] Since apprenticeship was certain to end in less than three years (the West Indians abolished it under considerable pressure from London in 1838), Buxton tried to alert the radicals to the importance of police regulations designed to curtail the freedom and movement of black workers but enacted under the pretext of preserving the public peace. In fact, by 1840 the British and Foreign Anti-Slavery Society was vigorously protesting West Indian police and vagrancy acts that allowed a single magistrate to sentence workers who had committed no crime to two months of labor in chain gangs. The abolitionists were no less alarmed by various devices that would become familiar in the post–Civil War South: coercive contracts, the arbitrary ejection of workers from houses and grounds, a "truck system" that defrauded workers of wages by charging them 30 to 40 percent above market prices for the essential commodities they consumed.

The London abolitionists, who were increasingly reduced to a small core of professional lobbyists, continued to attack the government-sanctioned system of contract labor that enabled the planters of Mauritius and then of Trinidad, Jamaica, and British Guiana to import tens of thousands of East Indian "coolies" under conditions reminiscent of the African slave trade. The parallels were even more disturbing when shiploads of West African "immigrants" began arriving in the West Indies—in 1843, for example, virtually no females were listed among 1,056 African "labourers" unloaded in Jamaica, a large proportion of whom were boys under the age of fourteen. Meanwhile, the abolitionists were horrified to discover that British factories were openly manufacturing manacles and iron collars for the illegal slave trade; that British capitalists were supplying a large share of the credit as well as the firearms, liquor, and cheap cotton fabrics on which the slave trade depended; and that British investors were heavily involved in mining companies in Brazil and Cuba that employed slaveholding officers still on half-pay from the British army and navy. Above all, there was the inescapable fact that the cotton textile industry, the central engine of the British industrial economy, depended on the slave states of America for some 70 percent of its raw material. Wherever the abolitionists turned, the strands of Britain's expanding trade led to new networks of complicity. But in the 1840s the government was hardly more responsive than the company directors and shareholders with whom the abolitionists proposed to remonstrate "in a spirit of kindness and firmness."[165]

The remarkable point is that such sobering knowledge did nothing to tarnish Britain's self-image as the benevolent champion of universal emancipation or to diminish the faith shared by most abolitionists that Britain's expanding economic power, whatever the short-term consequences, would inevitably promote freedom and Christian civilization throughout the world. Although abolitionists had earlier emphasized personal guilt over their complicity in the British slave trade and in West Indian slavery, this sense of direct involvement waned with the nationalistic pride evoked by the emancipation act and the efforts of the British navy to suppress the slave trade of foreign states that continued to violate the obligations of treaties as well as the standards of civilized life. Hence in 1837 Buxton could announce that the slave trade was "going on worse than ever"—a conclusion that induced him to promote a disastrous imperial plan to civilize the Upper Niger River—and yet affirm that Englishmen could take comfort from the knowledge that they were no longer "sharers in the guilt." At the same time he could rejoice that "the grand experiment" of West Indian emancipation "has been and will be crowned with more complete success than the most sanguine of us anticipated." He balanced his "Black Case" against apprenticeship with a volume of evidence labeled "White Case," which documented the blacks' loyalty and peacefulness, the "alacrity" of their labor, their responsiveness to wage incentives, their declining rate of crime, and their responsible care of children who were no longer the property of their masters.[166]

Such contradictory images of postemancipation society were partly the reflections of contradictory empirical evidence. The geographic and socioeconomic diversity of the British Caribbean almost guaranteed evidence to support or challenge any generalization. In Jamaica, Trinidad, and Guiana, for example, the end of apprenticeship led to acute labor shortages as freedmen "deserted" the sugar estates for more attractive alternatives; in Antigua, Barbados, and Saint Kitts, where alternatives were as scarce as vacant land, planters had no difficulty recruiting an adequate labor force. But the important questions pertain to the uses made of such evidence. From 1833 through the 1840s, abolitionist expectations were strongly influenced by the need to present West Indian emancipation as a successful model for France, the United States, Cuba, and even British India. Late in 1843, for example, when the British and Foreign Anti-Slavery Society was vigorously attacking oppressive laws and labor conditions in the West Indies, the society could write a circular letter to India requesting specific information on the changes actually produced by the recent act abolishing slavery in British India, and then shamelessly claim that in the West Indies a "mass of glaring evils" had immediately been abolished "and a new state of things, of a most delightful kind, promptly appeared."[167] In short, the double vision of emancipation and progress could serve various ideological needs. The negative image of West Indian recalcitrance and of new forms of oppression could never detract from the sublime victory of 1833 or weaken confidence in the British government's irreversible commitment to liberty and moral progress.

In this respect West Indian emancipation greatly reinforced the symbolic purpose of parliamentary reform by demonstrating the disinterestedness with which the British aristocracy could wield power and respond to legitimate public opinion. In 1830 James Stephen the elder had warned that if the West Indians continued to deny antislavery a fair hearing in Parliament and to use money and intimidation to exlude antislavery arguments from the most influential newspapers, the "soundest part of the community" would become disillusioned with the British frame of government: "good men, and those who fear God among us," would then become reconciled to "hazardous innovations; for who can doubt that a purer and less aristocratical constitution of parliament, would long since have given victory to those sacred principles supported by the popular voice, which are now trampled down by the weight of colonial wealth and influence." As a conservative alarmed by the revolutionary rumblings of 1830, Stephen feared that times were at hand when the higher and wealthier classes would be in ever more need of "that best human safe-guard of social order, the moral and religious feelings of the people."[168] Because the Whig leaders were acutely sensitive to this very point, they avoided the portentous storms and calamities that Stephen foresaw. After 1833 the abolitionists could presume a continuing partnership with the nation's leaders—in marked contrast to the adversary relations between American abolitionists and the American government. Yet the Britons' long experience with law-defying governments such as the West Indian legislatures and the maritime nations that violated slave-trade treaties prepared them to believe that the United States was ruled by a ruthless Slave Power devoid of moral principle.

The faith in a common purpose between British abolitionists and British rulers brings us to a third and final level of analysis, which involves certain shared conceptions of order and moral progress, especially the connection, as Stephen put it, between "social order" and "the moral and religious feelings of the people." Any modern reader of the documents of British emancipation is struck by the extraordinary conjunction of two seemingly antithetical realms of language, thought, and rhetoric: the evangelical appeals to sin, guilt, retribution, and deliverance, which we have already examined from a number of perspectives; and a highly utilitarian analysis of punishment, nutrition, land use, labor incentives, productivity, and revenue, accompanied by the premise that such a rational calculus would enable the government to maximize the benefits at minimal cost to slaves, planters, merchants, taxpayers, and consumers. For reasons that were incomprehensible or at least misunderstood on the Continent, where abolitionism continued to be seen as a heritage of the secular Enlightenment, the emancipation issue enabled Britons to combine religious motives and expectations with an early form of applied social science. Although we have discussed certain aspects of this unique synthesis, such as the mixed perceptions of *kairos* and *chronos,* the final key may lie in emerging understandings of social order as embodied in specific proposals and blueprints for emancipation.

The starting point for such shared assumptions was the growing conviction that disorder and a defiance of law had led the British slave colonies to the brink of revolution and self-destruction. Early in 1832 Lord Howick informed the king that the Whig ministry had recognized the necessity for some kind of decisive change from the time it came into office. Knowing the king's fear that any attempt to emancipate the slaves would destroy the empire, Howick emphasized the planters' willful misrepresentation of the government's most cautious reforms and their threats to resist the king's authority by force. Echoing the arguments of James Stephen the younger (and of Goderich, the colonial secretary), Howick concluded that it was only natural for Jamaican slaves to interpret planter rebelliousness as proof that the king meant to free them, and that they had therefore risen in arms against their defiant masters. The government, faced with the prospect of further insurrections and of Parliament's "being hurried into some violent and precipitous course," was thus compelled to advance a moderate but unprecedented plan for social change.[169] Although government leaders were more fearful than abolitionists of making disastrous mistakes, they shared a commitment to the great dream of the era—revolutionary change without revolution, a controlled acceleration of the evolutionary stages that had supposedly converted British serfs and peasants into wage laborers.[170]

Buxton and other evangelical abolitionists sincerely believed that the moral and spiritual welfare of the Negroes was their only concern. "Immediate and total emancipation is our right," Buxton wrote Macaulay in 1832, and any concessions should be made for the sake of the Negro, not of the government, the economy, or the planter. Unlike their American counterparts, however, the British abolitionists were in a position to make concessions and to influence public policy. Indeed, it was the "moral and religious feelings of the people" they claimed to represent—the new sensibility that condemned public displays of cruelty, torture, coarseness, drunkenness, and physical disorder—that gave sanction to governmental experiments in social engineering.[171] Great Britain was the first nation in which a government responded to such modern sensibilities with modern and scientific formulas for social control. The merger of altruism and utilitarianism, in the test case of slave emancipation, meant that conceptions of the Negro's welfare could not be abstracted from the most immediate political and ideological concerns.

The Jamaican insurrection, for example, accentuated the possibility of black initiative and self-determination. The slaves ought to be freed instantly, Buxton agreed with a radical critic, "for I know *our* power of emancipating in one way or another is fast drawing to a close. I mean they will take the work into their own hands." There can be no doubt that this "Haitian argument" carried considerable weight. But the same precedent suggested that the danger of this "worst case" would subside if the government acted swiftly and unequivocally, putting an end to uncertainty and false hopes on all sides. In the important position paper "Immediate v. Gradual Emancipation," sent to the prime minister and the chancellor in March 1833, Howick acknowledged that danger would be "exceedingly great" during the time between the government's announcement of a date for emancipation and its actual accomplishment. But there were even worse risks, he predicted, in prolonging the present state of agitation and uncertainty. Even if the whites decided to resist a parliamentary act of emancipation, the blacks would simply laugh and walk off the plantations, knowing that their masters' discipline was worthless unless backed up by British military force. James Stephen the younger also minimized the danger that blacks would resort to violence in their opposition to the administrative controls of the postemancipation era. Slave insurrections, he pointed out, had always been "exceptions to a long protracted course of submission and orderly demeanour." By diminishing the need for coercive force, the abolition of slavery would also "weaken the motives for turbulent resistance." In a revealing mixture of inconsistencies, Stephen stressed the almost unequalled docility of black slaves; suggested that this otherwise barbarous and tyrannical system had prepared emancipated slaves, "in common with other free men," to "imbibe the sentiment of deference for an authority which though occasionally unequal in its exercise, is established for the common good of the whole Society, and is habitually exercised with no other view"; and then called for a military, naval, and constabulary force "at once so irresistible and so palpable as to repress whatever disposition to revolt may be manifested."[172]

White resistance or rebellion was a second concern that evoked revealing contradictions concerning order. From the late 1820s to 1833, relations between the Colonial Office and West Indian legislatures became increasingly adversary. Prodded by the younger James Stephen and Henry Taylor, colonial secretaries vetoed slave codes, ordered governors to investigate cases of religious persecution, and dismissed planter officials as well as Governor Belmore of Jamaica. It was the statistical and legal evidence amassed principally by Stephen—on religious persecution, on the causes of the Jamaican insurrection, on the correlation between the decrease in British Guiana's slave population and the severity and frequency of corporal punishment—that convinced government leaders of the impossibility of amelioration. It was such evidence of planter violence and lawlessness that led abolitionists to demand sufficient magistrates and police to keep both whites and blacks "in complete submission."[173]

When dismissing white West Indian threats of secession and civil war, abolitionist leaders sometimes invoked the presumed national loyalty of the colonies' large and critical population of "free coloureds," and the plan the abolitionists submitted to the government late in 1832 called for paid magistrates armed with a force of police including not only free blacks and mulattoes but also "the most intelligent and religious of the present slaves." In 1832 Stephen took it for granted that under free institutions the will of the black majority would eventually and inevitably prevail within West Indian legislatures. But despite their repeated affirmations that the Negroes' "moral, intellectual, and physical nature is substantially identical with our own," neither the abolitionists nor their friends in government gave serious consideration to substituting black for white authority. The avoidance of revolution necessitated at least a temporary acceptance of de facto racial distinctions, which amounted to an acceptance of white supremacy. Although the abolitionists' plan demanded equality under law "in most respects," it also recommended the treadmill as an appropriate punishment for black vagrancy or idleness. In 1834 Jamaica's governor Sligo could thus claim abolitionist sanction for promoting treadmills and "houses of correction," even though they were beyond the control of Britain's stipendiary magistrates. In January 1833 Stephen even applauded the Jamaican legislature's moves to create a system of police to prevent encroachments on land and to ensure "the punctual payment of Rent and the regular collection of the Land tax." Order and stability, in other words, took precedence over the planters' supposed incapacity for self-government. While patiently striving to create an independent and truly professional judiciary, Stephen knew that the success of all such reforms depended on "the zealous co-operation of the Colonial Legislature."[174] Despite the appearance of irreconcilable conflicts over slavery, Stephen and other government officials were confident that the colonists would begin to cooperate as soon as they recognized that emancipation was inevitable and that everyone had a common interest in ensuring order and maintaining productivity.

The third and major fear was that events would confirm the planters' worst predictions and warnings. For government leaders this nightmare was largely economic—a sharp drop in labor productivity, profits, and land values, accompanied by an accelerated exodus of whites and withdrawal of capital from the West Indies. One should add that there was a division of opinion on the significance of any decline in sugar exports; Stephen and Stanley, for example, maintained that the supply of British sugar had far outrun the European demand and that some decline in total production would increase the planters' profits within the protected British market, an argument hardly acceptable to free-traders or British consumers.[175] But for abolitionists, including Stephen, the worst dangers were moral. "If allowed to do as he liked," Stephen wrote, the freedman "would probably be distracted between the appetites, for basking in the Sun—for pork & Rum—for red waistcoats and the cast-off finery of the green room & the servants hall . . . with the occasional addition of a dance or a prayer meeting. . . ." Stephen was actually arguing against the more common prediction that in such circumstances the freedman would retreat to the forest or mountain hut, regress to subsistence agriculture, and having "no incentive to better his condition or to impose any but the slightest discipline on himself . . . might well become a more degraded being than his ancestors in Africa."[176]

Despite differences in motive and economic theory, there was virtually no dissent on the need to constrain freedmen within a civilizing environment of wholesome discipline, an environment equivalent to that which enlightened masters should have provided had they not shut their minds to amelioration and their own best interest. The assumptions underlying the abolitionists' own plans and testimony before the House of Lords committee were essentially identical with those Stephen embodied in a circular dispatch intended for colonial governors in January 1833, when the prevailing plan would have spurred colonial legislatures to enact their own emancipation measures within two or seven years. Everyone acknowledged the need for a vast educational program aimed at Christianizing and civilizing the freedmen, whose aspirations and habits of life should eventually sustain such a demand for the products of human industry "as can be gratified only by persevering and self-denying labour." Everyone also admitted that such education takes time and that meanwhile, as Stephen put it,

> measures must be adopted, tending more directly to counteract the disposition to sloth which may be expected to manifest itself, so soon as the coercive force of the Owners' Authority shall have been withdrawn. The manumitted Slaves must be stimulated to Industry by positive Laws which shall enhance the difficulty of obtaining a mere subsistence.[177]

Abolitionists recognized the apparent inconsistency of forcing freedmen to work for wages while also granting them the right to buy, rent, and cultivate land for their own subsistence. But, as Stephen pointed out, analogies with English wage labor overlooked a fundamental distinction:

> In England, manual Labour is redundant and Cheap. In the West Indies it is deficient and dear. Here men must either live by severe toil, or be supported as paupers: there, all dependence on the public may be avoided, and all the Necessaries of life obtained, by exertions comparatively light. . . . Can the same Rules with any reason be applied to regulate Labour in two cases, in the one of which it is accepted as a Boon, and eagerly solicited, and in the other rejected as a Burthen, or reluctantly undertaken?

Moreover, the habits of slavery had reinforced the effects of a tropical climate. Although abolitionists had repeatedly condemned the "grinding toil" on the sugar estates, it now appeared that the work performed by slaves

> is neither steadily nor assiduously done, but is executed in a manner so listless and reluctant, that the Exertions of the Slave in a given time Scarcely equal in intensity, one half the effort made by a free man working voluntarily in any similar task.

The various proposals for increasing labor productivity were seemingly less concerned with sugar output than with "creating habits of diligence, and converting to Individual gain and public advantage a leisure which might otherwise be devoted to unprofitable sloth or injurious dissipation." The debate over plans for West Indian reconstruction focused on the moral effects of labor and remuneration, especially on the minds of the slave elite who were best fitted, as Lord Howick observed, "to lead their fellows in an attempt to obtain their freedom by force."[178]

Howick, for example, strenuously objected to Henry Taylor's scheme for progressive emancipation and to a similar provision in Stanley's official plan. Taylor hoped to instill self-discipline while greatly reducing the public expense of emancipation: the government would compensate planters for two days of slave labor each week; from the wages earned on those days, slaves could then purchase a third and eventually more days, learning the rewards of labor as they bought by installment life's most precious commodity. For Howick such thinking evidenced a disastrous misunderstanding of human nature and the moral basis of freedom. It was absurd to make a work week half slave and half free. During the days of slavery only the cartwhip could prevent a worker from being as lazy as possible and conserving strength for his "own" days. But even on those days he would be deprived of the fruits of his labor in order to pay a debt that no one claimed he owed. The public goal of emancipation acknowledged the injustice of uncompensated labor and would hence sanction the Negro's accumulating grievances as he continued to work, under necessarily increased coercion, only for the benefit of others.[179]

The cabinet gave more serious consideration to Howick's own plan, which elicited numerous private commentaries and strongly influenced the thought of the younger James Stephen. From the early summer of 1832 to March 1833, Howick in effect presented a screen on which to project various scenarios regarding the effects of emancipation on social order. To this extent he defined the terms of the debate. The impracticability of his specific proposals for a land tax should not obscure the importance of his arguments or the significance to the emerging "official mind" of his main concerns. Howick's initial point was that the abolitionists' constricted focus on the moral and physical condition of the blacks had distracted attention from the fundamental issue of defining the conditions under which vacant land would be acquired, occupied, and cultivated. Although this question aroused the interest of various social theorists from Hume to Frederick Jackson Turner, Howick was most indebted to the explosive theories of Edward Gibbon Wakefield, who had launched a devastating attack against British penal and colonization policies after his own recent release from prison. Like Wakefield, Howick chose Australia, where "felons from this country supply the place of negroes from the coast of Africa," to prove that race and chattel slavery were incidental variants in the larger picture of colonization and labor control. The Australian example showed that as long as immigrant workers had access to free or cheap land, the cost of labor would remain unnaturally high, population would disperse, and attempts to coerce labor would lead to sullen resistance and low productivity. Until the West Indies were more densely settled with workers competing for subsistence, Howick argued, there was only one way to ensure the "combination of productive power" on which progress and civilization depended: making the use of land so expensive for freedmen that they would have no choice but to sell their labor in a competitive market.[180]

These assumptions would have far-reaching effects on future British policy, especially during Stephen's long term as permanent undersecretary of the Colonial Office (1836–47) and during Howick's (by then, the third Earl Grey) own critical term as colonial secretary (1846–52). Although Stephen sustained his family's concern for racial equity and distrust of planter legislators and justices of the peace, his close ties with Howick in 1832–33 reveal an agreement on the quite different principles by which the effects of emancipation would be shaped and judged.

In 1832, for example, Stephen feared that Howick's specific proposals for preventing subsistence farming and remitting the land tax to white proprietors depended on "too refined a view of human affairs to be made acceptable, or even intelligible, to those whose welfare it is intended to promote." Since an understanding of the plan required a scientific process of reasoning, Stephen felt it necessary "to mask the design," and Howick conceded that there was no need "to state publickly the theory of the proposed method of inducing the Slaves to continue after their emancipation to labour for hire." Stephen agreed with the fundamental point that families dispersed and "living entirely by the culture of the soil, will rather recede than advance in civilization and wealth." A comparison of Robinson Crusoe with the Manchester weaver confirmed Wakefield's point that a combination of labor must precede the division of labor and hence the creation and accumulation of wealth. Stephen predicted, however, that the black freedman's craving for town life and community would make him more amenable to civilization than "the North American Indian, the Arab, the Tartar, the aboriginal New Hollander, or the Backwoodsman of the United States" (though he added that the latter was really "a man of energy and enterprise, or of excited imagination, who consoles himself under the privations of to-day, by the dream of affluence tomorrow"). But the West Indian problem was complicated by the slaves' customary claims to provision grounds from which they derived subsistence and sufficient surplus to support their communal markets, and by the fact that colonies like Jamaica contained enough land to feed their inhabitants "even should they increase in geometrical progression for the next four or five generations." The answer to the problem, Stephen maintained, could be derived from the principle that "the Proprietors of the Soil in every Country are the arbiters of the condition of all the other Members of society. . . . They who hold the keys of the Granary may (so long as they can keep their hold) make what terms they please with the rest of the world."[181]

While cautioning Howick against any measure that might induce freedmen to emigrate to Cuba, Santo Domingo, or South America, Stephen accepted the principle that public policy should simulate the effects of a natural disaster:

> If all the soil which for the present, may be regarded as superfluous, were rendered barren or inaccessible until an increasing population should require encreased [*sic*] supplies, the alternative of industry or starving would be presented to the whole Body of the people, and there is no doubt what would be their choice. But that which we may not hope from nature, we may do for ourselves; and a discriminating land-tax may as effectually forbid the culture of the particular Districts affected by it, as though they were annually visited by the locust. The Owners of the privileged soils would thus have a virtual monopoly of food, and of all other necessaries & comforts of life. . . . The manumitted Slave must therefore not only cease to indulge himself in a life of idleness, but must betake himself to that description of labour in which the land-holder of the privileged class, may be pleased to find him employment. The dread of starving is thus substituted for the dread of being flogged. A liberal motive takes the place of a servile one. The "Emancipist" undergoes a transition from the brutal to the rational predicament; and the Planter incurs no other loss than that of finding his whips, stocks and manacles deprived of their use & value.[182]

In this remarkable statement Stephen felt no need to "mask" his endorsement of the "refined" principle whereby the dread of starving becomes a "liberal motive" and a "rational predicament." That these views were not a temporary aberration can be seen from his memoranda and dispatches recommending the legal enforcement of contracts for labor exceeding the statutory requirement, and measures "to discourage the occupation of land by those whose single object it was to consume the produce they might raise for their own subsistence." It is true that these economic objectives clashed with Stephen's abiding fear that the West Indian planters, unless constantly checked by independent magistrates and the Colonial Office, would reestablish slavery in substance if not name. When Stephen acquired extraordinary powers during Lord Glenelg's tenure as colonial secretary (1835–39), he virtually dictated the standards for colonial legislation regarding vagrancy, marriage, police, militia, and labor contracts—standards considered so lenient in protecting the individual liberties of freedmen that his interventionism contributed to the constitutional crisis of 1839, which resulted in Glenelg's resignation, a victory for the Jamaican assembly, and a new British policy of colonial conciliation. When judged by the emerging standards of the 1840s, Stephen seemed excessively moralistic and doctrinaire, a symbol of Clapham Sect self-righteousness in his insistence on the sovereignty of African states; in his scruples against labor contracts made in Asia or Africa for an unseen New World employer; in his criticisms of indentured immigration; and in his advocacy of suffrage and other political rights for qualified freedmen.[183] But what made these controversies so explosive was Stephen's conviction, shared and supported by the antislavery lobby, that former slaveholders could not be trusted; and the colonists' opposing conviction that anyone committed to the destruction of slavery could only be an enemy to the colonies' best interests. Given the furor over defining the narrow line between acceptable and unacceptable forms of coercion, and over who would do the defining, it is easy to overlook the points on which virtually all white authorities agreed.

Stephen epitomized this emerging Western consensus when he defined moral progress as a "transition from the brutal to the rational predicament," a transition that would nullify the value of whips, stocks, and manacles while enhancing the value of land and other capital. The debate over the precise nature and mixture of wages, labor contracts, rents, taxes, and restrictions governing plantation provision grounds and crown land presupposed a common goal of maximizing incentives for plantation labor. With few exceptions, even the abolitionists and missionaries who supported the freedmen's claims to provision grounds or "free villages" agreed that the success of emancipation in the eyes of the world would ultimately depend on the ability of free labor to produce cheaper sugar than that produced by the slaves of Cuba, Brazil, the United States, and other competitive nations. Stephen frankly acknowledged, in the words of William A. Green, "that a collapse of the free West Indian sugar economy might prolong the bondage of slaves elsewhere in the Americas."[184] Moreover, as previous quotations have indicated, even abolitionists valued wage labor on plantations as a moral and educational force that would prevent Negroes from regressing to the imagined barbarous life of their African ancestors. In short, the criteria for judging the freedmen's moral progress were closely linked with the success or failure of the plantation regime.

By the early 1840s, however, it was clear that the local and imperial efforts to maintain an adequate labor force had failed, at least in the critical colonies of Jamaica, Trinidad, Guiana, Saint Vincent, Tobago, Grenada, and Montserrat. Ironically, the market forces that Howick so highly esteemed encouraged the freedmen's acquisition of small freeholds as an alternative to wage labor on plantations. In Guiana, for example, where cotton planters had succumbed to a long and losing competition with low-cost American cotton, there were numerous abandoned estates available for subdivision and sale at low price. The growing abandonment of coffee and sugar plantations in Jamaica, Trinidad, and elsewhere subverted the government's attempts to restrict the acquisition or occupation of crown lands, which were often occupied in any event by defiant squatters. Even as apprentices, many freedmen had accumulated sufficient savings to buy land, individually or sometimes collectively. But as Douglas Hall and others have emphasized, most ex-slaves were strongly attached to their familial houses, gardens, and grounds and would probably have preferred remaining on the estates if rents had not been linked with wages and with coercive labor requirements. Because freedmen refused to accept the prescribed system of rents and obligatory labor, the plantation labor force soon declined by more than 50 percent in several colonies, and officials complained that former slaves were independent enough to work "but very few hours and perhaps not more than three days in the week." After considering a mass of verbal and documentary evidence in 1842, a parliamentary select committee first praised the gratifying moral benefits of emancipation exemplified by, among other things, the Negro's "improved morals" and "increasing desire for religious and general instruction," and then proceeded to confirm the worst fears that Howick and Stephen had expressed a decade earlier: the overabundance and cheapness of fertile land had allowed freedmen to demand high wages and "to live in comfort and to acquire wealth without, for the most part, labouring on the estates of the planters for more than three or four days in a week. . . ." The result had been a disastrous rise in labor costs, decline in sugar and other staple exports, and depreciation in land values. The only solution, the committee concluded, was to promote the immigration of "a fresh labouring population, to such an extent as to create competition for employment."[185]

The earlier forms of double vision now became fixed in two official and contradictory dogmas: the "moral" success of emancipation, and an interpretation of economic failure that not only cast doubt on moral success but also justified an oppressive system of indentured immigration, long-term labor contracts, discriminatory taxes, and falling wage rates. For the elder James Stephen, the Special Providences of God had guaranteed that moral progress and national interest would coincide. The weakening of such faith is suggested by Henry Reeve's claim that in 1853 Stephen's son privately expressed regret over emancipation, contending that "slavery alone perpetuates the black race out of Africa."[186] The most significant point, however, was Britain's unwillingness to extend the capitalist ethic to the freedmen's remarkable enterprise and economic achievements of the postapprenticeship years.

Wherever possible, blacks rejected the kind of regimented plantation labor, especially for women, that abolitionists had always described as inhumanly degrading. In Guiana, communities of freedmen purchased large estates and collectively managed the drainage, irrigation, and upkeep needed for sugar cultivation. In Saint Lucia former slaves profitably cultivated their own coffee and sugar, inventing ingenious contrivances for crushing the cane. In general, however, freedmen gradually moved out of the sugar and export sector of the economy, stimulating and taking advantage of a spectacular growth of internal markets. It is impressive to note that by 1851 well over one-half of Guiana's former slaves were living and working on their own land. Even in Barbados, where vacant or abandoned land was very scarce, the number of freeholds increased in three years from 26 to an estimated 1,630. Besides feeding themselves, these small farmers made profits from selling livestock, poultry, ginger, arrowroot, coconuts, honey, and a variety of provisions. In addition, thousands of freedmen acquired skilled trades or retail shops in towns, or huckstered goods in local markets. Such achievements, however, not only were contrary to British expectations but were made in spite of local and imperial governmental policies that had succeeded by the 1840s in lowering wages, retarding the growth of the internal economy, limiting freedmen's opportunities, and ending British public support for Negro education—even if they were unable to protect the sugar economy from the devastating effects of free trade and European subsidies to beet sugar.[187]

One might easily conclude that British emancipation was deceptive because the planters' predictions proved to be far more accurate than those of the abolitionists. This was a fact of considerable importance to slaveholders in other societies for whom statistics on exports, profits, land values, and mortgage foreclosures counterbalanced tons of humanitarian rhetoric. One might also point to the continuing discrepancy between the realities of postemanicpation society and the millennial images and expectations of the British religious public. But British emancipation was deceptive in a profounder sense because it was, as the saying goes, too good to be true. The decision to free 780,000 colonial slaves and to compensate their owners was not the result of some Machiavellian design to disguise an ulterior goal. It was the response of a conservative government, representing a defensive aristocracy, to the competing claims that reformers and planters voiced against a backdrop of economic crisis and potential revolution. What distinguished the abolitionist reformers was not their blindness to closer and more visible evils but their determination to plead the grievances of a distant people with whom they shared no familial, ethnic, racial, or economic interests. This abstracted concern for human rights ran counter to the normal assumptions and procedures of law and has hardly been a prominent theme in human history. Nevertheless, by 1838, conservative and practical-minded statesmen had met virtually all the initial demands of even the more radical antislavery crusaders. Here it is worth noting that Charles Stuart's most famous and inflammatory tract of 1832 had assured planters that immediate emancipation meant lower labor costs and higher profits: "We are not going to take from you your laborers, or any lawful power over your laborers; we are only going to deprive you of the power of insulting, and polluting, and plundering, and abusing them, with impunity." If the consequences of emancipation diverged from the scenario projected by Stuart, Stephen, and other well-wishers, there was no revolution or mass slaughter. Order prevailed. Freedmen were denied political, economic, and social equality, but they succeeded in expanding their own peasant economy and perpetuating their own syncretic Afro-Caribbean culture. Planters suffered from a shortage of dependent and tractable labor, and in some colonies the sugar economy never recovered from the effects of emancipation, free trade, and bounty-supported beet-sugar production in western Europe. But especially in British Guiana, thanks to massive immigration, long indentures, and stringent labor controls, sugar production soared in the 1850s, and by the 1860s and 1870s exports had far surpassed those of the pre-emancipation era.[188] The Anglo-American abolitionists who continued to praise the success of Britain's noble experiment and to cite encouraging statistics on the value of West Indian exports, imports, and land could well ask what other moral crusades had produced such tangible evidence of human progress.

It was Britain's success in avoiding revolution, usually envisioned as a replay of the horrors of Saint Domingue, that challenged the assumptions of slaveholders throughout the New World. This was the fact that initially impressed the French Ministry of the Navy and Colonies, the conservative leaders of the American Colonization Society, and numerous other observers who had no sympathy with abolition movements. The results of Britain's experiment were closely scrutinized for decades to come, and provoked an international debate that we cannot begin to analyze here. Until further research on this subject appears, it is sufficient to summarize some of the illusions bequeathed by British emancipation.

We have frequently noted a kind of double vision or conceptual dualism arising from the unique British mixture of redemptive religion and utilitarian science. Only an act of faith connected the "voice" of the religious public with public policy, or the edict proclaiming "liberty to the captives" with the regulations giving emancipation effect. But it was precisely this act of faith that supposedly removed Britain's burden of guilt and redeemed Christianity in the eyes of a skeptical and exploited pagan world. After a century of embattled and often reactionary defense, Christianity had at last proved that it could be far more "progressive" than the revolutions spawned by the infidel Enlightenment, even when measured by the Enlightenment's standards of secular freedom and happiness. In 1833 abolitionists expressed faith that God, in Buxton's words, had "turned the hearts of those who have influence & power, & [made] them to be labourers in the cause of the oppressed"; that West Indian planters would become more enlightened and charitable as they learned to benefit from free labor; and that the ex-slaves, as Charles Stuart affirmed, would forget their past grievances and perform their new duties with enduring gratitude and love.

While such faith enabled the abolitionists to exert effective influence, it also obscured the costs of their alliance with the state. The payment of monetary compensation, the assurance that planters would define the practical details of apprenticeship, the continuing primacy given to sugar production and the maintenance of the plantation system—these were not incidental flaws that might have been avoided by more consistent moral pressure; they were essential parts of a great political compromise. Despite the appearance of a "Jubilee," a dramatic break with the past, British abolitionists soon reverted to the pattern of the earlier era of slave amelioration, pressuring the government to overcome planter resistance and to fulfill its moral commitment. But this continuing crusade coincided with the growing popularity of laissez-faire ideology, a deepening concern over the decline of West Indian exports, and increasing public indifference to the fate of a population that had been liberated and could presumably look out for itself. In actuality, Buxton's men of influence and power had accumulated sufficient moral capital to resist new abolitionist demands that threatened to further undermine labor discipline and productivity. Planters gained a degree of sympathy by posing as injured martyrs to starry-eyed philanthropy, martyrs who now deserved every concession. The blacks' reaction to apprenticeship was probably summed up by Lord Seaford when he reported that when a group of slaves heard the details of emancipation, they professed to be indifferent, "saying it is not 'the sort of free' they expected."[189]

These circumstances, coupled with Britain's mission to set an example for the world, produced sharply bifurcated images: the picture of public opinion as an irresistible moral force, overcoming oppression and prejudice in a dramatic moment of national regeneration; and a growing body of empirical evidence that not only troubled abolitionists but often contradicted their claims as well. In France, to take the imperial power most closely attuned to the British experiment, attention focused almost exclusively on the utilitarian or cost-benefit aspects of freeing colonial slaves. This was partly because the French slave colonies could not avoid being affected by events in neighboring British territories, but also because French society was hardly receptive to the kind of Protestant evangelicalism that dominated British antislavery thought. Since we shall discuss French emancipation in a later chapter, it is sufficient here to note that the Ministry of the Navy and Colonies ordered detailed and comprehensive studies of the effects of British emancipation. Although these voluminous reports were biased in favor of planter interests, they embodied standards and modes of analysis that had been accepted by men like Cropper, Stephen, and Howick. Captain Layrle, writing in 1841, even commented on the freedmen's appreciable "progrès en moralisation," referring especially to the strengthening of family ties. Yet Layrle agreed with more hostile observers that British emancipation had been a tragic failure. The act had been irresponsibly hasty because apprenticeship had not prepared blacks to enjoy the benefits of liberty; it had also been unjust because it had sacrificed the interests of planters and their creditors without providing a smooth transition to free labor. It seems highly probable that these assessments influenced the French government's decision to postpone emancipation and to avoid Britain's mistakes. When emancipation came, in 1848, it was by the decree of a revolutionary regime.[190]

In the United States, as we have already suggested, abolitionists tended to ignore the economic arguments and theorizing of British antislavery leaders as well as the political negotiations that prepared the way for West Indian emancipation. Aside from stock complaints against the principles of compensation and apprenticeship, abolitionists publicized two momentous messages: America's monarchic "parent," the feared and fascinating embodiment of aristocratic privilege, had shamed her rebellious offspring by preempting the cause of human liberty; reassuringly, though, this was not a counterrevolution but rather the result of sustained and uncompromising public agitation, a model of responsible popular sovereignty that in effect fulfilled the American dream. This interpretation led to a number of conclusions that were no less illusory than the French government's image of economic ruin and reversion to African barbarism. For American reformers who focused on the transfiguring change in British public morality, it seemed self-evident that the United States, a land unfettered by aristocratic traditions and an established church, was capable of an even more dramatic moral regeneration. In a nation committed to popular sovereignty, nothing was needed beyond an appeal to the people—an appeal to moral principle that would eventually awaken the consciences of slaveholders and government officials.

It is misleading, of course, to contrast the responses of American abolitionists with those of French officials. The American government, unlike most abolitionists, knew that the southern states could not be compared with remote and politically weak colonies. And since slaveholders tended to dominate the executive branch of the American government, there was no interest in official investigations of British emancipation with an eye toward eventual emulation. It is true that prominent national leaders, mostly members of the American Colonization Society, initially praised Britain's decision and watched the results with care. For northern and border-state conservatives who feared that slavery and racial conflict threatened the ultimate survival of the Republic, West Indian emancipation presented an interesting experiment in controlled progress, even if inapplicable, in terms of the racial constituency of populations, to the United States. By the early 1840s, however, such political and religious leaders had reached conclusions similar to those of the French government: Britain had acted too hastily; black emancipation, though inevitable in the long run, required more time.

Reinforcing this conclusion was the significantly uncelebrated history of slave emancipation in the northern states. While Northerners took increasing pride in their own "free soil," even abolitionists curiously ignored the early political struggles that had cleansed the North of Negro slavery. Unlike the West Indies, the northern states had presumably been predestined for freedom by the virtue of their inhabitants or by geographic law. There had been no need for a Clarkson, a Sharp, a Wilberforce, or a Buxton. One implication of this prevalent assumption was that the South, like the West Indies, could be conceived essentially as a colony, a morally infected appendage that could be assimilated only after a heroic act of purgation; a second, more hidden implication, supposedly confirmed by the consequences of northern and West Indian emancipations, was that freed blacks, being incapable of the responsibilities of a truly free society, should remain in or migrate to such "colonial" regions.

The connections between emancipation and racist thought deserve more intensive study. It is clear that the freeing of slaves in the northern states, coupled with increasing working-class immigration from northwestern Europe, magnified prejudices that acutely embarrassed white abolitionists. It is also evident that the "failure" of West Indian emancipation, as judged by the British abolitionists' own standards and expectations, reinforced racist theories that were beginning to emerge from independent social and intellectual sources. Once freed, the West Indian blacks did not kneel in gratitude with eyes uplifted to their liberators, as prescribed by the famous abolitionist icon "Am I Not a Man and a Brother?" They fashioned, as best they could, a life of their own. The abolitionists, for all their rhetoric about the debilitating effects of bondage, could not conceal their disappointment or hide their fear that blacks were somehow predisposed to the cardinal sin of idleness. The need to explain such "backwardness" may not have diminished the British zeal for universal emancipation, but it encouraged a tolerance of new forms of coercion for unprogressive peoples.

But after the European revolutions of 1848, even the most reactionary regimes were eager to avoid the stigma of sanctioning chattel slavery. It was difficult enough to prove to the world that traditional forms of peasant service or new forms of factory labor were wholly distinct from the kind of plantation slavery dramatized by Anglo-American literature, and dramatized to an unprecedented international audience by Harriet Beecher Stowe. For a new era dominated by mass media and mobilized public opinion, the shortcomings of British emancipation were less important than Britain's lessons regarding the moral and ideological foundations of power. The decline of Jamaica, as the rulers of Europe and even czarist Russia surely observed, did not eclipse British influence in the rest of the world. After 1834 no European nation sought to extend chattel slavery to new colonial territories or even to defend its indefinite existence, as a "positive good," in existing colonies. European rulers may have taken a cynical view of British motives, but they knew that the British formula worked—that "emancipation," in one form or other, was the key to stable power.

PART THREE

Abolishing Slavery and Civilizing the World

"[Brazil], the last Christian Power that maintained the abominable institution of Slavery was freed from the blot that had so long defaced its escutcheon, and the year 1888, the Jubilee of the first Emancipation, saw the death of Slavery in its last stronghold in Christendom. To Mussulman and heathen countries, the crime of trading in human chattels and holding property in Slaves is now relegated. When will the Anti-Slavery chronicler be able to record the extinction of this abomination throughout the world?"

Anti-Slavery Reporter, Jan.–Feb. 1889, 11

1. THE WAR AGAINST BARBARISM: PART ONE

In 1835, when Thomas Babington Macaulay was building a personal fortune in India as legal member of the governor-general's council, he celebrated England's historical progress in an essay on the great Whig reformer Sir James Mackintosh. During the past seven centuries, he wrote, a

> wretched and degraded race have become the greatest and most highly civilised people that ever the world saw, have spread their dominion over every quarter of the globe, have scattered the seeds of mighty empires and republics over vast continents . . . have created a maritime power which would annihilate in a quarter of an hour the navies of Tyre, Athens, Carthage, Venice, and Genoa together, have carried the science of healing, the means of locomotion and correspondence, every mechanical art, every manufacture, every thing that promotes the convenience of life, to a perfection which our ancestors would have thought magical, have produced a literature which may boast of works not inferior to the noblest which Greece has bequeathed to us, have discovered the laws which regulate the motions of the heavenly bodies, have speculated with exquisite subtilty on the operations of the human mind, have been the acknowledged leaders of the human race in the career of political improvement.[1]

Although Macaulay was the son of a famous abolitionist and had made his public debut by attacking West Indian slavery in a speech at London's Freemason's Hall and in his first essay for the *Edinburgh Review,* he moved beyond such filial duties after participating as a young MP in the climactic debates on West Indian emancipation. As a leading ideologue of social and material improvement—of what later generations would call "modernization"—he illustrates the crucial point that the nation that called on the world for the universal emancipation of slaves was also the nineteenth century's archetype of progress and civilization. The first "world conventions" of antislavery delegates assembled in London, not in France, the northern United States, or the Hispanic American republics, all of which had preceded England in adopting emancipation measures. In the post-Napoleonic world the only nation seriously interested in suppressing the slave trade in every ocean, gulf, and bay was the nation that "ruled" the seas. For good or ill, the antislavery cause became closely identified with the first nation to achieve a sustained growth of per capita output, a truly industrialized economy, a rapidly urbanized population, and a prosperous middle class, which could enjoy the mechanical and cultural amenities that Macaulay so greatly esteemed. While such writers as Macaulay, Mill, and Charles Kingsley equated "progress" with the habits of thought and enterprise that had developed in England—and according to Kingsley, God had approved the Baconian method of science and improvement as the best instrument for "the glorious work which God seems to have laid on the English race, to replenish the earth and subdue it"[2]—even Anglophobes could not disregard the astronomical lead Britain had achieved by the 1830s in global wealth and power. Much as geographers and navigators measured longitude from the "prime" meridian of the Royal Observatory at Greenwich, so rival states and modernizing parties took envious note of British technology, metallurgy, iron and coal production, railway mileage, ship tonnage, steam power, and overseas investment and trade.

To be sure, the response to such material progress, both within Britain and without, was saturated with ambivalence. Americans, who tended to equate social and moral progress with technological improvements, agricultural yields per acre, the horsepower of steam engines, the value of exports, and the populousness of cities, were perplexed to see such incredible advances in a monarchy still committed to hereditary privilege, an established church, and hierarchical rule. They were also determined to avoid the class conflict and industrial degradation that British writers themselves publicized to the world. A host of sanguine prophets, mainly Whigs and Republicans, were confident that industrial technology could be harmoniously assimilated to a society of family farms, small towns, and independent craftsmen. Republican institutions, aided by the availability of western land, guaranteed that factories would bring prosperity and economic opportunity for all.

Edward Everett, the scholarly governor of Massachusetts and future American minister to Great Britain, was especially encouraged by the promise of labor-saving technology. Britain's steam engines, he noted in 1837, performed the work of one million men:

> What a population! so curiously organized that they need neither luxuries nor comforts; that they have neither vices nor sorrows; subject to an

> absolute control, without despotism; laboring night and day for their owners, without the crimes and woes of slavery; a frugal population that wastes nothing and consumes nothing unproductively; an orderly population, to which mobs and riots are unknown; among which the peace is kept without police, courts, prisons, or bayonets; and annually lavishing the product of one million pairs of hands, to increase the comforts of the fifteen or twenty millions of the human population.[3]

If the United States presented European critics with the first specimen of democratic government and majority rule, Britain dramatized the world's first experience with industrialization and thus gave rise to various forms of radical social theory as well as antimodern pessimism, aestheticism, medievalism, and nostalgia. Much as earlier travelers had groped for words adequate to describe the natural wonder of Niagara Falls, so writers like Carlyle, Dickens, Disraeli, Tocqueville, and Engels strove to find locutions to capture the unprecedented contradictions of Manchester. As Tocqueville put it:

> From this foul drain the greatest stream of human industry flows out to fertilize the whole world. From this filthy sewer pure gold flows. Here humanity attains its most complete development and its most brutish; here civilization works its miracles, and civilized man is turned back almost into a savage.[4]

But the descriptions of industrial barbarism, alienation, and dehumanization hardly deterred such nations as Belgium, Holland, France, Prussia, and the United States from scrambling to become next in line. "Anglicization" was once synonymous with the profound social transformations that accompanied industrialization; the term gradually changed to "Europeanization," "Westernization," and then "modernization."

The fact that the world's most advanced nation took the lead both in attempting to suppress the international slave trade and in a mass emancipation of her own slaves put all slaveholding societies on the defensive. From Virginia, Cuba, and Brazil to Sierra Leone, Zanzibar, and the Persian Gulf, slaveholders became aware that in British eyes they were in some way retrogressive and out of step with the times. They often responded to this verdict much as capitalists later responded to similar socialist verdicts—by pointing to the shortcomings, contradictions, and hypocrisy of their ideological foes. Southern defenders of slavery eagerly seized upon the blue books or parliamentary-commission reports documenting the horrors of women and children hauling barrows of coal in narrow mine shafts, of six-year-olds working sixteen hours a day in the mills, of tens of thousands of laborers living promiscuously in scabrous cellars. "When you look around you," South Carolina's governor James Henry Hammond asked in a public letter to the venerable

Thomas Clarkson, "how dare you talk to us before the world of Slavery? . . . If you are really humane, philanthropic, and charitable, here are objects for you. Relieve them. Emancipate them. Raise them from the condition of brutes, to the level of human beings—of American slaves, at least." In this long and devastating letter, Hammond also hammered at three points that recurred through French and Spanish as well as American anti-abolitionist literature: the supposedly proven and well-acknowledged failure of West Indian emancipation; Britain's even more disastrous efforts to suppress the African slave trade, which had simply become "more profitable and more cruel"; and Britain's attempt to disguise a revived slave trade to the West Indies by classifying the blacks as "immigrants" who would supposedly be sold into bondage for twenty-one years and then turned out after the prime of life to fend for themselves. It was thus Britain, the champion of laissez-faire competition, the "cash nexus," and abstract humanitarian ideals, that had ushered in an age of true barbarism.[5]

Southerners doubtless gained collective reassurance from joining and drawing on the chorus of radical and conservative protest against the patent evils of early industrial capitalism. Proslavery writers were not troubled by the thought that such criticism originated and flourished in the very "free" societies they deplored, in marked contrast to the suppression of internal dissent in the southern states. Intellectual diversity and clashing "isms" were not part of the emerging ideal of an organic, harmonious, and chivalric society in which slavery, as George Fitzhugh put it, "educates, refines, and moralizes the masses by separating them from each other, and bringing them into continual intercourse with masters of superior minds, information, and morality." The leading proslavery spokesmen found themselves in the curious position of repudiating the apologies and compromises of their fathers' generation, of invoking ideals of the feudal past, and of claiming to have discovered the only principles that could ensure genuine social progress—principles that would eventually lead even England to reject such half-way devices as coolie labor and to "reinstate African slavery," as Fitzhugh said, "in its old and mildest form." Even in their most rebellious moods, most West Indian planters had acknowledged their dependence on the metropolitan society and had relied on the sanctity of property, the government's contractual obligations, and predictions that severe pecuniary loss and disorder would result from rash reforms. Latin American slaveholders appealed to centuries of religious and legal tradition, to the fear of revolution, and to a patriotic desire to resist what they perceived as British pressure to weaken foreign competitors for the benefit of her own colonies. Of all the slaveholding peoples along the "periphery" that supplied raw materials to industrial Europe and America, only the American South presumed to be an innovative "center" that could save Europe not only from starving but from the cannibalism of class warfare as well. Fitzhugh's conviction that "Southern thought and Southern example must rule the world" was, of course, a variant on the older British and American themes of historic mission.[6]

Unlike Caribbean and Brazilian slaveholders, Southerners had long enjoyed the moral benefit of being insulated from the Atlantic slave trade. Because they could count on a naturally increasing labor force and on an internal flow of slaves from the Upper South to the cotton states, they long accepted the Revolutionary ideology that had blamed the British or a less enlightened age for whatever crimes had been committed in Africa or on the high seas. Southern leaders fully concurred with the Congress of Vienna's pious proclamation that the African slave trade was "repugnant to the principles of humanity and universal morality." In 1820 they supported an ineffectual American law declaring the trade piracy and prescribing capital punishment for any citizens engaged in it. Even when attacking British slave-trade-suppression policies as a cloak for anti-American imperialism, the *Southern Literary Messenger* conceded as late as 1842 the purity of the original abolitionists' motives: "Though Wilberforce and other great and good men and as pure philanthropists as the world ever saw, have earnestly and devoutly labored for the suppression of the African slave-trade . . . there are those in the English government who have used this noble and generous feeling of the *people* at large, as an instrument merely of national aggrandizement, and as a cloak for their designs upon America."[7]

In fact, the first generation of British abolitionists had decided as a matter of tactics to confine their campaign to the African slave trade. But the effect was to magnify and publicize evils that Southerners could soon dismiss as wholly irrelevant to their own social order. The African slave trade suggested a world of international warfare, outlawry, uprootedness, and unscrupulous buying and selling; it illustrated the depths to which New England and especially Liverpool and Bristol merchants would sink in order to make a profit. Plantation slavery, on the other hand, could be likened to the benign and protective institutions of premodern paternalism. Ironically, southern writers insisted that as soon as slavery was cut off from the corrupting supply of fresh captives, as the British abolitionists had originally hoped, the institution became subject to the ameliorative currents of human progress.

As we have seen, British abolitionists abandoned such hopes with respect to the British West Indies, which were subject to direct parliamentary intervention. Yet the British government and much of the antislavery public continued to view the African slave trade as the most intolerable of evils. Its effective suppression would open the way to universal emancipation and the civilization of Africa. This faith was partly a matter of patriotic tradition dating back to William Pitt's memorable plea in 1792 to make "an atonement for our long and cruel injustice towards Africa," to set an example for the nations of Europe, and to open the Dark Continent to the beams of science, pure religion, and legitimate commerce, to "those blessings which have descended so plentifully upon us." Having atoned for her guilt in 1807 by relinquishing the lion's share of the slave trade, Britain was determined to prevent unrepentant nations from rushing in to seize the sinful spoils. The treaties exacted from dependent and weaker nations at the conclusion of the Napoleonic wars provided a legal framework for restricting and eventually destroying the slave trade while simultaneously promoting legitimate British commerce.[8]

It is clear that Britain's dogged pursuit of foreign slavers was largely unsuccessful and often contrary to the nation's immediate political and economic interests. But the suppression policy did not endanger Britain's vital relations with the cotton-producing South until 1836, when the proclamation of Texan independence from Mexico raised the prospect of a new North American market for African slaves. Although there is evidence that a significant number of Africans were reexported from Cuba to the new Republic of Texas,[9] Texans were far too preoccupied with securing American annexation or recognition and commercial treaties from England and France to openly defy what the Congress of Vienna had termed "the public voice in all civilised countries" that supposedly demanded the slave trade's "prompt suppression." Lord Palmerston, the aggressive foreign secretary who was as determined to destroy the slave trade as to extend British commerce to the uncivilized corners of the world, blamed the United States for giving covert protection to the illicit slave trade to Cuba. He could be counted on to demand slave-trade prohibition as a price for any treaty with Texas or mediation with Mexico. There is no need here to describe the international diplomacy to preserve Texan independence and block American expansion. Palmerston and his Tory successor, Lord Aberdeen, were well aware that any direct attempt to undermine slavery in Texas would jeopardize British-American relations, the interests of British investors, and the goal of promoting a new cotton supply that would lessen British dependence on the United States. Yet the British government could not ignore the pressure from abolitionists who argued that Texans had reinstituted slavery in defiance of Mexican law, that the expansion of the institution threatened to negate the effects of British West Indian emancipation, and that Texas, being so sparsely settled, offered an ideal field for British immigration and free-labor plantations. Aberdeen's chargé d'affaires in Texas, Capt. Charles Elliot, became involved in abolitionist intrigues, and in 1843 Aberdeen himself tried to sound out Mexico on a proposal linking recognition of Texan independence with slave emancipation.[10]

President John Tyler and his secretaries of state Abel P. Upshur and John C. Calhoun became increasingly alarmed by the exaggerated reports from American and Texan agents in England who warned that slave-trade abolition had become the entering wedge for a plot to undermine slavery in Texas, Cuba, and then the United States. As the Texan minister to Britain wrote Calhoun, "I sincerely believe that the ultimate purpose is to make Texas a refuge for runaway slaves from the United States, and eventually a negro nation, a sort of Hayti on the continent . . . under the protection of the British Government." Of course, Texan and American annexationists were eager to exploit such Anglophobia as the most promising means of overcoming the American political resistance that had long reconciled many Texans to an independent course. But there can be no doubt that the Tyler administration and much of the American press believed that British philanthropy had become a pretext for subverting republican government and ensuring Britain's control of foreign markets and dominion over the world. Although Lord Aberdeen was anxious to resolve conflicts with Britain's most valuable foreign customer, and publicly disavowed any intention of intervening in the internal affairs of Texas or disturbing the "tranquility" of slavery in the United States, he also affirmed that "Great Britain desires and is constantly exerting herself to procure, the general abolition of slavery throughout the world." When Calhoun became secretary of state, early in 1844, he seized upon an official dispatch in which Aberdeen sought to explain the above words and reassure the American government. Even by expressing the hope to see slavery abolished in Texas, Calhoun maintained, the British Foreign Office had posed a grave challenge to the security of the United States. In lecturing Britain on the failure of emancipation in the northern states (employing faulty statistics from the 1840 census), Calhoun equated Texas annexation with promoting the welfare and progress of the Negro race.[11]

As we shall see in a moment, the menace of a British antislavery and antirepublican conspiracy induced some Southerners to reconsider the presumed evils of the African slave trade. American abolitionists had long maintained that the sins of enslavement and slaveholding were inseparable, that the kindliest master was guilty every moment of perpetuating afresh the original crime. Conversely, if slavery was a blessing for the African and a "positive good" for all concerned, why should American warships patrol the African coast in search of "pirates" who were in effect rescuing blacks from hopeless barbarism? In the eyes of southern leaders, British intervention in Cuba showed that slave-trade suppression could become a lighted fuse leading to a powderkeg on every plantation.

In 1817, when Spain was struggling desperately to pacify her rebellious colonies, Britain had coerced and bribed the Spanish crown into signing a treaty designed to outlaw the African slave trade by 1820. When British officials arrived in Havana to serve on a mixed commission court to enforce the treaty, they were regarded by Cuban planters and government leaders as agents of revolution and members of an "inquisitorial tribunal of foreigners." Cuba had already entered a period of plantation expansion stimulated by a rising world demand for cane sugar, coffee, and other tropical or subtropical staples. This boom was later accelerated by the decline in British sugar production following the abolition of British slavery and apprenticeship, and in the late 1840s by the lowering of British duties on foreign sugar. From 1820 Cuban sugar output doubled by 1835, quadrupled by 1847, and increased more than eightfold by 1859. Since there was a net natural decrease in the Cuban slave population, these gains in production depended on the illegal importation by 1843 of well over 250,000 African slaves—a trade that brought Cuba some 25,000 annual slave imports as late as 1859.[12]

In 1840, Cuban planters were understandably alarmed by reports that Spain, convulsed by rebellion and civil war, might accede to British demands for an effective registration system that could lead to the emancipation of illegally imported slaves. In accordance with a new treaty of 1835, Britain appointed as superintendent of liberated Africans R. R. Madden, an abolitionist magistrate who had struggled against the apprenticeship system in Jamaica. Cuban suspicions of a revolutionary plot were fueled by Madden's attempts to exploit political grievances against Spain, by Lord Palmerston's disregard of Spanish requests for Madden's recall, and by the anchorage in Havana harbor of a British transport hulk manned by black British troops who were intended to escort to British colonies the Africans liberated from slave ships. In 1840 Palmerston blatantly experimented with antislavery imperialism by appointing the British and Foreign Anti-Slavery Society's candidate, David Turnbull, as the government's consul to Cuba. A crusading reformer with a single-minded vision, Turnbull had recently publicized a plan for eradicating the slave trade by undermining planter demand. Cuba, which he had visited in 1838, provided the ideal testing ground since suits might be brought before courts of mixed commission challenging the legal title to most slave property. Such a "radical and practical change in the legal condition of the imported African," Turnbull predicted, would shatter planter confindence, depress the monetary value of slaves, and necessitate a shift to other forms of labor. After winning endorsement from British abolitionists and from the somewhat skeptical 1840 World Anti-Slavery Convention, Turnbull persuaded Palmerston that it would at least be useful to present the plan to the precarious Spanish government and to make the most of Spain's existing treaty obligations.[13]

Turnbull pictured himself as the agent of philanthropy and civilization striking at the most vulnerable prop of New World barbarism. As consul he hoped to command a corps of British agents backed by a British warship and to coerce Spanish compliance by threatening to promote Cuban independence. Turnbull's appointment provoked predictable outrage in Spain and hysteria in Cuba. After a series of stormy conflicts with Cuban leaders and British officials whom Turnbull accused of slave dealing, the abolitionist finally sought refuge for two months on board the British hulk in Havana harbor. But later, in 1842, the indefatigable Turnbull returned to Cuba as a private citizen, accompanied by a crew of free blacks from Nassau. Cubans and many Americans held Turnbull directly responsible for the slave plots and rebelliousness that culminated in 1844 with the uncovering of an alleged mass conspiracy. Whatever the nature of Turnbull's mission, his activities encouraged harsh repressive measures against slaves and free blacks as well as Cuban flirtations with the expanisve United States. Ironically, the fear of American annexation led not only to new Spanish laws ensuring the security of Cuban slave property but also to the temporary acquiescence of a British administration alarmed by American expansion and increasingly committed to competitive free trade.[14]

American leaders, however, seemed unaware that the British antislavery movement had been disastrously divided and weakened by the issue of free trade or that Britain's economic interests might lie in lowering the labor costs of competing foreign suppliers of raw materials. The Cuban slave conspiracy, coupled with British pressure on Texas and Brazil, seemed to prove that Britain was determined to destroy New World slavery by any available means. This view was shared by northern diplomats and editors such as Alexander Everett and John L. O'Sullivan, but it was probably developed with the most consistent logic by Secretary of State Calhoun. Writing at considerable length to America's minister to France, William R. King, Calhoun acknowledged that Britain had initially acted on humanitarian motives, assuming that tropical products could be produced more cheaply by free African and East Indian labor than by slaves. West Indian emancipation had been "calculated to combine philanthropy with profit and power, as is not unusual with fanaticism." But this experiment had proved to be catastrophic. British statesmen could read the statistics that showed how far Cuba, Brazil, and the United States had outstripped all the British tropical possessions in the production of coffee, cotton, and sugar. The British understood as well as anyone that "the great source of the wealth, prosperity, and power, of the more civilized nations of the temperate zone, especially Europe, where the arts have made the greatest advance, depends in a great degree on the exchange of their products with those of the tropical regions." The most progressive nations, Calhoun emphasized, had become so productive that the fate of their commerce, manufactures, wealth, and power depended on finding markets in the tropical regions and "the more newly settled portions of the globe."

In order to regain and keep her superiority, Calhoun affirmed, Britain was pursuing two simultaneous objectives. First, she aimed to restore her own capacity to produce tropical staples by exploiting nominally free labor in the West Indies, East Africa, and her East India possessions. But this capital investment could never succeed unless Britain also destroyed the rival slave societies that "have refused to follow her suicidal policy" and that could therefore keep the prices of tropical staples "so low as to prevent their cultivation with profit, in the possessions of Great Britain, by what she is pleased to call free labor." Calhoun drew a sharp distinction between Britain's own experiment with emancipation and the violent upheavals that would result from her subversive instigations in Cuba, Brazil, and the United States. The former example, however fatal to the plantation economy, had benefited from a firm authority that assured social order and "the political and social ascendency of their former masters over their former slaves." The abolitions that Britain now promoted could only result in the kind of racial warfare that had desolated Saint Domingue. Calhoun grounded his argument on foreseeable results, not on immediate tactics or motives:

> It matters not how or for what motive it may be done, whether it be by diplomacy, influence, or force—by secret or open means; and, whether the motive be humane or selfish, without regard to manner, means, or motive, the thing itself, should it be accomplished, would put down all rivalry, and give her the undisputed supremacy in supplying her own wants and those of the rest of the world, and thereby more than fully retrieve what she has lost by her errors. It would give her the monopoly of tropical productions. . . .[15]

James Hammond's two letters to Clarkson, written less than a year after Calhoun's letter to King, captured in restrained and punctilious prose the growing fury that Southerners felt toward the whole self-righteous tradition of British philanthropy. Hammond professed no desire to defend the African slave trade, calling it "no longer a question." The slaveholder's rights rested on the solid rock of inheritance and prescription. It was as absurd to appeal to ancient wars and kidnappings in Africa as it would be to demand that New England abolitionists restore their farms to the descendants of slaughtered Indians or to impeach the title of English estates originally seized by Norman conquerors. Yet, after acknowledging the probable barbarities of the slave trade that Clarkson and his co-workers had exposed to the world more than half a century earlier, Hammond noted, "If I might judge of the truth of transactions stated as occurring in this trade, by that of those reported as transpiring among us, I should not hesitate to say, that a large proportion of the stories in circulation are unfounded, and most of the remainder highly colored." Moreover, the evils of the illicit slave trade showed that Clarkson's lifelong crusade had been in vain:

> If kidnapping, both secretly and by war made for the purpose, could be by any means prevented in Africa, the next greatest blessing you could bestow upon that country would be to transport its actual slaves in comfortable vessels across the Atlantic. Though they might be perpetual bondsmen, still they would emerge from darkness to light—from barbarism into civilization—from idolatry to Christianity—in short from death to life.[16]

This was precisely the argument advanced in the 1850s by Leonidas W. Spratt, Robert Barnwell Rhett, Edmund Ruffin, Henry Hughes, James De Bow, and other young "fire-eaters" who called for a reopening of the African slave trade to the southern states. Hammond, by then a senator counting on an alliance with northern Democrats to head off attacks on the South, denounced this agitation as "abolitionism in disguise," which could only serve to divide and isolate the slave states. By any pragmatic standard, the pro-slave-trade movement was bound to be self-defeating. If the aim was to alienate northern Democrats and provoke secession, the cause was also certain to alienate Virginia and the Upper South, which would lose its profitable monopoly as a supplier of labor to the cotton states. Much of the South's incipient antislavery sentiment had been appeased by the southwestward migration of slaves and the racist hope that the black population would become increasingly dispersed. If large steamships began unloading thousands of new African slaves, as in contemporary Cuba, the racism of the nonslaveholding whites, exemplified by Hinton R. Helper's incendiary book *The Impending Crisis of the South,* might well crystallize in an antislavery form of southern "nativism."[17]

In any event, the Lower South possessed no navy or merchant marine. Although the North built and outfitted ships for the illegal Cuban trade, sectional conflict would almost certainly lead, as it did in 1862, to compliance with British demands for an effective slave-trade-suppression treaty including the right of search. Everything would therefore depend on the response of the nation that in 1850–51 had not only imposed an anti-slave-trade blockade on the Brazilian coast but had also captured and sunk suspected ships within Brazilian harbors. At that time William E. Gladstone, the son of a West Indian merchant and slaveholder and anything but an abolitionist, had told the House of Commons that under international law "we have now a perfect right to go to Brazil and call upon her to emancipate every slave imported since 1830, and, upon refusal, to make war with them even to extermination." When South Carolina was later about to secede, the British consul in Charleston warned Robert Barnwell Rhett that Britain would demand a commitment not to reopen the slave trade—a credible threat in view of Britain's treaties with the Latin American republics, Spain, the Republic of Texas, Brazil, Zanzibar, and the states on the Persian Gulf. The fate of the new Confederacy hinged on European recognition and aid. As one might expect, the Montgomery Constitutional Convention of 1861 adopted a provision that not only prohibited the importation of African slaves from any foreign country but also required the new Confederate Congress to enact enabling legislation. What is surprising is the militancy of the opposition and the widespread sense of betrayal.[18]

If the South was to become a "slave republic" and what Leonidas Spratt termed "a chosen people" charged with the global mission of harmoniously unifying two unequal races, it was essential to legitimate historical origins that had fallen into universal disrepute. According to Spratt, the Charleston editor who became widely known as "the philosopher of the new African slave trade," restrictions on the slave trade or on the "further union of the races" necessarily implied that slavery itself was wrong—and had historically served to isolate the South, sap its morale, and retard its economic and political growth. Since Britain had made slave-trade abolition into a kind of totem symbolizing legitimate commercial power, there was a certain brilliance in throwing off all restraints and violating "civilization's" most pious taboo. The producers of raw materials would at last confront British and northern customers with a vision of progress wholly antithetical to that of "exploitive," consumer societies. For a few Southerners who saw themselves besieged by an ideologically hostile world, defending the slave trade became a self-vindicating ritual that would test the integrity of their cause as well as the expected opportunism of capitalist nations that could not survive without cotton and whose tenderness for human rights, as Spratt put it, did not prevent them from crushing India, Algeria, and Poland or from tolerating the trade in white Circassian slaves to the markets of Constantinople.[19]

Spratt maintained that Negro slavery was so superior to white "hireling" labor that the system would have spread throughout the North if the African trade had not been closed. Indeed, it was "the most efficient form of labor this world has ever known." Like some modern economists, Spratt argued that black slaves were eminently suited for skilled trades and "mechanical employments" and were concentrated in agriculture simply because cotton planters could pay higher prices for a supply of labor that was always insufficient. The North, having deprived itself of the benefits of African labor, had then imported millions of "paupers" from Europe and had begun to suffer the turmoil and instability of a democratic society. Spratt regarded the ensuing conflict between free and slave societies as inevitable and irrepressible: "Like twin lobsters in a single shell . . . the natural expansion of the one must be inconsistent with the existence of the other. . . . The great tendency to social conflict pre-existed; it was in the heart of the North—it was in the very structure of Northern society."[20]

Lincoln, Seward, and the abolitionists were thus the mere "instruments" of broad social forces moving toward the destruction of a competitive social order. For Spratt the question was not whether to resist such aggression but whether the South, which could become a center of "imperial power and grandeur," would make Negro slavery its "sole exclusive social system." Spratt was deeply disturbed by the prevalence of free white labor in the Upper South, by the immigration of European workers to the coastal towns, and, above all, by the increasing inability of most whites to pay the skyrocketing price for a black slave. Renewed importations from Africa would soothe class unrest by enabling most whites to become slaveholders. Expansion of the slave population would also stimulate southern industry and provide a sufficient labor force for settling new territories. For Spratt and his followers, imperial expansion would be essential if the South was to retain control of the world's production of cotton and thus test Europe's professed commitment to sentiment as opposed to interest. In 1861 Spratt repeated a prediction he had made three years before to a Montgomery commercial convention: a strong and independent South would be "singlularly favoured—crowns would bend before her; kingdoms and empires would break a lance to win the smile of her approval; and, quitting her free estate, it would be in her option to become the bride of the world, rather than, as now, the miserable mistress of the North." He went on to warn, however, that if the new constitutional prohibition was confirmed out of deference to the moral sentiment of the world, all would be lost. A slave republic filled with self-doubt and unsure of its principles could never fulfill its daring mission, "in the grand drama of human history," of "erecting a nationality upon a union of races, where other nations have but one."[21]

When in 1862 John Elliott Cairnes prepared a revised, second edition of his *The Slave Power: Its Character, Career and Probable Designs,* he added numerous quotations from Leonidas Spratt and even reprinted as an appendix Spratt's "The Philosophy of Secession," a long protest against the constitutional prohibition of the slave trade. Before taking the professorship of political economy and jurisprudence at Queen's College, Galway, Cairnes had delivered lectures on American slavery at Trinity College, Dublin. He intended the contemporary subject to show that the course of history was "largely determined by the action of economic causes." John Stuart Mill, his friend and mentor, had then encouraged him to rework the lectures into a book, which displayed, in Mill's words, the mind of a "first-rate political economist" as well as "the higher character of a moral and political philosopher." Although Cairnes regarded political economy as a science concerned with facts alone, he intended this work to counteract what the *Spectator* called "the extraordinary tide of sympathy with the South which the clever misrepresentations of Southern advocates" had set in motion, and to present the British public with "the true nature of the issues involved" in the American Civil War.[22]

One way to refute the prevalent British view that slavery had nothing to do with the American war was to show that "a party claiming admission as an equal member into the community of Christian nations" had in fact settled on a plan "of reviving in the full light of modern civilization a scandal which has long lain under its ban." According to Cairnes, Spratt had given voice to the true designs of the Confederacy and his arguments had been sanctioned by the southern press and by southern society. The constitutional prohibition of the slave trade was "a mere abstract proposition" adopted for expediency but destined for repeal, like the Missouri Compromise and all other measures restricting the ambitions of the Slave Power, once peace and independence had been achieved.[23]

While *The Slave Power* was a political tract arguing against European intervention in the Civil War, it also synthesized ideas that were passing from the realm of partisan struggle into the sphere of social science. An analysis of Cairnes's thought will therefore help to illuminate the strategy of redefining the problem of slavery as a problem of modernization—of dealing with what Mill termed "barbarous nations." Yet it is impossible to understand Cairnes without first giving some attention to the unexpected British response to the Civil War—not to the intricate diplomacy involving British neutrality but to the sudden upswell of opinion hostile to the northern cause.

Even Southerners confident of the economic power of "King Cotton" had been fearful that the British antislavery tradition, as John Floyd put it, "will fix upon us forever the badge of inferiority which we are now ready to destroy the Union to escape. . . ." Anglophile New Englanders, who for generations had looked to Britain both for models and certifications of civilized life, were devastated to discover that their mother country refused to believe that they had taken on the ultimate "battle of civilization." The hurt and bewilderment extended to abolitionists who had earlier toured Britain attacking the Consitution, American racism, and the hopelessness of the American political system, but who had failed to convey the reasons for their more recent change of heart. To his admiring American correspondent Sarah Blake Shaw, Cairnes himself blamed British ignorance and the inflammatory press of both nations, especially the Anglophobe papers of the northern Democrats. But by the second year of war there could be no doubt that from the *Times* to the *Edinburgh Review,* the most respected British newspapers and journals vehemently opposed the Lincoln administration's attempt to conquer the South. This view was shared not only by the aristocracy but also by much of the middle class, Lancashire workers, and even abolitionists who were appalled by the carnage of a modern war that bore no apparent relation to slave emancipation or any idealistic cause. "A very general apprehension prevails here," Cairnes wrote Mrs. Shaw in July 1862, "that the ruling motive of the North in the war is ambition purely, and that slavery abolition is only regarded as an effectual expedient for crushing its antagonist in the last resort. I wish I could believe that there was no foundation for this impression." To his profound horror, one year later Mrs. Shaw's only son, Robert Gould Shaw, would lose his life leading the black troops of the Massachusetts Fifty-fourth Regiment in a gallant assault on Fort Wagner.[24]

No one described the paradox more eloquently than Mill:

> What is the meaning of this? Why does the English nation, which has made itself memorable to all time as the destroyer of negro slavery, which has shrunk from no sacrifices to free its own character from that odious stain, and to close all the countries of the world against the slave merchant; why is it that the nation which is at the head of abolitionism, not only feels no sympathy with those who are fighting against the slave-

> holding conspiracy, but actually desires its success? Why is the general voice of our press, the general sentiment of our people, bitterly reproachful to the North, while for the South, the aggressors in the war, we have either mild apologies or direct and downright encouragement? and this not only from the Tory and anti-democratic camp, but from Liberals, or *soi-disant* such?[25]

Mill might also have noted the eagerness with which the British exploited the familiar charge that Europeans and Americans had directed against Britain's own policies: antislavery was a "cloak" or pretext for imperialism. Having indignantly rejected such aspersions for half a century, why did the pragmatic British challenge the purity of humanitarian motives when harnessed to America's political and military needs and opportunities?

Contemporaries, like later historians, pointed to some obvious answers. Despite a long history of "cultural exchange" and economic interdependence, the "Anglo-American connection" had been punctuated with recurring crises and grievances. Charles Francis Adams, America's minister to Britain, shared his father's and grandfather's mistrust of perfidious Albion; memories of the War of 1812 were even fresher in the mind of Lord Palmerston, the elderly prime minister who now confronted across the Channel another Napoleon and the possibility that an American war would lead to an anti-British alliance or unleash Continental ambitions that would shatter the balance of power that had served British interests so well. From Secretary of State Seward as well as from the northern press, there were sufficient intimations that a restored and toughened Union would seek by various means to humble Britain's power. Cairnes and Mill were addressing a public that equated the North's subjugation of the South with the aggrandizing behavior that had recently won the United States hegemony over the entire North American continent. Talk and even preparations for war had erupted over America's intervention in the Canadian rebellion of 1837; the violent dispute over the boundary of Maine; America's truculent demand for all the Pacific Northwest to the latitude 54°40′; and, most recently, the armed seizure and removal of two Confederate agents from the British mail steamer *Trent*.[26]

Aside from such symbolic tests of power, it was clear by 1861 that Britain had failed to prevent the rapid industrialization of rival states, including the North, or to find an adequate alternative to southern slave-grown cotton. Although the effects of the war-induced "cotton famine" were initially delayed and also compensated for by a stimulus to other export industries, there could be no mistaking that a northern victory would jeopardize Lancashire's main supply of cotton, result in permanent tariff barriers to British manufactures, and intensify competition in exports to Asia, Latin America, and other distant markets that were becoming more essential as Europe was becoming more industrially self-sufficient. Given this larger setting, it seemed plausible, as Lord John Russell said, that the North and South were contending, "as so many states in the Old World have contended, the one side for empire and the other for independence."[27]

As the war began to paralyze the cotton textile industry, bringing mass unemployment in Lancashire, even antislavery writers found reasons to believe that southern independence would hasten emancipation or at least lead to the "euthanasia of slavery," as the Confederacy found itself wholly dependent on "progressive" free-labor nations. Thus far, so the argument went, slaveholders had been protected by the racist North, reinforced by hordes of ignorant, Anglophobic Irish immigrants. Northern Democrats attributed every antislavery proposal and even John Brown's raid to an English conspiracy to subvert the Union. Independence would deprive the South of this political and ideological support, which American abolitionists had always condemned as indispensable for slavery's continued existence. For Britons who had heard vivid accounts of anti-abolition mobs, race riots, and legalized segregation in the North, there could be little surprise in learning that federal troops had returned fugitive slaves to their southern owners, that Lincoln had ensured the security of slave property in the border states, or that draft rioters in New York, mostly Irish-Americans, had tortured and murdered untold numbers of free blacks. The baffling question was why such figures as Charles Sumner, Harriet Beecher Stowe, and even William Lloyd Garrison defended the forcible restoration of such a Union.

But after granting these points and making allowance for the skill of Henry Hotze, James Spence, James Murry Mason, and other pro-Confederate propagandists, certain mysteries remain. As we have seen, British abolitionism and eventually British public policy had worked from the premise that West Indian planters could never be trusted to ameliorate the condition of their slaves or move toward effective emancipation measures. During the 1850s the supposedly liberalizing influence of British commerce had done nothing to weaken black slavery in Cuba, Brazil, or the American South; the striking rise in slave prices in all three regions suggested that planters were anything but pessimistic about the future.[28] Why should an independent Confederacy be more susceptible to the fragmented and languishing British antislavery organizations of the early 1860s?

We have also seen that the British emancipation act of 1833 was a highly qualified measure attuned to political and economic expediency. Yet most of the British press greeted Lincoln's emancipation proclamation with scorn and derision. As the antislavery *Spectator* put it, "the principle asserted is not that a human being cannot own another, but that he cannot own him unless he is loyal to the United States." While John Bright, Harriet Martineau, and a few newspapers hailed the proclamation as a decisive turning point, even Cairnes reported rather condescendingly to Sarah Shaw:

> The grand objection that is urged on all hands is that the proclamation fails to assert the *principle* of freedom. For my part, while I admit and deplore the failure, I regard the objection as scarcely reasonable. To expect the average American politician, of which I take it, the President is a fair specimen, to be *at once* converted into a far-sighted and philanthropic statesman, is I think more than childish, and with such a weapon as emancipation in the armoury of the Unionism, it was vain to expect that it wd not be used as a war-measure.

As George William Curtis, Mrs. Shaw's son-in-law, replied to Cairnes, the British expectation rested on a gross misconception of the American Constitution and the powers of the commander-in-chief. Neither Lincoln nor Congress was empowered to emancipate a single slave as a matter of principle or public policy; yet in the cause of self-defense "an immense social and moral change which under our system in peace could have been but indirectly and gradually effected, is wrought in war at a blow."[29]

The dominant British response is put in better perspective by the remarkable assessment in the Vienna *Presse* of 12 October 1862, written by Karl Marx:

> [Lincoln] always gives the most significant of his acts the most commonplace form. Where another man, acting for the sake of so many "square feet of land" declaims about "the struggle for an idea," Lincoln, even when he is acting for the sake of an idea, speaks only in terms of "square feet of land."
>
> Indecisively, against his will, he reluctantly performs the *bravura aria* of his role as though asking pardon for the fact that circumstances are forcing him to "play the hero." The most formidable decrees which he hurls against the enemy and which will never lose their historic significance, resemble—as the author intends them to—ordinary summonses sent by one lawyer to another on the opposing side. . . . And this is the character the recent Proclamation bears—the most important document of American history since the founding of the Union, a document that breaks away from the old American Constitution—Lincoln's manifesto on the abolition of slavery. . . .
>
> In the history of the United States and in the history of humanity, Lincoln occupies a place beside Washington! Truly in our day, when every

> little happening on this side of the Atlantic assumes an air of melodramatic portent, is there no meaning in the fact that everything of significance taking shape in the New World makes its appearance in such everyday form?
>
> . . . Never yet has the New World scored a greater victory than in this instance, through its demonstration that, thanks to its political and social organization, ordinary people of good will can carry out tasks which the Old World would have to have a hero to accomplish![30]

Marx's eagerness to view the Civil War as a revolutionary struggle helps to explain the diffidence of British liberals who feared that Lincoln's proclamation would ignite a servile insurrection leading to racial warfare and "rivers of blood." Forgetting that West Indian planters had raised similar warnings against any interference with the slave trade or colonial race relations, even British abolitionists had come to think of slave emancipation as an example of peaceful and gradual progress implemented by planters in response to the moral influence of the "civilized world." As we shall see later on, the failure of West Indian blacks to meet the reformers' expectations tended to reinforce racist stereotypes propagated by popular minstrel shows and pseudoscientific anthropology. Fear of "inferior" races was considerably aggravated by the Indian mutinies and uprisings of 1857–58, particularly the massacre at Cawnpore of over two hundred British women and children. As the London *Times* put it, "there is no society which cannot be destroyed by the process of setting loose those 'dangerous classes' which are always to be found in every community whether urban or rural." Although the British press had castigated Lincoln for spurning antislavery principles, the prospect of freeing slaves as a military measure evoked images of Cawnpore and Haiti, of childlike barbarians, "under the promptings and goadings of superior power," as the *Saturday Review* put it, bursting "into the frenzy of a young tiger which now for the first time smells blood." Even Richard Cobden feared a servile insurrection until July 1863, when he reassured himself that the docility and religious training of blacks would prevent them from rising up and committing "dreadful crimes."[31]

On a deeper level, British responses to the American war reflected anxieties over domestic class conflict and the strains of social change. Though America had long served as a "beacon of freedom" for British reformers, the reports of travelers had also dramatized the argument that American democracy was precisely what Britain had most to fear. Universal suffrage, it was tirelessly repeated, had led in France to the despotism of the First and Second republics; in America "to a society of tobacco-chewers, political duelists, and border ruffians—in a word, to anarchy." And to impudent servants who did not know their place.

Worst of all, as the historian Sir Archibald Alison moaned during the Civil War, "England is already becoming Americanized, with destructive effects horrible to behold." The North, in particular, represented the frenetic pursuit of gain, collapse of deference, demagoguery, and vulgarity of manners that had already begun to shred the fabric of British society. For this reason the romanticized and underdog South became a counterpoise for the uglier side of democratization. Even Union sympathizers like Monckton Milnes privately acknowledged that "the lower civilization, as represented by the South, is so much braver & cunninger & daringer than the cultivated shopkeepers of the North." The southern planter, transmogrified into a Stonewall Jackson, commanded at least the covert admiration of a self-doubting "nation of shopkeepers."[32]

This is not to say that Britons were ever prepared to believe that the slaveholding Confederacy represented the wave of the future or that it could defy the moral juggernaut of universal emancipation. Historians were long misled by the myth that Lancashire textile workers rallied selflessly to the Union cause, but there can be no doubt that in 1863 the London Emancipation Society and similar provincial groups orchestrated mass demonstrations against British recognition of the Confederacy. Cobden and Bright were not alone in recognizing that a Union defeat would shatter prospects for electoral reform in Britain; as the war progressed, an increasing number of intellectuals, evangelicals, and labor reformers agreed with Goldwin Smith "that the Union cause was not that of the negro alone, but of civilization, Christian morality, the rights of labour, and the rights of man."[33] This was the ideology that Cairnes helped to shape—the Emancipation Society distributed thousands of copies of one of his pamphlets, and his *Slave Power* had a decisive impact on such figures as Mill, Darwin, Leslie Stephen, and Harriet Martineau. Though evangelicals regretted that such "rectification of public opinion" should come from a writer so little concerned with Christianity, Cairnes clearly sought to revive the quiescent antislavery public by addressing the momentous issue of global progress and retrogression, fusing the seemingly impartial approach of the political scientist with secularized imagery of Christian civilization confronting the Antichrist.

Cairnes's critique of southern "barbarism" was in part a compendium of the arguments of such Republican party publicists as Salmon P. Chase, Charles Sumner, John G. Palfrey, and Horace Greeley, who in the 1850s had transformed fears of a "slave power conspiracy," a legacy of abolitionist struggles against the annexation of Texas and the "gag law" of the late 1830s, into an effective political weapon. Despite the explosive debates in America following the Kansas-Nebraska Act and the Dred Scott decision, the very idea of the "Slave Power" seems to have been something of a novelty to the British public in 1862, doubtless a sign of the declining interest in antislavery agitation. For the impartial, scientific mind, the crucial question was why the South should be any more barbarous or impervious to moral and material progress than the North?

Alexis de Tocqueville, on whom Cairnes relied heavily, had addressed this question in some unforgettable passages in *Democracy in America.* In July 1831 the French traveler had abandoned his earlier hypothesis that geography had been the primary force shaping the diversities of American society. Joel Poinsett, the South Carolinian statesman and diplomat who had traveled widely in Europe and Latin America, prepared Tocqueville for the contrast he would find between Kentucky and Ohio during his forthcoming descent of the Ohio River. Poinsett, like Josiah Quincy, John Quincy Adams, and other northeastern advisers, stressed the differences in manners and customs, including slaveholding, of the Virginian and New England settlers. Southern backwardness and "underdevelopment" had been a stock theme of northern Federalist writing. In 1821 Justice Joseph Story, whose writings Tocqueville absorbed, had attributed the contrast between Kentucky and Ohio to "the structure of land titles"—the former state having allowed individuals to appropriate land "by entries and descriptions of their own, without any previous survey under public authority, and without any such boundaries as were precise, permanent, and unquestionable."[34]

Still pondering the effects of climate, geography, *moeurs,* history, and slavery, Tocqueville discovered in Cincinnati and beyond exactly what he had been prepared to see:

> On the left bank of the river the population is sparse; from time to time one sees a troop of slaves loitering through half-deserted fields; the primeval forest is constantly reappearing; one might say that society had gone to sleep; it is nature that seems active and alive, whereas man is idle.
>
> But on the right bank a confused hum proclaims from afar that men are busily at work; fine crops cover the fields; elegant dwellings testify to the taste and industry of the workers; on all sides there is evidence of comfort; man appears rich and contented; he works.

The states on both sides of the river, Tocqueville observed, had been settled by migrants of the same European race. They had originally shared the same habits, laws, and civilization. The soil on both shores of the river promised inexhaustible riches to the farmer; the air was equally wholesome and the climate mild. Yet the state of Ohio, founded twelve years after Kentucky, could boast of such public improvements as a canal connecting Lake Erie with the distant Ohio River, and of a population that exceeded Kentucky's by nearly one-quarter million. In his final assessment Tocqueville had no hesitation in attributing the contrast, which extended to character, ambition, and the quality of life, to Negro slavery:

> On the left bank of the Ohio work is connected with the idea of slavery, but on the right with well-being and progress; on the one side it is degrading, but on the other honorable; on the left bank no white laborers are to be found, for they would be afraid of being like the slaves; for work people must rely on the Negroes; but one will never see a man of leisure on the right bank; the white man's intelligent activity is used for work of every sort.[35]

Although this famous contrast was a "fact" that no political economist could ignore, Cairnes overlooked the almost identical imagery used by Lord Durham, whose travels in 1838 along the Canadian-American border resulted in the following report:

> By describing one side, and reversing the picture, the other would be also described. On the American side, all is activity and bustle. The forest has been widely cleared; every year numerous settlements are formed, and thousands of farms are created out of the waste; the country is intersected by common roads; canals and railroads are finished . . . the ways of communication and transportation are crowded with people, and enlivened by numerous carriages and large steamboats. . . . Good houses, warehouses, mills, inns, villages, towns, and even great cities, are almost seen to spring up out of the desert. Every village has its schoolhouse and place of worship. . . . On the British side of the line, with the exception of a few favored spots, where some approach to American prosperity is apparent, all seems waste and desolate. . . .
>
> There, on the side of both the Canadas, and also of New Brunswick and Nova Scotia, a widely scattered population, poor and apparently unenterprising, though hardy and industrious, separated from each other by tracts of intervening forest, without towns and markets, almost without roads, living in mean houses, drawing little more than subsistence from ill-cultivated land, and seemingly incapable of improving their condition, present the most instructive contrast to their enterprising and thriving neighbors on the American side.[36]

Whereas Lord Durham was concerned with the effects of misgovernment in failing to check the wasteful disperison of the Canadian population, Cairnes sought to establish the causal links between black slavery and the unprogressive South. By what specific means did slave labor blight an entire region and insulate white Americans from the "spontaneous process" of self-improvement? Although drawing on many sources, including the extraordinarily informative Orleanist journal *Revue des deux mondes,* Cairnes found the most valuable clues in Frederick Law Olmsted's *Journey in the Seaboard Slave States* and other works. During his trips through the South in the 1850s as a correspondent for the *New-York Daily Times* and then for the *New York Daily Tribune,* Olmsted had visited surprisingly few plantations but had compiled a series of richly detailed observations that helped to shape the dominant Republican view of the retrogressive "Slave Power." Though his original letters to the *Times* presented a more benign picture of master-slave relations than did his later books, a letter of 12 January 1854 epitomized Olmsted's interpretation of the "immense quiet influence" that slavery exerted on the character of the master class.[37]

In this typical report Olmsted argued that "from early intimacy with the negro (an association fruitful in other respects of evil) [the master] has acquired much of his ready, artless and superficial benevolence, good nature and geniality." As a result, slaveholders became indifferent to minor failings, ready impulsively to punish or forgive, but incredibly tolerant of "the frequent disobedience and constant indolence, forgetfulness and carelessness, and the blundering, awkward, brute-like manner of work of the plantation-slave." Such a psychological environment explained the Southerner's antipathy toward progress:

> The southerner has no pleasure in labor except with reference to a result. He enjoys life in itself. He is content with being. Here is the grand distinction between him and the Northerner; for the Northerner enjoys progress in itself. He finds his happiness in doing. Rest, in itself, is irksome and offensive to him, and however graceful or beatific that rest may be, he values it only with reference to the power of future progress it will bring him. Heaven itself will be dull and stupid to him, if there is no work to be done it it—nothing to struggle for—if he reaches perfection at a jump, and has no chance to make an improvement.[38]

Cairnes was inspired by this ideal of progress and by Olmsted's vision of a bipolar America. But as a professional economist he was alert to the problem of dramatizing the peril to civilization of a "Slave Power" rotting in indolence, self-indulgence, and wasted resources. How could such a barbarous society, which Cairnes himself likened to the uncivilized regions of the world, defeat powerful Union armies and threaten disaster to the industrial economies of western Europe? Unlike Olmsted, Cairnes readily acknowledged certain economic advantages of slave labor: since the employer enjoyed absolute power over his workers, the system permitted "the most complete organization, that is to say, it may be combined on an extensive scale, and directed by a controlling mind to a single end, and its cost can never rise above that which is necessary to maintain the slave in health and strength." Given the fortuitous circumstances of an almost unlimited expanse of fertile soil, of freedom to move or sell slaves to the most productive frontiers, and of an international demand for crops that could be most efficiently produced by large-scale combinations of labor, slavery could yield temporary wealth and power. It is interesting to note that Marx, in his critique of Adam Smith's theory of capital formation, quoted Edward Gibbon Wakefield to similar effect:

> The labour of slaves being combined, is more productive than the much divided labour of freemen. The labour of freemen is more productive than that of slaves, only when it comes to be combined *by means of greater dearness of land and the system of hiring for wages*. . . . In countries where land remains very cheap, either all the people are in a state of barbarism, or some of them are in a state of slavery.[39]

Cairnes insisted, however, that the economic gains of slave labor had been achieved at a ghastly cost, indeed, "by blasting every germ from which national well-being and general civilization may spring." To justify his arguments linking social consequences to the "economic necessities" of slave labor, Cairnes invoked the example of the comparative anatomist who, presented with the fragment of a tooth or bone, could reconstruct by deductive reasoning "the form, dimensions, and habits of the creature to which it belonged."[40] The anatomical key to slave societies was the pursuit of wealth and power without an incentive for improvement of any kind. The latter defect, as Olmsted had suggested, originated with the slave himself.

Like most antislavery writers, Cairnes fell into a binary mode of thought that left no place for the coercive aspects of wage labor or the positive incentives compatible with human bondage. He assumed that proportional rewards induced free workers to exert themselves willingly and to develop their most productive skills as they strove to rise above their individual competitors. By contrast, fear alone could stimulate the slave. And as Jeremy Bentham had pointed out, Cairnes reminded his readers, fear "leads the labourer to hide his powers, rather than to show them; to remain below, rather than to surpass himself. . . . By displaying superior capacity, the slave would only raise the measure of his ordinary duties; by a work of supererogation he would only prepare punishment for himself."[41]

In stressing the unskillfulness and lack of versatility of slave labor, Cairnes took pains, as Olmsted did not, to refute the popular racist argument that blacks were inherently indolent. He cited recent evidence from the British West Indies to show that free blacks could be as industrious and enterprising as any people. Under slavery, however, blacks had been deprived of an incentive for careful and diligent work, and in the South had been systematically barred from even the rudiments of learning. Here Cairnes quoted Tocqueville's observation that "the only means by which the ancients maintained slavery were fetters and death; the Americans of the South of the Union have discovered more intellectual securities for the duration of their power. They have employed their despotism and their violence against the human mind." In America racial antipathy had aggravated the dehumanizing effects of bondage, removing the barest hope of the only reward that mattered—freedom.[42]

Such debased and apathetic labor was almost worthless except on land of exceptional fertility, where, as Cairnes put it, "nature does so much as to leave little room for art." But this was a temporary partnership in which nature was the perishing resource. Because slaves were incapable of learning the skills required for rotating crops, planters accepted the necessity of becoming "land-killers" and exhausted the soil by harvesting in successive years a single crop of cotton, tobacco, sugar, or rice. They then abandoned the land and moved on to new clearings. Reports from Brazil and the West Indies showed that slavery had produced the same effects throughout the New World. Cairnes presented a long quotation from Herman Merivale's *Lectures on Colonization and the Colonies* describing a uniform cycle that began with the "rude prosperity" of free proprietors, moved on to consolidated estates and gangs of slaves, and ended with burned-out colonies succumbing to the ruinous competition of new settlements on fresh soil. "The life of artificial and anti-social communities may be brilliant for a time," Merivale concluded, "but it is necessarily a brief one, and terminates either by rapid decline, or still more rapid revolution."[43]

Yet, as Cairnes repeatedly emphasized, the southern states had won an indefinite reprieve from the inherent forces of decline. Unlike the insular or coastal colonies in the tropics, they had long ago acquired sufficient political power to ensure the annexation of an almost inexhaustible expanse of virgin land. Virginia and Maryland had thus escaped most of the *economic* penalties of soil depletion by becoming "breeding states" for the infamous internal slave trade to the Gulf states and the Southwest. Profits from breeding slaves had united the suppliers and consumers of labor in a common political interest. But the continual dispersion of population—as the theories of Wakefield and Merivale predicted—had also inhibited the growth of capital and the development of towns, canals, railroads, schools, and all institutions for civic, moral, and intellectual improvement. While the system encouraged the increasing accumulation of land and slaves by a few wealthy planters, it also ensured the degradation of the mass of "mean whites," who could compete neither with planters nor with slaves. Cairnes believed that it was "as demonstrable as any proposition in Euclid" that in the long run "slavery has acted injuriously on every class and every interest in the South, and that its continued maintenance is absolutely incompatible with the full development of the resources of the country." He was no less certain, however, that American slaveholders could never be induced voluntarily to abolish their retrogressive institution.[44]

The main reason, Cairnes maintained, was that the system made slaveholders "the sole depositaries of social prestige and political power. . . . Abolish slavery, and you introduce a new order of things, in which the ascendancy of the men who now rule in the South would be at an end." Cairnes did not seem to mean a revolutionary redistribution of land. He referred instead to an expected immigration of new men and the emergence of new political interests and combinations that would break the almost magic spell by which a few large planters had captivated the South. The small oligarchy that constituted the Slave Power had "directed the career of the American Union" for over half a century and was now determined to establish a slave republic powerful enough to dictate terms to industrial consumers.[45]

Cairnes was especially eager to dispel the common British prejudice that attributed America's blustering expansionism, arrogance, and braggadocio to democratic institutions. Like later liberals explaining the excesses of socialist nations, he made it clear he was no "admirer of democracy as it exists in the Northern States," but insisted that American aggression from the seizure of Florida to the filibustering expeditions in Cuba and Nicaragua was the result of institutions diametrically opposed to democracy. Cairnes failed to note that this had been a common theme in American politics, especially from the time of the Liberty party's birth in 1839. But he went on to argue that Englishmen blamed the United States, now represented by the North, for a provocative foreign policy that had in fact been conceived and implemented by the Slave Power. If freed from further restraints, the ambitious designs of the new Confederacy would in all probability extend to the Caribbean and the entire tropical region of the New World, for only such expansion could save southern slavery from the laws of internal decay. In promoting such conquests, the planter oligarchy could rely on millions of whites who were accustomed to violence and to the use of arms, "a population ignorant, averse to systematic industry, and prone to irregular adventure. A system of society more formidable for evil, more menacing to the best interests of the human race, it is difficult to conceive."[46]

Cairnes was especially troubled by the ideology, or what Engels would call the "false consciousness," of southern leaders. They no longer regarded slavery as a "barbarous institution" or as an unfortunate "inheritance from a ruder age." This was the point ignored by the *Economist* and other journals that contended that slave emancipation would be better promoted by southern independence than by northern conquest and reunion. On the contrary, Southerners looked upon the system as "admirable for its intrinsic excellence, worthy to be upheld and propagated, the last and completest result of time." One could manage or even aid backward peoples who were conscious of their own moral or material inferiority. But the southern Confederacy had the effrontery to put itself forward as a model of philanthropy and civilized progress; it "calmly awaits the tardy applause of mankind." It was this arrogance and self-assurance that made the Slave Power

> the most formidable antagonist to civilized progress which has appeared for many centuries, representing a system of society at once retrograde and aggressive, a system which, containing within it no germs from which improvement can spring, gravitates inevitably towards barbarism, while it is impelled by exigencies, inherent in its position and circumstances, to constant extension of its territorial domain.[47]

Cairnes acknowledged that the maxims of political morality as applied to "the ordinary practice of civilized nations" would not justify the North in totally subjugating the South. But the laws of civilized states could not be allowed to protect a would-be nation that sought political independence in order to revive the African slave trade, subject an entire race to barbarous tyranny, and extend "the worst form of human servitude which mankind has ever seen, over the fairest portions of the New World." When Cairnes faced the liberals' dilemma of imposing liberty on the unfree portions of the world, he cited the righteous precedent of British rule in India and quoted Mill on the necessity of suspending the law of nations when dealing with barbarous peoples. Mill spoke of slaveholders in abstract terms that could be applied to any "barbarians" unfit for self-determination. His words, which illuminate the various themes of this chapter—particularly the power conveyed by harnessing antislavery to progress—must be quoted at some length:

> To suppose that the same international customs, and the same rules of international morality, can obtain between one civilized nation and another, and between civilized nations and barbarians, is a grave error, and one which no statesman can fall into, however it may be with those who, from a safe and unresponsible position, criticize statesmen. . . . In the first place, the rules of ordinary international morality imply reciprocity. But barbarians will not reciprocate. They cannot be depended on for observing any rules. Their minds are not capable of so great an effort,

> nor their will sufficiently under the influence of distant motives. In the next place, nations which are still barbarous have not got beyond the period during which it is likely to be for their benefit that they should be conquered and held in subjection by foreigners. Independence and nationality, so essential to the due growth and development of a people further advanced in improvement, are generally impediments to theirs. . . . To characterize any conduct whatever towards a barbarous people as a violation of the law of nations, only shows that he who so speaks has never considered the subject. A violation of great principles of morality it may easily be; but barbarians have no rights as a *nation* except the right to such treatment as may, at the earliest possible period, fit them for becoming one. The only moral laws for the relation between a civilized and a barbarous government, are the universal rules of morality between man and man.[48]

Despite waning antislavery zeal and persisting British sympathy for the South, Mill and Cairnes helped to assimilate the Union cause to Britain's own emancipating and civilizing mission. The century's leading philosopher of liberty justified the subjugation of slaveholders in terms almost identical to those slaveholders invoked to justify the continuing subjugation of "barbarians." Where Cairnes differed from Mill was in doubting the *expediency* of an unconditional victory, even while conceding that the North had as clear a right to conquer the South as to put down murder or piracy—or as Britain had a right to suppress the slave trade. Fearing that the defeated South could not be governed except by a prolonged military despotism, Cairnes foresaw many of the difficulties of Reconstruction, including the hostility toward "missionaries of a new social and political faith" and the likelihood that unredeemed planters would regain political sway. He therefore favored a military victory sufficient to crush the ambitions of the Slave Power, seal off the Mississippi River, and enclose the Deep South within a narrow domain where it would be subject to self-decay. The border states could then be reconstructed upon principles of freedom and reincorporated within the Union. Shut off by a cordon sanitaire, the Confederate planters would ultimately be forced to follow their true self-interest, "no longer overborne by passion or pride." After assessing the generally favorable results of West Indian emancipation, Cairnes concluded that the blacks would ultimately benefit more from the genuine self-interest of their former masters than from external decrees compromised by the racism of American society and the absence of effective "protectors." In this vision, faith in long-term forces of progress took precedence over antislavery principles.[49]

2. THE WAR AGAINST BARBARISM: PART TWO

Northern abolitionists, journalists, clergymen, and Republican ideolgues had popularized similar if less systematic diagnoses of the Slave Power. But whereas John Elliott Cairnes appealed ultimately to a utilitarian standard, "the best interests of mankind," Northerners increasinly invoked America's world mission. They also expressed fury over Britain's hypocrisy and betrayal of the cause of freedom, epitomized by the London *Times'* early verdict that "the United States of North America have ceased to be."[50] The unexpected attacks on the Union by the British press helped to reanimate the rhetoric of the American Revolution as well as the conviction that Americans had been chosen by divine Providence to lead the world toward "a millennium of republicanism." With respect to the theme of progress, Cairnes's writings can be taken as a British restatement of the secular Republican interpretation of a war against barbarism. But if Cairnes's imagery sometimes suggested that the Slave Power was as figurative Antichrist, his mind seemed centuries removed from the American millenarian tradition. In much northern rhetoric, the Slave Power more explicitly approximated the Golden Calf, the Whore of Babylon, and the Seven-headed Beast.

Until the 1850s such views were confined to a small fringe of radical but religiously devout abolitionists. The dominant postmillennial faith—the belief that historical progress would gradually lead to a millennium of peace and brotherhood preceding the Second Coming of Christ—encouraged a conciliatory approach to southern Christians. It is true that most radical abolitionists were also postmillennialists who believed that militant agitation was the only means of bringing the nation to repentance and avoiding either a secular cataclysm or divine retribution. Yet the leading spokesmen for northern Protestantism had deplored abolitionism as a danger to the Union and thus to America's transcendent cause. They had also deplored the evils of southern slavery but were convinced that such a relic of barbarism could not withstand the elevating influence of religious revivals, national benevolent societies, technological improvements, and free institutions. This faith was finally eroded by the Mexican War and the specter of the Slave Power's seizing new territories and arming itself against external influence or internal dissent. But whether responding to abolitionism or the Slave Power conspiracy, the northern clergy merged secular mission with religious eschatology, using the "American Jeremiad" as a means of alerting the nation to moral peril, of instilling a sense of collective responsibility and destiny, and of inspiring faith that steam power, the telegraph, and other technological marvels were part of a divine plan for redeeming the world.[51]

The views of Leonard Bacon, the influential pastor of the First Congregational Church of New Haven, illustrate the dilemmas of an embattled and divided clergy struggling to maintain their traditional "office" as moral custodians of the nation. Bacon became preoccupied with the slavery issue in 1823, when he was a student at Andover Seminary and eagerly read the pamphlets of British abolitionists. Twenty-three years later he said that aside from his official duties and professional studies, no other subject had absorbed so much of his attention. By 1833, however, Bacon had become an outspoken critic of American abolitionism and New England's leading defender of the American Colonization Society. From his conservative persepective, the British model was simply not applicable to American society or American institutions. In Britain the doctrine of immediate emancipation had arisen in response to West Indian resistance to any ameliorative measures. In Britain it was possible to demand "that a new constitution of society, a new body of laws, a new system of relations between capital and labor, and between landholder and peasant, should be imposed upon dependent and vassal colonies by the omnipotence of the Imperial Parliament." In America, however, immediatism challenged the organic foundations of law and authority without regard to the public interest, the welfare of the slave, or the fate of republican institutions. At a time when various self-appointed moralists infringed upon the church's traditional domain, nothing could be more dangerous than abstract doctrines divorced from concrete circumstance and social responsibility. To make matters worse, any New Englander who questioned the wisdom of abolitionist dogma was branded as " ' proslavery' and as sacrificing duty to expediency."[52]

In a statement that echoed the Scottish moral philosopher James Beattie and that would later be adapted by Abraham Lincoln, Bacon affirmed that if slavery and the system that supported it in the southern states was not wrong, "nothing is wrong." The moral issue on which he and the majority of northern evangelical ministers disagreed with the abolitionists was whether slaveholding was sinful per se, regardless of the character, piety, or circumstances of the slave owner. Even in 1833 Bacon acknowledged that it was "invariably sinful" to treat a fellow human being as a piece of property or as a "thing" destitute of personal rights. He also agreed with the abolitionists that there was an immediate duty to cease from the sin "of claiming and treating men as chattels." What he protested was the verbal legerdemain by which abolitionists imputed this absolute sin to the particular situation of *all* southern slaveholders and equated the cessation of sin with "an immediate discharge of the slave from all special guardianship and government, and his immediate investiture with the power of self-control."[53]

Bacon perceptively noted that it was this "certain logical sleight-of-hand" that perplexed, irritated, and inflamed the public as the abolitionists shifted from moral abstractions to specific denunciations and popular harangues. By courting opposition, he charged, the abolitionists had encourage southern intransigence while cutting themselves off from the religious, educational, and benevolent institutions that offered at least some hope of improving the condition of southern slaves; of promoting the welfare of northern free blacks, who wandered "like fugitives and outcasts, in the land which gave them birth"; and of spreading Christiantity and enlightenment in Africa. Bacon typified the northern moderates who regarded the evils of American slavery as self-evident but who were less troubled by injustice to the slave than by three other problems: the plight of conscientious masters who might be counted on for effective reform but who "found the negroes among them, in a degraded state, incapable either of appreciating or enjoying liberty"; the dangers to law and order inherent in any but the most gradual transition from bondage to liberty; and the seemingly hopeless prospects of free blacks who were "separated by obstacles which they did not create, and which they cannot surmount, from all the institutions and privileges to which the other portions of the community owe their superiority." In the terms of our previous discussion of British emancipation, Bacon and his counterparts (whether colonizationists or not) were defenders of *chronos:* they were prepared to tolerate injustice as long as the American Union and its vast network of voluntary societies appeared to be the divinely appointed instruments for gradual but irreversible progress.[54]

As we have seen, the violent persecution of missionaries and the Jamaican slave insurrection of 1831 helped mobilize British opinion behind "immediate emancipation." The sectional crises of the 1850s evoked no comparable northern demand for direct intervention. There was a parallel, however, in the way the crises undermined faith in the indirect influence of religion, market forces, and liberal institutions. The Fugitive Slave Law of 1850 led even moderates like Bacon to endorse the doctrine of a "higher law," supreme over all the human constitutions and enactments that might force Northerners to become accomplices in southern despotism. The Kansas-Nebraska Act and the government's subsequent attempts to legalize slavery in Kansas revolutionized the rhetoric of leading Protestant journals that had previously decried abolitionism. The need to maintain that a Christian could own slaves in good conscience gave way to the higher priority of defending the reputation of Christianity against a diabolical force that seemed to threaten the very essence of America's mission. By 1857 Bacon could denounce President Pierce's state of the union message as a "great treason against the Constitution and the people of the Union." He and innumerable other northern clergy adopted substantially the same view of a Slave Power conspiracy that permeated Republican speeches and that Cairnes later integrated with formal economic theory. But for the clergy and their evangelical weeklies, "the signs of the times" also revivifed ancient apocalyptic imagery. The appearance of an Antichrist had always provided the occasion for collective repentance and dedication. The worse the peril, the greater the hope.

The struggle over Kansas dramatized the first act of the Miltonic scenario of the Great American Epic. When passage of the Kansas-Nebraska Act repealed the Missouri Compromise's restrictions on slavery and empowered the settlers of the territory to prohibit or sanction human bondage, Sen. William H. Seward confidently accepted the southern "challenge" to "engage in competition for the virgin soil of Kansas." Eli Thayer had already obtained a charter for the Massachusetts Emigrant Aid Company, and Horace Greeley's New York *Tribune* broadcast to the nation extravagant visions of an army of free-soil migrants converting the West into a magnified replica of northeastern family farms, small towns, and artisanal shops and mills. Three years later Thayer, undeterred by failures in Kansas, helped organize the North American Emigrant Aid Company for the purpose of colonizing enterprising Northerners in western Virginia. Whether such efforts could succeed in eradicating slavery at strategic locations or would have to await the destruction of the Slave Power, Republican leaders agreed that the South must ultimately be "Northernized." As the *Nation* summed up the ideal three months after Appomattox, a stream of northern colonists would be essential "to renew [its] soil, to raise unheard-of crops, to clear the forest and drain the swamp, to impress the water-power into service, to set up the cotton-mill alongside of the corn-field, to build highways, to explore mines, and in short to turn the slothful, shiftless Southern world upside down."[55]

But this bold goal was closely related to the obverse, apocalyptic vision of the Slave Power conquering the West and finally annihilating liberty and mankind's last hope in the North. Predictions that the South would destroy democracy and establish a slave market at the base of Bunker Hill cannot be dismissed as the inflamed rhetoric of a few fanatics. The Fugitive Slave Act gave federal support to "slave-catchers" who roamed the streets of northern cities. Seward, Lincoln, and eventually even Stephen Douglas feared that a "second Dred Scott decision" would implement the South's ambition to legalize slavery in every state. In Lincoln's famous words, the house divided "will become *all* one thing, or *all* the other." Joshua Giddings expressed in 1856 a widespread Republican conviction when he privately wrote Salmon P. Chase "that northern liberty or southern slavery must fall." Such fears harked back to the flagrant attempts in the 1830s to suppress the abolitionists' civil liberties; the fears gained strength when the Pierce and Buchanan administrations defied the will of the majority of Kansas settlers and recognized a proslavery territorial legislature established by brutish "Pukes" or "Border Ruffians" from Missouri who warred, according to popular accounts, against the schools, churches, free press, and other progressive institutions of the New England Emigrant Aid Society. The Dred Scott decision, depriving free blacks of citizenship and prohibiting Congress from even conferring to territorial legislatures the power to deprive citizens of slave property, made the issues clear-cut. It was a struggle, said Frederick Frothingham in 1857, not only "of Religion and Irreligion, of Order with Disorder, of Self-sacrifice with Selfishness, of Civilization with Barbarism . . . [but] of God with Satan." Slavery was a black Goliath defying the Lord. "If David [should] fall," Frothingham predicted, "the progress of mankind is turned backward, the lessons of history are unlearned, and the human race for centuries to come must wander in darkness, and wade through seas of blood to regain the point where it now stands."[56]

"Are you for God," Senator Sumner asked a crowded audience at Faneuil Hall, "or are you for the Devil?" In his "Landmark of Freedom" speech opposing the Kansas-Nebraska Act's repeal of the Missouri Compromise, Sumner emphasized that the Senate was not considering a proposition to abolish slavery in any region "but, on the contrary, a proposition to abolish freedom." Slaveholding, he went on to argue, inevitably corrupted the manners and morals of white Southerners, presenting children with examples of "the most boisterous passions, the most unremitting despotism," in Jefferson's often-quoted words, and depriving them of the discipline to control their temper, lust, and craving for power. Southern barbarism was thus rooted in the character defects of a people who had been trained to command and to inflict violence on anyone who prevented the instant gratification of their desires. In 1854 Sumner could still appeal to contractual obligations and the "common ground" of America's "political fabric." But his increasing verbal aggression seemed designed to test his theory of southern self-control.[57]

In 1856 Sumner made no references to a fraternal bond in his vituperative two-day speech entitled "The Crime against Kansas"—"the rape of a virgin territory, compelling it to the hateful embrace of slavery." His continuing impeachment of South Carolina's military record in the Revolution provoked a heated debate on the heroism or cowardice of forefathers who had resisted British tyranny. Speakers from Massachusetts and South Carolina challenged the patriotism and symbolic heritage that provided each state with a sense of historical identity and republican mission. Sumner's speech also identified the South with the barbarism of medieval Europe and slave-catching Africa: in Kansas the Slave Power had revived on American soil the "border incursions" of medieval robbers and the crimes of African kidnappers. As a result of the government's concerted conspiracy, Sumner charged, "slavery stands erect, clanking its chains on the Territory of Kansas, surrounded by a code of death, and trampling upon all cherished liberties, whether of speech, the press, the bar, the trial by jury, or the electoral franchise." Sumner's personal attacks on southern leaders and their northern allies prompted Stephen Douglas to remark, "That damn fool will get himself killed by some other damn fool." This was the speech that led South Carolina's representative Preston Brooks to conclude that words alone could no longer vindicate southern honor and that the time had come for a punitive act to stop the "coarse abuse" of abolitionists. Brooks thereupon attacked Sumner in the Senate chamber and beat him senseless with a gold-headed cane. The wild applause that Brooks received throughout the South, coupled with the indignant outrage in the North, suggests a public ritual confirming the annulment of any "common ground."[58]

On a different level, the verbal and physical attacks in the nation's supreme forum confirmed the stereotypes of two modes of power: the calculated verbal abuse that demeaned and humiliated an "unprogressive" opponent; and the "manly" if primitive response of an aggrieved society that had been insulted beyond endurance. As Sumner himself lapsed into three years of invalidism, the debates on Brooks's expulsion presented the occasion for extravagant speeches comparing the virtues and vices of North and South. From the southern perspective, Sumner's reckless slanders were symptomatic of a society careening toward anarchy and class warfare, a society whose leaders had joined in an imperialistic crusade against the South in order to distract attention from their own domestic ills. Northern speakers expanded on the glories of religion and civilization in Sumner's Massachusetts, a state that led the nation in economic modernity, educational and humanitarian institutions, and universal improvement. It would be a mistake, however, to conclude that this imagery reinforced an essentially pacifist or "feminine" northern self-image. Brooks's resort to violence confirmed widespread conceptions of southern barbarism, but it also sharpened northern criticism of compromising politicians who seemed cowed by southern threats and bluster. Wendell Phillips was by no means alone in extolling the stiff-necked Puritans as men of action, not speculation: "The Puritan did not stop to think; he recognized God in his soul, and *acted*." And for Phillips it was John Brown, "the impersonation of God's order and God's law," who reawakened the Puritan spirit of New England. It was this stiff old Puritan, a "Lord High Admiral of the Almighty, with his commission to sink every pirate he meets on God's ocean of the nineteenth century," who in a week taught the nation more than any statesman could have done in seventy years. As Phillips added, "Virginia herself looks into his face, and melts; she has nothing but praises. She tries to scan his traits; they are too manly, and she bows."[59]

These telling remarks suggest that abolitionists had not been "manly" enough and that Virginia had not "melted" in the face of Christian exhortation or shaming abuse. Historians have often commented on the inconsistency of self-proclaimed pacifists' shipping Sharps rifles to Kansas and eulogizing John Brown as a second Christ. Yet the radical abolitionists, the most notable of whom endorsed nonresistance, had always relied on surrogates to implement their goals. Originally, they had hoped that as soon as the duty of immediate emancipation was understood, southern planters or national legislators would devise the necessary means to cleanse the nation of sin. While the Garrisonians sought to preserve the purity of their own moral vision by dissociating themselves from insitutions based on violence, they encouraged less conscientious citizens to vote for the most promising candidates and to choose between the lesser of worldly evils. Similarly, radical abolitionists held that if violence could ever by justified, it would be in the case of a slave's attempted escape—and, by extension, of a forcible seizure of freedom, as in French Saint Domingue. Reformers who insisted on the sanctity of private judgment swept away the kind of reverence for social order and organic institutions that made conservatives like Leonard Bacon shudder at the thought of outlaw slaves. Of course, nonresistants like Henry Clarke Wright resolutely denied that their doctrines could ever incite slaves to revolt. Like Garrison, Wright thought of himself as laboring for a millennium in which "a kiss for a blow" would establish, in Lewis Perry's words, the universal "supremacy of love and martyrdom over revenge and conquest." But because Wright also believed that violence in the sinful world necessarily begets violence, he could paint a fantasy in which "a baptism of blood" would convert masters into the slaves of their former bondsmen, "their wives and daughters consigned to the negro's harem, unless they willingly and penitently let their slaves go free."[60]

Wright imagined that the black slaves themselves would be the agents of such just retribution. Charles B. Stearns, who went to Kansas as the correspondent for the *Liberator* and *National Anti-Slavery Standard,* hoped at first to remain personally true to his nonresistant principles. But the sights of border warfare convinced him that Missourians were not human beings but "*drunken* ourang-outans" or "demons from the bottomless pit and may be shot with impunity." As Perry remarks, the notion that one "could pronounce his neighbor subhuman" and then kill him resembled certain justifications for slavery, and Sterns applied to white Missourians imagery that traditionally had been turned against blacks. But civil disobedience had already prepared Stearns to identify his own moral judgments with the will of God. The struggle against subhuman agents of the Slave Power was helping to deliver Kansas, "that 'Garden of Eden' from Slavery's blackened touch." Stearns well knew that the settlers of Kansas feared the "blackened touch" of free Negroes as much as that of slaves.[61] There is sharp irony in the fact that this supposed battleground between freedom and slavery—the western territories—had long been cherished as the homeland for white eastern workers who, without such a land of promise, would become the "wage slaves" of early industrialization.

It was not the secession crisis, then, that converted nonresistants to support a holy war against southern traitors and barbarians. By the late 1850s radical abolitionists agreed that slavery was treason against God, the only treason that mattered, and they were ready to support John Brown or other activists in whatever efforts were necessary to overthrow the Slave Power. This did not mean that secession evoked an immediate demand for war. Early in 1857 a group of Garrisonians and radical Republicans had themselves called for disunion. The secession crisis simply confirmed their claim that the Union was a hopeless failure and could no longer hold together two antagonistic forms of society. The South's withdrawal, inconceivable in 1857, was hailed as good riddance. The South's declaration of independence, Wendell Phillips predicted, "is the jubilee of the Slave." What most alarmed the radicals was the likelihood that Republican leaders would stoop to any unholy compromise in an attempt to restore the Union. Then the bombardment of Fort Sumter suddenly transformed the world. The North was electrified. The surge of nationalism and antisouthern fury soon convinced the most radical abolitionists that the Union cause was their own, a providential agency designed to destroy the Slave Power. Slaveholders were now rebels against the United States as well as against the abolitionists' God.[62]

Conceptions of progress were profoundly transformed by the unexpected outbreak of armed conflict and the gradual recognition that both the North and South were doomed to suffer the consequences of a prolonged and unconditional war. The secession crisis had initially provoked riots against abolitionist speakers, who were accused of subverting the Union. White mobs continued to persecute northern blacks who challenged the presumption that this was "a white man's war" that had no bearing on their own fate. Yet the war soon rehabilitated the abolitionists as patriots and prophets, providing them with new forums in which they pressed their demands for slave emancipation, the enlistment of black troops, and federal support for the civil and political rights of freedmen. The changing fortunes of war brought fluctuating spasms of hope and despair that can only be touched upon here. For example, both black and white abolitionists were deeply discouraged by Lincoln's long refusal to accept black volunteers or to sanction the emancipation edicts of such field commanders as Generals John C. Frémont and David Hunter. Sometimes they feared that decisive northern victories might encourage a peace settlement that would allow slavery to endure. Yet a pervasive faith that the war had been decreed by Providence dissipated temporary disappointments and emboldened reformers to make the most of opportune moments. For example, in the summer of 1861 James McCune Smith's *Anglo-African* exhorted its black readers to prepare themselves for battle or face the peril of enslavement:

> In aiding the Federal government in whatever way we can, we are aiding to secure our own liberty; for this war can only end in the subjugation of the North or of the South. We do not affirm that the North is fighting in behalf of the black man's rights, as such—if this was the single issue, we even doubt whether they would fight at all. But circumstances have been so arranged by the decrees of Providence, that in struggling for their own nationality they are forced to defend our rights. . . .[63]

Decrees of Providence had always been the domain of the Protestant clergy. Even when calling for a peaceful resolution of the secession crisis, northern clerical leaders had assured their countrymen that all signs pointed to the imminent day when they would see "the Son of Man taking to Himself the power over the nations." By allowing the apostate South to resort to arms, God had signaled that the new Israel could not expect to advance toward the millennium without first expatiating in blood for the nation's sins. While the clergy closed ranks in denouncing southern leaders as traitors who threatened to destroy the principle of legitimate authority and hence America's promise to save the world, they also agreed that the war was a divine chastisement of the entire nation. As President Lincoln put it when calling, on 30 March 1863, for a day of national humiliation, fasting, and prayer, could the calamity of civil war not be seen as "a punishment, inflicted upon us, for our presumptuous sins, to the needful end of our national reformation as a whole People?"

> We have been the recipients of the choicest bounties of Heaven. We have been preserved, these many years, in peace and prosperity. We have grown in numbers, wealth and power, as no other nation has ever grown. But we have forgotten God. We have forgotten the gracious hand which preserved us in peace, and multiplied and enriched and strengthened us; and we have vainly imagined, in the deceitfulness of our hearts, that all these blessings were produced by some superior wisdom and virtue of our own. Intoxicated with unbroken success, we have become too self-sufficient to feel the necessity of redeeming and preserving grace, too proud to pray to the God that made us![64]

Lincoln's words played on the themes of half a century of evangelical revivalism and were echoed in countless fast-day jeremiads that linked confessions of sin with visions of redemption and high mission. "We have sinned," intoned the Reverend Byron Sunderland, "while holding in trust the noblest heritage ever held by any people, while having charge in effect of the last and most precious hopes of human nature." Such sermons were more than an excuse to enhance the clergy's status or reiterate the traditional catalog of America's moral failings. Revivals had always aimed at counteracting the greed and selfishness generated by "universal liberty and boundless prosperity." The great dilemma facing evangelical leaders was how to give practical effect to the ideal of disinterested benevolence without becoming so engaged in the whirl of modern life as to become indistinguishable from every other competing demand. More than any peacetime revival or even foreign mission, the war presented a field for tangible sacrifice and purgation, an outlet for disciplined action in behalf of an ennobling cause. And the cause, as Lincoln made clear in his Gettysburg Address, involved the fate of free institutions throughout the world. Religious and political mission thus found their ultimate fulfillment on the field of battle. In *A Sermon on the Christian Necessity of War,* William Goodrich invoked history to show that though the "precious seed" of progress was sown by the church, "in the establishment of great rights, and the overthrow of great wrongs, there has always come a point where the issue must be fought out in battle." Again and again the northern clergy anticipated Lincoln's grim prediction, in his second inaugural address, that the Lord might will the slaughter to continue "until all the wealth piled by the bond-man's two hundred and fifty years of unrequited toil shall be sunk, and until every drop of blood drawn with the lash, shall be paid by another drawn with the sword."[65]

It was only in the second year of war that the North began to accept the abolitionists' doctrine that slavery itself was the national sin that had brought the American people to Armageddon. Military reverses finally made it impossible to ignore the abolitionists' reminders that in 1842 John Quincy Adams had maintained that, in the event of war, the commander-in-chief would be constitutionally empowered to free the slaves of the enemy. Slavery, Frederick Douglass insisted from the outset, was "a tower of strength" to the Confederacy: "The negro is the key of the situation—the pivot upon which the whole rebellion turns. . . . To fight against slaveholders, without fighting against slavery, is but a half-hearted business, and paralyzes the hands engaged in it." As Douglass predicted, an "inexorable logic of events" forced the North to come to terms with the fundamental issue. Far from being passive onlookers, thousands of slaves sought protection behind Union lines; thousands of blacks clamored to fight as the number of white volunteers declined. Despite continuing outbursts of racism, northern blacks saw a new era of hope in the fall of 1862 when Lincoln issued his preliminary emancipation proclamation and the Union army began enlisting black troops. The blacks of Harrisburg, Pennsylvania, for example, noted that the emancipation proclamation "was not made as an act of philanthropy, or as a great deed of justice due to those suffering in bonds, but simply as a war measure." Still, they recognized "the hand of God" in this edict, which marked 1 January 1863 "as a new era in our country's history—a day in which injustice and oppression were forced to flee and cower before the benign principles of justice and righteousness." As black troops captured Jacksonville and finally led the way into the charred streets of Charleston and Richmond, it appeared that the Union forces had providentially become an army of liberation.[66]

But religious imagery of an American apocalypse and day of Jubilee far outran the national will for effective slave emancipation. On 6 March 1862 Lincoln futilely proposed to Congress that compensation be given to "any state which may adopt gradual abolishment of slavery," at the same time renouncing any claim of federal authority to interfere with "the absolute control" over slavery within state limits. On 1 December 1862, a month before Lincoln was scheduled to implement the emancipation of slaves in rebel territory, the president's annual message to Congress supported the colonization of free blacks and proposed a constitutional amendment intended to restore the Union by rational compromise. The first article of the amendment promised to compensate with government bonds every slaveholding state that completed emancipation by 1 January 1900. Lincoln argued that in thirty-seven years an anticipated growth in population from 31.4 million to 103.2 million would make it easier to pay this national debt, which would also be much lower than the continuing costs of war. The prolonged time would, moreover, spare living slaves "from the vagrant destitution which must largely attend immediate emancipation in localities where their numbers are very great," while giving them "the inspiring assurance that their posterity shall be free forever." There was the added advantage that the southern whites most opposed to emancipation "will have passed away before its consummation." The second article confirmed the "actual freedom" won by slaves "by chances of war," but provided compensation to all owners "who shall not have been disloyal." Although Lincoln glorified the growth of population and expected the ending of hostilities to encourage immigration, his third article empowered Congress to appropriate money for colonizing free blacks "with their own consent, at any place or places without the United States." Dedicated above all to preserving the Union, Lincoln saw no inconsistency between this proffered "carrot" and the impending "stick" of confiscating the rebels' slave property. It is true that he became determined to prevent the courts or a future Congress from annulling the emancipation proclamation. Yet as late as June 1864, after years of abolitionist petitioning, the Thirteenth Amendment failed to win the needed two-thirds majority in the House of Representatives.[67]

On the level of religious rhetoric, however, slavery had long since become the Antichrist, whose death struggles betokened the emptying of the seven "vials" described in the Book of Revelation. In the eyes of numerous clergymen and missionaries, the purgation of American slavery coincided with portentous events in world history, such as the decline of the Turkish empire, the Italian risorgimento, and the disintegration of the Papal States, preparing the way for the United States as a "modern Israel" to proclaim to the world a "year of Jubilee to all that still are bound." Preaching on the theme "Our Country's Mission, or the Present Suffering of the Nation Justified by Its Future Glory," J. W. Hough prophesied that after the war had perfected the nation, "its voice will be heard around the world; it will stir the peoples of Italy and Germany and Hungary; it will echo from the Ural heights to the Chinese Wall; it will penetrate even the jungles of Africa, proclaiming everywhere 'liberty to the captives, and the opening of prison to them that are bound.' " In this and innumerable other eschatological visions, the liberation of slaves purified older concepts of America's Manifest Destiny, which had been based at least implicitly on the expansion of the southern slaveholding system. Both versions of Manifest Destiny shared the vague belief that a republican world would depend on the guidance of the American Anglo-Saxon race. But earlier expansionists like William Gilmore Simms had hailed black slavery as "the "medium & great agent for rescuing and recovering to freedom and civilization all the vast tracts of Texas, Mexico &c." For the Unionist clergy during the Civil War, it was the military destruction of slavery that would prepare a Christian army to "renew and unite the world." As the Methodist chaplain and future bishop Gilbert Haven put it: "To save ourselves, we may be compelled to save others. We shall then be the inspiring and molding nation that they have long needed. . . . We are the only great nation that represents the sovereignty of the people. We may be compelled to maintain that sovereignty everywhere with the sword."[68]

Yet, unlike their British predecessors, American abolitionists showed little initiative in promoting emancipation throughout the world. This was partly because the British had already preempted the field and because there was no issue like suppressing the slave trade that could divert attention from the problems of Reconstruction, problems that were far more central and critical in the United States than in other post-emancipation societies. President Grant aroused little enthusiasm for his ardent drive to annex the Dominican Republic, despite his confident assurances that such expansion would ensure the abolition of slavery in Puerto Rico, Cuba, and probably even Brazil. Sen. Charles Sumner attacked Grant's "imperial system" and compared the annexation plan to the government's attempts in the 1850s to impose slavery on Kansas. Most American abolitionists and their disciples continued to oppose imperialistic ventures, even those advertised as liberationist and humanitarian. At the turn of the twentieth century, for example, Garrison's sons took a leading part in exposing the connections between the entrenchment of Jim Crow in the South and America's attempt to "enslave" the brave Filipinos.[69]

From a Confederate or states' rights perspective, however, Lincoln's wartime proclamation had led to an imperialistic subversion of the federal system. The United States had traditionally been committed to the premise that the federal government could not interfere with slavery, radical discrimination, or rules governing suffrage in the several states. It required a constitutional amendment, the first in sixty-one years, to legitimate the uncompensated emancipation of four million slaves. Not content with imposing this Thirteenth Amendment on the defeated South as a condition for readmission into the Union, the Republicans had blocked the seating in Congress of elected southern representatives and had then embodied in the Fourteenth Amendment provisions that barred most Confederate leaders from holding public office; that redefined citizenship to include all races; and that prohibited states from depriving any person of life, liberty, or property without due process of law or from denying any person the equal protection of the laws. Although the Fourteenth Amendment was a compromise that failed to meet the radicals' objectives, it went well beyond the measures that accompanied other nations' acts of emancipation. America's Reconstruction was unique in depriving the former slaveholding elite of political power and of a political role in defining the consequences of emancipation. This punitive policy was, of course, essential for preserving a precarious Republican hegemony that could easily have been overthrown by a reunited Democratic party. It was also the response to a costly and bloody "rebellion," and was fueled by a sense of national catharsis and historic mission.

To mobilize support for the Fourteenth Amendment, Pennsylvania Republicans stressed the duty "to gather the legitimate fruits of the war, in order that our Constitution may come out of the rebellion purified, our institutions strengthened, and our national life prolonged." As David Montgomery has shown, the radicals merged nationalism, utilitarianism, and a faith in human perfectibility in a way that exalted the sovereignty of the people and proscribed political or civil inequalities based on race or local custom. For a regenerated and expansive Union, dedicated to promoting the welfare of all the people, there could be no place for decentralized satrapies that denied to a given class the rights of full citizenship. In 1870 President Grant noted the remarkable contrast between the Dred Scott decision of 1857 and the new Fifteenth Amendment, which prevented states from denying or abridging the right of citizens to vote "on account of race, color, or previous condition of servitude." According to Grant, this third Reconstruction amendment was "a measure of grander importance than any other act of the kind from the foundation of our free government to the present day." Montgomery adds that "the crowning tribute to the work of the Radicals in this area came two years later when both Presidential candidates espoused equal rights and equal suffrage regardless of race."[70]

Political history seemed to confirm Angelina Grimké's prediction, in an 1863 address to the soldiers "of Our Second Revolution" on behalf of one thousand of their loyal northern sisters, that "the army of the North will thus become the angel of deliverance, rescuing the nation from the shifting sands of compromise and refounding it upon the rock of justice." The crucial question, as Grimké well knew, was whether the white soldiers she was urging to reenlist could be convinced that racial prejudice was an offspring of slavery and that the South was waging "a war upon the working-classes, whether white or black; a war against *Man*, the world over." At a time when the North was resorting to the draft and when state and local governments were forced to pay increasingly high bounties to secure enlistments, abolitionists like Grimké warned that "*all* who contend for the rights of labor, for free speech, free schools, free suffrage, and a free government, securing to *all* life, liberty, and the pursuit of happiness, are driven to do battle in defense of these or to fall with them, victims of the same violence that for two centuries has held the black man a prisoner of war."[71]

Massachusetts abolitionists, including William Lloyd Garrison, supported labor's demand for an eight-hour day on the same grounds that they opposed the exploitation of slaves. By 1865 Massachusetts workingmen and middle-class reformers had united in a common front, and some labor reformers endorsed the philosophy Angelina Grimké had expressed. The 1866 Baltimore Program of the National Labor Union affirmed "that the interests of labor are one; that their should be no distinction of race or nationality." But though the mass of northern workers were loyal to the Union cause, they shared the pervasive fears and prejudices of whites toward blacks. Moreover, as labor reformers attacked the wage system as a species of slavery, they moved beyond the middle-class radicals' ideals of nationalism, social harmony, and equal rights for all citizens. At the moment when radical Republicans seemed to have secured universal civil and political equality, they discovered to their dismay that various groups of citizens were invoking radical principles in the pursuit of class, racial, and ethnic interests. Once regenerated by the catharsis of war, the nation appeared to lapse again into selfish materialism. Faced with an upthrust of agitation from the working class, Republican leaders began retreating from their vision of a unified and egalitarian social order.[72]

Without becoming engaged in the historiographical debate over the successes and failures of Reconstruction, we should draw attention to a central paradox that illuminates changing concepts of progress. Clearly, wartime emancipation fostered the impression of *kairos*, a new dispensation resulting from a total break from the constraints and processes of the past. The millennial visions were not wholly illusory. A nation steeped in Negrophobia committed itself to the civil and political equality of its most despised and "unwanted" population. Southern slaves looked in awe upon black liberators in Union army uniforms. Although black reactions to freedom varied widely, thousands of Charleston blacks joined in a Jubilee parade that presented a mock slave auction as well as a black-draped coffin with the inscription "Slavery Is Dead," followed by mourners dressed in black. Hundreds of missionaries, philanthropists, and educators moved into the South, beginning a prolonged campaign to aid, educate, and uplift the more than four million freedmen. When southern provisional legislatures enacted Black Codes designed to keep blacks in a state of quasi-servitude, radical and moderate Republicans united to block President Johnson's attempt to reconstruct the Union without ensuring federal protection of the freedmen's rights. After adopting the Civil Rights Act of 1866 and the Fourteenth Amendment, Congress made Negro suffrage a condition for the readmission of most of the former Confederate states. Such revolutionary moves would have been ineffective without black initiative and leadership in resisting the Black Codes, assembling southern conventions, and drafting liberal constitutions. In no other white-controlled society, including that of the northern states themselves, did former slaves win full legal and political equality and sit in legislative halls. From 1867 to 1876 more than half the state and federal officeholders elected in South Carolina, the seedbed of the former Confederacy, were black. No less revolutionary than blacks' being sent to the United States Congress and Senate was the initiative of the ex-slaves of Port Royal who bought town houses at Beaufort and who collectively purchased and managed a Sea Island plantation. From the perspective of 1860 or any preceding year, these were all inconceivable events, a revolutionary transformation that plunged far beyond the will of the majority.[73]

But as in the British Caribbean, severe limits were imposed on the economic freedom of former slaves. The priorities became clear in the Union's first free-labor experiment, on the Sea Islands of South Carolina, a strategic base that an expeditionary force had captured in November 1861. This venture was intended from the outset to supply the Treasury Department with revenue, and northern factories with high-quality cotton. In Republican ideology there was no conflict whatever between restoring the productivity of this rich cotton-producing region and sending a corps of abolitionist missionaries and teachers to prepare the "contraband" slaves for the responsibilities of eventual freedom. Indeed, in the eyes of such entrepreneur-philanthropists as Edward Philbrick, the success of the experiment depended on proving to northern investors that free black labor could be profitable. After the slaves had been freed by Lincoln's emancipation proclamation, the abolitionist and teacher William Channing Gannett warned that it would be *"Most unwise and injurious"* to give them free lands: "Let all the laws of labor, wages, competition, etc., come into play,—and the sooner will habits of responsibility, industry, self-dependence, and manliness be developed." Accordingly, the first message the evangels preached to their new wards, on whom they relied for the technical knowledge of how to produce a cotton crop, was the dignity and godliness of work. One black patriarch complained that "the Yankees preached nothing but cotton, cotton!" Ironically, these reformers found themselves approximating the role of slaveholders dedicated to labor discipline and one-crop agriculture.[74]

In the aftermath of a war that burdened the nation with an undreamed-of public debt, the agricultural economy of the South was far more vital to the United States than the sugar colonies had ever been to Britain. Cotton exports were essential for earning credits abroad and restoring the nation's fiscal stability. From this perspective, the rich lands of the South would be worthless without a complaint and reliable labor force. It is true that such radicals as Thaddeus Stevens and Charles Sumner insisted on land grants for freedmen and that Congress debated various proposals for sweeping agrarian reform. But hostility toward the defeated rebel oligarchy was not sufficient to overcome constitutional and ideological scruples respecting private property. Freedmen's Bureau agents tried to explain to black workers that the forthcoming constitutional conventions would have no power to confiscate land or interfere with private property, a position also endorsed by leaders of the black convention movement who generally restricted their demands to full equality before the law. The Freedmen's Bureau, which prevented mass starvation and helped lay the foundations for black education in the South, also strove to convince freedmen that they could not be supported in idleness and would have to move from congested towns to regions short of labor, where they should sign one-year labor contracts. Though blacks resisted such contracts and understandably felt betrayed when evicted from abandoned lands on which they had been officially encouraged to settle and farm, their leaders repeatedly pointed to the dangers of white paternalism, urging that the freedmen be allowed to work out their own destiny free from interference. Unfortunately, the weakness of federal protection meant that most ex-slaves would be dependent either on southern whites or on northern entrepreneurs who monopolized the land.[75]

With the benefit of hindsight, the continuities of plantation agriculture from slavery to tenant farming look less surprising than the legal and constitutional innovations of Radical Reconstruction. It was fairly predictable that southern landowners, when dealing with black workers, would demand in initial contracts the same "true and faithful service as they had done when they were slaves." In return for rations, clothing, medical care, and a portion of the crop, southern planters expected blacks to accept the same social relations—the surveillance, restrictions on movement, and control over leisure-time behavior—that had characterized slavery. Stripped of legal claims to land, food, tools, and assistance in illness or old age, most freedmen had little with which to bargain except the knowledge that their labor was essential for the survival of the usually indebted landowners. As in the British West Indies, blacks exercised some degree of choice by refusing to sign contracts that replicated bondage, by staging strikes and slowdowns, by struggling to maintain family integrity, and by withdrawing women from heavy field labor. The impossibility of restoring the punitive system of large-scale gang labor contributed to a sharp decline in labor productivity, profits, and regional per capita income. From 1860 to 1880 real per capita income nearly doubled in the North; in the South, despite fifteen years of recovery from wartime devastation, real per capita income was still 15 percent below the 1860 level. This widening gap in economic performance reinforced the image of a stagnating society impervious to the currents of progress. Although the blacks had freed themselves from the brutalizing coercions of slave labor, they became locked, along with the mass of small white farmers, into an exploitive system of tenancy, crop liens, and declining agricultural self-sufficiency.[76]

What is so anomalous about this mixture of continuity and radical change is the criteria by which the ex-slaves were judged. The defeat of the Antichrist raised expectations of a national regeneration, not least among the blacks themselves. Radicals countered the virulent racism of old-line Democrats by arguing that the freedmen, once liberated from the corruptions of slavery, would in time become diligent, trustworthy workers, as intent on self-improvement as any whites. Many radicals agreed with Gilbert Haven that "the complete removal of this curse from our land" depended on a bold stand supporting the divine doctrine of "the perfect unity of the human race." Yet such friends of the blacks were always put in the defensive position of having to deny the economic benefits and emphasize the debilitating effects of bondage. The published letters and reports describing the Port Royal experiment minimized the culture shock and disappointments the evangels experienced. They exaggerated the cheerful industriousness of the blacks in the field, the eagerness of freedmen for Christian education, their noble impulses, elevated intellect, and progress in manners and morals. These inflated expectations merged with the widespread assumption that blacks could ultimately prove their worthiness for freedom only by approximating their economic performance as slaves. For most white Americans the success of emancipation would be judged not by the freedmen's demands for self-determination but by their response to the incentives of an extremely restricted market and by their willingness to open their minds and souls to the white Protestant ethic. Given these assumptions, any "failure" of the blacks to progress could be ascribed only to inherent racial limitations.[77]

In some ways, racial ideology had a life of its own. There were no direct ties, for example, between the politics of emancipation and the racial theories that began to preoccupy the international scientific community by the mid-nineteenth century. Britain, which could justly pride itself on an absence of discrimination against individual blacks, was swept with degrading stereotypes of colored peoples which ranged from the mania for comic black-faced minstrelsy to sober scientific treatises. Disillusion over the consequences of West Indian emancipation mixed with a broader reaction against sentimental reformers and "Nigger Philanthropy." This heightened racial consciousness appealed to workingmen who felt they suffered far worse hardships than the supposedly coddled blacks of the New World, and also to the upper classes who feared that sympathy for downtrodden slaves had already been extended dangerously close to their own proletariat. For reasons that have not yet been fully explained, most of the Western world began accepting racist theories that had earlier lacked the sanction of science and that had generally been limited to the United States. It was largely in vain that black writers and white abolitionists appealed to the accomplishments of ancient "black" Egyptians and modern black Americans or argued that European slave traders were responsible for the centuries of African "barbarism." Popular prejudices, which had once shocked foreign travelers to the United States, became rationalized as the official wisdom of the West. As Alfred Russel Wallace summed up the most distinguished and moderate scientific opinion, "no one had denied—that the negro is very inferior in intellectual capacity to the European. The only question to be determined was, how far that inferiority extends."[78]

This verdict was accepted by most Republican leaders who for a variety of motives demanded universal Negro suffrage and equal civil rights. As in England, few voices challenged the prevailing dogma that blacks as a race were incapable of attaining the progress that whites, especially Anglo-Saxon whites, could achieve. Some apologists spoke of the blacks' compensatory virtues—their spirituality, kindliness, lightheartedness, and "effeminate" submissiveness and patience, traits much needed to balance what the American Freedmen's Inquiry Commission described as "a certain hardness, a stubborn will, only moderate geniality, a lack of habitual cheerfulness" in the progressive Anglo-Saxon race. The romantic Uncle Tom image became fused with the ancient theory, now sanctioned by Louis Agassiz and other eminent scientists, that mulattoes were largely infertile and would become, without further white admixture, a perishing race. Needless to say, only a few extreme radicals like the Methodist bishop Gilbert Haven advocated further white admixture. And since pure-blooded Africans could supposedly survive only in a semitropical climate, racial ideology fulfilled the collective northern wish for distance and removal. The abrasive qualities of northern enterprise would have to be softened indirectly by a new genre of southern literature.[79]

Relieved that freed slaves had not swarmed into the labor-scarce Midwest, most Republican spokesmen tended to agree with Ignatius Donnelly, a young radical congressman from Minnesota, who in 1865–66 argued that blacks in the South deserved the chance of achieving "the fullest development of which they are capable but that if, after a fair trial, the black "proves himself an unworthy savage and brutal wretch, condemn him, but not till then."[80] For many Britons the fair trial ended in a cataclysm of violence at Morant Bay, Jamaica. In October 1865 a typical dispute over blacks squatting on uncultivated land led to a minor insurrection and to the shooting or execution of 439 alleged rebels, an act of savage reprisal that far exceeded the slaughter of blacks in Memphis and New Orleans the following year. Gov. Edward John Eyre's bloody repression of the Jamaican uprising provoked a stormy controversy that gave vent to the high tensions of contemporary British politics and class relations. Although the controversy divided the intelligentsia and failed to diminish Britain's official antislavery commitment, the liberal *Examiner* probably expressed the popular consensus when it reversed its initial judgment and concluded that "the negroes of our West Indies, free for a generation, . . . are still, despite of generous hopes and vaticinations to the contrary, barbarians of Africa who have but changed their sky." The crisis at Morant Bay contributed to the growing Anglo-American conviction that freed slaves and their descendants, like permanent children, must be carefully governed by a superior race.[81]

White Southerners, like their earlier West Indian counterparts, had the bitter satisfaction of watching the emancipationist world discover the "truths" they had once preached to unreceptive ears. What they themselves had failed to see was that slavery itself was not indispensable for white supremacy, that nominal emancipation could prepare the way for a kind of colonialism based on a sharp distinction between legal and economic freedom. "Reconciliation" would be founded on a primal recognition that both North and South had been right—that Southerners, while fighting valiantly for a retrogressive cause, had understood the realities of race relations. In the national mythology that endured beyond the Second World War, the Civil War remained America's noblest moment of heroism, sacrifice, and new birth. Reconstruction, interpreted as a misguided departure from the principles that had ensured national progress, represented America's greatest disgrace.

3. A CENTURY OF PROGRESS

The spring and summer of 1933 marked the centennial of the British emancipation act and the death of the pioneer emancipator William Wilberforce. In Britain an outpouring of popular books, articles, and radio broadcasts reviewed the historical struggle against black slavery as a means of focusing attention on the task of the immediate future—the liberation of the estimated five million slaves who still suffered in large parts of Africa, the Mideast, and Asia. Historical commemorations repeatedly stressed that slavery was not yet a thing of the past and that a glorious "century of progress"—the title also chosen for the 1933 Chicago World's Fair—should inspire the world to fulfill the dreams of the first abolitionists.[82]

By 1933 a decade of British pressure had finally persuaded the assembly of the League of Nations to establish an advisory committee of experts to help implement the League's convention of 1926, which had bound its signatories to bring about "progressively and as soon as possible the complete abolition of Slavery in all its forms." Sir John Harris, Viscount Cecil, Lady Kathleen Simon, Lord Noel-Buxton, and other abolitionist leaders were heartened by the momentum gained since the mid-1920s. In a hazardous military expedition Sir Harcourt Butler had reportedly freed some 8,000 slaves in Burma. Invoking the British model of 1833, the ruler of Nepal had liberated 57,000 bondsmen. And the Colonial Office, responding to public outrage over the discovery that slavery still persisted in the protectorate of Sierra Leone, had freed

215,000 blacks in Britain's oldest African colony. Attention now focused on the two most recalcitrant and independent parts of Africa, Liberia and Ethiopia, the only countries governed by black Africans. The task ahead, Harris warned, was in some ways more formidable than that which Wilberforce had faced. Where slavery remained in the world, it took highly diverse forms and was often a deeply entrenched custom beyond the reach of any single government. Yet antislavery was now an international cause linked with the international mechanism for preserving world peace. When serving as foreign secretary and delegate to the League's council and assembly, Sir Austen Chamberlain said that the British government doubted whether any civilized country would wish to challenge the general consensus that slavery could be regarded "in a peculiar degree" as one of the "crimes against the human race." For Harris and the other neo-abolitionists the key to securing the total abolition of slavery throughout the world lay in arousing an "international conscience, vocal in every country attached to the League of Nations." But 1933 was an inauspicious year for inaugurating a second age of progress. Harris could not recognize that the rise of Hitler and the deepening global depression already presaged a war that would destroy his paternalistic vision of "the great principle of Trusteeship" leading to the final emancipation of "child races, backward races, native races from systems either of slavery or of oppression under which they the weaker races have been in the past and are still to-day exploited for selfish ends."[83]

From the perspective of the centennial year, the struggle against slavery appeared to have been a single, continuous crusade extending from Granville Sharp's successful campaign to outlaw slavery in England to recent British efforts to help Emperor Haile Selassie find ways to suppress the institution in Ethiopia. According to the standard historical accounts, the initiative of Wilberforce, Clarkson, and Buxton had led irresistibly to the French and Danish emancipation laws of 1848; to the freeing of four million blacks in the American Civil War; to the abolition of slavery in Cuba in 1886 and in Brazil in 1888; and to the endeavors of David Livingstone, Sir John Kirk, Sir Bartle Frere, and other philanthropist-adventurers who had undermined the slave trade at its source, in darkest Africa. Both Harris and Sir Reginald Coupland, Beit Professor of Colonial History at Oxford, recognized that enslavement in African and Asian societies differed in many respects from enslavement to white planters in New World or Indian Ocean colonies. Yet their conception of a continuous antislavery movement sustained by British Quakers and such prominent families as the Buxtons suggested that the target was essentially the same. As William Pitt had prophesied in 1792, in a speech Coupland quoted with obvious national pride, Britain's renunciation of the slave trade would become truly meaningful only when it led to the substitution of legitimate commerce and to the civilization of Africa's most benighted and slave-infested regions.[84]

Although Harris and Coupland saw a direct link between the progress of emancipation and Britain's imperial expansion, we will not involve ourselves in the stormy debate over the nature and causes of imperialism. The crucial point is that antislavery ideology held that the gradual eradication of coerced labor was synonymous with the material and moral progress of humanity as a whole and was the noblest mission and achievement of the nineteenth century. This transcendent belief stirred abolitionists in the United States during the antebellum and Civil War periods, in France during the 1840s, in Cuba during the Ten Years' War (1868–78), and in Brazil during the 1880s. In every country, however, it was necessary to overcome the deeply rooted fear that antislavery was a cloak for British national interests. Although Britain tried from 1788 and especially from 1814 onward to internationalize the slave-trade issue, no other government rivaled its initiative or sustained commitment to antislavery policies. It now appears that these policies often ran counter to Britain's economic, political, and strategic interests by raising the cost of tropical produce, constricting markets for investment and manufactures, alienating clients or potential allies, and encouraging expensive and unwanted intervention in regions that offered little prospect of profit. In reality, "legitimate commerce" flourished alongside the slave trade; Britain's industrial and commercial expansion, reinforced by free trade, stimulated the slave-trading systems of Cuba, Brazil, and East Africa that British officials were committed to suppress.[85] Yet antislavery policies also sanctioned and extended British influence. In an era of intensified European rivalry and expansion, antislavery goals inevitably became intertwined with the control of labor supplies and with various commercial and diplomatic strategies. From the Congress of Vienna to the League of Nations, British statesmen invoked the moral expectations of the British public as a transcendent standard that the rest of the world was obliged to respect. Other peoples, particularly the French, may have been irritated by this self-image of high-minded decency, but they knew it was a potent weapon. It raised the momentous issue of whether a nation-state can ever be the altruistic agent of progress and civilization.

From the time of France's humiliating defeats in 1814 and 1815, the French viewed the suppression of the slave trade as one of the obsessive quirks of their victorious rival, a nation that combined self-righteous piety with Machiavellian schemes to police the seas and cripple the production of Spanish, Dutch, Portuguese, and French colonies. Although antislavery had acquired a supranational character during the late Enlightenment and the early years of the French Revolution, the traumatic loss of Saint Domingue helped to popularize the white colonists' claims that the *Amis des noirs* had been the agents of a British plot to destroy the French tropical empire. Because Britain could rely on the inexhaustible human and natural resources of India, so the argument went, it could afford to abandon the African slave trade and pose as the champion of global philanthropy in order to keep foreign colonies from acquiring the continuous supply of manpower essential for agricultural productivity. Britain's diplomatic pressure to secure from each maritime nation the right of search was also interpreted as a means of harassing the commerce of competitors and of perpetuating Britannia's wartime rule of the seas.[86]

But if Restoration France tended to associate abolitionism with British guile and earlier French fanaticism, public opinion and British naval hegemony precluded any official sanction of the African slave trade—in 1802 Napoleon had reinstituted both colonial slavery and the slave trade, but in 1815, during the Hundred Days, he had outlawed the slave trade in an effort to win British favor. France warded off Britain's insistence on the right of search by committing her own naval squadron to the supposedly common cause of slave-trade suppression. From 1818 onward, the French sought to play the British game and to reassert their naval power under a humanitarian banner. The cruisers, while protecting the growing French commerce with Africa, actually captured an increasing number of slavers but failed in the 1820s to curb the illegal French slave trade. French sailors, attuned to the traditional interests of the colonies and port towns, hardly had the zeal of British abolitionists. Nor were their activities closely watched by a government sensitive to the expectations of an aroused and evangelical public.[87]

Nevertheless, by the revolution of 1830, antislavery principles suffused the emerging ideology of progress. The works of French political economists, supplemented by translations of Adam Smith and a growing body of humanitarian literature, persuaded a rising group of leaders not only that slave labor was morally retrogressive, inefficient, unproductive, and dangerous but also that the system exacted intolerable costs from French taxpayers and consumers. Such views were congenial to many of the Orleanist officials who came to power with the July Monarchy and who looked to Britain for moral and diplomatic support. Since 1822 a moderate brand of antislavery had been sustained by the *Société de la morale chrétienne,* an Anglophile reform society composed of a disproportionate number of eminent Protestants such as the duc de Broglie, who became minister of foreign affairs and president of the council in the Orleanist regime. In 1831 and 1833 the French government made a serious commitment to suppress the slave trade, concluding treaties with Britain that embodied a limited right of search. Meanwhile, the British emancipation act posed a direct threat to the French colonies, particularly to those like Martinique and Guadeloupe that lay close to neighboring "free soil." Once again French officials were forced to look across the Channel for innovative leadership. On the other hand, the British experiment, which French leaders generally interpreted as hasty and ill-prepared, offered a social laboratory for careful observation and study. Despite public apathy, the French government watched with the keenest interest the consequences of British emancipation and apprenticeship.[88]

The voluminous reports on the British colonies confirmed the cautious outlook of the Orleanist government. The French observers recognized the diverse results of emancipation and admitted that it had generally improved the physical and moral condition of the blacks and had failed to provoke the predicted riots and disorder. But they concluded that the experiment, conducted under the most favorable circumstances, had proved to be an economic disaster. Plantation owners had been deprived of an adequate supply of reliable labor, and the British government had been forced to turn to contract labor from Africa and India, a brutal expedient that exposed the hypocrisy of official abolitionist pretensions. When French slavery was considered by itself, Captain Layrle pointed out, apart from the fate of the colonies, ports, commerce, and sea power, there could be no question that the institution was immoral and unjust. It might also be costly and retrogressive, but its abrupt termination could be more costly still. Determined not to repeat Britain's mistakes, the July Monarchy contented itself with commissions, reports, and postponement. Virtually everyone agreed that the years of slavery were numbered, but as late as 1847 there was no prospect of hastening the institution's demise.[89]

Two developments complicated this general picture of institutionalized delay. Beginning in 1840, conflict with England over Egypt and the Mideast revived the Anglophobia and fantasies of conspiratorial philanthropy that had characterized the Restoration period. Outraged by the British seizure of a French ship transporting contract labor, or *engagés libres,* from Senegal, and by the reported mistreatment of the captain of a detained French merchant vessel, the press and public helped to prevent the government from ratifying an 1841 multipower treaty that extended Britain's right of search. While strengthening their own anti-slave-trade squadron, the French then suspended their earlier agreements with Britain regarding the right of search. At the same time, radical republicans took up the emancipation cause as part of their general demands for a total restructuring of French society. Aroused by Victor Schoelcher and other leaders of the left, a broad-based coalition including Protestants and liberal Catholics, women and urban workers, called for the immediate emancipation of slaves.[90]

French slaves were not freed in conformity with a British model. Emancipation came by a decree of the provisional republican government in 1848. It came in a reassuringly French way, at the hands of the left, led by Schoelcher, an atheist untainted by British evangelicalism, echoing the events of the Revolution of 1789, and in response to both domestic and colonial turmoil. But this temporary merger of domestic and colonial reform also meant that there was nothing comparable to the continuing British public concern with the fate of oppressed alien peoples. Britain's resort to African and Asian contract labor evoked intense opposition from British abolitionists, who continued to demand strict regulations and the shortest possible indentures. The French government was much freer to develop a massive program of "ransoming" and liberating African slaves to meet the labor needs occasioned by colonial emancipation. For a time, Napoleon III's officials were able to dismiss British protests that this "free emigration" policy encouraged slaving raids in Africa and provided a thin veneer for a revived Middle Passage, especially to the French colonies in the Indian Ocean.[91]

Moreover, as Serge Daget has observed, "the germ of [French] imperialist thought developed in the heart of the abolitionist ethic." The Institut d'Afrique, for example, was a cosmopolitan organization that called for Anglo-French cooperation, in an epoch of humanitarian progress, to wipe out the last traces of slave trading in Africa. For the institut the antislavery cause was inseparable from promoting European colonization, uprooting barbarism and ignorance, and introducing to the darkest corners of Africa the light of Christian civilization. Philanthropists, the institut was confident, would hail the French conquest of Algeria as part of civilization's conquest of barbarism. Pointing with pride to their own revolutionary tradition—in response to the question whether emancipation was "une idée anglaise"—the French saw themselves as the liberators and civilizers of Africa. Yet emancipation increasingly played a secondary role to the institut's schemes for promoting European colonization. As they moved outward from Algeria and Senegal, the French understood that their national interests often required cooperation with slave-trading states and that their long-range mission could be subverted by sentimental zeal.[92]

The British had always represented the abolition of slavery and especially the suppression of the slave trade as objectives of universal value to humanity, transcending the interests of any religion, class, or nation. This view received some support from the French and Danish emancipations of 1848, the businesslike concurrence of the Dutch in 1863, the abolition of Russian serfdom in 1861, and the dramatic outcome of the American Civil War. Despite repressive restrictions and censorship under the Second Empire, an international antislavery conference convened in Paris in 1867, attended by Garrison, John Gorham Palfrey, and other Americans as well as by a galaxy of British reformers. With a truly global outlook, such publications as the *Annales de l'Institut d'Afrique* and the *Anti-Slavery Reporter* dutifully applauded every report of progress toward the eradication of bondage and the uplifting of backward peoples. Unfortunately, the liberation of plantation slaves led to acute labor problems, to declining productivity, and to a growing disillusionment over the capacity of blacks for civilization. Outside Britain, popular abolitionism seldom survived the enthusiastic moment of emancipation. Even in Britain the antislavery tradition was maintained less by widespread public interest than by the continuing collaboration between a small but knowledgeable pressure group and public officials and exalted patrons, including the prince consort and Prince of Wales. Among colonial nations Britain led the way in assimilating antislavery to an imperial self-image, linking humanitarianism in the most subtle ways to strategic and commercial interests. All of these factors complicated the choices open to Spain and Brazil, the nations that governed slavery's last two bastions in the New World.

We have already seen how Britain's anti-slave-trade policies led in the 1840s to what Spain, Cuba, and Brazil perceived as flagrant violations of national sovereignty. In Havana an abolitionist consul, David Turnbull, threatened to encourage Cuban independence as a means of coercing antislavery concessions from Spain; when Brazil refused to continue a slave-trade treaty beyond 1845, Lord Aberdeen secured a law from Parliament unilaterally empowering the British navy to seize suspected Brazilian ships and bring them before British vice-admiralty courts for trial. Britain's persistent attempts to suppress the Cuban slave trade were matched only by Cuba's persistent evasion of treaty commitments. Starting in the latter years of the Napoleonic wars, Spain played a difficult diplomatic game of meeting Britain's minimal but escalating demands while maintaining the trust of Cuban merchants and planters whose economic world depended on a continuing labor supply from Africa. The slave system provided a crucial bond between Spain and loyalist Cuba; according to one Spanish minister, the presence of slaves in Cuba was worth an army of one hundred thousand men for maintaining colonial loyalty to Spain. For Spaniards and Cubans alike, resistance to foreign reformers became an antidote to the kind of revolutionary forces that had destroyed most of Spain's American empire. The slave-trade treaties of 1817 and 1835 were thus interpreted as humiliating, if necessary, concessions to an ally on which the Spanish crown unfortunately relied. The Cuban plantation system was distinguished not only by its increasing productivity and wealth but also by its officially sanctioned illegality. A fast fleet of slavers, often flying the United States flag on outbound voyages to Africa, ensured the replacement of an otherwise rapidly depleting labor force. As late as 1875 *bozales,* or African-born slaves, constituted 42 percent of the workers on the sugar estates in one district of Santa Clara Province; on some estates the proportion rose to as high as 66 percent, over 70 percent of whom were male. To disguise such facts, Cubans became adept at manipulating census data and obscuring the fate of *emancipados*—the Africans captured by British cruisers and entrusted to the Cuban government by the court of mixed commission. Despite British militancy and more conscientious efforts by the Spanish government in the 1850s, the slave trade flourished well into the 1860s, when the Anglo-American suppression treaty coincided with a decisive shift in public policy in both Cuba and Spain.[93]

Although the trends of Cuban demography indicated that slavery could not survive indefinitely without a renewing supply of Africans, the large importations of the late 1850s and early 1860s provided a labor base for many decades to come. In 1862 there were still over 368,000 slaves in Cuba, and there was nothing inevitable about the timing or manner in which the institution would disappear. Spanish and Cuban officials were pledged to preserve the plantation economy, which in 1868 supplied over 40 percent of the cane sugar in the world market. And that economy depended at harvest time on intense, concentrated labor that could be extracted only by some form of coercion. We have just begun to appreciate the resiliency and flexibility of the Cuban slave system. In the western provinces, where large plantations were integrated with mechanized and steam-powered mills for the manufacture of sugar, slave labor seemed to be fully compatible with the most sophisticated technology. It is true that the declining supply of Africans forced planters to rely increasingly on Chinese coolies, who as debt peons were treated almost like slaves. Yet slavery prospered where it coexisted with the labor of indentured coolies, convicts, and task-paid or free wage workers. The effects on slavery of technology and free labor are still a matter of debate, but Cuban slavery was most entrenched and profitable precisely where the forces of modernization were most evident.[94]

Although Cuban and Spanish writers were increasingly sensitive to the censure of world opinion and to accusations of economic and moral backwardness, they repeatedly protested that Cuban slavery had long been softened by Hispanic and Catholic traditions of justice and humanity and was in no way comparable to the exploitive systems of the British and North Americans. Justo Zaragoza, a liberal-minded historian, characteristically attacked the peculiar British mixture of greed and puritanism that had led to the extremes of brutal colonial slavery and abolitionist manifestos. British hypocrisy accounted for the disastrous results of emancipation, which had uprooted an idle class of blacks while leaving the land under control of white proprietors. Zaragoza and others also pointed to the anarchy of American Reconstruction and to the imperialist motives that had led the North to free southern slaves without preparation or responsible planning. If Britain, France, and the United States were the world's most "progressive" nations, their acts of emancipation showed what Spain must at all costs avoid. The crucial question, complicated by growing Cuban resentment of Spanish political and economic domination, was whether the transition from slavery to freedom could be protracted in a way that would avoid social disruption and allow blacks to be gradually replaced by white immigrant labor.[95]

It is difficult to exaggerate the profound conservatism of the nineteenth-century Hispanic world. Long traumatized by the effects of the French Revolution and the loss of an empire, officials in both Spain and Cuba were obsessed by the fear of abolitionist subversion. Only in 1811 and 1845 did the Spanish Cortes break the understood taboo against debating the issue of colonial slavery; in Cuba, where censors tried to suppress news of the French revolution of 1848 and the emancipation decree, discussion of abolition was more dangerous than in antebellum Mississippi. It was impossible, however, to blunt the impact of the American Civil War and the violent destruction of the slaveholding South. In the fields slaves reportedly sang:

> Advance, Lincoln, advance.
> You are our hope.

Although the Cuban government tightened restrictions and even banned racial intermarriage, the northern victory encouraged liberals in Cuba and especially in Puerto Rico who for decades had cautiously advocated free trade, free labor, white immigration, and local autonomy.[96]

Except in Puerto Rico, where the proportion of slaves was much smaller than in Cuba and where after 1850 the sugar economy was forced to make greater use of free labor, few of these reformers were avowed abolitionists. José Antonio Saco, the exiled Cuban patriot and historian of slavery from ancient to modern times, disclaimed the label even in 1868, at the moment of Spain's "Glorious Revolution," although he cited his long record of favoring an extremely gradual emancipation attuned to the long-range interests of slaves, their owners, and the state. Saco had preceded more radical critics in arguing that slavery impeded white immigration, debased the dignity of labor, retarded public improvements, and prolonged Spain's despotic colonial rule. On the other hand, he looked upon slaves as semisavages who would invade Cuba's cities if freed prematurely and without adequate safeguards. Late in 1864 Julio Vizcarrondo and other Puerto Ricans launched a genuine abolitionist movement in Spain. Most of these reformers were anticlerical and antimonarchal republicans whose influence was severely limited before the revolution of 1868. The rash of emancipation plans stimulated by the American Union victory—especially those proposed at a reform convention assembled in 1866 by the Spanish government—aimed at avoiding the anticipated calamities of immediate freedom. Whether they favored a lottery scheme or liberating newborn children after a certain date, most reformers agreed with Don Francisco Montaos y Robillard that freedom should come gradually, "without disturbing the habits of subordination and respect instilled in the slaves . . . nor introducing great disturbances in the labor system. " Yet despite the desire to "calm the execration and hate of the abolitionist centers of Europe," the Spanish convention failed to accept even the most cautious proposals. Indeed, the preamble to Spain's 1866 anti-slave-trade law stated that "slavery has to exist in the islands of Cuba and Puerto Rico as a pre-existing fact."[97]

The facts were decisively altered in 1868 by the liberal revolution in Spain and especially by a rebellion in eastern Cuba which became known as the Ten Years' War against Spanish rule. As in Haiti, the Spanish-American republics, and the southern American states, military needs helped to undermine the institution of black slavery. With an eye to world opinion and United States recognition, the Cuban insurgents, led by small planters, decreed a qualified emancipation of slaves under their control. The fighting opened the way for black military initiative as well as for mass desertions from eastern estates. To counter the rebels' ideological appeal, Spanish authorities proclaimed freedom to all the slaves of rebels and to others who loyally served the cause of Spain. Yet, in trying to match the rebels' appeal to blacks, the Spanish faced a serious dilemma. Some kind of commitment to emancipation would be in keeping with the principles of the Spanish revolution and might forestall intervention by the United States, where the antislavery fervor of

Radical Reconstruction fed new imperialistic ambitions associated with popular sympathy for the Cuban insurgents. On the other hand, any measures threatening the prosperous sugar planters of western Cuba, who were far removed from the insurrection, could provoke an even more dangerous kind of resistance. In 1870 the Cortes settled for a cautious preparatory law, proposed by Segismundo Moret, a vice-president of the Spanish Abolitionist Society, which freed all slaves at sixty and all children born since 18 September 1868, the date of the Glorious Revolution. These freeborn *patrocinados* were to work without pay until the age of eighteen and at half-wages until the age of twenty-two, which really meant that they would largely pay the compensation for their own emancipation. The law portrayed the arrangement in terms of tutelage by a paternalistic *patrón*, ensuring that freeborn blacks would "assimilate themselves to the culture and civilization of Spain," not to that of Afro-Cuba. On slavery itself, including corporal punishment, the Moret law had no effect. Moret reminded the more radical abolitionists that "the great Lincoln did not want to abolish slavery until 1900"; his law looked forward to an act of gradual and indemnified emancipation once the insurrection had been suppressed. Meanwhile, western planters received some comfort from the fact that in Cuba publication of the Moret law was delayed for two years and that enforcement lay in slaveholder hands.[98]

Britain, concerned over American expansionism and wishing to ensure continued Spanish control over Cuba, muted abolitionist appeals for immediate emancipation. By 1873, however, Spain was unable to ignore mounting pressure from the Grant administration as well as from abolitionist leaders in the short-lived Spanish Republic who saw a common cause with the Republican victors of the American Civil War. Puerto Rican reformers were eager to move beyond the Moret law, and in 1873 the Spanish Republic freed Puerto Rican slaves with compensation for their owners. Despite this commitment to principle, Spanish officials insisted on delaying further action in Cuba until hostilities had ceased, a policy aided by the monarchic restoration and by lessening antislavery zeal in the United States. By 1879, when peace had been restored and Cuban sugar production had reached its peak of the decade, a Spanish subcommission recommended a "scientific" approach that could avoid the mistakes of Britain, France, and the United States and follow the more "successful" path of Brazil, which in 1871 had enacted a complicated law freeing newborn children, protecting the interests of masters, and providing for the slow but continuous evolution from slave to free labor. "Modern science counsels this solution," the Spanish commissioners concluded, "by demonstrating that there is no solid progress . . .

unless it is through evolutions." To this doctrine the governor of Cuba added the common fear that slaves set free without some form of *patronato* "would run off to the woods and live like savages." Yet the 1880 Spanish law actually went a good bit further than the Brazilian law of free birth. It abolished slavery outright, without indemnity, and substituted an eight-year *patronato,* during which the *patrocinados,* or apprentices, would be subject to slavelike discipline and working conditions. Abolitionists in Spain as well as England attacked the *patronato* as slavery by another name. But though the experiment retained the most objectionable features of slavery, it also failed to ensure the complaint labor force planters demanded. In 1877 China had halted the further emigration of contract laborers, depriving Cuban planters of an important alternative to coerced black workers. In 1883 Spain restricted the use of corporal punishment. Most important, black slaves and *patrocinados* increasingly took advantage of reform provisions and unsettled conditions, resisting planter authority, seeking legal redress, and pooling their resources to purchase freedom. When Spain finally ended the *patronato* by royal decree, in 1886, two years before its scheduled expiration date, the system had already disintegrated. Black workers were now free but were hardly less dependent on the owners of land or less vulnerable to a devastating depression in world sugar prices that impoverished free Jamaica as well as the slave economy of northeastern Brazil.[99]

Despite the Ten Years' War and the political turmoil in Spain, there was a remarkable continuity in the Cuban plantation system as planters struggled to preserve the social relationships needed to produce cheap sugar for the North American and European markets. There were no abrupt changes until the economic and political dislocations associated with emancipation set in motion forces that severed Spain's ties with her last American colonies. Hispanic liberals, sensitive to the world's progressive opinion and to the "backwardness" of their own societies, tried valiantly to devise an evolutionary program that would prevent foreign intervention, preserve productivity, and avoid the mistakes of other slaveholding nations. Identifying themselves with international abolitionism, they made heroes of Wilberforce, Garrison, and Lincoln while uneasily merging the legend of humanitarian Catholic precedents with anticlerical rationalism. Yet emancipation, when it came, was less the outcome of abolitionist agitation than of antipeninsular Creole nationalism, which gave blacks themselves the chance to subvert the system. Hispanic emancipation brought no sense of an apocalypse, of collective rebirth, or of the self-purgation of deep national guilt.

Nevertheless, early in 1887 the British and Foreign Anti-Slavery Society had good reason to congratulate the handful of surviving British abolitionists who had struggled against slavery in the British colonies and who had helped to create "that strong public opinion, before which the Cuban Slave-holder is now compelled to yield up his claim for the right to hold property in his fellow man." The society trusted "that not a few amongst the younger members of the Committee may live, in like manner, to witness the termination of Slavery, not only in Brazil, but also in the blood-stained districts of Central Africa, though at present the prospect is not very hopeful." The society's *Anti-Slavery Reporter* was not particularly sanguine even about Brazil, although there the long-awaited triumph lay hardly a year away.[100]

In Brazil, but not in other Iberian New World societies, a strong commitment to slavery survived national independence. It was as if the southern United States alone had won independence from Britain and had then been governed by a resident British monarch, a stabilizing force equivalent to the emperor of Brazil. The relationship between master and slave was deeply embedded in Brazilian life and customs, intertwined with conceptions of authority, honor, and family status. Although Brazilians associated slavery with patriarchal tradition, they also adapted the institution to the needs of economic change. As the nineteenth century progressed, the coffee-growing plantations of the south-central provinces rapidly supplanted the sugar-producing Northeast as the driving engine of a slave economy. The stagnant sugar regions of the Northeast, which in 1822 contained almost 70 percent of Brazil's slaves, found it difficult to compete with Cuban cane sugar and the growing production of European beet sugar. But Brazil increasingly dominated the expanding market for coffee, especially in the United States, and by the early 1880s the four major coffee provinces held some 65 percent of the nation's slaves. Black slaves worked at a variety of occupations throughout the empire, but it was the southwestward-moving coffee boom that kept reinvigorating a tradition-bound institution.[101]

These circumstances deepened Brazil's ambivalence toward "modernization" and its nineteenth-century exemplar, Great Britain. For it was the world's mortal foe of slavery that financed the coffee boom and distributed its product. British firms controlled much of the Brazilian export trade, major banks and insurance companies, and even urban public utilities. British investors and entrepreneurs were largely responsible for the railroads that linked interior coffee *fazendas* with such port towns as Santos. For Brazilians of all social classes, the modern world was first represented by British-made tools, textiles, hardware, and other manufactures that in value far exceeded the imports of any competitors. Brazilian intellectuals were no less dazzled by the writings of Macaulay, Mill, Spencer, and especially the non-English but progressive-minded Comte, and a new class of urban engineers, bureaucrats, journalists, and professionals increasingly equated "progress" with the values of European and North American elites. Yet, according to Joaquim Nabuco, a reformer who belonged to an elite northeastern dynasty and who became a parliamentary leader of Brazilian abolitionism, "those who wish to see Brazil linked to the progress of our century . . . are always pointed to as foreign agents." As an Anglophile continually denounced as a traitor to his class and country, Nabuco was incensed in 1886 when a respected English writer, Goldwin Smith, criticized the Massachusetts abolitionists for having tried to enlist the aid of British public opinion. Defending the patriotism of William Lloyd Garrison (and by implication himself), Nabuco referred to "those countries whose progress, culture, enthusiasms, and ideas do influence our social growth, or which are, so to say, the intellectual highlands whose waters run down to us," and emphasized the need of bringing slavery, "that doomed institution[,] under the influence of foreign progress, so as to contrast moral death within with moral life abroad." Like the earlier Garrison, Nabuco failed to appreciate how images of moral death within and moral life abroad could feed the very currents of nationalism and xenophobia he wished to combat.[102]

There was no automatic connection between antislavery and the more "progressive" groups in Brazil. As in the United States, lawyers, doctors, bankers, engineers, and bureaucrats owned household servants and opposed the abolitionists. Even British residents adapted themselves to prevailing social norms and, contrary to British law, either owned slaves or managed companies that relied on slave labor. By the mid-nineteenth century the region most identified with economic progress was the province of São Paulo, especially the frontier of Paulista West, where the number of slaves continued to increase until the mid-1880s. Paulista planters were modern capitalists attuned to railroads, the ideology of progress, and even republicanism. Unlike American planters of the Old Southwest, they were not ideologically committed to slavery as a permanent system and in the 1850s experimented with free contract laborers from Germany and Switzerland. But when the indentured immigrants resisted slavelike labor discipline, the Paulistas reverted to their dependence on blacks and on the military arm of the government to keep the blacks subdued. Until 1887, when the slaves took matters into their own hands, the Paulista *fazendeiros* were as hostile as Mississippi planters to the most moderate antislavery proposals.

Rio de Janeiro, the imperial capital, became a sharply divided center of abolitionist agitation, but the surrounding province was dominated by debt-ridden but recently affluent coffee planters who remained the nation's most die-hard defenders of human bondage. Yet an indigenous emancipation movement suddenly erupted in the slave-exporting Northeast, especially in drought-stricken Ceará, where the value and quality of slaves had steadily diminished and where indigent freemen from the backcountry presented an alternative form of labor. In 1881 thousands of Cearense massed on the beaches of Fortaleza and other ports to block the shipping of slaves to other provinces. Within the next three years the Cearense ruling class supported the abolitionist societies, which either persuaded masters to manumit their slaves or raised funds to free nearly every black in the province.[103]

During the first half of the nineteenth century, even moderate abolitionism had been alien to Brazilian thought and society. In 1850 and 1851 Brazil stopped importing Africans largely because British naval attacks humiliated national pride and threatened vital interests. It is true that the Brazilian government insisted that it had acted spontaneously, in spite of British aggression, and that by 1850 many Brazilians were becoming alarmed by the dangers of "Africanization," insurrection, and indebtedness incurred as a result of heavy slave importations. Yet there was so little concern for the fate of the *emancipados,* the Africans freed by the court of mixed commission and turned over to the Brazilian government, that in 1863 it required British reprisals against Brazilian shipping, a six-day blockade of Rio, and a break in diplomatic relations before Brazil finally granted the *emancipados* genuine freedom. In theory, all Africans imported since 1831 were legally free, and British abolitionists and ministers to Brazil kept pressing for an accurate census and vigorous steps to liberate this army of illegally bound captives.[104]

Brazilian leaders had no intention of destroying the empire's economy but were keenly aware that the labor force was not self-reproducing and that the interprovincial slave trade could only temporarily meet the labor demands of expanding regions. The suppression of the African trade prompted much debate but no decision regarding government support for massive Chinese coolie, "free" African, and European immigration. The American Civil War was instrumental in eliciting cautious emancipationist sympathies from Emperor Pedro II, a leader sensitive to world opinion and determined to prevent, with respect to slavery, the kind of humiliating coercion that had cut off Brazil's supply of Africans. The course favored by Dom Pedro and his spokesmen was "emancipation of the womb," or the freeing of all newborn children after a fixed date. Yet, as the British and Foreign Anti-Slavery Society later concluded, the emperor had a genius for encouraging abolitionist hopes while assuring slaveholders that all their "vested interests" would be protected: "He talks of his hopes for the emancipation of the future, and of his fears of the disorganization of labour and society. He would have all slaves freed, and yet is unwilling to break their bonds."[105]

The law of free birth of 1871 was a response less to abolitionist pressure, which was then still minimal, than to slave unrest, world opinion, and domestic radicalism. As a "definitive solution" to the slavery problem, enacted by the conservative Rio Branco ministry with the support of northeastern legislators but against the bitter opposition of southern coffee barons, the law was intended to deprive radicals of an incendiary issue while giving some hope to slaves, who had begun to challenge the system. The government rejected the idea of setting a fixed date for ending slavery (one councilor suggested 1930) but adopted an unwieldly system of registration, classification councils, and selective manumission financed by an emancipation fund. Vulnerable to evasion and delay, these measures, including protections for the *ingenuos,* or freeborn children, were hardly more effective than Brazil's earlier commitments against the African slave trade. By allowing masters to demand and even sell the "services" of *ingenuos* for twenty-one years, the law "respected the past," as the minister of agriculture put it, "and corrected only the future." It enabled Brazilians to project a progressive self-image—we have already mentioned the law's influence on an 1879 Spanish committee—to profess a ritualistic commitment to the ideal of ultimate freedom while simultaneously repeating most of the arguments of Caribbean and North American planters concerning the necessity and blessings of bondage and the unfitness of blacks for liberty. The evidence confirms Joaquim Nabuco's conclusion that the Rio Branco law led to "another epoch of indifference for the fate of the slave, during which even the government could forget to comply with the law which it had passed." On the other hand, by nullifying the master's property rights in the offspring of female slaves, the measure eroded the slaveholders' financial credit and undermined the ideological legitimacy of the slave system.[106]

With the debatable exception of France, Brazil was the only non-English-speaking country in which abolitionism developed into a mass movement. Abolitionist history was compressed essentially into the nine years from 1879, when Jeronymo Sodré called on the chamber of deputies to move beyond the disgraceful gradualism of the Rio Branco law, to the final and uncompromising emancipation of 1888. Although 1880 marked the founding of the Brazilian Anti-Slavery Society and of a militant abolitionist press, hostile public reaction nearly extinguished the movement and in 1881 resulted in a resounding electoral defeat of antislavery candidates. It was not until 1884 that the dramatic "liberation" of Ceará led to a sudden proliferation of abolitionist clubs and to organized efforts to purge Amazonas, Rio Grande do Sul, and the city of Rio de Janeiro of slaveholding. The movement penetrated the smallest towns and attracted a wide range of social, political, occupational, and racial groups. But the abolitionists soon reached discouraging limits both in influencing legislation and in promoting voluntary manumissions.

By 1886 the most significant outcome of popular agitation, reinforced by the example of Cuban emancipation, was the abolition of whipping as a legal punishment for slaves. This relaxation of official discipline, coupled with legal decisions favoring slave plaintiffs, made it easier for thousands of Paulista slaves to desert the coffee *fazendas.* Nothing in the history of slavery approximates this astonishing and wholly unanticipated exodus, which soon spread on a minor scale to other provinces. It was precipitated in 1886 by the underground activism of Antônio Bento, a conspiratorial zealot inspired by the image of Christ the Redeemer and the vision of Brazil's redemption from bondage. Working in a secret network, Bento's black and white followers encouraged slaves to flee the planations, sheltered them on trains and in shanty towns, and even found them work as free laborers. Early in 1887 São Paulo Province faced a crisis more threatening than a general strike. Amid increasing turmoil and violence, the police and armed forces were either unwilling or powerless to chase down runaways. At this point the Paulista planters underwent a sudden "conversion" to emancipationist doctrine. They began freeing their slaves, often in exchange for service contracts, as a desperate means of preserving a labor force for the harvest. As some fugitives began returning to the plantations, the province abolished slavery altogether. Farther north, especially in the Paraíba valley, recalcitrant planters continued to resist the irreversible forces that were finally confirmed in May 1888 when, amid national jubilation, the government granted all slaves their immediate and unconditional freedom. Although emancipation worsened economic hardship in many regions, the provincial government of São Paulo had already begun to subsidize the immigration of Europeans, especially Italians, who rapidly began displacing blacks in the coffee fields and artisan trades. This influx, amounting to some ninety thousand immigrants in 1888, smoothed the transition to free labor and sustained São Paulo's economic growth and prosperity. One result of this unforeseen "progress" was that black freedmen remained in the lowest-paid and most-marginal positions in society.[107]

The question arises whether Brazilian emancipation was the result of a single, worldwide movement, as British abolitionists assumed. Certainly Nabuco, José Ferreira de Menezes, José do Patrocínio, and other Brazilian reformers saw it that way. They pictured themselves reenacting against a common enemy the earlier battles fought by British and American heroes. Ferreira, the mulatto founder of the influential abolitionist daily *Gazeta da Tarde,* hailed the American Civil War as a decisive turning point in civilization's triumph over barbarism. From an American veteran he obtained a list of the immortal names that should be honored as promoters of human social evolution, and in 1880 he paid tribute to Lucretia Mott, Harriet Beecher Stowe, Garrison, Greeley, Phillips, Sumner, Joshua Giddings, Samuel May, Edward Everett, Whittier, Seward, and the Christ-like martyr Lincoln. The pantheon expanded to include Franklin, Penn, Sharp, Wilberforce, Clarkson, and Buxton as the newspaper presented inspiring but garbled accounts of a legitimating antislavery tradition. As part of their effort to associate slavery with Portuguese colonialism, Brazilian abolitionists also invoked the heroes of national independence, such as the Pernambucan rebels of 1817 and José Bonifácio de Andrada e Silva. But even Patrocínio, the mulatto radical who in 1881 took over the *Gazeta da Tarde* and who became the charismatic leader of the national movement, referred constantly to the North American example and to prestigious Anglo-American precedents. The *Gazeta da Tarde* quoted Lord Stanley on the economic, social, and religious improvements that had resulted almost immediately from British West Indian emancipation. The United States supposedly demonstrated that the "cancer" of slavery could be easily cured and followed by an era of recovery, health, and vigor. According to Patrocínio, if there had been no Civil War, immigrants would have shunned the great Mississippi valley, and American industry would have languished. By 1883 Cuba was following the American path and entering a new period of prosperity. The lesson should be clear for São Paulo, the region most suited by climate and European connections for genuine progress, and yet it was brave Ceará that was leading the way.[108]

This orientation received strong support from the English-speaking world. Joaquim Nabuco had close ties with British abolitionists, was a corresponding member of the British and Foreign Anti-Slavery Society, and even wrote his major reform tract, *O abolicionismo,* while living in London in self-imposed exile. The *Anti-Slavery Reporter* frequently reprinted accounts from the *Rio News,* a newspaper published by an American, Andrew Jackson Lamoureux, and devoted to commercial, shipping, and financial news as well as to abolitionist propaganda. According to the admiring *Gazeta da Tarde,* the *Rio News* contained information on everything relating to the prosperity of Brazil and was read by the entire English-speaking colony as well as by many Brazilians. Most

British businessmen had no desire to become involved in a battle that could threaten their well-being, but the *Rio News* argued that since foreigners owned about one-half the investment in Brazilian railroads, steamship lines, cables, commercial and industrial enterprises, and the public debt, they had a right to speak out against proslavery policies that jeopardized "this enormous capital." One foreigner who spoke out boldly was Henry Washington Hilliard, the American minister to Brazil. Hilliard's words carried special weight since he was a former slaveholder and Confederate commissioner and colonel (although a Unionist until Lincoln called for troops), who responded to a letter from Nabuco by describing the great blessings emancipation had brought to the South. He assured Brazilians that there had been no economic ruin or loss of plantation labor, and urged the adoption of a cautious program including compensation to masters. Nabuco and his associates embraced Hilliard, made him an honorary member of their Anti-Slavery Society, and held a banquet at which Jefferson Davis's former commissioner could gaze on a portrait of Lincoln freeing the slaves.[109]

Despite this sense of a common cause, Brazilians could hardly accept the complacent view of many British commentators who assumed that Brazilians, having been taught a lesson by Palmerston and the British navy, had done little more than follow an inspiring example. Brazilian abolitionism bore a distinctive stamp even apart from its parades, flower-strewn performances, and "Carnaval spirit." Public subscriptions to free individual slaves violated Anglo-American abolitionist principles opposing any recognition of property rights in human beings. Unlike their Anglo-American counterparts, Brazilian abolitionists faced slaveholders on the same street and managed campaigns to bring pressure on individual masters and to liberate territory block by block. Brazilians were stirred by tales of the "underground railroad" to Canada, and for a time looked upon Ceará as a similar potential refuge. But in subversive activities they went far beyond the North Americans, and their fugitives were protected and welcomed by a far less racist society. Even more than in Cuba or Civil War America, slaves played a critical part in their own liberation. For it was the slaves themselves, responding to the collapse of the planters' ideological legitimacy, who turned the tide. Yet, after acknowledging these distinctive aspects of Brazilian emancipation, one is still left with the crucial and pervasive belief that slavery had become an obstacle to every progressive force that could improve Brazilian life. Brazilians were eager, as Nabuco wrote the British, "to imitate every European progress, and possess each new material—moral, intellectual, or social improvement of civilization." They were humiliated when Europeans, including the heir to the British throne, referred to them as the last *Christian* nation that tolerated slavery, and then put them on a level with the Turks. The growing conviction that a Brazilian institution was founded on provincial prejudice and was contrary to universal forces of betterment shook the confidence of all but the most resolute planters.[110]

One of the most revealing celebrations of Brazilian emancipation occurred in the small British colony of Lagos, in West Africa. This island colony had absorbed over three thousand Brazilian "repatriates," who were either African-born *emancipados* or Afro-Brazilians eager to resettle in a secure commercial post near Yorubaland. As in Sierra Leone and other coastal points, the "repatriates" had mostly been Westernized and often traveled through the interior as merchants or Christian missionaries, though in the villages of Sierra Leone they were sometimes reenslaved by other freed slaves. The six-day commemoration began with a procession of the Brazilian emigrants and a solemn high mass of thanksgiving at the Roman Catholic church and ended with a carnaval and ball. An address to the British governor signed by thirty repatriate members of the Brazilian Emancipation Committee praised England as "the prime mover [and] precursor in this Philanthropic act of emancipation" and expressed gratitude for "the privileges we have from time to time enjoyed under the British Government." The committee in charge of festivities similarly expressed thanks to God, "who has disposed the hearts of the Philanthropists of Great Britain to lay the foundation of the temple of Liberty by their endeavours to abolish the foreign slave trade and finally to emancipate Our Countrymen in all the British Colonies." After reviewing the history of human slavery and paying tribute to Granville Sharp, "the Morning Star of Negro freedom . . . [who] awakened the British Nation from its Criminal Supineness to behold the horrors attendant on the slave trade," this second address went on to applaud the Brazilian senate and especially Emperor Dom Pedo, who "was much impressed with the information given respecting the progress made by Africans under the British flag." Looking to the future, the committee suggested that Brazilian emancipation marked "a new Era to the Negro race" and would result in "the addition of valuable Civilizing Centres into our midst, by the emigration of repatriates now longing to return to the bosom of their fatherland: and no one, here present, I venture to say is more alive to the importance to the Colony of such valuable Civilizing Centres than your Excellency." Since the preceding six years had witnessed intense Anglo-French and Anglo-German competition for the control of West African markets, British administrators and governors were very much alive to the idea of "civilizing centres."[111]

In his own speech Gov. Cornelius Alfred Moloney first quoted Prince Albert, who had occupied "a similar position" when addressing the 1840 World Anti-Slavery Convention. He then recalled the 1884 "Jubilee year" celebration of West Indian emancipation, an event given added resonance by Queen Victoria's great Jubilee of 1887. It should be noted that this proliferation of fifty-year commemorations—in 1888 the British and Foreign Anti-Slavery Society emphasized that Brazil's noble act coincided with the "Jubilee of the first emancipation," meaning the abolition of West Indian apprenticeship—diluted the euphoria originally associated with a jubilee as a new dispensation, and focused attention on the backward regions still in need of British tutelage. At the 1884 celebration the Prince of Wales, the royal patron of the British and Foreign Anti-Slavery Society, had observed that "our example was followed in many other countries, though I regret to say that still in Brazil slavery exists, as well as in Mohammedan and heathen countries." Governor Moloney had no doubt that this censure from Britain's heir apparent "helped on what we are assembled this evening to commemorate." He was similarly confident that the repatriates, their numbers augmented by Brazilian emancipation, would become a "formidable contingent" in helping to liberate the African mainland from slavery. He reminded his listeners that the British government had annexed Lagos in order "to assist, defend, and protect the inhabitants, to put an end to the slave trade not only here but in the neighboring countries, and to prevent the destructive intertribal wars so frequently undertaken, mainly for the capture of slaves." In fact, the British motives for seizing Lagos had been considerably more complex, and a fear of disturbing trade with the interior had prevented curbs against the importation of young children, who were in much demand in Lagos as domestic servants.[112]

From the founding of Sierra Leone, in 1787, antislavery had been intermeshed with the acquisition of European outposts in Africa, despite the strong reluctance of most British abolitionists to encourage the annexation of more colonies. During the "scramble for Africa" the British and Foreign Anti-Slavery Society explained why it would stand aloof from the "wild schemes . . . of armed crusaders from England and other countries, to attack the Slave-hunters in the hidden recesses of the Dark Continent." Having devoted increasing attention to missionary reports on the horrors of African slavery, the society nevertheless insisted that the evil could be conquered not by the sword "but by a mightier and keener weapon—the indignant protest of a united public opinion of the whole civilised world—before which, eventually, even Mussulman stolidity will have to give way." The abolitionists did not explain how the agents of such opinion were to be protected from hostile Arab traders, whose resistance had prompted Cardinal Lavigerie's appeal for "armed crusaders." And how was one to prevent the indignant protest of a united public opinion from becoming a justification for European political and military control?[113]

This is not to suggest that antislavery became nothing more than a cloak for imperialistic ambitions. The celebration at Lagos suggests how antislavery rhetoric and ritual could become an integral part of the processes of power. For a large segment of the British governing elite, including the royal family, cabinet members, MPs, prominent churchmen, experts on Africa, and officials in the field like Sir John Kirk, suppressing the slave trade was the linchpin of Britain's mission to pacify the seas and spread the blessings of free trade, civilization, and progress throughout the non-Christian world. Until the 1880s these objectives were seldom associated with the acquisition of colonies. Indeed, the Foreign Office repeatedly rejected opportunities to annex territory for the purpose of closing slave markets and promoting legitimate trade. When British officials first extended the slave-trade-treaty network to Asian and African rulers, they sought only to stop the flow of black slaves to European colonies, particularly in the Mascarene Islands and western India. It is true that slave-trade agreements with "barbarous chiefs," as at Lagos, opened the way for British commercial and political hegemony and for imposing order on a war-torn and unsettled economy, and that the exposure of French and Portugese complicity with slave-trading societies helped to extend British moral influence and jeopardize the supply of nominally free labor to rival colonies. But during most of the nineteenth century British leaders assumed that by extending and enforcing treaties, they could seal off slave exports—an objective, as Sir Robert Peel put it, that would convince "the black population of Africa of the moral superiority of their European fellow men" and enable Africa "to effect its own advancement."[114]

British interest in eastern and central Africa was considerably heightened by David Livingstone's expeditions of the 1850s and early 1860s, which revealed the ghastly depredations of Arab and pagan slave traders. Livingstone's dramatic indictment of Arab traders, coupled with his vision of regenerating Africa with Christianity, commerce, and civilization, "attracted an England obsessed with the idea of progress," as Roland Oliver has put it, and Livingstone's revolutionary ideas "did much to promote the wider than ecclesiastical policies which missions came to pursue." The government was unprepared to annex the Shiré country, as Livingstone proposed, but it heartily supported missions that gave refuge to liberated or escaped slaves and that created social environments hostile to the surrounding slave-trading systems. An exalted moral purpose increasingly accentuated the superiority of British culture and justified the persistent bullying of British clients, such as the sultans of Zanzibar.[115]

Ruled by Arabs from Oman, Zanzibar had long been the main entrepôt for Afro-Asian trade and the leading slave market in East Africa. In 1822 Britain had sought by treaty to restrict to the northwestern quarter of the Indian Ocean the ancient maritime slave trade, thereby limiting the market to non-Europeans in the Mideast and the Persian Gulf. In 1845 Lord Aberdeen finally succeeded in pressuring Sayyid Sa'id, the ruler of Muscat, Oman, and Zanzibar, to outlaw the entire oceanic slave trade, without however infringing on the vital supply of slave labor to the islands of Zanzibar and Pemba. This latter coastal trade made it impossible for British cruisers to stop the smuggling of slaves to the Persian Gulf. By 1871, two years after the opening of the Suez Canal, British patience was exhausted. A select committee of the House of Commons, appointed to investigate the entire question of slave trading in East Africa, heard testimony from naval officers and missionaries and concluded that the sultan of Zanzibar should be compelled to abolish the traffic throughout his dominions, including his tenous claims on the East African coast. Barghash ibn Sa'id, the new sultan, saw the British demands as an unacceptable threat to his people's economy and to his own authority. "We are a poor and narrow-minded people," he told Bartle Frere, the special envoy sent to negotiate a treaty, "and require time to see our way." The British government then presented an ultimatum, transmitted in 1873 by Sir John Kirk, a botanist and medical officer on Livingstone's Zambesi expedition who had become vice-consul at Zanzibar: unless Barghash prohibited slave exports from the coast and closed slave markets in the islands, he would face a naval blockade. After surrendering to coercion, the sultan traveled to England, where he further learned the meaning of progress and power. The 1873 treaty gave Kirk the opportunity to conduct a vigorous anti-slave-trade campaign in the sultan's name. According to the leading historian of the subject, he used Barghash as "the instrument of informal empire, the agent who would suppress the slave trade and promote legitimate commerce, and with it British influence, at little cost to the imperial treasury."[116]

It is nevertheless clear that Britain's fixation on the slave trade often worked against British interests, damaging or straining relations with Muslim rulers in an era of Islamic insurgency and nationalistic discontent. As Frederick Cooper has observed with respect to labor policies in East Africa, "the British seem to have followed the path of greatest resistance. . . ." Western conceptions of slave and "free" labor were wholly alien to Asian and African societies, where bondage took a variety of forms and seldom fit the paradigm of New World plantation slavery. In 1840, when Palmerston was exerting pressure on the Ottoman Empire, Iran, and the maritime Arabian states as well as on Brazil and the Republic of Texas, Viscount Ponsonby, the ambassador to Turkey, told the sultan that the whole British nation unanimously sought to end the cruel practice of making slaves and that the sultan's refusal would seriously damage Turkey's reputation and weaken British interest in Turkey's welfare. Ponsonby reported that this message was heard "with extreme astonishment accompanied with a smile at a proposition for destroying an institution closely interwoven with the frame of society in this country, and intimately connected with the Law and with the habits and even the religion of all classes, from the Sultan himself down to the lowest peasant." Ponsonby further observed that in the Ottoman Empire slave mothers produced most of the generals and ministers of state: "The Turks may believe us to be their superiors in the Sciences, in arts, and in Arms, but they are very far from thinking our wisdom or our morality greater than their own." Since Britain had a long-term interest in guarding her lifeline to India and in propping up a crumbling Turkish empire against Russian and other encroachments, foreign ministers learned to act with caution and to accept concessions on the slave trade that were unenforceable in North Africa and many Ottoman possessions. When Britain finally invaded and occupied Egypt, in 1882, the Foreign Office considered abolishing slavery as a way of destroying a crucial segment of the African slave trade. But Sir Evelyn Baring, the consul general, successfully resisted this pressure in order to preserve stability and tranquillity along England's strategic route to India.[117]

Officially, the British drew a distinction between the criminal export of slaves and systems of "domestic" slavery with which they had no right to interfere. The distinction harked back to the early history of the antislavery movement and may well have been reinforced by divided opinion on the consequences of rapid emancipation. For Asian and African rulers, however, domestic servitude was inseparable from its source of supply. And British missionaries and consuls, acting as self-appointed policemen in the midst of "lawless" societies, made clear their expectation that once the trade had been shut off, African "natives" would cease selling one another and would settle down to produce legitimate commodities for export. Such attitudes undermined the authority of Muslim and pagan clients and often opened the way for French, Portuguese, or German encroachments. British antislavery policies also encouraged slaves to seek refuge on British warships or in missions, consulates, and protectorates; when asylum was granted, the surrounding populace viewed the British as slave stealers—or as slave buyers, if indemnity was paid. Unless British settlers and British Indian merchants circumvented the law, they were at a competitive disadvantage in not being able to employ slave labor. Of course, British policies were based on the persistent assumption that market forces would increasingly reward rulers and employers who turned to free labor. Yet the internal African slave trade continued to flourish alongside the expanded export of ivory, palm oil, and cloves. Indeed, the growth of legitimate trade and the availability of cheaper European products stimulated the demand for labor in areas where slaves constituted the only supply. The colonizing nations, including Britain, tapped the same source when they recruited labor for such productive zones as the Mascarenes, Comoros, Madagascar, São Tomé, and South Africa. Contrary to the dogmas that equated moral and material progress, slave labor became more brutal and unrelenting when drawn into production for the world market, as on the great clove plantations of Zanzibar and Pemba.[118]

But if antislavery policies produced a tangle of contradictions and conflicting interests, they enhanced Britain's moral prestige and contributed to what Jawaharlal Nehru referred to as "the calm assurance of always being in the right."[119] They not only certified Britain's "service to mankind" and commitment to human progress but also legitimated its right to determine the best interests of backward peoples and to define what forms "progress" would take. The key to this ideological power lay in the fusion of humanitarian and worldly interests, in the fact that a seemingly idealistic and even quixotic cause was promoted by practical-minded administrators, naval officers, and empire builders who represented the world's mightiest industrial nation. As various Muslim leaders made concessions in exchange for commercial and political support, the defense of the slave trade, which had once been associated with the cosmopolitan interchange of cultures, became increasingly linked with the hopeless defense of local autonomy and imperiled traditions. Western-oriented rulers, such as the khedive Ismail of Egypt, understood the utility of suppressing the slave trade as an aid in extending centralized power. To win British backing for his scheme of building an Egyptian empire extending up the Nile to Central Africa, Ismail promised to eradicate the slave trade, appointed Col. Charles George Gordon governor general of the Sudan, and appealed to the British and Foreign Anti-Slavery Society for moral reinforcement. As it turned out, Gordon's anti-slave-trade campaign nourished the anti-Egyptian grievances of the Sudanese and helped bring on the Mahdist revolt and fall of Khartoum in 1885. Yet Gordon's death as an antislavery martyr evoked widespread support for further British intervention.[120]

British abolitionists had long cultivated an ecumenical spirit that made it easier for other colonizing nations to take up the cause. In November 1839 Thomas Fowell Buxton had been sent by Palmerston as the queen's secret ambassador to solicit Pope Gregory XVI's cooperation in forming a "Christian league" to combat the slave trade and to diffuse "schools & Bibles & literature, & railroads—& Civilisation & Christianity" among the Africans. In December the pope had issued a cautious encyclical condemning the African slave trade as then practiced.[121] Pope Gregory's successors, besieged by the revolutionary forces of mid-century, marked time until the advent of Brazilian emancipation, when Leo XIII sought to rehabilitate a Catholic antislavery tradition and put the church at the forefront of African emancipation. The force behind this belated Catholic crusade was Cardinal Lavigerie, archbishop of Algiers and founder of the White Fathers, who devoted heroic efforts to the cause of civilizing and Christianizing Central Africa. Hoping to restore the moral leadership of the Roman Catholic church, Lavigerie promoted African education, especially in medicine, and established a chain of missions and orphanages that recruited ransomed slave children. Because his missions around the African lakes were vulnerable to Arab raids, Lavigerie sought to fortify his outposts of progress with military force. The British government had long encouraged Catholic missions in Africa, and French armies had provided precedents for Lavigerie's armed camps by establishing *villages de liberté* in the western Sudan, where freed slaves were compelled to work for the military occupation. Lavigerie found a receptive audience in France, Britain, and the rest of the western Europe when in 1888 he began preaching a new crusade against the Islamic infidel, a crusade that would send out Christian knights to destroy the internal African slave trade. In England, where he was received by Lord Salisbury and the Prince of Wales, Lavigerie applauded Britain's noble antislavery tradition and invoked David Livingstone's dying wish to wipe slavery from the face of the earth. In Belgium he joined forces with Leopold II, whose private Congo Independent State had been advertised to the world as a philanthropic and antislavery venture.[122]

It was Lavigerie's crusade to recruit an "army of apostles" that prompted Britain to propose the alternative of an international conference on the slave trade, which was to be a purely humanitarian sequel to the Berlin West African conference of 1884–85. With the scramble for Africa under way, slave-trade suppression was becoming the required shibboleth for imperialists like Leopold II, who had no qualms about using armed power and forced labor to extract more rubber, ivory, and minerals from the Zaire basin. Henry Morton Stanley, the famous explorer who opened up the Zaire and who was employed by King Leopold, was a corresponding member of the British and Foreign Anti-Slavery Society and the star speaker at the 1884 Jubilee antislavery celebration in Manchester. A few weeks after Stanley's recital of the horrors of an expanding slave trade on the Zaire, the Foreign Office recognized that Britain could "carry off all the honours" at the impending Berlin West African conference by being the first to propose an international declaration making the traffic in slaves a crime against the law of nations. In this way Britain retained the moral, if not political, leadership at the meeting that devised the formula for partitioning West Africa. At Berlin the European powers not only condemned the internal as well as maritime slave trade but also committed themselves to care for the moral and material improvement of "native tribes" and to help in suppressing slavery itself in the Zaire basin. This was the kind of international sanction Britain had been striving for since the Congress of Vienna, but abolitionists had not foreseen that it would be accompanied by imperialistic rule.[123]

By 1889 antislavery had become so much a part of the scramble that no international conference on the slave trade could possibly exclude territorial ambitions and rivalries. In 1888 a rebellion against high-handed German actions in East Africa persuaded even Bismarck that suppressing the slave trade would be the ideal pretext for a joint Anglo-German blockade. On the other hand, as Suzanne Miers points out, no state, including Turkey, Iran, and Zanzibar, "could risk the odium of failing to co-operate in a great humanitarian cause." Britain urged Belgium to sponsor the conference in order to minimize French and Portuguese suspicions. King Leopold recognized that such a meeting could help him extend his own empire. He was also eager to refurbish his image as a humanitarian, which had been somewhat tarnished when he had given the governorship at Stanley Falls to Tippu Tip, the most powerful slave and ivory dealer in eastern Zaire. The delegates from seventeen nations who met at Brussels in the winter of 1889–90 generally approved Leopold's Congo State as an instrument of civilization and progress. They replaced Britain's obsolete treaty system with a comprehensive act drafted with the intention "of putting an end to the crimes and devastations engendered by the traffic in African slaves, of efficiently protecting the aboriginal population of Africa, and of securing for that vast continent the benefits of peace and civilization."[124]

The Brussels conference approved detailed provisions regarding the repression of slave trading at places of origin, along inland caravan routes, and at sea. In lieu of Leopold's more obligatory proposals, the treaty merely sanctioned a blueprint for conquest that included "strongly occupied stations in the interior," the construction of roads, "and in particular of railways, connecting the advanced stations with the coast, and permitting easy access to the inland waters," steamboats on the inland navigable waters and lakes, telegraph lines linking "administrative centres," and fortified posts that would initiate Africans "in agricultural labour and in the industrial arts so as to increase their welfare; to raise them to civilization and bring about the extinction of barbarous customs, such as cannibalism, and human sacrifices." Restrictions were also placed on the zones in which modern arms and distilled liquors could be sold—colonizers were naturally interested in limiting the weapons that could be used to resist European occupation, and humanitarians had long deplored the traffic in arms and liquor as adjuncts to the slave trade. The ostensible purpose of this grandiose scheme was "purely humanitarian," and much attention was given to the protection of fugitive and liberated slaves. Although the European powers seized the occasion to censure and patronize Muslim states, they were silent with respect to the persistence of slavery in their own territories, to say nothing of protection for the slaves who were nominally freed and transformed into contract laborers. Viewed from one angle, the Brussels Act was a formalization of the merger of antislavery and imperialism. It used the maritime traffic as an excuse to take military action against peoples engaged in internal slave trading, and the latter actions as an excuse to develop a colonial infrastructure more suitable for economic exploitation than for the protection and uplift of "native peoples." Viewed from another angle, the Brussels Act was a significant step toward "international trusteeship" and the institutionalization of moral standards that had gradually won dominance in the Western world. Two years after the ending of black slavery in the New World, even Turkey and Iran were members of a convention that agreed to cooperate in eradicating the slave trade, in punishing offenders, and in exchanging documents and statistical information that would be accessible at international offices in Brussels and in Zanzibar. Although divisions among the Christian powers enabled Turkey to block proposals for more interference in Islamic lands, the Brussels conference prompted Turkey to take more vigorous action against slave dealers in her provinces, a precedent that was not followed by states in the Arabian Peninsula.[125]

The signing of the Brussels Act of 1890 marked the ironic climax of a century of abolitionist agitation that had always been torn between a vision of self-determination and a desire to guarantee the tractability and productivity of former slaves. Despite the pacifist and anti-imperialist leanings of many abolitionists, the problem of emancipation had proved to be inseparable from imperial power. Instead of dealing with embattled white planters, emancipators and modernizers now confronted highly diverse groups of African and Asian slaveholders who were connected in varying degrees to the capitalist world economy and were subject to direct or indirect European control. When discussing British West Indian emancipation, we emphasized the importance of an act of faith that linked redemptive religion with utilitarian science, a proclamation of "liberty to the captives" with regulations giving emancipation effect. Half a century of experience had eroded the exuberant faith of the 1830s. Although statesmen and reformers would continue to work for slave emancipation and to regard the emancipations of the nineteenth century as the surest evidence of moral and social progress, the 1890s witnessed a decisive lowering of expectations. Here it is sufficient to mention the waning commitment to the idea of progress itself, a disenchantment encouraged by the excesses of industrialism, imperialism, and nationalistic rivalry, and bitterly confirmed by the First World War. The degradation of antislavery rhetoric can be seen in the efforts of British Conservatives to justify the Boer War as "the last great slave war," a struggle to save blacks from a despotism worse than that which Lincoln overcame, and in Lloyd George's opposing argument that British troops were shedding blood in order to restore slavery under the British flag.[126]

More important in the 1890s was the pervasive racism that confined the possibilities of progress to the white or even to the Anglo-Saxon race, a tendency exemplified in extreme form by the rigid formalization of Jim Crow in the southern United States. The African explorer Joseph Thomson expressed a relatively moderate and hopeful view when he cautioned his readers that no one should expect that European civilization could be grafted "on to the low mind of the negro in either one or two generations," and affirmed that Islam, an inferior religion, was better suited than Christianity to the Africans' "low undeveloped mind." Even Sir Frederick Lugard, the African explorer, empire builder, and abolitionist who fought Arab slave traders and promoted the cause of emancipation from British Africa to the League of Nations, warned that the American example showed the dangers of extending too much liberty to slaves in East Africa, and instructed officials in northern Nigeria to give no jobs or land to slaves who deserted their masters. Opponents of jingoism and imperialistic exploitation, such as the Aborigines Protection Society (which merged in 1909 with the Anti-Slavery Society), spoke increasingly of their duty to protect "child races" from the worst evils of civilization, such as alcohol.[127] In this paternalistic outlook there was little place for either social or economic self-determination. On the other hand, recognition of such ideological limitations should not lead us to make the fatal and ahistorical mistake of assuming that all who absorbed racist dogmas thought alike. Even the most infectious racism failed to deter British reformers and administrators who fervently believed, often against their best empirical judgment, that legalized slavery could no longer be tolerated—and who could be counted on, if they were still alive, to deflate the hypocrisies of our own, professedly antiracist age.

Once the British had established political control in strategic parts of Africa, officials faced the dilemma of meeting the minimal criteria of free-labor ideology without disrupting the social order or destroying the basis for a productive economy. Here the relevant precedent was not the Caribbean but British India, where in 1843 the government had annulled all legal sanctions for slavery without taking direct steps to destroy the institution. This was the policy adopted in 1874 for the Gold Coast, where slaves had few options that could induce them to leave their masters but where the British governor still considered the move "too rapid and peremptory." In 1890 the British showed more caution after annexing Zanzibar and Pemba. They quietly ignored a decree that the sultan had been forced to issue freeing all slave children born after 1 January 1890, since they feared that owners would not care for children whom no one was prepared to support. The slaves in Zanzibar and Pemba produced most of the world's supply of cloves, and production reached a record level five years after British annexation. In 1897, under humanitarian pressure and with the gravest forebodings, Britain finally abolished the legal status of slavery in Zanzibar and Pemba. In deference to Muslim sensibilities, concubines were excluded. In Kenya, where British rule was far less secure, a similar measure was delayed until 1907.[128]

Arthur Hardinge, the consul and administrator general, articulated precisely the same concerns and remedies that had preoccupied Lord Howick and the younger James Stephen in 1832–33. The problem, which no experiment in emancipation had really solved, was how to prevent plantation slaves from working for themselves whenever they wished. If one dispensed with the whip and such coercive substitutes for slavery as apprenticeship or *patronato,* how could landowners maintain the kind of sustained and predictable labor indispensable for the production of tropical staples? As Howick had predicted, any access to land in climates where it was easy to subsist would prevent replicating the conditions of industrial labor markets where "free labor" had proved so beneficial. Only fiscal and legal restrictions could compel former slaves to make the transition, as Stephen had put it, "from the brutal to the rational predicament," substituting the fear of starvation for the fear of the whip. After Howick, by then Earl Grey, became colonial secretary in 1846, he translated his theories of using taxes to force the poor to work for wages into a comprehensive system of tropical development. Despite the general failure of Grey's plans for regressive taxation, British administrators continued to insist that the restriction of economic freedom was the only solution for ensuring progress in the tropics. As one historian has recently summarized Hardinge's recommendations to the Foreign Office, the freed slaves of Zanzibar "should be made to pay rent; the tax burden on clove producers should be shifted to ex-slaves; movement of ex-slaves should be restricted; and labor during the harvest, although it would be paid, should be compulsory."[129]

In view of the history of other "reconstructions," it is hardly surprising that British officials and businesses had no intention of replacing slavery with a wage-labor system freely regulated by the forces of supply and demand. For political as well as economic ends, they wished to shore up and protect the interests of an Arab planter elite while gradually instilling in ex-slaves a new respect for property and the rectitude of diligent work. But in Zanzibar and coastal Kenya the British failed to create the kind of rigid system of labor control that developed in the mining and agricultural districts of southern Africa. Despite efforts to immobilize workers with vagrancy laws and punitive contracts, officials complained

> that certain Arabs of the old regime, anxious to maintain their former prestige as landed gentry, suffer financially by allowing ex-slaves and their descendants to continue to live on their plantations without demanding labour or any form of rent in exchange. Such ex-slaves and their descendants, especially the latter, lead an idle parasitical life and are addicted to stealing the produce of their ex-masters' estates.

British development in Kenya also created a demand for caravan porters and railroad construction workers, lowly occupations that provided a certain independence from the plantation system. As in other post-emancipation societies, the freedmen became a landless and powerless people who nevertheless acquired some freedom to live as squatters and to refuse to work like slaves. When the Kenya government adopted harsh measures to mobilize forced labor, as in 1919, it produced an outcry from the Anti-Slavery Society, religious leaders, and criticis in Parliament who succeeded in modifying the way labor was recruited. Such continuing protests against remnants of slavery or a reversion to slave-like practices defined the minimal standards for a "voluntary labor system" and had the unintended effect of legitimating the prevailing system of land ownership and corporate wealth and power.[130]

Although slavery was an extremely minor concern for the victorious

Allies who sought in 1919 to reorder the world, the conventions signed at Saint-Germain-en-Laye, which replaced the Berlin and Brussels acts, contained a brief clause announcing that the signatory powers would "endeavour to secure the complete suppression of slavery in all its forms, and of the slave trade by land and sea." This was a sweeping and unprecedented commitment, unsupported, however, by any supervisory machinery or even by an international office. The covenant of the League of Nations mentioned suppression of slavery and the slave trade only in connection with some of the former German and Turkish territories mandated to the Allied powers. The British mandate for Tanganyika, for example, provided for as "speedy an elimination of domestic and other slavery as social conditions will allow," and prohibited all forms of forced labor "except for essential public works and services, and then only in return for adequate remuneration." But while League members professed to recognize the mandate standards defining the protection of native peoples as "a sacred trust of civilisation," such colonial nations as Holland and Portugal resisted Britain's efforts to extend to all colonies the recommendations regarding forced labor. Indeed, it was only persistent British pressure and the continuing difficulty of obtaining reliable information that finally moved the League's council to appoint in 1924 the Temporary Slavery Commission. The commission's findings, reinforced by a draft treaty submitted by the British Foreign Office, led the League, as "a trustee for humanity," to sponsor the 1926 International Convention on Slavery, to which the United States and eight other non-League members were invited.[131]

It should be stressed that the meetings of the Temporary Commission, the International Convention, and the subsequent Committee of Experts and Advisory Committee of Experts in the 1930s were landmark efforts to arrive at international agreements protecting human rights. Although recent history had lowered expectations regarding the progress of "less-advanced races," the world hegemony of the Allied powers encouraged hopes that prudent social engineering could assure "the final eradication of the slave system," as Sir Reginald Coupland put it, "except perhaps in remote and unsettled regions of the world beyond the present reach of civilised opinion . . . in no long space of time." The earlier abolitionists' moralism and sense of identity with suffering slaves had gradually given way to a faith in scientific administration, investigatory commissions, and experts like Sir Frederick Lugard, the former governor general of Nigeria, and Albrecht Gohr, the former Belgian director general for the colonies, both of whom sat on the League's Temporary Commission and later Committee of Experts. Obviously, the most knowledgeable authorities on slavery were administrators with wide experience in the British, French, Belgian, Dutch, Portuguese, and Spanish colonies; the implementation of their proposed reforms, which extended to all forms of compulsory labor and to conditions "analogous to slavery," such as debt peonage and the purchase of girls when disguised as a dowery payment, would depend on the will of colonial governments.[132]

The reports submitted to the League by the colonial powers reveal the extraordinary difficulties reformers faced. Each nation celebrated its history of enlightened colonial rule, its perseverance in promoting freedom and education, in overcoming obstacles of ignorance, laziness, and superstition. France claimed to have championed emancipation and equality since 1848, and in Togoland and the Cameroons to have counteracted the effects of proslavery German decrees. Portugal outdid every other nation by proudly citing "the civilising policy" she had consistently followed "from the fifteenth century onwards," a policy devoid of racial prejudice and aimed at bringing about "a Christian brotherhood of native peoples, their moral improvement and their general betterment." Although Portugal, like other nations, had "admittedly tolerated" the traffic in African slaves, both slavery and the slave trade had "always been fortuitous and incidental, and limited in extent," in the continents and seas that Portugal had discovered! This astounding assertion, coupled with the claim that "Portugal is still in the van of progress," that "her laws and rulers have alike been dominated by the idea of the equality of man and by a constant desire to defend, protect and educate the natives," was clearly addressed to British critics who throughout the 1920s pointed to slave raids in Angola and to the cruel treatment and ghastly mortality of compulsory labor throughout Portuguese Africa.[133]

Along with the rosy picture of humanitarian accomplishments, the colonial nations presented excuses for the persistence of "domestic slavery" and the necessity of certain forms of compulsory labor. That such arguments were still being advanced and even approved by an international body in the third decade of the twentieth century would have amused and gratified slaveholding planters in the British West Indies, the antebellum South, and mid-nineteenth century Cuba and Brazil. It now appeared, according to H. A. Grimshaw, the representative of the International Labor Office on the Temporary Commission, that it was not possible to abolish a slave economy "by a stroke of the pen" and that there were grave dangers "lest the social system adopted in substitution for it might not, at least temporarily, lead to worse evils for the working population." The commission's 1925 report agreed:

> Wherever slaves have been freed by a stroke of the pen, serious troubles have almost always arisen: an economic crisis caused by diminution of production leading to general impoverishment and even famine, owing

> to the fact that the freed slaves have regarded their emancipation as meaning the right to do no work; a social crisis, for they sought by irregular and often criminal means to satisfy their daily needs; a political crisis, for poverty and disorder made the Government unpopular.[134]

Understandably, the sixth committee of the Sixth League of Nations Assembly, which prepared the way for the 1926 convention, underscored the importance of the adverb "progressively" in the proposal that the contracting powers undertake in the territories placed under their jurisdiction, protection, or tutelage "to bring about, progresssively and as soon as possible, the complete abolition of slavery in all its forms." Moving progressively was synonymous with maintaining the fundamental structure of the previous social order. The sixth committee recognized that "in certain cases in the past the attempt to do away with slavery and other similar conditions in an abrupt manner, although noble in its inspiration, had resulted in unforseen hardships for the individuals whose condition it was sought to alleviate, and even in grave social upheavals."[135]

The colonial powers agreed that such upheavals were likely whenever Europeans directly interfered with ancestral customs or with slaves, as the Belgians put it, who "voluntarily" accepted their work. The British admitted that if servants in Tanganyika or Ashanti were closely questioned, they would still say they were slaves when in reality they were not only well treated but also free to leave their master any time. Slaves would not voluntarily give up their only means of subsistence, at least not until they had been educated to take advantage of what the Temporary Commission called "the civilising influence of Colonial powers." Fortunately, as the Belgian government observed, European industrial and agricultural enterprises were in search of labor and could offer "wages and material advantages which the native masters can never give." Hence the contract that a domestic slave concluded with a European employer "is equivalent to his final emancipation."[136]

Of course, many Africans viewed such employers, whether public or private, as the owners of slaves. The Portuguese proudly described the pass book that all native males would be required to carry as "an identity document substantiating all their rights and obligations and a register for their labour contracts." But far from creating a form of slavery, Portugal argued, such policies merely implemented the basic law that "in an organized society it is an obligation upon all citizens to work for the advancement of civilisation and the continuance of progress." What was true for fully developed societies was all the more mandatory for societies "in the process of formation, like the colonial communities. It is essential, in the general interest of mankind, to carry out the principle that the natives must cultivate their lands and exploit their resources." In actuality, natives had little claim to "their" land and resources; in Mozambique the Portuguese forcibly recruited blacks to be sent to work in South African mines. But in striking contrast with South Africa, Portugal coupled defenses of compulsory labor with pious denunciations of racial prejudice. Belgium even emphasized the need for respecting the customs of social organization of native tribes while gradually relocating them in labor-starved industrial and mining centers. Given the time and delicacy required for such progressive change, Belgium rejected Norway's proposal for annual reports on slavery within the borders of each empire: "If traces of slavery subsist in native institutions, they are in the process of natural and gradual disappearance under the influence of European penetration, and it would manifestly be impossible to determine with any exactitude the stage reached by this evolution each year."[137]

The most innovative step the Temporary Commission took was to expand its agenda to include systems of forced labor in the European colonies. This question, Gohr and Lugard surmised, was more likely than slavery itself to affect the development of "backward races." It was also the most controversial question the commission and convention faced. Though recognizing that abuses could easily convert forced labor into "a more or less disguised form of slavery," the commission watered down Lugard's original proposal, omitting the requirement of "adequate remuneration" for "essential public works and services." Article 5 of the 1926 convention even sanctioned forced labor for private purposes during a "transition period" but rejected a Belgian amendment authorizing the coerced labor of natives in the interests of their own "education and social welfare." None of these proposals infringed upon the right of each colonial power to define "forced labor" or "public purposes" as it saw fit. There was clearly greater sensitivity to colonies where Europeans made use of indigenous forms of servitude than to South Africa, where a system of industrial and racial servitude had developed long after the abolition of slavery. It is significant that the Committee of Experts appointed in 1931 and the Advisory Committee of Experts approved the following year expressly excluded questions of forced labor related to Article 5 of the 1926 convention. These were now the province of the International Labor Office, not of experts on slavery.[138]

Yet distinctions were becoming increasingly complicated as the old world order began to collapse. In February 1931 the British House of Lords held a full-scale debate on "slave labor" in Soviet Russia, especially in timber camps that produced wood for the British market. The bishop of Durham maintained that the whole theory of Russian communism implied "a brutal contempt of elementary individual rights" and that "the very core and essence of slavery is precisely that contempt of individual rights." The League of Nations had defined slavery as "the status or condition of a person over whom any or all the powers attaching to the right of ownership are exercised"—a definition that could be extended to family members in many of the world's societies but not to the inmates of Soviet labor camps. Lord Parmoor objected, however, that if he were ordered to work in a Russian forest or mine, "it would not be the smallest consolation for me to be told that I was not a slave but a free citizen in the Soviet State who was undergoing forced labour. . . . I would prefer to be a Liberian, because . . . in that case I should have the support of the League of Nations and of the British Labour Party. . . ." Lord Newton concluded that documentary evidence left no doubt that "free labour in Soviet Russia no longer exists, and that the State is practically, although not technically, a slave State. . . . Every citizen in the Soviet Republic who is not a military conscript is an industrial conscript."[139]

While the International Labor Office studied ways to prevent forced labor from developing into "conditions analogous to slavery," the neo-abolitionists had difficulties enough in trying to mobilize effective action against genuine slavery in Portuguese Africa and the Sahara, the traffic in women and children in the New Hebrides, the "Colour Bar Bill" in South Africa, slave raids from Ethiopia into adjacent territories, the continuing slave trade from Africa to the Arabian Peninsula, and the ancient Chinese custom of *mui tsai,* or the selling of female children for "adoption" as domestic servants, a practice that flourished in British Hong Kong and was finally replaced by a no less exploitive system of child industrial labor. Where it was not a question of prodding colonial governments to enforce their own antislavery laws, reformers thought the central problem lay in breaking the crust of ignorance and traditionalism that protected self-perpetuating retardation. Sir George Maxwell, Britain's delegate on the Advisory Committee of Experts, summed up the matured ideology of slavery and progress in his 1934 report on the Arabian Peninsula, the last citadel of legalized human bondage. Admitting that the poor classes of Europe would welcome the security of Muslim domestic slavery, Maxwell emphasized that the Arabian slave,

> who is completely dependent upon a master, and who, having been fed and clothed and told what work to do, is, as a general rule, so incapable of thinking for himself or herself, that he or she would be quite unable to earn an independent living by the exercise of personal energy and initiative, if suddenly called upon to do so.

It followed that genuine progress was impossible in any country so permeated by the degrading slave mentality and master mentality. No advance could be made until

> the labourers—upon whom the real wealth of every country depends—are free, wage-earning, intelligent, and intent upon increasing their wage-earning capacity by the exercise of their labour. The government revenue of every country depends directly upon the wage-earning capacity of its labouring-class, and no country which is dependent upon slave labour can ever expect to be prosperous.[140]

Similar beliefs had guided the antislavery movement for more than a century, and in 1925 Sir Frederick Lugard had called attention to the primary object of eradicating the "servile mentality." Yet how could this be done without creating in the process a new dependency? Lugard had suggested that the goal could best be furthered "by giving the native communities a share in the control of their own domestic affairs so that the freed slave may have new aspirations." After much discussion, the Temporary Commission adopted a text listing three strategies for eliminating "the servile attitude of mind among the backward races": "(1) by encouraging a system of education fully adapted to the conditions of native life; (2) by permitting native communities to participate in the conduct of their own domestic affairs; (3) by allowing them to participate in the working enterprises, conducted by the more advanced races and giving them a share in the profits." In 1925 this was remarkably enlightened paternalism, based on an explicit rejection of the racist view that natives should be confined "within the narrow limits of their present civilisation." The 1926 convention omitted the whole question of apportioning rights and power, and what the Temporary Commission had termed the transition from servile labor to "free-wage labour or independent production." Yet this had always been at the heart of the problem of emancipation. When the British Anti-Slavery Society reported in 1938 that Mussolini's military occupation had finally begun to suppress slavery in Ethiopia, they confronted the ultimate paradox of emancipators who intentionally or unintentionally enslave.[141]

EPILOGUE

Although the events of the past half-century fall beyond the scope of this study, it is important to emphasize that slavery did not expire with the League of Nations. Indeed, even chattel slavery thrived in Saudi Arabia as British naval patrols were shifted to wartime duty and, after the war, as American pilots flew shipments of young boys from Africa to Riyadh, where wealth from oil created a growing demand for slaves as well as Cadillacs. In 1960 Lord Shackleton reported to the House of Lords that African Muslims on pilgrimages to the Mideast still sold slaves upon arrival, "using them as living traveller's cheques." Meanwhile, Nazi Germany had brought a wholly new dimension to compulsory labor. Along with unprecedented crimes of genocide, the Nazis shipped hundreds of thousands of Jews and other concentration-camp inmates to work and often die in the factories of I. G. Farben, Krupp, Telefunken, Friedrich Flick, and other industrial firms that considered the laborers wholly expendable. This was one of the most ghastly forms of slavery the world had yet known, enthusiastically condoned by some of the world's most "advanced" industrial leaders. While all forms of bondage were theoretically proscribed by the United Nations' 1948 Universal Declaration of Human Rights, postwar international agencies faced three quite different varieties of modern slavery: (1) indigenous and traditional forms of chattel slavery, debt bondage, and related institutions that survived in many parts of the Third World; (2) systems of forced or virtually forced labor supported by racial subordination in European colonies or Commonwealth nations like South Africa; (3) compulsory labor in Communist states where, as the British Anti-Slavery Society succinctly put it, "slavery has been taken out of private ownership."[1]

Spurred on by the Society of Friends and such "Non-governmental Organizations" as the Anti-Slavery Society (which now added "for the Protection of Human Rights" to its title), the UN Economic and Social

Council sought to reactivate the antislavery enterprises of the League of Nations. From the late 1940s, however, the issue became entangled in ideological disputes generated by Third World anticolonialism and the cold war. In 1949, for example, the Soviet delegate argued that the League had "worked in an academic atmosphere and achieved no concrete results," and insisted that the council should investigate "colonial and dependent territories, where forms of slavery still flourished vigorously." Predictably, he also called attention to the plight of workers in capitalist countries who were "subjected to what amounted to hired slavery since they were compelled to accept work on any conditions in order to secure a livelihood." The British representative deplored such propaganda, said he would refrain from further clouding the issue by requesting an investigation of the situation in the Soviet Union, and pointed out that colonial powers had been almost exclusively responsible for the effort to abolish slavery in Africa and had taken the initiative against slavery in both the League and the United Nations. Such ideological divisions precluded agreement on a satisfactory definition of modern slavery and made it extremely difficult for UN agencies to secure candid information from member governments. The detailed reports of the Working Group of Experts on Slavery, appointed only in 1975, would rely for information on the Anti-Slavery Society and other "consultative" organizations. On the other hand, the Economic and Social Council and its Ad Hoc Committee on Slavery, which met in 1950, generally agreed that the definition of slavery should be expanded to correspond with modern conditions. The UN Supplementary Convention of 1956, ultimately signed by most member states, was designed to abolish not only slavery as defined by the League of Nations but also serfdom, debt bondage, and institutions similar to slavery affecting women and children. A growing concern for women's rights led to mounting protests against traditional practices of selling daughters as wives, servants, and prostitutes. By 1970, however, attention was focused increasingly on "the Slavery-like Practices of Apartheid and Colonialism."[2]

As Conor Cruise O'Brien has pointed out, the United Nations is political theater dominated by an institutional tone of "lofty morality" perfectly suited for the dramatic exploitation of guilt—in particular, "Western guilt feelings toward the non-white world." The influx of new African states enabled the nonwhite members to win hegemonic control over the "moral conscience of mankind." Unfortunately, condemnations of colonialism and apartheid as the twentieth-century equivalents of slavery sometimes served to shield forms of oppression for which whites bore no responsibility. In a complacent report of 1965, the Republic of Mali contended that a benign, paternalistic servitude had preceded European colonization and that national independence, accompanied by genuine social democracy, had brought the final abolition of slavery and similar institutions. Yet slave-trading continued to flourish in Mauritania, Mali, Niger, and Chad, along the drought-stricken southern fringe of the Sahara. Historical mythology minimizing or denying African and Arab involvement in the slave trade has fostered the false assumption that slavery depended for its survival on colonial regimes. Western sensitivity to African nationalism and especially to the goodwill of Arab oil-producing states compounded the difficulties of obtaining reliable information and publicizing known facts about the sale and treatment of black slaves. There can be no doubt, however, that the prevalence of chattel slavery declined dramatically in the 1960s. The institution was finally outlawed by Saudi Arabia in 1962 and by the Sultanate of Muscat and Oman in 1970. Although prohibition must be distinguished from genuine abolition, the twelve reports submitted in the mid-1970s by the Anti-Slavery Society to the Working Group of Experts on Slavery dealt not with the traditional bastions of chattel slavery but with such diverse problems as the slaughter or capture of Aché Indians in Paraguay; the political and economic oppression of indigenous peasants in Guatemala, El Salvador, Honduras, and Nicaragua; the condition of tin miners in Bolivia; and the plight of forced laborers in Namibia and Equatorial Guinea.[3]

During the postwar years the small but indefatigable Anti-Slavery Society, still listing as officers several descendants of Wilberforce and Buxton, came to regard slavery less as an isolated evil to be "suppressed" than as a part of a wider problem of protecting human rights in a world plagued by destitution, growing inequality, and political tyranny. In the view of Col. Patrick Montgomery, the society's energetic secretary, "slavery will cease only when human rights in general are effectively protected." It thus made little sense to debate the juridical limits of the term "slavery" when five-year-old Moroccan girls were working in carpet factories seventy-two-hours a week for no pay except their midday meals; or when Guatemalan death squads were exterminating peasants who resisted being uprooted from their land and compelled to work in "unspeakable conditions." While the Portuguese government charged that the Anti-Slavery Society was a Soviet agent, the Soviet Union in 1977 accused the organization, along with Amnesty International and the International League for Human Rights, of systematically abusing its UN consultative status "in order to slander socialist countries." Needless to say, the past decades have not been glorious chapters in the historical struggle for human rights. Isolated cases of slavery have survived even in the United States, where government prosecutors have proved that exploiters of migrant labor have flagrantly violated the Thirteenth Amendment. But despite frequent and depressing reports of compulsory labor, the absolute ownership of one person by another has become as rare as Wilberforce, Buxton, or Garrison could ever have hoped. This virtually unnoticed process of extinction is what generations of abolitionists would have applauded as "human progress."[4]

NOTES

INTRODUCTION

1. Robert William Fogel and Stanley L. Engerman, *Time on the Cross: The Economics of American Negro Slavery* (Boston, 1974), 4–6, 191–232.

2. Quoted in Ronald Sanders, *Lost Tribes and Promised Lands: The Origins of American Racism* (Boston, 1978), 60.

3. R. W. Beachey, ed., *A Collection of Documents on the Slave Trade of Eastern Africa* (New York, 1976), 19.

4. Frederick Cooper, *Plantation Slavery on the East Coast of Africa* (New Haven, 1977), 45–46.

PART ONE

Epigraphs: Aristotle, *Politics,* 1, 5, trans. Thomas Wiedemann, in Wiedemann, ed., *Greek and Roman Slavery* (Baltimore: Johns Hopkins University Press, 1981), 18, 19. George D. Whitney, D.V.M., *The Health and Happiness of Your Old Dog* (New York: Wm. Morrow & Co., 1975), 3.

1. There is conflicting or ambiguous evidence concerning most of the details of the Zanj revolt, a subject freighted with ideological controversy. For a full bibliography and a careful survey of the evidence, see Alexandre Popovic, *La révolte des esclaves en Iraq au III*[e]*/IX*[e] *siècle* (Paris, 1976). I have also drawn on Popovic's paper "Les facteurs économiques et la révolte des Zang"; Gernot Rotter, *Die Stellung des Negers in der islamisch-arabischen Gesellschaft bis zum XVI. Jahrhundert* (Bonn, 1967), 35–37, 105–11; Theodor Nöldeke, *Sketches from Eastern History,* trans. John Sutherland Black (London, 1892), 146–75; and the articles "Zandj," by L. Massignon, and " ʿAli b. Muhammad," by Bernard Lewis, in *Encyclopedia of Islam,* 4 (Leiden, 1934); 1 (n.s., Leiden, 1960). For use of the term "Zanj" in relation to Arab conceptions of geography, see Paulo Fernando de Moraes Farias, "Models of the World and Categorical Models: The 'Enslavable Barbarian' as a Mobile Classificatory Label," *Slavery and Abolition: A Journal of Comparative Studies,* 1 (1980), 115–31. Ghada Hashem Talhami, "The Zanj Rebellion Reconsidered," *International Journal of African Historical Studies,* 10 (1977), 443–61, challenges the traditional assumption that the black slaves near Basra were East Africans who had been transported by Arab sea merchants; he argues, though mostly from the silence of known sources, that Zanj did not designate a distinct place of origin.

In transcribing Arabic names and words, I have avoided vowel marks except in quotations.

2. The pitfalls and deceptive selectivity of early Islamic sources are described in Patricia Crone, *Slaves on Horses: The Evolution of the Islamic Polity* (Cambridge, Eng., 1980), 3–16. Some historians have concluded that a slave trade from the Zanzibar region to Mesopotamia antedated Islam. As Popovic points out, reports of Zanj uprisings in 689–90

and 694–95 indicate that a slave trade by ship and caravan must have commenced much earlier. But given the sparseness and ambiguity of sources, Popovic concludes that it is impossible to say when the maritime trade began (Popovic, *La révolte,* 60–61; Rotter, *Die Stellung des Negers,* 35–37, 105–6). In view of Talhami's critique, even greater caution would seem advisable ("Zanj Rebellion," 444–46, 460–61).

3. William McKee Evans, "From the Land of Canaan to the Land of Guinea: The Strange Odyssey of the 'Sons of Ham,'" *American Historical Review,* 85 (1980), 28. While slavery in antiquity was not associated with skin color, representations of blacks frequently suggest captivity and servile employments. See Jean Vercoutter et al., *The Image of the Black in Western Art,* vol. 1, *From the Pharaohs to the Fall of the Roman Empire* (New York, 1976). For a critique of conventional assumptions concerning slavery and Islam, see Frederick Cooper, "Islam and Cultural Hegemony: The Ideology of Slaveholders on the East African Coast," in Paul Lovejoy, ed., *The Ideology of Slavery in Africa* (Beverly Hills, 1981), 271–304.

4. M. I. Finley, *Ancient Slavery and Modern Ideology* (New York, 1980), 42–44, 150–51 n. 7; Giovanni Abignente, *La schiavitù nei suoi rapporti colla chiesa e col laicato . . .* (Turin, 1890); John K. Ingram, *History of Slavery and Serfdom* (London, 1895); Ettore Ciccotti, *Il tramonto della schiavitù nel mondo antico* (Turin, 1899); Charles Jean Marie Letourneau, *L'évolution de l'esclavage dans les diverses races humaines* (Paris, 1897); H. J. Nieboer, *Slavery as an Industrial System* (The Hague, 1900).

5. Bernard Siegel's functionalist comparison of slavery among the Northwest Coast Indians, the Creek Indian Confederacy, and various West African groups appeared in *American Anthropologist,* 47 (1945), 357–92. One should add that the 1920s and 1930s produced important studies of non-Western slavery by W. C. Macleod, Richard Thurnwald, Melville J. Herskovits, Gunnar Landtman, and a few others.

6. Claude Meillassoux, ed., *L'esclavage en Afrique précoloniale* (Paris, 1975), 20.

7. Orlando Patterson, *Slavery and Social Death* (Cambridge, Mass., 1982), 1–14. I am most grateful to Professor Patterson and to Aida Donald, of Harvard University Press, for sending me proof of this monumental work just as I was completing my own manuscript. Though our purposes are very different, Patterson and I have used many of the same sources and have arrived at many similar conclusions. Fortunately, I have been able to clarify and expand a number of important points as a result of reading Patterson's work. For a sampling of earlier theoretical and empirical approaches, see Orlando Patterson, "The Structural Origins of Slavery: A Critique of the Nieboer-Domar Hypothesis from a Comparative Perspective," *Annals of the New York Academy of Science,* 292 (1977), 12–34; Gunnar Landtman, *The Origin of the Inequality of the Social Classes* (London, 1938); Evsey Domar, "The Causes of Slavery and Serfdom: A Hypothesis," *Journal of Economic History,* 30 (1970), 18–31; Robert A. Padgug, "Problems in the Theory of Slavery and Slave Society," *Science and Society,* 40 (1976), 3–27; Frederic L. Pryor, "A Comparative Study of Slave Societies," *Journal of Comparative Economics,* 1 (1977), 25–49; Edmund Leach, "Caste, Class and Slavery: The Taxonomic Problem," in Anthony de Reuck and Julie Knight, eds., *Caste and Race: Comparative Approaches* (London, 1967), 5–16; Stanley L. Engerman, "Some Considerations Relating to Property Rights in Man," *Journal of Economic History,* 33 (1973), 43–65; Stanley L. Engerman, "The Realities of Slavery: A Review of Recent Evidence," *International Journal of Comparative Sociology,* 20, nos. 1–2 (1979), 46–66; Yoram Barzel, "An Economic Analysis of Slavery," *Journal of Law and Economics,* 20 (1977), 87–109; Richard Hellie, "Muscovite Slavery in Comparative Perspective," *Russian History,* 6 (1979), 133–209; Suzanne Miers and Igor Kopytoff, "African 'Slavery' as an Institution of Marginality," in Miers and Kopytoff, eds., *Slavery in Africa: Historical and Anthropological Perspectives* (Madison, Wis., 1977), 3–78; James L. Watson, ed., *Asian and African Systems of Slavery* (Berkeley, 1980); Lovejoy, *Ideology of Slavery in Africa.*

8. See esp. Sidney Mintz, *Caribbean Transformations* (Chicago, 1974).

9. Eugene D. Genovese, *Roll, Jordan, Roll: The World the Slaves Made* (New York, 1974), 48.

10. Ibid.; Herbert G. Gutman, *The Black Family in Slavery and Freedom, 1750–1925* (New

York, 1976); John W. Blassingame, *The Slave Community: Plantation Life in the Antebellum South,* rev. and enl. ed. (New York, 1979); Lawrence W. Levine, *Black Culture and Black Consciousness: Afro-American Folk Thought from Slavery to Freedom* (New York, 1977); Albert J. Raboteau, *Slave Religion: The "Invisible Institution" in the Antebellum South* (New York, 1978).

11. Genovese, *Roll, Jordan, Roll,* 5; Patterson, *Slavery and Social Death,* 4; Daniel Pipes, *Slave Soldiers and Islam: The Genesis of a Military System* (New Haven, 1981), 18. Patterson presents a penetrating analysis of the merger of power, servility, and dishonor in the persons of Janissaries, Mamluks, and especially palatine eunuchs (*Slavery and Social Death,* chap. 11).

12. Miers and Kopytoff, "African 'Slavery,'" 57.

13. Isaac Mendelsohn, *Slavery in the Ancient Near East: A Comparative Study of Slavery in Assyria, Syria, and Palestine, from the Middle of the Third Millennium to the End of the First Millennium* (New York, 1949), 1–5, 34, 40–42, 50; Jack Goody, "Slavery in Time and Space," in Watson, *Asian and African Systems of Slavery,* 18–20; 'Abd el-Moshen Bakir, *Slavery in Pharaonic Egypt* (Cairo, 1952); Patterson, *Slavery and Social Death,* 57, 60, 168–69. Though Patterson occasionally mentions the similar treatment received by slaves and domestic animals, he never elaborates upon an association that was probably as important sociologically as conceptually and metaphorically.

14. Goody, "Slavery in Time and Space," 18; Patterson, *Slavery and Social Death,* 27–32; Thomas Wiedemann, ed., *Greek and Roman Slavery* (Baltimore, 1981), 19, 24. Prof. Dirk Hartog, of the Indiana University School of Law, has helped me understand that property law starts with the power of one individual over another, a point that Patterson develops, but too often by sheer assertion. The complex relation between slavery and changing conceptions of property still requires much study and clarification.

15. Goody, "Slavery in Time and Space," 20–21; Mendelsohn, *Slavery in the Ancient Near East,* 1–5; Miers and Kopytoff, "African 'Slavery,'" 16 n. 3, 17, 22–26, 30; Patterson, *Slavery and Social Death,* 39–44, 63–65; James L. Watson, "Slavery as an Institution: Open and Closed Societies," in Watson, *Asian and African Systems of Slavery,* 9–15; Lionel Caplan, "Power and Status in South Asian Society," ibid., 169–94; Nancy E. Levine, "Opposition and Interdependence: Demographic and Economic Perspectives on Nyinba Slavery," ibid., 195–222. Some African societies, such as the Ibo of Nigeria, were relatively "closed"; some Asian societies, such as the Melanau of Sarawak, were "open" and absorbtive. Patterson draws a valuable distinction between an "intrusive" mode of representing the social death of outsiders and an "extrusive" mode, typified by eighteenth-century Russia and the Northern Dynasties period of China, in which the locally recruited slave became "an internal exile, who had been deprived of all claims of community" (*Slavery and Social Death,* 38–45). I am almost wholly concerned with the "intrusive" mode, since it was most commonly associated with commercial and religious "progress."

16. Patterson, *Slavery and Social Death,* 51, 302.

17. Miers and Kopytoff, "African 'Slavery,'" 17. For the point on early Saxon law, I am indebted to a personal communication from Robert S. Lopez.

18. Patterson, *Slavery and Social Death,* 62–65, 209–49. An exception should be made for Muslim military slaves, who, as Daniel Pipes shows, often freed themselves through "a gradual shift in relations with their master" and evolved "from being his subordinates into being an independent military force" (Pipes, *Slave Soldiers and Islam,* 10, and passim).

19. 1 Cor. 7:20–22; 12:1; David Brion Davis, *The Problem of Slavery in Western Culture* (Ithaca, N.Y., 1966), 63–66, 78–90.

20. David Brion Davis, *The Problem of Slavery in the Age of Revolution, 1770–1823* (Ithaca, N.Y., 1975), 558–64; Davis, *Problem of Slavery in Western Culture,* 72–90; Patterson, *Slavery and Social Death,* 97–101, 336–42. Patterson is clearly right in challenging the assumption of Hegel (and of many other social theorists, including Marx) that the slave was typically a *laborer;* in various societies, as Patterson and numerous predecessors have pointed out, slaves were expensive and unproductive symbols of luxury and power. This was true of a small minority of slaves even in the plantation colonies and southern states of the

New World. It is important to add, however, that Hegel and his followers were thinking of the functions of the vast majority of bondsmen in ancient Greece, Rome, and the New World.

21. William McKee Evans, "Race, Class and Myth in Slaveholding Societies" (Paper presented at the 1981 meeting of the Southern Historical Assocation). Patterson makes the crucial but paradoxical point that slave-based honorific cultures were possible only where "a substantial free population" was able to adopt and share "the collective honor of the master class." In extreme cases such as the Caribbean colonies and the Dutch East Indian colonies in the Banda group of spice islands, masters abandoned all pretense of culture and civilization and "simply indulged their appetites," approaching Hegel's "crisis of honor and recognition" (*Slavery and Social Death,* 99–100). While Patterson overstates his case, at least with respect to the West Indies, I agree with the thrust of his argument. The essentially abolitionist image of West Indian planter depravity, though no doubt grounded in reality, must be treated with almost the same caution as abolitionist and anti-abolitionist images of "primitive" Africa.

22. E. E. Urbach, "The Laws Regarding Slavery as a Source for Social History of the Period of the Second Temple, the Mishnah and Talmud," *Papers of the Institute of Jewish Studies,* ed. J. G. Weiss, vol. 1 (Jerusalem, 1964), 31–49.

23. Ibid., 50–56.

24. George Frederick Holmes, "Ancient Slavery," *De Bow's Review,* 19 (1855), quoted in Drew Gilpin Faust, *A Sacred Circle: the Dilemma of the Intellectual in the Old South, 1840–1860* (Baltimore, 1979), 119; William Henry Holcombe, *The Alternative: A Separate Nationality, or the Africanization of the South* (New Orleans, 1860), 6–8.

25. See below, pp. 111–14; and also Finley, *Ancient Slavery and Modern Ideology.*

26. My purpose and approach are thus very different from those of John U. Nef's *War and Human Progress: An Essay on the Rise of Industrial Civilization* (Cambridge, Mass., 1950), a study that tries to demonstrate that war is "a disease of human nature" (113) that has always tended to retard economic productivity and scientific progress, even while becoming more destructive as a result of such progress. For an interesting argument that New World slavery retarded technological innovation on plantations but stimulated innovations in the gathering, merchandising, and transport of slaves, see Henry A. Gemery and Jan S. Hogendorn, "Technological Change, Slavery, and the Slave Trade," in Clive Dewey and A. G. Hopkins, eds., *The Imperial Impact: Studies in the Economic History of Africa and India* (London, 1978), 243–58. Since I am an agnostic with respect to "progress," I should emphasize that my own use of the term is not limited to the arguable benefits of technological innovation; I assume that the concept is relative, double-edged, and shaped in oppositional ways by a total culture, including science and technology.

27. Ludwig Edelstein, *The Idea of Progress in Classical Antiquity* (Baltimore, 1967); Robert Nisbet, *History of the Idea of Progress* (New York, 1980), 10–76; Eric R. Dodds, *The Ancient Concept of Progress and Other Essays on Greek Literature and Belief* (Oxford, 1973), 1–25; From the enormous literature on definitions and concepts of progress, I have drawn especially on W. Warren Wagar, ed., *The Idea of Progress since the Renaissance* (New York, 1969), esp. the essay by Georg G. Iggers, "The Idea of Progress: A Critical Reassessment"; John Passmore, *The Perfectibility of Man* (London, 1970); Ruth Macklin, "Moral Progress," *Ethics,* 87 (1977), 370–82; Sidney Pollard, *The Idea of Progress: History and Society* (London, 1968); Nathan Rotenstreich, "The Idea of Historical Progress and Its Assumptions," *History and Theory,* 10 (1971), 197–221; Hans Blumenberg, "On a Lineage of the Idea of Progress," *Social Research,* 41 (1974), 6–27; Roy S. Wolper, "The Rhetoric of Gunpowder and the Idea of Progress," *Journal of the History of Ideas,* 31 (1970), 589–98. From J. B. Bury to Robert Nisbet, virtually none of the authorities on "the idea of progress" mentions the subject of slavery, despite the shelves of nineteenth-century literature that equate historical progress with the irresistible force of global emancipation.

28. Wiedemann, *Greek and Roman Slavery,* 80–81.

29. Aristotle, *Politics,* 1.7.9–10; quotations are from Wiedemann, *Greek and Roman Slavery,* 17. See also my discussion of slavery and ancient political philosophy in *Problem of Slavery*

in Western Culture, 66–83; and Piero A. Milani, *La schiavitù nel pensiero politico, dai Greci al basso medio evo* (Milan, 1972), 49–236.

30. Xenophon *Poroi* 1, quoted in Wiedemann, *Greek and Roman Slavery,* 96–97, 133–38.

31. Livy 6.27.8 and 8.28.1–9, quoted in Wiedemann, *Greek and Roman Slavery,* 40–42; see also 91–93, 136–38, 177; Dodds, *Ancient Concept of Progress,* 8–17; Davis, *Problem of Slavery in Western Culture,* 72–83; Milani, *La schiavitù nel pensiero politico,* 155–236. It should be noted that freemen also worked under brutal conditions in Roman mines.

32. Keith Hopkins, *Conquerors and Slaves: Sociological Studies in Roman History* (Cambridge, Eng., 1978), 1–14, 32, 99–101, 113–14; M. I. Finley, *The Ancient Economy* (Berkeley, 1973), 70–79. For the difficulties in estimating the number of slaves in Greco-Roman societies and in distinguishing them from other forms of labor, see Finley, *Ancient Slavery and Modern Ideology,* 78–90, and E. Badian's review of this book, "The Bitter History of Slave History," *New York Review of Books,* 22 Oct. 1981, 49–53. With respect to Islamic conquests, Patricia Crone describes the massive, if temporary, enslavement of prisoners of war and emphasizes the need to consult enemy Greek, Armenian, Hebrew, Aramaic, Syriac, and Coptic sources (*Slaves on Horses,* 6–16, 50–55). In tropical Africa, however, where Islam was later spread more peacefully by Muslim traders, slaves were generally purchased like ivory, gold, ostrich feathers, and other luxuries. See Nehemia Levtzion, "Patterns of Islamization in West Africa," in Levtzion, ed., *Conversion to Islam* (New York, 1979), 207–12; I. M. Lewis, ed., *Islam in Tropical Africa: Studies Presented and Discussed at the Fifth International African Seminar, Ahmadu Bello University, Zaria* (Oxford, 1966); Philip D. Curtin, *Economic Change in Precolonial Africa: Senegambia in the Era of the Slave Trade* (Madison, Wis., 1975), 4–5, 47–51, 66–83. For an unusually detailed account of the magnitude of the Spaniards' enslavement of Amerindians, in a small and isolated sector of the New World, see William L. Sherman, *Forced Native Labor in Sixteenth-Century Central America* (Lincoln, Neb., 1979), 9–59, 82.

33. Finley, *Ancient Economy,* 70–83. The following discussion also draws on M. I. Finley, ed., *Slavery in Classical Antiquity: Views and Controversies* (Cambridge, Eng., 1960); William L. Westermann, *The Slave Systems of Greek and Roman Antiquity* (Philadelphia, 1955); William V. Harris, *War and Imperialism in Republican Rome, 327–70 B.C.* (Oxford, 1979); Susan Treggiari, *Roman Freedmen during the Late Republic* (Oxford, 1969); William W. Buckland, *The Roman Law of Slavery* (Cambridge, Eng., 1908); Bernard Lewis, ed. and trans., *Islam from the Prophet Muhammad to the Capture of Constantinople,* vol. 1, *Politics and War* (London, 1974); Pipes, *Slave Soldiers and Islam;* Paul Forand, "The Relation of the Slave and the Client to the Master or Patron in Medieval Islam," *International Journal of Middle East Studies,* 2 (1971), 59–66; R. Brunschvig, "*'Abd,*" in *Encyclopedia of Islam,* 1 (n.s., Leiden, 1960); David Ayalon, *Gunpowder and Firearms in the Mamluk Kingdom: A Challenge to Medieval Society* (London, 1956); Stanley Lane-Poole, *A History of Egypt in the Middle Ages* (London, 1901); Charles R. Boxer, *The Portuguese Seaborne Empire, 1415–1825* (London, 1969); J. H. Elliott, *The Old World and the New, 1492–1650* (Cambridge, Eng., 1970); Gavin Hambly, "A Note on the Trade in Eunuchs in Mughul Bengal," *Journal of the American Oriental Society,* 94 (1974), 125–30. I am especially indebted to Gavin R. G. Hambly, a former colleague, for giving me copies of his extremely informative essays "Slavery in Islam" (Paper read at Yale University, 1973) and "The Problem of Slavery in Indian History" (Paper read at Yale University, 1973).

34. Harris, *War and Imperialism,* 81–82; William V. Harris, "Towards a Study of the Roman Slave Trade," in J. H. D'Arms and E. C. Kopff, eds., *The Seaborne Commerce of Ancient Rome: Studies in Archaeology and History, Memoirs of the American Academy in Rome,* vol. 36 (Rome, 1980), 117–40; Alan W. Fisher, "Muscovy and the Black Sea Slave Trade," *Canadian-American Slavic Studies,* 6 (1972), 579–84. Though estimates by Polish and Soviet historians of the number of Tatar captives range to well over one million, Fisher concludes that it is impossible to arrive at an accurate figure. Since the Roman demand for slaves exceeded even the huge supply of captives taken in almost yearly conquests from 327 to 70 B.C., Harris argues, it is implausible that slaves were merely an incidental result

of war and expansion, a point that would seem to support Finley's view that the demand for slaves and especially the agrarian conditions creating such a demand preceded "the enormous leap" in supply following the Second Punic War (*Ancient Slavery and Modern Ideology,* 83–86). But like Harris, Ramsay MacMullen also emphasizes the social importance in later centuries of enslaving small children who would otherwise have died from exposure (*Roman Social Relations, 50 B.C. to A.D. 284* [New Haven, 1974], 92).

35. Hopkins, *Conquerers and Slaves,* 1–4, 109, 114–15; Wiedemann, *Greek and Roman Slavery,* 133–35. While Finley and Hopkins acknowledge the continued use of free unskilled labor throughout the Roman Empire, Ramsay MacMullen goes further and contends that the free poor were really at the bottom of the social pyramid in standard of living and were worse off than many slaves (*Roman Social Relations,* 92–93). P. A. Brunt also stresses the availability of a large pool of displaced free labor, including peasants who had migrated to Rome, who were employed by the state in large-scale construction and other public works. The use of slaves in agriculture and manufacturing enterprises requiring *continuous* employment presumably reduced the wages of such free workers ("Free Labor and Public Works at Rome," *Journal of Roman Studies,* 70 [1980], 81–98). For the Romans' use of slaves as prostitutes for both heterosexual and homosexual relations, a practice no less common in Islamic societies, see John Boswell, *Christianity, Social Tolerance, and Homosexuality: Gay People in Western Europe from the Beginning of the Christian Era to the Fourteenth Century* (Chicago, 1980), 77–80.

36. Charles Verlinden, *L'esclavage dans l'Europe médiévale,* vol. 1, *Péninsule ibérique, France* (Bruges, 1955), 615–32, 835–41; Verlinden, *The Beginnings of Modern Colonization: Eleven Essays with an Introduction,* trans. Yvonne Freccero (Ithaca, N.Y., 1970), 39–40; Crone, *Slaves on Horses,* 49–50; Forand, "Relation of the Slave," 60–62, 65–66; Alan G. B. Fisher and Humphrey J. Fisher, *Slavery and Muslim Society in Africa: The Institution in Saharan and Sudanic Africa and the Trans-Saharan Trade* (Garden City, N.Y., 1971); Hambly, "Slavery in Islam."

37. Pipes, *Slave Soldiers and Islam,* xxi, 5–16, 20–35, 45–102, 193–94; Kenneth R. Andrews, *The Spanish Caribbean: Trade and Plunder, 1530–1630* (New Haven, 1978), 20, 31–36, 49–50, 140–46.

38. Hopkins, *Conquerers and Slaves,* 114.

39. Henri Pirenne, *Economic and Social History of Medieval Europe* (Harvest paperback ed., New York, n.d.), 17–23; Iris Origo, "The Domestic Enemy: The Eastern Slaves in Tuscany in the Fourteenth and Fifteenth Centuries," *Speculum,* 30 (1955), 321–55; Alberto Tenenti, "Gli schiavi de Venezia alla fine del cinquecento," *Revista storica italiana,* 67 (1955), 52–54, 60; Charles Verlinden, "La colonie vénitienne de Tana, centre de la traite des esclaves au XIVe et au debut du XVe siècles," in *Studi in onore di Gino Luzzatto* (Milan, 1950), 1–25; Verlinden, "Les origines coloniales de la civilisation atlantique: antécédents et types de structure," *Cahiers d'histoire mondiale,* 1 (1953), 378–98; Verlinden, *Beginnings of Modern Colonization,* 79–97; Verlinden, *L'esclavage dans l'Europe médiévale,* I, 320–43, 370, 427; vol. 2, *Italie—Colonies italiennes du Levant—Levant latin—Empire byzantin* (Gent, 1977), 137–55, 236–38, 282, 348–58, 360–84, 427–61, 550–659, 713–814, 878, 884–92, 978–1010; Robert Lopez, Harry Miskimin, and Abraham Udovitch, "England to Egypt, 1350–1500: Long-term Trends and Long-distance Trade," in M. A. Cook, ed., *Studies in the Economic History of the Middle East* (London, 1970), 119–27; Udovitch, "Introduction," ibid., 10.

40. Verlinden, *Beginnings of Modern Colonization,* 21–22; T. Bentley Duncan, *Atlantic Islands: Madeira, the Azores, and the Cape Verdes in Seventeenth-Century Commerce and Navigation* (Chicago, 1972), 9–11; Sidney M. Greenfield, "Madeira and the Beginnings of New World Sugar Cane Cultivation and Plantation Slavery: A Study in Institution Building," in Vera Rubin and Arthur Tuden, eds., *Comparative Perspectives on Slavery in New World Plantation Societies* (New York, 1977), 536–52. The effects of slave labor on economic and technological innovation are still a matter of controversy and fall beyond the scope of this book, but M. I. Finley observes that it was not until the fourteenth century that wheat production in England and France regularly matched the apparent yield on slave-worked

estates in ancient Italy, and that "one can point to some technological progress precisely where slavery showed its most brutal and oppressive face, in the Spanish mines and on the Roman *latifundia*" (*Ancient Economy,* 83). Without pretending to resolve this debate, one should also note the large number of slaves in various ancient and modern societies who have worked as skilled artisans and mechanics. Rebecca Scott has recently shown that in mid-nineteenth century Cuba slaves were used extensively on the most advanced plantations and in the most fully mechanized sugar mills ("Slave Emancipation and the Transition to Free Labor in Cuba, 1868–1895" [Ph.D. diss., Princeton University, 1981], 1–17, 111, 123–24). Lynn White, Jr., even suggests that slaves from Central Asia were probably responsible for introducing into fifteenth-century Italy such technological innovations as the verticle-axle windmill, the hot-air turbine, and especially the ball-and-chain governor (*Medieval Technology and Social Change* [Oxford, 1964], 116).

41. Bernard J. Siegel, "Some Methodological Considerations for a Comparative Study of Slavery," 390 n. 67; Dev Raj Chanana, *Slavery in Ancient India, as Depicted in Pali and Sanskrit Texts* (New Delhi, 1960), 19, 22, 94, 105–6, 108–9.

42. Verlinden, *L'esclavage dans l'Europe médiévale,* II, 797–98, 999–1010; Verlinden, *Beginnings of Modern Colonization,* 35–36; Evans, "From the Land of Canaan," 24; Davis, *Problem of Slavery in Western Culture,* 59–60; Brunschvig, "*'Abd*"; Leon Carl Brown, "Color in Northern Africa," in John Hope Franklin, ed., *Color and Race* (Boston, 1968), 192–93; Bernard Lewis, *Race and Color in Islam* (New York, 1971), 64. Orlando Patterson argues that "perceived racial differences between masters and slaves" have been common to a significant number of slaveholding societies throughout the world, as has the assumption that slaves belong to an innately inferior group. He also emphasizes that the "sambo" stereotype has been universal, "an ideological imperative of all systems of slavery" (*Slavery and Social Death,* 58, 96–97, 176–77). One should add that even within a single racial group, landlords have commonly regarded serfs and peasants as innately inferior, distinguished by repulsive physical features as well as by a fawning, "sambo" character.

43. Stephen Jay Gould, *The Mismeasure of Man* (New York, 1981). See also Reginald Horsman, *Race and Manifest Destiny: The Origins of American Racial Anglo-Saxonism* (Cambridge, Mass., 1981); and for cultural variations in the perception of racial differences, Mintz, *Caribbean Transformations,* 20–32.

44. Philip Curtin, Steven Feierman, Leonard Thompson, and Jan Vansina, *African History* (Boston, 1978), 9–27, 44, 80–86, 95; Nehemia Levtzion, *Ancient Ghana and Mali* (London, 1973), 3–4, 11–14.

45. Vercoutter et al., *Image of the Black,* I, 33–132. Egyptian artists did differentiate long-haired Nubians in Egyptian dress from Kushites and other Africans wearing only loincloths. Vercoutter, noting the resemblance between the present inhabitants of Darfur and Kordofan and Egyptian representations of the fourteenth century B.C., speculates on the possibility of an extremely ancient slave trade from Darfur to Lower Nubia and the Nile, a well-traveled route for slaves from early Islamic to modern times (63). Curtin et al., who find no evidence of an extensive trans-Saharan caravan trade until camels were introduced in the early Christian era, stress that dense vegetation in the Upper Nile blocked easy access from Egypt to the East African highlands (43, 53).

46. Vercoutter et al., *Image of the Black,* I, 89–245; Frank M. Snowden, Jr., *Blacks in Antiquity: Ethiopians in the Greco-Roman Experience* (Cambridge, Mass., 1970); A. N. Sherwin-White, *Racial Prejudice in Imperial Rome* (Cambridge, Eng., 1967).

47. Richard W. Bulliet, *The Camel and the Wheel* (Cambridge, Mass., 1975), 20–22, 36, 56, 87–99, 111–19, 124–38, 219; E. W. Bovill, *The Golden Trade of the Moors* (London, 1958); Levtzion, *Ancient Ghana and Mali,* 6–9, 124, 175–76. Bulliet's brilliant study says nothing about the significance of camel caravans for the long history of black slavery; on the other hand, Ralph A. Austen seems to take the camel for granted in "The Trans-Saharan Slave Trade: A Tentative Census," in Henry A. Gemery and Jan S. Hogendorn, eds., *The Uncommon Market: Essays in the Economic History of the Atlantic Slave Trade* (New York, 1979), 23–71. In Rome times there were some chariot roads across North Africa and there was some trade with the Garmantes of the Fezzan for gold, slaves, and other

commodities, but only a few recorded crossings of the Sahara. From premodern times there are no accounts of the way slaves were transported across the Sahara, but Levtzion surmises that conditions might well have resembled those described in the 1820s by R. Caillié, who traveled in a caravan of 1,400 camels: "Slaves were put on camels which carried loads of lesser weight such as ostrich feathers and cloth; others went on foot. They were given very little water and suffered more than others from the heat. Some of the Moors in Caillié's caravan treated the slaves very harshly" (*Ancient Ghana and Mali,* 175–76).

48. Ephraim Isaac, "Genesis, Judaism, and the 'Sons of Ham,'" *Slavery and Abolition,* 1 (1980), 7–9, 15–16; Song of Songs 1:5; Psalms 68:31; Jean Marie Courtès, "The Theme of 'Ethiopia' and 'Ethiopians' in Patristic Literature," in Jean Devisse, *The Image of the Black in Western Art,* vol. 2, *From the Early Christian Era to the "Age of Discovery,"* pt. 1, *From the Demonic Threat to the Incarnation of Sainthood* (New York, 1979), 14–16. For Origen, as one might expect, the conversion and symbolic "whitening" of Ethiopia also signified a repudiation of the "black" synagogue.

49. Acts 8:26–40; Courtès, "Theme of 'Ethiopia,'" 21–25; Jean Devisse, "Christians and Black," in *Image of the Black,* II, pt. 1, 38–43.

50. Courtès, "Theme of 'Ethiopia'" 11–16; Snowden, *Blacks in Antiquity,* 206–7; Lewis, *Race and Color in Islam,* 6–9.

51. Courtès and Devisse, *Image of the Black,* II, pt. 1, 19–20, 27–28, 46–80, 96; Rotter, *Die Stellung des Negers,* 156, 176–77.

52. Ladislas Bugner, introd. to *Image of the Black,* I, 22; II, pts. 1 and 2.

53. Here and in the following discussion, I have drawn particularly on Bernard Lewis, *Islam in History: Ideas, Men and Events in the Middle East* (New York, 1973); Lewis, *Race and Color in Islam;* Forand, "Relation of Slave and Client," 59–66; Brunschvig, "*'Abd*"; Fisher and Fisher, *Slavery and Muslim Society;* Levtzion, *Conversion to Islam;* I. M. Lewis, introd. to *Islam in Tropical Africa;* Crone, *Slaves on Horses;* Hambly, "Slavery in Islam"; Lovejoy, introd. to *Ideology of Slavery in Africa,* 16–22; Paul E. Lovejoy, Igor Kopytoff, and Frederick Cooper, "Indigenous African Slavery" [paper and commentaries], in Michael Craton, ed., *Roots and Branches: Current Directions in Slave Studies* (Toronto, 1979), 19–83.

54. Peter Brown, "Understanding Islam," *New York Review of Books,* 22 Feb. 1979, 30–33.

55. Bernard Lewis, *Islam in History,* 92–93; Lewis, *Race and Color in Islam,* 28.

56. André Miquel, *La géographie humaine du monde musulman jusqu'au milieu du 11ᵉ siècle,* vol. 2 (Paris, 1975), 3–11, 58, 90–126.

57. Miquel, *La géographie humaine,* II, 127–33, 153–88, 203; Moraes Farias, "Models of the World," 115–28. Even such experienced travelers as Ibn Battuta assumed that the Upper Niger was a branch of the Nile.

58. Rotter, *Die Stellung des Negers,* 155–58; Miquel, *La géographie humaine,* II, 141, 151–52; Lewis, *Race and Color in Islam,* 34–35. According to Lewis, Mas'udi noted that Galen included in his catalog "merriment," which "dominated the black man because of his defective brain, whence also the weakness of his intelligence."

59. Rotter, *Die Stellung des Negers,* 158, 165–66; Bryan Edwards, *The History Civil and Commercial of the British Colonies in the West Indies* (Philadelphia, 1806), II, 218–21.

60. Lewis, *Race and Color in Islam,* 11–14; Rotter, *Die Stellung des Negers,* 89. I have used the wording of both Lewis's and Rotter's translations.

61. Rotter, *Die Stellung des Negers,* 141–52; Miquel, *La géographie humaine,* II, 142; Evans, "From the Land of Canaan," 32–34. The continuing emphasis on hair tends to confirm Orlando Patterson's thesis that perceived differences in hair type were at least as important as skin color. In premodern societies it was common to shave the heads of captive slaves, a ritual symbolizing not only dishonor but also the loss of manliness, beauty, power, and freedom. Patterson surmises that the African hair type, which was more enduring genetically than skin color, became a similar badge of servility. Whites therefore had no need to shave the heads of African captives (*Slavery and Social Death,* 60–61).

62. Rotter, *Die Stellung des Negers,* 158–61, 182; Lewis, *Race and Color in Islam,* 34–38.

63. Lewis, *Race and Color in Islam,* 38 (the words in brackets are Lewis's); Rotter, *Die Stellung des Negers,* 162–63. Nehemia Levtzion points out that the Arabic word *nakhkhās* applied to traders in slaves and horses, as distinguished from traders in inanimate objects. In Ifriqiya, as in other regions, horses were frequently exchanged for slaves from the south (*Ancient Ghana and Mali,* 178).

64. Brunschvig, "*'Abd.*"

65. Lewis, *Race and Color in Islam,* 15–18; Miquel, *La géographie humaine,* II, 143–44.

66. Ibn Battuta, *Travels in Asia and Africa, 1325–1354,* trans. and selected by H. A. R. Gibb (London, 1929), 317–37. It should be noted that the kingdom of Mali included such groups as the Malinke, Bambara, Soninke, and Fulbe, but that "Malinke" properly refers simply to the Mande language of Mali, even though such speakers of Mande were commonly labeled "Malinke" or "Mandingo."

67. Austen, "Trans-Saharan Slave Trade," 30–32, 43–69; Austen, "The Islamic Slave Trade out of Africa (Red Sea and Indian Ocean): An Effort at Quantification" (Paper presented at the Conference on Islamic Africa: Slavery and Related Institutions, Princeton University, June 1977), 27–30, table V. An obvious question arises concerning the "missing" descendants of such an enormous black diaspora. As Austen points out, the Islamic world continually needed large numbers of imported slaves because the transport and "seasoning" to a new disease environment created a high mortality, because female slaves greatly outnumbered males (many of whom were eunuchs), and because the offspring of the females were often manumitted and regarded as "white." We know that over the course of two centuries large populations of African slaves virtually "disappeared" in Mexico and Peru. For the Asian diaspora, see Joseph E. Harris, *The African Presence in Asia: Consequences of the East African Slave Trade* (Evanston, Ill., 1971); Lewis, *Race and Color in Islam,* 88–89; and Raymond Mauny, *Les siècles obscurs de l'Afrique noir* (Paris, 1971).

It is also possible that by the sixteenth and seventeenth centuries Asian blacks were absorbed and drowned out by the massive influx of Russian, Polish, and other Caucasian slaves from the Ottoman-controlled Black Sea (Fischer, "Muscovy and the Black Sea Slave Trade," 575–94). As Austen readily acknowledges, though, statistics for the premodern period are anything but certain. Verlinden's figures on blacks in fifteenth-century Naples, Sicily, and Aragon-Catalonia suggest a larger diaspora to Europe than has usually been imagined, but Talhami ("The Zanj Rebellion Reconsidered," 443–61) questions the very existence of an Indian Ocean slave trade before the twelfth or thirteenth century.

68. I. M. Lewis, introd. to *Islam in Tropical Africa;* Levtzion, "Patterns of Islamization," 207–8; R. W. Beachey, *The Slave Trade of Eastern Africa* (New York, 1976); Frederick Cooper, *Plantation Slavery on the Coast of East Africa* (New Haven, 1977), 23–79.

69. For a now classic argument that Muslim ideology did not prevent Muslim societies from taking a capitalist path of development, see Maxime Rodinson, *Islam and Capitalism,* trans. Brian Pearce (London, 1974), esp. 99–117.

70. Charles-Emmanuel Dufourcq, *L'Espagne catalane et le Maghrib aux XIIIe et XIVe siècles* (Paris, 1966), 21–23, 71–81; Stephen Clisshold, *The Barbary Slaves* (London, 1977); Fernand Braudel, *The Mediterranean and the Mediterranean World in the Age of Philip II,* trans. Siân Reynolds (New York, 1972), II, 865–91; Norman R. Bennett, "Christian and Negro Slavery in Eighteenth-Century North Africa," *Journal of African History,* 1 (1960), 65–82; Hambly, "Slavery in Islam." As Clisshold points out, however, in the sixteenth, seventeenth, and eighteenth centuries most of the Christian "Barbary slaves" died in captivity if they refused to convert to Islam.

71. Lewis, *Race and Color in Islam,* 64–65, 68. These remarks, even as qualified above, in note 70, apply only to western Europeans. Like the sub-Saharan Africans, Christian Slavs captured by Tatars in the sixteenth and seventeenth centuries suffered from terrible brutality, disease, and mortality in the long transport from Galicia, Poland, the Ukraine, and southern Russia to markets in Caffa and Istanbul and often thence to buyers in Anatolia, Egypt, Iran, North Africa, Abyssinia, and even western Europe. But at least a small minority of these Christian slaves were ransomed either by wealthy friends or by the

Muscovite government; others were converted and more or less assimilated into Islamic society (Fisher, "Muscovy and the Black Sea Slave Trade," 582–93).

72. A translation of the principal text appears in Bernard Lewis, ed. and trans., *Islam: From the Prophet Muhammad to the Capture of Constantinople,* vol. 1 *Politics and War* (London, 1976), 232–34. Reports differed on whether the Nubians were to supply 400 or 360 slaves a year; according to one account they delivered only 40 slaves in the first year of the "pact."

73. Levtzion, *Ancient Ghana and Mali,* 3, 10, 18–27, 136–37, 174–75, 200. Levtzion, "Patterns of Islamization," 210–13; I. M. Lewis, introd. to *Islam in Tropical Africa;* Lovejoy, *The Ideology of Slavery in Africa;* Fisher and Fisher, *Slaves and Muslim Society in Africa;* Terence Walz, *Trade between Egypt and Bilād Sudan, 1700–1820* (Cairo, 1978); Curtin, *Economic Change in Precolonial Africa,* xx–xxi, 4–5, 46–50, 66–68.

74. Levtzion, *Ancient Ghana and Mali,* 34–54, 115–16, 126–29, 150–64, 175; Dufourcq, *L'Espagne catalane,* 138; Bovill, *Golden Trade of the Moors;* Curtin discusses the weakening of Mali and the rise of other states in the Senegambia region after the mid-fifteenth century (*Economic Change in Precolonial Africa,* 8–12).

75. Levtzion, *Ancient Ghana and Mali,* 129–32; Dufourcq, *L'Espagne catalane,* 32; Robert S. Lopez, "The Dawn of Modern Banking," in Center for Medieval and Renaissance Studies, Univeristy of California, Los Angeles, *The Dawn of Modern Banking* (New Haven, 1979), 14–15, 17–19; Michael Prestwich, "Italian Merchants in England," ibid., 84; John H. Munro, "Bullionism and the Bill of Exchange in England," ibid., 185–87. For the shift from the earlier Sudanese gold trade to the Portuguese gold trade from West Africa, see Braudel, *Mediterranean,* I, 466–74.

76. Ronald Sanders, *Lost Tribes and Promised Lands: The Origins of American Racism* (Boston, 1978), 3–12.

77. Dufourcq, *L'Espagne catalane,* 15–26, 34–36, 61, 68, 138–44, 543–46, 572–88; Levtzion, *Ancient Ghana and Mali,* 149–52, 168–79. Levtzion suggests that by spreading a moral repugnance to nudity, Islam helped to promote a market for textiles. The insatiable demand for salt was a response to Sudanese heat.

78. Levtzion, *Ancient Ghana and Mali,* 168–69. My own focus is on European enslavers and emancipators, not on African history. I am, of course, aware of recent efforts to "decolonize" African history and to minimize the importance of European influences, including slave trading, before the mid-nineteenth century. It is appropriate here to refer to Gemery and Hogendorn's interesting analysis of the ways European technology affected the gathering and merchandizing of slaves in Africa and their transport to the New World ("Technological Change, Slavery, and the Slave Trade," 243–58). The subtle complexities of this process, including the effects on indigenous institutions of long-distance trade, are illuminated for the central Zaire basin by Robert W. Harms, *River of Wealth, River of Sorrow: the Central Zaire Basin the Era of the Slave and Ivory Trade, 1500–1891* (New Haven, 1981). See also Curtin, *Economic Change in Precolonial Africa,* 3, 45–46, 153–87.

79. David Eltis, "Free and Coerced Transatlantic Migrations: Some Comparisons," *American Historical Review,* 88 (1983), 251–56; Verlinden, *L'esclavage dans l'Europe médiévale,* I, 847–52, II, 1029–46; Braudel, *Mediterranean,* II, 754–55, 865–91; Tenenti, "Gli schiavi de Venezia," 52–54, 61–69; Alberto Tenenti, *Cristoforo da Canal: La marine vénitienne avant Lépante* (Paris, 1962); Hellie, "Muscovite Slavery," 133–209; Richard Hellie, *Slavery in Russia, 1450–1725* (Chicago, 1982), 1–26, 679–720; Fisher, "Muscovy and the Black Sea Slave Trade," 575–94; Jerome Blum, *The End of the Old Order in Rural Europe* (Princeton, 1978), 35–46, and passim; John H. Langbein, *Torture and the Law of Proof: Europe and England in the Ancien Regime* (Chicago, 1977), 30–31; Paul W. Bamford, "Slaves for the Galleys of France, 1665 to 1700," in *Merchants and Scholars: Essays in the History of Exploration and Trade* (Minneapolis, 1965), 173–88; Clissold, *Barbary Slaves;* David W. Galenson, *White Servitude in Colonial America: An Economic Analysis* (Cambridge, Eng., 1981), ix.

80. Robert S. Lopez, *The Commercial Revolution of the Middle Ages, 950–1350* (Englewood Cliffs, N.J., 1971), 60–61, 109–11, and passim; Lopez, *The Birth of Mordern Europe*

(London, 1966), 56–61, 109, 111; Rodney Hilton, "The Transition from Feudalism to Capitalism," *Science and Society,* 17 (1953), 340–48.

81. Robert S. Lopez, "Market Expansion: The Case of Genoa," in *Su e giù per la storia di Genova* (Genoa, 1975), 45.

82. Ibid., 44–62; Jacques Heers, *Gênes au XVe siècle: Activité économique et problèmes sociaux* (Paris, 1961), 313–14; Origo, "Domestic Enemy," 326–27. Lopez emphasizes, however, that "the westward expansion of the fifteenth century was mostly the work of powerful companies" and that economic opportunities contracted as both capital and credit became concentrated in the hands of the few (p. 61). Braudel also affirms that the spectacular symbols of "progress" after 1450, such as the scale of construction and the amount of public building, did not mean a rise in living standards for most of the population: "During every period, until at least the eighteenth century, economic progress was inevitably at the expense of the ever-increasing masses, the victims of 'social massacres' " (*Mediterranean,* II, 893–95).

83. Verlinden, *Beginnings of Modern Colonization,* 5–6, 31, 80–97; Verlinden, "La colonie vénitienne de Tana," 1–25; Verlinden, "Esclaves alains en Italie et dans les colonies italiennes au XIVe siècle," *Revue belge de philologie et d'histoire,* 36 (1958), 451–57; Verlinden, *L'esclavage dans l'Europe médiévale,* II, 132, 137, 155, 220–31, 427–61, 550, 712–99, 910–14, 924–48; Heers, *Gênes au XVe siècle,* 370ff. For the selling of slaves by Swedish merchants and by the merchants and princes of Kievan Russia, see George Vernadsky, *A History of Russia,* vol. 2, *Kievan Russia* (New Haven, 1948), 15–18, 30, 111, 126, 146; vol. 3, *The Mongols and Russia* (New Haven, 1953), 336–37; M. Tikhomirov, *The Towns of Ancient Rus* (Moscow, 1959), 149–62; B. Grekov, *Kiev Rus* (Moscow, 1959), 224–51.

84. Verlinden, *Beginnings of Modern Colonization,* x–xviii, 6–12, 21–25, 71–72, 98–157; Charles Verlinden, "Le problème de la continuité en histoire coloniale: De la colonisation médiévale à la colonisation moderne," *Revista de Indias,* 11 (1951), 219–36; Verlinden, "Le influenze italiana nella colonizzazione iberica," *Nuova revista storica,* 36 (1952), 265–70; Verlinden, *L'esclavage dans l'Europe médiévale,* II, 356–58; Heers, *Gênes au XVe siècle,* 494–98; Lopez, "Market Expansion," 53, 56–62.

85. Origo, "Domestic Enemy," 321–29; Verlinden, *L'esclavage dans l'Europe médiévale,* II, 360–84, 460–61, 566–666. Population decline brought a sharp drop in the price of grain and other foodstuffs and a rising urban demand for luxuries, including domestic servants (Harry A. Miskimin, *The Economy of Later Renaissance Europe, 1460–1600* [Cambridge, Eng., 1977], 21–22).

86. Verlinden, *Beginnings of Modern Colonization,* 79–97; Verlinden, *L'esclavage dans l'Europe médiévale,* II, 133–234, 802ff., 844ff. Modern historians sometimes forget that the European words for "Negro" are derived from *niger,* the Latin word for "black." The Romans, however, never classified all sub-Saharan Africans or "Ethiopians" as "blacks." It was only in the fifteenth century that Europeans, possibly following Arabic precedents, began to identify sub-Saharan Africans not simply as "black Saracens" but as "blacks."

By the sixteenth century, Fernand Braudel contends, even the richest of the Mediterranean islands had been blighted by the effects of sugar monoculture and continual warfare, piracy, and banditry. While piracy and banditry were common to the entire Mediterranean region, the islands were in effect "besieged territories." Though Braudel sometimes attributes the islands' poverty to the destruction and insecurity of war, he also equates their prosperity with piracy and privateering (*Mediterranean,* I, 153–55, II, 734–54, 865–91).

87. Charles Verlinden, "La Crète, débouché et plaque tournante de la traite des esclaves," in *Studi in onore di Amintore Fanfani* (Milan, 1962), III, 593–669; Verlinden, "L'esclavage en Sicile au bas moyen âge," *Institut historique belge de Rome,* 35 (1963), 13–113; Verlinden, *L'esclavage dans l'Europe médiévale,* II, 155–358. Although there are no adequate statistics for estimating the proportion of slaves in Sicily, a Majorcan tax list of 1428 leads Verlinden to estimate a minimum of 18 percent. Using the same methods and assumptions regarding sex ratio in analyzing a tax list of 1328, before the Black Death, he arrives at the figure of 36 percent (pp. 282, 348–51, 357–58).

88. Verlinden, "L'esclavage en Sicile," 42–43, 68–79, 90–93; Charles Verlinden, "L'esclavage noir en France méridionale et courants de traite en Afrique," *Annales du Midi,* 78 (1966), 335–343; Verlinden, *L'esclavage dans l'Europe médiévale,* II, 208–220, 233–38, 329–30, 353–54.

89. Sidney M. Greenfield, "Plantations, Sugar Cane and Slavery," in Craton, *Roots and Branches,* 96.

90. Verlinden, *L'esclavage dans l'Europe médiévale,* I, 550, 621.

91. Greenfield, "Plantations, Sugar Cane and Slavery," 96–108; Boxer, *Portuguese Seaborne Empire,* 16–70, 98. Late in 1980 there was a magnificent exhibit of such Japanese screens at the Musée Cernuschi in Paris. Some have been reproduced in various collections, such as Bradley Smith, *Japan: A History in Art* (New York, 1964), 148–57.

92. Noel Deerr, *The History of Sugar* (London, 1949–50), I, 69–70, II, 259, and passim.

93. Verlinden, *Beginnings of Modern Colonization,* 5, 18–19, 196–240; Greenfield, "Plantations, Sugar Cane and Slavery," 90–91.

94. Greenfield, "Plantations, Sugar Cane and Slavery," 91, 108; Verlinden, *Beginnings of Modern Colonization,* 19–21, 109–11, 124–25, 135–57; Heers, *Gênes au XVᵉ siècle,* 494–98; Miskimin, *Economy of Later Renaissance Europe,* 21–22, 74–75. Braudel notes that in 1625 Naples imported "the unbelievable quantity" of 1,500 tons of sugar, much of which was apparently exported in the form of various food commodites (*Mediterranean,* I, 347). Although Europe began importing substantial quantities of tea and coffee in the seventeenth century, sugar was still a luxury in France in the eighteenth century (Braudel, *Capitalism and Material Life, 1400–1800,* trans. Miriam Kochan [New York, 1973], 157–58, 179–86).

95. A. J. R. Russell-Wood, "Iberian Expansion and the Issue of Black Slavery: Changing Portuguese Attitudes, 1440–1770," *American Historical Review,* 83 (1978), 16–18, 27–28; Verlinden, *L'esclavage dans l'Europe médiévale,* I, 617–20; John Francis Maxwell, *Slavery and the Catholic Church: The History of Catholic Teaching Concerning the Moral Legitimacy of the Institution of Slavery* (Chichester, Eng., 1975), 53–54; Sanders, *Lost Tribes and Promised Lands,* 59–60.

96. Verlinden, *L'esclavage dans l'Europe médiévale,* I, 615–16, 621; Verlinden, *Beginnings of Modern Colonization,* 132–57; Russell-Wood, "Iberian Expansion," 20; Anthony Luttrell, "Slavery and Slaving in the Portuguese Atlantic (to about 1500)," in Christopher Fyfe, ed., "The Transatlantic Slave Trade from West Africa" (Mimeographed Proceedings of a Seminar Held in the Centre of African Studies, University of Edinburgh, 4 and 5 June 1965), 65–69, 74–75; Greenfield, "Madeira and the Beginnings of New World Sugar Cane Cultivation," 536–52; Curtin, *Economic Change in Precolonial Africa,* 59–75, 95–100; Boxer, *Portuguese Seaborne Empire,* 68–70.

97. Russell-Wood, "Iberian Expansion," 20–22; Verlinden, *L'esclavage dans l'Europe médiévale,* I, 615–32. Agrarian interests in Portugal, strongly represented in the Cortes, feared that the export of black slaves would raise the costs of labor, but finally lost out to the king and commercial interests. Philip D. Curtin estimates that only fifty thousand African slaves were imported into Portugal and the rest of Europe during the entire era of the Atlantic slave trade (*The Atlantic Slave Trade: A Census* [Madison, Wis., 1969], 18–20).

98. Greenfield, "Madeira and the Beginnings of New World Sugar Cane Cultivation," 536–52; Greenfield, "Plantations, Sugar Cane and Slavery," 85–88, 98–119; Duncan, *Atlantic Islands,* 9–11; Virginia Rau and Jorge de Macedo, *O açúcar da Madeira nos fins do século XV: Problemas de produção e comércio* (Funchal, Madeira, 1962), 9–15; Heers, *Gênes au XVᵉ siècle,* 494–98; Miskimin, *Economy of Later Renaissance Europe,* 125–28.

99. Duncan, *Atlantic Islands,* 17–22; Verlinden, *Beginnings of Modern Colonization,* 161–80.

100. Duncan, *Atlantic Islands,* 58–59, 195–96; Greenfield, "Plantations, Sugar Cane and Slavery," 114–16; Calvin Martin, *Keepers of the Game: Indian-Animal Relationships and the Fur Trade* (Berkeley, 1978), 41; Curtin, *Atlantic Slave Trade,* 20–21, 99, 115–16. Although Curtin indicates that a significant proportion of the estimated 75,000 slaves imported into São Tomé in the sixteenth century were reexported to Brazil, he implies that most of the

44,000 who arrived before 1550 remained on the island. On the other hand, according to Miskimin, who follows the 1970 caculations of F. Mauro, São Tomé produced only 324 U.S. tons of sugar in 1580 and 648 tons in 1600, compared with Madeira's more than 3,239 tons in 1570 (Miskimin, *Economy of Later Renaissance Europe,* 133). Yet, according to Curtin's estimates, Madeira and the other Atlantic islands, excluding São Tomé, imported only 15,000 slaves in the first half of the sixteenth century. Further research is needed to clarify this discrepancy.

101. Deerr, *History of Sugar,* 101–6; Boxer, *Portuguese Seaborne Empire,* 89–112; Miskimin, *Economy of Later Renaissance Europe,* 132–35; Andrews, *Spanish Caribbean,* 37–40, 72–133, 171–97; Colin A. Palmer, *Slaves of the White God: Blacks in Mexico, 1570–1650* (Cambridge, Mass., 1976), 8–35.

102. Philip D. Curtin, "Epidemiology and the Slave Trade," *Political Science Quarterly,* 83 (1968), 190–216; K. G. Davies, "The Living and the Dead: White Mortality in West Africa, 1684–1732," in Stanley L. Engerman and Eugene D. Genovese, eds., *Race and Slavery in the Western Hemisphere: Quantitative Studies* (Princeton, 1975), 83–98; Curtin et al., *African History,* 186, 214–15; Herbert S. Klein, *The Middle Passage: Comparative Studies in the Atlantic Slave Trade* (Princeton, 1978), 193–202, 229–38; Joseph C. Miller, "Mortality in the Atlantic Slave Trade: Statistical Evidence on Causality," *Journal of Interdisciplinary History,* 11 (1981), 385–423.

103. Sherburne F. Cook and Woodrow Borah, *Essays in Population History: Mexico and the Caribbean,* vol. 1 (Berkeley, 1971), viii, 82, 392–410; Alfred W. Crosby, Jr., "Virgin Soil Epidemics as a Factor in the Aboriginal Depopulation of America," *William and Mary Quarterly,* 33 (1976), 289–99; Crosby, *The Columbian Exchange: Biological and Cultural Consequences of 1492* (Westport, Conn., 1972); Martin, *Keepers of the Game,* 43–65, and passim. Martin provides a valuable guide to the literature on Amerindian depopulation (197–99).

104. Philip D. Curtin, "Slavery and Empire," in Rubin and Tuden, *Comparative Perspectives,* 9; Peter H. Wood, *Black Majority: Negroes in South Carolina, from 1670 through the Stono Rebellion* (New York, 1974), 35–91.

105. Richard S. Dunn, *Sugar and Slaves: The Rise of the Planter Class in the English West Indies, 1624–1713* (Chapel Hill, 1972), 52–55, 155, 303, 312–13, 325–34; Galenson, *White Servitude in Colonial America,* 150, 216–18, 265 n. 16; Gary Puckrein, "The Political Demography of Colonial Barbados (1627–1800)" (Paper, Shelby Cullom Davis Center, Princeton University); Richard N. Bean and Robert P. Thomas, "The Adoption of Slave Labor in British America," in Gemery and Hogendorn, *Uncommon Market,* 381–94.

106. Edmund S. Morgan, *American Slavery, American Freedom: The Ordeal of Colonial Virginia* (New York, 1975), 157–61; Galenson, *White Servitude in Colonial America,* 152–53. For conflicting explanations of the shift from white indentured servants to black slaves, see Morgan, *American Slavery,* 295–315; Bean and Thomas, "Adoption of Slave Labor," 377–98; Russell R. Menard, "From Servants to Slaves: The Transformation of the Chesapeake Labor System," *Southern Studies,* 16 (1977), 355–90; Galenson, *White Servitude in Colonial America,* 141–68. Despite differences on technical details, recent scholarship emphasizes the central importance of labor costs and changes in the conditions and elasticity of the supply both of white servants and of black slaves.

107. Miller, "Mortality in the Atlantic Slave Trade," 385–423; Philip D. Curtin, "The African Diaspora," in Craton, *Roots and Branches,* 14–16; Dunn, *Sugar and Slaves,* 314–25. There is a growing literature on New World slave morbidity and mortality, which was, of course, affected by factors other than disease. For the diseases associated with black slavery, see especially Richard B. Sheridan, "Mortality and the Medical Treatment of Slaves in the British West Indies," in Engerman and Genovese, *Race and Slavery,* 285–310; Sheridan, *Sugar and Slavery: An Economic History of the British West Indies, 1623–1775* (Baltimore, 1974); David L. Chandler, *Health and Slavery in Colonial Colombia,* Dissertations in European Economic History (New York, 1981); Kenneth F. Kiple and Virginia H. Kiple, "Deficiency Diseases in the Caribbean," *Journal of Interdisciplinary History,* 11 (1980), 197–215; Kiple and Kiple, "Black Yellow Fever Immunities, Innate and Acquired, as Revealed in the American South," *Social Science History,* 1 (1977), 419–36; Kenneth F. Kiple

and Virginia Himmelsteib King, *Another Dimension to the Black Diaspora: Diet, Disease, and Racism* (Cambridge, Eng., 1981).

108. Andrews, *Spanish Caribbean,* 6, 12, 20–21, 38; Palmer, *Slaves of the White God,* 6–10; Patterson, *Slavery and Social Death,* 481, table N11; Davis, *Problem of Slavery in Western Culture,* 128–30; Sherman, *Forced Native Labor,* ix.

109. Palmer, *Slaves of the White God,* 9–30, 40, 45–47, 66–67; Frederick P. Bowser, *The African Slave in Colonial Peru, 1524–1650* (Stanford, 1974), 25–51, 75; Andrews, *Spanish Caribbean,* 20, 31–32.

110. Andrews, *Spanish Caribbean,* 54–84, 108–33, 245–55; Bowser, *African Slave in Colonial Peru,* 37, 272–334; Davis, *Problem of Slavery in Western Culture,* 128–32, 241, 281–88; Palmer, *Slaves of the White God,* 167–90. Although the temporary union of Portugal and Spain removed many obstacles to the slave trade to Hispanic America, the bureaucracies of the two nations remained separate, and the Spanish crown relied on selling a contract, for a specific number of slaves, to an *asentista,* who would then sell a valid export license to a slave trader. The complexities and difficulties of the system are explained by Bowser (*African Slave Trade in Colonial Peru,* 26–37).

111. Patterson, *Slavery and Social Death,* 113; Elliott, *Old World and the New,* 4, 51, 103.

112. Patterson, *Slavery and Social Death,* 171; Braudel, *Mediterranean,* II, 871.

113. Sherman, *Forced Native Labor,* 20–82. After considering higher estimates by Murdo MacLeod and others, Sherman concludes by saying, "I would be surprised if the total number of chattel slaves made in all of Central America between 1524 and 1549 surpassed a hundred and fifty thousand, no more than a third of whom were shipped out to other lands" (82). The Spanish crown tried to regulate the branding of Amerindians, and even hoped that the use of branding irons could be supervised by the bishop or the governor, but Sherman sums up the significance of early reforms in one unforgettable scene: "When a ship put in at a Nicaraguan port loaded with illegally enslaved encomienda Indians, the governor freed them and sent them home. But first the natives, some of whom were women and suckling children, had their face brands canceled. Fresh letters spelling 'libre' were burned into their scarred faces. That same year, 1532, the Crown ruled that no one was to dare brand an Indian on the face" (64–65).

114. Various scholars have revised Philip D. Curtin's pioneering estimates of the volume of the Atlantic slave trade, some insisting on a total importation into the Americas of at least 12 or 13 million slaves. In the most careful review and analysis of current evidence, Paul E. Lovejoy raises some of Curtin's estimates but lowers others, and arrives at the figures of about 11.7 million Africans exported and 9.8 million imported into the Americas and Atlantic basin between 1450 and 1900. See Lovejoy, "The Volume of the Atlantic Slave Trade: A Synthesis," *Journal of African History,* 23 (1982), 473–501.

115. Rau and Macedo, *O açúcar da Madeira,* 9–10; Boxer, *Portuguese Seaborne Empire,* 84–85, 97–104; Richard Price, ed., *Maroon Societies: Rebel Slave Communities in the Americas* (Garden City, N.Y., 1973), 170–224; Greenfield, "Plantations, Sugar Cane and Slavery," 118–19; Miskimin, *Economy of Later Renaissance Europe,* 133. *Mocambos,* later called *quilombos,* appeared in Brazil as early as 1575 and reached the apogee with the famous "Negro Republic" of Palmares, which flourished from the early seventeenth century until finally destroyed, in 1694, by thousands of *bandeirantes* reinforced by troops from Pernambuco.

116. Boxer, *Portuguese Seaborne Empire,* 87–93, 105–13; Deerr, *History of Sugar,* I, 102–7; Arnold Wiznitzer, *Jews in Colonial Brazil* (New York, 1970), 9–10. Philip II's war against the Protestants in the Low Countries resulted in the destruction of much of Antwerp's sugar industry (Nef, *War and Human Progress,* 77).

117. Andrews, *Spanish Caribbean,* 224–49; Dunn, *Sugar and Slaves,* 3–83.

118. Dunn, *Sugar and Slaves,* 17, 226; Winthrop D. Jordan, *White over Black: American Attitudes toward the Negro, 1550–1812* (Chapel Hill, 1968), 63–68; Richard Pares, *War and Trade in the West Indies, 1739–1763* (Oxford, 1936). Many of the Caribbean islands changed hands several times during the Anglo-French wars from 1756 to 1815. Saint Lucia, for example, was captured by the British no fewer than four times before being officially

added to the empire in 1814. For the most up-to-date figures on the soaring slave population in the eighteenth-century Caribbean, see Patterson, *Slavery and Social Death,* 477–82.

119. Eric Williams, *Capitalism and Slavery* (Chapel Hill, 1944); Roger Anstey, "Capitalism and Slavery: A Critique," *Economic History Review,* 2d ser., 21 (1968), 307–20; Anstey, "The Volume and Profitability of the British Slave Trade, 1761–1807," in Engerman and Genovese, *Race and Slavery in the Western Hemisphere,* 3–31; Stanley L. Engerman, "The Slave Trade and British Capital Formation in the Eighteenth Century: A Comment on the Williams Thesis," *Business History Review,* 46 (1972), 430–43; Richard B. Sheridan, "The Wealth of Jamaica in the Eighteenth Century," *Economic History Review,* 2d ser., 18 (1965), 292–311; R. P. Thomas, "The Sugar Colonies of the Old Empire: Profit or Loss for Great Britain?" *Economic History Review,* 2d ser., 21 (1968), 30–45; Stanley L. Engerman, "Notes on the Patterns of Economic Growth in the British North American Colonies in the Seventeenth, Eighteenth, and Nineteenth Centuries," in Paul Bairoch and Maurice Lévy-Leboyer, eds., *Disparities in Economic Development since the Industrial Revolution* (London, 1981), 46–57; Eltis, "Free and Coerced Transatlantic Migration," 251–56.

120. My calculations on colonial exports are from Engerman, "Notes on the Patterns of Economic Growth," 48, table 5. The figures for 1725–34 apply to England and Wales for West Indian exports, and to England alone for mainland colony exports; the figures for 1765–74 apply to Great Britain for the West Indies, and to England and Scotland for the mainland colonies. For non-European shares of British exports, see Seymour Drescher, *Econocide: British Slavery in the Era of Abolition* (Pittsburgh, 1977), 23, table 4.

121. Drescher, *Econocide,* 16–37, esp. tables 1–4. Drescher vigorously disputes the other side of the "Williams thesis," namely, that the British West Indies entered a period of long-term decline after the Seven Years' War and that Britain's abolition of the slave trade and its emancipation of black slaves were thus "profit-maximizing or loss-minimizing" operations motivated largely by economic self-interest. Drescher rightly points out that the assumption of economic decline has been accepted, in one form or another, by Lowell J. Ragatz (in 1928), Richard Pares, Elsa Goveia, Sidney Mintz, Richard B. Sheridan, C. Duncan Rice, Alan Adamson, Michael Craton, and numerous other historians, including myself. In view of Roger Anstey's work on the abolition of the British slave trade and Drescher's compelling arguments and statistics on the West Indian share of British trade, I would no longer maintain, as I did in 1966, that "there can be little doubt that colonial slavery was of greater importance to the British economy in 1750 than in 1789, or that the reverse was true of France"; or that "it is . . . difficult to get around the simple fact that no country thought of abolishing the slave trade until its economic value had considerably declined" (*Problem of Slavery in Western Culture,* 153). On the other hand, no one has shown that abolition of the slave trade retarded British economic growth or was perceived at the time (except by a few merchants, planters, and naval officers) as endangering vital national interests. The debate over the West Indies' relative "decline" involves a good bit more than the value of overseas trade, as the works of Craton, Goveia, Sheridan, Mintz, and other Caribbean specialists amply show.

122. Gary B. Nash, *The Urban Crucible: Social Change, Political Consciousness, and the Origins of the American Revolution* (Cambridge, Mass., 1979), 13; Davis, *Problem of Slavery in Western Culture,* 126.

123. Marcel Trudel, *L'esclavage au Canada français: Histoire et conditions de l'esclavage* (Quebec, 1960), 20–35; Nash, *Urban Crucible,* 13–14, 107; Edward Channing, *The Narragansett Planters* (Boston, 1886), 8–10; Lorenzo J. Green, *The Negro in Colonial New England, 1660–1776* (New York, 1942), 28–29, 74, 76, 99, 103; Edgar J. McManus, *Black Bondage in the North* (Syracuse, N.Y., 1973).

124. Ira Berlin, "Time, Space, and the Evolution of Afro-American Society on British Mainland North America," *American Historical Review,* 85 (1980), 46–54; Nash, *Urban Crucible,* 14, 107–9; Edgar J. McManus, *A History of Negro Slavery in New York* (Syracuse, N.Y., 1966), 23–57, 197–200; James G. Lydon, "New York and the Slave Trade, 1700 to

1774," *William and Mary Quarterly,* 35 (1978), 375–94; Galenson, *White Servitude,* 119–20, tables 8.1 and 8.2; Jeanne Chase, "Fugitive Space and Judicial Boundaries in Provincial New York" (Paper, La Maison des Sciences de l'Homme, Paris).

125. Galenson, *White Servitude,* 117–68; Nash, *Urban Crucible,* 109–10; Gary B. Nash, "Slaves and Slaveowners in Colonial Philadelphia," *William and Mary Quarterly,* 30 (1973), 226–52; Darold D. Wax, "The Demand for Slave Labor in Colonial Pennsylvania," *Pennsylvania History,* 34 (1967), 331–45.

126. Lydon, "New York and the Slave Trade," 382, table IV; Menard, "From Servants to Slaves," 355–90; Allan Kulikoff, "The Colonial Chesapeake: Seedbed of Antebellum Southern Culture?" *Journal of Southern History,* 45 (1979), 525–26.

127. Berlin, "Time, Space, and the Evolution of Afro-American Society," 71–77; Bureau of the Census, *Historical Statistics of the United States, Colonial Times to 1970,* pt. 2 (Washington, 1975), 1168–72; Bureau of the Census, *Negro Population, 1790–1915* (Washington, 1918), 45; Morgan, *American Slavery, American Freedom;* Kulikoff, "Colonial Chesapeake," 520–21, 532–36.

128. Alice Hanson Jones, *Wealth of a Nation to Be: The American Colonies on the Eve of the Revolution* (New York, 1980), 95–101; Engerman, "Notes on Patterns of Economic Growth," 50–56, esp. tables 5.4 and 5.5

129. Engerman, "Notes on Patterns of Economic Growth," 51–52.

130. Patterson, *Slavery and Social Death,* 481, table N11; David Geggus, "The British Government and the Saint Domingue Slave Revolt, 1791–1793," *English Historical Review,* 96 (1981), 285–305; Drescher, *Econocide,* 46–54, 76–91; Gavin Wright, *The Political Economy of the Cotton South: Households, Markets, and Wealth in the Nineteenth Century* (New York, 1978).

131. Gemery and Hogendorn, "Technological Change, Slavery, and the Slave Trade," 243–58; Gemery and Hogendorn, "The Economic Costs of West African Participation in the Atlantic Slave Trade," in *Uncommon Market,* 143–61; Walter Rodney, *A History of the Upper Guinea Coast, 1545–1800* (Oxford, 1970).

132. Davis, *Problem of Slavery in Western Culture,* 211–22, 291–493; Davis, *Problem of Slavery in the Age of Revolution,* 164–468; David Bertelson, *The Lazy South* (New York, 1967); Linda K. Kerber, *Federalists in Dissent: Imagery and Ideology in Jeffersonian America* (Ithaca, N.Y., 1970), 23–66. Eighteenth-century British and American writers anticipated most of the themes and imagery that were later woven into the "Republican critique of the South," which has been masterfully described by Eric Foner (*Free Soil, Free Labor, Free Men: The Ideology of the Republican Party before the Civil War* [New York, 1970], 11–72).

133. For blacks in Britain, see esp. James Walvin, *Black and White: The Negro and English Society, 1555–1945* (London, 1973), 46–156. For the *Somerset* case involving the freeing of slaves in England, see William M. Wiecek, *The Sources of Antislavery Constitutionalism in America, 1760–1848* (Ithaca, N.Y., 1977), 20–39; and Davis, *Problem of Slavery in the Age of Revolution,* 469–522.

134. *Connecticut Courant,* 14 Aug. 1797.

135. Ella McKenna Friend Mielziner, *Moses Mielziner, 1828–1903: A Biography with a Bibliography of his Writings . . . a Reprint of His 'Slavery amongst the Ancient Hebrews' and Other Works* (New York, 1931), 64–65, and passim.

136. Ibid., 212–50; Morris U. Schappes, *A Documentary History of the Jews in the United States, 1654–1875,* 3d ed. (New York, 1971), 405–18, 682–84; Bertram Wallace Korn, *American Jewry and the Civil War* (Philadelphia, 1951), chap. 2.

137. New York Manumission Society MS Minutes, New York Historical Society; Jonathan D. Sarna, *Jacksonian Jew: The Two Worlds of Mordecai Noah* (New York, 1981), 108–17, and passim; Robert D. Meade, *Judah P. Benjamin* (New York, 1943).

138. Urbach, "Laws regarding Slavery," 2–3, 39–40, 93–94.

139. Deut. 15:12–15; Lev. 15:35–55 (I have used the phrasing from *The Holy Scriptures according to the Masoretic Text,* new ed. [Philadelphia, 1955]).

140. Personal communication from Frank Moore Cross, Hancock Professor of Hebrew and Other Oriental Languages, Harvard University, 20 Dec. 1979.

141. Joseph Klausner, "The Economy of Judea in the Period of the Second Temple," in Michael Avi-yonah et al., eds., *The Herodian Period,* vol. 7 of *The World History of the Jewish People,* ed. Cecil Roth (New Brunswick, N.J., 1975), 189–93; Urbach, "Laws regarding Slavery," 3–31, 88–93.

142. Urbach, "Laws regarding Slavery," 14–17, 67–87; Mendelsohn, *Slavery in the Ancient Near East,* 85–90; Treggiari, *Roman Freedmen during the Late Republic,* 206; Joshua Starr, *The Jew in the Byzantine Empire, 641–1204* (Athens, 1939), 32–33; S. D. Goitein, *A Mediterranean Society: The Jewish Communities of the Arab World as Portrayed in the Documents of the Cairo Geniza* (Berkeley, 1967–71), I, 65, 144–46.

143. Isaac, "Genesis, Judaism, and the 'Sons of Ham,'" 5–6. The ideological need to invalidate the Canaanites' claim to Palestine is best revealed in a passage that Isaac quotes from the Ethiopic version of the book of Jubilees. Isaac emphasizes that "the concept of 'curse and blessings' is applied not only to the Canaanites but even to the Israelites themselves if they transgress the law. . . . Inasmuch as the Israelites who sin against God can be accursed, the Canaanites who obey God can be blessed; in other words, there is no dogmatic view on the curse of Canaan" (6–7).

144. Gerhard Von Rad, *Genesis: A Commentary,* trans. John H. Marks (Philadelphia, 1961), 131–33; Isaac, "Genesis, Judaism, and the 'Sons of Ham,'" 3–17; Milani, *La schiavitù nel pensiero politico,* 292, 300, 316, 355–57, 377 n. 16. The apologetic tradition represented by Moses Mielziner has been more than counterbalanced by recent and less careful Jewish and gentile historians who, searching for the origins of modern racism, have pounced upon quotations extracted arbitrarily from the Babylonian Talmud and other rabbinic sources. Ephraim Isaac, an Ethiopian scholar, no doubt overstates his case; but his exhaustive scholarship fills in the context and variant texts of what turn out to be misquotations and misinterpretations. His footnotes also provide the best tentative guide I have seen to the later misappropriation of the "Hamitic myth." Although I have learned much from the pioneering research of William McKee Evans ("From the Land of Canaan to the Land of Guinea"), I am convinced that the "Hamitic myth" played a relatively minor role in justifying black slavery until the late eighteenth and the nineteenth centuries, when slaveholders were able to identify the "rationalist" challenge to Holy Scripture with an attack upon a divinely ordained institution. Before then, for Jews, Christians, and Muslims alike, it was sufficient that blacks were Gentiles, pagans, or infidels, and the Noachian curse served as an occasional, if forceful, obiter dictum.

145. Urbach, "Laws regarding Slavery," 17, and passim.

146. Ibid., 51–60, 83–84; Boaz Cohen, *Jewish and Roman Law: A Comparative Study* (New York, 1966), I, 128, 153, 161–62, 209, 213.

147. Moses ben Maimon, *The Code of Maimonides,* bk. 12, *The Book of Acquisition,* trans. Isaac Klein (New Haven, 1955), 276–82.

148. Solomon Grayzel, *The Church and the Jews in the XIIIth Century* (Philadelphia, 1933), 10–24, 52–53, 75, and passim; Jacob R. Marcus, *The Colonial American Jew, 1492–1776* (Detroit, 1970), I, 11.

149. Lopez, *Commercial Revolution of the Middle Ages,* 60–61.

150. Goitein, *Mediterranean Society,* I, 65–66, II, passim.

151. Verlinden, *L'esclavage dans l'Europe médiévale,* II, 93–94, 136, 251.

152. Starr, *The Jew in the Byzantine Empire;* Salo Wittmayer Baron, *A Social and Religious History of the Jews,* 2d ed., vol. 4 (New York, 1957), 187.

153. Goitein, *Mediterranean Society.*

154. Ibid., I, 134–35; Baron, *Social and Religious History,* IV, 188–89, 193–94; Grayzel, *Church and the Jews,* 24–25; Davis, *Problem of Slavery in Western Culture,* 99.

155. Davis, *Problem of Slavery in Western Culture,* 99; Baron, *Social and Religious History,* IV, 188; Grayzel, *Church and the Jews,* 22–23, 113; Verlinden, "L'esclavage en Sicile," 101–6; Verlinden, *L'esclavage dans l'Europe médiévale,* II, 251–56.

156. "Slavery and the Slave Trade," *Encyclopedia Judaica* (Jerusalem, 1971); Origo, "Domestic Enemy," 323; Verlinden, *L'esclavage dans l'Europe médiévale,* II, 121–23, 128–29; Baron, *Social and Religious History,* III, 214, IV, 191–93, 336–37.

157. Bovill, *Golden Trade of the Moors,* 53, 110–15; Levtzion, *Ancient Ghana and Mali,* 132–36, 149; Dufourcq, *L'Espagne catalane,* 57–58, 61, 139–44; Sanders, *Lost Tribes and Promised Lands,* 3–52, 112–22.

158. Goitein, *Mediterranean Society,* I, 125–26; "Sugar," *Encyclopedia Judaica;* Braudel, *Mediterranean,* II, 815–20; Sanders, *Lost Tribes and Promised Lands,* 113; Wiznitzer, *Jews in Colonial Brazil,* 9–10, 40.

159. Marcus, *Colonial American Jew,* I, 49–52; Braudel, *Mediterranean,* II, 807. For various information on the Marranos and the "Nacion" that developed in Brazil and the Caribbean, I am much indebted to the Nahum Goldmann Museum of the Jewish Diaspora, Tel-Aviv University.

160. Wiznitzer, *Jews in Colonial Brazil,* 1–40; Marcus, *Colonial American Jew,* I, 35–52.

161. Wiznitzer, *Jews in Colonial Brazil,* 45–72, 130; Marcus, *Colonial American Jew,* I, 71–77.

162. Wiznitzer, *Jews in Colonial Brazil,* 140–41; Marcus, *Colonial American Jew,* I, 81.

163. Isaac S. Emmanuel and Suzanne A. Emmanuel, *History of the Jews of the Netherlands Antilles* (Cincinnati, 1970), I, 7, 37, 65, 75–80, 226–28; Marcus, *Colonial American Jew,* I, 176–85.

164. Alan H. Adamson, *Sugar without Slaves: The Political Economy of British Guiana, 1838–1904* (New Haven, 1972), 3–33.

165. Marcus, *Colonial American Jew,* I, 150–65, 205; and exhibits at the Nahum Goldmann Museum of the Jewish Diaspora.

166. Marcus, *Colonial American Jew,* I, 86–95; Dorothy Burne Goebel, "The 'New England Trade' and the French West Indies, 1763–1774: A Study in Trade Policies," *William and Mary Quarterly,* 20 (1963), 332–72.

167. Marcus, *Colonial American Jew,* I, 101–2, 113–21, 704; Dunn, *Sugar and Slaves,* 106–8. With respect to Sunday markets, Sidney W. Mintz discusses the dilemma faced by Edward Long, a noted eighteenth-century Jamaican historian: "The slaves of Christians received 86 days per year free from plantation labor (except in cases of 'very urgent business'), which included every Sunday and, normally, half of every Saturday. The slaves of Jews, however, received at least 111 days per year for themselves. Long shrewdly calculated how these additional days not only improved the slaves' morale, but also increased significantly their ability to accumulate capital for themselves. But he recognized that few Christians were Christian enough to give their slaves two free days a week. At the same time, since markets had to be held on Sunday—the one day on which the majority of slaves were entirely free—the larger part of the market trade was engrossed by Jewish merchants. In order for Christian shopkeepers to compete with the Jews for the slaves' custom, the market day ought to have been changed to some day other than Sunday. Yet that would have meant a significant loss of labor to Christian slave owners. Long aruges for the addition of Thursday to Sunday as a free day, both to improve the slaves' morale, and to afford Christian shopkeepers a firmer purchase on the buying-power of the slaves." ("Currency Problems in Eighteenth-Century Jamaica and Gresham's Law," in Robert A. Manners, ed., *Process and Pattern in Culture* [Chicago, 1964], 263 n. 4).

168. Marcus, *Colonial American Jew,* I, 702–3; Jay Coughtry, *The Notorious Triangle: Rhode Island and the African Slave Trade, 1700–1807* (Philadelphia, 1981), 45–46, 47, 88–89, 183, 192.

PART TWO

Epigraph: Kenneth Burke, *Towards a Better Life: Being a Series of Epistles or Declarations* (Berkeley: University of California Press, 1966, originally published 1932), 4.

1. These points are discussed in some detail in David Brion Davis, *The Problem of Slavery in Western Culture* (Ithaca, N.Y., 1966), pt. 3. See also William B. Cohen, *The French Encounter with Africans: White Response to Blacks, 1530–1880* (Bloomington, 1980), 60–99.

2. John Stuart Mill, "Representative Government," in *Utilitarianism, Liberty and Representative Government* (London, 1948), 183–84.

3. Ralph Waldo Emerson, "Address Delivered in Concord on the Anniversary of the Emancipation of the Negroes in the British West Indies, August 1, 1844," in *Complete Works of Emerson* (New York, 1903–04), XI, 125–27.

4. Alexis de Tocqueville, "On the Emancipation of Slaves" (1843), in Seymour Drescher, ed. and trans., *Tocqueville and Beaumont on Social Reform* (New York, 1968), 138.

5. Ibid., 149–51; Tocqueville, "De l'émancipation des esclaves," *Le Siècle*, 9 Nov. 1843.

6. Quoted in M. I. Finley, *Ancient Slavery and Modern Ideology* (New York, 1980), 12.

7. Ralph Wardlaw, *The Jubilee: A Sermon Preached in West George-Street Chapel, Glasgow, on Friday, August 1st, 1834, the Memorable Day of Negro Emancipation in the British Colonies* (Glasgow, 1834), 4. For examples of earlier abolitionists' apologies for biblical slavery, see David Brion Davis, *The Problem of Slavery in the Age of Revolution, 1770–1823* (Ithaca, N.Y., 1975), 533–551.

8. Finley, *Ancient Slavery*, 19–26. Finley's pioneering work points to the need for a reasonably comprehensive study of the historiography of slavery from the late Enlightenment to the early twentieth century. It is a modern illusion to think that scholarly interest in slavery first emerged as a faddish response to the civil rights movements of the 1960s. In fact, nineteenth-century writers became almost obsessed with the place of slavery and emancipation in the "progress of civilization," or in what Edouard Biot termed "la plus grande révolution qui signale *la marche de la civilisation humaine*" (*De l'abolition de l'esclavage ancien en occident* [Paris, 1840], vii). The student of popular conceptions of world history should not overlook such ambitious macrohistories as José Antonio Saco, *Historia de la esclavitud desde los tiempos mas remotos hasta nuestros dias*, 2d ed. (Havana, 1936–45); W. O. Blake, *The History of Slavery and the Slave Trade, Ancient and Modern . . .* (New York, 1860); A. Tourmagne, *Histoire de l'esclavage ancien et moderne* (Paris, 1880); and Henri Wallon, *Histoire de l'esclavage dans l'antiquité* (Paris, 1847).

9. William Blair, *An Inquiry into the State of Slavery amongst the Romans: From the Earliest Period, till the Establishment of the Lombards in Italy* (Edinburgh, 1833), 197–98; Wallon, *Histoire*, II, 438, as quoted in Joseph Vogt, *Ancient Slavery and the Ideal of Man*, trans. Thomas Wiedemann (Oxford, 1974), 174. For a more detailed discussion of Wallon and Auguste Comte, see Davis, *Problem of Slavery in Western Culture*, 17–21.

10. Finley, *Ancient Slavery*, 36–38; John Millar, *The Origin of the Distinction of Ranks: or, An Inquiry into the Circumstances Which Give Rise to Influence and Authority in the Different Members of Society*, 3d ed. (London, 1781), 4–13, 67–71, 112, 123, 133–69, 295–312, 320–44.

11. Benjamin Franklin, "Observations concerning the Increase of Mankind," in *The Papers of Benjamin Franklin*, ed. Leonard W. Labaree et al. (New Haven, 1959–), IV, 229–31; David Hume, *Essays, Moral, Political, and Literary* (Edinburgh, 1817), 377–419; Auguste Comte, *Cours de philosophie positive* (Paris, 1840–42), V, 186–93, VI, 133–36; Finley, *Ancient Slavery*, 40–41.

12. Augustin Cochin, *The Results of Slavery* (Boston, 1863), 345; Biot, as quoted by Finley, *Ancient Slavery*, 32–33.

13. *Declaration of the Objects of the Liverpool Society for Promoting the Abolition of Slavery, 25th March, 1823* (Liverpool, 1823), 3.

14. *The Tourist: A Literary and Anti-Slavery Journal*, 28 Jan. 1833, 180; 4 Feb. 1833, 196.

15. Porteus MS 2104, 91, 98, 102, Lambeth Palace Library, London.

16. Thomas Clarkson, *The History of the Rise, Progress and Accomplishment of the Abolition of the African Slave-Trade by the British Parliament* (London, 1808), II, 580–85.

17. Ibid., 565–68, 581–83.

18. Ibid., 586.

19. Thomas Clarkson to William Smith, 1 Sept. 1833, Smith Papers, Duke University Library.

20. Izhak Gross, "The Abolition of Negro Slavery and British Parliamentary Politics,

1832–3," *Historical Journal,* 23 (1980), 63–85; Gross, "Commons and Empire, 1833–1841" (D.Phil. diss., Oxford University, 1975), 102–8.

21. This point is clearly revealed in a letter from Lord Goderich, whom Stanley replaced in the Colonial Office and who afterwards became the earl of Ripon, to Lord Brougham, 4 Apr. 1838, Brougham Papers, 14439, University College, London. See also Stanley to Goderich, 28 Mar. 1833, British Library, Add. MSS 40863, fol. 47.

22. Elie Halévy, *The Triumph of Reform, 1830–1841,* trans. E. I. Watkin (London, 1950), 135.

23. Wardlaw, *Jubilee,* 35–36.

24. Ibid., 13, 16–17, 20.

25. Ibid., 26–37.

26. Steven B. Webb has shown that the small minority of thirty MPs who opposed the harshest provisions of the New Poor Law "had significantly above *average* anti-slavery indices," according to a careful statistical analysis. But, as Webb hastens to point out, the same Parliament passed both the emancipation bill and the New Poor Law by overwhelming majorities. Both measures "intended to have labor allocated through as nearly a free market as possible." Both appealed for different reasons to reformers, administrators, and aristocratic landlords whose assumptions led as logically to the New Poor Law as to new forms of labor discipline in the West Indies (Webb, "Saints or Cynics: A Statistical Analysis of Parliament's Decision for Emancipation in 1833," forthcoming essay, kindly sent to me by Robert William Fogel). For a contrary view, see Seymour Drescher, "Cart Whip and Billy Roller: Antislavery and Reform Symbolism in Industrializing Britain," *Journal of Social History,* 15 (1981), 23–24 n. 69.

27. Buxton Papers, MSS Brit. Emp. S.444, IV, 279, Rhodes House, Oxford. Although the final number of emancipated slaves turned out to be closer to 800,000, abolitionists sometimes spoke of 700,000. Buxton had hoped to reserve 1 August 1834 for "a season of deep retirement of Soul—of earnest prayer—& of close communion with my God." To his surprise, however, his daughter Priscilla, who had been his co-worker and confidante on abolitionist matters, chose that day for her wedding!

28. Buxton Papers, X, 75–76, II, 289, II, 65–72.

29. Ibid., XXV, 37–40. Buxton's scrapbooks are filled with similar reports, some of which appeared in the parliamentary papers.

30. Emerson, "Address Delivered in Concord," 99, 115–16, 135.

31. Benjamin Quarles, *Black Abolitionists* (New York, 1970), 121–29. As late as 1914, Marcus Garvey chose 1 August as the date for launching his Universal Negro Improvement Association.

32. Anthony F. C. Wallace, "Revitalization Movements," *American Anthropologist,* 58 (1956), 270.

33. Buxton to Joseph John Gurney, 25 June 1837, Buxton Papers, II, 131–37. The most famous account of West Indian emancipation, written by Henry Bleby, was characteristically entitled *Death Struggles of Slavery* (London, 1853).

34. *The Bow in the Cloud: or, The Negro's Memorial* (London, 1834), viii, 273–75, and passim.

35. Ibid., 321–61. In 1934 the Jamaicans are debating whether to erect the next statue to Sharp or Clarkson. In V. S. Naipaul's novel *A Bend in the River,* an East Indian trader who is living in the heart of Africa concludes that "the Europeans could do one thing and say something quite different; and they could act in this way because they had an ideal of what they owed to their civilization. It was their great advantage over us. The Europeans wanted gold and slaves, like everybody else; but at the same time they wanted statues put up to themselves as people who had done good things for the slaves. Being an intelligent and energetic people, and at the peak of their powers, they could express both sides of their civilization; and they got both the slaves and the statues" ([New York, 1980], 17).

36. J. Laplanche and J. B. Pontalis, *The Language of Psycho-Analysis,* trans. Donald Nicholson-Smith, with an introd. by Daniel Lagache (New York, 1973), 349–55.

37. M. H. Abrams, *Natural Supernaturalism: Tradition and Revolution in Romantic Literature* (New York, 1971), 363; G. W. F. Hegel, *The Phenomenology of Mind,* trans. J. B. Baillie, 2d ed. (New York, 1964); Davis, *Problem of Slavery in the Age of Revolution,* 558–64.

38. British and Foreign Anti-Slavery Society, petition to Lord Palmerston, 9 Nov. 1839, MSS Brit. Emp. S.20 E 2/19, 6, Rhodes House, Oxford.

39. Buxton Papers, XXXVII (7 Apr. 1839), 51.

40. Paul Tillich, "The Decline and the Validity of the Idea of Progress," in Jerald C. Bauer, ed., *The Future of Religions* (New York, 1966), 75–77.

41. S. T. Kimball, discussing Arnold Van Gennep's *Les rites de passage,* quoted in Victor Turner, "Process, System, and Symbol: A New Anthropological Synthesis," *Daedalus,* Summer 1977, 67; and Turner, 68; Turner, *Dramas, Fields, and Metaphors: Symbolic Action in Human Society* (Ithaca, N.Y., 1974).

42. Tocqueville, "Emancipation of Slaves," 148.

43. Quoted in Peter Gay, *The Enlightenment: An Interpretation,* vol. 1, *The Rise of Modern Paganism* (New York, 1967), 324, 342–46, 391. It is interesting to note that Gay chooses Granville Sharp's grandfather, the archbishop of York, to epitomize the bland, self-satisfied, latitudinarian Christianity that evoked contempt from deists and a thirst for revitalization from later evangelicals.

44. For a more extended discussion of the Enlightenment and slavery, see Davis, *Problem of Slavery in Western Culture,* 333–445; *Problem of Slavery in the Age of Revolution,* 164–212, 343–85; and Cohen, *French Encounter with Africans,* 60–99.

45. David Hume, footnote added to 1753–54 ed. of his "Of National Characters," *Essays Moral, Political, and Literary,* ed. T. H. Green and T. H. Grose (London, 1889), I, 252.

46. John Wesley, *Thoughts upon Slavery* (Philadelphia, 1774), 10–14, 23, 51–58; James Ramsay, *An Essay on the Treatment and Conversion of African Slaves in the British Sugar Colonies* (London, 1784), 198–245; Granville Sharp to William Dillwyn, 25 July 1774, Sharp Papers, British and Foreign Bible Society; James Beattie, *An Essay on the Nature and Immutability of Truth . . . ,* 7th ed. (London, 1807), 56–57, 424–28; Beattie, *Elements of Moral Science* (Edinburgh, 1793), II, 164. The influence of Beattie's argument can be seen from the following assertion by Leonard Bacon, an eminent American Congregationalist, colonizationist, and anti-abolitionist who adhered to the Scottish moral-sense philosophy: "If that form of government, that system of social order is not wrong—if those laws of the southern states, by virtue of which it is, are not wrong—nothing is wrong"; and if the wrongness of slavery is not self-evident, "what elementary idea of right and wrong can that man have?" (*Slavery Discussed in Occasional Essays, from 1833 to 1846* [New York, 1846], ix–x). In Abraham Lincoln's more famous and succinct phrase, "If slavery is not wrong, nothing is wrong."

47. "Negro," in *Encyclopaedia Britannica: or A Dictionary of Arts, Sciences and Miscellaneous Literature,* 3d ed. (Edinburgh, 1797), XII, 794–98.

48. Ibid.

49. [Henry Brougham], "Examen de l'esclavage en général, et particulièrement de l'esclavage des négres dans les colonies françaises de l'Amérique, par V.D.C. ancient avocat et colon de St. Domingue," *Edinburgh Review,* 6 (1805), 326–50.

50. Ibid.

51. Ibid., 327, 347–50.

52. In addition to the articles cited in *Encyclopaedia Britannica,* this paragraph has been influenced by Richard H. Popkin, "The Philosophical Basis of Eighteenth-Century Racism," in *Racism in the Eighteenth Century: Studies in Eighteenth-Century Culture,* vol. 3 (Cleveland and London, 1973), 245–62; and H. M. Bracken, "Essence, Accident and Race," *Hermathena: A Dublin University Review,* 16 (1973), 81–95.

53. James D. Essig, *The Bonds of Wickedness: American Evangelicals against Slavery, 1770–1808* (Philadelphia, 1982), 43–52, 55–56, 71–72; Davis, *Problem of Slavery in the Age of Revolution,* 196–254.

54. [Benjamin Rush], *An Address to the Inhabitants of the British Settlements in America, upon Slave-Keeping* (Philadelphia, 1773), 9–11; Rush to Granville Sharp, 1 May 1773; Rush to

William Gordon, 10 Oct. 1773, in *Letters of Benjamin Rush,* ed. L. H. Butterfield (Princeton, 1951), I, 80–82; David Freeman Hawke, *Benjamin Rush: Revolutionary Gadfly* (Indianapolis, 1971), 51, 78, 137–39, 388; Granville Sharp, *The Just Limitations of Slavery in the Laws of God . . .* (London, 1776), 26n.

55. Davis, *Problem of Slavery in Western Culture,* 366–71, 385–87; *Problem of Slavery in the Age of Revolution,* 286–99; Essig, *Bonds of Wickedness.* I have learned much from James Essig's fine study, which supplements and qualifies my own earlier treatment of the antislavery evangelicals in America. Unfortunately, even William G. McLoughlin's monumental *New England Dissent, 1630–1833: The Baptists and the Separation of Church and State* (Cambridge, Mass., 1971), fails to explain why Baptists in the northern states lagged so far behind their brethren in the South and in Britain in speaking out against Negro slavery.

56. Davis, *Problem of Slavery in the Age of Revolution,* 361–66, 373–74, 432–36. My understanding of these aspects of British abolition has been greatly enriched by the papers of Roger Anstey, G. M. Ditchfield, and James Walvin published in *Anti-Slavery, Religion, and Reform: Essays in Memory of Roger Anstey,* ed. Christine Bolt and Seymour Drescher (Folkestone, Eng., 1980), and by the papers of Anstey, Walvin, and Howard Temperley published in *The Abolition of the Atlantic Slave Trade: Origins and Effects in Europe, Africa, and the Americas,* ed. David Eltis and James Walvin, with the collaboration of Svend E. Green-Pederson (Madison, Wis., 1981).

57. Clarkson, *History,* I, 8.

58. Ibid., 179–80, 262–63.

59. Quoted by Reginald Coupland, *Wilberforce: A Narrative* (Oxford, 1923), 240–41, from Wilberforce's immensely influential *A Practical View of the Prevailing Religious System of Professed Christians.*

60. *Letters and Addresses by George Thompson, during his Mission in the United States* (Boston, 1837), 84–85.

61. *The Christian Advocate,* reprinted in *Tourist,* 22 Apr. 1833, 300.

62. *Letters and Addresses by George Thompson,* 107; C. C. Burleigh, ed., *Reception of George Thompson in Great Britain* (Boston, 1836), 68.

63. *Liberator,* 30 Jan. 1846, quoted by Aileen Kraditor, *Means and Ends in American Abolitionism: Garrison and His Critics on Strategy and Tactics, 1834–1850* (New York, 1969), 94.

64. Lewis Perry, *Childhood, Marriage, and Reform: Henry Clarke Wright, 1797–1870* (Chicago, 1980), 1–26, 41, 144–46, 152–53.

65. Ibid., 152–54.

66. Ibid., 25–41, 132–41, 152–63.

67. James Stephen, *The Slavery of the British West India Colonies Delineated, As It Exists Both in Law and Practice, and Compared with the Slavery of Other Countries, Antient and Modern* (London, 1824–30), I, xix; Perry, *Henry Clarke Wright,* 28; William Lloyd Garrison, *The "Infidelity" of Abolition* (New York, 1860), 3.

68. Garrison, *"Infidelity,"* 7–11.

69. *Letters of Theodore Dwight Weld, Angelina Grimké Weld, and Sarah Grimké, 1822–1844,* ed. Gilbert H. Barnes and Dwight L. Dumond (1934; reprint, Gloucester, Mass., 1965), I, 143–44.

70. Elizabeth Heyrick, *Immediate, Not Gradual Abolition: or An Inquiry into the Shortest, Safest, and Most Effectual Means of Getting Rid of West Indian Slavery* (London, 1824), 36; British Anti-Slavery Society, *An Address to the Public of Great Britain and Ireland . . . June 27, 1834* (London, 1834), 3–4; William Lloyd Garrison, ed., *Lectures of George Thompson, with a Full Report of the Discussion between Mr. Thompson and Mr. Barthwick* (Boston, 1836), xviii; Buxton Papers, VI, 1–2, Rhodes House, Oxford; Wilberforce to Buxton, 24 May 1821, Bodleian Library, Oxford, C. 106/4.

71. Perry, *Henry Clarke Wright,* 21–22. An interesting example of the orthodox suspicion of attempts to dissociate the necessary evils of corporal punishment from the supposed "innocence" of less coercive forms of correction is Joseph Hale's *Rejoinder to the "Reply" of the Hon. Horace Mann* (Boston, 1845).

72. Weld to Garrison, 2 Jan. 1833, *Weld-Grimké Letters,* I, 98; George Allen, *Mr. Allen's*

Report of a Declaration of Sentiments on Slavery, December 5, 1837 (Worcester, Mass., 1838), 6.

73. As developed from the original formulations by Freud and Melanie Klein, "splitting" has acquired a variety of technical meanings and can refer to normal and necessary thought processes. See esp. André Green, "The Borderline Concept," and Otto F. Kernberg, "The Structural Diagnosis of Borderline Personality Organization," in Peter Hartocollis, ed., *Borderline Personality Disorders* (New York, 1978). One may note that insofar as splitting is linked with an impairment of superego integration, "normal guilt" and "successful" superego regulation would in a slave society serve to support the slaveholding norms—a point Mark Twain brilliantly exposed in *Huckleberry Finn.*

74. Abrams, *Natural Supernaturalism,* 356–72.

75. Perry, *Henry Clarke Wright,* 263.

76. Ibid., 99.

77. Ibid., 86, 146, 155–66, 232–36, 274.

78. Thomas Clarkson, *An Essay on the Slavery and Commerce of the Human Species* (Philadelphia, 1786), v–vi; Clarkson, *History,* I, 30–42. Such assumptions help explain the extraordinary importance Clarkson attached to his audience in 1814 with Emperor Alexander of Russia, as well as his naïve faith that Alexander, Talleyrand, Louis XVIII, and the duke of Wellington would unite in redeeming the world from its most flagrant sin.

79. David Walker, *Appeal, in Four Articles, Together with a Preamble to the Colored Citizens of the World. . . ,* 3d ed. (Boston, 1830, originally published 1829), 24–29; Wendell Phillips Garrison and Francis Jackson Garrison, *William Lloyd Garrison, 1805–1879: The Story of His Life Told by His Children* (London, 1885), II, 145–48.

80. William Goodell, *Slavery and Anti-Slavery: A History of the Great Struggle in Both Hemispheres, with a View to the Slavery Question in the United States* (New York, 1853), 121–32.

81. Parallels between the jeremiads of abolitionists and those of proslavery southern evangelicals can be seen in Anne C. Loveland, *Southern Evangelicals and the Social Order, 1800–1860* (Baton Rouge, 1980), 125–29.

82. Goodell, *Slavery and Anti-Slavery,* 125–26.

83. Ibid., 3, 136–40, 143–219, 583–86.

84. Ibid., 558, 584–93.

85. Ibid., 561–62.

86. See, e.g., Charles Van Doren, *The Idea of Progress* (New York, 1967). Mortimer Adler, in the introduction, defends the study of ideas without regard for the intention of the thinkers or historical context, "as if all the documents represented the voices of participants confronting one another in actual discussion" (p. x).

87. C. Duncan Rice, "Controversies over Slavery in Eighteenth- and Nineteenth-Century Scotland," in Lewis Perry and Michael Fellman, eds., *Antislavery Reconsidered: New Perspectives on the Abolitionists* (Baton Rouge, 1979), 24–48; Rice, *The Scots Abolitionists, 1833–1861* (Baton Rouge, 1981).

88. Robert Nisbet, *History of the Idea of Progress* (New York, 1980); Sidney Pollard, *The Idea of Progress: History and Society* (London, 1968); Ruth Macklin, "Moral Progress," *Ethics,* 87 (1977), 370–82; Raymond Aron, *Progress and Disillusion: The Dialectics of Modern Society* (New York, 1968); W. Warren Wagar, ed., *The Idea of Progress since the Renaissance* (New York, 1969); Nathan Rotenstreich, "The Idea of Historical Progress and Its Assumptions," *History and Theory,* 10 (1971), 197–221.

89. Marie Jean Antoine Nicolas de Caritat, marquis de Condorcet, *Esquisse d'un tableau historique des progrès de l'esprit humain,* texte revu et présenté par O. H. Prior (Paris, n.d.); M. Schwartz [pseud.], *Réflexions sur l'esclavage des nègres* (Paris, 1788).

90. Davis, *Problem of Slavery in Western Culture,* chap. 10.

91. Ronald S. Crane, "Anglican Apologetics and the Idea of Progress, 1699–1745," *Modern Philology,* 31 (1934), 281–99, 349–67; Arthur O. Lovejoy, *The Great Chain of Being: A Study of the History of an Idea* (New York, 1960), 268; James Ramsay, "A MS Volume, Entirely in Ramsay's Hand. . . ," Phillips MS 17780, fols. 69–71, 95, Rhodes House, Oxford.

92. James Ramsay, *An Essay on the Treatment and Conversion of African Slaves in the British*

Sugar Colonies (London, 1784), 1–3, 9–18, 107–8, 172–75, 184–88; [Condorcet], *Adresse de la société des amis des noirs, à l'assemblée nationale . . .* (Paris, 1791), 107–8; Schwartz, *Réflexions*, 28–53.

93. Davis, *Problem of Slavery in the Age of Revolution*, 322; Essig, *Bonds of Wickedness*, 86–88.

94. Noah Webster, *Effects of Slavery, on Morals and Industry* (Hartford, 1793, originally published 1791), 34–37.

95. [Grímur Jónsson Thorkelin], *An Essay on the Slave Trade* (London, 1788), 15–19, 28–30. See also Robert Norris, *A Short Account of the African Slave Trade*, 2d ed. (London, 1789), 182–83, and passim.

96. Henry Thornton to John Clarkson, 30 Dec. 1791, British Library Add. MS 41,262A, fol. 39. John Clarkson was Thomas Clarkson's brother.

97. *A Letter to Granville Sharp, Esq., on the Proposed Abolition of the Slave Trade* (London, 1788), 42–47.

98. Ibid., 48.

99. Adam Smith, *An Inquiry into the Nature and Causes of the Wealth of Nations*, ed. Edwin Cannan (New York, 1937), 365–66. With regard to Smith's "sanctification" of economic man, one should note that the tradition of moral philosophy extending from Shaftesbury and Hutcheson to Smith and beyond had always been concerned with refuting the "dangerous" and amoral views of self-interest advanced by Hobbes and Mandeville.

100. Jonathan Elliott, ed., *The Debates in the Several State Conventions . . .* (Philadelphia, 1891), II, 451–52; Jonathan Edwards, *The Injustice and Impolicy of the Slave-Trade . . .* (Providence, 1792, originally published 1791), 34–37; *Journal of the Times*, 7 Nov. 1828; Garrison, *William Lloyd Garrison*, I, 135.

101. George M. Fredrickson, *White Supremacy: A Comparative Study in American and South African History* (New York, 1981), 154–55; Howard A. Ohline, "Slavery, Economics, and Congressional Politics, 1790," *Journal of Southern History*, 46 (1980), 335–60.

102. Davis, *Problem of Slavery in the Age of Revolution*, 196–212, 326–42; Essig, *Bonds of Wickedness;* John Michael Shay, "The Antislavery Movement in North Carolina" (Ph.D. diss., Princeton University, 1971); H. Shelton Smith, *In His Image, But . . . Racism in Southern Religion, 1780–1910* (Durham, N.C., 1972); Philip Africa, "Slaveholding in the Salem Community, 1771–1851," *North Carolina Historical Review*, 54 (1977), 271–307; Donald G. Mathews, *Slavery and Methodism: A Chapter in American Morality, 1780–1845* (Princeton, 1965).

103. Davis, *Problem of Slavery in the Age of Revolution*, 386–468; *Parliamentary Debates*, 3d ser., vol. 17 (1833), col. 1194.

104. Henry Brougham, *A Concise Statement regarding the Abolition of the Slave Trade* (London, 1804), 60.

105. Thomas Clarkson, "Paper or Address to Country—to Interfere for Better Treatment of Negroes in W. Indies," and "Copy of Letter to William Wilberforce on Slave Trade Operation," Clarkson Papers, Henry E. Huntington Library.

106. Zachary Macaulay to Thomas Fowell Buxton, 11 Nov. 1823, Macaulay Papers, Henry E. Huntington Library. In actuality, the court of policy in Demerara had delayed in making Canning's order in council public; the slaves, knowing that some order had arrived, concluded that the colonists were depriving them of rights granted by the king. The other and more complex causes of the revolt have been admirably reconstructed by Michael Craton. While only 3 whites lost their lives in the uprising, about 250 slaves were killed, some of whose heads were exhibited on poles along the coast and in Georgetown. See Michael Craton, *Testing the Chains: Resistance to Slavery in the British West Indies* (Ithaca, N.Y., 1982), 267–90; and Alan H. Adamson, *Sugar without Slaves: The Political Economy of British Guiana, 1838–1904* (New Haven, 1972), 30.

107. I am much indebted to Prof. Ann M. Burton for allowing me to read in manuscript her illuminating article "James Stephen, the Maritime War and Abolition."

108. "Memoirs of James Stephen Written by Himself for the Use of His Children," British Library, Add. MSS 46443–46444, I, 1–11, 28–29, 35–36, 242, 289, 398–99, II,

450–83, 560–62; James Stephen, *The Slavery of the British West India Colonies Delineated* . . . (London, 1824–30), II, xiv–xvi, xix–xxiv, xxviii. James Stephen wrote his extraordinarily candid memoirs for the moral edification of his children. Their knowledge of the circumstances of the family's change of fortune may possibly account for the continuing antislavery activities of George and James the younger—a tradition notably absent in such famous progeny of the Clapham Sect as T. B. Macaulay and Wilberforce's sons. A fascinating study could be made of the way abolitionism was related to the "progress" of family dynasties, in America as well as Britain.

109. [James Stephen], *The Crisis of the Sugar Colonies* . . . (London, 1802); Stephen, *Slavery of the British West India Colonies,* II, xxxii, 4–5, 33. Stephen began working on his classic "delineation" of slavery early in the abolitionist struggle, and many of the basic assumptions are evident in such earlier works of his as *New Reasons for Abolishing the Slave Trade: Being the Last Section of a Larger Work, Now First Published, Entitled 'The Dangers of the Country.' By the Author of 'War in Disguise'* (London, 1807); [African Institution], *Reasons for Establishing a Registry of Slaves in the British Colonies* . . . (London, 1815); *A Defence of the Bill for the Registration of Slaves* . . . (London, 1816); *The Speech of James Stephen, Esq., at the Annual Meeting of the African Institution, at the Free-Masons' Hall, on the 26th March, 1817* (London, 1817).

110. Stephen to Wilberforce, 20 Sept. 1797, quoted by Burton, "James Stephen," 5.

111. Burton, "James Stephen"; [Stephen], *Crisis of the Sugar Colonies,* 121–22, 126, 151–61; Roger Anstey, *The Atlantic Slave Trade and British Abolition, 1760–1810* (London, 1975), 321–58; Davis, *Problem of Slavery in the Age of Revolution,* 418–19, 438–43; Seymour Drescher, *Econocide: British Slavery in the Era of Abolition* (Pittsburgh, 1977), 73–74, 134–35, 156–57.

112. Anstey, *Atlantic Slave Trade,* 321–402; Burton, "James Stephen." David Eltis has demonstrated the demographic significance of the acts limiting the transfer of slaves within the British West Indies, a policy formalized in 1823 by Stephen Lushington's Slave Trade Laws Consolidation Bill. See Eltis, "The Traffic in Slaves between the British West Indian Colonies, 1807–1833," *Economic History Review,* 2d ser., 25 (1972), 55–64. Stephen did envision the possibility of importing Africans to increase the population of Trinidad; once freed, they would become either a permanent military garrison or indentured servants (*Crisis of the Sugar Colonies,* 195); Henry Brougham publicly attacked this proposal (*Edinburgh Review,* 1 [1802], 232–36; *An Inquiry into the Colonial Policy of the European Powers* [Edinburgh, 1803], II, 426–29).

113. Stephen to Perceval, 13 Nov. 1807, Perceval Papers, British Library, Add. MSS 49183, fols. 11–14.

114. [Stephen], *Crisis of the Sugar Colonies,* 161–79; Eltis, "Traffic in Slaves," 55–64; Drescher, *Econocide,* 65–124, 170–77; D. J. Murray, *The West Indies and the Development of Colonial Government, 1801–1834* (Oxford, 1965), 71–79, 87, 93–94. Without debating all of Drescher's provocative arguments, one can no longer doubt that in strictly economic terms British policy made little sense or that Trinidad and Guiana offered extremely promising frontiers for the extension and strengthening of the slave system at a time of growing world demand for sugar, cotton, coffee, and other plantation staples.

It should be noted that the government that evolved for the British Guianese colonies was in some ways unique and that the crown colony system was extended mainly to non-American territories such as Ceylon and Mauritius. The legislative colonies in the West Indies included Barbados, Jamaica, Antigua, Saint Kitts, Nevis, Montserrat, Dominica, Tobago, Grenada, Saint Vincent, and the Virgin Islands.

115. Murray, *West Indies,* 121–29; Paul Knaplund, *James Stephen and the British Colonial System, 1813–1847* (Madison, Wis., 1953); Knaplund, "Sir James Stephen: The Friend of the Negroes," *Journal of Negro History,* 35 (1950), 368–407; Mary Reckord, "The Colonial Office and the Abolition of Slavery," *Historical Journal,* 14 (1971), 723–34. In 1801 most colonial business was transferred from the Home Department to the recently created third secretaryship of state. While the precise powers and jurisdiction of this Department for War and the Colonies were very slowly defined, the questions of slave-trade abolition and

slave amelioration provided unprecedented administrative duties requiring the aid of an expert legal counselor. Hence, in marked contrast to developments in the United States, British antislavery contributed directly to the growth of a bureaucratic structure within the Colonial Office—the third secretary of state delegating most of the colonial business and correspondence to undersecretaries. See, esp., Murray, *West Indies*, 109–15.

116. [Stephen], *Crisis of the Sugar Colonies*, 186–93.

117. Stephen, *A Defence of the Bill for the Registration of Slaves;* Stephen, *Slavery of the British West India Colonies*, I, xi–xii, II, 403; Sir George Stephen, *Anti-Slavery Recollections; in a Series of Letters Addressed to Mrs. Beecher Stowe*, 2d ed. (London, 1971, originally published 1853), 18–32. Sir George claimed that as a boy he had frequently been asked to copy antislavery correspondence, since the abolitionists feared employing an outsider who might leak secrets to their opponents.

118. T. J. Barron, "James Stephen, the 'Black Race' and British Colonial Administration, 1813–47," *Journal of Imperial and Commonwealth History*, 5 (1977), 133–47; William A. Green, "James Stephen and British West India Policy, 1834–1847," *Caribbean Studies*, 13, no. 4 (1974), 33–39; Stephen, *Slavery of the British West India Colonies*, II, 390–94, 399–403.

119. Stephen, *Slavery of the British West India Colonies*, II, 401–2.

120. Roger Anstey, "The Pattern of British Abolitionism in the Eighteenth and Nineteenth Centuries," in Christine Bolt and Seymour Drescher, eds., *Anti-Slavery, Religion, and Reform: Essays in Memory of Roger Anstey* (Folkestone, Eng., 1980), 24–25; Gross, "Abolition of Negro Slavery," 64–66; B. W. Higman, "The West India 'Interest' in Parliament, 1807–1833," *Historical Studies*, 13 (1967), 1–19.

121. James Stephen to James Cropper, 7 Nov. 1825, A.L. 345, Manuscript Division, University of London Library.

122. Ibid. Stephen was trying to persuade Cropper not to publish a pamphlet that he had heard about from Macaulay, their mutual friend. Cropper was especially close to Macaulay, who was a stockholder in the East India Company and an early supporter of Cropper's emphasis on the "impolicy" of slavery. Cropper's son Edward married Macaulay's daughter.

123. "Extracts from letters of the late James Cropper, transcribed for his grandchildren," fols. 4–17, British Library; Cropper to Macaulay, 12 July and 5 Aug. 1822, British Library, Add. MSS 41267A, fols. 108–9, 112–13. For detailed accounts of Cropper's contributions to the antislavery movement, see K. Charlton, "James Cropper and Liverpool's Contribution to the Anti-Slavery Movement," *Transactions of the Historic Society of Lancashire and Cheshire*, 123 (1972), 57–77; David Brion Davis, "James Cropper and the British Anti-Slavery Movement, 1821–1823," *Journal of Negro History*, 45 (1960), 241–58; Davis, "James Cropper and the British Anti-Slavery Movement, 1823–1833," ibid, 46 (1961), 154–73.

124. "Extracts," fols. 19–20; James Cropper, *Letters Addressed to William Wilberforce Recommending the Encouragement of the Cultivation of Sugar in Our Colonies in the East Indies as the Natural and Certain Means of Effecting the Total and General Abolition of the Slave Trade* (Liverpool, 1822); Cropper, *Letter Addressed to the Liverpool Society for Promoting the Abolition of Slavery* . . . (Liverpool, 1823); Cropper, *Relief for West Indian Distress* . . . (London, 1823); *The Correspondence between John Gladstone, Esq., M.P., and James Cropper, Esq.* . . . (Liverpool, 1824).

125. Davis, "James Cropper" (1960), 245–55; Charlton, "James Cropper," 58–62.

126. Davis, "James Cropper" (1961), 154–55, 160–61.

127. Charlton, "James Cropper," 64–65, and n. 42; Heyrick, *Immediate, Not Gradual Abolition.* On 8 June 1824 the London Anti-Slavery Committee instructed its secretary to procure a dozen copies of Heyrick's pamphlet, the first edition of which was anonymous, and to distribute them to members upon request. At the same time, the committee considered a letter written to Cropper dealing with the views of some of the members of the society regarding immediate emancipation. See Minutes of the Anti-Slavery Society, MSS Brit. Emp. S.20 E 2/1, 111–12, Rhodes House, Oxford.

128. Similar techniques had, of course, been used by the abolitionists in the 1790s and 1814, by Dissenters protesting various religious disabilities, and especially by Quakers. See N. C. Hunt, *Two Early Political Associations: The Quakers and the Dissenting Deputies in the Age of Sir Robert Walpole* (Oxford, 1961); Davis, *Problem of Slavery in the Age of Revolution,* chap. 5; Seymour Drescher, "Public Opinion and the Destruction of British Colonial Slavery," in James Walvin, ed., *Slavery and British Society, 1776–1846* (Baton Rouge, 1982), 22–48; James Walvin, "The Propaganda of Anti-Slavery," ibid., 49–68.

129. Davis, "James Cropper" (1961), 159–60; "Extracts," fols. 24–27, 37, 63–64; Cropper, *The Support of Slavery Investigated* (London, 1824), 5–16; K. Charlton, "The State of Ireland in the 1820s: James Cropper's Plan," *Irish Historical Studies,* 17 (1971), 320–39; Edward Gibbon Wakefield, *England and America: A Comparison of the Social and Political State of Both Nations* (New York, 1834), 27, 212–17, 224. The *Glasgow Courier,* after charging that the East India interest was behind both the Anti-Slavery Society and the Tropical Free Labour Society, expressed the hope that the crowds of ladies who attended an antislavery meeting in London were not burdening their consciences as well as their bodies with cotton clothing, "except of course cotton imported by Mr. Cropper" (5 May 1825).

130. Charlton, "James Cropper," 65–67 n. 47; Davis, "James Cropper" (1961), 161–62.

131. Anthony J. Barker, "Captain Charles Stuart and the British and American Abolition Movements, 1830–1834," *Slavery and Abolition: A Journal of Comparative Studies,* 1 (1980), 49, 51–52; Davis, "James Cropper," (1961), 163–71; Charlton, "James Cropper," 69–75; Minutes of the Anti-Slavery Society, 25 May 1831, E 2/3. According to the Agency Committee, toward the end of 1830 the general public was still ignorant of colonial slavery, especially of its most shocking features; West Indian money had closed most of the channels of printed communication, and most magazines and newspapers were opposed to the abolitionists (*Report of the Agency Committee of the Anti-Slavery Society, Established in June 1831, for the Purpose of Disseminating Information by Lectures on Colonial Slavery* (London, 1832), 1.

132. Barker, "Captain Charles Stuart," 46–59; Minutes of the Anti-Slavery Society, E 2/3, 105, 170; "Extracts," fols. 104–5; R. J. M. Blackett, *Building an Antislavery Wall: Black Americans in the Atlantic Abolitionist Movement, 1830–1860* (Baton Rouge, 1983), 52–60; James Cropper, *A Letter to Thomas Clarkson* (Liverpool, 1832); *The Letters of William Lloyd Garrison,* vol. 1, *I Will Be Heard! 1822–1835,* ed. Walter M. Merrill (Cambridge, Mass., 1971), 238–39.

133. Davis, "James Cropper" (1961), 170; *Letters of Garrison,* I, 230–33, 237–38; Charlton, "James Cropper," 72, 74.

134. Howard Temperley, *British Antislavery, 1833–1870* (Columbia, S.C., 1972), 23–25; Louis Billington, "Some Connections between British and American Reform Movements, 1830–1860, with Special Reference to the Anti-Slavery Movement" (M.A. diss., University of Bristol, 1966), 49–55, and passim.

135. *Letters of Garrison,* I, 232; *Parliamentary Debates,* 3d ser., vol. 17 (1833), cols. 1247–48. Howick's economic thought will be discussed more fully below. It should be added that Cropper strongly opposed entrusting such regulations to the colonial legislatures, at least during an apprenticeship period. He recognized the need for some laws protecting freedmen's rights until free-market conditions prevailed. But, like Howick, he placed his ultimate faith in the principle of competition. Charles Stuart similarly argued that if any "peculiar regulations" should be necessary, they should be limited by law to an early expiration date; like Cropper, Stuart equated free labor with lowered labor costs (*The West India Question* [London, 1832], 12).

136. "Extracts," fols. 126–27; Charlton, "James Cropper," 75.

137. Raymond English, "George Thompson and the Climax of Philanthropic Radicalism, 1830–1842" (Unpublished diss., Cambridge University, kindly lent to me by Mr. English many years ago), 348, 350–52; Joseph Pease, *On Slavery, and Its Remedy* (n.p. [London], 1841), 1–3; Temperley, *British Antislavery,* 93–110. Though the 1833 emancipation act did not extend to British India and Ceylon, abolitionists tended to assume that the

enslavement of Indians by fellow Indians was mild and "domestic" in character and that it would be ended by even the emasculated antislavery provisions of the 1833 East India Company Charter Bill. In view of Cropper's crusade to equalize sugar duties, it is ironic that Buxton suddenly feared that the actual equalization of 1836 would "convert gentle servitude [of the Indians] into grinding Slavery," unless the abolitionists took immediate action (Buxton to Joseph John Gurney, 25 June 1837, Buxton Papers, II, 131–37, Rhodes House, Oxford).

138. MS Minute Book, General Anti-Slavery Convention, 1840, MSS Brit. Emp. S.20 E 2/18, 55–64, Rhodes House, Oxford. Although the delegates significantly modified the wording of the free-labor committee's resolutions, they rejected a rider proposed by David Turnbull and Dr. R. R. Madden to the effect that the principles of free trade, however true in the abstract, "appear to be at variance with the anomalous facts connected with the cultivation of sugar. . . ." For divisions over sugar duties, see Temperley, *British Antislavery,* 153–83.

139. Minute Book, Committee of West India Planters and Merchants, Book 11, 22, 26, 29 April, 8 May, 5 June 1823, fols. 91–113, microfilm reel 4(1), Institute of Commonwealth Studies, London; Douglas Hall, *A Brief History of the West India Committee* (St. Lawrence, Barbados, 1971), 8–10; Lowell Joseph Ragatz, *The Fall of the Planter Class in the British Caribbean, 1763–1833* (New York, 1928), 413–20; Murray, *West Indies,* 127–33.

140. *Substance of the Debate in the House of Commons, on the 15th May, 1823, on a Motion for the Mitigation and Gradual Abolition of Slavery throughout the British Dominions . . .* (London, 1823), 1–21; CO 320/1, no. 209, Public Record Office, London. Thomas Clarkson, who tended to be the most gullible of abolitionists, wrote that while Canning's resolutions and Bathurst's order in council for Trinidad did not quite come up to his expectations, slavery had nevertheless *"received its Death wound"* in the six crown colonies and could linger only a few years more in the chartered colonies (undated letter, probably 1824, to the antislavery committees, British Library, Add. MSS 41267A, fols. 136–37). James Stephen later wrote that he would not say the West Indians had suggested the resolutions to Canning "for the purpose of dividing opinions, chilling popular feelings by delay, and postponing for an indefinite period, all effectual reformation; still less would I impute to that deceased minister, that he knowingly lent himself to such a purpose. But this has been the undeniable effect; and this, let me add, was the effect which I from the first foresaw and foretold" (*Slavery in the British West India Colonies,* II, 400). By 9 February 1824, Buxton heard a report that Canning would join the West Indians: "if he does we shall go to war with him in earnest" (Buxton Papers, I, 329–32).

141. CO 320/1, nos. 31, 42.

142. For example, Alexander M'Donnell, *Considerations on Negro Slavery . . .* (London, 1824); J. Clayton Jennyns, *An Appeal to Earl Bathurst . . .* (London, 1828); F. G. Smyth, *An Apology for West Indians, and Reflections on the Policy of Great Britain's Interference in the Internal Concerns of the West India Colonies* (London, 1824); John Foster, *Two Letters, on the State of the Negroes in the West Indies* (Bedford, 1824); *Correspondence between Gladstone and Cropper;* Alexander Barclay, *Effects of the Late Colonial Policy of Great Britain . . . ,* 2d ed. (London, 1830); *Actual State of the Question between our Colonial Slave Proprietors, and the Parliament and Abolitionists of this Country* (Glasgow, 1830); *Proceedings of the Honourable House of Assembly of Jamaica, in Relation to Those Which Took Place in the British House of Commons, on the 15th May Last . . .* (Jamaica, 1823).

143. MS Resolutions of the Standing Committee of West India Planters and Merchants, 11 May 1833; William Maxwell, MS plans for emancipation, 1830–33, to Grey and Goderich, 2 May 1833; MS from the Standing Committee, 25 Feb. 1833—all in Grey Papers, University of Durham, Department of Palaeography and Diplomatic (since the Grey Papers were being reorganized when I consulted them, I have omitted obsolete box and file numbers). From 1823 onward, the West India committee had placed the highest priority on indemnity for financial losses, including the declining value of slaves and estates (Minute Book, Committee of West India Merchants, 9 June 1823, fols. 274–78, microfilm reel 2[2]). By 1830 Buxton could affirm that the West India party candidly ac-

knowledged the physical and moral evils of slavery and expressed doubt whether "there remains one advocate of the old school—who rests his argument on the merits of slavery. . . ." Yet Buxton's own scrapbooks show that he was aware that positive defenses of slavery persisted into the 1830s (Buxton Papers, XX, 45–47). Lord Seaford emphasized to Lord Holland the sharp division in the West Indies between the loyal managers of great estates and the rabid resisters, usually men of "ruined fortune," who tended to dominate Jamaican politics (2 Aug. 1833, Grey Papers). For evidence that plantation managers felt a lessening interest in the properties under their control and that real interest rates were rapidly rising as a result of uncertainty over the colonies' future, see CO 320/1, no. 4.

144. Mary Reckord, "Missions in Jamaica before Emancipation," *Caribbean Studies,* 8, no. 1 (1968), 69–74; G. G. Findlay and W. W. Holdsworth, *The History of the Wesleyan Missionary Society* (London, 1921), II, 27, 37, 50–58, 69–75; Michael Craton, "Christianity and Slavery in the British West Indies, 1750–1865," *Historical Reflections/Réflexions historiques,* 5 (1978), 141–59.

145. Quoted in Craton, *Testing the Chains,* 246.

146. Reckord, "Missions in Jamaica," 69 n. 1; Craton, "Christianity and Slavery," 149. In the 1820s the Anglican church became active in baptizing slaves, but much of this was perfunctory; the Jamaican legislature paid a fee of 2*s.* 6*d.* per slave.

147. Michael Craton, "Proto-Peasant Revolts? The Late Slave Rebellions in the British West Indies, 1816–1832," *Past and Present,* no. 85 (1979), 99–125; Craton, *Testing the Chains,* 242–43, 247–53, 291–321. The insurrections in Barbados in 1816 and in Demerara in 1823 were encouraged by rumors that England had decreed emancipation. While slaves listened intently to the planters' threats and fulminations against the abolitionists and the British government, they also developed their own system of intelligence. For example, Jamaica's governor Mulgrave reported to the colonial secretary Goderich that from Hanover parish a well-informed physician had written "that by the very same packet, which then I recollected was the bearer of your Lordship's Confidential Communication to me, the Negroes of that distant County Parish had at the same time the intelligence diffused amongst them all that a Plan of Emancipation was about to be brought forward immediately, combined with a System of forced labour by Police, and he added that amongst the leaders the idea of such an attempt was generally scouted, and this I regret to say I have since had to a certain degree confirmed by Gentlemen in other parts of the Country" (CO 137/188, 26 Apr. 1833, fols. 324–29).

148. Craton, "Proto-Peasant Revolts?" 99–125; Craton, *Testing the Chains,* 291–321; B. W. Higman, *Slave Population and Economy in Jamaica, 1807–1834* (Cambridge, Eng., 1976), 227–32; Sidney W. Mintz and Douglas G. Hall, "The Origins of the Jamaican Internal Marketing System," *Yale Publications in Anthropology,* no. 57 (New Haven, 1960), 3–26.

149. John Shipman to Richard Watson, 3 Sept. 1823, Wesleyan Missionary Society Archives, Box 118/143, School of Oriental and African Studies, London; Shipman to Messrs. Taylor and Watson, 13 Sept. 1824, ibid., Box 122/110; William Rateliffe to Myles Morley Watson, 27 Jan. 1825, ibid., Box 121/28; MS Minutes of a District Committee Meeting Held in Kingston on Friday 23rd April 1824, ibid., Box 148; *At a Meeting of the Wesleyan Missionaries Held in Kingston, Jamaica, on the 6th Day of September 1824* . . . (printed circular, signed John Shipman); Richard Watson, *A Sermon Preached before the Wesleyan Methodist Missionary-Society* . . . (London, 1824), 14–17; *Methodist Magazine,* 3d ser., 48 (1825), 115–19.

150. Buxton Papers, I, 329–32.

151. For a discussion of the Williams case, see Reckord, "Colonial Office and the Abolition of Slavery," 726–31. I am indebted to John Walsh, of Jesus College, Oxford, for the point on Methodists' identifying planters with local Anglican squires.

152. Reckord, "Colonial Office and the Abolition of Slavery," 723–34; Findlay and Holdsworth, *History of Wesleyan Missionary Society,* II, 101–206; Benjamin Wiffin to John Crisp, 8 Aug. 1832, British Political Papers, 1717–1860, Duke University Library; [William Knibb and Peter Borthwick], *Colonial Slavery: Defence of the Baptist Missionaries from the Charge of Inciting the Late Rebellion in Jamaica* . . . (London, 1832); [Thomas F. Ab-

bott], *Narrative of Certain Events Connected with the Late Disturbances in Jamaica, and the Charges Preferred against the Baptist Missionaries in That Island* (London, 1832). By 1830 the Anti-Slavery Committee was working closely with Baptist and Methodist groups as well as with "Ladies' Anti-Slavery Associations," which had greatly multiplied since 1827. See Minutes of the Anti-Slavery Society, E 5/2; [Elizabeth Heyrick], *Apology for Ladies' Anti-Slavery Associations* (London, 1828), 8; *Report of the Agency Committee* (1832), 9–21; K. R. M. Short, "A Study in Political Nonconformity: The Baptists 1827–1845, with Particular Reference to Slavery" (D.Phil. diss., Oxford University, 1972), 41–42, 101–12, 126–31; A. F. Madden, "The Attitude of the Evangelicals to the Empire and Imperial Problems, 1820–50" (D.Phil. diss., Oxford University, 1950), 200–201.

153. MS observations on various matters, 3 Nov. 1830, Buxton Papers, XXII, 25–27. Buxton made much of the point that the Jamaican assembly had debated not whether females should be flogged but whether the flogging should be done decently or indecently—that is, on the naked body—and had resolved that it should be done indecently.

154. Minutes of the Anti-Slavery Society, E 5/3, 20–21, 27; Buxton Papers, III, 45–46; Stephen, *Anti-Slavery Recollections,* 112–87; Peter F. Dixon, "The Politics of Emancipation: The Movement for the Abolition of Slavery in the British West Indies, 1807–1833" (D.Phil. diss., Oxford University, 1971), 290–304.

155. Gross, "Abolition of Negro Slavery," 65; Gross, "Commons and Empire," 51; Dixon, "Politics of Emancipation," 315–25; Zachary Macaulay to William Wilberforce, 26 Nov. 1832, in *The Correspondence of William Wilberforce,* ed. Robert Isaac Wilberforce and Samuel Wilberforce, (London, 1840), II, 526.

156. Goderich to Mulgrave, confidential, 19 Jan. 1833, British Library, Add. MSS 40863, fols. 22–36; Minute of Conference, Standing Committee of West India Planters and Merchants, 28 Jan. 1833, Grey Papers; Acting Committee of West India Planters and Merchants to Earl Grey, 25 Feb. 1833, ibid.; William Burge to Committee of Correspondence, Assembly of Jamaica, 19 Jan., 9 Feb., 7, 23 Mar. 1833, Letterbook, vol. 6, Archives of Jamaica, Spanish Town; Earl of Ripon (Goderich) to Brougham, 4 Apr. 1838, Brougham Papers, 14439.

157. Stanley to Earl Grey, 8 Apr. 1833, Grey Papers; CO 318/116; Priscilla Buxton to Maria Buxton, 16 May 1833, Buxton Papers, II, 273–88; William Burge to Committee of Correspondence, 18 Apr., 4, 10 May 1833; Richard Barrett and Abraham Hodgson to Committee of Correspondence, 2, 11 May 1833, Letterbook, vol. 6. The West Indian "interest" had become increasingly divided into merchants and planters and into the representatives of the older and of the newer colonies; Stanley exploited these divisions and particularly outraged the Jamaican agents, who spoke for "those who were resident in the Colonies and whose lives, no less than property were involved in the measures. . . ." (Burge, letter of 18 Apr., reporting the interview with Stanley).

158. Buxton Papers, II, 271–88; *Parliamentary Debates,* 3d ser., vol. 17 (1833), cols. 1193–1231. On 14 May, Buxton had shown his own plan to Lord Althorp, who had not disapproved it.

159. *Parliamentary Debates,* 3d ser., vol. 17 (1833), cols. 1231–60.

160. George Stephen to Daniel O'Connell, 29 May 1833, George Stephen Papers (these were unidentified when I consulted them), the Hull Museums. In a letter of 3 June to Wilberforce, Stephen explained why he trusted O'Connell more than Buxton. Over a different dispute O'Connell fought a duel with Stanley.

161. Murray, *West Indies,* 201–4; William A. Green, *British Slave Emancipation: The Sugar Colonies and the Great Experiment, 1830–1865* (Oxford, 1976), 118–24; Gladstone Papers, British Library, Add. MS 44819. Green has calculated the annual cost to the Treasury of maintaining the special magistrates at £58,700 ("James Stephen and British West Indian Policy," 43 n. 38).

162. *Tourist,* 19 Nov. 1832, 84; 10 Dec. 1832, 114; 17 Dec. 1832, 124; George Stephen to Lord Suffield, 18 Jan. 1833, George Stephen Papers.

163. George Stephen to William Wilberforce, 20 June 1833; Stephen to Joseph Sturge,

20 June 1833, George Stephen Papers; Stephen, *Anti-Slavery Recollections,* 195–209; W. L. Burn, *Emancipation and Apprenticeship in the British West Indies* (London, 1937), 168–69.

164. Buxton Papers, XXIV; *Christian Advocate,* 20 Nov. 1837. For the complexities of ending apprenticeship and the discriminatory devices that followed it, see W. K. Marshall, "The Termination of Apprenticeship in Barbados and the Windward Islands: An Essay in Colonial Administration and Politics," *Journal of Caribbean History,* 2 (1971), 1–45; W. Emanuel Riviere, "Labour Shortage in the British West Indies after Emancipation," *Journal of Caribbean History,* 4 (1972), 1–28; Green, "James Stephen and British West India Policy," 3–56; Adamson, *Sugar without Slaves,* 34–56.

165. British and Foreign Anti-Slavery Society, Memorials and Petitions, MSS Brit. Emp. S.20 E 2/19, 12–17, 19–25, 51–53, 60–65; E 2/20, 56–59, 160, Rhodes House, Oxford; CO 140/138, 106–43; *The Friend of the Africans,* no. 27 (1845), 29–30; Minute Book, General Anti-Slavery Convention, 41–42, 71, 106–12, 121–22. For the history of indentured African immigration to the West Indies, see Johnson U. J. Asiegbu, *Slavery and the Politics of Liberation 1787–1861: A Study of Liberated African Emigration and British Anti-Slavery Policy* (New York, 1969), 34–135; and Monica Schuler, *"Alas, Alas, Kongo": A Social History of Indentured African Immigration into Jamaica, 1841–1865* (Baltimore, 1980). Neither of these studies makes use of the CO 140/138 file cited above.

166. Buxton to Joseph John Gurney, 25 June 1837, Buxton Papers, II, 131–37; Buxton Papers, XXIII, XXXII.

167. Riviere, "Labour Shortage," 9–24; Circular Letter to India, 26 Dec. 1843, Anti-Slavery Memorials and Petitions, E 2/20, 29–30.

168. Stephen, *Slavery of the British West India Colonies,* II, 412–13.

169. Howick to William IV, 5 Mar. 1832, Grey Papers; Lord Goderich's correspondence with William IV, Mar. 1832, British Library, Add. MSS 40862, fols. 327, 329–31, 345–46. The king, who feared that slave emancipation would result in the loss of the colonies, followed the debate very closely and exerted considerable pressure on Goderich, as is evident from Goderich's "most private" letter of 6 May 1832 to Henry Taylor, Goderich MSS, D/MH/9 O-152, Buckinghamshire County Record Office, Aylesbury.

170. For this point I have drawn on David Eltis's brilliant essay "Abolitionist Perceptions of Society after Slavery," in Walvin, ed., *Slavery and British Society,* esp. 202–3.

171. Buxton to Macaulay, 31 Dec. 1832, Buxton Papers, III, 45. On the new moral sensibility, I have learned much from the writings of James Walvin, esp. from a paper he kindly sent me, "The Refinement of Manners in England, 1780–1867"; but unlike Walvin, I am impressed by the connections between the public refinement in manners and the new prison system, asylums, workhouses, and other institutions for social control.

172. Buxton to Mr. East, 15 Oct. 1832, Buxton Papers, III, 31–32; Memo by Howick, 18 Mar. 1833, Grey Papers; Howick to Brougham, 21 Mar. 1833, Brougham Papers, 18371; *Parliamentary Debates,* 3d ser., vol. 17 (1833), cols. 1255–56; unpaged memorandum and draft of circular dispatch by Stephen, Jan. 1833, Grey Papers.

173. CO 320/1, nos. 2, 4, 5; Reckord, "Colonial Office and the Abolition of Slavery," 723–34; Capt. Charles Elliott, Protector of Slaves, British Guiana, MS Extract from Official Report for six months ending 31 Dec. 1831, Grey Papers; Zachary Macaulay to Wilberforce, Nov. 1832, *Correspondence of Wilberforce,* II, 525. On the basis of Elliott's figures of 194,744 lashes for 1830 and 199,507 for 1831, Buxton calculated an estimate for the West Indies as a whole of over two million cart-whip lashes a year.

174. Macaulay to Wilberforce, Nov. 1832, *Correspondence of Wilberforce,* II, 524–27; James Stephen, MS commentary on Howick's plan, 6 July 1832, Grey Papers; T. J. Barron, "James Stephen, the 'Black Race' and British Colonial Administration, 1813–47," *Journal of Imperial and Commonwealth History,* 5 (1977), 131–47; Burn, *Emancipation and Apprenticeship,* 193–94; Stephen, unpaged memo, Jan. 1833, Grey Papers. Although some Jamaican leaders like Richard Barrett had argued in the 1820s that the coloreds could be allies against the abolitionists and should be given the franchise, the legislature acted too slowly to win electoral support from the large colored population. For the politics of race in

Jamaica and the importance of British pressure in securing limited civil rights, see Gad J. Heuman, *Between Black and White: Race, Politics, and the Free Coloreds in Jamaica, 1792–1865* (Westport, Conn., 1981), 44–94.

175. James Stephen, Draft of answers to West Indian objections, 105–7, Grey Papers; *Parliamentary Debates,* 3d ser., vol. 17 (1833), cols. 1209–13; vol. 18 (1833), cols. 520–21.

176. Stephen, MS commentary on Howick's plan, 6 July 1832, Grey Papers; Burn, *Emancipation and Apprenticeship,* 105.

177. Macaulay to Wilberforce, Nov. 1832, *Correspondence of Wilberforce,* II, 524–27; Stephen, Draft of circular dispatch, Jan. 1833, 13–15, Grey Papers.

178. Stephen, Draft of circular dispatch, 103–4, and later, unnumbered pages; Stephen, Draft of answers to West Indian objections, 102, Grey Papers; *Parliamentary Debates,* 3d ser., vol. 17 (1833), cols. 1257–58.

179. Burn, *Emancipation and Apprenticeship,* 177–78; *Parliamentary Debates,* 3d ser., vol. 17 (1833), cols. 1235–58; Memo by Howick, 18 Mar. 1833, Grey Papers.

180. Printed Colonial Office confidential memo, written and initialed by Howick, 7 Jan. 1833, Grey Papers; Howick's draft of a plan, 3 July 1832, ibid.; two commentaries by James Stephen on Howick's plan, 6 July 1832, ibid.; notes by Earl Grey on Taylor's objections to land tax, 15 Aug. 1832, ibid.; Stephen, Draft of circular dispatch, Jan. 1833, ibid.; Normanby to Goderich, private and confidential, 2 Mar. 1833, ibid.; Howick to Goderich, n.d., and 4 Oct. 1832, Goderich MSS, D/MH/G O.58 and 58, Buckinghamshire County Record Office; Henry Taylor to Howick, 31 Dec. 1832, d7.ff.167–168, Sir Henry Taylor Papers, Bodleian Library, Oxford; Howick to Lord John Russell, 11 Jan. 1833, Russell Papers, 30322, Ic, fols. 111–14, Public Record Office; John Norman, *Edward Gibbon Wakefield: A Political Reappraisal* (Bridgeport, Conn., 1963), 4–8; R. Garnett, *Edward Gibbon Wakefield* (London, 1898), 144–47; *The Collected Works of Edward Gibbon Wakefield,* ed. M. F. Lloyd Pritchard (London, 1968).

181. James Stephen, two commentaries on Howick's plan, 6 July 1832, Grey Papers.

182. Ibid. The abolitionists looked upon Howick, in George Stephen's words, as "one of our firmest and ablest advocates, and one of the slave's best friends" (*Anti-Slavery Recollections,* 192–93). It is significant that William Burge, the Jamaican agent and former attorney general, had kind words for Howick's attack on Stanley's plan and concluded that Howick "exhibited a much more intimate acquaintance with the question, and a much more just sense of the difficulties of the Measure than Mr. Stanley possessed" (letter to the Committee of Correspondence, 21 May 1833, Letterbook, vol. 6, Archives of Jamaica). On the other hand, Lord Holland described Howick's impetuosity and ill temper, which made him extremely unpopular among government leaders (*The Holland House Diaries,* ed. A. D. Kriegel [London, 1977], II, 207–8).

183. Green, "James Stephen and British West India Policy," 35–55; Barron, "James Stephen, the 'Black Race' and British Colonial Administration," 131–50.

184. Green, "James Stephen and British West India Policy," 55.

185. Riviere, "Labour Shortage," 9–24; Douglas Hall, "The Flight from the Estates Reconsidered: The British West Indies, 1838–42," *Journal of Caribbean History,* 10 and 11 (1978), 7–24; Michael Moohr, "The Economic Impact of Slave Emancipation in British Guiana, 1832–1852," *Economic History Review,* 25 (1972), 588–606; Philip D. Curtin, *Two Jamaicans: The Role of Ideas in a Tropical Colony, 1830–1865* (1955; reprint, Westport, Conn., 1968), 101–57; K. O. Laurence, "The Evolution of Long-term Labour Contracts in Trinidad and British Guiana, 1834–1863," *Jamaican Historical Review,* 5 (1977), 131–47.

186. Quoted in Barron, "James Stephen, the 'Black Race' and British Colonial Administration," 132.

187. Hall, "Flight from the Estates," 7–24; Moohr, "Economic Impact of Slave Emancipation," 588–606; Sidney W. Mintz, "Slavery and the Rise of Peasantries," and commentary by Woodville K. Marshall, in Michael Craton, ed., *Roots and Branches: Current Directions in Slave Studies* (Toronto, 1979), 213–48; Mintz, *Caribbean Transformations* (Chicago, 1974), 131–250.

188. Stuart, *West India Question,* 39; Adamson, *Sugar without Slaves,* 160–88, 225–26.

Even British Guiana was devastated in 1884 by a collapse in sugar prices resulting from government-stimulated beet-root production in Europe.

189. Seaford to Lord Holland, 2 Aug. 1833, Grey Papers.

190. Archives Nationales, Section Outre-Mer, Généralités 165, Dossier 1336, 82–91; Dossier 1337.

PART THREE

1. Quoted in John Clive, *Macaulay: The Shaping of the Historian* (New York, 1973), 481–82.

2. Quoted in Walter E. Houghton, *The Victorian Frame of Mind, 1830–1870* (New Haven, 1957), 44–45.

3. Edward Everett, *Orations and Speeches on Various Occasions*, 6th ed. (Boston, 1860), II, 244–45.

4. Quoted in Steven Marcus, *Engels, Manchester, and the Working Class* (New York, 1977), 66.

5. Drew Gilpin Faust, ed., *The Ideology of Slavery: Proslavery Thought in the Antebellum South, 1830–1860* (Baton Rouge, 1981), 170–205. Hammond greatly exaggerated the length of indentures. The Colonial Office tried to limit indentures of Africans to one year, although children were apprenticed for five years (Monica Schuler, *"Alas, Alas, Kongo": A Social History of Indentured African Immigration into Jamaica, 1841–1865* [Baltimore, 1980], 51–53).

6. Faust, *Ideology of Slavery*, 274–99.

7. "Our Relations with England," reprinted from *Southern Literary Messenger*, 8 (1842), 387.

8. Roger Anstey, *The Atlantic Slave Trade and British Abolition, 1760–1810* (London, 1975); Betty Fladeland, "Abolitionist Pressures on the Concert of Europe, 1814–1822," *Journal of Modern History*, 38 (1966), 355–73; Leslie Bethell, *The Abolition of the Brazilian Slave Trade: Britain, Brazil and the Slave Trade Question, 1807–1869* (Cambridge, Eng., 1970); E. Phillip Le Veen, *British Slave Trade Suppression Policies, 1821–1865* (New York, 1977); David Eltis, "The Export of Slaves from Africa, 1821–1843," *The Journal of Economic History*, 37 (1977), 409–33; David R. Murray, *Odious Commerce: Britain, Spain and the Abolition of the Cuban Slave Trade* (Cambridge, Eng., 1980).

9. David Eltis, "The Direction and Fluctuation of the Transatlantic Slave Trade, 1821–1843: A Revision of the 1845 Parliamentary Paper," in Henry A. Gemery and Jan S. Hogendorn, eds., *The Uncommon Market: Essays in the Economic History of the Atlantic Slave Trade* (New York, 1979), 286.

10. David M. Pletcher, *The Diplomacy of Annexation: Texas, Oregon, and the Mexican War* (Columbia, Mo., 1973), 18–21, 82–83, 120–22; Frederick Merk, *Slavery and the Annexation of Texas* (New York, 1972), 23, 58; MSS Brit. Emp. E 2/19, 10–11, and passim, Rhodes House, Oxford; Madeleine B. Stern, "Stephen Pearl Andrews, Abolitionist, and the Annexation of Texas," *Southwestern Historical Quarterly*, 67 (1964), 491–523. In December 1840 the Foreign Office was remarkably defensive in justifying to the British and Foreign Anti-Slavery Society *any* commercial treaty with the Republic of Texas, which abolitionists perceived as "a wicked and cruel despotism."

11. Pletcher, *Diplomacy of Annexation*, 122–27, 134, 142–53; Merk, *Slavery*, 3–82, 187–92, 217–36, 257–64, 281–88; David Brion Davis, *The Slave Power Conspiracy and the Paranoid Style* (Baton Rouge, 1969), 43–47.

12. Manuel Moreno Fraginals, Herbert S. Klein, and Stanley L. Engerman, "The Level and Structure of Slave Prices on Cuban Plantations in the Mid-Nineteenth Century: Some Comparative Perspectives," *American Historical Review*, 88 (1983), 1201–18; Eltis, "Direction and Fluctuation of the Transatlantic Slave Trade," 281, 285–86, 290; Murray, *Odious Commerce*, 40–132; Arthur F. Corwin, *Spain and the Abolition of Slavery in Cuba, 1817–1886*

(Austin, 1967), 17–67. On the volume of the illegal slave trade to Cuba, David Eltis's careful estimates seem to be the most reliable.

13. Minute Book, General Anti-Slavery Convention 1840, MSS Brit. Emp. S.20 E 2/18, 85–92; E 2/19, 30; Murray, *Odious Commerce*, 114–80.

14. Murray, *Odious Commerce*, 133–207.

15. Calhoun to William R. King, 12 Aug. 1844, reprinted in Merk, *Slavery*, 281–88.

16. The most accessible text of the first of Hammond's widely reprinted letters is in Faust, *Ideology of Slavery*, 170–205.

17. Ronald T. Takaki, *A Pro-Slavery Crusade: The Agitation to Reopen the African Slave Trade* (New York, 1971); Drew Gilpin Faust, *James Henry Hammond and the Old South: A Design for Mastery* (Baton Rouge, 1982), 350; David M. Potter, *The Impending Crisis, 1848–1861*, comp. and ed. Don E. Fehrenbacher (New York, 1976), 395–401. The campaign to reopen the slave trade included some southern Unionists who wished to increase the political power of the slave states within the Union.

18. Takaki, *Pro-Slavery Crusade*, 230–39; Murray, *Odious Commerce*, 298–307; Bethell, *Abolition of the Brazilian Slave Trade*, 267–363; Richard Graham, *Britain and the Onset of Modernization in Brazil, 1850–1914* (Cambridge, Eng., 1968), 167–68; *The Constitution of the Confederate States of America*, 11 Mar. 1961, Art. I, Sec. 9 (1).

19. L. W. Spratt, *The Foreign Slave Trade the Source of Political Power—of Material Progress, of Social Integrity, and of Social Emanicpation to the South* (Charleston, 1858), 3–31; Spratt, "The Philosophy of Secession," repr. in John Elliott Cairnes, *The Slave Power: Its Character, Career and Probable Designs*, 2d ed. (London, 1863), 390–410.

20. Spratt, *Foreign Slave Trade;* Spratt, "Philosophy of Secession," 394–95; Takaki, *Pro-Slavery Crusade.*

21. Spratt, *Foreign Slave Trade*, 10–13, 27; Spratt, "Philosophy of Secession," 394–97, 405–8.

22. Cairnes, *Slave Power;* Adelaide Weinberg, *John Elliot [sic] Cairnes and the American Civil War: A Study in Anglo-American Relations* (London, n.d. [1968]), 16–20; [J. S. Mill], "The Slave Power," *Westminster Review*, n.s., 21 (1862), 490; William L. Miller, "J. E. Cairnes on the Economics of American Negro Slavery," *Southern Economic Journal*, 30 (1964), 333–41.

23. Cairnes, *Slave Power*, 282–98. Readers of Cairnes would never suspect that the pro-slave-trade cause had failed to win endorsement from a single state legislature and that it aroused strong opposition from nonslaveholders and, according to James Hammond, from nine-tenths of the southern population.

24. Brian Jenkins, *Britain and the War for the Union* (Montreal, 1974), I, 4, and passim; Donaldson Jordan and Edwin J. Pratt, *Europe and the American Civil War* (Boston, 1931), 10–38, 58; Mary Ellison, *Support for Secession: Lancashire and the American Civil War* (Chicago, 1972); Philip John Augar, "The Cotton Famine 1861–1865: A Study of the Principal Cotton Towns during the American Civil War" (Ph.D. diss., Clare College, Cambridge, 1979); Weinberg, *Cairnes*, 133–34. Though Cairnes had never met Sarah Shaw, in 1863 he named his newborn son after Robert Gould Shaw.

25. [Mill], "Slave Power," 503.

26. Jenkins, *Britain and the War for the Union*, provides the most comprehensive guide. In addition, I have drawn on Jordan and Pratt, *Europe and the American Civil War;* Ephraim Douglass Adams, *Great Britain and the American Civil War* (London, 1925); Kinley J. Brauer, "The Slavery Problem in the Diplomacy of the American Civil War," *Pacific Historical Review*, 46 (1977), 439–69; and P. J. Cain and A. G. Hopkins, "The Political Economy of British Expansion Overseas, 1750–1914," *Economic History Review*, 2d ser., 33 (1980), 463–90.

27. Quoted in Jordan and Pratt, *Europe and the American Civil War*, 24.

28. Fraginals, Klein, and Engerman, "Level and Structure of Slave Prices," 1205–9, 1217–18.

29. Jenkins, *Britain and the War for the Union*, II, 152–54; Richard Allen Heckman, "British Press Reaction to the Emancipation Proclamation," *Lincoln Herald*, 81 (1969), 150–

53; Weinberg, *Cairnes,* 144–45 and 144 n. 4. Replying in part to the London *Times,* the Saint Petersburg *Vedomosti* took a position similar to that of Cairnes, arguing that Lincoln's motives and principles had no bearing on the justice and significance of the deed itself (Belle Becker Sideman and Lillian Friedman, eds., *Europe Looks at the Civil War* [New York, 1960], 203–6).

30. Sideman and Friedman, *Europe Looks at the Civil War,* 190–91.

31. Douglas A. Lorimer, *Colour, Class and the Victorians: English Attitudes to the Negro in the Mid-Nineteenth Century* (New York, 1978), 164–73; Jenkins, *Britain and the War for the Union,* II, 156–58.

32. Jordan and Pratt, *Europe and the American Civil War,* 66–69; Jenkins, *Britain and the War for the Union,* II, 42–43, and passim.

33. Jenkins, *Britain and the War for the Union,* II, 214, and passim. Peter d'A. Jones has traced the history of the myth of working-class support for the Union in an appendix to Mary Ellison's valuable study *Support for Secession,* 199–219. Jenkins qualifies Ellison's conclusion that workers generally favored intervention to end the war, and Augar argues that pro-Confederate meetings were mostly organized by employers and their agents ("The Cotton Famine").

34. James T. Schleifer, *The Making of Tocqueville's "Democracy in America"* (Chapel Hill, 1980), 48, 50–55, 65–66; George Wilson Pierson, *Tocqueville in America* (Garden City, N.Y., 1959); Joseph Story, *An Address Delivered before the Members of the Suffolk Bar* (Boston, 1829), 18–21.

35. *Democracy in America,* ed. J. P. Mayer, trans. George Lawrence (Garden City, N.Y., 1969), 345–46. Although Cairnes quoted from these and other passages, I have chosen the most modern and accurate translation. (New York: Harper & Row, 1966).

36. *Lord Durham's Report on the Affairs of British North America,* ed. Sir C. P. Lucas (Oxford, 1912 [first edition by Charles Buller published in 1840]), II, 211–13.

37. *The Papers of Frederick Law Olmsted,* vol. 2, *Slavery and the South, 1825–1857,* ed. Charles E. Beveridge and Charles Capen McLaughlin (Baltimore, 1981), 238–45. In his introduction, Charles E. Beveridge points out that Olmsted was largely dependent on contacts with "persons connected with Yale College" and that on his first trip he gained access to only seven farms and plantations, aside from those providing accommodation for travelers using public conveyances; his second trip "was even more barren of opportunities to examine plantation slavery, and he seems to have had few letters of introduction for the purpose." Indeed, during his second trip, of nine months, he was able to investigate only one plantation and gained most of his knowledge "from conversation, observation along the road, and what he saw in the houses where he spent the night" (10–11).

38. Ibid., 239–40.

39. Cairnes, *Slave Power,* 43–44, 47–52, 62–68, 123–26; Karl Marx, *Grundrisse: Foundations of the Critique of Political Economy,* trans. Martin Nicolaus (New York, 1973), 615. Marx quoted from Wakefield's notes in the latter's edition of Adam Smith. Elsewhere, Marx argued that Negro slavery "*presupposes* wage labour, and if other, free states with wage labour did not exist alongside it, if, instead, the Negro states were isolated, then all social conditions there would immediately turn into pre-civilized forms" (ibid., 224). Cairnes took a very smiliar view.

40. Cairnes, *Slave Power,* 69, 94.

41. Ibid., 45. Olmsted's emphasis was somewhat different: "That slaves have to be 'humored' a great deal, and often cannot be made to do their master's will, is very evident,—I do not think they will do from fear nearly as much as Northern laborers will simply from respect to their contract or regard to their duty" (*Papers of Frederick Law Olmsted,* II, 106).

42. Cairnes, *Slave Power,* 116–17.

43. Ibid., 53, 61.

44. Ibid., 160–62, and passim.

45. Ibid., 162–63.

46. Ibid., 94–103, 277–80. See also Robert E. May, *The Southern Dream of a Caribbean Empire, 1854–1861* (Baton Rouge, 1973).

47. Cairnes, *Slave Power,* 18, 166–78, 190–91.

48. Ibid., 307–12.

49. Ibid., 314–350; [Mill], "Slave Power," 509–10. Mill seems, in retrospect, to have been far more naïve than Cairnes in predicting the consequences of an unconditional northern victory, although Cairnes later changed his mind and in 1865 humbly confessed his "mistake" to Mill. Igonring the fact that emancipation would *increase* the political representation of the South, Mill in 1862 foresaw no danger in restoring the southern states "to their old position in the Union": "It would be a diminished position, because the masters would no longer be allowed representatives in Congress in right of three-fifths of their slaves. The slaves once freed, and enabled to hold property, and the country thrown open to free colonization, in a few years there would be a free population in sympathy with the rest of the Union. The most actively disloyal part of the population, already diminished by the war, would probably in great part emigrate if the North were successful" (509).

50. *Christian Advocate and Journal,* 26 Sept. 1861; Henry B. Smith, "British Sympathy with America," *American Theological Review,* 4 (1862), 487–552.

51. For the American millenarian tradition, see esp. James West Davidson, *The Logic of Millennial Thought: Eighteenth-Century New England* (New Haven, 1977); Stephen J. Stein, introd. to *The Works of Jonathan Edwards,* vol. 5, *Apocalyptic Writings,* ed. Stephen J. Stein (New Haven, 1977); Ernest Lee Tuveson, *Redeemer Nation: The Idea of America's Millennial Role* (Chicago, 1968); Edward M. Burns, *The American Idea of Mission: Concepts of National Purpose and Destiny* (New Brunswick, N.J., 1957); Perry Miller, *The Life of the Mind in America: From the Revolution to the Civil War,* bk. 1 (New York, 1965); and George M. Marsden, *The Evangelical Mind and the New School Presbyterian Experience: A Case Study of Thought and Theology in Nineteenth Century America* (New Haven, 1970). I am also indebted to Sacvan Bercovitch, *The American Jeremiad* (Madison, Wis., 1978).

52. Leonard Bacon, *Slavery Discussed in Occasional Essays, from 1833 to 1846* (New York, 1846), iii–viii; Joel Bernard, "Leonard Bacon and the Conservative Antislavery Movement" (unpublished Paper); Timothy J. Sehr, "Leonard Bacon and the Myth of the Good Slaveholder," *New England Quarterly,* 49 (1976), 194–213. For a penetrating study of the way in which abolitionism impinged upon the critical transformation of the New England clergy's role, see Donald M. Scott, *From Office to Profession: The New England Ministry, 1750–1850* ([Philadelphia], 1978).

53. Bacon, *Slavery Discussed,* 57–79.

54. Bernard, "Leonard Bacon and the Conservative Antislavery Movement"; Bacon, *Slavery Discussed,* v, 176–87, and passim.

55. Daniel Aaron, *The Unwritten War: American Writers and the Civil War* (New York, 1973), xiii–xiv; Potter, *Impending Crisis,* 199–201; Eric Foner, *Free Soil, Free Labor, Free Men: The Ideology of the Republican Party before the Civil War* (New York, 1970), 53, and passim; Daniel T. Rodgers, *The Work Ethic in Industrial America, 1850–1920* (Chicago, 1978), 32.

56. Foner, *Free Soil,* 101–2; Paul Finkelman, *An Imperfect Union: Slavery, Federalism, and Comity* (Chapel Hill, 1981), 313–43; Michael Fellman, "Rehearsal for the Civil War: Antislavery and Proslavery at the Fighting Point in Kansas, 1854–1856," in Lewis Perry and Michael Fellman, eds., *Antislavery Reconsidered: New Perspectives on the Abolitionists* (Baton Rouge, 1979), 287–307; Frederick Forthingham, *Significance of the Struggle between Liberty and Slavery in America* (New York, 1857), 19–20.

57. Charles Sumner, *The Slave Oligarchy and Its Usurpations: Speech of Hon. Charles Sumner, November 2, 1855, in Faneuil Hall, Boston* (Boston, 1855), 1; Sumner, *The Landmark of Freedom: Speech of Hon Charles Sumner, against the Repeal of the Missouri Prohibition of Slavery . . .* (Boston, 1854); Harlan Joel Gradin, "Losing Control: The Caning of Charles Sumner and the Erosion of the 'Common Ground on Which Our Political Fabric Was Reared' ",

(M.A. thesis, University of North Carolina, Chapel Hill), 83–86. I am much indebted to Mr. Gradin for lending me a copy of this valuable dissertation.

58. Charles Sumner, "The Crime against Kansas," *Old South Leaflets,* vol. 4, no. 83 (Boston, n.d.), 1–24; David Donald, *Charles Sumner and the Coming of the Civil War* (New York, 1960), 282–311; Gradin, "Losing Control."

59. Gradin, "Losing Control," 163–79; Wendell Phillips, "The Puritan Principle and John Brown," in *Speeches, Lectures, and Letters,* 2d ser. (Boston, 1905), 294–308; "Harper's Ferry," ibid., 1st ser. (Boston, 1863), 263–88.

60. Lewis Perry, *Childhood, Marriage, and Reform: Henry Clarke Wright, 1797–1870* (Chicago, 1980), 84; Perry, *Radical Abolitionism: Anarchy and the Government of God in Antislavery Thought* (Ithaca, N.Y., 1973), 236.

61. Perry, *Radical Abolitionism,* 240–46.

62. Foner, *Free Soil,* 140–48; James M. McPherson, *The Struggle for Equality: Abolitionists and the Negro in the Civil War and Reconstruction* (Princeton, 1964), 29–55; George M. Fredrickson, *The Inner Civil War: Northern Intellectuals and the Crisis of the Union* (New York, 1965), 53–64.

63. James M. McPherson, ed., *The Negro's Civil War: How American Negroes Felt and Acted during the War for the Union* (New York, 1965), 31.

64. James H. Moorhead, *American Apocalypse: Yankee Protestants and the Civil War, 1860–1869* (New Haven, 1978), 33–41; *The Collected Works of Abraham Lincoln,* ed. Roy P. Basler (New Brunswick, N.J., 1953–55), VI, 156.

65. Moorhead, *American Apocalypse,* 45, 52, and passim; *Collected Works of Abraham Lincoln,* VIII, 333.

66. McPherson, *Struggle for Equality,* 61–69, 82–93, 117–22, 192–220; McPherson, *Negro's Civil War,* 49–53, 223–39; Leon F. Litwack, *Been in the Storm So Long: The Aftermath of Slavery* (New York, 1979), 64–103, 169.

67. *Collected Works of Abraham Lincoln,* V, 144–46, 520–21, 530–37; J. G. Randall, *Lincoln the President: Springfield to Gettysburg* (New York, 1946), II, 161–69; Harold M. Hyman, *A More Perfect Union: The Impact of the Civil War and Reconstruction on the Constitution* (New York, 1973), 174, 263–78.

68. Moorhead, *American Apocalypse,* 59–61, 73–76; Reginald Horsman, *Race and Manifest Destiny: The Origins of American Racial Anglo-Saxonism* (Cambridge, Mass., 1981), 167.

69. William S. McFeely, *Grant: A Biography* (New York, 1982), 336–52; James M. McPherson, *The Abolitionist Legacy, from Reconstruction to the NAACP* (Princeton, 1975), 324–32.

70. David Montgomery, *Beyond Equality: Labor and the Radical Republicans, 1862–1872* (New York, 1967), 78–85.

71. Angelina Grimké, "Address to the Soldiers of Our Second Revolution," repr. in Gerda Lerner, *The Grimké Sisters of South Carolina: Rebels against Slavery* (New York, 1967), 388–89.

72. Montgomery, *Beyond Equality,* 89, 96, 113, 123–25, 180, 230–31, 252–60, 335–36, 354–56.

73. Litwack, *Been in the Storm,* 177–78, 212–26; Joel Williamson, *After Slavery: The Negro in South Carolina during Reconstruction, 1861–1877* (Chapel Hill, 1965), 47–48; Thomas Holt, *Black over White: Negro Political Leadership in South Carolina during Reconstruction* (Urbana, 1977), 1, and passim; Willie Lee Rose, *Rehearsal for Reconstruction: The Port Royal Experiment* (Indianapolis, 1964), 314–15.

74. Rose, *Rehearsal for Reconstruction,* 79–80, 128, 215–16, 223.

75. Litwack, *Been in the Storm,* 521–23, 552–53; Kenneth M. Stampp, *The Era of Reconstruction, 1865–1877* (New York, 1966), 124–30; Rose, *Rehearsal for Reconstruction,* 357, and passim; Gerald David Jaynes, *Branches without Roots: Genesis of the Black Working-Class, 1860–80,* forthcoming, chaps. 4 and 5. I am much obliged to Professor Jaynes for allowing me to read this valuable study.

76. Jaynes, *Branches without Roots,* chap. 6; Robert William Fogel, *Without Consent or*

Contract: The Rise and Fall of American Slavery, forthcoming, chap. 5. I am grateful to Professor Fogel for sending me a copy of his important manuscript.

77. McPherson, *Struggle for Equality,* 135, 172–73; Rose, *Rehearsal for Reconstruction;* Jaynes, *Branches without Roots,* chap. 5.

78. Thomas F. Gossett, *Race: The History of an Idea in America* (Dallas, 1963), 54–175, 253–86; William Stanton, *The Leopard's Spots: Scientific Attitudes toward Race in America, 1815–59* (Chicago, 1960); Horsman, *Race and Manifest Destiny,* 43–186; George M. Fredrickson, *The Black Image in the White Mind: The Debate on Afro-American Character and Destiny, 1817–1914* (New York, 1971); Christine Bolt, *Victorian Attitudes to Race* (London, 1971); W. C. James Pennington, *A Test Book of the Origin and History, &c. &c. of the Colored People* (Hartford, 1841); McPherson, *Struggle for Equality,* 138–43; Lorimer, *Colour, Class and the Victorians,* 70, 86–91, 131–61.

79. Fredrickson, *Black Image,* 124, 161–86. The quoted section of the final report of the American Freedmen's Inquiry Commission was written by Robert Dale Owen.

80. Fredrickson, *Black Image,* 181 and n. 36.

81. Lorimer, *Colour, Class and the Victorians,* 178–200.

82. John H. Harris, "Slavery: World Abolition," *Contemporary Review,* 142 (1932), 308–14; Harris, *A Century of Emancipation* (London, 1933); "Slavery: the Uncompleted Task," *Spectator,* 150 (1933), 671–72; Lord Noel-Buxton, "A Century of Emancipation," *International Review of Missions,* 22 (1933), 323–30; *Listener,* 9 (1933), 645–47, 815–16, 855–57, 934–35; 10 (1933), 11–12, 29; *Times,* 10 May 1933, 19; 24 July 1933, 7; 25 July 1933, 16; 29 July 1933, 14; Kathleen Simon, "Slavery: Britain's Historic Decision," *Commonwealth and Empire Review,* 58 (1933), 72–77; Alice Law, "The Achievement of Wilberforce," *Fortnightly Review,* 139 (1933), 749–58; A. Mary Jeffrey, *The Knights and the Dragon: Stories of Slavery and Those Who Have Fought It* (London, 1933); Sir Reginald Coupland, *The British Anti-Slavery Movement* (Oxford, 1933). The year 1933 also marked the publication in the United States of Gilbert Hobbs Barnes's *The Antislavery Impulse, 1830–1844,* which emphasized the importance of the British example for American abolitionism.

83. Sir John Harris, "The Crime of Slavery," *Listener,* 9 (1933), 647 [Harris was knighted in 1933]; Lady Simon, "Slavery Today," *Listener,* 9 (1933), 815–16; Viscount Cecil of Chelwood, "The Final Blow at Slavery," *Listener,* 9 (1933), 934–35; Harris, *Century of Emancipation,* vii–viii, 229–30; "The Crusade against Slave Trading in Abyssinia," *Literary Digest,* 6 Jan. 1934, 15; Noel-Buxton, "Slavery in Abyssinia," *Contemporary Review,* 141 (1932), 698–707; M. A. Hallgren, "Liberia in Shackles," *Nation,* 137 (1933), 185–88; W. E. Burghardt Du Bois, "Liberia, the League, and the United States," *Foreign Affairs,* 11 (1933), 682–95.

84. Coupland, *Wilberforce: A Narrative* (Oxford, 1923), 168–71; Coupland, *British Anti-Slavery Movement,* 219–51.

85. David Eltis, "The British Contribution to the Nineteenth-Century Transatlantic Slave Trade," *Economic History Review,* 2d. ser., 32 (1979), 211–27; Eltis, MS on the abolition of the nineteenth-century slave trade. I am most grateful to Professor Eltis for allowing me to read a draft of this important work.

86. Yvan Debbasch, "Poésie et traite: L'opinion française sur le commerce négrier au début du XIXe siècle," *Revue française d'histoire d'outre-mer,* 49 (1961), 315–16, 319; Serge Daget, "A Model of the French Abolitionist Movement and Its Variations," in Christine Bolt and Seymour Drescher, eds., *Anti-Slavery, Religion and Reform: Essays in Memory of Roger Anstey* (Folkestone, Eng., 1980), 68–69; William B. Cohen, *The French Encounter with Africans: White Response to Blacks, 1530–1880* (Bloomington, 1980), 130–42, 182–88, 202.

87. Serge Daget, "France, Suppression of the Illegal Trade, and England, 1817–1850," in David Eltis and James Walvin, eds., *The Abolition of the Atlantic Slave Trade: Origins and Effects in Europe, Africa, and the Americas* (Madison, Wis., 1981), 193–217.

88. Daget, "Model of the French Abolitionist Movement," 71–72; Gaston Martin, *L'abolition de l'esclavage (27 avril 1848)* (Paris, 1948), 11–25; Christian Schnakenbourg, *Histoire de l'industrie sucrière en Guadeloupe aux XIXe et XXe siècles,* vol. 1, *La crise du système esclavagiste (1835–1847)* (Paris, 1980), 93–101; Debbasch, "Poésie et traite"; Lawrence C. Jen-

nings, "French Perceptions of British Slave Emancipation: A French Observer's Views on the Post-emancipation British Caribbean," *French Colonial Studies,* forthcoming; *Annales de l'Institut d'Afrique,* 1 (1841), 25–26, 33–35; Archives Nationales, Section Outre-Mer [hereafter SOM], Généralités 144, Dossier 1225; 165, Dossier 1336; 178, Dossiers 1418, 1419.

89. SOM, Généralités 169, Dossier 1374, general report of Capt. Layrle, Sept. 1842; 178, Dossier 1418, reports of Lt. Pardeilhan, 18 Apr. 1837 and 14 Aug. 1838, and Capt. Layrle, 1 July 1840; 165, Dossier 1336, report of Capt. Layrle, 15 Nov. 1841; 164, Dossiers 1329 and 1332, reports of Capt. Peltier and others; Lawrence C. Jennings, "French Reaction to the 'Disguised British Slave Trade': France and British African Emigration Projects, 1840–1864," *Cahiers d'études africaines,* 18 (1978), 201–13; Jennings, "French Perceptions." The British example also emboldened reformers like Tocqueville and Schoelcher (Cohen, *French Encounter,* 196–97).

90. Lawrence C. Jennings, "The French Press and Great Britain's Campaign against the Slave Trade, 1830–1848," *Revue française d'histoire d'outre-mer,* 67 (1980), 5–24; Johnson U. J. Asiegbu, *Slavery and the Politics of Liberation 1787–1861: A Study of Liberated African Emigration and British Anti-slavery Policy* (New York, 1969), 53–56; Seymour Drescher, "Two Variants of Anti-Slavery: Religious Organization and Social Mobilization in Britain and France, 1780–1870," in *Anti-Slavery, Religion and Reform,* 52; *Annales de l'Institut d'Afrique,* 4 (1844), 9; 7 (1847), 50–55; *Abolitionniste français,* 1 (1844), 6–9, 62–64; Victor Schoelcher, *Esclavage et colonisation* (Paris, 1948, originally published 1847), 138–39.

91. Martin, *L'abolition de l'esclavage,* 56–64; *Abolitionniste français,* 5 (1848), 16–45; *Annales de l'Institut d'Afrique,* 8 (1848), 17, 33–38; 18 (1858), 67–69; 19 (1859), 1–4; François Renault, *Liberation d'esclaves et nouvelle servitude* (n.p., 1976); Jennings, "French Reaction," 210. As late as 1887 the French government sought unsuccessfully to obtain sanction from the British Anti-Slavery Society for the reintroduction of Indian coolies into the sugar-producing island of Réunion, although such sanction was hardly necessary for the continuing use of contract labor (*Anti-Slavery Reporter,* Jan.–Feb. 1889, 11).

92. Daget, "Model of the French Abolitionist Movement," 75–77; *Annales de l'Institut d'Afrique,* 1 (1841), 1–2; 3 (1843), 49–51; 5 (1845), 17–18; 9 (1849), 1–2; 11 (1851), 16–21; *Abolitionniste français,* 1 (1844), 105–7; "Measures Taken by the French Government to Stamp Out Slavery," League of Nations, *Publications,* VI.B. A.25.1924.IV, 17–20; Cohen, *French Encounter,* 263–82.

93. Murray, *Odious Commerce,* 70–113, 185–207, 241–70, 282–97, 299–306, 316–24; Corwin, *Spain and the Abolition of Slavery,* 22, 28, 40–42, 51, 54–55, 61–66, 73, 112–13, 121, 147; Rebecca Scott, "Slave Emancipation and the Transition to Free Labor in Cuba, 1868–1895" (Ph.D. diss., Princeton University, 1981), 115–19. I am much indebted to Professor Scott for allowing me to read her extremely valuable dissertation.

94. Scott, "Slave Emancipation," 5, 14–17, 29–37, 108–24. For the contrary view that technology helped to undermine Cuban slavery, see Manuel Moreno Fraginals, *The Sugarmill: The Socioeconomic Complex of Sugar in Cuba, 1760–1860,* trans. Cedric Belfrage (New York, 1976).

95. Justo Zaragoza, *Las insurrecciones en Cuba: Apuntes para la historia política de esta isla en el presente siglo* (Madrid, 1872–73), II, 274–88; Vicente Vásquez Queipo, *Cuba, ses ressources, son administration, sa population, au point de vue de la colonisation européenne et de l'émancipation progressive des esclaves,* trans. Arthur d'Avrainville (Paris, 1851), 42, 108–23, and passim; Francisco de Armas y Céspedes, *De la esclavitud en Cuba* (Madrid, 1866), 88–115; Cristóbal Madan, *Llamamiento de la isla de Cuba a la nación española . . .* (New York, 1854), 107; Corwin, *Spain and the Abolition of Slavery,* 141, 149.

96. Corwin, *Spain and the Abolition of Slavery,* 51, 99–101, 140–43; Murray, *Odious Commerce,* 115–17, 203; Scott, "Slave Emancipation," 44.

97. José Antonio Saco, "La esclavitud en Cuba y la revolucion de España," in *Colección póstuma de papeles científicos, históricos, políticos . . .* (Havana, 1881), 443–45; Saco, *Memoria sobre la vagancia en la isla de Cuba* (Havana, 1846, originally published 1830); Saco, *Paralelo entre la isla de Cuba y algunas colonias inglesas* (Madrid, 1837), 17; Zaragoza, *Las insurrecciones en Cuba,* II, chap. 5; Corwin, *Spain and the Abolition of Slavery,* 149, 153–71, 181;

Scott, "Slave Emancipation," 46–49; Laird W. Bergad, "Recent Research on Slavery in Puerto Rico," *Plantation Society in the Americas*, 2 (1983), 99–109.

98. Franklin W. Knight, *Slave Society in Cuba during the Nineteenth Century* (Madison, Wis., 1970), 174–76, Scott, "Slave Emancipation," 75–76, 144–51, and passim; Corwin, *Spain and the Abolition of Slavery*, 233–34, 239, 246, 250, 280–81.

99. Murray, *Odious Commerce*, 323; British and Foreign Anti-Slavery Society, Minute Book, V (1 Jan. 1873), 13–14, Anti-Slavery Papers, E2/10, Rhodes House, Oxford; Corwin, *Spain and the Abolition of Slavery*, 255–72, 281–301; Knight, *Slave Society in Cuba*, 175; Scott, "Slave Emancipation"; *Anti-Slavery Reporter*, Mar. 1885, 323–24; Oct. 1885, 477–78.

100. *Anti-Slavery Reporter*, Jan.–Feb. 1887, 1–2.

101. Robert Conrad, *The Destruction of Brazilian Slavery, 1850–1888* (Berkeley, 1972), 3–19, 58–59; Emília Viotti da Costa, "The Political Emancipation of Brazil," in A. J. R. Russell-Wood, ed., *From Colony to Nation* (Baltimore, 1975), 43–88. The classic work on the Brazilian transition from slavery to free immigrant labor is Viotti da Costa, *Da senzala à colônia*, 2d ed. (São Paulo, 1982). I am much indebted to Professor da Costa for allowing me to read her extremely informative manuscript "Brazil: The Reform Era, 1870–1889," which is to appear in *The Cambridge History of Latin America*.

102. Graham, *Britain and the Onset of Modernization*, 24–39, 51–61, 73–110, 183; "Senhor Nabuco and Professor Goldwin Smith on the Morality of Slavery," *Anti-Slavery Reporter*, Aug.–Sept. 1886, 95–96.

103. Conrad, *Destruction of Brazilian Slavery*, xv, 40, 72, 125–28, 144–45, 173–82, 186–91; Warren Dean, *Rio Claro: A Brazilian Plantation System, 1820–1920* (Stanford, 1976), 50–51, 90–97, 110, 123–25; Viotti da Costa, *Da senzala*, 62–67, 108–13; Robert Brent Toplin, *The Abolition of Slavery in Brazil* (New York, 1972), 9–17, 97–98; Richard Graham, "Causes for the Abolition of Negro Slavery in Brazil: An Interpretive Essay," *Hispanic American Historical Review*, 46 (1966), 123–37. Both the *Rio News* and the *Anti-Slavery Reporter* are filled with complaints against Britons and other foreigners involved with the Brazilian slave system. It should be noted that Ceará contained less than 2 percent of the Brazilian slave population; that many of the slaves remaining in Ceará were old or sick; that the southern provinces tried to shut off the importation of slaves from the north, partly to prevent the political emergence of "free-soil" regions; and that the resulting decline in slave prices made many masters eager to manumit their slaves for a nominal sum in order to avoid the costs of maintenance and escalating taxes.

104. Bethell, *Abolition of the Brazilian Slave Trade*, 296–363; Graham, *Britain and the Onset of Modernization*, 167–70.

105. Conrad, *Destruction of Brazilian Slavery*, 72–74; *Anti-Slavery Reporter*, Aug.–Sept. 1886, 93–94.

106. Conrad, *Destruction of Brazilian Slavery*, 90–117, 167; *Rio News*, 15 June 1880; 5 Feb. 1881; Robert Brent Toplin, "The Specter of Crisis: Slaveholder Reactions to Abolitionism in the United States and Brazil," *Civil War History*, 18 (1972), 129–38; Dean, *Rio Claro*, 125–31.

107. Conrad, *Destruction of Brazilian Slavery*, 133–41, 143–50, 183–238, 242–62, 271; Viotti da Costa, *Da senzala*, 420–59; Toplin, *Abolition of Slavery in Brazil*, 61–110, 194–246; *Gazeta da Tarde*, 9 Sept. 1880; 31 May 1883; Graham, *Britain and the Onset of Modernization*, 171–73; Graham, "Causes for the Abolition of Negro Slavery," 123–37; Dean, *Rio Claro*, 142–55, 195.

108. *Gazeta da Tarde*, 11, 14, 17, 28 Sept. 1880; 31 May, 2 June, 25 Sept. 1883.

109. Toplin, *Abolition of Slavery in Brazil*, 72–73; Graham, *Britain and the Onset of Modernization*, 176–80, 184; *Gazeta da Tarde*, 17 Sept. 1880; *Anti-Slavery Reporter*, Dec. 1884, 239; Mar. 1885, 325; June 1885, 413; Oct. 1885, 462–64; Mar.–Apr. 1886, 32–33; Aug.–Sept. 1886, 92–93; *Rio News*, 15 Apr. 1883; Conrad, *Destruction of Brazilian Slavery*, 141–43.

110. Conrad, *Destruction of Brazilian Slavery*, 194; *Gazeta da Tarde*, 25 Sept. 1883; *Anti-Slavery Reporter*, Oct. 1885, 464.

111. *Programme of the Festivities in Honor of the Brazilian Slavery Emancipation,* and accompanying manuscript copies of addresses, MSS Brit. Emp. S.20, G, Rhodes House, Oxford; Philip Curtin et al., *African History* (Boston, 1978), 374–75; Suzanne Miers, *Britain and the Ending of the Slave Trade* (London, 1975), 162.

112. *Programme* and accompanying manuscripts; Miers, *Britain and the Ending of the Slave Trade,* 49–50, 159.

113. *Anti-Slavery Reporter,* Jan.–Feb. 1889, 13; A. P. Thornton, *The Imperial Idea and Its Enemies: A Study in British Power* (New York, 1966), 50. For an abolitionist attack on Britain's armed interference at Lagos, see *The Antislavery Watchman,* 2 (1853), 29–30. For the economic factors involved in the British expansion into West Africa, see A. G. Hopkins, "Economic Imperialism in West Africa: Lagos, 1880–1892," in Martin Klein and G. Wesley Johnson, eds., *Perspectives on the African Past* (Boston, 1972), 323–55.

114. Miers, *Britain and the Ending of the Slave Trade,* 21–25, 31–33, 35–37, 40, 47; J. B. Kelly, *Britain and the Persian Gulf, 1795–1880* (Oxford, 1968), 419–26; Ronald Robinson and John Gallagher, with Alice Denny, *Africa and the Victorians: The Climax of Imperialism in the Dark Continent* (New York, 1961), 27–41; Hopkins, "Economic Imperialism," 323–55; "First Anniversary Meeting of the Society for the Extinction of the Slave Trade, and for the Civilisation of Africa," *Times,* 2 June 1840, 6.

115. Roland Oliver, *The Missionary Factor in East Africa,* 2d ed. (London, 1965), 9, 53–82; Miers, *Britain and the Ending of the Slave Trade,* 88–89.

116. Reginald Coupland, *The Exploitation of East Africa, 1856–1890: The Slave Trade and the Scramble* (London, 1968, originally published 1939), 10–209, 227–52; Kelly, *Britain and the Persian Gulf,* 435–51, 579–85, 630–35; Miers, *Britain and the Ending of the Slave Trade,* 90–94.

117. Frederick Cooper, *From Slaves to Squatters: Plantation Labor and Agriculture in Zanzibar and Coastal Kenya, 1890–1925* (New Haven, 1980), 2; Kelly, *Britain and the Persian Gulf,* 585–86, 636; Miers, *Britain and the Ending of the Slave Trade,* 70–73, 84–86, 160; Robert L. Tignor, *Modernization and British Colonial Rule in Egypt, 1882–1914* (Princeton, 1966), chaps. 2 and 4. Kenneth Bourne argues forcefully that Palmerston was "a pragmatist, not a moralist," but his pragmatism in pursuing the suppression of the slave trade was more than matched by his conviction of the policy's rectitude (*Palmerston: The Early Years, 1784–1841* [New York, 1982], 621–24).

118. Miers, *Britain and the Ending of the Slave Trade,* 29, 41–42, 54, 69, 118, 147–51, 164–66; Coupland, *Exploitation of East Africa,* 360; Frederick Cooper, *Plantation Slavery on the East Coast of Africa* (New Haven, 1977); Ralph A. Austen, "From the Atlantic to the Indian Ocean: European Abolition, the African Slave Trade, and Asian Economic Structures," in Eltis and Walvin, *Abolition of the Atlantic Slave Trade,* 126–32.

119. Quoted in Thornton, *Imperial Idea,* 72.

120. Roland Oliver and Anthony Atmore, *Africa Since 1800,* 2d ed. (Cambridge, Eng., 1972), 86–89; Coupland, *Exploitation of East Africa,* 272–75; Miers, *Britain and the Ending of the Slave Trade,* 78–81.

121. Thomas Fowell Buxton to Priscilla Buxton, 18 Nov. 1839, Buxton Papers, II, 231–38, Rhodes House, Oxford. Buxton's trip to Italy was publicly announced as a vacation in the interest of his wife's health. I have no direct evidence on the connection between Buxton's secret mission in November and Pope Gregory's encyclical of 3 Dec. 1839.

122. François Renault, *Lavigerie, l'esclavage africain, et l'Europe, 1868–1892* (Paris, 1971), I, 162–70, 243–50, II, 11, 72–194; Oliver, *Missionary Factor,* 17–20, 47; Miers, *Britain and the Ending of the Slave Trade,* 163, 201–6.

123. Miers, *Britain and the Ending of the Slave Trade,* 169–73, 181, 208; *Anti-Slavery Reporter,* Nov. 1884, 195, 197, 203ff.

124. Miers, *Britain and the Ending of the Slave Trade,* 207–12, 235, 240–56; the text of the Brussels Act is printed on 346–63.

125. Ibid., 240–59, 263, 275–76, 292, 318–19, 346–63.

126. Bernard Porter, *Critics of Empire: British Radical Attitudes to Colonialism in Africa, 1895–1911* (London, 1968), 65–67.

127. Porter, *Critics of Empire,* 31; Cooper, *From Slaves to Squatters,* 31 n. 19; Miers, *Britain and the Ending of the Slave Trade,* 303.

128. Miers, *Britain and the Ending of the Slave Trade,* 157–59, 218–19, 248; League of Nations, *Publications* (hereafter LNP), VI.B. A.25(a).1924.VI, 8; Cooper, *From Slaves to Squatters,* 34, 58.

129. See above, pp. 203–4, 215–19; Philip D. Curtin, *The Image of Africa: British Ideas and Actions, 1780–1850* (Madison, Wis., 1964), 455–56; Cooper, *From Slaves to Squatters,* 37.

130. LNP,A.25(a).1924.IV, 6; Cooper, *From Slaves to Squatters,* 18, 48–59, 62–64, 86–89, 123–24.

131. Miers, *Britain and the Ending of the Slave Trade,* 310–14; "The Work of the League of Nations for the Suppression of Slavery," United Nations Economic and Social Council, E/AC.33/2, 23 Jan. 1950, 2–3; LNP, C.426.M.157.1925.VI, 71–74; Viscount Cecil of Chelwood, "The Final Blow at Slavery," *Listener,* 9 (1933), 934. Lord Chelwood helped draw up the draft treaty and was Britain's chief representative at Geneva.

132. Coupland, *British Anti-Slavery Movement,* 250.

133. LNP, A.25.1924.VI, 17–20; A.10(b).1926.VI, 1–3; A.17.1929. VI, 6–10; A.13(a).1930.VI, 2; *Anti-Slavery Reporter and Aborigines' Friend,* Apr. 1923, 27–34; Apr. 1924, 33–38; Apr. 1926, 34; Apr. 1927, 39–40.

134. LNP, A.18.1924.IV, 15; A.19.1925.VI, 11.

135. LNP, A.104.1926.VI, 1.

136. LNP, A.25.1924.IV, 7–8; A.25(a).1924.IV, 7–10.

137. LNP, A.17.1929.IV, 8; A.10(b).1926.VI, 8; George M. Fredrickson, *White Supremacy: A Comparative Study in American and South African History* (New York, 1981), 219; LNP, A.25.1924.IV, 13; A.10(a).1926.VI, 2.

138. LNP, C.426.M.157.1925.VI, 10, 71, 74; A.104.1926.VI, 2–3, 5; Fredrickson, *White Supremacy,* 185–98, and passim.

139. *Parliamentary Debates* (Lords), 5th ser., vol. 79 (1931), cols. 842–67; LNP, A.104.1926.VI, 5. The British Anti-Slavery Society was also concerned over reports of forced labor in Russian timber camps.

140. Marcia B. Libes, "The Abolition of the *Mui Tsai* System in Hong Kong" (Senior essay in history, Yale College, April 1980); Sir George Maxwell to Mr. Strang (or Stevenson), 7 Dec. 1934, FO 371/17822, Public Record Office, London.

141. LNP, A.19.1925.VI, 19; C.426.M.157.1925.VI, 80–81, 84; *Anti-Slavery Reporter,* Apr. 1939, 31–36. British abolitionists had shown great sympathy for Emperor Haile Selassie's efforts to abolish slavery.

EPILOGUE

1. United Nations, Economic and Social Council, 19th sess., 9 Feb. 1955, E/2673, 26; *Parliamentary Debates* (Lords), 5th ser., vol. 225 (1960), cols. 335, 341–43; Benjamin B. Ferencz, *Less Than Slaves: Jewish Forced Labor and the Question for Compensation* (Cambridge, Mass., 1979); Anti-Slavery Society for the Protection of Human Rights, printed leaflet, n.d. (1970).

2. Economic and Social Council, 9th sess., 22 July 1949, E/SR.298, 6–11, 24–25; 26 July 1949, E/SR.301, 5–12; Ad Hoc Committee on Slavery, 14 Feb. 1950, E/AC.33/SR.1, 4–8; 21 Feb. 1950, E/AC.33/SR.2, 2–5; Mohamed Awad, *Report on Slavery* (New York, 1966), E/4168/Rev.1, 95–99, 285, 294; Economic and Social Council, Commission on Human Rights, "Question of Slavery and the Slave Trade in All Their Practices and Manifestations, Including Slavery-like Practices of Apartheid and Colonialism," 30 Aug. 1978; *The Annual Report of the Anti-Slavery Society for the Protection of Human Rights for the Year Ended 31st March, 1978,* 3–4.

3. Conor Cruise O'Brien, "The Theater of Southern Africa," *New York Review of Books,* 23 Mar. 1978, 33; Awad, *Report,* 93–99; Jonathan Derrick, *Africa's Slaves Today* (New York,

1975); *Annual Report . . . 1978,* 3–4; Patrick Montgomery, "Slavery—Old Evil Lingers On," leaflet reprinted from *One World,* June 1977.

4. Patrick Montgomery, "The Antislavery Society in 1973," *Contemporary Review,* 223 (1973), 63–68; Montgomery, "Slavery in the Seventies," *Reconciliation Quarterly,* 6 (1976), 25–32; *Washington Post,* 18 Jan. 1982, p. A8; *Baptist Times,* 9 Jan. 1975, 5–8; *New York Times,* 18 Oct. 1980, 1, 58; *Newsday,* 23 Jan. 1982, 9.

INDEX

Abbasid Empire, 5-6
Aberdeen, George, 4th Earl, 123, 236-37, 285, 301
Abignente, Giovanni, 9
Abolition Committee (Manchester), 138
Abolitionism: progress of, 107-11, 280, 285, 296; promoted by British government, 127-28, 210, 211, 280-81, 285, 303; British and American compared, 141, 162-67, 175, 206-7, 210-11, 212, 260; incipient, 154; connections with government bureaucracy, 345-46 n.115. *See also* Imperialism, connections with antislavery
Abolitionists, 108, 109, 143-53
Abolition movement, 109; evangelical sources of, 136-41; history of, 139, 175, 189-90, 279-81; radical tendencies of, 141-43, 149, 166, 265-66, 273; inspired by God, 145; weakened in Britain by issue of free trade, 239, 348 n.138; links with labor movement, 273; in France, 284; in Spain, 288; in Brazil, 292-97
Aborigines Protection Society, 307
Abrams, M. H., 127, 148
Académie des Sciences Morales et Politiques, 114
Adams, Charles Francis, 246
Adams, John Quincy, 269
Africa: precolonial history of, 34-37; ideal of civilizing and Christianizing, 176, 180, 209, 236, 281, 284, 300-301, 304-6; scramble for, 299, 304-6. *See also* Imperialism, connections with antislavery
African Institution, 176, 196
Agassiz, Louis, 278
Agency Anti-Slavery Society (and Committee), 115, 141, 175, 186, 188, 200, 205, 207
Agobard, Archbishop, 91, 92
Algeria, 284
Ali b. Muhammad, 6-7
Alison, Sir Archibald, 250
Almoravids, 49
Althorp, Lord, 200
American Colonization Society, 186-87, 222, 225, 260. *See also* Colonization: of American blacks in Africa
American Freedmen's Inquiry Commission, 277
American Revolution, 77, 150, 178, 259
Amerindians: enslavement of, 28, 65, 67, 70, 71, 74, 334 n.113; depopulation of, 65, 70
Amis des noirs, 158
Amnesty International, 319
Andrade e Silva, José Bonifacio de, 296
Andrews, Kenneth R., 68
Anglophobia, 237, 245, 247, 282, 283
Angola, 71, 96, 311
Anstey, Roger, 172, 335 n.121
Anti-Semitism, 92, 93, 95
Antislavery. *See* Abolitionism
Anti-Slavery Committee (London), 179, 182, 183, 185, 186, 198, 200, 203. *See also* British Anti-Slavery Society; Society for the Mitigation and Gradual Abolition of Slavery
Antislavery movement. *See* Abolition movement
Antislavery societies. *See* Abolition Committee (Manchester); Agency Anti-Slavery Society; Anti-Slavery Committee (London); Anti-Slavery Society (20th century); Brazilian Anti-Slavery Society; British Anti-Slavery Society; London Emancipation Society; New England Anti-Slavery Society; Société de la morale chrétienne; Society for the Abolition of Slavery (Liverpool); Society for Effecting the Abolition of the Slave Trade (London); Society for the Mitigation and Gradual Abolition of Slavery (London); Spanish Abolitionist Society
Anti-Slavery Society (20th century), 307, 309, 315, 317-19
Apartheid, 318

Apprenticeship: in British West Indies, 118, 123, 124, 161, 205, 207, 208; in Cuba, 289-90. *See also* Slave emancipation, British: coupled with apprenticeship
Aquinas, Saint Thomas, 91
Aristotle, 3, 14, 23, 25, 40, 133
Asbury, Francis, 165-66
Athenaeus, 25
Augustine, Saint, 87
Austen, Ralph A., 45, 327-28 n.47, 329 n.67
Ayalon, David, 90

Bacon, Leonard, 260-62, 341 n.46
Bagehot, Walter, 24
Baptists, 136, 137, 139, 195-96
Barbados, 65-66, 72, 100, 197, 221
Barghash ibn Sa'id, 301
Baring, Sir Evelyn, 302
Baron, Salo W., 92
Bathurst, Lord, 193
Baxter, Richard, 139
Beattie, James, 131, 132, 171, 260
Benezet, Anthony, 136, 137
Benjamin, Judah P., 84
Bentham, Jeremy, 254
Bento, Antonio, 295
Berlin West African Conference (1884–85), 304-5
Beveridge, Charles E., 355 n.37
Biot, Edouard, 114, 339 n.8
Bismarck, Otto Edward Leopold von, 305
Black Codes, 274
Black Death, 54, 56, 59-60, 64
Blacks: as slaves in Muslim world, 5-8, 321 n.1, 321-22 n.2; as slaves in antiquity, 8, 327 n.45; as slaves in early modern Europe, 33, 55, 56, 57-58, 60, 61, 87; associated with ancient Egypt, 34; images of, 36-39, 42-45, 328 n.58, 331 n.86; in muslim world, 39-51; in free-labor societies, 80-81; response of to British emancipation, 124-25, 224; capacity of for progress, 131-35, 276-77, 307; response of to Civil War, 267, 269. *See also* Freedmen; Racism
Blackstone, William, 148
Blair, William, 112
Bodin, Jean, 156
Boer War, 307
Bonaparte, Napoleon, 131, 173, 282
Borah, Woodrow, 64, 65
Braudel, Fernand, 70, 95, 331 n.82, 331 n.86, 332 n.94
Brazilian Anti-Slavery Committee Society, 294
British and Foreign Anti-Slavery Committee Society, 186, 190, 208, 210, 290-91, 293, 296, 299, 303, 305
British and Foreign Bible Society, 124
British Anti-Slavery Society, 145, 186, 200
British Guiana, 174, 208, 220, 221, 222. *See also* Demerara
British India Society, 190
Broglie, duc de, 283
Brooks, Preston, 264
Brougham, Henry, 133-34, 135, 166, 197, 198, 199
Brown, John, 265-66
Brown, Peter, 40
Bruno, Giordano, 134
Brunt, P. A., 326 n.35
Brussels Act (1890), 306
Brussels Conference (1889–90), 305-6
Buchanan, James, 83
Bugner, Ladislas, 38
Bulliet, Richard W., 35, 327-28 n.47
Burge, William, 352 n.182
Burton, Ann M., 170, 172
Bury, John B., 24
Butler, Sir Harcourt, 279
Buxton, Priscilla, 186, 202, 203, 340 n.27
Buxton, Thomas Fowell, 123, 125, 128, 145, 148, 169, 192, 197, 198, 199, 200, 201, 202, 203, 205, 208, 209, 212, 223, 304, 347-48 n.137, 348-49 n.143

Ca da Mosto, Alvice da, 51
Cairnes, John Elliott, 244-45, 248, 250-58, 259, 356 n.49
Calhoun, John C., 237, 239-41
Calvinists, 146, 149, 151
Canaan, curse of, 21-22, 36, 39, 42-43, 83, 86-87, 337 n.144
Canary Islands, 54, 58, 60, 62, 70
Canning, George, 169, 192-93
Cape Verde Islands, 58, 61, 62, 63
Cartwright, Major John, 183
Catalan Atlas, 50, 94
Ceará, 293, 295, 296, 297, 360 n.103
Chamberlain, Sir Austen, 280
Christianity: role in abolishing European slavery, 110, 114, 157, 158, 159; revitalized by abolitionism, 119-22, 125, 129, 131, 135, 136-53, 153, 223. *See also* Slavery: Christian justifications of; Progress: as redemption from bondage, religious meanings of
Churchman, John, 136
Cicotti, Ettore, 9
Civil Rights Act (1866), 274
Civil War (U.S.): British response to, 244-50, 257-58, 355 n.33; providential meaning of, 267-71; Cuban response to, 287-88; Brazilian response to, 296
Clapham Sect, 140, 160, 170, 219
Clarkson, John, 160
Clarkson, Thomas, 117-18, 139, 140, 148, 150, 153, 167-68, 182, 187, 234, 240-41, 343 n.78, 348 n.140
Clisshold, Stephen, 329 n.70

Cobden, Richard, 249
Cochin, Augustine, 114
Coffee cultivation, 291
Colbert, Jean Baptiste, 100
Colonization: of American blacks in Africa, 186; of Brazilian blacks in Africa, 298
Columbus, Christopher, 62
Compromise of 1850, 153
Comte, Auguste, xiv, 113
Condorcet, Marie Jean, marquis de, 24, 156
Confederacy, 242, 247, 256-58
Congo Independent State, 304-5
Congress of Vienna, 235, 236
Contract labor: in British colonies, 208, 219, 221, 234, 283-84, 353 n.5; in the South, 275-76; in French colonies, 283-84, 359 n.91; in Cuba, 286, 290; in Brazil, 292; in Africa, 306; in Portuguese Africa, 312-13. *See also* Indentured servants
Cook, Sherburne F., 64, 65
Cooper, Frederick, 301, 322 n.3
Cotton cultivation, 78-79, 275
Coupland, Sir Reginald, 280-81, 310
Courtès, Jean Marie, 36, 37
Craton, Michael, 196, 344 n.106
Cresques, Abraham, 50, 94
Cresques, Jafuda, 94
Cresson, Elliott, 187
Cropper, Eliza, 185, 186
Cropper, James, 179-81, 199, 347 n.135
Cross, Frank Moore, 85
Crusades, 5, 53, 93
Cuba, 173, 174, 238-40, 285-91
Curaçao, 98
Curtin, Philip D., 65, 66, 67, 71, 332 n.97, 332-33 n.100, 334 n.114
Curtis, George William, 248

Daget, Serge, 284
Dante, 70
Davis, David Brion, 335 n.121
Declaration of Independence, 150, 151, 152
Deerr, Noel, 59
Demerara, 191, 197, 204
Devisse, Jean, 37-38
Diderot, Denis, 107
Didymus the Blind, 37
Disease environments, 64-65
Dodds, Eric R., 24
Dom Diniz, king of Portugal, 57
Dominican Republic, 271
Donnelly, Ignatius, 278
Douglas, Stephen A., 264
Douglass, Frederick, 269
Dred Scott decision, 263, 272
Drescher, Seymour, 74, 335 n.121, 340 n.26, 345 n.114
Dunn, Richard S., 67
Durham, bishop of, 313
Durham, Lord, 252
Dutch West India Company, 68-69

Edelstein, Ludwig, 24, 25
Edwards, Bryan, 42
Edwards, Jonathan, 138
Edwards, Jonathan, the younger, 151, 152, 163
Einhorn, David, 83, 84
Eleazar b. Simeon, R., 22
Elliott, J. H., 69
Eltis, David, 345 n.112, 353-54 n.12
Emancipation. *See* Freedmen; Manumission; Slave emancipation; Slave emancipation, British; Serfs (Russian), emancipation of
Emancipation Proclamation. *See* Slave emancipation: by Lincoln's proclamation
Emerson, Ralph Waldo, 110, 124
Encyclopaedia Britannica, 132, 135
Engels, Friedrich, xiv, 19
Engerman, Stanley L., xv, 77
Enlightenment, 129-30, 131, 132, 135, 137, 138, 141, 143, 148, 149, 211, 223; indictment of slavery, 108-9
Enlightenment, Scottish, 119, 155
Ethiopia, 280; as a religious symbol, 36-37, 328 n.48
Ethiopian eunuch, baptism of, 36-38
Evans, William McKee, 21, 322 n.3, 324, 337 n.144
Everett, Alexander, 239
Everett, Edward, 232
Eyre, Edward John, 278

Ferreira de Menezes, José, 296
Fifteenth Amendment, 272
Finley, M. I., 28, 325-26 n.34, 326-27 n.40, 339 n.8
Finney, Charles Grandison, 140, 187
Fisher, Alan W., 325-26 n.34
Fitzhugh, George, 234-35
Floyd, John, 245
Fogel, Robert William, xv
Foner, Eric, 336 n.132
Fourteenth Amendment, 272
Fox, Charles James, 117, 139
Fox, George, 139
Franklin, Benjamin, 107, 113, 137
Frederickson, George M., 164
Freedmen: regulations governing, 208, 214, 215, 219, 274, 276, 347 n.135; education of, 215; access to land, 216-18, 220, 274-75, 308. *See also* Slave emancipation; Blacks
Freedmen's Bureau, 275
Frémont, John C., 267
French Revolution, 115, 117, 132, 150, 151-52, 164

Frere, Sir Bartle, 280
Freud, Sigmund, 16
Frothingham, Frederick, 263
Fugitive Slave Act, 263
Fugitive Slave Law (1850), 261

Gaius, 14
Galen, 42, 328 n.58
Galenson, David W., 52
Gannett, William Channing, 274
Garrettson, Freeborn, 136, 137
Garrison, William Lloyd, 141, 142, 143-44, 145, 163-64, 187, 188, 189, 273, 292
Gay, Peter, 130
Gemery, Henry A., 79, 330 n.78
Genovese, Eugene D., 12, 13, 17
Gettysburg Address, 268
Ghana, Kingdom of, 48, 49
Giddings, Joshua, 263
Gladstone, John, 184
Gladstone, William E., 242
Glennelg, Lord, 218
Goderich, Lord, 201, 211
Godwyn, Morgan, 139
Gohr, Albrecht, 310, 313
Goitein, S. D., 90-91
Gomes, Diogo, 51
Goodell, William, 151-53, 154, 164
Goodrich, William, 268
Gordon, Charles George, 303
Gould, Stephen Jay, 33
Graham, Sir James, 200
Grant, Ulysses S., 271, 272
Great Awakening, 136, 137, 138
Green, William A., 219
Greenfield, Sidney M., 59, 62
Gregory XVI, pope, 304, 361 n.121
Grey, Charles, 2nd Earl, 119, 201, 202
Grimké, Angelina, 272-73
Grimshaw, H. A., 311
Guiana, 98-99, 174. *See also* British Guiana; Demerara

Haiti, 115-16, 134, 169. *See also* Saint Domingue
Hall, Douglas, 220
Ham. *See* Canaan, curse of
Hamerton, Atkins, xviii
Hamilton, Richard W., 125
Hamilton, Robert, 124
Hammond, James Henry, 233-34, 240-41
Hardinge, Arthur, 308-9
Harms, Robert W., 330 n.78
Harris, Sir John, 279-81
Harris, William V., 325-26 n.34
Hartog, Dirk, 323 n.14
Haven, Gilbert, 271, 276, 278
Hawkins, Sir John, 68
Heeren, Arnold, 111
Hegel, G. W. F., 20, 21, 127, 323 n.20
Helper, Hinton R., 241
Henriquez, Philippe, 98
Henry the Navigator, prince of Portugal, xvii, 58, 60
Heyrick, Elizabeth, 145, 183, 184
Hilliard, Henry Washington, 297
Hitler, Adolf, 280
Hobbes, Thomas, 21
Hogendorn, Jan S., 79, 330 n.78
Holcombe, William Henry, 23
Holland, Lord, 352 n.182
Holmes, George Frederick, 23
Hong Kong, 314
Hopkins, Keith, 29
Hopkins, Samuel, 151
Hough, J. W., 270
Howick, Henry G. G., Viscount (later 3rd Earl Grey), 189-90, 201, 203-4, 211, 212, 216-18, 308-9, 347 n.135, 352 n.182
Hume, David, 107, 113, 131, 132
Hunter, David, 267
Hutcheson, Francis, 107, 119

Ibn Battuta, 44-45, 48
Ibn Khaldun, 43
Imperialism, connections with antislavery, xvii-xviii, 128, 235, 237-42, 246, 257-58, 262, 271, 281, 284-85, 298-309, 310-12
Indentured servants, 52, 65-66, 76. *See also* Contract labor
Indian mutinies (1857–58), 249
Indians. *See* Amerindians
Industrialization, responses to, 232-34
Ingram, J. K., 9
Institut d'Afrique, 284
Insurrections. *See* Slave revolts
International Labor Office, 311, 313-14
International League for Human Rights, 319
Ireland, 184-85
Isaac, Ephraim, 36, 86-87, 337 n.144
Islam, early expansion of, 40-41, 46, 48-49. *See also* Slavery: in Muslim societies; Blacks: in Muslim world
Ismail Pasha (khedive of Egypt), 303

Jahiz of Basra, 44
Jamaica, 72, 73, 77, 123, 125-26, 193, 196-98, 208, 220, 278, 338 n.167
James, William, 206
Jefferson, Thomas, 132, 263
Jesus, 18-19
Jews: early rules regarding slaveholding, 21-22, 84-88, 89, 90, 91, 92; and 19th-century disputes over slavery, 82-84; ancient sanction of slavery, 84-88; perse-

cution of, 88, 89, 92, 93, 95-96; as slave traders, 89-93, 96, 97, 98, 99, 100-101; contributions to Atlantic slave system, 94-101; opportunities for in New World, 96-101; as sugar planters, 99-100; as slave labor in Nazi Germany, 317; as Jamaican slaveholders, 338 n.167
Joachim of Fiore, 157
Johnson, Andrew, 274
Jones, Alice Hanson, 77
Joseph, Biblical story of, 17
Journal des savants, 134
Joyce, Thomas A., 135
Jubilee, day of, 120-21, 123, 124, 144, 183, 205, 223, 229, 266, 269, 270, 274, 299
Judah, Moses, 83
July Monarchy (French), 282-83
Justinian Code, 20

Kansas-Nebraska Act, 262-63
Keane, A. H., 135
Kingsley, Charles, 232
Kirk, Sir John, 280, 300, 301
Kopytoff, Igor, 13, 14, 15
Kulikoff, Allan, 76

Labor. *See* Contract Labor; Slave labor, compared with free labor
Labor movement. *See* Abolition movement: links with labor movement
Lagos, 298-300
Lamoureux, Andrew Jackson, 296
Las Navas de Tolosa, battle of, 50
Lavigerie, Charles, Cardinal, 108, 300, 304
Layrle, Marie-Jean-François, 224, 283
League of Nations: Advisory Committee of Experts, 279, 310-13; International Convention on Slavery (1926), 279, 310-13, 315; Temporary Slavery Commission (1924), 310-13, 315
Leo XIII, pope, 108, 304
Leopold II, 304-6
Letourneau, C. J. M., 9
Levtzion, Nehemia, 46, 48, 327-28 n.47, 329 n.63
Lewis, Bernard, 42, 43, 44, 48
Lieber, Francis, 83
Lincoln, Abraham, 162, 247, 248-49, 260, 263, 267, 268-70, 287, 289, 296, 341 n.46
Livingstone, David, 280, 300, 304
Livy, 26
Lloyd George, David, 307
Locke, John, 20, 21, 107-8
London Emancipation Society, 250
London Missionary Society, 195
Long, Edward, 338 n.167
Lopez, Aaron, 101
Lopez, Robert S., 52, 53, 89, 331 n.82
Louis the Pious, Holy Roman Emperor, 91
Lovejoy, Paul E., 334 n.114
Lugard, Sir Frederick, 307, 310, 313, 315
Lundy, Benjamin, 186

Macaulay, Thomas Babington, 231-32
Macaulay, Zachary, 169-79, 202
MacFarquhar, Colin, 132
Mackintosh, Sir James, 231
MacMullen, Rasmay, 325-26 n.34, 326 n.35
Madden, R. R., 238
Madeira Islands, 58, 60, 62, 63, 71, 95, 96, 332-33 n.100
Mahdist revolt, 303
Maimonides, Moses, 88, 91
Majorca, 55, 56, 92, 94, 331 n.87
Mali, Kingdom of, 44-45, 46-48, 49, 50
Mali, Republic of, 319
Manchester, 233
Mansa Musa, 46-47, 50
Manumission, 17, 20-21, 39, 47, 69, 78, 107, 165, 192. *See also* Slave emancipation; Freedmen
Marcus, Jacob R., 95, 98, 100
Maroon communities, 7, 71, 72, 334 n.115. *See also* Slaves: fugitive
Marranos, 90, 94, 95, 96, 97, 98, 99, 100
Marx, Karl, xiv, 19, 113, 248-49, 254, 355 n.39
Maryland, 255
Mascarene Islands, 300
Massachusetts Emigrant Aid Company, 262
Mauritius, 208
Maxwell, Sir George, 314-15
Meacham, James, 136
Meillassoux, Claude, 9-10
Mercado, Raphael de, 100
Merivale, Herman, 255
Methodists, 136, 137, 138, 139, 196-97, 198
Meilziner, Moses, 82-84
Miers, Suzanne, 13, 14, 15, 305
Mill, John Stuart, 109-10, 244-46, 257-58, 356 n.49
Millar, John, xiv, 113, 137
Millennialism. *See* Progress: and millennialism
Milnes, Monckton, 250
Milton, John, 145, 148, 153
Mintz, Sidney W., 338 n.167
Miquel, André, 41, 42
Miskimin, Harry A., 332-33 n.100
Missionaries: to Africa, 121, 298, 300-301; in British West Indies, 195-98; persecution of, 185, 197-98, 213
Mitford, William, 112
Moloney, Cornelius Alfred, 299
Montacos y Robillard, Don Francisco, 288

Montesquieu, Charles de Secondat, baron de, 107
Montgomery, David, 272
Montgomery, Patrick, 319
Moraes Farias, Paulo Fernando, 41
Morant Bay (uprising), 278
Moravians, 195
Moret, Segismundo, 289
Morgan, Edmund S., 66, 77
Mui tsai, 314
Murray, Sir George, 199
Mussolini, Benito, 315

Nabuco, Joaquim, 292, 294, 296-97
Naipaul, V. S., 340 n.35
Nash, Gary B., 75
National Labor Union, 273
Nef, John U., 324 n.26
Negro. *See* Blacks
Nehru, Jawaharlal, 303
New England Anti-Slavery Society, 187
New England Emigrant Aid Society, 263
Newton, Lord, 314
Nieboer, H. J., 9
Nisbet, Robert, 24, 25
Noah, Mordecai M., 84
Norfolk, duke of, 116-17
Northwest Ordinance, 163
Noyes, John Humphrey, 150-51

O'Brien, Conor Cruise, 318
O'Connell, Daniel, 185, 202, 204, 207
Oliver, Roland, 300
Olmsted, Frederick Law, xv, 253-54, 355 n.37, 355 n.41
Origen, 36, 37, 328 n.48
O'Sullivan, John L., 239

Paine, Thomas, 137, 138, 142, 143, 151
Palmares, 334 n.115
Palmer, Colin A., 68
Palmerston, Henry John Temple, 3rd Viscount, xviii, 236, 238, 239, 246, 302
Paracelsus, Philippus Aureolus, 134
Parliament: Reform Bills of 1832, 118, 119, 200; New Poor Law of 1834, 122, 340 n.26; Canning resolutions of 1823, 193, 199, 348 n.140
Parmoor, Lord, 314
Patrocinio, José do, 296
Patterson, Orlando, 10-11, 13, 15, 17, 20-21, 69, 322n.7
Paul, Nathaniel, 187
Pease, Joseph, 190-91
Pedro II, emperor of Brazil, 293-95, 298
Peel, Sir Robert, 300
Perceval, Spencer, 173, 176
Perry, Lewis C., 142, 149, 265-66
Petrarch, 31
Pherecrates, 25
Philbrick, Edward, 274
Phillips, Ulrich Bonnell, xiii
Phillips, Wendell, 265-66
Philo of Alexandria, 19
Pipes, Daniel, 13, 323 n.18
Pitt, William, 236, 280-81
Plato, 26
Poinsett, Joel, 251
Ponsonby, Viscount, 302
Poor Law. *See* Parliament: New Poor Law of 1834
Popovic, Alexandre, 6, 321 n.1, 321-22 n.2
Posidonius, 26
Post-emancipation conditions, 161; in British West Indies, 122-23, 189-90, 204-5, 208, 209-10, 220-21, 222; in the South, 274-77; in Cuba, 290; in Brazil, 295; in colonial Africa, 309. *See also* Reconstruction; Apprenticeship
Presbyterians, 136, 137, 139
Prince of Wales (later Edward VII), 285, 297-98, 299
Progress: impeded by slavery, xi, xiii-xv, 67, 69, 70, 80-82, 109, 110, 112, 113, 154, 156, 168, 181, 184, 233, 252, 253-58, 288, 292, 296, 297-98, 315; furthered by slavery, xiv-xvi, xvii, 23-25, 30-32, 67, 69, 70-71, 73, 77, 79, 97, 101, 113, 234-235, 254; contrast of in North and South, xv, 251-53; ambiguities of, xv, 154-55, 324 n.26; ancient concepts of, xvii, 24-27; exemplified by England, xviii, 231-33, 291-92, 303; as redemption from bondage, 19-20; religious meanings of, 21, 39, 263; and Islam, 40-41, 43-44, 47; associated with Europe's expansion and prosperity, 49-51, 52-64; associated with New World settlement, 69; signified by slave-trade abolition and emancipation, 111, 116-21, 122, 124-29, 280-81, 320; as gradual evolution, 114-16, 157-62, 312-13; result of concerted effort, 115-16; as collective rebirth, 116, 117-22, 124-29, 152-53; and millennialism, 120-22, 157, 259-60, 265-66, 267-71; and racial prejudice, 126; as *chronos,* 128-29, 177, 178, 261; as *kairos,* 128-29, 153, 157, 158, 177, 178, 273; efforts to make scientific, 135, 217-19, 289-90; as an obstacle to emancipation, 154, 159; philosophies of, 154-58; laissez-faire views of, 160-62, 180-81, 183-85, 189-91; as social engineering, 178, 212, 215-20, 310; as revolutionary change without revolution, 212; proslavery views of, 241, 242-44; identified with Union cause, 250, 263, 267-71; contrast of in

Canada and United States, 252; declining faith in, 307. *See also* Slavery: and human redemption; and technology, and images of economic and social decay; Blacks: capacity for progress; Slave emancipation: equated with religious redemption, Slave emancipation, British: responses to
Proslavery arguments, 23, 193-94, 195-96, 233-35, 241, 294
Ptolemy, 41
Puerto Rico, 287-88

Quakers, 107, 108, 136-40, 157, 181, 182, 183, 280, 317
Quamina, 196
Queen Elizabeth I, of England, 68

Racism: in historical interpretations of slavery, xiv; absence of in ancient world, 33-37; historical origins of, 37-49, 327 n.42; in 18th century, 81, 132; and religious infidelity, 131-35; in 19th-century Britain, 135, 249, 277-78; and science, 135-36, 277-78; in 19th-century America, 164-65, 241, 247, 273; as obstacle to emancipation, 187, 255, 307-8; population of to emancipation, 226, 276-79
Ramsay, James, 131, 157-58
Raphall, Morris J., 83
Reconstruction, 258, 271-77, 279, 287, 289. *See also* Post-emancipation conditions: in the South
Reformation, Protestant, 143
Reform Bill. *See* Parliament: Reform Bills of 1832
Reid, Thomas, 119
Reitemeier, Johann Friedrich, 112-13
Revolution of 1848, 284, 287
Revolution of 1868 (Spain), 288
Rhett, Robert Barnwell, 242
Rice, C. Duncan, 155
Rice, David, 136, 158
Rio Branco law (1871), 294
Rivera, Jacob, 101
Rodinson, Maxime, 329 n.69
Rotter, Gernot, 38, 42, 43
Rousseau, Jean Jacques, 18, 107
Royal African Company, 107
Rush, Benjamin, 130, 137
Russell, Lord John, 247

Saco, José Antonio, 288
Saint Domingue, 6, 7, 72, 73, 78, 100, 158, 164, 169, 222, 265, 282. *See also* Haiti
Saint-Germain-en-Laye, Conventions (1919), 310
Saint Kitts, 170, 171
Saint Lucia, 221
Saint Maurice, 38
Saint Menas, 37
Saint Paul, 19
Sanders, Ronald, 94
São Paulo Province, 295, 296
São Tomé, 61, 63, 68, 71, 95, 96, 332-33 n.100
Schoelcher, Victor, 284
Scott, Rebecca, 326-27 n.40
Seaford, Lord, 224
Selassie, Haile, 280, 362 n.141
Seneca, 18, 24, 25
Serfs (Russian), emancipation of, 147, 285
Seward, William H., 246, 262
Shackleton, Lord, 317
Sharp, Granville, 81, 130, 131, 137, 138, 157, 298
Shaw, Robert Gould, 245
Shaw, Sarah Blake, 245, 248
Sherman, William L., 67, 334 n.113
Siegel, Bernard J., 9, 322 n.5
Sierra Leone, 160, 195, 299
Sierra Leone Company, 160
Simms, William Gilmore, 271
Slave emancipation: in Europe, 108, 113, 114, 157, 158, 159, 161; by gradual steps, 114, 134, 157-59, 163-64, 166, 169, 192-93, 270, 287-90, 294, 311-13; equated with religious redemption, 144, 157-58, 295; in northern United States, 163, 225; immediate, 177, 183, 198, 212, 260-61; by law of free birth, 198, 203, 289, 293-94, 308; in French colonies, 224, 284; by Lincoln's proclamation, 248-49, 269-70; in Burma, 279; in Nepal, 279; in Sierra Leone, 279-80; in Danish colonies, 285; in Dutch colonies, 285; in Cuba, 288-91; in Puerto Rico, 289; in Brazil, 295-99; in Muscat and Oman, 319; in Saudi Arabia, 319. *See also* Progress: signified by slave-trade abolition, as an obstacle to emancipation; Post-emancipation conditions; Reconstruction; Freedmen
Slave emancipation, British, 108; interpretations of, 109-10, 206, 209-10, 221, 224-25, 234, 240, 283, 287, 296 relation to parliamentary reform, 118-19, 178, 199, 200, 210; responses to, 118-29; political support for, 119, 200, 340 n.26; symbolic meanings of, 119-22, 124-29; moral validation of British power, 127-28, 209, 226; as a model for other nations, 169, 178, 189, 210, 219-20, 222, 225-26, 260, 283, 298, 359 n.89; double vision of, 177-78, 202, 203, 207, 210, 220-21, 223, 224; coupled with apprenticeship, 188, 201, 204; compensation to planters, 188,

Slave emancipation *(continued)*
204; in India, 190, 210, 308; plans for, 201, 202, 203, 204, 213-14, 216-19; details of final measure for, 204-5; role of free blacks in, 213-14, 351-52 n.174; fears concerning, 214-15, 216; Centennial of, 279-80; Jubilee of, 299, 305; in Gold Coast, 308; in Kenya, 308; in Zanzibar and Pemba, 308

Slave labor, compared with free labor, 15, 81-82, 113, 190-91, 215, 233-34, 253-54, 355 n.39, 355 n.41

Slave mortality, in New World, 333-34 n.107

Slave power, 211, 244, 250-51, 253, 256-58, 259, 262, 264, 266

Slave registration: in British West Indies, 176-77; in Cuba, 238; in Brazil, 294

Slave revolts: in Saint Domingue, 6, 7, 78, 115-16, 158, 164-65, 169, 222; in medieval Iraq, 6-8; in British West Indies, 122, 164-65, 213; in Demerara, 164, 169, 196, 197, 344 n.106, 349 n.147; in Barbados, 164, 177, 349 n.147; in Jamaica (1831), 196, 197-98, 200, 211, 212; fear of in American Civil War, 249

Slavery: in medieval Iraq, 6-8, 321 n.1, 321-22 n.2; in Muslim societies, 6-8, 18, 28, 29, 30, 31, 39, 41-51, 301-2, 306, 322 n.3, 323 n.18, 329 n.67, 329 n.70, 329-30 n.71; concepts and definitions of, 8-22, 314, 318-19; and technology, xi, 25-26, 31, 55, 62, 79, 286, 324 n.26, 326-27 n.40, 359 n.94; and industrial capitalism, xiv-xvi, 73, 79, 281, 291-92, 297; historiography of, xiv-xvi, 9, 12, 82-84, 339 n.8; and images of economic and social decay, xv, 79-81, 110, 251-58, 336 n.132; as an impetus to economic growth, xiv-xv; and European commercial expansion, xvii, 31-32, 49-51, 53-82, 73-79; in Zanzibar and Pemba, xviii, 303; in the British Caribbean, 11, 100-101; in the southern United States, 12, 251-58; in precolonial Africa, 13, 15, 45, 47, 49, 79-80, 323 n.15, 330 n.78; in ancient Mesopotamia, 13-14; in ancient Rome, 14, 15, 16, 26, 28, 29, 30, 112, 325-26 n.34, 326 n.35; metaphorical meanings of, 16; and human redemption, 20; related to concepts of freedom, 20-21; in ancient Palestine, 21-22, 84-88; in ancient Greece, 25-26, 111; and imperial expansion, 27-32; restricted to blacks, 30; in Renaissance Italy, 31, 54-56; decline of in early Middle Ages, 52; in Mediterranean basin, 55-57, 90-93, 331 n.87; in Portugal, 57-58, 60, 61; Christian justifications of, 60, 91-93, 107, 112, 146; beginnings of in New World, 64-73; in Hispanic America, 68-70; in colonial Brazil, 71, 97; in Dutch colonies, 71, 97-99; in French Canada, 74-75; in New England and the Middle Colonies, 74-76; in the Chesapeake Colonies, 76-77; as epitome of evil, 145-47, 153, 198, 260-61, 263-64, 341 n.46; amelioration of, 158, 159, 160, 162, 166, 169, 175-77, 192, 194-95; in British India, 190, 347-48 n.137; in the 20th century, 279-80; in Liberia, 280; in Ethiopia, 280, 315; in 19th-century Cuba, 286; in 19th-century Brazil, 291-95; in Ottoman Empire, 302; in Zaire basin, 305; in Soviet labor camps, 313-14; in 20th-century, 314-15, 317-20; in Nazi Germany, 317; in Saudi Arabia, 317. *See also* Slave labor, compared with free labor; Slave emancipation; Post-emancipation conditions

Slaves: aspirations of, xvii, 196, 349 n.147; fugitive, 7, 295, 297, 302-3, 306; marginality of, 11, 14-18; as "modern" people, 14-16; assimilation of, 15-18, 21-22; origin of the word for, 32-33; as distinct ethnic group, 32-33, 56-57; in European galleys, 52; religious conversion of, 195-96. *See also* Maroon communities

Slave trade: from Africa to Asia, 6, 45-46, 301-2, 321 n.1, 321-22 n.2, 329 n.67; from the Black Sea and Caucasia, 28, 33, 53-57, 90, 93, 243, 329 n.67, 329-30 n.71; trans-Saharan, 35-36, 39, 45-46, 48-49, 56, 327-28 n.47; related to gold trade, 49-51; to Atlantic Islands, 62, 63, 332-33 n.100; to New World, 51, 66-69, 73, 75-76; to Brazil, 71, 242, 285; to British Colonies, 76; in central Europe, 91-93; repudiation of in southern United States, 163, 235; to Cuba, 173, 174, 238, 285-86; within British West Indies, 173-74, 345 b.112; British support of in 19th century, 208-9; movement to reopen in southern United States, 241-44, 354 n.23; from Africa to Europe, 332 n.97; volume of to New World, 334 n.114

Slave-trade abolition: promoted by British diplomacy, xvii-xviii, 166, 174, 236-41, 242, 281-83, 285-86, 293, 300-306, 310; by Britain, 108, 116-18, 166, 173-74; by the United States, 118, 163; by Confederate States, 242; by France, 282-83; by Brazil, 293; by Zanzibar, 301; by Brussels Conference, 305-7

Sligo, Marquis of, 214

Smith, Adam, 113, 119, 157, 162, 180, 254, 282, 344 n.99

Smith, Goldwin, 250, 292

Smith, James McCune, 124, 267

Smith, John (missionary), 195-96, 197
Smith, William, 118, 139
Société da la morale chrétienne, 282
Society for Effecting the Abolition of the Slave Trade (London), 108
Society for the Abolition of Slavery (Liverpool), 115, 181, 186
Society for the Mitigation and Gradual Abolition of Slavery (London), 179, 183
Society of Friends. *See* Quakers
Society of West India Planters and Merchants, 192, 194
Sodré, Jeronymo, 294
Solon, 26
South Africa, 313-14, 317
South Carolina, 65, 163, 242, 274-75
Southern Literary Messenger, 235
Spanish Abolitionist Society, 289
Spratt, Leonidas W., 241-44
Stanley, Edward, 119, 123, 175, 201, 202-3, 204, 205, 206-7, 208, 214, 352 n.182
Stanley, Henry Morton, 305
Stearns, Charles B., 266
Stephen, George, 174-75, 177, 178, 186, 202, 204, 205-6, 207, 212-19
Stephen, James, 143, 168, 170-78, 179-80, 193, 201, 210, 211, 221, 344-45 n.108, 348 n.140
Stephen, Sir James, 174, 175, 177, 178, 189, 205, 208, 211, 212, 221, 308
Stevens, Thaddeus, 275
Story, Joseph, 251
Stowe, Harriet Beecher, 207, 226
Stowell, Lord, 195
Stuart, Charles, 186, 187, 188-89, 222, 223, 347 n.135
Sturge, Joseph, 185, 186, 190, 206, 208
Suffield, Lord, 189, 199, 205
Sugar cultivation, 54, 58-60, 61-62, 65-66, 71, 72, 94-95, 97-100, 191, 221, 222, 238, 286, 291, 332 n.94
Sumner, Charles, 263-64, 271, 275
Sunderland, Byron, 268
Surinam, 98, 99

Taharqa, 34
Talhami, Ghada Hashem, 321 n.2, 329 n.67
Tamerlane. *See* Timur
Tannenbaum, Frank, 9
Tarrant, Carter, 136
Taylor, Henry, 189, 201, 213, 216-18
Ten Years' War (Cuba), 288-89, 290
Texas, 236-37
Thayer, Eli, 262
The Wealth of Nations, 180
Thirteenth Amendment, 270-72, 320
Thompson, George, 140, 141, 145, 189, 190
Thomson, Joseph, 307
Thorkelin, G. J., 159
Thornton, Henry, 160
Thornwell, James Henley, 152
Tillich, Paul, 128
Timur, 55
Tippu Tip, 305
Tobacco cultivation, 65, 71-72, 76
Tocqueville, Alexis de, 110-11, 130, 131, 169, 233, 251-52, 255
Treaty of Alcáçovas, 61
Treaty of Tordesillas, 62
Trinidad, 174, 176, 193, 208, 220
Turgot, Anne Robert Jacques, 156
Turnbull, David, 238-39, 285
Turner, Frederick Jackson, 79
Tyler, John, 237

Uncle Tom's Cabin, 147
United Nations: Universal Declaraction of Human Rights, 317; Economic and Social Council, 318; Supplementary Convention (1956), 318; Working Group of Experts on Slavery, 318-19
Upshur, Abel P., 237
Urbach, E. E., 21, 84, 85, 88
Utilitarianism, 166, 211, 259, 272

Vaughan, James, 14
Verlinden, Charles, 54, 56, 57, 92, 331 n.87
Vesey, Denmark, 164
Virginia, 65-66, 75-77, 255
Vizcarrondo, Julio, 288
Voltaire (François Marie Arouet), 130, 131, 134, 135, 136, 142
Von Rad, Gerhard, 86-87

Wakefield, Edward Gibbon, 74, 185, 189, 216-17, 254
Wallace, Alfred Russel, 277
Wallace, Anthony F. C., 125
Wallon, Henri, 112, 114
Walvin, James, 351 n.171
Wardlaw, Ralph, 119-22, 124, 128
Watson, Richard, 197
Webb, Steven B., 340 n.26
Webster, Noah, 159
Weld, Theodore Dwight, 144-45, 146
Wellington, duke of, 201, 206
Wesley, John, 131, 136
Wesleyan Missionary Society, 197
West Indian faction, 178-79, 192-95, 200, 201, 202, 204, 205, 348-49 n.143, 350 n.157
White, Lynn Jr., 326-27 n.40
Whitney, George D., 3
Wiedermann, Thomas, 26
Wilberforce, William, 126, 138, 139-41, 145, 176-77, 206, 207, 279

William IV, of England, 199, 200, 201, 211
Williams, Eric, xiv, 9, 73, 335 n.121
Williams, Henry, 198
Wilson, James, 163
Wiznitzer, Arnold, 95, 97
Wood, Peter H., 65
Woolman, John, 136, 147
World Anti-Slavery Convention (1840), 191, 239, 299
Wright, Henry Clarke, 142-43, 146, 148, 149-50, 265-66

Xenophon, 26

Zaire basin, 305
Zanj, 6-8, 41, 43, 44, 321 n.2
Zanzibar, 301
Zaragoza, Justo, 287